WILD WALES

George Henry Borrow was born in 1803 at East Dereham, Norfolk. His father was a captain of militia and moved about Scotland, Ireland and many parts of England with his regiment during the Napoleonic war. When his father finally settled at Norwich, Borrow attended the grammar school there and subsequently spent five years articled to a firm of solicitors until 1823. Already his talent as a wordsmith was apparent and he was proficient in many languages, including Romany—the tongue of that strange race of which he was almost an adopted member.

On his father's death in 1824, Borrow attempted to seek his fortune in London, but in fact spent the next seven years wandering around England—sometimes in Gypsy company—as described in *Lavengro* and *The Romany Rye* to the delight of all Borrovians. In 1840 Borrow married a well-to-do widow and in 1843 he enjoyed an instant success with the publication of *The Bible in Spain*. During these years he settled down on his wife's small estate near Lowestoft from where he embarked on several travels, including the 1854 tour of Wales which gave rise to this delightful book.

Also available in the Century Travellers series:

A TRAMP ABROAD by Mark Twain
Introduction by Norman Lewis
EOTHEN by A. W. Kinglake
Introduction by Jonathan Raban
HOLY RUSSIA by Fitzroy Maclean
THE VALLEYS OF THE ASSASSINS by Freya Stark
THE SOUTHERN GATES OF ARABIA by Freya Stark
IN MOROCCO by Edith Wharton
A PERSON FROM ENGLAND by Fitzroy Maclean
FULL TILT by Dervla Murphy
A RIDE TO KHIVA by Fred Burnaby
Introduction by Eric Newby
SOUTHERN CROSS TO POLE STAR by A. F. Tschiffely
Introduction by Eric Newby
THE GOLDEN CHERSONESE by Isabella Bird
Introduction by Robin Hanbury-Tenison
VISITS TO MONASTERIES IN THE LEVANT
by Robert Curzon
Introduction by John Julius Norwich
THE TOMB OF TUTANKHAMEN by Howard Carter
Introduction by John Romer
LORDS OF THE ATLAS by Gavin Maxwell
Introduction by Geoffrey Moorhouse
SOUTH by Sir Ernest Shackleton
Introduction by Lord Hunt
ONE MAN'S MEXICO by John Lincoln
Introduction by Nicolas Cheetham
OLD CALABRIA by Norman Douglas
ISABEL AND THE SEA by George Millar
A WINTER IN ARABIA by Freya Stark
WHEN MEN AND MOUNTAINS MEET
by John Keay
A SULTAN IN OMAN by James Morris
GOOD MORNING AND GOOD NIGHT
by The Ranee Margaret of Sarawak

WILD WALES

The People, Language and Scenery

GEORGE BORROW

Introduction by Viscount Tonypandy

CENTURY PUBLISHING
LONDON

HIPPOCRENE BOOKS INC.
NEW YORK

Introduction copyright © Viscount Tonypandy 1984

All rights reserved

First published in Great Britain in three
volumes in 1862 by John Murray (Publishers) Ltd

This edition published in 1984 by Century Publishing Co. Ltd,
Portland House, 12–13 Greek Street, London W1V 5LE

Published in the United States of America by
Hippocrene Books Inc.
171 Madison Avenue
New York NY 10016

ISBN 0 7126 0448 0

Cover shows a detail of 'The River Llygwy, near
Capel Curig, North Wales' by Sidney Richard Percy
from the collection of K. G. Dervin Esq.

Reprinted in Great Britain by
Richard Clay (The Chaucer Press) Ltd,
Bungay, Suffolk

INTRODUCTION

The classics belong to every generation. Life would be incredibly the poorer without them. I count George Borrow's *Wild Wales* as one of those books which will continue to enrich the life of succeeding generations.

It is still possible to follow in Borrow's steps in Wales and to savour the tang of his writings. With a genius peculiar to himself, Borrow assesses not only the majesty of Welsh scenery, but also the rich variety of personalities in the truly Celtic areas which he enjoyed so much.

Every young person should regard *Wild Wales* as a treasure, to be enjoyed. It will challenge youth's spirit of adventure.

Older people who re-read Borrow's fanciful descriptions of his experiences in Wales, may well be spurred to use our modern comforts to travel at their leisure along the selfsame routes which he has immortalised by his writing. If they are so spurred they will find the scenery is as wild now, as it was for Borrow.

Thanks are due to Century Publishing Company for this timely reproduction of Borrow's masterpiece.

George Tonypandy

INTRODUCTION
TO THE 1906 EDITION

TALK ABOUT "WILD WALES"

BY

THEODORE WATTS-DUNTON

I

WHY "WILD WALES" IS A SIMPLE ITINERARY

I HAVE been invited by the editor of this series to say a few words upon Borrow's " Wild Wales." The invitation has come to me, he says, partly because during the latter days of Borrow's life I had the privilege as a very young man of enjoying his friendship, and partly because in my story, "Aylwin," and in my poem, " The Coming of Love," I have shown myself to be a true lover of Wales—a true lover, indeed, of most things Cymric.

Let me begin by saying that although the book is an entirely worthy compeer of " Lavengro " and " The Romany Rye," and although like them it is written in the autobiographic form, it belongs, as I propose to show further on, to an entirely different form of narrative from those two famous books. And it differs in this respect even from " The Bible in Spain." Unlike that splendid book, it is just a simple, uncoloured record of a walking tour through the Principality. As in any other itinerary, events in " Wild Wales " are depicted as they actually occurred, enriched by none of that glamour in which Borrow loved to disport himself. I remember once asking him why in this book he wrote an autobiographic narrative so fundamentally different from " Lavengro " and " The Romany Rye "—why he had made in this book none of those excursions into the realms of fancy which form so charming a part of his famous quasi-autobiographic narratives. It was entirely characteristic of him that he remained silent as he walked rather sulkily by my side. To find an answer to the queries, however, is not very difficult. Making a tour as he did on this occasion in the company of eye-witnesses—eye-witnesses of an extremely different temper from his own, eye-witnesses, moreover, whom he specially wished to satisfy and please—his wife and stepdaughter—he found it impossible to indulge in his bohemian proclivities and equally impossible to give his readers any of those romantic coincidences, those quaint arrangements of incidents to illustrate theories of life, which illuminate his other works. The tour was made in the summer and autumn of 1854; during the two or three years following, he seems to have been working upon this record of it. The book was announced for publication in 1857, but it was not until 1862 that his publisher, who had been so greatly disappointed by the reception given to " Lavengro " and " The Romany Rye," took courage to offer it to the public.

II

BORROW'S EQUIPMENT FOR WRITING UPON THE WELSH
LANGUAGE AND LITERATURE

IN 1860 Borrow's interest in Wales and Welsh literature had specially been shown by the publication of his English version of " Gweledigaethau y Bardd Cwsg," a curious kind of allegory in the form of a vision, written in the early years of the eighteenth century by a Welsh clergyman named Ellis Wynne. The English reader of Borrow's works will remember the allusion made to this book. As might have been expected, Borrow's translation of this Welsh prose classic is not very trustworthy, and it has been superseded by the translation of Mr. R. Gwyneddon Davies, published in 1897. A characteristic matter connected with Borrow's translation is that in the *Quarterly Review* for January 1861 he himself reviewed it anonymously, and not without appreciation of its merits—a method which may be recommended to those authors who are not in sympathy with their reviewers. The article showed a great deal of what may be called Borrovian knowledge of the Welsh language and Welsh literature, and perhaps it is not ungenerous to say a good deal of Borrovian ignorance too. For never was Nature's love of whim in the fashioning of individuals more delightfully exemplified than in the case of Borrow's irresistible desire for scholarship. Nothing whatever had he of the temperament of the true scholar—nothing whatever of the philologist's endowment, and yet to be recognized as a scholar was the great ambitious dream of his life. I wish I had time to compare his disquisitions upon the Welsh language and literature in this article with a very rare little book on the same subject, the "Sketch of the History of the Welsh Language and Literature," by a remarkable man as entirely forgotten now as Borrow is well remembered—Thomas Watts of the British Museum. In the one case we get nebulous speculation and fanciful induction based upon Borrovian knowledge ; in the other, a solid mass of real learning accompanied by the smallest possible amount of speculation or fanciful induction.

Borrow had a certain something of Mezzofanti's prodigious memory for words, accompanied by the great Italian's lack of philological science. It may be remembered in this connection that Mr. Thomas St. E. Hake in his reminiscences in *Notes and Queries* of a relation of mine, the late Mr. James Orlando Watts, says that the learned recluse used to express a good deal of humorous contempt of Borrow's "method of learning languages from dictionaries only," without any grammatical knowledge. And these strictures, if we consider them, will explain much in regard to the philological disquisitions in "Lavengro," "The Romany Rye," and "Wild Wales," where the knowledge Is all "dictionary knowledge." But it was not the shaky philology that caused "Wild Wales" to fall almost dead from the press. What, then, was the cause ? It arose from the fact, as I hinted above, that "Wild Wales" belongs to a different kind of autobiographic narrative from "Lavengro" and "The Romany Rye," and also, if the truth must be said, from "The Bible in Spain."

At the period when Borrow wrote this book the great and vigorous renascence of the Cymric idea, the new and deep interest that Welshmen are now taking in the preservation of the Welsh tongue, had not begun. That Borrow did not live to this day, when Welsh is much more spoken among the cultivated class than in his time, is to be lamented. With regard to this revival, whatever may become of it (whether the Welsh language can really be made to survive in the great linguistic struggle for life, which will be one of the principal features of the twentieth century), no one will deny that it is a language which from the poetic side as well as from the historic ought to survive. If I tread here upon dangerous ground, I may yet venture to say that one great obstacle against the spread of the Welsh language beyond Wales is the strange orthography. It is difficult for a person unacquainted with Welsh to believe that the sounds represented by such awkward arrangements of consonants as Welsh displays are otherwise than unmusical. And yet as a matter of fact those sounds are very musical. It may be remarked here that there is another language spoken in Europe which suffers from the same misfortune in regard to phonetics—the Magyar language. I have elsewhere in a novel, whose scene is partly laid in Hungary, made a character speak of the disappointment expressed by the traveller in Central Europe, when crossing the Austrian frontier into Hungary by rail, at the sight of the Hungarian names with which the stations become suddenly placarded. German is an ugly-looking language enough, but in this respect it is nothing to the Hungarian. And yet it would be hard to find in the whole of Europe a more musical tongue than that which is represented by the uncouth consonantal syllables. It is not a little striking too that between the Cymric race and the Magyar race there are many points of likeness ; one of these is the intense love of music displayed by the two, another is the blending of poetic imagination with practical sagacity. The Magyars have been called a race of lawyers, but their love of law-points and litigation is not greater than that of the Welsh, and yet how poetical is each race to the core !

With regard to languages—to survive will in the present century mean to spread. Languages that do not spread will be crushed out. People who talk glibly about the vast expansion of the English language all over the world do not seem to realize that it is not the excellence of a tongue which makes it survive and causes it to spread over the earth, but the energy, military or commercial, of the people who speak it. It is not the excellence of the tongue of Shakespeare and Milton that has carried it all round the globe, but the busy energy of the commonplace people who migrated for the most commonplace ends imaginable, and took the language with them, and then increased and multiplied, building up new English-speaking communities. It is for this reason that the English language seems destined to become, if not the "universal language," at least the *lingua franca* of the world. And nothing is more pathetic than to observe the dread among Continental nations that this will be the case in the future ; and nothing is more humorous than the passionate attempts to invent artificial languages, Volapük, Esperanto and what not, to do the work that the English language is already doing all over the sea, and will, apparently, soon be doing all over the land.

I dwell here upon this interesting subject in order to say that if Welsh does not survive it will not be because it is not a fine language, but simply because Destiny has decreed that it shall share the fate of many another language spoken at present much more widely than Welsh.

III

IS NOT "WILD WALES" WRITTEN BY A CELT AND NOT BY AN ANGLO-SAXON?

IN speaking of any one of Borrow's books it is always necessary to say a good deal about Borrow as a man. Besides being the very child of Nature's fantasy, he was the prince of literary egotists. Everything in human life and everything in nature upon which he looked was enveloped in a coloured atmosphere shed by the eccentric ego. That his love of Wales was genuine there can be no doubt whatever. For this there was perhaps a very special reason—a reason quite unrecognized by himself. I have somewhere—but I forget where—remarked upon a curious and common mistake in regard to Borrow— I mean the mistake of speaking of him as an East Anglian. Very gratifying was this mistake to Borrow himself. When walking with me in Richmond Park, or elsewhere, he would frequently stop, look round and murmur, "Beautiful England!" and then begin to declare eloquently that there was not in the world a country to be compared with it, and that the race which lived in this beloved land was equally incomparable in most things, especially in what he valued so much—athleticism in all its forms. This was merely because England was his place of birth. Born in East Anglia he was, to be sure; but Dr. Johnson long ago held to the opinion that a man born in a stable need not necessarily be described as a horse. When a man's father is pure Cornish (Celtic) and when his mother is mainly French, the fact of his having been born in Norfolk is not enough to make him an East Anglian. By an accident the regiment to which his father belonged was located in Norfolk at the time of his birth, just as by an accident it might have been located in Ireland or Scotland. In either of these cases he would have been George Borrow the Celt, or rather, George

Borrow the Unique, but not a Scotsman—not an Irishman. It is the blood in a man's veins, it is not the spot in which he is born, that decides the question of his race. Does one call the daughters of the Irishman, Patrick Brontë, who were Celtic to the marrow, Yorkshire girls because they were born at Thornton? Does one call Mr. Swinburne a Londoner because he, a Northumbrian by a long line of ancestors, chanced to be born within a stone's-throw of Belgrave Square? Does one call the Rossettis Londoners, because it was in London, and not in Italy, that they were born? To imagine any man more Celtic than Borrow is impossible. Not a single East Anglian characteristic exhibited by him do I remember—except perhaps his Norfolk accent, and his very worthy and exemplary passion for "boiled leg of mutton with turnips and caper sauce," which he pronounced to be "food for the gods." It was his own way of writing and talking about himself, however, that fostered if it did not originate the conception that Borrow was an East Anglian. There is no more unreasonable, as there is no more winsome, trait in human nature than the form of egotism which I will call provincial patriotism— a quality of which Borrow was so full. No matter what unlovely spot in any country had given Borrow birth, it would have become in his eyes sanctified because of the all-important fact that it gave birth to George Borrow, the "word-master." Rest assured that had he been a fenman he would have been as proud of his treeless, black-earthed fen as he would have been proud of the Swiss mountains had his birthplace chanced to be Switzerland. Rest assured that had he been born upon the barren soil of Damaraland he would have been proud of his desert, as proud as he would have been of any hilly district that had chanced to have the honour of giving him birth. But being born in East Anglia, to feel that he was the typical Anglo-Saxon of all Anglo-Saxons around him, gave him a mighty joy. At "The Bald-faced Stag" his eloquent addresses, to me and the little band of friends who loved him, about Norfolk ale were inspired by the same cause. Compared to that East Anglian nectar all other nectars were "swipes." I know East Anglia well; few men know it better—few men love it better. I say emphatically that a man more out of sympathy with the East Anglian temperament never lived than he who wished to be taken, and was taken, as the representative East Anglian. Moreover, one very potent reason why he was such a failure in

Norfolk—one very potent reason why he was such a failure in his contact with the Anglo-Saxon race generally—was this : he was a Celtic duckling hatched at Dereham, who took himself for a veritable Norfolk chicken. It is no wonder, therefore, that, without knowing it, his sympathy with the Celt, especially the Cymric Celt, which he himself fully believed to be philological, was racial.

The scenery of Wales had a very especial appeal for him, and no wonder ; for there is nothing like it in the world. Although I am familiar with the Alps and the other mountain ranges of Europe in their wildest and most beautiful recesses, it is with me as it was with Borrow : no hill scenery has the peculiar witchery of that around Eryri. It is unique in the scenery of Europe. Grander scenery there is on the Continent, no doubt—much grander—and scenery more soft and lovely ; but none in which grandeur and loveliness meet and mingle in so fascinating a way as in Wales. Moreover, to Borrow, as to all lovers of Wild Wales, beautiful as its scenery is, it is the romantic associations of that scenery which form so large a portion of its charm. For what race in Europe has a story so poetic, so romantic, so pathetic as the Welsh ? Over every inch of the Principality hovers that great Spirit who walks the earth hand in hand with his brother, the Spirit of Poetry, and throws a rainbow radiance over it—the Spirit of Antiquity. Upon this Borrow and the writer of these lines have often talked. No man ever felt more deeply than he that part and parcel of the very life of man is the atmosphere in which the Spirit of Antiquity lives. Irrational the sentiment about this Spirit may be, if you will, but stifled it will never be. Physical science strengthens rather than weakens the magical glamour of the Spirit of Antiquity. Even the most advanced social science, try to hate him as it may, cannot dim his glory. To the beloved poet of the socialists—William Morris—he was as dear, as great and as strong as to the most conservative poet that has ever lived. Those who express wonderment that in these days there should be the old human playthings as bright and captivating as ever— those who express wonderment at the survival of all the delightful features of the old European raree-show—have not realized the power of this Spirit and the power of the sentiment about him. What is the use of telling us that even in Grecian annals there is no kind of heroism recorded which you cannot match in the histories of modern countries—even of new countries, such as the United States and the Australias and Canada ? What is the use of telling us that the travels of Ulysses and of Jason are as nothing in point of real romance compared with Captain Phillip's voyage to the other side of the world, when he led his little convict-laden fleet to Botany Bay— a bay then as unknown almost as any bay in Laputa—that voyage which resulted in the founding of a cluster of great nations any one of whose mammoth millionaires could now buy up Ilium and the golden fleece combined ? The Spirit of Antiquity knows not that captain, and hence the Spirit of Poetry has nothing to say about him. In a thousand years' time, no doubt, these things may be as ripe for poetic treatment as the voyage of the Argonauts, or the voyage of the Cymric Prince Madoc, who the romantic lover of Wales, in spite of the arguments of Thomas Stephens, will still believe sailed westward with his fleet and discovered America before Columbus, —returned, and then sailed westward again into eternity. Now every peak and cliff of Snowdonia, and every matchless valley and dale of the land of the Druids, is very specially beloved by the Spirit of Antiquity. The land of Druidism —the land of that mysterious poetic religion which more than any other religion expresses the very voice of Nature, is the land painted in this delightful volume—Wild Wales. Compared with Druidism, all other religious systems have a sort of commonplace and modern ring, even those which preceded it by centuries. The scenic witchery of Wild Wales is great, no doubt, but it is enormously intensified by the memory of the heroic struggle of the unconquerable remnant of the ancient Britons with the brutal, physical power of Roman and Saxon. The history of Wales is an epic not to be surpassed for poetry and for romance. And even these things did not comprise all the points in connection with Wild Wales that delighted Borrow. For when the student of Welsh history and the lover of Welsh scenery is brought into contact with the contemporary Welsh people, the charm of the land does not fade, it is not fingered away by personal contact : it is, indeed, augmented tenfold. I have in "Aylwin" dwelt upon the poetry of Welsh common life, the passionate love of the Welsh people for a tiny strip of Welsh soil, the religion of hearth and home, the devotion to wife and children. In the Arvon edition of that book, dedicated to a Welsh poet, I have said what I had previously often said to Borrow, that, "although I have seen a good deal of the races of Europe, I put the Cymric race in many ways at the top of them all. They combine, as I think, the poetry, the music, the instinctive love of the fine arts, and the humour of the other Celtic peoples with the practicalness and bright-eyed sagacity of the very different race to which they were so closely linked by circumstance—the race whom it is the fashion to call the Anglo-Saxon. And as to the charm of the Welsh girls, no one who knows them as you and I do, can fail to be struck by it continually. Winifred Wynne I meant to be the typical Welsh girl as I have found her—affectionate, warm-hearted, self-sacrificing and brave."

IV

BORROW'S METHOD OF AUTOBIOGRAPHIC NARRATIVE COM-
PARED WITH THE METHODS OF DEFOE, WILKIE COLLINS,
DICKENS AND THE ABBÉ PRÉVOST

IT seems almost necessary that in this desultory talk upon " Wild Wales " I should, before proceeding any further, say a few words upon the book in its relations to two of Borrow's other autobiographic narratives, " Lavengro " and " The Romany Rye," and I do not know any literary subject more suggestive of interesting criticism.

Although Borrow always acknowledged Defoe as his master, he had, of course, qualities of his own that were as unlike Defoe's qualities as they were unlike those of any other writer. And as this speciality of his has, so far as I know, never been discussed, I should have liked, had space permitted, to give interest to my remarks upon " Wild Wales " by a thorough comparison between Borrow's imaginative works and Defoe's " Robinson Crusoe." This is impossible in the space at my command. And yet a few words upon the subject I cannot resist indulging in, for it relates to the very core and central light of Borrow's genius ; and I may now never have another opportunity of touching upon it.

I remember a long talk I once had with him upon the method of Defoe as contrasted and compared with his own method in " Lavengro," " The Romany Rye," and " Wild Wales," and the method of other writers who adopt the autobiographic form of fiction. He agreed with me that the most successful of all stories in the autobiographic form is " Robinson Crusoe,' although "Jane Eyre," "David Copperfield" and "Great Expectations" among English novels, and "Gil Blas" and "Manon Lescaut" among French novels, are also autobiographic in form. It is of all forms the most difficult. But its advantages, if they can be secured without making too many artistic sacrifices, are enormous. Flexibility is, of course, the one quality it lacks, but, lacking that, it cannot secure the variety of picture and the breadth of movement which is the special strength of the historic form.

The great pupils of Defoe—and by pupils I mean those writers who try to give as much commonplace ἀπάτη as possible to new and striking incidents—Edgar Poe, Wilkie Collins, Gaboriau and others, recognize the immense aid given to illusion by adopting the autobiographic form.

The conversation upon this subject occurred in one of my rambles with Borrow and Dr. Gordon Hake in Richmond Park, when I had been pointing out to the former certain passages in "Robinson Crusoe" where Defoe adds richness and piquancy to the incidents by making the reader believe that these incidents will in the end have some deep influence, spiritual or physical, upon the narrator himself.

Borrow was not a theorizer, and yet he took a quaint interest in other people's theorizings. He asked me to explain myself more fully. My reply in substance was something like this: Although in "Robinson Crusoe" the autobiographer is really introduced only to act as eye-witness for the purpose of bringing out and authenticating the incidents of the dramatic action, Defoe had the artistic craftiness to make it appear that this was not so—to make it appear that the incidents are selected by Crusoe in such a way as to exhibit and develop the emotions moving within his own breast. Defoe's *apparent* object in writing the story was to show the effect of a long solitude upon the human heart and mind ; but it was not so—it was simply to bring into fiction a series of incidents and adventures of extraordinary interest and picturesqueness—incidents such as did in part happen to Alexander Selkirk. But Defoe was a much greater artist than he is generally credited with being, and he had sufficient of the artistic instinct to know that, interesting as these external incidents were in themselves, they could be made still more interesting by humanizing them—by making it appear that they worked as a great life-lesson for the man who experienced them, and that this was why the man recorded them. Those moralizings of Crusoe upon the way in which the disasters of his life came upon him as " judgments," on account of his running away from his parents, seem to humanize the wheels of circumstance. They create in the reader's mind the interest in the man's personality which Defoe wished to create.

In reply to my criticism, Borrow said, " May not the same be said of Le Sage's ' Gil Blas '?"

And when I pointed out to him that there was a kind of kinship between the two writers in this particular he asked me to indicate in " Lavengro " and " The Romany Rye " such incidents in which Defoe's method had been followed by himself as had struck me. I pointed out several of them. Borrow, as a rule, was not at all given to frank discussion of his own artistic methods, indeed, he had a great deal of the instinct of the literary *histrio*—more than I have ever seen in any other writer—but he admitted that he had consciously in part and in part unconsciously adopted Defoe's method. The fact is, as I said to Borrow on that occasion, and as I have since had an opportunity of saying more fully in print, there are two kinds of autobiographic stories, and these two kinds are, if properly examined, really more unlike each other than the autobiographic form is unlike what is generally supposed to be its antithesis—the historic form. In one kind of autobiographic story, of which " Rob Roy " is a typical example, the narrator, though nominally the protagonist, is really not much more than the passive eye-witness of the dramatic action—not much more than the chorus to other characters who govern, or at least influence, the main issue. Inasmuch as he is an eye-witness of the dramatic action, he gives to it the authenticity of direct testimony. Through him the narrative gains a commonplace ἀπάτη such as is beyond the scope of the scattered forces of the historic form, howsoever powerfully handled. By the first-hand testimony of the eye-witness Frank Osbaldistone in Scott's fascinating novel, the more active characters, those who really control the main issue, Di Vernon, Rashleigh Osbaldistone, Rob, and Bailie Nicol Jarvie, are painted in much more vivid and much more authentic colours than the method of the historic form would allow.

It is in the nature of things that this kind of autobiographic fiction, howsoever strong may be the incidents, is not nearly so absorbing as is the other kind I am going to instance, the psychological, to which " Lavengro " and " The Romany Rye " belong ;

for in literature, as in life, the more interest we feel in the character, the more interest we feel in what befalls the character. Unlike the kind of autobiographic fiction typified by " Rob Roy," in which, as I have said, the main issue is little influenced and not at all controlled by the narrator but by other characters, or, if not by other characters, by the wheels of circumstance ;—in the psychological kind of autobiographic fiction, the personality of the narrator controls, or largely controls, the main issue of the dramatic action. In other words, the incidents in the latter kind of autobiographic fiction are selected and marshalled for the purpose of declaring the character of the narrator. The most superb exemplars of this kind of autobiographic narrative are stories which in all other respects are extremely unlike Borrow's—" Caleb Williams," " Manon Lescaut," " Jane Eyre," and " Villette."

A year or two ago I recurred to this subject in some comments I made upon some judgments of a well-known and admirable critic. I will take the liberty of referring here to one or two of the remarks I then made, for they seem to bear very directly upon Borrow's method as compared with Defoe's. The same artistic instinct which we see in Defoe and in Borrow's quasi autobiographic work is exhibited by the Abbé Prévost in " Manon Lescaut." The real object of the last-mentioned story (which, it will be remembered, is an episode in a much longer story) was to paint vivid pictures of the careless life of Paris at the period of the story, and especially to paint in vivid colours a kind of character which is essentially peculiar to Paris, the light-hearted, good-natured, unheeding *grisette*. But by making it appear that the incidents in Chevalier des Grieux's life are selected by him in order to show the effect of the life-lesson upon himself, Prévost gives to every incident the piquancy which properly belongs to this, the psychological form of autobiographic fiction. It must, however, be admitted that at its best the autobiographic form of fiction is rarely, very rarely, broad enough to be a satisfactory form of art, even when, as in " The Woman in White," the story consists of a series of autobiographic narratives stitched together. It was this difficulty which confronted Dickens when he wrote " Bleak House." When he was writing " David Copperfield " he had felt the sweetness and fascination of writing in the autobiographic form, and had seen the sweetness and fascination of reading it ; but he also felt how constricted the form is in regard to breadth, and it occurred to him that he could combine the two forms—that he could give in the same book the sweetness and the fascination and the authenticity of the autobiographic form and the breadth and variety of the historic form. To bring into an autobiographic narrative the complex and wide-spreading net that forms the story of "Bleak House" was, of course, impossible, and so he mixed up the chapters of Esther Summerson's autobiographic narrative with chapters of the history of the great Chancery suit and all that flowed from it. In order to minimize as much as possible the confusion of so very confused a scheme as this, he wrote the historic part of the book in the present tense ; and the result is the most oppressively-laboured novel that was ever produced by a great novelist.

I have dwelt at length upon this subject because if I were asked to name one of the greatest masters of the autobiographic form, in any language, I should, I think, have to name Borrow. In one variety of that form he gave us "Lavengro" and "The Romany Rye," in the other, "Wild Wales."

V

WHY ARE THE WELSH GYPSIES IGNORED IN "WILD WALES"?

"Wild Wales" seems to have disappointed Borrovians because it ignores the Welsh gypsies, the most superior branch of all the Romany race, except, perhaps, the gypsy musicians of Hungary. And certainly it is curious to speculate as to why he ignores them in that fashion. Readers of "The Romany Rye" wonder why, after his adventure with Mrs. Herne and her granddaughter, and his rescue by the Welshman, Peter Williams, on reaching the Welsh border, Borrow kept his mouth closed. Several reasons have occurred to me, one of which is that his knowledge of Welsh Romany was of the shakiest kind. Another reason might have been that in "The Romany Rye," as much of his story as could be told in two volumes being told, he abruptly broke off as he had broken off at the end of the third volume of "Lavengro." Or did the same reason that caused him to write, in "Wild Wales," an autobiographic narrative without any of the fantasies and romantic ornamentation which did so much to win popularity for his previous books, govern him when he decided to ignore the gypsies—the presence of his wife and stepdaughter ? There is a very wide class, including indeed the whole of British Philistia, that cherishes a positive racial aversion to the Romany—an aversion as strong as the Russian aversion to the Jew.

Anyhow, it was very eccentric to write a book upon Wales and to ignore so picturesque a feature of the subject as the Welsh gypsies. For, beyond doubt, the finest specimens of the Romany race are—or were in Borrow's time—to be found in Wales. And here I cannot help saying parenthetically, that as Borrow gave us no word about the Welsh Romanies and their language, the work of Mr. Sampson, the greatest master of the Welsh Romany that ever lived, is especially precious. So great is the work of that admirable scholar upon the subject that he told me when I last saw him that he was actually translating Omar Khayyám into Welsh Romany! Although the Welsh gypsies have a much greater knowledge of Welsh Romany than English gypsies have of English Romany, and are more intelligent, I am a little sceptical, as I told him, as to the Welsh Romanies taking that deep interest in the immortal quatrains which, it seems, atheists and Christians agree in doing among the gorgios.

VI

CELT *v* SAXON

THOSE who have seen much of the writing fraternity of London or Paris, know that the great mass of authors, whether in prose or in verse, have just as much and just as little individuality—have just as much and just as little of any new and true personal accent, as the vast flock of human sheep whose bleatings will soon drown all other voices over land and sea. They have the peculiar instinct for putting their thoughts into written words—that is all. This it is that makes Borrow such a memorable figure. If ever a man had an accent of his own that man was he. What that accent was I have tried to indicate here, in the remarks upon his method of writing autobiographic fiction. Vanity can make all, even the most cunning, simple on one side of their characters, but it made of Borrow a veritable child.

If Tennyson may be accepted as the type of the man without guile, what type does Borrow represent? In him guile and simplicity were blent in what must have been the most whimsical amalgam of opposite qualities ever seen on this planet. Let me give one instance out of a thousand of this.

Great as was his love of Wales and the Welsh, the Anglo-Saxonism—the John Bullism which he fondly cherished in that Celtic bosom of his, was so strong that whenever it came to pitting the prowess and the glories of the Welshman against those of the Englishman, his championship of the Cymric race would straightway vanish, and the claim of the Anglo-Saxon to superiority would be proclaimed against all the opposition of the world. This was especially so in regard to athletics, as was but natural, seeing that he always felt himself to be an athlete first, a writing man afterwards.

A favourite quotation of his was from Byron—

> "One hates an author that's *all author*—fellows
> In foolscap uniforms turned up with ink."

Frederick Sandys, a Norfolk man who knew him well, rarely spoke of Borrow save as a master in the noble art of self-defence.

It was as a swimmer I first saw him—one of the strongest and hardiest that ever rejoiced to buffet with wintry billows on the Norfolk coast. And to the very last did his interest in swimming, sparring, running, wrestling, jumping remain. If the Welshman would only have admitted that in athletics the Englishman stands first—stands easily first among the competitors of the world, he would have cheerfully admitted that the Welshman made a good second. General Picton used to affirm that the ideal—the topmost soldier in the world is a Welshman of five feet, eight inches in height. Such a man as the six-feet-three giant of Dereham knew well how to scorn such an assertion even though made by the great Picton himself. But suppose Borrow had been told, as we have lately been told, that the so-called "English archers" at Crecy and Agincourt were mainly made up of Welshmen, what a flush would have overspread his hairless cheek, what an indignant fire would have blazed from his eyes! Not even his indignation on being told, as we would sometimes tell him at "The Bald-faced Stag," that Scottish Highlanders had proved themselves superior to their English brothers-in-arms would have equalled his scorn of such talk about Crecy and Agincourt—scenes of English prowess that he was never tired of extolling.

But you had only to admit that Welshmen were superior to all others save Englishmen in physical prowess, and Borrow's championship of the Cymric athlete could be as enthusiastic and even as aggressive as the best and most self-assertive Welshman ever born in Arvon. Consequently I can but regret that he did not live to see the great recrudescence of Cymric energy which we are seeing at the present moment in " Cymru, gwlad y gân," —an energy which is declaring itself more vigorously every day, and not merely in pure intellectual matters, not merely in political matters, but equally in those same athletics which to Borrow were so important. Sparring has gone out of fashion as much in the Principality as in England and Scotland ; but that which has succeeded it, football, has taken a place in athleticism such as would have bewildered Borrow, as it would have bewildered most of his contemporaries. What would he have said, I wonder, had he been told that in this favourite twentieth-century game the Welsh would surpass all others in these islands, and save the honour of Great Britain ? No one would have enjoyed witnessing the great contest between the Welsh and the New Zealand athletes at the Cardiff Arms Park on the 16th of last December with more gusto than the admirer of English sparring and of the English pugilistic heroes, from Big Ben Bryan to Tom Spring. No one would have been more exhilarated than he by the song with which it opened—

"Mae hen wlad fy nhadau yn anwyl i mi." [1]

But one wonders what he would have said after the struggle was over—after Wales's latest triumph over the Saxon record of physical prowess. One can imagine, perhaps, his mixed feelings had he been a witness of that great athletic struggle which is going to be historic—the immortal contest in which after England had succumbed entirely to the Colonials, the honour of the old country was saved by Wales at the eleventh hour. His cheek would have glowed with admiration of the exploits of the only footballers whose names will be historic, and being historic must be mentioned in connection with his own Welsh pages,—I mean the names of Travers, of Bush, of Winfield, of Owen, of Jones, of Llewellyn, of Gabe, of Nicholls, of Morgan, of Williams, of Hodges, of Harding, of Joseph, and the names of the two Pritchards. Whatsoever might have been his after-emotions when provincial patriotism began to assert itself, Borrow would in that great hour of Cymric triumph have frankly admitted, I think, that for once England's honour was saved by Wales.

---

[1] " The old land of my father is dear unto me."

ITINERARY

CHAPTER		PAGE
I.	Proposed Excursion	5
II.	The Start, Peterborough, Birmingham	10
III.	Chester	14
IV.	Chester, Camp-meeting	19
V.	Chester, Book-Stall, Wrexham	24
VI.	Llangollen, the Dee	30
VII.	Llangollen, Lodgings	34
VIII.	The Robber's Leap	37
IX.	Llangollen, Pengwern	43
X.	The Berwyn	48
XI.	Pont Fadog	50
XII.	Pont y Cysswllt	58
XIII.	Llangollen, the Abbey of the Vale of the Cross	64
XIV.	Expedition to Ruthyn, the Column	69
XV.	The Turf Tavern, Ruthyn	74
XVI.	Return from Ruthyn, Agricola's Hill	80
XVII.	Llangollen, Plas Newydd, Llyn Ceiriog	84
XVIII.	Llangollen, the Parish Clerk	92
XIX.	Llangollen, the Vicar, the Pool of Catherine Lingo, Robber's Leap	100
XX.	The Valley of Ceiriog, Huw Morris's Chair, Pont y Meibion	107
XXI.	Pandy Teirw	116
XXII.	Llangollen Fair	124
XXIII.	Pont y Pandy, Glendower's Mount, Corwen	125
XXIV.	The Rock of Heroes, the Italian at the Inn	134
XXV.	On the way to Bangor, the Irishman	142

CHAPTER		PAGE
XXVI.	Pentre Voelas, the Conway, Swallow Falls, Capel Curig	149
XXVII.	Bangor	159
XXVIII.	Menai bridges	165
XXIX.	Snowdon, the Wyddfa	172
XXX.	Gronwy Owen	179
XXXI.	Anglesea, Pentraeth Coch	181
XXXII.	Llanfair Mathafarn Eithaf, the Birthplace of Gronwy Owen	186
XXXIII.	The Inn at Pentraeth Coch	199
XXXIV.	Conversation at the Inn	203
XXXV.	A Brilliant Morning	206
XXXVI.	Leaving Pentraeth Coch, Penmynnydd, Tomb of Owen Tudor	209
XXXVII.	Dyffryn Gaint	213
XXXVIII.	The Inn at L———	225
XXXIX.	Bound for Holy Head	231
XL.	Caer Gybi	237
XLI.	The Pier	240
XLII.	Town of Holy Head, Pen Caer Gybi . . .	244
XLIII.	Bangor, Port Dyn Norwig, Caernarvon . . .	251
XLIV.	Pont Bettws, Llyn Cwellyn	255
XLV.	Inn at Bethgelert	265
XLVI.	The Valley of Gelert	267
XLVII.	Tan y Bwlch, Festiniog	273
XLVIII.	Mynydd Mawr and Mynydd Bach, Tref y Talcot .	279
XLIX.	Bala	288
L.	The Tomen Bala	298
LI.	Back at Llangollen	300
LII.	Llangollen, Attempted Murder	304
LIII.	Pen y Coed	308
LIV.	Chirk	310
LV.	Llangollen, Some of the Inhabitants . . .	320
LVI.	Llangollen, News of the Fall of Sebastopol . .	324
LVII.	Pentré y Dwr	329
LVIII.	Sunday at Llangollen	334
LIX.	Llangollen, History of Twm O'r Nant . . .	338
LX.	Twm O'r Nant, his Interludes	348
LXI.	Walk to Wrexham, Methodistical Volume . .	354
LXII.	Rhiwabon Road	360
LXIII.	Last Night at Llangollen	364

CHAPTER		PAGE
LXIV.	Departure for South Wales	367
LXV.	Inn at Llan Rhyadr	373
LXVI.	Sycharth	378
LXVII.	Llan Silin	384
LXVIII.	Llan Silin Church, Tomb of Huw Morris	388
LXIX.	Church of Llan Rhyadr	393
LXX.	Rhyadr, Mountain Scenery	395
LXXI.	Wild Moors, Arrival at Bala	398
LXXII.	Bala, The White Lion	403
LXXIII.	Llyn Tegid	409
LXXIV.	Bala to Dinas Mawddwy	414
LXXV.	Inn at Mallwydd	423
LXXVI.	Mallwydd and its Church, Cemmaes	424
LXXVII.	The Vale of Dyfi	428
LXXVIII.	Machynlleth	432
LXXIX.	Machynlleth, Historic Events	438
LXXX.	Machynlleth to Esgyrn Hirion	442
LXXXI.	The Mining Compting Room	450
LXXXII.	Inn at Pont Erwyd	457
LXXXIII.	Conversation at the inn and on the way to the Devil's Bridge	465
LXXXIV.	The Devil's Bridge	474
LXXXV.	Dinner at the Hospice	477
LXXXVI.	Dafydd Ab Gwilym	481
LXXXVII.	Start for Plynlimmon	489
LXXXVIII.	Plynlimmon, and back to the Devil's Bridge	491
LXXXIX.	Hafod	499
XC.	Spytty Ystwyth	503
XCI.	Strata Florida, burial-place of Dafydd Ab Gwilym	507
XCII.	Rhyd Fendigaid to Tregaron	512
XCIII.	Tregaron Church	523
XCIV.	Llan Ddewi Brefi	527
XCV.	Lampeter to the Bridge of Twrch	532
XCVI.	Llandovery	539
XCVII.	Llandovery Church	544
XCVIII.	Llandovery to Gutter Vawr	553
XCIX.	Inn at Gutter Vawr	561
C.	Gutter Vawr to Swansea	568
CI.	Swansea	579
CII.	Swansea to Neath	581

CHAPTER		PAGE
CIII.	Town of Neath, the Glowing Mountain . . .	583
CIV.	Merthyr Tydvil	586
CV.	Start for Caerfili	589
CVI.	Pen y Glas to Caerfili	599
CVII.	Caerfili	602
CVIII.	Town of Newport	606
CIX.	Arrival at Chepstow	616

The following is a list of the works of George Borrow—

Faustus, His Life and Death [from the German of F. M. von Klinger], 1825; Romantic Ballads [from the Danish of Öhlenschläger, and from the Kiempé Viser], and miscellaneous pieces [from the Danish of Ewald and others], 1826 ; Targum, or Metrical Translations from Thirty Languages and Dialects, 1835 ; The Talisman of A. Pushkin, with other pieces [from Russian and Polish], 1835; New Testament (Luke), Embéo e Majaró Lucas . . . El Evangelio segun S. Lucas, traducido al Romani, 1837 ; The Bible in Spain, 3 vols., 1843 ; The Zincali (Gypsies of Spain), 2 vols., 1841 ; Lavengro : The Scholar—The Gypsy—The Priest, 3 vols., 1851 ; The Romany Rye, 2 vols., 1857 ; The Sleeping Bard, translated from the Cambrian British, 1860 ; Wild Wales, 3 vols., 1862 ; Romano Lavo-Lil : Word-Book of the Romany, 1874 ; Násr Al-Din, Khwájah, The Turkish Jester [from the Turkish], 1884 ; Death of Balder [from the Danish of Ewald], 1889.

The Life, Writings, and Correspondence of George Borrow, in 2 vols., by Dr. W. I. Knapp, appeared in 1899. Those who are specially interested in Borrow's philological acquirements, or deficiencies, will do well to consult the editions of "Lavengro" by Dr. Knapp (1900), and F. Hindes Groome (2 vols., 1901), and that of "Romany Rye," by John Sampson (1903). The "Isopel Berners" episode, excerpted from "Lavengro" and "Romany Rye," was edited and annotated by Thomas Seccombe in 1901.

WILD WALES

ITS PEOPLE, LANGUAGE, AND SCENERY

CHAPTER I

Proposed Excursion—Knowledge of Welsh—Singular Groom—
Harmonious Distich — Welsh Pronunciation — Dafydd Ab
Gwilym.

In the summer of the year 1854 myself, wife, and
daughter determined upon going into Wales, to pass
a few months there. We are country people of a
corner of East Anglia, and, at the time of which I am
speaking, had been residing so long on our own little
estate, that we had become tired of the objects around
us, and conceived that we should be all the better for
changing the scene for a short period. We were
undetermined for some time with respect to where
we should go. I proposed Wales from the first, but
my wife and daughter, who have always had rather a
hankering after what is fashionable, said they thought
it would be more advisable to go to Harrowgate or
Leamington. On my observing that those were
terrible places for expense, they replied that, though
the price of corn had of late been shamefully low, we
had a spare hundred pounds or two in our pockets,
and could afford to pay for a little insight into fashionable life. I told them that there was nothing I so
much hated as fashionable life, but that, as I was
anything but a selfish person, I would endeavour to
stifle my abhorrence of it for a time, and attend them
either to Leamington or Harrowgate. By this speech

I obtained my wish, even as I knew I should, for my wife and daughter instantly observed, that, after all, they thought we had better go into Wales, which, though not so fashionable as either Leamington or Harrowgate, was a very nice picturesque country, where, they had no doubt, they should get on very well, more especially as I was acquainted with the Welsh language.

It was my knowledge of Welsh, such as it was, that made me desirous that we should go to Wales, where there was a chance that I might turn it to some little account. In my boyhood I had been something of a philologist; had picked up some Latin and Greek at school; some Irish in Ireland, where I had been with my father, who was in the army; and subsequently whilst an articled clerk to the first solicitor in East Anglia—indeed I may say the prince of all English solicitors—for he was a gentleman, had learnt some Welsh, partly from books and partly from a Welsh groom, whose acquaintance I had made. A queer groom he was, and well deserving of having his portrait drawn. He might be about forty-seven years of age, and about five feet eight inches in height; his body was spare and wiry; his chest rather broad, and his arms remarkably long; his legs were of the kind generally known as spindle-shanks, but vigorous withal, for they carried his body with great agility; neck he had none, at least that I ever observed; and his head was anything but high, not measuring, I should think, more than four inches from the bottom of the chin to the top of the forehead; his cheek-bones were high, his eyes grey and deeply sunken in his face, with an expression in them, partly sullen, and partly irascible; his complexion was indescribable; the little hair which he had, which was almost entirely on the sides and the back part of his head, was of an iron-grey hue. He wore a leather hat on ordinary days, low at the crown, and with the side eaves turned up. A dirty pepper and salt coat, a waistcoat which had once been red, but which had lost its pristine colour, and looked brown; dirty yellow leather breeches, grey worsted stockings, and high-lows. Surely I was right when I said he was a very different groom to those of

the present day, whether Welsh or English? What
say you, Sir Watkin? What say you, my Lord of
Exeter? He looked after the horses, and occasionally
assisted in the house of a person who lived at the end
of an alley, in which the office of the gentleman to
whom I was articled was situated, and having to pass
by the door of the office half-a-dozen times in the day,
he did not fail to attract the notice of the clerks, who,
sometimes individually, sometimes by twos, sometimes
by threes, or even more, not unfrequently stood at
the door, bareheaded—mis-spending the time which
was not legally their own. Sundry observations, none
of them very flattering, did the clerks and, amongst
them, myself, make upon the groom, as he passed and
repassed, some of them direct, others somewhat
oblique. To these he made no reply save by looks,
which had in them something dangerous and menacing,
and clenching without raising his fists, which looked
singularly hard and horny. At length a whisper ran
about the alley that the groom was a Welshman; this
whisper much increased the malice of my brother clerks
against him, who were now whenever he passed the
door, and they happened to be there by twos or threes,
in the habit of saying something, as if by accident,
against Wales and Welshmen, and, individually or
together, were in the habit of shouting out "Taffy,"
when he was at some distance from them, and his back
was turned, or regaling his ears with the harmonious
and well-known distich of "Taffy was a Welshman,
Taffy was a thief: Taffy came to my house and stole
a piece of beef." It had, however, a very different
effect upon me. I was trying to learn Welsh, and the
idea occurring to me that the groom might be able to
assist me in my pursuit, I instantly lost all desire to
torment him, and determined to do my best to scrape
acquaintance with him, and persuade him to give me
what assistance he could in Welsh. I succeeded; how
I will not trouble the reader with describing: he and I
became great friends, and he taught me what Welsh he
could. In return for his instructions I persuaded my
brother clerks to leave off holloing after him, and to do
nothing further to hurt his feelings, which had been
very deeply wounded, so much so, that after the first

two or three lessons he told me in confidence that on the morning of the very day I first began to conciliate him he had come to the resolution of doing one of two things, namely, either to hang himself from the balk of the hayloft, or to give his master warning, both of which things he told me he should have been very unwilling to do, more particularly as he had a wife and family. He gave me lessons on Sunday afternoons, at my father's house, where he made his appearance very respectably dressed, in a beaver hat, blue surtout, whitish waistcoat, black trowsers and Wellingtons, all with a somewhat ancient look—the Wellingtons I remember were slightly pieced at the sides—but all upon the whole very respectable. I wished at first to persuade him to give me lessons in the office, but could not succeed : " No, no, lad," said he ; " catch me going in there : I would just as soon venture into a nest of parcupines." To translate from books I had already, to a certain degree, taught myself, and at his first visit I discovered, and he himself acknowledged, that at book Welsh I was stronger than himself, but I learnt Welsh pronunciation from him, and to discourse a little in the Welsh tongue. " Had you much difficulty in acquiring the sound of the ll?" I think I hear the reader inquire. None whatever : the double l of the Welsh is by no means the terrible guttural which English people generally suppose it to be, being in reality a pretty liquid, exactly resembling in sound the Spanish ll, the sound of which I had mastered before commencing Welsh, and which is equivalent to the English lh ; so being able to pronounce llano I had of course no difficulty in pronouncing Lluyd, which by the bye was the name of the groom.

I remember that I found the pronunciation of the Welsh far less difficult than I had found the grammar, the most remarkable feature of which is the mutation, under certain circumstances, of particular consonants, when forming the initials of words. This feature I had observed in the Irish, which I had then only learnt by ear.

But to return to the groom. He was really a remarkable character, and taught me two or three things besides Welsh pronunciation ; and to discourse a little in Cumraeg. He had been a soldier in his youth, and had served under Moore and Wellington in the Peninsular campaigns, and from him I learnt the details of many a bloody field and bloodier storm, of the sufferings of poor British soldiers, and the tyranny of haughty British officers; more especially of the two commanders just mentioned, the first of whom he swore was shot by his own soldiers, and the second more frequently shot at by British than French. But it is not deemed a matter of good taste to write about such low people as grooms, I shall therefore dismiss him with no observation further than that after he had visited me on Sunday afternoons for about a year he departed for his own country with his wife, who was an Englishwoman, and his children, in consequence of having been left a small freehold there by a distant relation, and that I neither saw nor heard of him again.

But though I had lost my oral instructor I had still my silent ones, namely, the Welsh books, and of these I made such use that before the expiration of my clerkship I was able to read not only Welsh prose, but, what was infinitely more difficult, Welsh poetry in any of the four-and-twenty measures, and was well versed in the compositions of various of the old Welsh bards, especially those of Dafydd ab Gwilym, whom, since the time when I first became acquainted with his works, I have always considered as the greatest poetical genius that has appeared in Europe since the revival of literature.

After this exordium I think I may proceed to narrate the journey of myself and family into Wales. As perhaps, however, it will be thought that, though I have said quite enough about myself and a certain groom, I have not said quite enough about my wife and daughter, I will add a little more about them. Of my wife I will merely say that she is a perfect paragon of wives—can make puddings and sweets and treacle posset, and is the best woman of business in Eastern Anglia—of my step-daughter—for such she is, though I generally call her daughter, and with good reason, seeing that she has always shown herself a daughter to me—that she has all kinds of good qualities, and

several accomplishments, knowing something of
conchology, more of botany, drawing capitally in the
Dutch style, and playing remarkably well on the
guitar—not the trumpery German thing so-called—but
the real Spanish guitar.

CHAPTER II

The Starting—Peterborough Cathedral—Anglo-Saxon Names—
Kæmpe Viser—Steam—Norman Barons—Chester Ale—Sion
Tudor—Pretty Welsh Tongue.

So our little family, consisting of myself, my wife
Mary, and my daughter Henrietta, for daughter I shall
persist in calling her, started for Wales in the afternoon of the 27th July, 1854. We flew through part of
Norfolk and Cambridgeshire in a train which we left
at Ely, and getting into another, which did not fly
quite so fast as the one we had quitted, reached the
Peterborough station at about six o'clock of a
delightful evening. We proceeded no farther on our
journey that day, in order that we might have an
opportunity of seeing the cathedral.

Sallying arm in arm from the Station Hotel, where
we had determined to take up our quarters for the
night, we crossed a bridge over the deep quiet Nen,
on the southern bank of which stands the station, and
soon arrived at the cathedral—unfortunately we were
too late to procure admission into the interior, and
had to content ourselves with walking round it and
surveying its outside.

It is named after, and occupies the site, or part
of the site, of an immense monastery, founded by the
Mercian King Peda in the year 665, and destroyed by
fire in the year 1116, which monastery, though
originally termed Medeshamsted, or the homestead on
the meads, was subsequently termed Peterborough,
from the circumstance of its having been reared by the
old Saxon monarch for the love of God and the honour
of Saint Peter, as the Saxon Chronicle says, a book
which I went through carefully in my younger days,

when I studied Saxon, for, as I have already told the
reader, I was in those days a bit of a philologist.
Like the first, the second edifice was originally a
monastery, and continued so till the time of the
Reformation; both were abodes of learning; for if
the Saxon Chronicle was commenced in the monkish
cells of the first, it was completed in those of the
second. What is at present called Peterborough Cathedral is a noble venerable pile, equal upon the whole
in external appearance to the cathedrals of Toledo,
Burgos, and Leon, all of which I have seen. Nothing
in architecture can be conceived more beautiful than
the principal entrance, which fronts the west, and
which, at the time we saw it, was gilded with the
rays of the setting sun.

After having strolled about the edifice surveying it
until we were weary, we returned to our inn, and after
taking an excellent supper retired to rest.

At ten o'clock next morning we left the capital of
the meads. With dragon speed, and dragon noise,
fire, smoke, and fury, the train dashed along its road
through beautiful meadows, garnished here and there
with pollard sallows; over pretty streams, whose
waters stole along imperceptibly; by venerable old
churches, which I vowed I would take the first opportunity of visiting : stopping now and then to recruit
its energies at places, whose old Anglo-Saxon names
stared me in the eyes from station boards, as specimens of which, let me only dot down Willy Thorpe,
Ringsted, and Yrthling Boro. Quite forgetting everything Welsh, I was enthusiastically Saxon the whole
way from Medeshampsted to Blissworth, so thoroughly
Saxon was the country, with its rich meads, its old
churches, and its names. After leaving Blissworth,
a thoroughly Saxon place by the bye, as its name
shows signifying the stronghold or possession of Bligh
or Blee, I became less Saxon; the country was rather
less Saxon, and I caught occasionally the word " by "
on a board, the Danish for a town; which " by "
waked in me a considerable portion of Danish enthusiasm, of which I have plenty, and with reason,
having translated the glorious Kæmpe Viser over the
desk of my ancient master, the gentleman solicitor of

East Anglia. At length we drew near the great work-shop of England, called by some Brummagem or Bromwicham, by others Birmingham, and I fell into a philological reverie, wondering which was the right name. Before, however, we came to the station, I decided that both names were right enough, but that Bromwicham was the original name; signifying the home on the Broomie moor, which name it lost in polite parlance for Birmingham, or the home of the son of Biarmer, when a certain man of Danish blood, called Biarming, or the son of Biarmer, got possession of it, whether by force, fraud, or marriage— the latter, by the bye, is by far the best way of getting possession of an estate—this deponent neither knoweth nor careth. At Birmingham station I became a modern Englishman, enthusiastically proud of modern Eng-land's science and energy; that station alone is enough to make one proud of being a modern Englishman. Oh, what an idea does that station, with its thousand trains dashing off in all directions, or arriving from all quarters, give of modern English science and energy. My modern English pride accompanied me all the way to Tipton; for all along the route there were wonder-ful evidences of English skill and enterprise; in chimneys high as cathedral spires, vomiting forth smoke, furnaces emitting flame and lava, and in the sound of gigantic hammers, wielded by steam, the Englishman's slave. After passing Tipton, at which place one leaves the great working district behind, I became for a considerable time a yawning, listless Englishman, without pride, enthusiasm or feeling of any kind, from which state I was suddenly roused by the sight of ruined edifices on the tops of hills. They were remains of castles built by Norman barons. Here, perhaps, the reader will expect from me a burst of Norman enthusiasm : if so he will be mistaken; I have no Norman enthusiasm, and hate and abominate the name of Norman, for I have always associated that name with the deflowering of helpless English-women, the plundering of English homesteads, and the tearing out of poor Englishmen's eyes. The sight of those edifices, now in ruins, but which were once the strongholds of plunder, violence, and lust, made me almost ashamed of being an Englishman, for they brought to my mind the indignities to which poor English blood had been subjected. I sat silent and melancholy, till looking from the window I caught sight of a long line of hills, which I guessed to be the Welsh hills, as indeed they proved, which sight causing me to remember that I was bound for Wales, the land of the bard, made me cast all gloomy thoughts aside and glow with all the Welsh enthusiasm with which I glowed when I first started in the direction of Wales.

On arriving at Chester, at which place we intended to spend two or three days, we put up at an old-fashioned inn in Northgate Street, to which we had been recommended; my wife and daughter ordered tea and its accompaniments, and I ordered ale, and that which always should accompany it, cheese. "The ale I shall find bad," said I; Chester ale had a villainous character in the time of old Sion Tudor, who made a first-rate englyn upon it, and it has scarcely improved since; "but I shall have a treat in the cheese, Cheshire cheese has always been reckoned excellent, and now that I am in the capital of the cheese country, of course I shall have some of the very prime." Well, the tea, loaf, and butter made their appearance, and with them my cheese and ale. To my horror the cheese had much the appearance of soap of the commonest kind, which indeed I found it much resembled in taste, on putting a small portion into my mouth. "Ah," said I, after I had opened the window and ejected the half-masticated morsel into the street; "those who wish to regale on good Cheshire cheese must not come to Chester, no more than those who wish to drink first-rate coffee must go to Mocha. I'll now see whether the ale is drinkable;" so I took a little of the ale into my mouth, and instantly going to the window, spirted it out after the cheese. "Of a surety," said I, "Chester ale must be of much the same quality as it was in the time of Sion Tudor, who spoke of it to the following effect :—

"'Chester ale, Chester ale! I could ne'er get it down,
'Tis made of ground-ivy, of dirt, and of bran,
'Tis as thick as a river below a huge town!
'Tis not lap for a dog, far less drink for a man.'

Well! if I have been deceived in the cheese, I have at

any rate not been deceived in the ale, which I expected to find execrable. Patience! I shall not fall into a passion, more especially as there are things I can fall back upon. Wife! I will trouble you for a cup of tea. Henrietta! have the kindness to cut me a slice of bread and butter.''

Upon the whole we found ourselves very comfortable in the old-fashioned inn, which was kept by a nice old-fashioned gentlewoman, with the assistance of three servants, namely, a "boots" and two strapping chambermaids, one of which was a Welsh girl, with whom I soon scraped acquaintance, not, I assure the reader, for the sake of the pretty Welsh eyes which she carried in her head, but for the sake of the pretty Welsh tongue which she carried in her mouth, from which I confess occasionally proceeded sounds which, however pretty, I was quite unable to understand.

CHAPTER III

Chester—The Rows—Lewis Glyn Cothi—Tragedy of Mold— Native of Antigua—Slavery and the Americans—The Tents —Saturday Night.

ON the morning after our arrival we went out together, and walked up and down several streets; my wife and daughter, however, soon leaving me to go into a shop, I strolled about by myself. Chester is an ancient town with walls and gates, a prison called a castle, built on the site of an ancient keep, an unpretending-looking red sandstone cathedral, two or three handsome churches, several good streets, and certain curious places called rows. The Chester row is a broad arched stone gallery running parallel with the street within the façades of the houses; it is partly open on the side of the street, and just one story above it. Within the rows, of which there are three or four, are shops, every shop being on that side which is farthest from the street. All the best shops in Chester are to be found in the rows. These rows, to which you ascend by stairs up narrow passages, were originally built for the security of the wares of the principal merchants against the Welsh. Should the mountaineers break into the town, as they frequently did, they might rifle some of the common shops, where their booty would be slight, but those which contained the more costly articles would be beyond their reach; for at the first alarm the doors of the passages, up which the stairs led, would be closed, and all access to the upper streets cut off, from the open arches of which missiles of all kinds, kept ready for such occasions, could be discharged upon the intruders, who would be soon glad to beat a retreat. These rows and the walls are certainly the most remarkable memorials of old times which Chester has to boast of.

Upon the walls it is possible to make the whole compass of the city, there being a good but narrow walk upon them. The northern wall abuts upon a frightful ravine, at the bottom of which is a canal. From the western one there is a noble view of the Welsh hills.

As I stood gazing upon the hills from the wall, a ragged man came up and asked for charity. "Can you tell me the name of that tall hill?" said I, pointing in the direction of the south-west. "That hill, sir," said the beggar, "is called Moel Vamagh; I ought to know something about it as I was born at its foot." "Moel," said I, "a bald hill; Vamagh, maternal or motherly. Moel Vamagh, the mother Moel." "Just so, sir," said the beggar; "I see you are a Welshman, like myself, though I suppose you come from the South—Moel Vamagh is the Mother Moel, and is called so because it is the highest of all the Moels." "Did you ever hear of a place called Mold?" said I. "Oh, yes, your honour," said the beggar; "many a time; and many's the time I have been there." "In which direction does it lie?" said I. "Towards Moel Vamagh, your honour," said the beggar, "which is a few miles beyond it; you can't see it from here, but look towards Moel Vamagh and you will see over it." "Thank you," said I, and gave something to the beggar, who departed, after first taking off his hat. Long and fixedly did I gaze in the direction of Mold. The reason which induced me to do so was the knowledge of an appalling tragedy transacted there in the old time, in which there is every reason to suppose a certain Welsh bard, called Lewis Glyn Cothi, had a share.

This man, who was a native of South Wales, flourished during the wars of the Roses. Besides being a poetical he was something of a military genius, and had a command of foot in the army of the Lancastrian Jasper Earl of Pembroke, the son of Owen Tudor, and half-brother of Henry the Sixth. After the battle of Mortimer's Cross, in which the Earl's forces were defeated, the warrior bard found his way to Chester, where he married the widow of a citizen and opened a shop, without asking the permission of the mayor, who with the officers of justice came and seized all his goods, which, according to his own account, filled nine sacks, and then drove him out of the town. The bard in a great fury indited an awdl, in which he invites Reinallt ap Grufydd ap Bleddyn, a kind of predatory chieftain, who resided a little way off in Flintshire, to come and set the town on fire, and slaughter the inhabitants, in revenge for the wrongs he had suffered, and then proceeds to vent all kinds of imprecations against the mayor and people of Chester, wishing, amongst other things, that they might soon hear that the Dee had become too shallow to bear their ships—that a certain cutaneous disorder might attack the wrists of great and small, old and young, laity and clergy—that grass might grow in their streets—that Ilar and Cyveilach, Welsh saints, might slay them—that dogs might snarl at them—and that the king of heaven, with the saints Brynach and Non, might afflict them with blindness—which piece, however ineffectual in inducing God and the saints to visit the Chester people with the curses with which the furious bard wished them to be afflicted, seems to have produced somewhat of its intended effect on the chieftain, who shortly afterwards, on learning that the mayor and many of the Chester people were present at the fair of Mold, near which place he resided, set upon them at the head of his forces, and after a desperate combat, in which many lives were lost, took the mayor prisoner, and drove those of his people who survived into a tower, which he set on fire and burnt, with all the un-

happy wretches which it contained, completing the
horrors of the day by hanging the unfortunate mayor.

Conversant as I was with all this strange history,
is it wonderful that I looked with great interest from
the wall of Chester in the direction of Mold?

Once did I make the compass of the city upon the
walls, and was beginning to do the same a second
time, when I stumbled against a black, who, with his
arms leaning upon the wall, was spitting over it, in
the direction of the river. I apologized, and contrived
to enter into conversation with him. He was tolerably
well dressed, had a hairy cap on his head, was about
forty years of age, and brutishly ugly, his features
scarcely resembling those of a human being. He told
me he was a native of Antigua, a blacksmith by trade,
and had been a slave. I asked him if he could speak
any language besides English, and received for answer
that besides English, he could speak Spanish and
French. Forthwith I spoke to him in Spanish, but he
did not understand me. I then asked him to speak to
me in Spanish, but he could not. "Surely you can
tell me the word for water in Spanish," said I; he,
however, was not able. "How is it," said I, "that,
pretending to be acquainted with Spanish, you do not
even know the word for water?" He said he could
not tell, but supposed that he had forgotten the Spanish
language, adding, however, that he could speak French
perfectly. I spoke to him in French—he did not understand me: I told him to speak to me in French, but he
did not. I then asked him the word for bread in
French, but he could not tell me. I made no observations on his ignorance, but inquired how he liked being
a slave? He said not at all; that it was very bad to
be a slave, as a slave was forced to work. I asked
him if he did not work now that he was free? He said
very seldom; that he did not like work, and that it did
not agree with him. I asked how he came into
England, and he said that wishing to see England, he
had came over with a gentleman as his servant, but
that as soon as he got there, he had left his master, as
he did not like work. I asked him how he contrived to
live in England without working? He said that any
black might live in England without working; that all

he had to do was to attend religious meetings, and speak against slavery and the Americans. I asked him if he had done so. He said he had, and that the religious people were very kind to him, and gave him money, and that a religious lady was going to marry him. I asked him if he knew anything about the Americans? He said he did, and that they were very bad people, who kept slaves and flogged them. "And quite right too," said I, "if they are lazy rascals like yourself, who want to eat without working. What a pretty set of knaves or fools must they be, who encourage a fellow like you to speak against negro slavery, of the necessity for which you yourself are a living instance, and against a people of whom you know as much as of French or Spanish." Then leaving the black, who made no other answer to what I said, than by spitting with considerable force in the direction of the river, I continued making my second compass of the city upon the wall.

Having walked round the city for the second time, I returned to the inn. In the evening I went out again, passed over the bridge, and then turned to the right in the direction of the hills. Near the river, on my right, on a kind of green, I observed two or three tents resembling those of gypsies. Some ragged children were playing near them, who, however, had nothing of the appearance of the children of the Egyptian race, their locks being not dark, but either of a flaxen or red hue, and their features not delicate and regular, but coarse and uncouth, and their complexions not olive, but rather inclining to be fair. I did not go up to them, but continued my course till I arrived near a large factory. I then turned and retraced my steps into the town. It was Saturday night and the streets were crowded with people, many of whom must have been Welsh, as I heard the Cambrian language spoken on every side.

CHAPTER IV

Sunday Morning—Tares and Wheat—Teetotalism—Hearsay—
Irish Family—What Profession?—Sabbath Evening—Priest
or Minister—Give us God.

ON the Sunday morning, as we sat at breakfast, we
heard the noise of singing in the street; running to
the window, we saw a number of people, bareheaded,
from whose mouths the singing or psalmody proceeded.
These, on inquiry, we were informed, were Methodists,
going about to raise recruits for a grand camp-meeting,
which was to be held a little way out of the town. We
finished our breakfast, and at eleven attended divine
service at the cathedral. The interior of this holy
edifice was smooth and neat, strangely contrasting
with its exterior, which was rough and weather-beaten.
We had decent places found us by a civil verger, who
probably took us for what we were—decent country
people. We heard much fine chanting by the choir,
and an admirable sermon, preached by a venerable pre-
bend, on "Tares and Wheat." The congregation was
numerous and attentive. After service, we returned to
our inn, and at two o'clock dined. During dinner, our
conversation ran almost entirely on the sermon, which
we all agreed was one of the best sermons we had ever
heard, and most singularly adapted to country people
like ourselves, being on "Wheat and Tares." When
dinner was over, my wife and daughter repaired to a
neighbouring church, and I went in quest of the camp-
meeting, having a mighty desire to know what kind of
a thing Methodism at Chester was.

I found about two thousand people gathered together
in a field near the railroad station; a waggon stood
under some green elms at one end of the field, in which
were ten or a dozen men with the look of Methodist
preachers; one of these was holding forth to the multitude when I arrived, but he presently sat down, I having, as I suppose, only come in time to hear the fag-
end of his sermon. Another succeeded him, who, after
speaking for about half an hour, was succeeded by

another. All the discourses were vulgar and fanatical, and in some instances unintelligible, at least to my ears. There was plenty of vociferation, but not one single burst of eloquence. Some of the assembly appeared to take considerable interest in what was said, and every now and then showed they did by devout hums and groans; but the generality evidently took little or none, staring about listlessly, or talking to one another. Sometimes, when anything particularly low escaped from the mouth of the speaker, I heard exclamations of " How low ! well, I think I could preach better than that," and the like. At length a man of about fifty, pock-broken and somewhat bald, began to speak : unlike the others who screamed, shouted, and seemed in earnest, he spoke in a dry, waggish style, which had all the coarseness and nothing of the cleverness of that of old Rowland Hill, whom I once heard. After a great many jokes, some of them very poor, and others exceedingly threadbare, on the folly of those who sell themselves to the Devil for a little temporary enjoyment, he introduced the subject of drunkenness, or rather drinking fermented liquors, which he seemed to consider the same thing; and many a sorry joke on the folly of drinking them did he crack, which some half-dozen amidst the concourse applauded. At length he said—

" After all, brethren, such drinking is no joking matter, for it is the root of all evil. Now, brethren, if you would all get to heaven, and cheat the enemy of your souls, never go into a public-house to drink, and never fetch any drink from a public-house. Let nothing pass your lips, in the shape of drink, stronger than water or tea. Brethren, if you would cheat the Devil, take the pledge and become teetotalers. I am a teetotaler myself, thank God—though once I was a regular lushington."

Here ensued a burst of laughter in which I joined, though not at the wretched joke, but at the absurdity of the argument; for, according to that argument, I thought my old friends the Spaniards and Portuguese must be the most moral people in the world, being almost all water-drinkers. As the speaker was proceeding with his nonsense, I heard some one say behind me—" A pretty fellow, that, to speak against drinking and public-houses : he pretends to be reformed, but he is still as fond of the lush as ever. It was only the other day I saw him reeling out of a gin-shop."

Now that speech I did not like, for I saw at once that it could not be true, so I turned quickly round and said—

" Old chap, I can scarcely credit that !"

The man whom I addressed, a rough-and-ready-looking fellow of the lower class, seemed half disposed to return me a savage answer; but an Englishman of the lower class, though you call his word in question, is never savage with you, provided you call him old chap, and he considers you by your dress to be his superior in station. Now I, who had called the word of this man in question, had called him old chap, and was considerably better dressed than himself ; so, after a little hesitation, he became quite gentle, and something more, for he said in a half-apologetic tone—" Well, sir, I did not exactly see him myself, but a particular friend of mine heer'd a man say, that he heer'd another man say, that he was told that a man heer'd that that fellow——"

" Come, come !" said I, " a man must not be convicted on evidence like that; no man has more contempt for the doctrine which that man endeavours to inculcate than myself, for I consider it to have been got up partly for fanatical, partly for political purposes ; but I will never believe that he was lately seen coming out of a gin-shop; he is too wise, or rather too cunning, for that."

I stayed listening to these people till evening was at hand. I then left them, and without returning to the inn strolled over the bridge to the green, where the tents stood. I went up to them : two women sat at the entrance of one ; a man stood by them, and the children, whom I had before seen, were gambolling near at hand. One of the women was about forty, the other some twenty years younger ; both were ugly. The younger was a rude, stupid-looking creature, with red cheeks and redder hair, but there was a dash of intelligence and likewise of wildness in the countenance of the elder female, whose complexion and hair were rather dark. The man was about the same age as the elder woman; he had rather a sharp look, and was dressed in hat, white frock-coat, corduroy breeches, long stockings and shoes. I gave them the seal of the evening.

" Good evening to your haner," said the man. " Good evening to you, sir," said the woman; whilst the younger mumbled something, probably to the same effect, but which I did not catch.

" Fine weather," said I.

" Very, sir," said the elder female. " Won't you please to sit down?" and reaching back into the tent, she pulled out a stool which she placed near me.

I sat down on the stool. " You are not from these parts?" said I, addressing myself to the man.

" We are not, your haner," said the man; " we are from Ireland."

" And this lady," said I, motioning with my head to the elder female, " is, I suppose, your wife."

" She is, your haner, and the children which your haner sees are my children."

" And who is this young lady?" said I, motioning to the uncouth-looking girl.

" The young lady, as your haner is pleased to call her, is a daughter of a sister of mine who is now dead, along with her husband. We have her with us, your haner, because if we did not she would be alone in the world."

" And what trade or profession do you follow?" said I.

" We do a bit in the tinkering line, your haner."

" Do you find tinkering a very profitable profession?" said I.

" Not very, your haner; but we contrive to get a crust and a drink by it."

" That's more than I ever could," said I.

" Has your haner then ever followed tinkering?" said the man.

" Yes," said I, " but I soon left off."

" And became a minister," said the elder female. " Well, your honour is not the first indifferent tinker, that's turn'd out a shining minister."

" Why do you think me a minister?"

" Because your honour has the very look and voice of one. Oh, it was kind of your honour to come to us here in the Sabbath evening, in order that you might bring us God."

" What do you mean by bringing you God?" said I.

" Talking to us about good things, sir, and instructing us out of the Holy Book."

" I am no minister," said I.

" Then you are a priest; I am sure that you are either a minister or a priest; and now that I look on you, sir, I think you look more like a priest than a minister. Yes, I see you are a priest. Oh, your Reverence, give us God! pull out the crucifix from your bosom, and let us kiss the face of God!"

" Of what religion are you?" said I.

" Catholics, your Reverence, Catholics are we all."

" I am no priest."

" Then you are a minister; I am sure you are either a priest or a minister. O sir, pull out the Holy Book, and instruct us from it this blessed Sabbath evening. Give us God, sir, give us God!"

" And would you, who are Catholics, listen to the voice of a minister?"

" That would we, sir; at least I would. If you are a minister, and a good minister, I would as soon listen to your words as those of Father Toban himself."

" And who is Father Toban?"

" A powerful priest in these parts, sir, who has more than once eased me of my sins, and given me God upon the cross. Oh, a powerful and comfortable priest is Father Toban."

" And what would he say if he were to know that you asked for God from a minister?"

" I do not know, and do not much care; if I get God, I do not care whether I get Him from a minister or a priest; both have Him, no doubt, only give Him in different ways. O sir, do give us God; we need Him, sir, for we are sinful people; we call ourselves tinkers, but many is the sinful thing——"

" Bi-do-hosd," said the man: Irish words tantamount to " Be silent!"

" I will not be hushed," said the woman, speaking English. " The man is a good man, and he will do us no harm. We are tinkers, sir; but we do many things besides tinkering, many sinful things, especially in Wales, whither we are soon going again. Oh, I want to be eased of some of my sins before I go into Wales again, and so do you Tourlough, for you know how you are sometimes haunted by Devils at night in those dreary Welsh hills. O sir, give us comfort in some shape or other, either as priest or minister; give us God! give us God!"

"I am neither priest nor minister," said I, "and can only say: Lord have mercy upon you!" Then getting up I flung the children some money and departed.

"We do not want your money, sir," screamed the woman after me; "we have plenty of money. Give us God! give us God!"

"Yes, your haner," said the man, "Give us God! we do not want money;" and the uncouth girl said something, which sounded much like Give us God! but I hastened across the meadow, which was now quite dusky, and was presently in the inn with my wife and daughter.

CHAPTER V

Welsh Book-Stall—Wit and Poetry—Welsh of Chester—Beautiful Morning—Noble Fellow—The Coiling Serpent—Wrexham Church—Welsh or English?—Codiad yr Ehedydd.

ON the afternoon of Monday I sent my family off by the train to Llangollen, which place we had determined to make our headquarters during our stay in Wales. I intended to follow them next day, not in train, but on foot, as by walking I should be better able to see the country, between Chester and Llangollen, than by making the journey by the flying vehicle. As I returned to the inn from the train I took refuge from a shower in one of the rows or covered streets, to which, as I have already said, one ascends by flights of steps; stopping at a book-stall I took up a book which chanced to be a Welsh one—the proprietor, a

short red-faced man, observing me reading the book,
asked me if I could understand it. I told him that I
could.

"If so," said he, "let me hear you translate the two
lines on the title-page."

"Are you a Welshman?" said I.

"I am!" he replied.

"Good!" said I, and I translated into English the
two lines which were a couplet by Edmund Price, an
old archdeacon of Merion, celebrated in his day for wit
and poetry.

The man then asked me from what part of Wales I
came, and when I told him that I was an Englishman
was evidently offended, either because he did not
believe me, or, as I more incline to think, did not
approve of an Englishman's understanding Welsh.

The book was the life of the Rev. Richards, and was
published at Caerlleon, or the city of the legion, the
appropriate ancient British name for the place now
called Chester, a legion having been kept stationed
there during the occupation of Britain by the Romans.

I returned to the inn and dined, and then yearning
for society, descended into the kitchen and had some
conversation with the Welsh maid. She told me that
there were a great many Welsh in Chester from all
parts of Wales, but chiefly from Denbighshire and
Flintshire, which latter was her own county. That a
great many children were born in Chester of Welsh
parents, and brought up in the fear of God and love
of the Welsh tongue. That there were some who had
never been in Wales, who spoke as good Welsh as herself, or better. That the Welsh of Chester were of
various religious persuasions; that some were Baptists,
some Independents, but that the greater parts were
Calvinistic-Methodists; that she herself was a Calvinistic-Methodist; that the different persuasions had
their different chapels, in which God was prayed to
in Welsh; that there were very few Welsh in Chester
who belonged to the Church of England, and that the
Welsh in general do not like Church of England
worship, as I should soon find if I went into Wales.

Late in the evening I directed my steps across the
bridge to the green, where I had discoursed with the

Irish itinerants. I wished to have some more conversation with them respecting their way of life, and, likewise, as they had so strongly desired it, to give them a little Christian comfort, for my conscience reproached me for my abrupt departure on the preceding evening. On arriving at the green, however, I found them gone, and no traces of them but the mark of their fire and a little dirty straw. I returned, disappointed and vexed, to my inn.

Early the next morning I departed from Chester for Llangollen, distant about twenty miles; I passed over the noble bridge and proceeded along a broad and excellent road, leading in a direction almost due south through pleasant meadows. I felt very happy—and no wonder; the morning was beautiful, the birds sang merrily, and a sweet smell proceeded from the new-cut hay in the fields, and I was bound for Wales. I passed over the river Allan and through two villages called, as I was told, Pulford and Marford, and ascended a hill; from the top of this hill the view is very fine. To the east are the high lands of Cheshire, to the west the bold hills of Wales, and below, on all sides a fair variety of wood and water, green meads and arable fields.

"You may well look around, Measter," said a waggoner, who, coming from the direction in which I was bound, stopped to breathe his team on the top of the hill; "you may well look around—there isn't such a place to see the country from, far and near, as where we stand. Many come to this place to look about them."

I looked at the man, and thought I had never seen a more powerful-looking fellow; he was about six feet two inches high, immensely broad in the shoulders, and could hardly have weighed less than sixteen stone. I gave him the seal of the morning, and asked whether he was Welsh or English.

"English, Measter, English; born t'other side of Beeston, pure Cheshire, Measter."

"I suppose," said I, "there are few Welshmen such big fellows as yourself."

"No, Measter," said the fellow, with a grin, "there are few Welshmen so big as I, or yourself either, they

are small men mostly, Measter, them Welshers, very
small men—and yet the fellows can use their hands.
I am a bit of a fighter, Measter, at least I was before
my wife made me join the Methodist connexion, and I
once fit with a Welshman at Wrexham, he came from
the hills, and was a real Welshman, and shorter than
myself by a whole head and shoulder, but he stood up
against me, and gave me more than play for my money,
till I gripped him, flung him down and myself upon
him, and then of course 'twas all over with him.''

"You are a noble fellow," said I, "and a credit to
Cheshire. Will you have sixpence to drink?"

"Thank you, Measter, I shall stop at Pulford, and
shall be glad to drink your health in a jug of ale.''

I gave him sixpence, and descended the hill on one
side, while he, with his team, descended it on the
other.

"A genuine Saxon," said I; "I dare say just like
many of those who, under Hengist, subdued the plains
of Lloegr and Britain. Taliesin called the Saxon race
the Coiling Serpent. He had better have called it
the Big Bull. He was a noble poet, however : what
wonderful lines, upon the whole, are those in his
prophecy, in which he speaks of the Saxons and
Britons, and of the result of their struggle—

> "A serpent which coils,
>   And with fury boils,
> From Germany coming with arm'd wings spread,
>   Shall subdue and shall enthrall
>   The broad Britain all,
> From the Lochlin ocean ro Severn's bed.

> "And British men
>   Shall be captives then
> To strangers from Saxonia's strand ;
>   They shall praise their God, and hold
>   Their language as of old,
> But except wild Wales they shall lose their land."

I arrived at Wrexham, and having taken a very
hearty breakfast at the principal inn, for I felt rather
hungry after a morning's walk of ten miles, I walked
about the town. The town is reckoned a Welsh town,
but its appearance is not Welsh—its inhabitants have
neither the look nor language of Welshmen, and its

name shows that it was founded by some Saxon adventurer, Wrexham being a Saxon compound, signifying the home or habitation of Rex or Rag, and identical, or nearly so, with the Wroxham of East Anglia. It is a stirring bustling place, of much traffic, and of several thousand inhabitants. Its most remarkable object is its church, which stands at the south-western side. To this church, after wandering for some time about the streets, I repaired. The tower is quadrangular, and is at least one hundred feet high; it has on its summit four little turrets, one at each corner, between each of which are three spirelets, the middlemost of the three the highest. The nave of the church is to the east; it is of two stories, both crenelated at the top. I wished to see the interior of the church, but found the gate locked. Observing a group of idlers close at hand with their backs against a wall, I went up to them and addressing myself to one, inquired whether I could see the church. " O yes, sir," said the man; " the clerk who has the key lives close at hand; one of us shall go and fetch him; by the bye, I may as well go myself." He moved slowly away. He was a large bulky man of about the middle age, and his companions were about the same age and size as himself. I asked them if they were Welsh. " Yes, sir," said one, " I suppose we are, for they call us Welsh." I asked if any of them could speak Welsh. " No, sir," said the man, " all the Welsh that any of us know, or indeed wish to know, is Cwrw da." Here there was a general laugh. Cwrw da signifies good ale. I at first thought that the words might be intended as a hint for a treat, but was soon convinced of the contrary. There was no greedy expectation in his eyes, nor, indeed, in those of his companions, though they all looked as if they were fond of good ale. I inquired whether much Welsh was spoken in the town, and was told very little. When the man returned with the clerk I thanked him. He told me I was welcome, and then went and leaned with his back against the wall. He and his mates were probably a set of boon companions enjoying the air after a night's bout at drinking. I was subsequently told that all the people of Wrexham are fond of good ale. The clerk unlocked the church door, and conducted me in. The interior was modern, but in no respects remarkable. The clerk informed me that there was a Welsh service every Sunday afternoon in the church, but that few people attended, and those few were almost entirely from the country. He said that neither he nor the clergyman were natives of Wrexham. He showed me the Welsh Church Bible, and at my request read a few verses from the sacred volume. He seemed a highly intelligent man. I gave him something, which appeared to be more than he expected, and departed, after inquiring of him the road to Llangollen.

I crossed a bridge, for there is a bridge and a stream too at Wrexham. The road at first bore due west, but speedily took a southerly direction. I moved rapidly over an undulating country; a region of hills or rather of mountains lay on my right hand. At the entrance of a small village a poor sickly-looking woman asked me for charity.

"Are you Welsh or English?" said I.

"Welsh," she replied; "but I speak both languages, as do all the people here."

I gave her a halfpenny; she wished me luck, and I proceeded. I passed some huge black buildings which a man told me were collieries, and several carts laden with coal, and soon came to Rhiwabon, a large village about half way between Wrexham and Llangollen. I observed in this place nothing remarkable, but an ancient church. My way from hence lay nearly west. I ascended a hill, from the top of which I looked down into a smoky valley. I descended, passing by a great many collieries, in which I observed grimy men working amidst smoke and flame. At the bottom of the hill near a bridge I turned round. A ridge to the east particularly struck my attention; it was covered with dusky edifices, from which proceeded thundering sounds, and puffs of smoke. A woman passed me going towards Rhiwabon; I pointed to the ridge and asked its name; I spoke English. The woman shook her head and replied, "Dim Saesneg."

"This is as it should be," said I to myself; "I now feel I am in Wales." I repeated the question in Welsh.

"Cefn Bach," she replied—which signifies the little ridge.

"Diolch iti," I replied, and proceeded on my way.

I was now in a wide valley—enormous hills were on my right. The road was good, and above it, in the side of a steep bank, was a causeway intended for foot passengers. It was overhung with hazel bushes. I walked along it to its termination, which was at Llangollen. I found my wife and daughter at the principal inn. They had already taken a house. We dined together at the inn; during the dinner we had music, for a Welsh harper stationed in the passage played upon his instrument "Codiad yr ehedydd." "Of a surety," said I, "I am in Wales!"

CHAPTER VI

Llangollen—Wyn Ab Nudd—The Dee—Dinas Bran.

THE northern side of the vale of Llangollen is formed by certain enormous rocks, called the Eglwysig rocks, which extend from east to west, a distance of about two miles. The southern side is formed by the Berwyn hills. The valley is intersected by the River Dee, the origin of which is a deep lake near Bala, about twenty miles to the west. Between the Dee and the Eglwysig rises a lofty hill, on the top of which are the ruins of Dinas Bran, which bear no slight resemblance to a crown. The upper part of the hill is bare with the exception of what is covered by the ruins; on the lower part there are inclosures and trees, with, here and there, a grove or farm-house. On the other side of the valley, to the east of Llangollen, is a hill caled Pen y Coed, beautifully covered with trees of various kinds; it stands between the river and the Berwyn, even as the hill of Dinas Bran stands between the river and the Eglwysig rocks—it does not, however, confront Dinas Bran, which stands more to the west.

Llangollen is a small town or large village of white houses with slate roofs, it contains about two thousand inhabitants, and is situated principally on the southern

side of the Dee. At its western end it has an ancient
bridge and a modest unpretending church nearly in its
centre, in the chancel of which rest the mortal remains
of an old bard called Gryffydd Hiraethog. From some
of the houses on the southern side there is a noble view
—Dinas Bran and its mighty hill forming the principal
objects. The view from the northern part of the town,
which is indeed little more than a suburb, is not quite
so grand, but is nevertheless highly interesting. The
eastern entrance of the vale of Llangollen is much wider
than the western, which is overhung by bulky hills.
There are many pleasant villas on both sides of the
river, some of which stand a considerable way up the
hill; of the villas the most noted is Plas Newydd at the
foot of the Berwyn, built by two Irish ladies of high
rank, who resided in it for nearly half-a-century, and
were celebrated throughout Europe by the name of
the Ladies of Llangollen.

The view of the hill of Dinas Bran, from the
southern side of Llangollen, would be much more complete were it not for a bulky excrescence, towards its
base, which prevents the gazer from obtaining a complete view. The name of Llangollen signifies the church
of Collen, and the vale and village take their name
from the church, which was originally dedicated to
Saint Collen, though some, especially the neighbouring
peasantry, suppose that Llangollen is a compound of
Llan a church and Collen a hazel-wood, and that the
church was called the church of the hazel-wood from the
number of hazels in the neighbourhood. Collen, according to a legendary life, which exists of him in
Welsh, was a Briton by birth, and of illustrious
ancestry. He served for some time abroad as a soldier
against Julian the Apostate, and slew a Pagan
champion who challenged the best man amongst the
Christians. Returning to his own country, he devoted
himself to religion, and became Abbot of Glastonbury,
but subsequently retired to a cave on the side of a
mountain, where he lived a life of great austerity. Once
as he was lying in his cell he heard two men out abroad
discoursing about Wyn Ab Nudd, and saying that he
was king of the Tylwyth Teg or Fairies, and lord of
Unknown, whereupon Collen thrusting his head out of

his cave told them to hold their tongues, for that Wyn
Ab Nudd and his host were merely devils.   At dead of
night he heard a knocking at the door, and on his asking who was there, a voice said : " I am a messenger
from Wyn Ab Nudd, king of Unknown, and I am come
to summon thee to appear before my master to-morrow,
at midday, on the top of the hill."

Collen did not go.   The next night there was the same
knocking and the same message.   Still Collen did not
go.   The third night the messenger came again and
repeated his summons, adding that if he did not go it
would be the worse for him.   The next day Collen made
some holy water, put it into a pitcher and repaired to
the top of the hill, where he saw a wonderfully fine
castle, attendants in magnificent liveries, youths and
damsels dancing with nimble feet, and a man of
honourable presence before the gate, who told him that
the king was expecting him to dinner.   Collen followed
the man into the castle, and beheld the king on a throne
of gold, and a table magnificently spread before him.
The king welcomed Collen, and begged him to taste of
the dainties on the table, adding that he hoped that
in future he would reside with him.   " I will not eat of
the leaves of the forest," said Collen.

" Did you ever see men better dressed?" said the
king, " than my attendants here in red and blue?"

" Their dress is good enough," said Collen, " considering what kind of dress it is."

" What kind of dress is it?" said the king.

Collen replied : " The red on the one side denotes
burning, and the blue on the other side denotes freez-
ing."   Then drawing forth his sprinkler, he flung the
holy water in the faces of the king and his people,
whereupon the whole vision disappeared, so that there
was neither castle nor attendants, nor youth nor damsel, nor musician with his music, nor banquet, nor anything to be seen save the green bushes.

The valley of the Dee, of which the Llangollen district forms part, is called in the British tongue Glyndyfrdwy—that is, the valley of the Dwy or Dee.   The
celebrated Welsh chieftain, generally known as Owen
Glendower, was surnamed after the valley, the whole
of which belonged to him, and in which he had two or

three places of strength, though his general abode was a castle in Sycharth, a valley to the south-east of the Berwyn, and distant about twelve miles from Llangollen.

Connected with the Dee there is a wonderful Druidical legend to the following effect. The Dee springs from two fountains, high up in Merionethshire, called Dwy Fawr and Dwy Fach, or the great and little Dwy, whose waters pass through those of the lake of Bala without mingling with them, and come out at its northern extremity. These fountains had their names from two individuals, Dwy Fawr and Dwy Fach, who escaped from the Deluge, when all the rest of the human race were drowned, and the passing of the waters of the two fountains through the lake, without being confounded with its flood, is emblematic of the salvation of the two individuals from the Deluge, of which the lake is a type.

Dinas Bran, which crowns the top of the mighty hill on the northern side of the valley, is a ruined stronghold of unknown antiquity. The name is generally supposed to signify Crow Castle, bran being the British word for crow, and flocks of crows being frequently seen hovering over it. It may, however, mean the castle of Bran or Brennus, or the castle above the Bran, a brook which flows at its foot.

Dinas Bran was a place quite impregnable in the old time, and served as a retreat to Gruffydd, son of Madawg, from the rage of his countrymen, who were incensed against him because, having married Emma, the daughter of James Lord Audley, he had, at the instigation of his wife and father-in-law, sided with Edward the First against his own native sovereign. But though it could shield him from his foes, it could not preserve him from remorse and the stings of conscience, of which he speedily died.

At present the place consists only of a few ruined walls, and probably consisted of little more two or three hundred years ago : Roger Cyffyn, a Welsh bard who flourished at the beginning of the seventeenth century, wrote an englyn upon it, of which the following is a translation :—

" Gone, gone are thy gates, Dinas Bran on the height !
  Thy warders are blood-crows and ravens, I trow ;
Now no one will wend from the field of the fight
  To the fortress on high, save the raven and crow. "

CHAPTER VII

Poor Black Cat—Dissenters—Persecution—What Impudence !

THE house or cottage, for it was called a cottage though it consisted of two stories, in which my wife had procured lodgings for us, was situated in the northern suburb. Its front was towards a large perllan or orchard, which sloped down gently to the banks of the Dee; its back was towards the road leading from Wrexham, behind which was a high bank, on the top of which was a canal called in Welsh the Camlas, whose commencement was up the valley about two miles west. A little way up the road, towards Wrexham, was the vicarage, and a little way down was a flannel factory, beyond which was a small inn, with pleasure grounds, kept by an individual who had once been a gentleman's servant. The mistress of the house was a highly respectable widow, who with a servant maid was to wait upon us. It was as agreeable a place in all respects as people like ourselves could desire.

As I and my family sat at tea in our parlour, an hour or two after we had taken possession of our lodgings, the door of the room and that of the entrance to the house being open, on account of the fineness of the weather, a poor black cat entered hastily, sat down on the carpet by the table, looked up towards us, and mewed piteously. I never had seen so wretched a looking creature. It was dreadfully attenuated, being little more than skin and bone, and was sorely afflicted with an eruptive malady. And here I may as well relate the history of this cat previous to our arrival, which I subsequently learned by bits and snatches. It had belonged to a previous vicar of Llangollen, and had been left behind at his departure. His successor brought with him dogs and cats, who conceiving that the late vicar's cat had no business at the vicarage, drove it

forth to seek another home, which, however, it could
not find. Almost all the people of the suburb were dissenters, as indeed were the generality of the people of
Llangollen, and knowing the cat to be a church cat,
not only would not harbour it, but did all they could
to make it miserable; whilst the few who were not dissenters, would not receive it into their houses, either
because they had cats of their own, or dogs, or did not
want a cat, so that the cat had no home, and was
dreadfully persecuted by nine-tenths of the suburb. O,
there never was a cat so persecuted as that poor Church
of England animal, and solely on account of the
opinions which it was supposed to have imbibed in the
house of its late master, for I never could learn that
the dissenters of the suburb, nor indeed of Llangollen
in general, were in the habit of persecuting other cats;
the cat was a Church of England cat, and that was
enough: stone it, hang it, drown it! were the cries of
almost everybody. If the workmen of the flannel factory, all of whom were Calvinistic Methodists, chanced
to get a glimpse of it in the road from the windows of
the building, they would sally forth in a body, and with
sticks, stones, or for want of other weapons, with clots
of horse-dung, of which there was always plenty on the
road, would chase it up the high bank or perhaps over
the Camlas—the inhabitants of a small street between
our house and the factory leading from the road to the
river, all of whom were dissenters, if they saw it moving
about the perllan, into which their back windows looked,
would shriek and hoot at it, and fling anything of no
value, which came easily to hand at the head or body
of the ecclesiastical cat. The good woman of the house,
who though a very excellent person, was a bitter dis-
senter, whenever she saw it upon her ground or heard
it was there, would make after it, frequently attended
by her maid Margaret, and her young son, a boy about
nine years of age, both of whom hated the cat, and
were always ready to attack it, either alone or in company, and no wonder, the maid being not only a dis-
senter, but a class teacher, and the boy not only a dis-
senter, but intended for the dissenting ministry. Where
it got its food, and food it sometimes must have got,
for even a cat, an animal known to have nine lives,

cannot live without food, was only known to itself, as was the place where it lay, for even a cat must lie down sometimes; though a labouring man who occasionally dug in the garden told me he believed that in the spring-time it ate freshets, and the woman of the house once said that she believed it sometimes slept in the hedge, which hedge, by the bye, divided our perllan from the vicarage grounds, which were very extensive. Well might the cat after having led this kind of life for better than two years look mere skin and bone when it made its appearance in our apartment, and have an eruptive malady, and also a bronchitic cough, for I remember it had both. How it came to make its appearance there is a mystery, for it had never entered the house before, even when there were lodgers; that it should not visit the woman, who was its declared enemy, was natural enough, but why if it did not visit her other lodgers, did it visit us? Did instinct keep it aloof from them? Did instinct draw it towards us? We gave it some bread-and-butter, and a little tea with milk and sugar. It ate and drank and soon began to purr. The good woman of the house was horrified when on coming in to remove the things she saw the church cat on her carpet. "What impudence!" she exclaimed, and made towards it, but on our telling her that we did not expect that it should be disturbed, she let it alone. A very remarkable circumstance was, that though the cat had hitherto been in the habit of flying not only from her face, but the very echo of her voice, it now looked her in the face with perfect composure, as much as to say, " I don't fear you, for I know that I am now safe and with my own people." It stayed with us two hours and then went away. The next morning it returned. To be short, though it went away every night, it became our own cat, and one of our family. I gave it something which cured it of its eruption, and through good treat-ment it soon lost its other ailments and began to look sleek and bonny.

CHAPTER VIII

The Mowers—Deep Welsh—Extensive View—Old Celtic Hatred
—Fish-Preserving—Smollett's Morgan.

NEXT morning I set out to ascend Dinas Bran; a
number of children, almost entirely girls, followed me.
I asked them why they came after me. "In the hope
that you will give us something," said one in very good
English. I told them that I should give them nothing,
but they still followed me. A little way up the hill I
saw some men cutting hay. I made an observation to
one of them respecting the fineness of the weather; he
answered civilly, and rested on his scythe, whilst the
others pursued their work. I asked him whether he was
a farming man; he told me that he was not; that he
generally worked at the flannel manufactory, but that
for some days past he had not been employed there,
work being slack, and had on that account joined the
mowers in order to earn a few shillings. I asked him
how it was he knew how to handle a scythe, not being
bred up a farming man; he smiled, and said that,
somehow or other, he had learnt to do so.

"You speak very good English," said I, "have you
much Welsh?"

"Plenty," said he; "I am a real Welshman."

"Can you read Welsh?" said I.

"O, yes!" he replied.

"What books have you read?" said I.

"I have read the Bible, sir, and one or two other
books."

"Did you ever read the *Bardd Cwsg*?" said I.

He looked at me with some surprise.

"No," said he, after a moment or two, "I have
never read it. I have seen it, but it was far too deep
Welsh for me."

"I have read it," said I.

"Are you a Welshman?" said he.

"No," said I; "I am an Englishman."

"And how is it," said he, "that you can read Welsh
without being a Welshman?"

"I learned to do so," said I, "even as you learned to mow, without being bred up to farming work."

"Ah!" said he, "but it is easier to learn to mow than to read the *Bardd Cwsg*."

"I don't know that," said I; "I have taken up a scythe a hundred times, but I cannot mow."

"Will your honour take mine now, and try again?" said he.

"No," said I, "for if I take your scythe in hand I must give you a shilling, you know, by mowers' law."

He gave a broad grin, and I proceeded up the hill. When he rejoined his companions he said something to them in Welsh, at which they all laughed. I reached the top of the hill, the children still attending me.

The view over the vale is very beautiful; but on no side, except in the direction of the west, is it very extensive, Dinas Bran being on all other sides overtopped by other hills : in that direction, indeed, the view is extensive enough, reaching on a fine day even to the Wyddfa or peak of Snowdon, a distance of sixty miles, at least as some say, who perhaps ought to add, to very good eyes, which mine are not. The day that I made my first ascent of Dinas Bran was very clear, but I do not think I saw the Wyddfa then from the top of Dinas Bran. It is true I might see it without knowing it, being utterly unacquainted with it, except by name; but I repeat I do not think I saw it, and I am quite sure that I did not see it from the top of Dinas Bran on a subsequent ascent, on a day equally clear, when if I had seen the Wyddfa I must have recognized it, having been at its top. As I stood gazing around the children danced about upon the grass, and sang a song. The song was English. I descended the hill; they followed me to its foot, and then left me. The children of the lower class of Llangollen are great pests to visitors. The best way to get rid of them is to give them nothing : I followed that plan, and was not long troubled with them.

Arrived at the foot of the hill, I walked along the bank of the canal to the west. Presently I came to a barge lying by the bank; the boatman was in it. I entered into conversation with him. He told me that the canal and its branches extended over a great part of England. That the boats carried slates—that he had frequently gone as far as Paddington by the canal—that he was generally three weeks on the journey—that the boatmen and their families lived in the little cabins aft—that the boatmen were all Welsh—that they could read English, but little or no Welsh—that English was a much more easy language to read than Welsh—that they passed by many towns, among others Northampton, and that he liked no place so much as Llangollen. I proceeded till I came to a place where some people were putting huge slates into a canal boat. It was near a bridge which crossed the Dee, which was on the left. I stopped and entered into conversation with one, who appeared to be the principal man. He told me amongst other things that he was a blacksmith from the neighbourhood of Rhiwabon, and that the flags were intended for the flooring of his premises. In the boat was an old bareheaded, bare-armed fellow, who presently joined in the conversation in very broken English. He told me that his name was Joseph Hughes, and that he was a real Welshman and was proud of being so; he expressed a great dislike for the English, who he said were in the habit of making fun of him and ridiculing his language; he said that all the fools that he had known were Englishmen. I told him that all Englishmen were not fools. "But the greater part are," said he. "Look how they work," said I. "Yes," said he, "some of them are good at breaking stones for the road, but not more than one in a hundred." "There seems to be something of the old Celtic hatred to the Saxon in this old fellow," said I to myself, as I walked away.

I proceeded till I came to the head of the canal, where the navigation first commences. It is close to a weir, over which the Dee falls. Here there is a little floodgate, through which water rushes from an oblong pond or reservoir, fed by water from a corner of the upper part of the weir. On the left, or south-west side, is a mound of earth fenced with stones which is the commencement of the bank of the canal. The pond or reservoir above the floodgate is separated from the weir by a stone wall on the left, or south-west side. This pond has two floodgates, the one already mentioned, which opens into the canal, and another, on the other side of the stone mound, opening to the lower part of the weir. Whenever, as a man told me who was standing near, it is necessary to lay the bed of the canal dry in the immediate neighbourhood for the purpose of making repairs, the floodgate to the canal is closed, and the one to the lower part of the weir is opened, and then the water from the pond flows into the Dee, whilst a sluice, near the first lock, lets out the water of the canal into the river. The head of the canal is situated in a very beautiful spot. To the left or south is a lofty hill covered with wood. To the right is a beautiful slope or lawn, on the top of which is a pretty villa, to which you can get by a little wooden bridge over the floodgate of the canal, and indeed forming part of it. Few things are so beautiful in their origin as this canal, which, be it known, with its locks and its aqueducts, the grandest of which last is the stupendous erection near Stockport, which by the bye filled my mind when a boy with wonder, constitutes the grand work of England, and yields to nothing in the world of the kind, with the exception of the great canal of China.

Retracing my steps some way I got upon the river's bank and then again proceeded in the direction of the west. I soon came to a cottage nearly opposite a bridge, which led over the river, not the bridge which I have already mentioned, but one much smaller, and considerably higher up the valley. The cottage had several dusky outbuildings attached to it, and a paling before it. Leaning over the paling in his shirt-sleeves was a dark-faced, short, thickset man, who saluted me in English. I returned his salutation, stopped, and was soon in conversation with him. I praised the beauty of the river and its banks : he said that both were beautiful and delightful in summer, but not at all in winter, for then the trees and bushes on the banks were stripped of their leaves, and the river was a frightful torrent. He asked me if I had been to see the place called the Robber's Leap, as strangers generally went to see it. I inquired where it was.

" Yonder," said he, pointing to some distance down the river.

" Why is it called the Robber's Leap?" said I.

" It is called the Robber's Leap, or Llam y Lleidyr,"
said he, " because a thief pursued by justice once
leaped across the river there and escaped. It was an
awful leap, and he well deserved to escape after taking
it." I told him that I should go and look at it on some
future opportunity, and then asked if there were many
fish in the river. He said there were plenty of salmon
and trout, and that owing to the river being tolerably
high, a good many had been caught during the last
few days. I asked him who enjoyed the right of fishing
in the river. He said that in these parts the fishing
belonged to two or three proprietors, who either preserved the fishing for themselves, as they best could
by means of keepers, or let it out to other people; and
that many individuals came not only from England,
but from France and Germany and even Russia for the
purpose of fishing, and that the keepers of the proprietors from whom they purchased permission to fish went
with them, to show them the best places, and to teach
them how to fish. He added that there was a report
that the river would shortly be rhydd, or free, and open
to any one. I said that it would be a bad thing to fling
the river open, as in that event the fish would be killed
at all times and seasons, and eventually all destroyed.
He replied that he questioned whether more fish would
be taken then than now, and that I must not imagine
that the fish were much protected by what was called
preserving; that the people to whom the lands in the
neighbourhood belonged, and those who paid for fishing
did not catch a hundredth part of the fish which were
caught in the river : that the proprietors went with their
keepers, and perhaps caught two or three stone of fish,
or that strangers went with the keepers, whom they
paid for teaching them how to fish, and perhaps caught
half-a-dozen fish, and that shortly after the keepers
would return and catch on their own account sixty
stone of fish from the very spot where the proprietors
or strangers had great difficulty in catching two or
three stone or the half-dozen fish, or the poachers would
go and catch a yet greater quantity. He added that
gentry did not understand how to catch fish, and that
to attempt to preserve was nonsense. I told him that
if the river was flung open everybody would fish; he

said that I was much mistaken, that hundreds who were now poachers would then keep at home, mind their proper trades, and never use line or spear; that folks always longed to do what they were forbidden, and that Shimei would never have crossed the brook provided he had not been told he should be hanged if he did. That he himself had permission to fish in the river whenever he pleased, but never availed himself of it, though in his young time, when he had no leave, he had been an arrant poacher.

The manners and way of speaking of this old personage put me very much in mind of those of Morgan, described by Smollett in his immortal novel of *Roderick Random*. I had more discourse with him : I asked him in what line of business he was—he told me that he sold coals. From his complexion, and the hue of his shirt, I had already concluded that he was in some grimy trade. I then inquired of what religion he was, and received for answer that he was a Baptist. I thought that both himself and part of his apparel would look all the better for a good immersion. We talked of the war then raging—he said it was between the false prophet and the Dragon. I asked him who the Dragon was—he said the Turk. I told him that the Pope was far worse than either the Turk or the Russian, that his religion was the vilest idolatry, and that he would let no one alone. That it was the Pope who drove his fellow religionists the Anabaptists out of the Netherlands. He asked me how long ago that was. Between two and three hundred years, I replied. He asked me the meaning of the word Anabaptist; I told him ; whereupon he expressed great admiration for my understanding, and said that he hoped he should see me again.

I inquired of him to what place the bridge led ; he told me that if I passed over it, and ascended a high bank beyond, I should find myself on the road from Llangollen to Corwen, and that if I wanted to go to Llangollen I must turn to the left. I thanked him, and passing over the bridge, and ascending the bank, found myself upon a broad road. I turned to the left, and walking briskly, in about half-an-hour reached our cottage in the northern suburb, where I found my family and dinner awaiting me.

CHAPTER IX

The Dinner—English Foibles—Pengwern—The Yew-Tree—Carn-
Lleidyr—Applications of a Term.

FOR dinner we had salmon and leg of mutton; the
salmon from the Dee, the leg from the neighbouring
Berwyn. The salmon was good enough, but I had
eaten better; and here it will not be amiss to say, that
the best salmon in the world is caught in the Suir, a
river that flows past the beautiful town of Clonmel in
Ireland. As for the leg of mutton, it was truly wonderful; nothing so good had I ever tasted in the shape of
a leg of mutton. The leg of mutton of Wales beats the
leg of mutton of any other country, and I had never
tasted a Welsh leg of mutton before. Certainly I shall
never forget the first Welsh leg of mutton which I
tasted, rich but delicate, replete with juices derived from
the aromatic herbs of the noble Berwyn, cooked to a
turn, and weighing just four pounds.

> " O its savoury smell was great,
>   Such as might well tempt, I trow,
>   One that's dead to lift his brow."

Let any one who wishes to eat leg of mutton in perfection go to Wales, but mind you to eat leg of mutton
only. Welsh leg of mutton is superlative; but with the
exception of the leg, the mutton of Wales is decidedly
inferior to that of many other parts of Britain.

Here, perhaps, as I have told the reader what we ate
for dinner, it will be as well to tell him what we drank
at dinner. Let him know, then, that with our salmon
we drank water, and with our mutton ale, even ale of
Llangollen; but not the best ale of Llangollen; it was
very fair; but I subsequently drank far better Llangollen
ale than that which I drank at our first dinner in our
cottage at Llangollen.

In the evening I went across the bridge and strolled
along in a south-east direction. Just as I had cleared
the suburb a man joined me from a cottage, on the top
of a high bank, whom I recognized as the mower with

C

whom I had held discourse in the morning. He saluted me and asked me if I were taking a walk. I told him I was, whereupon he said that if I were not too proud to wish to be seen walking with a poor man like himself, he should wish to join me. I told him I should be glad of his company, and that I was not ashamed to be seen walking with any person, however poor, who conducted himself with propriety. He replied that I must be very different from my countrymen in general, who were ashamed to be seen walking with any people who were not, at least, as well-dressed as themselves. I said that my country-folk in general had a great many admirable qualities, but at the same time a great many foibles, foremost amongst which last was a crazy admiration for what they called gentility, which made them sycophantic to their superiors in station, and extremely insolent to those whom they considered below them. He said that I had spoken his very thoughts, and then asked me whether I wished to be taken the most agreeable walk near Llangollen.

On my replying by all means, he led me along the road to the south-east. A pleasant road it proved : on our right at some distance was the mighty Berwyn; close on our left the hill called Pen y Coed. I asked him what was beyond the Berwyn?

"A very wild country, indeed," he replied, "consisting of wood, rock, and river; in fact, an anialwch."

He then asked if I knew the meaning of anialwch.

"A wilderness," I replied, "you will find the word in the Welsh Bible."

"Very true, sir," said he, "it was there I met it, but I did not know the meaning of it, till it was explained to me by one of our teachers."

On my inquiring of what religion he was, he told me he was a Calvinistic Methodist.

We passed an ancient building which stood on our right. I turned round to look at it. Its back was to the road : at its eastern end was a fine arched window like the oriel window of a church.

"That building," said my companion, "is called Pengwern Hall. It was once a convent of nuns; a little time ago a farm-house, but is now used as a barn, and a place of stowage. Till lately it belonged to the

Mostyn family, but they disposed of it, with the farm on which it stood, together with several other farms, to certain people from Liverpool, who now live yonder," pointing to a house a little way farther on.   I still looked at the edifice.

"You seem to admire the old building," said my companion.

"I was not admiring it," said I; "I was thinking of the difference between its present and former state. Formerly it was a place devoted to gorgeous idolatry and obscene lust; now it is a quiet old barn in which hay and straw are placed, and broken tumbrils stowed away : surely the hand of God is visible here?"

"It is so, sir," said the man in a respectful tone, "and so it is in another place in this neighbourhood. About three miles from here, in the north-west part of the valley, is an old edifice.   It is now a farm-house, but was once a splendid abbey, and was called——"

"The abbey of the vale of the cross," said I; "I have read a deal about it.   Iolo Goch, the bard of your celebrated hero, Owen Glendower, was buried somewhere in its precincts."

We went on : my companion took me over a stile behind the house which he had pointed out, and along a path through hazel coppices.   After a little time I inquired whether there were any Papists in Llangollen.

"No," said he, "there is not one of that family at Llangollen, but I believe there are some in Flintshire, at a place called Holywell, where there is a pool or fountain, the waters of which it is said they worship."

"And so they do," said I, "true to the old Indian superstition, of which their religion is nothing but a modification.   The Indians and sepoys worship stocks and stones, and the river Ganges, and our Papists worship stocks and stones, holy wells and fountains."

He put some questions to me about the origin of nuns and friars.   I told him they originated in India, and made him laugh heartily by showing him the original identity of nuns and nautch-girls, begging priests and begging Brahmins.   We passed by a small house with an enormous yew-tree before it; I asked him who lived there.

" No one," he replied, " it is to let. It was originally a cottage, but the proprietors have furbished it up a little, and call it yew-tree villa."

" I suppose they would let it cheap," said I.

" By no means," he replied, " they ask eighty pounds a year for it."

" What could have induced them to set such a rent upon it?" I demanded.

" The yew-tree, sir, which is said to be the largest in Wales. They hope that some of the grand gentry will take the house for the romance of the yew-tree, but somehow or other nobody has taken it, though it has been to let for three seasons."

We soon came to a road leading east and west.

" This way," said he, pointing in the direction of the west, " leads back to Llangollen, the other to Offa's Dyke and England."

We turned to the west. He inquired if I had ever heard before of Offa's Dyke.

" O yes," said I, " it was built by an old Saxon king called Offa, against the incursions of the Welsh."

" There was a time," said my companion, " when it was customary for the English to cut off the ears of every Welshman who was found to the east of the dyke, and for the Welsh to hang every Englishman whom they found to the west of it. Let us be thankful that we are now more humane to each other. We are now on the north side of Pen y Coed. Do you know the meaning of Pen y Coed, sir?"

" Pen y Coed," said I, " means the head of the wood. I suppose that in the old time the mountain looked over some extensive forest, even as the nunnery of Pengwern looked originally over an alder-swamp, for Pengwern means the head of the alder-swamp."

" So it does, sir; I shouldn't wonder if you could tell me the real meaning of a word, about which I have thought a good deal, and about which I was puzzling my head last night as I lay in bed."

" What may it be?" said I.

" Carn-lleidyr," he replied: " now, sir, do you know the meaning of that word?"

" I think I do," said I.

" What may it be, sir?"

" First let me hear what you conceive its meaning to be," said I.

" Why, sir, I should say that Carn-lleidyr is an out-and-out thief—one worse than a thief of the common sort. Now, if I steal a matrass I am a lleidyr, that is a thief of the common sort; but if I carry it to a person, and he buys it, knowing it to be stolen, I conceive he is a far worse thief than I; in fact, a carn-lleidyr."

" The word is a double word," said I, " compounded of carn and lleidyr. The original meaning of carn is a heap of stones, and carn-lleidyr means properly a thief without house or home, and with no place on which to rest his head, save the carn or heap of stones on the bleak top of the mountain. For a long time the word was only applied to a thief of that description, who, being without house and home, was more desperate than other thieves, and as savage and brutish as the wolves and foxes with whom he occasionally shared his pillow, the carn. In course of time, however, the original meaning was lost or disregarded, and the term carn-lleidyr was applied to any particular dishonest person. At present there can be no impropriety in calling a person who receives a matrass, knowing it to be stolen, a carn-lleidyr, seeing that he is worse than the thief who stole it, or in calling a knavish attorney a carn-lleidyr, seeing that he does far more harm than a common pick-pocket; or in calling the Pope so, seeing that he gets huge sums of money out of people by pretending to be able to admit their souls to heaven, or to hurl them to the other place, knowing all the time that he has no such power; perhaps, indeed, at the present day the term carn-lleidyr is more applicable to the Pope than to any one else, for he is certainly the arch-thief of the world. So much for Carn-lleidyr. But I must here tell you that the term carn may be applied to any one who is particularly bad or disagreeable in any respect, and now I remember, has been applied for centuries both in prose and poetry. One Lewis Glyn Cothi, a poet, who lived more than three hundred years ago, uses the word carn in the sense of arrant or exceedingly bad, for in his abusive ode to the town of Chester, he says that the women of London itself were never more carn strumpets than those of Chester, by which he means that there were never more arrant harlots in the world than those of the cheese capital. And the last of your great poets, Gronwy Owen, who flourished about the middle of the last century, complains in a letter to a friend, whilst living in a village of Lancashire, that he was amongst Carn Saeson. He found all English disagreeable enough, but those of Lancashire particularly so—savage, brutish louts, out-and-out John Bulls, and therefore he called them Carn Saeson."

"Thank you, sir," said my companion; "I now thoroughly understand the meaning of carn. Whenever I go to Chester, and a dressed-up madam jostles against me, I shall call her carn-butein. The Pope of Rome I shall in future term carn-lleidyr y byd, or the arch-thief of the world. And whenever I see a stupid, brutal Englishman swaggering about Llangollen, and looking down upon us poor Welsh, I shall say to myself, Get home, you carn Sais! Well, sir, we are now near Llangollen; I must turn to the left. You go straight forward. I never had such an agreeable walk in my life. May I ask your name?"

I told him my name, and asked him for his.

"Edward Jones," he replied.

CHAPTER X

The Berwyn—Mountain Cottage—The Barber's Pole.

On the following morning I strolled up the Berwyn on the south-west of the town, by a broad winding path, which was at first very steep, but by degrees became less so. When I had accomplished about three parts of the ascent I came to a place where the road, or path, divided into two. I took the one to the left, which seemingly led to the top of the mountain, and presently came to a cottage from which a dog rushed barking towards me; an old woman, however, coming to the door, called him back. I said a few words to her in Welsh, whereupon in broken English she asked me to enter the cottage and take a glass of milk. I went in and sat down on a chair which a sickly-looking young woman handed to me. I asked her in English who she was, but she made no answer, whereupon the old woman told me that she was her daughter and had no English. I then asked her in Welsh what was the matter with her; she replied that she had the cryd or ague. The old woman now brought me a glass of milk, and said in the Welsh language that she hoped that I should like it. What further conversation we had was in the Cambrian tongue. I asked the name of the dog, who was now fondling upon me, and was told that his name was Pharaoh. I inquired if they had any books, and was shown two, one a common Bible printed by the Bible Society, and the other a volume in which the Book of Prayer of the Church of England was bound up with the Bible, both printed at Oxford, about the middle of the last century. I found that both mother and daughter were Calvinistic Methodists. After a little further discourse I got up and gave the old woman twopence for the milk; she accepted it, but with great reluctance. I inquired whether by following the road I could get to the Pen y bryn or the top of the hill. They shook their heads and the young woman said that I could not, as the road presently took a turn and went down. I asked her how I could get to the top of the hill. "Which part of the top?" said she. "I'r gor-uchaf," I replied. "That must be where the barber's pole stands," said she. "Why does the barber's pole stand there?" said I. "A barber was hanged there a long time ago," said she, "and the pole was placed to show the spot." "Why was he hanged?" said I. "For murdering his wife," said she. I asked her some questions about the murder, but the only information she could give me was, that it was a very bad murder and occurred a long time ago. I had observed the pole from our garden at Llangollen, but had concluded that it was a common flagstaff. I inquired the way to it. It was not visible from the cottage, but they gave me directions how to reach it. I bade them farewell, and in about a quarter of an hour reached the pole on the top of the hill. I imagined that I should have a glorious view of the vale of Llangollen from the spot where it stood; the view, however, did not answer my expectations. I returned to Llangollen by nearly the same way by which I had come.

The remainder of the day I spent entirely with my family, whom at their particular request I took in the evening to see Plas Newydd, once the villa of the two ladies of Llangollen. It lies on the farther side of the bridge, at a little distance from the back part of the church. There is a thoroughfare through the grounds, which are not extensive. Plas Newydd, or the New Place, is a small, gloomy mansion, with a curious dairy on the right-hand side, as you go up to it, and a remarkable stone pump. An old man whom we met in the grounds, and with whom I entered into conversation, said that he remembered the building of the house, and that the place where it now stands was called before its erection Pen y maes, or the head of the field.

CHAPTER XI

Welsh Farm-house—A Poet's Grandson—Hospitality—Mountain Village—Madoc—The Native Valley—Corpse Candles—The Midnight Call.

My curiosity having been rather excited with respect to the country beyond the Berwyn, by what my friend, the intelligent flannel-worker, had told me about it, I determined to go and see it. Accordingly on Friday morning I set out. Having passed by Pengwern Hall I turned up a lane in the direction of the south, with a brook on the right running amongst hazels. I presently arrived at a small farm-house standing on the left with a little yard before it. Seeing a woman at the door I asked her in English if the road in which I was would take me across the mountain. She said it would, and forthwith cried to a man working in a field, who left his work and came towards us. " That is my husband," said she; " he has more English than I."

The man came up and addressed me in very good English: he had a brisk, intelligent look, and was about sixty. I repeated the question which I had put to his wife, and he also said that by following the road

I could get across the mountain. We soon got into conversation. He told me that the little farm in which he lived belonged to the person who had bought Pengwern Hall. He said that he was a good kind of gentleman, but did not like the Welsh. I asked him if the gentleman in question did not like the Welsh why he came to live among them. He smiled, and I then said that I liked the Welsh very much, and was particularly fond of their language. He asked me whether I could read Welsh, and on my telling him I could, he said that if I would walk in he would show me a Welsh book. I went with him and his wife into a neat kind of kitchen, flagged with stone, where were several young people, their children. I spoke some Welsh to them which appeared to give them great satisfaction. The man went to a shelf and taking down a book put it into my hand. It was a Welsh book, and the title of it in English was *Evening Work of the Welsh*. It contained the lives of illustrious Welshmen, commencing with that of Cadwalader. I read a page of it aloud, while the family stood round and wondered to hear a Saxon read their language. I entered into discourse with the man about Welsh poetry, and repeated the famous prophecy of Taliesin about the Coiling Serpent. I asked him if the Welsh had any poets at the present day. "Plenty," said he, "and good ones—Wales can never be without a poet." Then after a pause he said that he was the grandson of a great poet.

"Do you bear his name?" said I.

"I do," he replied.

"What may it be?"

"Hughes," he answered.

"Two of the name of Hughes have been poets," said I—"one was Huw Hughes, generally termed the Bardd Coch, or red bard; he was an Anglesea man, and the friend of Lewis Morris and Gronwy Owen—the other was Jonathan Hughes, where he lived I know not."

"He lived here, in this very house," said the man; "Jonathan Hughes was my grandfather!" and as he spoke his eyes flashed fire.

"Dear me!" said I; "I read some of his pieces thirty-two years ago when I was a lad in England. I think I can repeat some of the lines." I then repeated a quartet which I chanced to remember.

" Ah !" said the man, " I see you know his poetry. Come into the next room and I will show you his chair." He led me into a sleeping-room on the right hand, where in a corner he showed me an antique three-cornered arm-chair. "That chair," said he, " my grandsire won at Llangollen, at an Eisteddfod of Bards. Various bards recited their poetry, but my grandfather won the prize. Ah, he was a good poet. He also won a prize of fifteen guineas at a meeting of bards in London."

We returned to the kitchen, where I found the good woman of the house waiting with a plate of bread-and-butter in one hand, and a glass of buttermilk in the other—she pressed me to partake of both—I drank some of the buttermilk, which was excellent, and after a little more discourse shook the kind people by the hand and thanked them for their hospitality. As I was about to depart the man said that I should find the lane farther up very wet, and that I had better mount through a field at the back of the house. He took me to a gate, which he opened, and then pointed out the way which I must pursue. As I went away he said that both he and his family should be always happy to see me at Ty yn y Pistyll, which words, interpreted, are the house by the spout of water.

I went up the field with the lane on my right, down which ran a runnel of water, from which doubtless the house derived its name. I soon came to an unenclosed part of the mountain covered with gorse and whin, and still proceeding upward reached a road, which I subsequently learned was the main road from Llangollen over the hill. I was not long in gaining the top, which was nearly level. Here I stood for some time looking about me, having the vale of Llangollen to the north of me, and a deep valley abounding with woods and rocks to the south.

Following the road to the south, which gradually descended, I soon came to a place where a road diverged from the straight one to the left. As the left-hand road appeared to lead down a romantic valley I followed it. The scenery was beautiful—steep hills on each side. On the right was a deep ravine, down which ran a brook; the hill beyond it was covered towards the top with a wood, apparently of oak, between which and the ravine were small green fields. Both sides of the ravine were fringed with trees, chiefly ash. I descended the road which was zig-zag and steep, and at last arrived at the bottom of the valley, where there was a small hamlet. On the farther side of the valley to the east was a steep hill on which were a few houses —at the foot of the hill was a brook crossed by an antique bridge of a single arch. I directed my course to the bridge, and after looking over the parapet, for a minute or two, upon the water below, which was shallow and noisy, ascended a road which led up the hill : a few scattered houses were on each side. I soon reached the top of the hill, where were some more houses, those which I had seen from the valley below. I was in a Welsh mountain village, which put me much in mind of the villages which I had strolled through of old in Castile and La Mancha; there were the same silence and desolation here as yonder away—the houses were built of the same material, namely stone. I should perhaps have fancied myself for a moment in a Castilian or Manchegan mountain pueblicito, but for the abundance of trees which met my eyes on every side.

In walking up this mountain village I saw no one, and heard no sound but the echo of my steps amongst the houses. As I returned, however, I saw a man standing at a door—he was a short figure, about fifty. He had an old hat on his head, a stick in his hand, and was dressed in a duffel great coat.

" Good day, friend," said I ; " what may be the name of this place?"

" Pont Fadog, sir, is its name, for want of a better."

" That's a fine name," said I ; " It signifies in English the bridge of Madoc."

" Just so, sir ; I see you know Welsh."

" And I see you know English," said I.

" Very little, sir; I can read English much better than I can speak it."

" So can I Welsh," said I. " I suppose the village is named after the bridge."

" No doubt it is, sir."

" And why was the bridge called the bridge of Madoc?" said I.

" Because one Madoc built it, sir."

" Was he the son of Owain Gwynedd?" said I.

" Ah, I see you know all about Wales, sir. Yes, sir; he built it, or I dare say he built it, Madawg ap Owain Gwynedd. I have read much about him—he was a great sailor, sir, and was the first to discover Tir y Gorllewin, or America. Not many years ago his tomb was discovered there with an inscription in old Welsh—saying who he was, and how he loved the sea. I have seen the lines which were found on the tomb."

" So have I," said I ; " or at least those which were said to be found on a tomb : they run thus in English :—

" ' Here, after sailing far, I, Madoc, lie,
Of Owain Gwynedd lawful progeny :
The verdant land had little charms for me ;
From earliest youth I loved the dark-blue sea.' "

" Ah, sir," said the man, " I see you know all about the son of Owain Gwynedd. Well, sir, those lines, or something like them, were found upon the tomb of Madoc in America."

" That I doubt," said I.

" Do you doubt, sir, that Madoc discovered America?"

" Not in the least," said I ; " but I doubt very much that his tomb was ever discovered with the inscription which you allude to upon it."

" But it was, sir, I do assure you, and the descendants of Madoc and his people are still to be found in a part of America speaking the pure iaith Cymraeg better Welsh than we of Wales do."

" That I doubt," said I. " However, the idea is a pretty one ; therefore cherish it. This is a beautiful country."

" A very beautiful country, sir ; there is none more beautiful in all Wales."

" What is the name of the river, which runs beneath the bridge?"

" The Ceiriog, sir."

" The Ceiriog," said I ; " the Ceiriog !"

" Did you ever hear the name before, sir?"

" I have heard of the Eos Ceiriog," said I ; " the Nightingale of Ceiriog."

" That was Huw Morris, sir; he was called the Nightingale of Ceiriog."

" Did he live hereabout?"

" O no, sir; he lived far away up towards the head of the valley, at a place called Pont y Meibion."

" Are you acquainted with his works?" said I.

" O yes, sir, at least with some of them. I have read the Marwnad on Barbara Middleton; and likewise the piece on Oliver and his men. Ah, it is a funny piece that—he did not like Oliver nor his men."

" Of what profession are you?" said I; " are you a schoolmaster or apothecary?"

" Neither, sir, neither; I am merely a poor shoemaker."

" You know a great deal for a shoemaker," said I.

" Ah, sir; there are many shoemakers in Wales who know much more than I."

" But not in England," said I. " Well, farewell."

" Farewell, sir. When you have any boots to mend, or shoes, sir—I shall be happy to serve you."

" I do not live in these parts," said I.

" No, sir; but you are coming to live here."

" How do you know that?" said I.

" I know it very well, sir; you left these parts very young, and went far away—to the East Indies, sir, where you made a large fortune in the medical line, sir; you are now coming back to your own valley, where you will buy a property, and settle down, and try to recover your language, sir, and your health, sir; for you are not the person you pretend to be, sir; I know you very well, and shall be happy to work for you."

" Well," said I, " if I ever settle down here, I shall be happy to employ you. Farewell."

I went back the way I had come, till I reached the little hamlet. Seeing a small public-house, I entered it —a good-looking woman, who met me in the passage, ushered me into a neat sanded kitchen, handed me a chair and inquired my commands; I sat down, and told her to bring me some ale; she brought it, and then seated herself by a bench close by the door.

" Rather a quiet place this," said I. " I have seen but two faces since I came over the hill, and yours is one."

" Rather too quiet, sir," said the good woman; " one would wish to have more visitors."

" I suppose," said I, " people from Llangollen occasionally come to visit you."

" Sometimes, sir, for curiosity's sake; but very rarely —the way is very steep."

" Do the Tylwyth Teg ever pay you visits?"

" The Tylwyth Teg, sir?"

" Yes; the fairies. Do they never come to have a dance on the green sward in this neighbourhood?"

" Very rarely, sir; indeed, I do not know how long it is since they have been seen."

" You have never seen them?"

" I have not, sir; but I believe there are people living who have."

" Are corpse candles ever seen on the bank of that river?"

" I have never heard of more than one being seen, sir, and that was at a place where a tinker was drowned a few nights after—there came down a flood, and the tinker in trying to cross by the usual ford was drowned."

" And did the candle prognosticate, I mean fore-show his death?"

" It did, sir. When a person is to die, his candle is seen a few nights before the time of his death."

" Have you ever seen a corpse candle?"

" I have, sir; and as you seem to be a respectable gentleman, I will tell you all about it. When I was a girl, I lived with my parents, a little way from here. I had a cousin, a very good young man, who lived with his parents in the neighbourhood of our house. He was an exemplary young man, sir, and having a consider-able gift of prayer, was intended for the ministry; but he fell sick, and shortly became very ill indeed. One evening when he was lying in this state, as I was re-turning home from milking, I saw a candle proceeding from my cousin's house. I stood still and looked at it. It moved slowly forward for a little way, and then mounted high in the air above the wood, which stood not far in front of the house, and disappeared. Just three nights after that my cousin died."

" And you think that what you saw was his corpse candle?"

" I do, sir ! what else should it be?"

" Are deaths prognosticated by any other means than corpse candles?"

" They are, sir; by the knockers, and by a supernatural voice heard at night."

" Have you ever heard the knockers, or the supernatural voice?"

" I have not, sir; but my father and mother, who are now dead, heard once a supernatural voice, and knocking. My mother had a sister who was married like herself, and expected to be confined. Day after day, however, passed away, without her confinement taking place. My mother expected every moment to be summoned to her assistance, and was so anxious about her that she could not rest at night. One night, as she lay in bed, by the side of her husband, between sleeping and waking, she heard of a sudden, a horse coming stump, stump, up to the door. Then there was a pause —she expected every moment to hear some one cry out, and tell her to come to her sister, but she heard no farther sound, neither voice nor stump of horse. She thought she had been deceived, so, without awakening her husband, she tried to go to sleep, but sleep she could not. The next night, at about the same time, she again heard a horse's feet coming stump, stump, up to the door. She now waked her husband and told him to listen. He did so, and both heard the stumping. Presently, the stumping ceased, and then there was a loud " Hey !" as if somebody wished to wake them. " Hey !" said my father, and they both lay for a minute, expecting to hear something more, but they heard nothing. My father then sprang out of bed, and looked out of the window; it was bright moonlight, but he saw nothing. The next night, as they lay in bed both asleep, they were suddenly aroused by a loud and terrible knocking. Out sprang my father from the bed, flung open the window, and looked out, but there was no one at the door. The next morning, however, a messenger arrived with the intelligence that my aunt had had a dreadful confinement with twins in the night, and that both she and the babes were dead."

" Thank you," said I; and paying for my ale, I returned to Llangollen.

CHAPTER XII

A Calvinistic Methodist—Turn for Saxon—Our Congregation—
Pont y Cyssylltau—Catherine Lingo.

I HAD inquired of the good woman of the house in which we lived whether she could not procure a person to accompany me occasionally in my walks, who was well acquainted with the strange nooks and corners of the country, and who could speak no language but Welsh; as I wished to increase my knowledge of colloquial Welsh by having a companion, who would be obliged, in all he had to say to me, to address me in Welsh, and to whom I should perforce have to reply in that tongue. The good lady had told me that there was a tenant of hers who lived in one of the cottages, which looked into the perllan, who, she believed, would be glad to go with me, and was just the kind of man I was in quest of. The day after I had met with the adventures which I have related in the preceding chapter, she informed me that the person in question was awaiting my orders in the kitchen. I told her to let me see him. He presently made his appearance. He was about forty-five years of age, of middle stature, and had a good-natured open countenance. His dress was poor, but clean.

"Well," said I to him in Welsh, "are you the Cumro who can speak no Saxon?"

"In truth, sir, I am."

"Are you sure that you know no Saxon?"

"Sir! I may know a few words, but I cannot converse in Saxon, nor understand a conversation in that tongue."

"Can you read Cumraeg?"

"In truth, sir, I can."

"What have you read in it?"

"I have read, sir, the Ysgrythyr-lan, till I have it nearly at the ends of my fingers."

"Have you read anything else besides the Holy Scripture?"

"I read the newspaper, sir, when kind friends lend it to me."

" In Cumraeg?"

" Yes, sir, in Cumraeg.   I can read Saxon a little,
but not sufficient to understand a Saxon newspaper."

" What newspaper do you read?"

" I read, sir, *Yr Amserau.*"

" Is that a good newspaper?"

" Very good, sir; it is written by good men."

" Who are they?"

" They are our ministers, sir."

" Of what religion are you?"

" A Calvinistic Methodist, sir."

" Why are you of the Methodist religion?"

" Because it is the true religion, sir."

" You should not be bigoted.   If I had more Cumraeg than I have, I would prove to you that the only
true religion is that of the Lloegrian Church."

" In truth, sir, you could not do that; had you all
the Cumraeg in Cumru you could not do that."

" What are you by trade?"

" I am a gwehydd, sir."

" What do you earn by weaving?"

" About five shillings a week, sir."

" Have you a wife?"

" I have, sir."

" Does she earn anything?"

" Very seldom, sir; she is a good wife, but is generally sick."

" Have you children?"

" I have three, sir."

" Do they earn anything?"

" My eldest son, sir, sometimes earns a few pence,
the others are very small."

" Will you sometimes walk with me, if I pay you?"

" I shall be always glad to walk with you, sir,
whether you pay me or not."

" Do you think it lawful to walk with one of the
Lloegrian Church?"

" Perhaps, sir, I ought to ask the gentleman of the
Lloegrian Church whether he thinks it lawful to walk
with the poor Methodist weaver."

" Well, I think we may venture to walk with one
another.   What is your name?"

" John Jones, sir."

" Jones ! Jones ! I was walking with a man of that name the other night."

" The man with whom you walked the other night is my brother, sir, and what he said to me about you made me wish to walk with you also."

" But he spoke very good English."

" My brother had a turn for Saxon, sir; I had not. Some people have a turn for the Saxon, others have not. I have no Saxon, sir, my wife has digon iawn— my two youngest children speak good Saxon, sir, my eldest son not a word."

" Well, shall we set out?"

" If you please, sir."

" To what place shall we go?"

" Shall we go to the Pont y Cyssylltau, sir?"

" What is that?"

" A mighty bridge, sir, which carries the Camlas over a valley on its back."

" Good ! let us go and see the bridge of the junction, for that I think is the meaning in Saxon of Pont y Cyssylltau."

We set out; my guide conducted me along the bank of the Camlas in the direction of Rhiwabon, that is towards the east. On the way we discoursed on various subjects, and understood each other tolerably well. I asked if he had ever been anything besides a weaver. He told me that when a boy he kept sheep on the mountain. " Why did you not go on keeping sheep?" said I; " I would rather keep sheep than weave."

" My parents wanted me at home, sir," said he; " and I was not sorry to go home; I earned little, and lived badly."

" A shepherd," said I, " can earn more than five shillings a week."

" I was never a regular shepherd, sir," said he. " But, sir, I would rather be a weaver with five shillings a week in Llangollen, than a shepherd with fifteen on the mountain. The life of a shepherd, sir, is perhaps not exactly what you and some other gentlefolks think. The shepherd bears much cold and wet, sir, and he is very lonely; no society save his sheep and dog. Then, sir, he has no privileges. I mean gospel privileges. He does not look forward to Dydd Sul, as a day of llawenydd, of joy and triumph, as the weaver does; that is if he is religiously disposed. The shepherd has no chapel, sir, like the weaver. Oh, sir, I say again that I would rather be a weaver in Llangollen with five shillings a week, than a shepherd on the hill with fifteen."

" Do you mean to say," said I, "that you live with your family on five shillings a week?"

" No, sir. I frequently do little commissions by which I earn something. Then, sir, I have friends, very good friends. A good lady of our congregation sent me this morning half-a-pound of butter. The people of our congregation are very kind to each other, sir."

"That is more," thought I to myself, "than the people of my congregation are; they are always cutting each other's throats." I next asked if he had been much about Wales.

" Not much, sir. However, I have been to Pen Caer Gybi, which you call Holy Head, and to Bethgelert, sir."

" What took you to those places?"

" I was sent to those places on business, sir; as I told you before, sir, I sometimes execute commissions. At Bethgelert I stayed some time. It was there I married, sir; my wife comes from a place called Dol Gellyn near Bethgelert."

"What was her name?"

" Her name was Jones, sir."

" What, before she married?"

" Yes, sir, before she married. You need not be surprised, sir; there are plenty of the name of Jones in Wales. The name of my brother's wife, before she married, was also Jones."

" Your brother is a clever man," said I.

" Yes, sir, for a Cumro he is clebber enough."

" For a Cumro?"

" Yes, sir, he is not a Saxon, you know."

" Are Saxons then so very clever?"

" O yes, sir; who so clebber? The clebberest people in Llangollen are Saxons; that is, at carnal things—for at spiritual things I do not think them at all clebber. Look at Mr. A., sir."

" Who is he?"

"Do you not know him, sir? I thought everybody knew Mr. A. He is a Saxon, sir, and keeps the inn on the road a little way below where you live. He is the clebberest man in Llangollen, sir. He can do everything. He is a great cook, and can wash clothes better than any woman. O, sir, for carnal things, who so clebber as your countrymen!"

After walking about four miles by the side of the canal we left it, and bearing to the right presently came to the aqueduct, which strode over a deep and narrow valley, at the bottom of which ran the Dee. "This is the Pont y Cysswllt, sir," said my guide; "it's the finest bridge in the world, and no wonder, if what the common people say be true, namely that every stone cost a golden sovereign." We went along it; the height was awful. My guide, though he had been a mountain shepherd, confessed that he was somewhat afraid. "It gives me the pendro, sir," said he, "to look down." I too felt somewhat dizzy, as I looked over the parapet into the glen. The canal which this mighty bridge carries across the gulf is about nine feet wide, and occupies about two-thirds of the width of the bridge and the entire western side. The footway is towards the east. From about the middle of the bridge there is a fine view of the forges on the Cefn Bach and also of a huge hill near it called the Cefn Mawr. We reached the termination, and presently crossing the canal by a little wooden bridge we came to a village. My guide then said, "If you please, sir, we will return by the old bridge, which leads across the Dee in the bottom of the vale." He then led me by a romantic road to a bridge on the west of the aqueduct, and far below. It seemed very ancient. "This is the old bridge, sir," said my guide; "it was built a hundred years before the Pont y Cysswllt was dreamt of." We now walked to the west, in the direction of Llangollen, along the bank of the river. Presently we arrived where the river, after making a bend, formed a pool. It was shaded by lofty trees, and to all appearance was exceedingly deep. I stopped to look at it, for I was struck with its gloomy horror. "That pool, sir," said john Jones, "is called Llyn y Meddwyn, the drunkard's pool. It is called so, sir, because a drunken man once

fell into it, and was drowned. There is no deeper pool
in the Dee, sir, save one, a little below Llangollen,
which is called the pool of Catherine Lingo. A girl of
that name fell into it, whilst gathering sticks on the
high bank above it. She was drowned, and the pool
was named after her. I never look at either without
shuddering, thinking how certainly I should be drowned
if I fell in, for I cannot swim, sir."

"You should have learnt to swim when you were
young," said I, "and to dive too. I know one who
has brought up stones from the bottom, I dare say,
of deeper pools than either, but he was a Saxon, and
at carnal things, you know, none so clebber as the
Saxons."

I found my guide a first-rate walker, and a good
botanist, knowing the names of all the plants and trees
in Welsh. By the time we returned to Llangollen I had
formed a very high opinion of him, in which I was subsequently confirmed by what I saw of him during the
period of our acquaintance, which was of some duration. He was very honest, disinterested, and exceedingly good-humoured. It is true, he had his little skits
occasionally at the Church, and showed some marks of
hostility to the church cat, more especially when he
saw it mounted on my shoulders; for the creature soon
began to take liberties, and in less than a week after
my arrival at the cottage, generally mounted on my
back, when it saw me reading or writing, for the sake
of the warmth. But setting aside those same skits at
the Church and that dislike of the church cat, venial
trifles after all, and easily to be accounted for, on the
score of his religious education, I found nothing to
blame and much to admire in John Jones the Calvinistic
Methodist of Llangollen.

CHAPTER XIII

Divine Service—Llangollen Bells—Iolo Goch—The Abbey—Twm
o'r Nant—Holy Well—Thomas Edwards.

SUNDAY arrived—a Sunday of unclouded sunshine. We attended Divine service at church in the morning. The congregation was very numerous, but to all appearance consisted almost entirely of English visitors, like ourselves. There were two officiating clergymen, father and son. They both sat in a kind of oblong pulpit on the southern side of the church, at a little distance below the altar. The service was in English, and the elder gentleman preached; there was good singing and chanting.

After dinner I sat in an arbour in the perllan thinking of many things, amongst others, spiritual. Whilst thus engaged the sound of the church bells calling people to afternoon service, came upon my ears. I listened and thought I had never heard bells with so sweet a sound. I had heard them in the morning, but without paying much attention to them, but as I now sat in the umbrageous arbour I was particularly struck with them. O, how sweetly their voice mingled with the low rush of the river, at the bottom of the perllan. I subsequently found that the bells of Llangollen were celebrated for their sweetness. Their merit indeed has even been admitted by an enemy; for a poet of the Calvinistic-Methodist persuasion, one who calls himself Einion Du, in a very beautiful ode, commencing with—

" Tangnefedd i Llangollen,"

says that in no part of the world do bells call people so sweetly to church as those of Llangollen town.

In the evening, at about half-past six, I attended service again, but without my family. This time the congregation was not numerous, and was composed principally of poor people. The service and sermon were now in Welsh, the sermon was preached by the younger gentleman, and was on the building of the second temple, and, as far as I understood it, appeared to me to be exceedingly good.

On the Monday evening myself and family took a walk to the abbey. My wife and daughter, who are fond of architecture and ruins, were very anxious to see the old place. I too was anxious enough to see it, less from love of ruins and ancient architecture, than from knowing that a certain illustrious bard was buried in its precincts, of whom perhaps a short account will not be unacceptable to the reader.

This man, whose poetical appellation was Iolo Goch, but whose real name was Llwyd, was of a distinguished family, and Lord of Llechryd. He was born and generally resided at a place called Coed y Pantwn, in the upper part of the Vale of Clwyd. He was a warm friend and partisan of Owen Glendower, with whom he lived, at Sycharth, for some years before the great Welsh insurrection, and whom he survived, dying at an extreme old age beneath his own roof-tree at Coed y Pantwn. He composed pieces of great excellence on various subjects; but the most remarkable of his compositions are decidedly certain ones connected with Owen Glendower. Amongst these is one in which he describes the Welsh chieftain's mansion at Sycharth, and his hospitable way of living at that his favourite residence; and another in which he hails the advent of the comet, which made its appearance in the month of March, fourteen hundred and two, as of good augury to his darling hero.

It was from knowing that this distinguished man lay buried in the precincts of the old edifice that I felt so anxious to see it. After walking about two miles we perceived it on our right hand.

The abbey of the vale of the cross stands in a green meadow, in a corner near the north-west end of the valley of Llangollen. The vale or glen, in which the abbey stands, takes its name from a certain ancient pillar or cross, called the pillar of Eliseg, and which is believed to have been raised over the body of an ancient British chieftain of that name, who perished in battle against the Saxons, about the middle of the tenth century. In the Papist times the abbey was a place of great pseudo-sanctity, wealth and consequence. The territory belonging to it was very extensive, comprising, amongst other districts, the vale of Llangollen and the mountain region to the north of it, called the Eglwysig Rocks, which region derived its name Eglwysig, or ecclesiastical, from the circumstance of its pertaining to the abbey of the vale of the cross.

We first reached that part of the building which had once been the church, having previously to pass through a farm-yard, in which was abundance of dirt and mire.

The church fronts the west and contains the remains of a noble window, beneath which is a gate, which we found locked. Passing on we came to that part where the monks had lived, but which now served as a farm-house; an open door-way exhibited to us an ancient gloomy hall, where was some curious old-fashioned furniture, particularly an ancient rack, in which stood a goodly range of pewter trenchers. A respectable dame kindly welcomed us and invited us to sit down. We entered into conversation with her, and asked her name, which she said was Evans. I spoke some Welsh to her, which pleased her. She said that Welsh people at the present day were so full of fine airs that they were above speaking the old language—but that such was not the case formerly, and that she had known a Mrs. Price, who was housekeeper to the Countess of Mornington, who lived in London upwards of forty years, and at the end of that time prided herself upon speaking as good Welsh as she did when a girl. I spoke to her about the abbey, and asked if she had ever heard of Iolo Goch. She inquired who he was. I told her he was a great bard, and was buried in the abbey. She said she had never heard of him, but that she could show me the portrait of a great poet, and going away, presently returned with a print in a frame.

"There," said she, "is the portrait of Twm o'r Nant, generally called the Welsh Shakespear."

I looked at it. The Welsh Shakespear was represented sitting at a table with a pen in his hand; a cottage-latticed window was behind him, on his left hand; a shelf with plates and trenchers behind him, on his right. His features were rude, but full of wild, strange expression; below the picture was the following couplet :—

" Llun Gwr yw llawn gwir Awen ;
Y Byd a lanwodd o'i Ben."

" Did you ever hear of Twm o'r Nant?" said the old dame.

" I never heard of him by word of mouth," said I; " but I know all about him—I have read his life in Welsh, written by himself, and a curious life it is. His name was Thomas Edwards, but he generally called himself Twm o'r Nant, or Tom of the Dingle, because he was born in a dingle, at a place called Pen Porchell in the vale of Clwyd—which, by the bye, was on the estate which once belonged to Iolo Goch, the poet I was speaking to you about just now. Tom was a carter by trade, but once kept a toll-bar in South Wales, which, however, he was obliged to leave at the end of two years, owing to the annoyance which he experienced from ghosts and goblins, and unearthly things, particularly phantom hearses, which used to pass through his gate at midnight without paying, when the gate was shut."

" Ah," said the Dame, " you know more about Twm o'r Nant than I do; and was he not a great poet?"

" I dare say he was," said I, " for the pieces which he wrote, and which he called Interludes, had a great run, and he got a great deal of money by them, but I should say the lines beneath the portrait are more applicable to the real Shakespear than to him."

" What do the lines mean?" said the old lady; " they are Welsh, I know, but they are far beyond my understanding."

" They may be thus translated," said I:

" God in his head the Muse instill'd,
And from his head the world he fill'd."

" Thank you, sir," said the old lady; " I never found any one before who could translate them." She then said she would show me some English lines written on the daughter of a friend of hers who was lately dead, and put some printed lines in a frame into my hand. They were an Elegy to Mary, and were very beautiful. I read them aloud, and when I had finished she thanked me and said she had no doubt that if I pleased I could put them into Welsh. She then sighed and wiped her eyes.

On our inquiring whether we could see the interior

of the abbey she said we could, and that if we rang a bell at the gate a woman would come to us, who was in the habit of showing the place. We then got up and bade her farewell—but she begged that we would stay and taste the dwr santaidd of the holy well.

" What holy well is that?" said I.

" A well," said she, " by the road's side, which in the time of the popes was said to perform wonderful cures."

" Let us taste it by all means," said I; whereupon she went out, and presently returned with a tray on which were a jug and tumbler, the jug filled with the water of the holy well; we drank some of the dwr santaidd, which tasted like any other water, and then after shaking her by the hand, we went to the gate, and rang at the bell.

Presently a woman made her appearance at the gate; she was genteelly drest, about the middle age, rather tall, and bearing in her countenance the traces of beauty. When we told her the object of our coming she admitted us, and after locking the gate conducted us into the church. It was roofless, and had nothing remarkable about it, save the western window, which we had seen from without. Our attendant pointed out to us some tombs, and told us the names of certain great people whose dust they contained. " Can you tell us where Iolo Goch lies interred?" said I.

" No," said she; " indeed I never heard of such a person."

" He was the bard of Owen Glendower," said I, " and assisted his cause wonderfully by the fiery odes, in which he incited the Welsh to rise against the English."

" Indeed!" said she; " well, I am sorry to say that I never heard of him."

" Are you Welsh?" said I.

" I am," she replied.

" Did you ever hear of Thomas Edwards?"

" O, yes," said she; " I have frequently heard of him."

" How odd," said I, " that the name of a great poet should be unknown in the very place where he is buried, whilst that of one certainly not his superior, should be well known in that same place, though he is not buried there."

" Perhaps," said she, " the reason is that the poet, whom you mentioned, wrote in the old measures and language which few people now understand, whilst Thomas Edwards wrote in common verse and in the language of the present day."

" I dare say it is so," said I.

From the church she led us to other parts of the ruin —at first she had spoken to us rather cross and loftily, but she now became kind and communicative. She said that she resided near the ruins, which she was permitted to show; that she lived alone, and wished to be alone—there was something singular about her, and I believe that she had a history of her own. After showing us the ruins she conducted us to a cottage in which she lived; it stood behind the ruins by a fish-pond, in a beautiful and romantic place enough—she said that in the winter she went away, but to what place she did not say. She asked us whether we came walking, and on our telling her that we did, she said that she would point out to us a near way home. She then pointed to a path up a hill, telling us we must follow it. After making her a present we bade her fare-well, and passing through a meadow crossed a brook by a rustic bridge, formed of the stem of a tree, and ascending the hill by a path which she had pointed out, we went through a corn field or two on its top, and at last found ourselves on the Llangollen road, after a most beautiful walk.

CHAPTER XIV

Expedition to Ruthyn—The Column—Slate Quarries—The Gwyddelod—Nocturnal Adventure.

NOTHING worthy of commemoration took place during the two following days, save that myself and family took an evening walk on the Wednesday up the side of the Berwyn, for the purpose of botanizing, in which we were attended by John Jones. There, amongst other plants, we found a curious moss which our good friend said was called in Welsh Corn Carw, or deer's horn, and which he said the deer were very fond of. On the Thursday he and I started on an expedition on foot to Ruthyn, distant about fourteen miles, proposing to return in the evening.

The town and castle of Ruthyn possessed great interest for me from being connected with the affairs of Owen Glendower. It was at Ruthyn that the first and not the least remarkable scene of the Welsh insurrection took place by Owen making his appearance at the fair held there in fourteen hundred, plundering the English who had come with their goods, slaying many of them, sacking the town and concluding his day's work by firing it; and it was at the castle of Ruthyn that Lord Grey dwelt, a minion of Henry the Fourth and Glendower's deadliest enemy, and who was the principal cause of the chieftain's entering into rebellion, having in the hope of obtaining his estates in the vale of Clwyd poisoned the mind of Henry against him, who proclaimed him a traitor, before he had committed any act of treason, and confiscated his estates, bestowing that part of them upon his favourite, which the latter was desirous of obtaining.

We started on our expedition at about seven o'clock of a brilliant morning. We passed by the abbey and presently came to a small fountain with a little stone edifice, with a sharp top above it. " That is the holy well," said my guide : " Llawer iawn o barch yn yr amser yr Pabyddion yr oedd i'r fynnon hwn—much respect in the times of the Papists there was to this fountain."

" I heard of it," said I, " and tasted of its water the other evening at the abbey." Shortly after we saw a tall stone standing in a field on our right hand at about a hundred yards distance from the road. " That is the pillar of Eliseg, sir," said my guide. " Let us go and see it," said I. We soon reached the stone. It is a fine upright column about seven feet high, and stands on a quadrate base. " Sir," said my guide, " a dead king lies buried beneath this stone. He was a mighty man of valour and founded the abbey. He was called Eliseg." " Perhaps Ellis," said I, " and if his name was Ellis his stone was very properly called

Colofn Eliseg, in Saxon the Ellisian column." The
view from the column is very beautiful, below on the
south-east is the venerable abbey, slumbering in its
green meadow. Beyond it runs a stream, descending
from the top of a glen, at the bottom of which the old
pile is situated; beyond the stream is a lofty hill. The
glen on the north is bounded by a noble mountain,
covered with wood. Struck with its beauty I inquired
its name. "Moel Eglwysig, sir," said my guide.
"The Moel of the Church," said I. "That is hardly
a good name for it, for the hill is not bald (moel)."
"True, sir," said John Jones. "At present its name
is good for nothing, but estalom (of old) before the hill
was planted with trees its name was good enough.
Our fathers were not fools when they named their
hills." "I dare say not," said I, "nor in many other
things which they did, for which we laugh at them,
because we do not know the reasons they had for
doing them." We regained the road; the road tended
to the north up a steep ascent. I asked John Jones the
name of a beautiful village, which lay far away on our
right, over the glen, and near its top. "Pentref y dwr,
sir" (the village of the water). It is called the village
of the water, because the river below comes down
through part of it. I next asked the name of the hill up
which we were going, and he told me Allt Bwlch; that
is, the high place of the hollow road.

This bwlch, or hollow way, was a regular pass, which
put me wonderfully in mind of the passes of Spain.
It took us a long time to get to the top. After resting
a minute on the summit we began to descend. My
guide pointed out to me some slate-works, at some distance on our left. "There is a great deal of work
going on there, sir," said he: "all the slates that you
see descending the canal at Llangollen come from
there." The next moment we heard a blast, and then
a thundering sound: "Llais craig yn syrthiaw; the
voice of the rock in falling, sir," said John Jones;
"blasting is dangerous and awful work." We reached
the bottom of the descent, and proceeded for two or
three miles up and down a rough and narrow road; I
then turned round and looked at the hills which we
had passed over. They looked bulky and huge.

We continued our way, and presently saw marks of a fire in some grass by the side of the road. " Have the Gipsiaid been there?" said I to my guide.

" Hardly, sir; I should rather think that the Gwyddeliad (Irish) have been camping there lately."

" The Gwyddeliad?"

" Yes, sir, the vagabond Gwyddeliad, who at present infest these parts much, and do much more harm than the Gipsiaid ever did."

" What do you mean by the Gipsiaid?"

" Dark, handsome people, sir, who occasionally used to come about in vans and carts, the men buying and selling horses, and sometimes tinkering, whilst the women told fortunes."

" And they have ceased to come about?"

" Nearly so, sir; I believe they have been frightened away by the Gwyddelod."

" What kind of people are these Gwyddelod?"

" Savage, brutish people, sir; in general without shoes and stockings, with coarse features and heads of hair like mops."

" How do they live?"

" The men tinker a little, sir, but more frequently plunder. The women tell fortunes, and steal whenever they can."

" They live something like the Gipsiaid."

" Something, sir; but the hen Gipsiaid were gentle-folks in comparison."

" You think the Gipsiaid have been frightened away by the Gwyddelians?"

" I do, sir; the Gwyddelod made their appearance in these parts about twenty years ago, and since then the Gipsiaid have been rarely seen."

" Are these Gwyddelod poor?"

" By no means, sir; they make large sums by plundering and other means, with which, 'tis said, they retire at last to their own country or America, where they buy land and settle down."

" What language do they speak?"

" English, sir; they pride themselves on speaking good English, that is to the Welsh. Amongst them-selves they discourse in their own Paddy Gwyddel."

" Have they no Welsh?"

" Only a few words, sir; I never heard of one of them speaking Welsh, save a young girl—she fell sick by the roadside, as she was wandering by herself— some people at a farm-house took her in, and tended her till she was well. During her sickness she took a fancy to their quiet way of life, and when she was re-covered she begged to stay with them and serve them. They consented; she became a very good servant, and hearing nothing but Welsh spoken, soon picked up the tongue."

" Do you know what became of her?"

" I do, sir; her own people found her out, and wished to take her away with them, but she refused to let them, for by that time she was perfectly reclaimed, had been to chapel, renounced her heathen crefydd, and formed an acquaintance with a young Methodist who had a great gift of prayer, whom she afterwards married —she and her husband live at present not far from Mineira."

" I almost wonder that her own people did not kill her."

" They threatened to do so, sir, and would doubtless have put their threat into execution, had they not been prevented by the Man on High."

And here my guide pointed with his finger reverently upward.

" Is it a long time since you have seen any of these Gwyddeliaid?"

" About two months, sir, and then a terrible fright they caused me."

" How was that?"

" I will tell you, sir; I had been across the Berwyn to carry home a piece of weaving work to a person who employs me. It was night as I returned, and when I was about half-way down the hill, at a place which is called Allt Paddy, because the Gwyddelod are in the habit of taking up their quarters there, I came upon a gang of them, who had come there and camped and lighted their fire, whilst I was on the other side of the hill. There were nearly twenty of them, men and women, and amongst the rest was a man standing naked in a tub of water with two women stroking him down with clouts. He was a large fierce-looking fellow, and his body, on which the flame of the fire glittered, was nearly covered with red hair. I never saw such a sight. As I passed they glared at me and talked violently in their Paddy Gwyddel, but did not offer to molest me. I hastened down the hill, and right glad I was when I found myself safe and sound at my house in Llangollen, with my money in my pocket, for I had several shillings there, which the man across the hill had paid me for the work which I had done."

CHAPTER XV

The Turf Tavern—Don't Understand—The Best Welsh—The Maids of Merion — Old and New — Ruthyn — The Ash Yggdrasill.

WE now emerged from the rough and narrow way which we had followed for some miles, upon one much wider, and more commodious, which my guide told me was the coach road from Wrexham to Ruthyn, and going on a little farther we came to an avenue of trees which shaded the road. It was chiefly composed of ash, sycamore, and birch, and looked delightfully cool and shady. I asked my guide if it belonged to any gentleman's house. He told me that it did not, but to a public-house, called Tafarn Tywarch, which stood near the end, a little way off the road. "Why is it called Tafarn Tywarch?" said I, struck by the name, which signifies " the tavern of turf."

" It was called so, sir," said John, " because it was originally merely a turf hovel, though at present it consists of good brick and mortar."

" Can we breakfast there," said I, " for I feel both hungry and thirsty?"

" O, yes, sir," said John, " I have heard there is good cheese and cwrw there."

We turned off to the " tafarn," which was a decent public-house of rather an antiquated appearance. We entered a sanded kitchen, and sat down by a large oaken table. " Please to bring us some bread, cheese and ale," said I in Welsh to an elderly woman, who was moving about.

" Sar?" said she.

" Bring us some bread, cheese and ale," I repeated in Welsh.

" I do not understand you, sar," said she in English.

" Are you Welsh?" said I in English.

" Yes, I am Welsh!"

" And can you speak Welsh?"

" O, yes, and the best."

" Then why did you not bring what I asked for?"

" Because I did not understand you."

" Tell her," said I to John Jones, " to bring us some bread, cheese and ale."

" Come, aunt," said John, " bring us bread and cheese and a quart of the best ale."

The woman looked as if she was going to reply in the tongue in which he addressed her, then faltered, and at last said in English that she did not understand.

" Now," said I, " you are fairly caught : this man is a Welshman, and moreover understands no language but Welsh."

" Then how can he understand you?" said she.

" Because I speak Welsh," said I.

" Then you are a Welshman?" said she.

" No I am not," said I, " I am English."

" So I thought," said she, " and on that account I could not understand you."

" You mean that you would not," said I. " Now do you choose to bring what you are bidden?"

" Come, aunt," said John, " don't be silly and cenfigenus, but bring the breakfast."

The woman stood still for a moment or two, and then biting her lips went away.

" What made the woman behave in this manner?" said I to my companion.

" O, she was cenfigenus, sir," he replied; " she did not like that an English gentleman should understand Welsh; she was envious; you will find a dozen or two like her in Wales; but let us hope not more."

Presently the woman returned with the bread, cheese and ale, which she placed on the table.

" Oh," said I, " you have brought what was bidden, though it was never mentioned to you in English, which shows that your pretending not to understand was all a sham. What made you behave so?"

" Why I thought," said the woman, " that no Englishman could speak Welsh, that his tongue was too short."

" Your having thought so," said I, " should not have made you tell a falsehood, saying that you did not understand, when you knew that you understood very well. See what a disgraceful figure you cut."

" I cut no disgraced figure," said the woman : " after all, what right have the English to come here speaking Welsh, which belongs to the Welsh alone, who in fact are the only people that understand it."

" Are you sure that you understand Welsh?" said I.

" I should think so," said the woman, " for I come from the vale of Clwyd, where they speak the best Welsh in the world, the Welsh of the Bible."

" What do they call a salmon in the vale of Clwyd?" said I.

" What do they call a salmon?" said the woman.

" Yes," said I, " when they speak Welsh."

" They call it—they call it—why a salmon."

" Pretty Welsh!" said I. " I thought you did not understand Welsh."

" Well, what do you call it?" said the woman.

" Eawg," said I, " that is the word for a salmon in general—but there are words also to show the sex— when you speak of a male salmon you should say cemyw, when of a female hwyfell."

" I never heard the words before," said the woman, " nor do I believe them to be Welsh."

" You say so," said I, " because you do not understand Welsh."

" I not understand Welsh!" said she. " I'll soon show you that I do. Come, you have asked me the word for salmon in Welsh, I will now ask you the word for salmon-trout. Now tell me that, and I will say you know something of the matter."

" A tinker of my country can tell you that," said I. " The word for salmon-trout is gleisiad."

The countenance of the woman fell.

"I see you know something about the matter," said she; "there are very few hereabouts, though so near

to the vale of Clwyd, who know the word for salmon-
trout in Welsh. I shouldn't have known the word
myself, but for the song which says :

> " ' Glân yw'r gleisiad yn y llyn.' "

" And who wrote that song?" said I.

" I don't know," said the woman.

" But I do," said I ; " one Lewis Morris wrote it."

" Oh," said she, " I have heard all about Huw
Morris."

" I was not talking of Huw Morris," said I, " but
Lewis Morris, who lived long after Huw Morris. He
was a native of Anglesea, but resided for some time in
Merionethshire, and whilst there composed a song
about the Morwynion bro Meirionydd, or the lasses
of County Merion, of a great many stanzas, in one of
which the gleisiad is mentioned. Here it is in English :

> " ' Full fair the gleisiad in the flood,
>   Which sparkles 'neath the summer's sun,
> And fair the thrush in green abode
>   Spreading his wings in sportive fun,
> But fairer look if truth be spoke,
> The maids of County Merion.' "

The woman was about to reply, but I interrupted
her.

" There," said I, " pray leave us to our breakfast,
and the next time you feel inclined to talk nonsense
about no Englishman's understanding Welsh, or knowing anything of Welsh matters, remember that it was
an Englishman who told you the Welsh word for
salmon, and likewise the name of the Welshman who
wrote the song in which the gleisiad is mentioned."

The ale was very good, and so were the bread and
cheese. The ale indeed was so good that I ordered a
second jug. Observing a large antique portrait over
the mantel-piece I got up to examine it. It was that
of a gentleman in a long wig, and underneath it was
painted in red letters " Sir Watkin Wynn 1742." It
was doubtless the portrait of the Sir Watkin who in
1745 was committed to the Tower under suspicion of
being suspected of holding Jacobite opinions, and
favouring the Pretender. The portrait was a very
poor daub, but I looked at it long and attentively as
a memorial of Wales at a critical and long past time.

When we had dispatched the second jug of ale, and I had paid the reckoning, we departed and soon came to where stood a turnpike house at a junction of two roads, to each of which was a gate.

"Now, sir," said John Jones, "the way straight forward is the ffordd newydd and the one on our right hand is the hen ffordd. Which shall we follow, the new or the old?"

"There is a proverb in the Gerniweg," said I, "which was the language of my forefathers, saying, 'ne'er leave the old way for the new,' we will therefore go by the hen ffordd."

"Very good, sir," said my guide, "that is the path I always go, for it is the shortest." So we turned to the right and followed the old road. Perhaps, however, it would have been well had we gone by the new, for the hen ffordd was a very dull and uninteresting road, whereas the ffordd newydd, as I long subsequently found, is one of the grandest passes in Wales. After we had walked a short distance my guide said, "Now, sir, if you will turn a little way to the left hand I will show you a house built in the old style, such a house, sir, as I dare say the original turf tavern was." Then leading me a little way from the road he showed me, under a hollow bank, a small cottage covered with flags.

"That is a house, sir, built yn yr hen dull in the old fashion, of earth, flags and wattles, and in one night. It was the custom of old when a house was to be built, for the people to assemble, and to build it in one night of common materials, close at hand. The custom is not quite dead. I was at the building of this myself, and a merry building it was. The cwrw da passed quickly about among the builders, I assure you." We returned to the road, and when we had ascended a hill my companion told me that if I looked to the left I should see the vale of Clwyd.

I looked and perceived an extensive valley pleasantly dotted with trees and farm-houses, and bounded on the west by a range of hills.

"It is a fine valley, sir," said my guide, "four miles wide and twenty long, and contains the richest land in all Wales. Cheese made in that valley, sir, fetches a penny a pound more than cheese made in any other valley."

"And who owns it?" said I.

"Various are the people who own it, sir, but Sir Watkin owns the greater part."

We went on, passed by a village called Craig Vychan, where we saw a number of women washing at a fountain, and by a gentle descent soon reached the vale of Clwyd.

After walking about a mile we left the road and proceeded by a footpath across some meadows. The meadows were green and delightful, and were intersected by a beautiful stream. Trees in abundance were growing about, some of which were oaks. We passed by a little white chapel with a small graveyard before it, which my guide told me belonged to the Baptists, and shortly afterwards reached Ruthyn.

We went to an inn called the Crossed Foxes, where we refreshed ourselves with ale. We then sallied forth to look about, after I had ordered a duck to be got ready for dinner, at three o'clock. Ruthyn stands on a hill above the Clwyd, which in the summer is a mere brook, but in the winter a considerable stream, being then fed with the watery tribute of a hundred hills. About three miles to the north is a range of lofty mountains, dividing the shire of Denbigh from that of Flint, amongst which, almost parallel with the town, and lifting its head high above the rest, is the mighty Moel Vamagh, the mother heap, which I had seen from Chester. Ruthyn is a dull town, but it possessed plenty of interest for me, for as I strolled with my guide about the streets I remembered that I was treading the ground which the wild bands of Glendower had trod, and where the great struggle commenced, which for fourteen years convulsed Wales, and for some time shook England to its centre. After I had satisfied myself with wandering about the town we proceeded to the castle.

The original castle suffered terribly in the civil wars; it was held for wretched Charles, and was nearly demolished by the cannon of Cromwell, which were planted on a hill about half-a-mile distant. The present castle is partly modern and partly ancient. It belongs to a family of the name of W——, who reside in the modern part, and who have the character of being kind, hospitable, and intellectual people. We only visited the ancient part, over which we were shown by a woman, who hearing us speaking Welsh, spoke Welsh herself during the whole time she was showing us about.   She showed us dark passages, a gloomy apartment in which Welsh kings and great people had been occasionally confined, that strange memorial of the good old times, a drowning pit, and a large prison room, in the middle of which stood a singular looking-column, scrawled with odd characters, which had of yore been used for a whipping-post, another memorial of the good old baronial times, so dear to romance readers and minds of sensibility. Amongst other things which our conductor showed us, was an immense onen or ash; it stood in one of the courts, and measured, as she said, pedwar y haner o ladd yn ei gwmpas, or four yards and a half in girth. As I gazed on the mighty tree I thought of the Ash Yggdrasill mentioned in the Voluspa, or prophecy of Vola, that venerable poem which contains so much relating to the mythology of the ancient Norse.

We returned to the inn and dined. The duck was capital, and I asked John Jones if he had ever tasted a better. "Never, sir," said he, "for to tell you the truth, I never tasted a duck before." "Rather singular," said I. "What that I should not have tasted duck? O, sir, the singularity is, that I should now be tasting duck. Duck in Wales, sir, is not fare for poor weavers. This is the first duck I ever tasted, and though I never taste another, as I probably never shall, I may consider myself a fortunate weaver, for I can now say I have tasted duck once in my life. Few weavers in Wales are ever able to say as much."

CHAPTER XVI

Baptist Tomb-Stone—The Toll-Bar—Rebecca—The Guitar.

THE sun was fast declining as we left Ruthyn. We retraced our steps across the fields. When we came to the Baptist chapel I got over the wall of the little yard to look at the gravestones. There were only three. The inscriptions upon them were all in Welsh. The following stanza was on the stone of Jane, the daughter of Elizabeth Williams, who died on the second of May, 1843 :—

> " Er myn'd i'r oerllyd annedd
> Dros dymher hir i orwedd,
> Cwyd i'r lan o'r gwely bridd
> Ac hyfryd fydd ei hagwedd,"

which is

> " Though thou art gone to dwelling cold,
> To lie in mould for many a year,
> Thou shalt, at length, from earthy bed,
> Uplift thy head to blissful sphere."

As we went along I stopped to gaze at a singular-looking hill forming part of the mountain range on the east. I asked John Jones what its name was, but he did not know. As we were standing talking about it, a lady came up from the direction in which our course lay. John Jones, touching his hat to her, said :

"Madam, this gwr boneddig wishes to know the name of that moel; perhaps you can tell him."

" Its name is Moel Agrik," said the lady, addressing me in English.

" Does that mean Agricola's hill?" said I.

" It does," said she; " and there is a tradition that the Roman general Agricola, when he invaded these parts, pitched his camp on that moel. The hill is spoken of by Pennant."

" Thank you, madam," said I; " perhaps you can tell me the name of the delightful grounds in which we stand, supposing they have a name."

" They are called Oaklands," said the lady.

" A very proper name," said I, " for there are plenty of oaks growing about. But why are they called by a Saxon name, for Oaklands is Saxon."

" Because," said the lady, " when the grounds were first planted with trees they belonged to an English family."

" Thank you," said I, and, taking off my hat, I departed with my guide. I asked him her name, but he could not tell me. Before she was out of sight, however, we met a labourer, of whom John Jones inquired her name.

"Her name is W——s," said the man, " and a good lady she is."

" Is she Welsh?" said I.

" Pure Welsh, master," said the man. " Purer Welsh flesh and blood need not be."

Nothing farther worth relating occurred till we reached the toll-bar at the head of the hen ffordd, by which time the sun was almost gone down. We found the master of the gate, his wife, and son seated on a bench before the door. The woman had a large book on her lap, in which she was reading by the last light of the departing orb. I gave the group the seal of the evening in English, which they all returned, the woman looking up from her book.

" Is that volume the Bible?" said I.

" It is, sir," said the woman.

" May I look at it?" said I.

" Certainly," said the woman, and placed the book in my hand. It was a magnificent Welsh Bible, but without the title-page.

" That book must be a great comfort to you," said I to her.

" Very great," said she. " I know not what we should do without it in the long winter evenings."

" Of what faith are you?" said I.

" We are Methodists," she replied.

" Then you are of the same faith as my friend here," said I.

" Yes, yes," said she, " we are aware of that. We all know honest John Jones."

After we had left the gate I asked John Jones whether he had ever heard of Rebecca of the toll-gates.

" O, yes," said he; " I have heard of that chieftainess."

" And who was she?" said I.

" I cannot say, sir: I never saw her, nor any one who had seen her. Some say that there were a hundred Rebeccas, and all of them men dressed in women's clothes, who went about at night, at the head of bands to break the gates. Ah, sir, something of the kind was almost necessary at that time. I am a friend of peace, sir; no head-breaker, house-breaker, nor gate-breaker, but I can hardly blame what was done at that time, under the name of Rebecca. You have no idea how the poor Welsh were oppressed by those gates, aye, and the rich too. The little people and farmers could not carry their produce to market owing to the exactions at the gates, which devoured all the profit and sometimes more. So that the markets were not half supplied, and people with money could frequently not get what they wanted. Complaints were made to government, which not being attended to, Rebecca and her byddinion made their appearance at night, and broke the gates to pieces with sledge-hammers, and everybody said it was gallant work, everybody save the keepers of the gates and the proprietors. Not only the poor, but the rich said so. Aye, and I have heard that many a fine young gentleman had a hand in the work, and went about at night at the head of a band dressed as Rebecca. Well, sir, those breakings were acts of violence, I don't deny, but they did good, for the system is altered; such impositions are no longer practised at gates as were before the time of Rebecca."

"Were any people ever taken up and punished for those nocturnal breakings?" said I.

"No, sir; and I have heard say that nobody's being taken up was a proof that the rich approved of the work and had a hand in it."

Night had come on by the time we reached the foot of the huge hills we had crossed in the morning. We toiled up the ascent, and after crossing the level ground on the top, plunged down the bwlch between walking and running, occasionally stumbling, for we were nearly in complete darkness, and the bwlch was steep and stony. We more than once passed people who gave us the n's da, the hissing night salutation of the Welsh. At length I saw the abbey looming amidst the darkness, and John Jones said that we were just above the fountain. We descended, and putting my head down, I drank greedily of the dwr santaidd, my guide following my example. We then proceeded on our way, and in about half-an-hour reached Llangollen. I took John Jones home with me. We had a cheerful cup of tea. Henrietta played on the guitar, and sang a Spanish song, to the great delight of John Jones, who at about ten o'clock departed contented and happy to his own dwelling.

CHAPTER XVII

John Jones and his Bundle—A Good Lady—The Irishman's Dingle—Ab Gwilym and the Mist—The Kitchen—The Two Individuals—The Horse-Dealer—I can manage him—The Mist again.

THE following day was gloomy. In the evening John Jones made his appearance with a bundle under his arm, and an umbrella in his hand.

"Sir," said he, "I am going across the mountain with a piece of weaving work, for the man on the other side, who employs me. Perhaps you would like to go with me, as you are fond of walking."

"I suppose," said I, "you wish to have my company for fear of meeting Gwyddelians on the hill."

John smiled.

"Well, sir," said he, "if I do meet them I would sooner be with company than without. But I dare venture by myself, trusting in the Man on High, and perhaps I do wrong to ask you to go, as you must be tired with your walk of yesterday."

"Hardly more than yourself," said I. "Come; I shall be glad to go. What I said about the Gwyddelians was only in jest."

As we were about to depart John said,

"It does not rain at present, sir, but I think it will. You had better take an umbrella."

I did so, and away we went. We passed over the bridge, and turning to the right went by the back of the town through a field. As we passed by the Plas Newydd John Jones said:

"No one lives there now, sir; all dark and dreary; very different from the state of things when the ladies lived there—all gay then and cheerful. I remember the ladies, sir, particularly the last, who lived by herself after her companion died. She was a good lady, and very kind to the poor; when they came to her gate they were never sent away without something to cheer them.

She was a grand lady too—kept grand company, and used to be drawn about in a coach by four horses. But she too is gone, and the house is cold and empty; no fire in it, sir; no furniture. There was an auction after her death; and a grand auction it was and lasted four days. O, what a throng of people there was, some of whom came from a great distance, to buy the curious things, of which there were plenty."

We passed over a bridge, which crosses a torrent, which descends from the mountain on the south side of Llangollen, which bridge John Jones told me was called the bridge of the Melin Bac, or mill of the nook, from a mill of that name close by. Continuing our way we came to a glen, down which the torrent comes which passes under the bridge. There was little water in the bed of the torrent, and we crossed easily enough by stepping-stones. I looked up the glen; a wild place enough, its sides overgrown with trees. Dreary and dismal it looked in the gloom of the closing evening. John Jones said that there was no regular path up it, and that one could only get along by jumping from stone to stone, at the hazard of breaking one's legs. Having passed over the bed of the torrent, we came to a path, which led up the mountain. The path was very steep and stony; the glen with its trees and darkness on our right. We proceeded some way. At length John Jones pointed to a hollow lane on our right, seemingly leading into the glen.

"That place, sir," said he, "is called Pant y Gwyddel —the Irishman's dingle, and sometimes Pant Paddy, from the Irish being fond of taking up their quarters there. It was just here, at the entrance of the pant, that the tribe were encamped, when I passed two months ago at night, in returning from the other side of the hill with ten shillings in my pocket, which I had been paid for a piece of my work, which I had carried over the mountain to the very place where I am now carrying this. I shall never forget the fright I was in, both on account of my life, and my ten shillings. I ran down what remained of the hill as fast as I could, not minding the stones. Should I meet a tribe now on my return I shall not run; you will be with me, and I shall not fear for my life nor for my money, which will be now more than ten shillings, provided the man over the hill pays me, as I have no doubt he will."

As we ascended higher we gradually diverged from the glen, though we did not lose sight of it till we reached the top of the mountain. The top was nearly level. On our right were a few fields enclosed with stone walls. On our left was an open space where whin, furze and heath were growing. We passed over the summit, and began to descend by a tolerably good, though steep road. But for the darkness of evening and a drizzling mist, which, for some time past, had been coming on, we should have enjoyed a glorious prospect down into the valley, or perhaps I should say that I should have enjoyed a glorious prospect, for John Jones, like a true mountaineer, cared not a brass farthing for prospects. Even as it was, noble glimpses of wood and rock were occasionally to be obtained. The mist soon wetted us to the skin, notwithstanding that we put up our umbrellas. It was a regular Welsh mist, a niwl, like that in which the great poet Ab Gwilym lost his way, whilst trying to keep an assignation with his beloved Morfydd, and which he abuses in the following manner :—

" O ho ! thou villain mist, O ho !
What plea hast thou to plague me so !
I scarcely know a scurril name,
But dearly thou deserv'st the same ;
Thou exhalation from the deep
Unknown, where ugly spirits keep !
Thou smoke from hellish stews uphurl'd
To mock and mortify the world !
Thou spider-web of giant race,
Spun out and spread through airy space !
Avaunt, thou filthy, clammy thing,
Of sorry rain the source and spring !
Moist blanket dripping misery down,
Loathed alike by land and town !
Thou watery monster, wan to see,
Intruding 'twixt the sun and me,
To rob me of my blessed right,
To turn my day to dismal night.
Parent of thieves and patron best,
They brave pursuit within thy breast !
Mostly from thee its merciless snow
Grim January doth glean, I trow.
Pass off with speed, thou prowler pale,
Holding along o'er hill and dale,

Spilling a noxious spittle round,
Spoiling the fairies' sporting ground !
Move off to hell, mysterious haze ;
Wherein deceitful meteors blaze ;
Thou wild of vapour, vast, o'ergrown,
Huge as the ocean of unknown."

As we descended the path became more steep; it was
particularly so at a part where it was overshadowed
with trees on both sides. Here finding walking very
uncomfortable, my knees suffering much, I determined
to run. So shouting to John Jones, "Nis gallav
gerdded rhaid rhedeg," I set off running down the
pass. My companion followed close behind, and luckily
meeting no mischance, we presently found ourselves on
level ground, amongst a collection of small houses. On
our turning a corner a church appeared on our left
hand on the slope of the hill. In the churchyard, and
close to the road, grew a large yew-tree which flung
its boughs far on every side. John Jones stopping by
the tree said, that if I looked over the wall of the yard
I should see the tomb of a Lord Dungannon, who had
been a great benefactor to the village. I looked, and
through the lower branches of th yew, which hung
over part of the churchyard, I saw what appeared to be
a mausoleum. Jones told me that in the church also
there was the tomb of a great person of the name of
Tyrwhitt.

We passed on by various houses till we came nearly
to the bottom of the valley. Jones then pointing to a
large house, at a little distance on the right, told me
that it was a good gwesty, and advised me to go and
refresh myself in it, whilst he went and carried home
his work to the man who employed him, who he said
lived in a farm-house a few hundred yards off. I asked
him where we were.

"At Llyn Ceiriog," he replied.

I then asked if we were near Pont Fadog; and
received for answer that Pont Fadog was a good way
down the valley, to the north-east, and that we could
not see it owing to a hill which intervened.

Jones went his way and I proceeded to the gwestfa,
the door of which stood invitingly open. I entered a
large kitchen, at one end of which a good fire was
burning in a grate, in front of which was a long table,

and a high settle on either side. Everything looked very comfortable. There was nobody in the kitchen : on my calling, however, a girl came whom I bade in Welsh to bring me a pint of the best ale. The girl stared, but went away apparently to fetch it. Presently came the landlady, a good-looking middle-aged woman. I saluted her in Welsh and then asked her if she could speak English. She replied " Tipyn bach," which interpreted, is, a little bit. I soon, however, found that she could speak it very passably, for two men coming in from the rear of the house she conversed with them in English. These two individuals seated themselves on chairs near the door, and called for beer. The girl brought in the ale, and I sat down by the fire, poured myself out a glass, and made myself comfortable. Presently a gig drove up to the door, and in came a couple of dogs, one a tall black greyhound, the other a large female setter, the coat of the latter dripping with rain, and shortly after two men from the gig entered, one who appeared to be the principal was a stout bluff-looking person between fifty and sixty dressed in a grey stuff coat and with a slouched hat on his head. This man bustled much about, and in a broad Yorkshire dialect ordered a fire to be lighted in another room, and a chamber to be prepared for him and his companion ; the landlady, who appeared to know him, and to treat him with a kind of deference, asked if she should prepare two beds ; whereupon he answered " No ! As we came together, and shall start together, so shall we sleep together ; it will not be for the first time."

His companion was a small mean-looking man dressed in a black coat, and behaved to him with no little respect. Not only the landlady but the two men, of whom I have previously spoken, appeared to know him and to treat him with deference. He and his companion presently went out to see after the horse. After a little time they returned, and the stout man called lustily for two fourpennyworths of brandy and water— " Take it into the other room !" said he, and went into a side room with his companion, but almost immediately came out saying that the room smoked and was cold, and that he preferred sitting in the kitchen. He then took his seat near me, and when the brandy was

brought drank to my health. I said thank you : but
nothing farther. He then began talking to the men
and his companion upon indifferent subjects. After a
little time John Jones came in, called for a glass of ale,
and at my invitation seated himself between me and the
stout personage. The latter addressed him roughly in
English, but receiving no answer said, " Ah, you no
understand. You have no English and I no Welsh."

" You have not mastered Welsh yet, Mr. ——" said
one of the men to him.

" No !" said he : " I have been doing business with
the Welsh forty years, but can't speak a word of their
language. I sometimes guess at a word, spoken in the
course of business, but am never sure."

Presently John Jones began talking to me, saying
that he had been to the river, that the water was very
low, and that there was little but stones in the bed of
the stream.

I told him if its name was Ceiriog no wonder there
were plenty of stones in it, Ceiriog being derived from
Cerrig, a rock. The men stared to hear me speak
Welsh.

" Is the gentleman a Welshman?" said one of the
men, near the door, to his companion; " he seems to
speak Welsh very well."

" How should I know?" said the other, who appeared to be a low working man.

" Who are those people?" said I to John Jones.

" The smaller man is a workman at a flannel manufactory," said Jones. " The other I do not exactly
know."

" And who is the man on the other side of you?"
said I.

" I believe he is an English dealer in gigs and
horses," replied Jones, " and that he is come here
either to buy or sell."

The man, however, soon put me out of all doubt with
respect to his profession.

" I was at Chirk," said he, " and Mr. So-and-so
asked me to have a look at his new gig and horse, and
have a ride. I consented. They were both brought out
—everything new : gig new, harness new, and horse
new. Mr. So-and-so asked me what I thought of his

turn-out. I gave a look and said, ' I like the car very well, harness very well, but I don't like the horse at all : a regular bolter, rearer, and kicker, or I'm no judge; moreover, he's pigeon-toed.' However, we all got on the car—four of us, and I was of course complimented with the ribbons. Well, we hadn't gone fifty yards before the horse, to make my words partly good, began to kick like a new 'un. However, I managed him, and he went on for a couple of miles till we got to the top of the hill, just above the descent with the precipice on the right hand. Here he began to rear like a very devil.

" ' O dear me !' says Mr. So-and-so; ' let me get out !'

" ' Keep where you are,' says I, ' I can manage him.'

" However, Mr. So-and-so would not be ruled, and got out; coming down, not on his legs, but his hands and knees. And then the two others said—

" ' Let us get out !'

" ' Keep where you are,' said I, ' I can manage him.'

" But they must needs get out, or rather tumble out, for they both came down on the road hard on their backs.

" ' Get out yourself,' said they all, ' and let the devil go, or you are a done man.'

" ' Getting out may do for you young hands,' says I, ' but it won't do for I; neither my back nor bones will stand the hard road.'

" Mr. So-and-so ran to the horse's head.

" ' Are you mad?' says I, ' if you try to hold him he'll be over the pree-si-pice in a twinkling, and then where am I? Give him head; I can manage him.'

" So Mr. So-and-so got out of the way, and down flew the horse right down the descent, as fast as he could gallop. I tell you what, I didn't half like it ! A pree-si-pice on my right, the rock on my left, and a devil before me, going, like a cannon-ball, right down the hill. However, I contrived, as I said I would, to manage him; kept the car from the rock and from the edge of the gulf too. Well, just when we had come to the bottom of the hill out comes the people running from the inn, almost covering the road.

" ' Now get out of the way,' I shouts, ' if you don't

wish to see your brains knocked out, and what would
be worse, mine too.'

" So they gets out of the way, and on I spun, I and
my devil. But by this time I had nearly taken the devil
out of him. Well, he hadn't gone fifty yards on the
level ground, when, what do you think he did? why,
went regularly over, tumbled down regularly on the
road, even as I knew he would some time or other,
because why? he was pigeon-toed. Well, I gets out of
the gig, and no sooner did Mr. So-and-so come up than
I says—

" ' I likes your car very well, and I likes your harness, but —— me if I likes your horse, and it will be
some time before you persuade me to drive him
again.' "

I am a great lover of horses, and an admirer of good
driving, and should have wished to have some conversation with this worthy person about horses and their
management. I should also have wished to ask him
some questions about Wales and the Welsh, as he
must have picked up a great deal of curious information
about both in his forty years' traffic, notwithstanding
he did not know a word of Welsh, but John Jones prevented my farther tarrying by saying that it would be
as well to get over the mountain before it was entirely
dark. So I got up, paid for my ale, vainly endeavoured
to pay for that of my companion, who insisted upon
paying for what he had ordered, made a general bow,
and departed from the house, leaving the horse-dealer
and the rest staring at each other and wondering who
we were, or at least who I was. We were about to
ascend the hill when John Jones asked me whether I
should not like to see the bridge and the river. I told
him I should. The bridge and the river presented
nothing remarkable. The former was of a single arch;
and the latter anything but abundant in its flow.

We now began to retrace our steps over the mountain. At first the mist appeared to be nearly cleared
away. As we proceeded, however, large sheets began
to roll up the mountain sides, and by the time we
reached the summit we were completely shrouded in
vapour. The night, however, was not very dark, and
we found our way tolerably well, though once in de-

scending I had nearly tumbled into the nant or dingle,
now on our left hand. The bushes and trees, seen indistinctly through the mist, had something the look of
goblins, and brought to my mind the elves, which Ab
Gwilym of old saw, or thought he saw, in a somewhat
similar situation :—

> " In every hollow dingle stood
> Of wry-mouth'd elves a wrathful brood."

Drenched to the skin, but uninjured in body and limb,
we at length reached Llangollen.

CHAPTER XVIII

Venerable Old Gentleman—Surnames in Wales—Russia and
Britain—Church of England—Yriarte—The Eagle and his
Young—Poets of the Gael—The Oxonian—Master Salisburie.

MY wife had told me that she had had some conversation upon the Welsh language and literature with a
venerable old man, who kept a shop in the town, that
she had informed him that I was very fond of both,
and that he had expressed a great desire to see me.
One afternoon I said : " Let us go and pay a visit to
your old friend of the shop. I think from two or three
things which you have told me about him, that he must
be worth knowing." We set out. She conducted me
across the bridge a little way ; then presently turning to
the left into the principal street, she entered the door
of a shop on the left-hand side, over the top of which
was written : " Jones ; provision dealer and general
merchant." The shop was small, with two little
counters, one on each side. Behind one was a young
woman, and behind the other a venerable-looking old
man.

" I have brought my husband to visit you," said my
wife, addressing herself to him.

" I am most happy to see him," said the old gentleman, making me a polite bow.

He then begged that we would do him the honour
to walk into his parlour, and led us into a little back
room, the window of which looked out upon the Dee a

few yards below the bridge. On the left side of the
room was a large case, well stored with books. He
offered us chairs, and we all sat down. I was much
struck with the old man. He was rather tall, and
somewhat inclined to corpulency. His hair was grey;
his forehead high; his nose aquiline; his eyes full of intelligence; whilst his manners were those of a perfect
gentleman. I entered into conversation by saying that
I supposed his name was Jones, as I had observed that
name over the door.

"Jones is the name I bear at your service, sir," he
replied.

I said that it was a very common name in Wales,
as I knew several people who bore it, and observed
that most of the surnames in Wales appeared to be
modifications of Christian names; for example Jones,
Roberts, Edwards, Humphreys, and likewise Pugh,
Powel, and Probert, which were nothing more than the
son of Hugh, the son of Howel, and the son of Robert.
He said I was right, that there were very few real surnames in Wales; that the three great families, however,
had real surnames; for that Wynn, Morgan, and Bulk-
ley were all real surnames. I asked him whether the
Bulkleys of Anglesea were not originally an English
family. He said they were, and that they settled down
in Anglesea in the time of Elizabeth.

After some minutes my wife got up and left us. The
old gentleman and I had then some discourse in Welsh;
we soon, however, resumed speaking English. We got
on the subject of Welsh bards, and after a good deal of
discourse the old gentleman said :

"You seem to know something about Welsh poetry;
can you tell me who wrote the following line?

"'There will be great doings in Britain, and I shall have no
concern in them.'"

"I will not be positive," said I, "but I think from
its tone and tenor that it was composed by Merddyn,
whom my countrymen call Merlin."

"I believe you are right," said the old gentleman,
"I see you know something of Welsh poetry. I met
the line, a long time ago, in a Welsh grammar. It then
made a great impression upon me and of late it has

always been ringing in my ears. I love Britain. Britain
has just engaged in a war with a mighty country, and
I am apprehensive of the consequences. I am old,
upwards of fourscore, and shall probably not live to see
the evil, if evil happens, as I fear it will—'There will
be strange doings in Britain, but they will not concern
me.' I cannot get the line out of my head.''

I told him that the line probably related to the progress of the Saxons in Britain, but that I did not
wonder that it made an impression upon him at the
present moment. I said, however, that we ran no risk
from Russia; that the only power at all dangerous to
Britain was France, which though at present leagued
with her against Russia, would eventually go to war
with and strive to subdue her, and then of course
Britain could expect no help from Russia, her old
friend and ally, who, if Britain had not outraged her,
would have assisted her, in any quarrel or danger, with
four or five hundred thousand men. I said that I
hoped neither he nor I should see a French invasion,
but I had no doubt one would eventually take place,
and that then Britain must fight stoutly, as she had no
one to expect help from but herself; that I wished she
might be able to hold her own, but——

"Strange things will happen in Britain, though they
will concern me nothing,'' said the old gentleman with
a sigh.

On my expressing a desire to know something of his
history, he told me that he was the son of a small
farmer, who resided at some distance from Llangollen;
that he lost his father at an early age, and was obliged
to work hard, even when a child, in order to assist his
mother who had some difficulty, after the death of his
father, in keeping things together; that though he was
obliged to work hard he had been fond of study, and
used to pore over Welsh and English books by the
glimmering light of the turf fire at night, for that his
mother could not afford to allow him anything in the
shape of a candle to read by; that at his mother's
death he left rural labour, and coming to Llangollen,
commenced business in the little shop in which he was
at present; that he had been married and had children,
but that his wife and family were dead; that the young

woman whom I had seen in the shop, and who took
care of his house, was a relation of his wife; that
though he had always been attentive to business, he
had never abandoned study; that he had mastered his
own language, of which he was passionately fond, and
had acquired a good knowledge of English and of some
other languages. That his fondness for literature had
shortly after his arrival at Llangollen attracted the
notice of some of the people, who encouraged him in
his studies, and assisted him by giving him books; that
the two celebrated ladies of Llangollen had particularly
noticed him; that he held the situation of church clerk
for upwards of forty years, and that it was chiefly
owing to the recommendation of the " great ladies "
that he had obtained it. He then added with a sigh,
that about ten years ago he was obliged to give it up,
owing to something the matter with his eyesight, which
prevented him from reading, and that his being obliged
to give it up was a source of bitter grief to him, as he
had always considered it a high honour to be permitted
to assist in the service of the Church of England, in
the principles of which he had been bred, and in whose
doctrines he firmly believed.

Here shaking him by the hand I said that I too had
been bred up in the principles of the Church of England; that I too firmly believed in its doctrines, and
would maintain with my blood, if necessary, that there
was not such another church in the world.

" So would I," said the old gentleman; " where is
there a church in whose liturgy there is so much
Scripture as in that of the Church of England?"

" Pity," said I, " that so many traitors have lately
sprung up in its ministry."

" If it be so," said the old church clerk, " they have
not yet shown themselves in the pulpit at Llangollen.
All the clergymen who have held the living in my time
have been excellent. The present incumbent is a model
of a Church-of-England clergyman. O, how I regret
that the state of my eyes prevents me from officiating
as clerk beneath him."

I told him that I should never from the appearance
of his eyes have imagined that they were not excellent
ones.

" I can see to walk about with them, and to distinguish objects," said the old gentleman; " but see to read with them I cannot. Even with the help of the most powerful glasses I cannot distinguish a letter. I believe I strained my eyes at a very early age, when striving to read at night by the glimmer of the turf fire in my poor mother's chimney corner. O what an affliction is this state of my eyes! I can't turn my books to any account, nor read the newspapers; but I repeat that I chiefly lament it because it prevents me from officiating as under preacher."

He showed me his books. Seeing amongst them *The Fables of Yriarte* in Spanish, I asked how they came into his possession.

" They were presented to me," said he, " by one of the ladies of Llangollen, Lady Eleanor Butler."

" Have you ever read them?" said I.

" No," he replied; " I do not understand a word of Spanish; but I suppose her ladyship, knowing I was fond of languages, thought that I might one day set about learning Spanish, and that then they might be useful to me."

He then asked me if I knew Spanish, and on my telling him that I had some knowledge of that language he asked me to translate some of the fables. I translated two of them, which pleased him much.

I then asked if he had ever heard of a collection of Welsh fables compiled about the year thirteen hundred. He said that he had not, and inquired whether they had ever been printed. I told him that some had appeared in the old Welsh magazine called *The Greal*.

" I wish you would repeat one of them," said the old clerk.

" Here is one," said I, " which particularly struck me :—

" It is the custom of the eagle, when his young are sufficiently old, to raise them up above his nest in the direction of the sun; and the bird which has strength enough of eye to look right in the direction of the sun, he keeps and nourishes, but the one which has not, he casts down into the gulf to its destruction. So does the Lord deal with His children, in the Catholic Church Militant : those whom He sees worthy to serve Him in

godliness and spiritual goodness He keeps with Him
and nourishes, but those who are not worthy from
being addicted to earthly things He casts out into utter
darkness, where there is weeping and gnashing of
teeth."

The old gentleman after a moment's reflection said
it was a clever fable, but an unpleasant one. It was
hard for poor birds to be flung into a gulf for not
having power of eye sufficient to look full in the face
of the sun, and likewise hard that poor human creatures
should be lost for ever, for not doing that which they
had no power to do.

"Perhaps," said I, "the eagle does not deal with
his chicks, or the Lord with His creatures as the fable
represents."

"Let us hope at any rate," said the old gentleman,
"that the Lord does not."

"Have you ever seen this book?" said he, and put
Smith's *Sean Dana* into my hand.

"O yes," said I, "and have gone through it. It
contains poems in the Gaelic language by Oisin and
others, collected in the Highlands. I went through it a
long time ago with great attention. Some of the poems
are wonderfully beautiful."

"They are so," said the old clerk. "I too have
gone through the book; it was presented to me a great
many years ago by a lady to whom I gave some lessons
in the Welsh language. I went through it with the
assistance of a Gaelic grammar and dictionary which
she also presented to me, and I was struck with the
high tone of the poetry."

"This collection is valuable indeed," said I; "it
contains poems, which not only possess the highest
merit, but serve to confirm the authenticity of the
poems of Ossian, published by Macpherson, so often
called in question. All the pieces here attributed to
Ossian are written in the same metre, tone, and spirit
as those attributed to him in the other collection, so if
Macpherson's Ossianic poems, which he said were collected by him in the Highlands, are forgeries, Smith's
Ossianic poems, which according to his account, were
also collected in the Highlands, must be also forged,
and have been imitated from those published by the

other. Now as it is well known that Smith did not
possess sufficient poetic power to produce any imitation
of Macpherson's Ossian with a tenth part the merit
which the *Sean Dana* possess, and that even if he had
possessed it his principles would not have allowed him
to attempt to deceive the world by imposing forgeries
upon it, as the authentic poems of another, he being a
highly respectable clergyman, the necessary conclusion
is that the Ossianic poems which both published are
genuine and collected in the manner in which both
stated they were."

After a little more discourse about Ossian the old
gentleman asked me if there was any good modern
Gaelic poetry. "None very modern," said I : "the
last great poets of the Gael were Macintyre and
Buchanan, who flourished about the middle of the last
century. The first sang of love and of Highland
scenery; the latter was a religious poet. The best
piece of Macintyre is an ode to Ben Dourain, or the Hill
of the Water-dogs—a mountain in the Highlands. The
masterpiece of Buchanan is his La Breitheanas or Day
of Judgment, which is equal in merit, or nearly so, to
the Cywydd y Farn or Judgment Day of your own immortal Gronwy Owen. Singular that the two best
pieces on the Day of Judgment should have been written
in two Celtic dialects, and much about the same time;
but such is the fact."

"Really," said the old church clerk, "you seem to
know something of Celtic literature."

"A little," said I; "I am a bit of a philologist; and
when studying languages dip a little into the literature
which they contain."

As I had heard him say that he had occasionally
given lessons in the Welsh language, I inquired
whether any of his pupils had made much progress in
it. "The generality," said he, "soon became tired of
its difficulties, and gave it up without making any
progress at all. Two or three got on tolerably well.
One however acquired it in a time so short that it might
be deemed marvellous. He was an Oxonian, and came
down with another in the vacation in order to study
hard against the yearly collegiate examination. He and
his friend took lodgings at Pengwern Hall, then a farm-

house, and studied and walked about for some time, as other young men from college, who come down here, are in the habit of doing. One day he and his friend came to me who was then clerk, and desired to see the interior of the church. So I took the key and went with them into the church. When he came to the altar he took up the large Welsh Common Prayer Book which was lying there and looked into it.

" ' A curious language this Welsh,' said he; ' I should like to learn it.'

" ' Many have wished to learn it, without being able,' said I ; ' it is no easy language.'

" ' I should like to try,' he replied; ' I wish I could find some one who would give me a few lessons.'

" ' I have occasionally given instructions in Welsh,' said I, ' and shall be happy to oblige you.'

" Well, it was agreed that he should take lessons of me; and to my house he came every evening, and I gave him what instructions I could. I was astonished at his progress. He acquired the pronunciation in a lesson, and within a week was able to construe and converse. By the time he left Llangollen, and he was not here in all more than two months, he understood the Welsh Bible as well as I did, and could speak Welsh so well that the Welsh, who did not know him, took him to be one of themselves, for he spoke the language with the very tone and manner of a native. O, he was the cleverest man for language that I ever knew; not a word that he heard did he ever forget."

" Just like Mezzofanti," said I, " the great cardinal philologist. But whilst learning Welsh, did he not neglect his collegiate studies?"

" Well, I was rather apprehensive on that point," said the old gentleman, " but mark the event. At the examination he came off most brilliantly in Latin, Greek, mathematics, and other things too; in fact, a double first class man, as I think they call it."

" I have never heard of so extraordinary an individual," said I. " I could no more have done what you say he did, than I could have taken wings and flown. Pray what was his name?"

" His name," said the old gentleman, " was Earl."

I was much delighted with my new acquaintance, and

paid him frequent visits; the more I saw him the more he interested me. He was kind and benevolent, a good old Church of England Christian, was well versed in several dialects of the Celtic, and possessed an astonishing deal of Welsh heraldic and antiquarian lore. Often whilst discoursing with him I almost fancied that I was with Master Salisburie, Vaughan of Hengwrt, or some other worthy of old, deeply skilled in everything remarkable connected with wild " Camber's Lande."

CHAPTER XIX

The Vicar and his Family—Evan Evans—Foaming Ale—Llam y Lleidyr—Baptism—Joost Van Vondel—Over to Rome—The Miller's Man—Welsh and English.

WE had received a call from the Vicar of Llangollen and his lady; we had returned it, and they had done us the kindness to invite us to take tea with them. On the appointed evening we went, myself, wife, and Henrietta, and took tea with the vicar and his wife, their sons and daughters, all delightful and amiable beings—the eldest son a fine intelligent young man from Oxford, lately admitted into the Church, and now assisting his father in his sacred office. A delightful residence was the vicarage, situated amongst trees in the neighbourhood of the Dee. A large open window in the room, in which our party sat, afforded us a view of a green plat on the top of a bank running down to the Dee, part of the river, the steep farther bank covered with umbrageous trees, and a high mountain beyond, even that of Pen y Coed clad with wood. During tea Mr. E. and I had a great deal of discourse. I found him to be a first-rate Greek and Latin scholar, and also a proficient in the poetical literature of his own country. In the course of discourse he repeated some noble lines of Evan Evans, the unfortunate and eccentric Prydydd Hir, or tall poet, the friend and correspondent of Gray, for whom he made literal translations from the Welsh, which the great English genius afterwards wrought into immortal verse.

" I have a great regard for poor Evan Evans," said
Mr. E., after he had finished repeating the lines, " for
two reasons : first, because he was an illustrious genius,
and second, because he was a South-Wallian like
myself."

" And I," I replied, " because he was a great poet,
and like myself fond of a glass of cwrw da."

Some time after tea the younger Mr. E. and myself
took a walk in an eastern direction along a path cut
in the bank, just above the stream. After proceeding a
little way amongst most romantic scenery I asked my
companion if he had ever heard of the pool of Catherine
Lingo—the deep pool, as the reader will please to remember, of which John Jones had spoken.

" O yes," said young Mr. E. : " my brothers and
myself are in the habit of bathing there almost every
morning. We will go to it if you please."

We proceeded, and soon came to the pool. The pool
is a beautiful sheet of water, seemingly about one hundred and fifty yards in length, by about seventy in
width. It is bounded on the east by a low ridge of
rocks forming a weir. The banks on both sides are
high and precipitous, and covered with trees, some of
which shoot their arms for some way above the face of
the pool. This is said to be the deepest pool in the
whole course of the Dee, varying in depth from twenty
to thirty feet. Enormous pike, called in Welsh pen-
hwiaid, or ducks'-heads, from the similarity which the
head of a pike bears to that of a duck, are said to be
tenants of this pool.

We returned to the vicarage and at about ten we all
sat down to supper. On the supper-table was a mighty
pitcher full of foaming ale.

" There," said my excellent host, as he poured me
out a glass, " there is a glass of cwrw, which Evan
Evans himself might have drunk."

One evening my wife, Henrietta, and myself, attended by John Jones, went upon the Berwyn a little
to the east of the Geraint or Barber's Hill to botanize.
Here we found a fern which John Jones called Coed
llus y Brân, or the plant of the Crow's berry. There
was a hard kind of berry upon it, of which he said the
crows were exceedingly fond. We also discovered two

or three other strange plants, the Welsh names of which our guide told us, and which were curious and descriptive enough. He took us home by a romantic path which we had never before seen, and on our way pointed out to us a small house in which he said he was born.

The day after, finding myself on the banks of the Dee in the upper part of the valley, I determined to examine the Llam Lleidyr or Robber's Leap, which I had heard spoken of on a former occasion. A man passing near me with a cart, I asked him where the Robber's Leap was. I spoke in English, and with a shake of his head he replied, "Dim Sæsneg." On my putting the question to him in Welsh, however, his countenance brightened up.

"Dyna Llam Lleidyr, sir!" said he, pointing to a very narrow part of the stream a little way down.

"And did the thief take it from this side?" I demanded.

"Yes, sir, from this side," replied the man.

I thanked him, and passing over the dry part of the river's bed, came to the Llam Lleidyr. The whole water of the Dee in the dry season gurgles here through a passage not more than four feet across, which, however, is evidently profoundly deep, as the water is as dark as pitch. If the thief ever took the leap he must have taken it in the dry season, for in the wet the Dee is a wide and roaring torrent. Yet even in the dry season it is difficult to conceive how anybody could take this leap, for on the other side is a rock rising high above the dark gurgling stream. On observing the opposite side, however, narrowly, I perceived that there was a small hole a little way up the rock, in which it seemed possible to rest one's foot for a moment. So I supposed that if the leap was ever taken, the individual who took it darted the tip of his foot into the hole, then springing up seized the top of the rock with his hands, and scrambled up. From either side the leap must have been a highly dangerous one—from the farther side the leaper would incur the almost certain risk of breaking his legs on a ledge of hard rock, from this of falling back into the deep, horrible stream, which would probably suck him down in a moment.

From the Llam y Lleidyr I went to the canal and
walked along it till I came to the house of the old man
who sold coals, and who had put me in mind of
Smollett's Morgan; he was now standing in his little
coal yard, leaning over the pales. I had spoken to him
on two or three occasions subsequent to the one on
which I made his acquaintance, and had been every
time more and more struck with the resemblance which
his ways and manners bore to those of Smollett's
character, on which account I shall call him Morgan,
though such was not his name. He now told me that
he expected that I should build a villa and settle down
in the neighbourhood, as I seemed so fond of it. After
a little discourse, induced either by my questions or
from a desire to talk about himself, he related to me
his history, which though not one of the most wonderful
I shall repeat. He was born near Aberdarron, in Caernarvonshire, and in order to make me understand the
position of the place, and its bearing with regard to
some other places, he drew marks in the coal-dust on
the earth. His father was a Baptist minister, who
when Morgan was about six years of age went to live
at Canol Lyn, a place at some little distance from Port
Heli. With his father he continued till he was old
enough to gain his own maintenance, when he went to
serve a farmer in the neighbourhood. Having saved
some money, young Morgan departed to the foundries
at Cefn Mawr, at which he worked thirty years, with
an interval of four, which he had passed partly working
in slate quarries, and partly upon the canal. About
four years before the present time he came to where he
now lived, where he commenced selling coals, at first
on his own account, and subsequently for some other
person. He concluded his narration by saying that he
was now sixty-two years of age, was afflicted with
various disorders, and believed that he was breaking
up.

Such was Morgan's history; certainly not a very remarkable one. Yet Morgan was a most remarkable
individual, as I shall presently make appear.

Rather affected at the bad account he gave me of his
health, I asked him if he felt easy in his mind. He
replied perfectly so, and when I inquired how he came

to feel so comfortable, he said that his feeling so was owing to his baptism into the faith of Christ Jesus. On my telling him that I too had been baptized, he asked me if I had been dipped; and on learning that I had not, but only been sprinkled, according to the practice of my church, he gave me to understand that my baptism was not worth three-halfpence. Feeling rather nettled at hearing the baptism of my church so undervalued, I stood up for it, and we were soon in a dispute, in which I got rather the worst, for though he spuffled and sputtered in a most extraordinary manner, and spoke in a dialect which was neither Welsh, English, nor Cheshire, but a mixture of all three, he said two or three things rather difficult to be got over. Finding that he had nearly silenced me, he observed that he did not deny that I had a good deal of book learning, but that in matters of baptism I was as ignorant as the rest of the people of the church were, and had always been. He then said that many church people had entered into argument with him on the subject of baptism, but that he had got the better of them all; that Mr. P., the minister of the parish of L., in which we then were, had frequently entered into argument with him, but quite unsuccessfully, and had at last given up the matter as a bad job. He added that a little time before, as Mr. P. was walking close to the canal with his wife and daughter and a spaniel dog, Mr. P. suddenly took up the dog and flung it in, giving it a good ducking, whereupon he, Morgan, cried out: "Dyna y gwir vedydd! That is the right baptism, sir! I thought I should bring you to it at last!" at which words Mr. P. laughed heartily, but made no particular reply.

After a little time he began to talk about the great men who had risen up amongst the Baptists, and mentioned two or three distinguished individuals.

I said that he had not mentioned the greatest man who had been born amongst the Baptists.

"What was his name?" said he.

"His name was Joost Van Vondel," I replied.

"I never heard of him before," said Morgan.

"Very probably," said I; "he was born, bred, and died in Holland."

"Has he been dead long?" said Morgan.

" About two hundred years," said I.

" That's a long time," said Morgan, " and maybe is the reason that I never heard of him. So he was a great man?"

" He was indeed," said I. " He was not only the greatest man that ever sprang up amongst the Baptists, but the greatest, and by far the greatest, that Holland ever produced, though Holland has produced a great many illustrious men."

" O, I dare say he was a great man if he was a Baptist," said Morgan. " Well, it's strange I never read of him. I thought I had read the lives of all the eminent people who lived and died in our communion."

" He did not die in the Baptist communion," said I.

" Oh, he didn't die in it," said Morgan. " What, did he go over to the Church of England? a pretty fellow!"

" He did not go over to the Church of England," said I, " for the Church of England does not exist in Holland; he went over to the Church of Rome."

" Well, that's not quite so bad," said Morgan; " however, it's bad enough. I dare say he was a pretty blackguard."

" No," said I; " he was a pure, virtuous character, and perhaps the only pure and virtuous character that ever went over to Rome. The only wonder is that so good a man could ever have gone over to so detestable a church; but he appears to have been deluded."

" Deluded indeed!" said Morgan. " However, I suppose he went over for advancement's sake."

" No," said I; " he lost every prospect of advancement by going over to Rome: nine-tenths of his countrymen were of the reformed religion, and he endured much poverty and contempt by the step he took."

" How did he support himself?" said Morgan.

" He obtained a livelihood," said I, " by writing poems and plays, some of which are wonderfully fine."

" What," said Morgan, " a writer of Interludes? One of Twm o'r Nant's gang! I thought he would turn out a pretty fellow." I told him that the person in question certainly did write Interludes, for example

Noah, and Joseph at Goshen, but that he was a highly respectable, nay venerable character.

"If he was a writer of Interludes," said Morgan, "he was a blackguard; there never yet was a writer of Interludes, or a person who went about playing them, that was not a scamp. He might be a clever man, I don't say he was not. Who was a cleverer man than Twm o'r Nant with his Pleasure and Care, and Riches and Poverty, but where was there a greater blackguard? Why, not in all Wales. And if you knew this other fellow—what's his name—Fondle's history, you would find that he was not a bit more respectable than Twm o'r Nant, and not half so clever. As for his leaving the Baptists I don't believe a word of it; he was turned out of the connection, and then went about the country saying he left it. No Baptist connection would ever have a writer of Interludes in it, not Twm o'r Nant himself, unless he left his ales and Interludes and wanton hussies, for the three things are sure to go together. You say he went over to the Church of Rome; of course he did, if the Church of England were not at hand to receive him, where should he go but to Rome? No respectable church like the Methodist or the Independent would have received him. There are only two churches in the world that will take in anybody without asking questions, and will never turn them out however bad they may behave; the one is the Church of Rome, and the other the Church of Canterbury; and if you look into the matter you will find that every rogue, rascal, and hanged person since the world began has belonged to one or other of those communions."

In the evening I took a walk with my wife and daughter past the Plas Newydd. Coming to the little mill called the Melyn Bac, at the bottom of the gorge, we went into the yard to observe the water-wheel. We found that it was turned by a very little water, which was conveyed to it by artificial means. Seeing the miller's man, a short dusty figure, standing in the yard, I entered into conversation with him, and found to my great surprise that he had a considerable acquaintance with the ancient language. On my repeating to him verses from Taliesin he understood them, and to show me that he did translated some of the lines into

English. Two or three respectable-looking lads, probably the miller's sons, came out, and listened to us.
One of them said we were both good Welshmen. After
a little time the man asked me if I had heard of Huw
Morris. I told him that I was well acquainted with his
writings, and inquired whether the place in which he
had lived was not somewhere in the neighbourhood.
He said it was; and that it was over the mountains not
far from Llan Sanfraid. I asked whether it was not
called Pont y Meibion. He answered in the affirmative,
and added that he had himself been there, and had sat
in Huw Morris's stone chair, which was still to be seen
by the road's side. I told him that I hoped to visit the
place in a few days. He replied that I should be quite
right in doing so, and that no one should come to these
parts without visiting Pont y Meibion, for that Huw
Morris was one of the columns of the Cumry.

"What a difference," said I to my wife, after we
had departed, " between a Welshman and an Englishman of the lower class. What would a Suffolk miller's
swain have said if I had repeated to him verses out of
Beowulf or even Chaucer, and had asked him about the
residence of Skelton?"

CHAPTER XX

Huw Morris—Immortal Elegy—The Valley of Ceiriog—Tangled
Wilderness—Perplexity—Chair of Huw Morris—The Walking-stick—Huw's Descendant—Pont y Meibion.

Two days after the last adventure I set off, over the
Berwyn, to visit the birth-place of Huw Morris under
the guidance of John Jones, who was well acquainted
with the spot.

Huw Morus or Morris, was born in the year 1622
on the banks of the Ceiriog. His life was a long one,
for he died at the age of eighty-four, after living in six
reigns. He was the second son of a farmer, and was
apprenticed to a tanner, with whom, however, he did
not stay till the expiration of the term of his apprenticeship, for not liking the tanning art, he speedily returned
to the house of his father, whom he assisted in hus-

E

bandry till death called the old man away. He then
assisted his elder brother, and on his elder brother's
death, lived with his son. He did not distinguish himself as a husbandman, and appears never to have been
fond of manual labour. At an early period, however,
he applied himself most assiduously to poetry, and
before he had attained the age of thirty was celebrated,
throughout Wales, as the best poet of his time. When
the war broke out between Charles and his parliament,
Huw espoused the part of the king, not as a soldier, for
he appears to have liked fighting little better than tanning
or husbandry, but as a poet, and probably did the king
more service in that capacity, than he would if he had
raised him a troop of horse, or a regiment of foot, for
he wrote songs breathing loyalty to Charles, and
fraught with pungent satire against his foes, which ran
like wild fire through Wales, and had a great influence
on the minds of the people. Even when the royal cause
was lost in the field, he still carried on a poetical war
against the successful party, but not so openly as before,
dealing chiefly in allegories, which, however, were easy
to be understood. Strange to say the Independents,
when they had the upper hand, never interfered with
him, though they persecuted certain Royalist poets of
far inferior note. On the accession of Charles the
Second he celebrated the event by a most singular piece
called the Lamentation of Oliver's men, in which he
assails the Roundheads with the most bitter irony. He
was loyal to James the Second, till that monarch
attempted to overthrow the Church of England, when
Huw, much to his credit, turned against him, and
wrote songs in the interest of the glorious Prince of
Orange. He died in the reign of good Queen Anne.
In his youth his conduct was rather dissolute, but
irreproachable and almost holy in his latter days—a
kind of halo surrounded his old brow. It was the
custom in those days in North Wales for the congregation to leave the church in a row with the clergyman at
their head, but so great was the estimation in which old
Huw was universally held, for the purity of his life and
his poetical gift, that the clergyman of the parish
abandoning his claim to precedence, always insisted
on the good and inspired old man's leading the file,

himself following immediately in his rear. Huw wrote
on various subjects, mostly in common and easily
understood measures. He was great in satire, great in
humour, but when he pleased could be greater in pathos
than in either; for his best piece is an elegy on Barbara
Middleton, the sweetest song of the kind ever written.
From his being born on the banks of the brook Ceiriog,
and from the flowing melody of his awen or muse, his
countrymen were in the habit of calling him Eos
Ceiriog, or the Ceiriog Nightingale.

So John Jones and myself set off across the Berwyn
to visit the birth-place of the great poet Huw Morris.
We ascended the mountain by Allt Paddy. The morning was lowering, and before we had half got to the
top it began to rain. John Jones was in his usual good
spirits. Suddenly taking me by the arm he told me to
look to the right across the gorge to a white house,
which he pointed out.

" What is there in that house?" said I.

" An aunt of mine lives there," said he.

Having frequently heard him call old women his
aunts, I said, " Every poor old woman in the neighbourhood seems to be your aunt."

" This is no poor old woman," said he, " she is
cyfoethawg iawn, and only last week she sent me and
my family a pound of bacon, which would have cost
me sixpence-halfpenny, and about a month ago a
measure of wheat."

We passed over the top of the mountain, and descending the other side, reached Llansanfraid, and stopped
at the public-house where we had been before, and
called for two glasses of ale. Whilst drinking our ale
Jones asked some questions about Huw Morris of the
woman who served us; she said that he was a famous
poet, and that people of his blood were yet living upon
the lands which had belonged to him at Pont y Meibion.
Jones told her that his companion, the gwr boneddig,
meaning myself, had come in order to see the birth-
place of Huw Morris, and that I was well acquainted
with his works, having gotten them by heart in Lloegr,
when a boy. The woman said that nothing would give
her greater pleasure than to hear a Sais recite poetry
of Huw Morris, whereupon I recited a number of his

lines addressed to the Gôf Du, or blacksmith. The woman held up her hands, and a carter who was in the kitchen, somewhat the worse for liquor, shouted applause. After asking a few questions as to the road we were to take, we left the house, and in a little time entered the valley of Ceiriog. The valley is very narrow, huge hills overhanging it on both sides, those on the east side lumpy and bare, those on the west precipitous, and partially clad with wood; the torrent Ceiriog runs down it, clinging to the east side; the road is tolerably good, and is to the west of the stream. Shortly after we had entered the gorge, we passed by a small farm-house on our right hand, with a hawthorn hedge before it, upon which seems to stand a peacock, curiously cut out of thorn. Passing on we came to a place called Pandy uchaf, or the higher Fulling mill. The place so called is a collection of ruinous houses, which put me in mind of the Fulling mills mentioned in Don Quixote. It is called the Pandy because there was formerly a fulling mill here, said to have been the first established in Wales; which is still to be seen, but which is no longer worked. Just above the old mill there is a meeting of streams : the Tarw from the west rolls down a dark valley into the Ceiriog.

At the entrance of this valley and just before you reach the Pandy, which it nearly overhangs, is an enormous crag. After I had looked at the place for some time with considerable interest we proceeded towards the south, and in about twenty minutes reached a neat kind of house, on our right hand, which John Jones told me stood on the ground of Huw Morris. Telling me to wait, he went to the house, and asked some questions. After a little time I followed him and found him discoursing at the door with a stout dame about fifty-five years of age, and a stout buxom damsel of about seventeen, very short of stature.

"This is the gentleman," said he, "who wishes to see anything there may be here connected with Huw Morris."

The old dame made me a curtsey and said in very distinct Welsh, "We have some things in the house which belonged to him, and we will show them to the gentleman willingly."

" We first of all wish to see his chair," said John Jones.

" The chair is in a wall in what is called the hen ffordd (old road)," said the old gentlewoman; " it is cut out of the stone wall; you will have maybe some difficulty in getting to it, but the girl shall show it to you." The girl now motioned to us to follow her, and conducted us across the road to some stone steps, over a wall to a place which looked like a plantation.

" This was the old road," said Jones; " but the place has been enclosed. The new road is above us on our right hand beyond the wall."

We were in a maze of tangled shrubs, the boughs of which, very wet from the rain which was still falling, struck our faces, as we attempted to make our way between them; the girl led the way, bare-headed and bare-armed, and soon brought us to the wall, the boundary of the new road. Along this she went with considerable difficulty, owing to the tangled shrubs, and the nature of the ground, which was very precipitous, shelving down to the other side of the enclosure. In a little time we were wet to the skin, and covered with the dirt of birds, which they had left whilst roosting in the trees; on went the girl, sometimes creeping, and trying to keep herself from falling by holding against the young trees; once or twice she fell and we after her, for there was no path, and the ground, as I have said before, very shelvy; still as she went her eyes were directed towards the wall, which was not always very easy to be seen, for thorns, tall nettles, and shrubs were growing up against it. Here and there she stopped, and said something, which I could not always make out, for her Welsh was anything but clear; at length I heard her say that she was afraid we had passed the chair, and indeed presently we came to a place where the enclosure terminated in a sharp corner.

" Let us go back," said I; " we must have passed it."

I now went first, breaking down with my weight the shrubs nearest to the wall.

" Is not this the place?" said I, pointing to a kind of hollow in the wall, which looked something like the shape of a chair.

"Hardly," said the girl, "for there should be a slab, on the back, with letters, but there's neither slab nor letters here."

The girl now again went forward, and we retraced our way, doing the best we could to discover the chair, but all to no purpose; no chair was to be found. We had now been, as I imagined, half-an-hour in the enclosure, and had nearly got back to the place from which we had set out, when we suddenly heard the voice of the old lady exclaiming, "What are ye doing there?—the chair is on the other side of the field; wait a bit, and I will come and show it you." Getting over the stone stile, which led into the wilderness, she came to us, and we now went along the wall at the lower end; we had quite as much difficulty here, as on the other side, and in some places more, for the nettles were higher, the shrubs more tangled, and the thorns more terrible. The ground, however, was rather more level. I pitied the poor girl who led the way and whose fat naked arms were both stung and torn. She at last stopped amidst a huge grove of nettles, doing the best she could to shelter her arms from the stinging leaves.

"I never was in such a wilderness in my life," said I to John Jones, "is it possible that the chair of the mighty Huw is in a place like this; which seems never to have been trodden by human foot. Well does the Scripture say 'Dim prophwyd yw yn cael barch yn ei dir ei hunan.'"

This last sentence tickled the fancy of my worthy friend, the Calvinistic Methodist; he laughed aloud and repeated it over and over again to the females with amplifications.

"Is the chair really here," said I, "or has it been destroyed? if such a thing has been done it is a disgrace to Wales."

"The chair is really here," said the old lady, "and though Huw Morus was no prophet, we love and reverence everything belonging to him. Get on, Llances, the chair can't be far off;" the girl moved on, and presently the old lady exclaimed "There's the chair, Diolch i Duw!"

I was the last of the file, but I now rushed past John Jones, who was before me, and next to the old lady, and sure enough there was the chair, in the wall, of him who was called in his day, and still is called by the mountaineers of Wales, though his body has been below the earth in the quiet church-yard, one hundred and forty years, Eos Ceiriog, the Nightingale of Ceiriog, the sweet caroller Huw Morus, the enthusiastic partizan of Charles, and the Church of England, and the never-tiring lampooner of Oliver and the Independents, there it was, a kind of hollow in the stone wall, in the hen ffordd, fronting to the west, just above the gorge at the bottom of which murmurs the brook Ceiriog, there it was, something like a half-barrel chair in a garden, a mouldering stone slab forming the seat, and a large slate stone, the back, on which were cut these letters—

H. M. B.

signifying Huw Morus Bard.

"Sit down in the chair, Gwr Boneddig," said John Jones, "you have taken trouble enough to get to it."

"Do, gentleman," said the old lady; "but first let me wipe it with my apron, for it is very wet and dirty."

"Let it be," said I; then taking off my hat I stood uncovered before the chair, and said in the best Welsh I could command, "Shade of Huw Morus, supposing your shade haunts the place which you loved so well when alive—a Saxon, one of the seed of the Coiling Serpent, has come to this place to pay that respect to true genius, the Dawn Duw, which he is ever ready to pay. He read the songs of the Nightingale of Ceiriog in the most distant part of Lloegr, when he was a brown-haired boy, and now that he is a grey-haired man he is come to say in this place that they frequently made his eyes overflow with tears of rapture."

I then sat down in the chair, and commenced repeating verses of Huw Morris. All which I did in the presence of the stout old lady, the short, buxom, and bare-armed damsel, and of John Jones, the Calvinistic weaver of Llangollen, all of whom listened patiently and approvingly though the rain was pouring down upon them, and the branches of the trees and the tops of the tall nettles, agitated by the gusts from the mountain hollows, were beating in their faces, for enthusiasm is never scoffed at by the noble, simple-minded, genuine

Welsh, whatever treatment it may receive from the coarse-hearted, sensual, selfish Saxon.

After some time our party returned to the house—which put me very much in mind of the farm-houses of the substantial yeomen of Cornwall, particularly that of my friends at Penquite; a comfortable fire blazed in the kitchen grate, the floor was composed of large flags of slate. In the kitchen the old lady pointed to me the ffon, or walking-stick, of Huw Morris; it was supported against a beam by three hooks. I took it down and walked about the kitchen with it; it was a thin polished black stick, with a crome cut in the shape of an eagle's head; at the end was a brass fence. The kind creature then produced a sword without a scabbard; this sword was found by Huw Morris on the mountain—it belonged to one of Oliver's officers who was killed there. I took the sword, which was a thin two-edged one, and seemed to be made of very good steel. It put me in mind of the blades which I had seen at Toledo—the guard was very slight like those of all rapiers, and the hilt the common old-fashioned English officer's hilt; there was no rust on the blade, and it still looked a dangerous sword. A man like Thistlewood would have whipped it through his adversary in a twinkling. I asked the old lady if Huw Morris was born in this house; she said no, but a little farther on at Pont y Meibion; she said, however, that the ground had belonged to him, and that they had some of his blood in their veins. I shook her by the hand, and gave the chubby bare-armed damsel a shilling, pointing to the marks of the nettle stings on her fat bacon-like arms; she laughed, made me a curtsey and said, "Llawer iawn o diolch."

John Jones and I then proceeded to the house at Pont y Meibion, where we saw two men, one turning a grindstone, and the other holding an adze to it. We asked if we were at the house of Huw Morris, and whether they could tell us anything about him; they made us no answer but proceeded with their occupation; John Jones then said that the Gwr Boneddig was very fond of the verses of Huw Morris, and had come a great way to see the place where he was born—the wheel now ceased turning, and the man with the adze turned his face full upon me—he was a stern-looking, dark man, with black hair, of about forty; after a moment or two he said, that if I chose to walk into the house, I should be welcome. He then conducted us into the house, a common-looking stone tenement, and bade us be seated. I asked him if he was a descendant of Huw Morus; he said he was; I asked him his name, which he said was Huw ——. " Have you any of the manuscripts of Huw Morus?" said I.

"None," said he; " but I have one of the printed copies of his works."

He then went to a drawer, and taking out a book, put it into my hand, and seated himself in a blunt, careless manner. The book was the first volume of the common Wrexham edition of Huw's works; it was much thumbed—I commenced reading aloud a piece which I had much admired in my boyhood. I went on for some time, my mind quite occupied with my reading; at last lifting up my eyes, I saw the man standing bolt upright before me, like a soldier of the days of my childhood, during the time that the adjutant read prayers; his hat was no longer upon his head, but on the ground, and his eyes were reverently inclined to the book. After all, what a beautiful thing it is, not to be, but to have been a genius. Closing the book, I asked him whether Huw Morris was born in the house where we were, and received for answer that he was born about where we stood, but that the old house had been pulled down, and that of all the premises only a small outhouse was coeval with Huw Morris. I asked him the name of the house, and he said Pont y Meibion. " But where is the bridge?" said I.

" The bridge," he replied, " is close by, over the Ceiriog. If you wish to see it, you must go down yon field; the house is called after the bridge."

Bidding him farewell, we crossed the road, and going down the field speedily arrived at Pont y Meibion. The bridge is a small bridge of one arch which crosses the brook Ceiriog; it is built of rough moor stone; it is mossy, broken, and looks almost inconceivably old; there is a little parapet to it about two feet high. On the right-hand side it is shaded by an ash. The brook, when we viewed it, though at times a roaring torrent, was stealing along gently. On both sides it is over-grown with alders; noble hills rise above it to the east and west; John Jones told me that it abounded with trout. I asked him why the bridge was called Pont y Meibion, which signifies the bridge of the children. "It was built originally by children," said he, "for the purpose of crossing the brook."

"That bridge," said I, "was never built by children."

"The first bridge," said he, "was of wood, and was built by the children of the houses above."

Not quite satisfied with his explanation, I asked him to what place the road across the little bridge led, and was told that he believed it led to an upland farm. After taking a long and wistful view of the bridge and the scenery around it, I turned my head in the direction of Llangollen. The adventures of the day were, how-ever, not finished.

CHAPTER XXI

The Gloomy Valley—The Lonely Cottage—Happy Comparison—
Clogs—the Alder Swamp—The Wooden Leg—The Militiaman—Death-bed Verses.

ON reaching the ruined village where the Pandy stood I stopped, and looked up the gloomy valley to the west, down which the brook which joins the Ceiriog at this place descends, wherupon John Jones said, that if I wished to go up it a little way he should have great pleasure in attending me, and that he would show me a cottage built in the hen ddull, or old fashion, to which he frequently went to ask for the rent; he being em-ployed by various individuals in the capacity of rent-gatherer. I said that I was afraid that if he was a rent-collector, both he and I should have a sorry wel-come. "No fear," he replied, "the people are very good people, and pay their rent very regularly," and without saying another word he led the way up the valley. At the end of the village, seeing a woman standing at the door of one of the ruinous cottages, I asked her the name of the brook, or torrent, which

came down the valley. " The Tarw," said she, " and
this village is called Pandy Teirw."

" Why is the streamlet called the bull?" said I. " Is
it because it comes in winter weather roaring down the
glen and butting at the Ceiriog?"

The woman laughed, and replied that perhaps it was.
The valley was wild and solitary to an extraordinary
degree, the brook or torrent running in the middle of it
covered with alder trees. After we had proceeded about
a furlong we reached the house of the old fashion. It
was a rude stone cottage standing a little above the
road on a kind of platform on the right-hand side of
the glen; there was a paling before it with a gate, at
which a pig was screaming, as if anxious to get in.
" It wants its dinner," said John Jones, and opened the
gate for me to pass, taking precautions that the
screamer did not enter at the same time. We entered
the cottage, very glad to get into it, a storm of wind
and rain having just come on. Nobody was in the
kitchen when we entered. It looked comfortable enough,
however; there was an excellent fire of wood and coals,
and a very snug chimney-corner. John Jones called
aloud, but for some time no one answered; at last a
rather good-looking woman, seemingly about thirty,
made her appearance at a door at the farther end of
the kitchen. " Is the mistress at home," said Jones,
" or the master?"

" They are neither at home," said the woman; " the
master is abroad at his work, and the mistress is at
the farm-house of —— three miles off, to pick feathers
(trwsio plu)." She asked us to sit down.

" And who are you?" said I.

" I am only a lodger," said she; " I lodge here with
my husband, who is a clog-maker."

" Can you speak English?" said I.

" O yes," said she, " I lived eleven years in England,
at a place called Bolton, where I married my husband,
who is an Englishman."

" Can he speak Welsh?" said I.

" Not a word," said she. " We always speak
English together."

John Jones sat down, and I looked about the room.
It exhibited no appearance of poverty; there was plenty

of rude but good furniture in it; several pewter plates and trenchers in a rack, two or three prints in frames against the wall, one of which was the likeness of no less a person than the Rev. Joseph Sanders; on the table was a newspaper. " Is that in Welsh?" said I.

" No," replied the woman, " it is the *Bolton Chronicle;* my husband reads it."

I sat down in the chimney-corner. The wind was now howling abroad, and the rain was beating against the cottage panes—presently a gust of wind came down the chimney, scattering sparks all about. " A cataract of sparks!" said I, using the word Rhaiadr.

" What is Rhaiadr?" said the woman; " I never heard the word before."

" Rhaiadr means water tumbling over a rock," said John Jones—" did you never see water tumble over the top of a rock?"

" Frequently," said she.

" Well," said he, " even as the water with its froth tumbles over the rock, so did sparks and fire tumble over the front of that grate when the wind blew down the chimney. It was a happy comparison of the Gwr Boneddig, and with respect to Rhaiadr it is a good old word, though not a common one; some of the Saxons who have read the old writings, though they cannot speak the language as fast as we, understand many words and things which we do not."

" I forgot much of my Welsh, in the land of the Saxons," said the woman, " and so have many others; there are plenty of Welsh at Bolton, but their Welsh is sadly corrupted."

She then went out and presently returned with an infant in her arms and sat down. " Was that child born in Wales?" I demanded.

" No," said she, " he was born at Bolton about eighteen months ago—we have been here only a year."

" Do many English," said I, " marry Welsh wives?"

" A great many," said she. " Plenty of Welsh girls are married to Englishmen at Bolton."

" Do the Englishmen make good husbands?" said I.

The woman smiled and presently sighed.

" Her husband," said Jones, " is fond of a glass of ale and is often at the public-house."

"I make no complaint," said the woman, looking somewhat angrily at John Jones.

"Is your husband a tall bulky man?" said I.

"Just so," said the woman.

"The largest of the two men we saw the other night at the public-house at Llansanfraid," said I to John Jones.

"I don't know him," said Jones, "though I have heard of him, but I have no doubt that was he."

I asked the woman how her husband could carry on the trade of a clog-maker in such a remote place—and also whether he hawked his clogs about the country.

"We call him a clog-maker," said the woman, "but the truth is that he merely cuts down the wood and fashions it into squares; these are taken by an under-master who sends them to the manufacturer at Bolton, who employs hands, who make them into clogs."

"Some of the English," said Jones, "are so poor that they cannot afford to buy shoes; a pair of shoes cost ten or twelve shillings, whereas a pair of clogs cost only two."

"I suppose," said I, "that what you call clogs are wooden shoes."

"Just so," said Jones—"they are principally used in the neighbourhood of Manchester."

"I have seen them at Huddersfield," said I, "when I was a boy at school there; of what wood are they made?"

"Of the gwern, or alder tree," said the woman, "of which there is plenty on both sides of the brook."

John Jones now asked her if she could give him a tamaid of bread; she said she could, "and some butter with it."

She then went out, and presently returned with a loaf and some butter.

"Had you not better wait," said I, "till we get to the inn at Llansanfraid?"

The woman, however, begged him to eat some bread and butter where he was, and cutting a plateful, placed it before him, having first offered me some, which I declined.

"But you have nothing to drink with it," said I to him.

"If you please," said the woman, "I will go for a pint of ale to the public-house at the Pandy; there is better ale there than at the inn at Llansanfraid. When my husband goes to Llansanfraid he goes less for the ale than for the conversation, because there is little English spoken at the Pandy, however good the ale."

John Jones said he wanted no ale—and attacking the bread and butter speedily made an end of it; by the time he had done the storm was over, and getting up I gave the child twopence, and left the cottage with Jones. We proceeded some way farther up the valley, till we came to a place where the ground descended a little. Here Jones, touching me on the shoulder, pointed across the stream. Following with my eye the direction of his finger, I saw two or three small sheds with a number of small reddish blocks, in regular piles beneath them. Several trees felled from the side of the torrent were lying near, some of them stripped of their arms and bark. A small tree formed a bridge across the brook to the sheds.

"It is there," said John Jones, "that the husband of the woman with whom we have been speaking works, felling trees from the alder swamp and cutting them up into blocks. I see there is no work going on at present or we would go over—the woman told me that her husband was at Llangollen."

"What a strange place to come to work at," said I, "out of crowded England. Here is nothing to be heard but the murmuring of waters and the rushing of wind down the gulleys. If the man's head is not full of poetical fancies, which I suppose it is not, as in that case he would be unfit for any useful employment, I don't wonder at his occasionally going to the public-house."

After going a little farther up the glen and observing nothing more remarkable than we had seen already, we turned back. Being overtaken by another violent shower just as we reached the Pandy I thought that we could do no better than shelter ourselves within the public-house, and taste the ale, which the wife of the clog-maker had praised. We entered the little hostelry which was one of two or three shabby-looking houses, standing in contact, close by the Ceiriog. In a kind of little back room, lighted by a good fire and a window, which looked up the Ceiriog valley, we found the landlady, a gentlewoman with a wooden leg, who on perceiving me got up from a chair, and made me the best curtsey that I ever saw made by a female with such a substitute for a leg of flesh and bone. There were three men, sitting with jugs of ale near them on a table by the fire, two were seated on a bench by the wall, and the other on a settle with a high back, which ran from the wall just by the door, and shielded those by the fire from the draughts of the doorway. He of the settle no sooner beheld me than he sprang up and placing a chair for me by the fire bade me in English be seated, and then resumed his own seat. John Jones soon finding a chair came and sat down by me, when I forthwith called for a quart of cwrw da. The landlady bustled about on her wooden leg and presently brought us the ale with two glasses, which I filled, and taking one, drank to the health of the company, who returned us thanks, the man of the settle in English rather broken. Presently one of his companions, getting up, paid his reckoning and departed, the other remained, a stout young fellow dressed something like a stone-mason, which indeed I soon discovered that he was—he was far advanced towards a state of intoxication and talked very incoherently about the war, saying that he hoped it would soon terminate for that if it continued he was afraid he might stand a chance of being shot, as he was a private in the Denbighshire Militia. I told him that it was the duty of every gentleman in the militia, to be willing at all times to lay down his life in the service of the Queen. The answer which he made I could not exactly understand, his utterance being very indistinct, and broken; it was, however, made with some degree of violence, with two or three Myn Diawls, and a blow on the table with his clenched fist. He then asked me whether I thought the militia would be again called out. " Nothing more probable," said I.

" And where would they be sent to?"

" Perhaps to Ireland," was my answer, whereupon he started up with another Myn Diawl, expressing the greatest dread of being sent to Iwerddon.

" You ought to rejoice in your chance of going

there," said I, " Iwerddon is a beautiful country, and abounds with whiskey."

" And the Irish?" said he.

" Hearty, jolly fellows," said I, " if you know how to manage them, and all gentlemen."

Here he became very violent, saying that I did not speak truth, for that he had seen plenty of Irish camping amidst the hills, that the men were half naked and the women were three parts so, and that they carried their children on their backs. He then said that he hoped somebody would speedily kill Nicholas, in order that the war might be at an end and himself not sent to Iwerddon. He then asked if I thought Cronstadt could be taken. I said I believed it could, provided the hearts of those who were sent to take it were in the right place.

" Where do you think the hearts of those are who are gone against it?" said he—speaking with great vehemence.

I made no other answer than by taking my glass and drinking.

His companion now looking at our habiliments, which were in rather a dripping condition, asked John Jones if he had come from far.

" We have been to Pont y Meibion," said Jones, " to see the chair of Huw Morris," adding that the Gwr Boneddig was a great admirer of the songs of the Eos Ceiriog.

He had no sooner said these words than the intoxicated militiaman started up, and striking the table with his fist, said : " I am a poor stone-cutter—this is a rainy day and I have come here to pass it in the best way I can. I am somewhat drunk, but though I am a poor stone-mason, a private in the militia, and not so sober as I should be, I can repeat more of the songs of the Eos than any man alive, however great a gentleman, however sober—more than Sir Watkin, more than Colonel Biddulph himself."

He then began to repeat what appeared to be poetry, for I could distinguish the rhymes occasionally, though owing to his broken utterance it was impossible for me to make out the sense of the words. Feeling a great desire to know what verses of Huw Morris the intoxi-

cated youth would repeat I took out my pocket-book
and requested Jones, who was much better acquainted
with Welsh pronunciation, under any circumstances,
than myself, to endeavour to write down from the mouth
of the young fellow any verses uppermost in his mind.
Jones took the pocket-book and pencil and went to the
window, followed by the young man scarcely able to
support himself. Here a curious scene took place, the
drinker hiccuping up verses, and Jones dotting them
down, in the best manner he could, though he had
evidently great difficulty to distinguish what was said
to him. At last, methought, the young man said—
" There they are, the verses of the Nightingale, on his
death-bed."

I took the book and read aloud the following lines
beautifully descriptive of the eagerness of a Christian
soul to leave its perishing tabernacle, and get to Paradise and its Creator :—

> " Myn'd i'r wyl ar redeg,
> I'r byd a heryi chwaneg,
> I Beradwys, y ber wiw deg,
> Yn Enw Duw yn union deg."

" Do you understand those verses?" said the man
on the settle, a dark swarthy fellow with an oblique
kind of vision, and dressed in a pepper-and-salt coat.

" I will translate them," said I; and forthwith put
them into English—first into prose and then into rhyme,
the rhymed version running thus :—

> " ' Now to my rest I hurry away,
> To the world which lasts for ever and aye,
> To Paradise, the beautiful place,
> Trusting alone in the Lord of Grace.' "

" Well," said he of the pepper-and-salt, " if that isn't
capital I don't know what is."

A scene in a public-house, yes! but in a Welsh
public-house. Only think of a Suffolk toper repeating
the death-bed verses of a poet; surely there is a considerable difference between the Celt and the Saxon.

CHAPTER XXII

Llangollen Fair—Buyers and Sellers—The Jockey—
The Greek Cap.

On the twenty-first was held Llangollen Fair. The day
was dull with occasional showers. I went to see the
fair about noon. It was held in and near a little square
in the south-east quarter of the town, of which square
the police-station is the principal feature on the side of
the west, and an inn, bearing the sign of the Grapes,
on the east. The fair was a little bustling fair, attended
by plenty of people from the country, and from the
English border, and by some who appeared to come
from a greater distance than the border. A dense row
of carts extended from the police-station, half across
the space. These carts were filled with pigs, and had
stout cord nettings drawn over them, to prevent the
animals escaping. By the sides of these carts the principal business of the fair appeared to be going on—
there stood the owners male and female, higgling with
Llangollen men and women, who came to buy. The
pigs were all small, and the price given seemed to vary
from eighteen to twenty-five shillings. Those who
bought pigs generally carried them away in their arms ;
and then there was no little diversion ; dire was the
screaming of the porkers, yet the purchaser invariably
appeared to know how to manage his bargain, keeping
the left arm round the body of the swine and with the
right hand fast griping the ear—some few were led
away by strings. There were some Welsh cattle, small
of course, and the purchasers of these seemed to be
Englishmen, tall burly fellows in general, far exceeding
the Welsh in height and size.

Much business in the cattle-line did not seem, however, to be going on. Now and then a big fellow made
an offer, and held out his hand for a little Pictish
grazier to give it a slap—a cattle bargain being concluded by a slap of the hand—but the Welshman
generally turned away, with a half-resentful exclama-

tion. There were a few horses and ponies in a street leading into the fair from the south.

I saw none sold, however. A tall athletic figure was striding amongst them, evidently a jockey and a stranger, looking at them and occasionally asking a slight question of one or another of their proprietors, but he did not buy. He might in age be about eight-and-twenty, and about six feet and three-quarters of an inch in height; in build he was perfection itself—a better-built man I never saw. He wore a cap and a brown jockey coat, trowsers, leggings and highlows, and sported a single spur. He had whiskers—all jockeys should have whiskers—but he had what I did not like, and what no genuine jockey should have, a moustache, which looks coxcombical and Frenchified—but most things have terribly changed since I was young. Three or four hardy-looking fellows, policemen, were gliding about in their blue coats and leather hats, holding their thin walking-sticks behind them; conspicuous amongst whom was the leader, a tall lathy North Briton with a keen eye and hard features. Now if I add there was much gabbling of Welsh round about, and here and there some slight sawing of English—that in the street leading from the north there were some stalls of ginger-bread and a table at which a queer-looking being with a red Greek-looking cap on his head, sold rhubarb, herbs, and phials containing the Lord knows what, and who spoke a low vulgar English dialect,—I repeat, if I add this, I think I have said all that is necessary about Llangollen Fair.

CHAPTER XXIII

An Expedition—Pont y Pandy—The Sabbath—Glendower's Mount—Burial-place of Old—Corwen—The Deep Glen—The Grandmother—The Roadside Chapel.

I WAS now about to leave Llangollen, for a short time, and to set out on an expedition to Bangor, Snowdon, and one or two places in Anglesea. I had determined to make the journey on foot, in order that I might have perfect liberty of action, and enjoy the best opportunities of seeing the country. My wife and daughter were to meet me at Bangor, to which place they would repair by the railroad, and from which, after seeing some of the mountain districts, they would return to Llangollen by the way they came, where I proposed to rejoin them, returning, however, by a different way from the one I went, that I might traverse new districts. About eleven o'clock of a brilliant Sunday morning I left Llangollen, after reading the morning-service of the Church to my family. I set out on a Sunday because I was anxious to observe the general demeanour of the people, in the interior of the country, on the Sabbath.

I directed my course towards the west, to the head of the valley. My wife and daughter after walking with me about a mile bade me farewell, and returned. Quickening my pace I soon left Llangollen valley behind me and entered another vale, along which the road which I was following, and which led to Corwen and other places, might be seen extending for miles. Lumpy hills were close upon my left, the Dee running noisily between steep banks, fringed with trees, was on my right; beyond it rose hills which form part of the wall of the vale of Clwyd; their tops bare, but their sides pleasantly coloured with yellow corn-fields and woods of dark verdure. About an hour's walking, from the time when I entered the valley, brought me to a bridge over a gorge, down which water ran to the Dee. I stopped and looked over the side of the bridge nearest to the hill. A huge rock about forty feet long, by twenty broad, occupied the entire bed of the gorge, just above the bridge, with the exception of a little gullet to the right, down which between the rock and a high bank, on which stood a cottage, a run of water purled and brawled. The rock looked exactly like a huge whale lying on its side, with its back turned towards the runnel. Above it was a glen with trees. After I had been gazing a little time a man making his appearance at the door of the cottage just beyond the bridge, I passed on, and drawing nigh to him, after a slight salutation, asked him in English the name of the bridge.

"The name of the bridge, sir," said the man, in very good English, "is Pont y Pandy."

" Does not that mean the bridge of the fulling mill?"

" I believe it does, sir," said the man.

" Is there a fulling mill near?"

" No, sir, there was one some time ago, but it is now a sawing mill."

Here a woman, coming out, looked at me steadfastly.

" Is that gentlewoman your wife?"

" She is no gentlewoman, sir, but she is my wife."

" Of what religion are you?"

" We are Calvinistic Methodists, sir."

" Have you been to chapel?"

" We are just returned, sir."

Here the woman said something to her husband, which I did not hear, but the purport of which I guessed from the following question which he immediately put.

" Have you been to chapel, sir?"

" I do not go to chapel; I belong to the Church."

" Have you been to church, sir?"

" I have not—I said my prayers at home, and then walked out."

" It is not right to walk out on the Sabbath day, except to go to church or chapel."

" Who told you so?"

" The law of God, which says you shall keep holy the Sabbath day."

" I am not keeping it unholy."

" You are walking about, and in Wales when we see a person walking idly about, on the Sabbath day, we are in the habit of saying Sabbath breaker; where are you going?"

" The Son of Man walked through the fields on the Sabbath day, why should I not walk along the roads?"

" He who called Himself the Son of Man was God, and could do what He pleased, but you are not God."

" But He came in the shape of a man to set an example. Had there been anything wrong in walking about on the Sabbath day, He would not have done it."

Here the wife exclaimed, " How worldly-wise these English are!"

" You do not like the English," said I.

" We do not dislike them," said the woman; " at present they do us no harm, whatever they did of old."

" But you still consider them," said I, " the seed of
Y Sarfes cadwynog, the coiling serpent."

" I should be loth to call any people the seed of the
serpent," said the woman.

" But one of your great bards did," said I.

" He must have belonged to the Church, and not to
the chapel then," said the woman. " No person who
went to chapel would have used such bad words."

" He lived," said I, " before people were separated
into those of the Church, and the chapel; did you ever
hear of Taliesin Ben Beirdd?"

" I never did," said the woman.

" But I have," said the man; " and of Owain
Glendower too."

" Do people talk much of Owen Glendower in these
parts?" said I.

" Plenty," said the man, " and no wonder, for when
he was alive he was much about here—some way
farther on there is a mount, on the bank of the Dee,
called the mount of Owen Glendower, where it is said
he used to stand and look out after his enemies."

" Is it easy to find?" said I.

" Very easy," said the man, " it stands right upon
the Dee and is covered with trees; there is no mis-
taking it."

I bade the man and his wife farewell, and proceeded
on my way. After walking about a mile, I perceived a
kind of elevation which answered to the description of
Glendower's mount, which the man by the bridge had
given me. It stood on the right hand, at some distance
from the road, across a field. As I was standing looking
at it a man came up from the direction in which I
myself had come. He was a middle-aged man plainly
but decently dressed, and had something of the appearance of a farmer.

" What hill may that be?" said I in English, pointing to the elevation.

" Dim Saesneg, sir," said the man, looking rather
sheepish, " Dim gair o Saesneg."

Rather surprised that a person of his appearance
should not have a word of English I repeated my
question in Welsh.

" Ah, you speak Cumraeg, sir," said the man,

evidently surprised that a person of my English appearance should speak Welsh. "I am glad of it! What hill is that, you ask—Dyna Mont Owain Glyndwr, sir."

"Is it easy to get to?" said I.

"Quite easy, sir," said the man. "If you please I will go with you."

I thanked him, and opening a gate he conducted me across the field to the mount of the Welsh hero.

The mount of Owen Glendower stands close upon the southern bank of the Dee, and is nearly covered with trees of various kinds. It is about thirty feet high from the plain, and about the same diameter at the top. A deep black pool of the river, which here runs far beneath the surface of the field, purls and twists under the northern side, which is very steep, though several large oaks spring out of it. The hill is evidently the work of art, and appeared to me to be some burying-place of old.

"And this is the hill of Owain Glyndwr?" said I.

"Dyma Mont Owain Glyndwr, sir, lle yr oedd yn sefyll i edrych am ei elynion yn dyfod o Gaer Lleon. This is the hill of Owen Glendower, sir, where he was in the habit of standing to look out for his enemies coming from Chester."

"I suppose it was not covered with trees then?" said I.

"No, sir; it has not been long planted with trees. They say, however, that the oaks which hang over the river are very old."

"Do they say who raised this hill?"

"Some say that God raised it, sir; others that Owain Glendower raised it. Who do you think raised it?"

"I believe that it was raised by man, but not by Owen Glendower. He may have stood upon it, to watch for the coming of his enemies, but I believe it was here long before his time and that it was raised over some old dead king by the people whom he had governed."

"Do they bury kings by the side of rivers, sir?"

"In the old time they did, and on the tops of mountains; they burnt their bodies to ashes, placed them in pots and raised heaps of earth or stones over them.

Heaps like this have frequently been opened, and found to contain pots with ashes and bones."

" I wish all English could speak Welsh, sir."

" Why?"

" Because then we poor Welsh who can speak no English could learn much which we do not know."

Descending the monticle, we walked along the road together. After a little time I asked my companion of what occupation he was and where he lived.

" I am a small farmer, sir," said he, " and live at Llansanfraid Glyn Dyfrdwy across the river."

" How comes it," said I, " that you do not know English?"

" When I was young," said he, " and could have easily learnt it, I cared nothing about it, and now that I am old and see its use, it is too late to acquire it."

" Of what religion are you?" said I.

" I am of the Church," he replied.

I was about to ask him if there were many people of his persuasion in these parts; before, however, I could do so he turned down a road to the right which led towards a small bridge, and saying that was his way home, bade me farewell and departed.

I arrived at Corwen, which is just ten miles from Llangollen and which stands beneath a vast range of rocks at the head of the valley up which I had been coming, and which is called Glyndyfrdwy, or the valley of the Dee water. It was now about two o'clock, and feeling rather thirsty I went to an inn very appropriately called the Owen Glendower, being the principal inn in the principal town of what was once the domain of the great Owen. Here I stopped for about an hour refreshing myself and occasionally looking into a newspaper in which was an excellent article on the case of poor Lieutenant P. I then started for Cerrig y Drudion, distant about ten miles, where I proposed to pass the night. Directing my course to the north-west, I crossed a bridge over the Dee water and then proceeded rapidly along the road, which for some way lay between corn-fields, in many of which sheaves were piled up, showing that the Welsh harvest was begun. I soon passed over a little stream the name of which I was told was Alowan. " O, what a blessing it is to be able to speak

Welsh!" said I, finding that not a person to whom I
addressed myself had a word of English to bestow upon
me. After walking for about five miles I came to a
beautiful but wild country of mountain and wood with
here and there a few cottages. The road at length
making an abrupt turn to the north I found myself with
a low stone wall on my left on the verge of a profound
ravine, and a high bank covered with trees on my right.
Projecting out over the ravine was a kind of looking-
place, protected by a wall, forming a half-circle, doubtless made by the proprietor of the domain for the use
of the admirers of scenery. There I stationed myself,
and for some time enjoyed one of the wildest and most
beautiful scenes imaginable. Below me was the deep
narrow glen or ravine down which a mountain torrent
roared and foamed. Beyond it was a mountain rising
steeply, its nearer side, which was in deep shade, the
sun having long sunk below its top, hirsute with all
kinds of trees, from the highest pinnacle down to the
torrent's brink. Cut on the top surface of the wall,
which was of slate and therefore easily impressible by
the knife, were several names, doubtless those of
tourists, who had gazed from the look-out on the
prospect, amongst which I observed in remarkably
bold letters that of T. . . .

"Eager for immortality, Mr. T.," said I; "but you
are no H. M., no Huw Morris."

Leaving the looking-place I proceeded, and after
one or two turnings, came to another, which afforded
a view if possible yet more grand, beautiful and wild,
the most prominent objects of which were a kind of
devil's bridge flung over the deep glen and its foaming
water, and a strange-looking hill beyond it, below
which, with a wood on either side, stood a white farm
house—sending from a tall chimney a thin misty reek
up to the sky. I crossed the bridge, which however
diabolically fantastical It looked at a distance, seemed
when one was upon it capable of bearing any weight,
and soon found myself by the farm-house past which
the way led. An aged woman sat on a stool by the
door.

"A fine evening," said I in English.

"Dim Saesneg," said the aged woman.

" O, the blessing of being able to speak Welsh,"
said I; and then repeated in that language what I had
said to her in the other tongue.

" I dare say," said the aged woman, " to those who
can see."

" Can you not see?"

" Very little. I am almost blind."

" Can you not see me?"

" I can see something tall and dark before me; that
is all."

" Can you tell me the name of the bridge?"

" Pont y Glyn blin—the bridge of the glen of
trouble."

" And what is the name of this place?"

" Pen y bont—the head of the bridge."

" What is your own name?"

" Catherine Hughes."

" How old are you?"

" Fifteen after three twenties."

" I have a mother three after four twenties; that is
eight years older than yourself."

" Can she see?"

" Better than I—she can read the smallest letters."

" May she long be a comfort to you!"

" Thank you—are you the mistress of the house?"

" I am the grandmother."

" Are the people in the house?"

" They are not—they are at the chapel."

" And they left you alone?"

" They left me with my God."

" Is the chapel far from here?"

" About a mile."

" On the road to Cerrig y Drudion?"

" On the road to Cerrig y Drudion."

I bade her farewell and pushed on—the road was
good, with high rocky banks on each side. After walking about the distance indicated by the old lady, I
reached a building, which stood on the right-hand side
of the road, and which I had no doubt was the chapel
from a half-groaning, half-singing noise which proceeded from it. The door being open I entered, and
stood just within it, bare-headed. A rather singular
scene presented itself. Within a large dimly-lighted

room a number of people were assembled, partly seated in rude pews, and partly on benches. Beneath a kind of altar, a few yards from the door, stood three men— the middlemost was praying in Welsh in a singular kind of chant, with his arms stretched out. I could distinguish the words, " Jesus descend among us ! sweet Jesus descend among us—quickly.'' He spoke very slowly, and towards the end of every sentence dropped his voice, so that what he said was anything but distinct. As I stood within the door a man dressed in coarse garments came up to me from the interior of the building, and courteously and in excellent Welsh asked me to come with him and take a seat. With equal courtesy but far inferior Welsh, I assured him that I meant no harm, but wished to be permitted to remain near the door, whereupon with a low bow he left me. When the man had concluded his prayer the whole of the congregation began singing a hymn ; many of the voices were gruff and discordant, two or three, however, were of great power, and some of the female ones of surprising sweetness—at the conclusion of the hymn another of the three men by the altar began to pray, just in the same manner as his comrade had done, and seemingly using much the same words. When he had done there was another hymn, after which seeing that the congregation was about to break up I bowed my head towards the interior of the building, and departed.

Emerging from the hollow way I found myself on a moor over which the road lay in the direction of the north. Towards the west at an immense distance rose a range of stupendous hills, which I subsequently learned were those of Snowdon—about ten minutes' walking brought me to Cerrig y Drudion, a small village near a rocky elevation, from which, no doubt, the place takes its name, which interpreted, is the Rock of Heroes.

CHAPTER XXIV

Cerrig y Drudion—The Landlady—Doctor Jones—" Coll Gwynfa "
The Italian—Men of Como—Disappointment—Weather-
Glasses—Filicaia.

THE inn at Cerrig y Drudion was called the Lion—
whether the white, black, red or green Lion I do not
know, though I am certain that it was a lion of some
colour or other. It seemed as decent and respectable a
hostelry as any traveller could wish to refresh and
repose himself in, after a walk of twenty miles. I
entered a well-lighted passage and from thence a well-
lighted bar room, on the right hand, in which sat a
stout, comely, elderly lady dressed in silks and satins,
with a cambric coif on her head, in company with a
thin, elderly man with a hat on his head, dressed in a
rather prim and precise manner. " Madam !" said I,
bowing to the lady, " as I suppose you are the mistress
of this establishment, I beg leave to inform you that
I am an Englishman walking through these regions in
order fully to enjoy their beauties and wonders. I
have this day come from Llangollen, and being somewhat hungry and fatigued hope I can be accommodated
here with a dinner and a bed."

" Sir !" said the lady, getting up and making me a
profound curtsey, " I am as you suppose the mistress
of this establishment, and am happy to say that I shall
be able to accommodate you—pray sit down, sir ;" she
continued handing me a chair, " you must indeed be
tired, for Llangollen is a great way from here."

I took the seat with thanks, and she resumed her
own.

" Rather hot weather for walking, sir !" said the
precise-looking gentleman.

" It is," said I ; " but as I can't observe the country
well without walking through it I put up with the
heat."

" You exhibit a philosophic mind, sir," said the
precise-looking gentleman—" and a philosophic mind
I hold in reverence."

" Pray, sir," said I, " have I the honour of address-ing a member of the medical profession?"

" Sir," said the precise-looking gentleman, getting up and making me a bow, " your question does honour to your powers of discrimination—a member of the medical profession I am, though an unworthy one."

" Nay, nay, doctor," said the landlady briskly; " say not so—every one knows that you are a credit to your profession—well would it be if there were many in it like you—unworthy? marry come up! I won't hear such an expression."

" I see," said I, " that I have not only the honour of addressing a medical gentleman, but a doctor of medicine—however, I might have known as much by your language and deportment."

With a yet lower bow than before he replied, with something of a sigh, " No, sir, no, our kind landlady and the neighbourhood are in the habit of placing doctor before my name, but I have no title to it—I am not Doctor Jones, sir, but plain Geffery Jones at your service," and thereupon with another bow he sat down.

" Do you reside here?" said I.

" Yes, sir, I reside here in the place of my birth—I have not always resided here—and I did not always expect to spend my latter days in a place of such obscurity, but, sir, misfortunes—misfortunes . . ."

" Ah," said I, " misfortunes! they pursue every one, more especially those whose virtues should exempt them from them. Well, sir, the consciousness of not having deserved them should be your consolation."

" Sir," said the doctor, taking off his hat, " you are infinitely kind."

" You call this an obscure place," said I—" can that be an obscure place that has produced a poet? I have long had a respect for Cerrig y Drudion because it gave birth to, and was the residence of a poet of considerable merit."

" I was not aware of that fact," said the doctor, " pray what was his name?"

" Peter Lewis," said I; " he was a clergyman of Cerrig y Drudion about the middle of the last century, and amongst other things wrote a beautiful song called

'Cathl y Gair Mwys,' or the melody of the ambiguous word."

"Surely you do not understand Welsh?" said the doctor.

"I understand a little of it," I replied.

"Will you allow me to speak to you in Welsh?" said the doctor.

"Certainly," said I.

He spoke to me in Welsh and I replied.

"Ha, ha," said the landlady in English; "only think, doctor, of the gentleman understanding Welsh —we must mind what we say before him."

"And are you an Englishman?" said the doctor.

"I am," I replied.

"And how came you to learn it?"

"I am fond of languages," said I, "and studied Welsh at an early period."

"And you read Welsh poetry?"

"O yes."

"How were you enabled to master its difficulties?"

"Chiefly by going through Owen Pugh's version of 'Paradise Lost' twice, with the original by my side. He has introduced into that translation so many of the poetic terms of the old bards that after twice going through it, there was little in Welsh poetry that I could not make out with a little pondering."

"You pursued a very excellent plan," said the doctor, "a very excellent plan indeed. Owen Pugh!"

"Owen Pugh! The last of your very great men," said I.

"You say right, sir," said the doctor. "He was indeed our last great man—Ultimus Romanorum. I have myself read his work, which he called 'Coll Gwynfa,' the 'Loss of the Place of Bliss'—an admirable translation, sir; highly poetical, and at the same time correct."

"Did you know him?" said I.

"I had not the honour of his acquaintance," said the doctor—"but, sir, I am happy to say that I have made yours."

The landlady now began to talk to me about dinner, and presently went out to make preparations for that very important meal. I had a great deal of conversation with the doctor, whom I found a person of great and varied information, and one who had seen a vast deal of the world. He was giving me an account of an island in the West Indies, which he had visited, when a boy coming in whispered into his ear; whereupon, getting up he said; "Sir, I am called away. I am a country surgeon, and of course an accoucheur. There is a lady who lives at some distance, requiring my assistance. It is with grief I leave you so abruptly, but I hope that some time or other we shall meet again." Then making me an exceedingly profound bow, he left the room, followed by the boy.

I dined upstairs in a very handsome drawing-room communicating with a sleeping apartment. During dinner I was waited upon by the daughter of the landlady, a good-looking merry girl of twenty. After dinner I sat for some time thinking over the adventures of the day, then feeling rather lonely and not inclined to retire to rest, I went down to the bar, where I found the landlady seated with her daughter. I sat down with them and we were soon in conversation. We spoke of Doctor Jones—the landlady said that he had his little eccentricities, but was an excellent and learned man. Speaking of herself, she said that she had three daughters, that the youngest was with her and that the two eldest kept the principal inn at Ruthyn. We occasionally spoke a little Welsh. At length the landlady said, "There is an Italian in the kitchen who can speak Welsh too. It's odd the only two people not Welshmen I have ever known who could speak Welsh, for such you and he are, should be in my house at the same time."

"Dear me," said I, "I should like to see him."

"That you can easily do," said the girl; "I dare say he will be glad enough to come in if you invite him."

"Pray take my compliments to him," said I, "and tell him that I shall be glad of his company."

The girl went out and presently returned with the Italian. He was a short, thick, strongly-built fellow of about thirty-seven, with a swarthy face, raven-black hair, high forehead, and dark deep eyes, full of intelligence and great determination. He was dressed in a velveteen coat, with broad lappets, red waistcoat, velveteen breeches, buttoning a little way below the knee; white stockings, apparently of lamb's-wool, and highlows.

"Buona sera?" said I.

"Buona sera, signore!" said the Italian.

"Will you have a glass of brandy and water?" said I in English.

"I never refuse a good offer," said the Italian.

He sat down, and I ordered a glass of brandy and water for him and another for myself.

"Pray speak a little Italian to him," said the good landlady to me. "I have heard a great deal about the beauty of that language, and should like to hear it spoken."

"From the Lago di Como?" said I, trying to speak Italian.

"Si, signore! but how came you to think that I was from the Lake of Como?"

"Because," said I, "when I was a ragazzo I knew many from the Lake of Como, who dressed much like yourself. They wandered about the country with boxes on their backs and weather-glasses in their hands, but had their head-quarters at N. where I lived."

"Do you remember any of their names?" said the Italian.

"Giovanni Gestra and Luigi Pozzi," I replied.

"I have seen Giovanni Gestra myself," said the Italian, "and I have heard of Luigi Pozzi. Giovanni Gestra returned to the Lago—but no one knows what is become of Luigi Pozzi."

"The last time I saw him," said I, "was about eighteen years ago at Coruña, in Spain; he was then in a sad drooping condition, and said he bitterly repented ever quitting N."

"E con ragione," said the Italian, "for there is no place like N. for doing business in the whole world. I myself have sold seventy pounds' worth of weather-glasses at N. in one day. One of our people is living there now, who has done bene, molto bene."

"That's Rossi," said I, "how is it that I did not mention him first? He is my excellent friend, and a finer cleverer fellow never lived, nor a more honourable man. You may well say he has done well, for he is now the first jeweller in the place. The last time I was there I bought a diamond of him for my daughter Henrietta. Let us drink his health!"

"Willingly!" said the Italian. "He is the prince of the Milanese of England—the most successful of all, but I acknowledge the most deserving. Che viva."

"I wish he would write his life," said I; "a singular life it would be—he has been something besides a travelling merchant, and a jeweller. He was one of Buonaparte's soldiers and served in Spain, under Soult, along with John Gestra. He once told me that Soult was an old rascal, and stole all the fine pictures from the convents, at Salamanca. I believe he spoke with some degree of envy, for he is himself fond of pictures, and has dealt in them, and made hundreds by them. I question whether if in Soult's place he would not have done the same. Well, however that may be, che viva."

Here the landlady interposed, observing that she wished we would now speak English, for that she had quite enough of Italian, which she did not find near so pretty a language as she had expected.

"You must not judge of the sound of Italian from what proceeds from my mouth," said I. "It is not my native language. I have had little practice in it, and only speak it very imperfectly."

"Nor must you judge of Italian from what you have heard me speak," said the man of Como; "I am not good at Italian, for the Milanese speak amongst themselves a kind of jargon composed of many languages, and can only express themselves with difficulty in Italian. I have been doing my best to speak Italian but should be glad now to speak English, which comes to me much more glibly."

"Are there any books in your dialect, or jergo, as I believe you call it?" said I.

"I believe there are a few," said the Italian.

"Do you know the word slandra?" said I.

"Who taught you that word?" said the Italian.

"Giovanni Gestra," said I—"he was always using it."

"Giovanni Gestra was a vulgar illiterate man," said the Italian; "had he not been so he would not have used it. It is a vulgar word; Rossi would not have used it."

"What is the meaning of it?" said the landlady eagerly.

"To roam about in a dissipated manner," said I.

"Something more," said the Italian. "It is considered a vulgar word even in jergo."

"You speak English remarkably well," said I; "have you been long in Britain?"

"I came over about four years ago," said the Italian.

"On your own account?" said I.

"Not exactly, signore; my brother, who was in business in Liverpool, wrote to me to come over and assist him. I did so, but soon left him, and took a shop for myself at Denbigh, where, however, I did not stay long. At present I travel for an Italian house in London, spending the summer in Wales and the winter in England."

"And what do you sell?" said I.

"Weather-glasses, signore—pictures and little trinkets, such as the country people like."

"Do you sell many weather-glasses in Wales?" said I.

"I do not, signore. The Welsh care not for weather-glasses; my principal customers for weather-glasses are the farmers of England."

"I am told that you can speak Welsh," said I; "is that true?"

"I have picked up a little of it, signore."

"He can speak it very well," said the landlady; "and glad should I be, sir, to hear you and him speak Welsh together."

"So should I," said the daughter, who was seated nigh us; "nothing would give me greater pleasure than to hear two who are not Welshmen speaking Welsh together."

"I would rather speak English," said the Italian; "I speak a little Welsh, when my business leads me amongst people who speak no other language, but I see no necessity for speaking Welsh here."

" It is a pity," said I, " that so beautiful a country as Italy should not be better governed."

" It is, signore," said the Italian; " but let us hope that a time will speedily come when she will be so."

" I don't see any chance of it," said I. " How will you proceed in order to bring about so desirable a result as the good government of Italy?"

" Why, signore, in the first place we must get rid of the Austrians."

" You will not find it an easy matter," said I, " to get rid of the Austrians: you tried to do so a little time ago, but miserably failed."

" True, signore; but the next time we try perhaps the French will help us."

" If the French help you to drive the Austrians from Italy," said I, " you must become their servants. It is true you had better be the servants of the polished and chivalrous French, than of the brutal and barbarous Germans, but it is not pleasant to be a servant to anybody. However, I do not believe that you will ever get rid of the Austrians, even if the French assist you. The Pope for certain reasons of his own favours the Austrians, and will exert all the powers of priestcraft to keep them in Italy. Alas, alas, there is no hope for Italy! Italy, the most beautiful country in the world, the birthplace of the cleverest people, whose very pedlars can learn to speak Welsh, is not only enslaved, but destined always to remain enslaved."

" Do not say so, signore," said the Italian, with a kind of groan.

" But I do say so," said I, " and what is more, one whose shoe-strings, were he alive, I should not be worthy to untie, one of your mighty ones, has said so. Did you ever hear of Vincenzio Filicaia?"

" I believe I have, signore; did he not write a sonnet on Italy?"

" He did," said I; " would you like to hear it?"

" Very much, signore."

I repeated Filicaia's glorious sonnet on Italy, and then asked him if he understood it.

" Only in part, signore; for it is composed in old Tuscan, in which I am not much versed. I believe I should comprehend it better if you were to say it in English."

"Do say it in English," said the landlady and her daughter; "we should so like to hear it in English."

"I will repeat a translation," said I, "which I made when a boy, which though far from good, has, I believe, in it something of the spirit of the original :—

> "'O Italy! on whom dark Destiny
> The dangerous gift of beauty did bestow,
> From whence thou hast that ample dower of wo,
> Which on thy front thou bear'st so visibly.
> Would thou hadst beauty less or strength more high,
> That more of fear, and less of love might show,
> He who now blasts him in thy beauty's glow,
> Or woos thee with a zeal that makes thee die;
> Then down from Alp no more would torrents rage
> Of armed men, nor Gallic coursers hot
> In Po's ensanguin'd tide their thirst assuage;
> Nor girt with iron, not thine own, I wot,
> Wouldst thou the fight by hands of strangers wage,
> Victress or vanquish'd slavery still thy lot.'"

CHAPTER XXV

Lacing up Highlows—The Native Village—Game Leg—"Croppies Lie Down"—Keeping Faith—Processions—"Croppies Get Up"—Daniel O'Connell.

I SLEPT in the chamber communicating with the room in which I had dined. The chamber was spacious and airy, the bed first-rate, and myself rather tired, so that no one will be surprised when I say that I had excellent rest. I got up, and after dressing myself went down. The morning was exceedingly brilliant. Going out I saw the Italian lacing up his highlows against a step. I saluted him, and asked him if he was about to depart.

"Yes, signore; I shall presently start for Denbigh."

"After breakfast I shall start for Bangor," said I.

"Do you propose to reach Bangor to-night, signore?"

"Yes," said I.

"Walking, signore?"

"Yes," said I; "I always walk in Wales."

"Then you will have rather a long walk, signore, for Bangor is thirty-four miles from here."

I asked him if he was married.

"No, signore; but my brother in Liverpool is."

"To an Italian?"

"No, signore; to a Welsh girl."

"And I suppose," said I, "you will follow his example by marrying one; perhaps that good-looking girl the landlady's daughter we were seated with last night?"

"No, signore; I shall not follow my brother's example. If ever I take a wife she shall be of my own village, in Como, whither I hope to return, as soon as I have picked up a few more pounds."

"Whether the Austrians are driven away or not?" said I.

"Whether the Austrians are driven away or not—for to my mind there is no country like Como, signore."

I ordered breakfast; whilst taking it in the room above I saw through the open window the Italian trudging forth on his journey, a huge box on his back, and a weather-glass in his hand—looking the exact image of one of those men his country people, whom forty years before I had known at N. I thought of the course of time, sighed and felt a tear gather in my eye.

My breakfast concluded, I paid my bill, and after inquiring the way to Bangor, and bidding adieu to the kind landlady and her daughter, set out from Cerrig y Drudion. My course lay west, across a flat country, bounded in the far distance by the mighty hills I had seen on the preceding evening. After walking about a mile I overtook a man with a game leg, that is a leg, which either by nature or accident not being so long as its brother leg, had a patten attached to it, about five inches high, to enable it to do duty with the other —he was a fellow with red shock hair and very red features, and was dressed in ragged coat and breeches, and a hat which had lost part of its crown, and all its rim, so that even without a game leg he would have looked rather a queer figure. In his hand he carried a fiddle.

"Good morning to you," said I.

"A good marning to your hanner, a merry afternoon

and a roaring joyous evening—that is the worst luck I
wish to ye.''

"Are you a native of these parts?'' said I.

"Not exactly, your hanner—I am a native of the city
of Dublin, or, what's all the same thing, of the village
of Donnybrook which is close by it.''

"A celebrated place,'' said I.

"Your hanner may say that; all the world has heard
of Donnybrook, owing to the humours of its fair.
Many is the merry tune I have played to the boys at
that fair.''

"You are a professor of music, I suppose?''

"And not a very bad one as your hanner will say if
you will allow me to play you a tune.''

"Can you play 'Croppies Lie Down'?''

"I cannot, your hanner; my fingers never learnt to
play such a blackguard tune; but if ye wish to hear
'Croppies Get Up' I can oblige ye.''

"You are a Roman Catholic, I suppose?''

"I am nat, your hanner—I am a Catholic to the
backbone, just like my father before me. Come, your
hanner, shall I play ye 'Croppies Get Up'?''

"No,'' said I; "It's a tune that doesn't please my
ears. If, however, you choose to play 'Croppies Lie
Down,' I'll give you a shilling.''

"Your hanner will give me a shilling?''

"Yes,'' said I, "if you play 'Croppies Lie Down':
but you know you cannot play it, your fingers never
learned the tune.''

"They never did, your hanner; but they have heard
it played of ould by the blackguard Orange fiddlers of
Dublin on the first of July, when the Protestant boys
used to walk round Willie's statue on College Green—
so if your hanner gives me the shilling they may
perhaps bring out something like it.''

"Very good,'' said I; "begin!''

"But, your hanner, what shall we do for the words?
Though my fingers may remember the tune, my tongue
does not remember the words—that is unless . . .''

"I give another shilling,'' said I; "but never mind
you the words; I know the words, and will repeat
them.''

" And your hanner will give me a shilling?"

" If you play the tune," said I.

" Hanner bright, your hanner?"

" Honour bright," said I.

Thereupon the fiddler, taking his bow and shoulder-ing his fiddle, struck up in first-rate style the glorious tune, which I had so often heard with rapture in the days of my boyhood in the barrack yard of Clonmel; whilst I walking by his side as he stumped along, caused the welkin to resound with the words, which were the delight of the young gentlemen of the Protestant academy of that beautiful old town.

" I never heard those words before," said the fiddler, after I had finished the first stanza.

" Get on with you," said I.

" Regular Orange words!" said the fiddler, on my finishing the second stanza.

" Do you choose to get on?" said I.

" More blackguard Orange words I never heard!" cried the fiddler, on my coming to the conclusion of the third stanza. " Divil a bit farther will I play; at any rate till I get the shilling."

"Here it is for you," said I; " the song is ended and of course the tune."

" Thank your hanner," said the fiddler, taking the money, " your hanner has kept your word with me, which is more than I thought your hanner would. And now, your hanner, let me ask you why did your hanner wish for that tune, which is not only a blackguard one, but quite out of date; and where did your hanner get the words?"

" I used to hear the tune in my boyish days," said I, " and wished to hear it again, for though you call it a blackguard tune, it is the sweetest and most noble air that Ireland, the land of music, has ever produced. As for the words, never mind where I got them; they are violent enough, but not half so violent as the words of some of the songs made against the Irish Protestants by the priests."

" Your hanner is an Orange man, I see. Well, your hanner, the Orange is now in the kennel, and the Croppies have it all their own way."

" And perhaps," said I, " before I die, the Orange

will be out of the kennel and the Croppies in, even as they were in my young days."

"Who knows, your hanner? and who knows that I may not play the ould tune round Willie's image in College Green, even as I used some twenty-seven years ago?"

"O then you have been an Orange fiddler?"

"I have, your hanner. And now as your hanner has behaved like a gentleman to me I will tell ye all my history. I was born in the city of Dublin, that is in the village of Donnybrook, as I tould your hanner before. It was to the trade of bricklaying I was bred, and bricklaying I followed till at last, getting my leg smashed, not by falling off the ladder, but by a row in the fair, I was obliged to give it up, for how could I run up the ladder with a patten on my foot, which they put on to make my broken leg as long as the other. Well, your hanner; being obliged to give up my bricklaying, I took to fiddling, to which I had always a natural inclination, and played about the streets, and at fairs, and wakes, and weddings. At length some Orange men getting acquainted with me, and liking my style of playing, invited me to their lodge, where they gave me to drink, and tould me that if I would change my religion and join them, and play their tunes, they would make it answer my purpose. Well, your hanner, without much stickling I gave up my Popery, joined the Orange lodge, learned the Orange tunes, and became a regular Protestant boy, and truly the Orange men kept their word, and made it answer my purpose. O the meat and drink I got, and the money I made by playing at the Orange lodges and before the processions when the Orange men paraded the streets with their Orange colours. And O, what a day for me was the glorious first of July when with my whole body covered with Orange ribbons I fiddled 'Croppies Lie Down'—'Boyne Water,' and the 'Protestant Boys' before the procession which walked round Willie's figure on horseback in College Green, the man and horse all ablaze with Orange colours. But nothing lasts under the sun, as your hanner knows; Orangeism began to go down; the Government scowled at it, and at last passed a law preventing the Protestant boys dressing up the figure on the first of July, and walking round it. That was the death-blow of the Orange party, your hanner; they never recovered it, but began to despond and dwindle, and I with them, for there was scarcely any demand for Orange tunes. Then Dan O'Connell arose with his emancipation and repale cries, and then instead of Orange processions and walkings, there were Papist processions and mobs, which made me afraid to stir out, lest knowing me for an Orange fiddler, they should break my head, as the boys broke my leg at Donnybrook fair. At length some of the repalers and emancipators knowing that I was a first-rate hand at fiddling came to me, and tould me, that if I would give over playing 'Croppies Lie Down' and other Orange tunes, and would play 'Croppies Get Up,' and what not, and become a Catholic and a repaler, and an emancipator, they would make a man of me—so as my Orange trade was gone, and I was half-starved, I consinted, not however till they had introduced me to Daniel O'Connell, who called me a credit to my country, and the Irish Horpheus, and promised me a sovereign if I would consint to join the cause, as he called it. Well, your hanner, I joined with the cause and became a Papist, I mane a Catholic once more, and went at the head of processions, covered all over with green ribbons, playing 'Croppies Get Up,' 'Granny Whale,' and the like. But, your hanner; though I went the whole hog with the repalers and emancipators, they did not make their words good by making a man of me. Scant and sparing were they in the mate and drink, and yet more sparing in the money, and Daniel O'Connell never gave me the sovereign which he promised me. No, your hanner, though I played 'Croppies Get Up,' till my fingers ached, as I stumped before him and his mobs and processions, he never gave me the sovereign : unlike your hanner who gave me the shilling ye promised me for playing 'Croppies Lie Down,' Daniel O'Connell never gave me the sovereign he promised me for playing 'Croppies Get Up.' Och, your hanner, I often wished the ould Orange days were back again. However as I could do no better I continued going the whole hog with the emancipators and repalers and Dan O'Connell; I went the whole animal with them till they had got emancipation; and I went the whole animal with them till they nearly got repale—when all of a sudden they let the whole thing drop—Dan and his party having frighted the Government out of its seven senses, and gotten all they thought they could get, in money and places, which was all they wanted, let the whole hullabaloo drop, and of course myself, who formed part of it. I went to those who had persuaded me to give up my Orange tunes, and to play Papist ones, begging them to give me work; but they tould me very civilly that they had no farther occasion for my services. I went to Daniel O'Connell reminding him of the sovereign he had promised me, and offering if he gave it me to play ' Croppies Get Up ' under the nose of the lord-lieutenant himself; but he tould me that he had not time to attend to me, and when I persisted, bade me go to the Divil and shake myself. Well, your hanner, seeing no prospect for myself in my own country, and having incurred some little debts, for which I feared to be arrested, I came over to England and Wales, where with little content and satisfaction I have passed seven years."

" Well," said I, "thank you for your history—farewell."

" Stap, your hanner; does your hanner think that the Orange will ever be out of the kennel, and that the Orange boys will ever walk round the brass man and horse in College Green as they did of ould?"

" Who knows?" said I. " But suppose all that were to happen, what would it signify to you?"

" Why then Divil be in my patten if I would not go back to Donnybrook and Dublin, hoist the Orange cockade, and become as good an Orange boy as ever."

" What," said I, "and give up Popery for the second time?"

" I would, your hanner; and why not? for in spite of what I have heard Father Toban say, I am by no means certain that all Protestants will be damned."

" Farewell," said I.

" Farewell, your hanner, and long life and prosperity to you! God bless your hanner and your Orange face. Ah, the Orange boys are the boys for keeping faith. They never served me as Dan O'Connell and his dirty gang of repalers and emancipators did. Farewell, your hanner, once more; and here's another scratch of the illigant tune your hanner is so fond of, to cheer up your hanner's ears upon your way."

And long after I had left him I could hear him playing on his fiddle in first-rate style the beautiful tune of "Down, down, Croppies Lie Down."

CHAPTER XXVI

Ceiniog Mawr—Pentre Voelas—The Old Conway—Stupendous Pass—The Gwedir Family—Capel Curig—The Two Children —Bread—Wonderful Echo—Tremendous Walker.

I WALKED on briskly over a flat uninteresting country, and in about an hour's time came in front of a large stone house. It stood near the road, on the left-hand side, with a pond and pleasant trees before it, and a number of corn-stacks behind. It had something the appearance of an inn, but displayed no sign. As I was standing looking at it, a man with the look of a labourer, and with a dog by his side, came out of the house and advanced towards me.

" What is the name of this place?" said I to him in English as he drew nigh.

" Sir," said the man, " the name of the house is Ceiniog Mawr."

" Is it an inn?" said I.

" Not now, sir; but some years ago it was an inn, and a very large one at which coaches used to stop; at present it is occupied by an amaethwr—that is a farmer, sir."

" Ceiniog Mawr means a great penny," said I, " why is it called by that name?"

" I have heard, sir, that before it was an inn it was a very considerable place, namely, a royal mint at which pennies were made, and on that account it was called Ceiniog Mawr."

I was subsequently told that the name of this place was Cernioge Mawr. If such be the real name the legend about the mint falls to the ground, Cernioge having nothing to do with pence. Cern in Welsh means a jaw. Perhaps the true name of the house is Corniawg, which interpreted is a place with plenty of turrets or chimneys. A mile or two further the ground began to rise, and I came to a small village at the entrance of which was a water-wheel—near the village was a gentleman's seat almost surrounded by groves. After I had passed through the village, seeing a woman seated by the roadside knitting, I asked her in English its name. Finding she had no Saesneg I repeated the question in Welsh, whereupon she told me that it was caled Pentre Voelas.

"And whom does the 'Plas' belong to yonder amongst the groves?" said I.

"It belongs to Mr. Wynn, sir, and so does the village and a great deal of the land about here. A very good gentleman is Mr. Wynn, sir; he is very kind to his tenants and a very good lady is Mrs. Wynn, sir; in the winter she gives much soup to the poor."

After leaving the village of Pentre Voelas I soon found myself in a wild hilly region. I crossed a bridge over a river which brawling and tumbling amidst rocks shaped its course to the north-east. As I proceeded the country became more and more wild; there were dingles and hollows in abundance, and fantastic-looking hills some of which were bare and others clad with trees of various kinds. Came to a little well in a cavity dug in a high bank on the left-hand side of the road, and fenced by rude stone work on either side; the well was about ten inches in diameter, and as many deep. Water oozing from the bank upon a slanting tile fastened into the earth fell into it. After damming up the end of the tile with my hand and drinking some delicious water I passed on and presently arrived at a cottage just inside the door of which sat a good-looking middle-aged woman engaged in knitting, the general occupation of Welsh females.

"Good-day," said I to her in Welsh. "Fine weather."

"In truth, sir, it is fine weather for the harvest."

"Are you alone in the house?"

"I am, sir, my husband has gone to his labour."

" Have you any children?"

" Two, sir; but they are out at service."

" What is the name of this place?"

" Pant Paddock, sir."

" Do you get your water from the little well yonder?"

" We do, sir, and good water it is."

" I have drunk of it."

" Much good may what you have drunk do you, sir!"

" What is the name of the river near here?"

" It is called the Conway, sir."

" Dear me; is that river the Conway?"

" You have heard of it, sir?"

" Heard of it! it is one of the famous rivers of the world. The poets are very fond of it—one of the great poets of my country calls it the old Conway."

" Is one river older than another, sir?"

" That's a shrewd question. Can you read?"

" I can, sir."

" Have you any books?"

" I have the Bible, sir."

" Will you show it me?"

" Willingly, sir."

Then getting up she took a book from a shelf and handed it to me at the same time begging me to enter the house and sit down. I declined and she again took her seat and resumed her occupation. On opening the book the first words which met my eye were " Gad i mi fyned trwy dy dir!" Let me go through your country. Numbers xx. 22.

" I may say these words," said I, pointing to the passage. " Let me go through your country."

" No one will hinder you, sir, for you seem a civil gentleman."

" No one has hindered me hitherto. Wherever I have been in Wales I have experienced nothing but kindness and hospitality, and when I return to my own country I will say so."

" What country is yours, sir?"

" England. Did you not know that by my tongue?"

" I did not, sir. I knew by your tongue that you were not from our parts—but I did not know that you were an Englishman. I took you for a Cumro of the south country."

Returning the kind woman her book, and bidding her farewell I departed, and proceeded some miles through a truly magnificent country of wood, rock, and mountain. At length I came down to a steep mountain gorge down which the road ran nearly due north, the Conway to the left running with great noise parallel with the road, amongst broken rocks, which chafed it into foam. I was now amidst stupendous hills, whose paps, peaks, and pinnacles seemed to rise to the very heaven. An immense mountain on the right side of the road particularly struck my attention, and on inquiring of a man breaking stones by the roadside I learned that it was called Dinas Mawr or the large citadel, perhaps from a fort having been built upon it to defend the pass in the old British times. Coming to the bottom of the pass I crossed over by an ancient bridge and passing through a small town found myself in a beautiful valley with majestic hills, on either side. This was the Dyffryn Conway, the celebrated Vale of Conway, to which in the summer time fashionable gentry from all parts of Britain resort for shade and relaxation. When about midway down the valley I turned to the west up one of the grandest passes in the world, having two immense door-posts of rock at the entrance, the northern one probably rising to the altitude of nine hundred feet. On the southern side of this pass near the entrance were neat dwellings for the accommodation of visitors with cool apartments on the ground-floor with large windows, looking towards the precipitous side of the mighty northern hill; within them I observed tables, and books, and young men, probably English collegians, seated at study.

After I had proceeded some way up the pass down which a small river ran, a woman who was standing on the right-hand side of the way, seemingly on the look-out, begged me in broken English to step aside and look at the fall.

"You mean a waterfall, I suppose?" said I.

"Yes, sir."

"And how do you call it?" said I.

"The Fall of the Swallow, sir."

" And in Welsh?" said I.

" Rhaiadr y Wennol, sir."

" And what is the name of the river?" said I.

" We call the river the Lygwy, sir."

I told the woman I would go, whereupon she conducted me through a gate on the right-hand side and down a path, overhung with trees to a rock projecting into the river. The Fall of the Swallow is not a majestic single fall, but a succession of small ones. First there are a number of little foaming torrents, bursting through rocks about twenty yards above the promontory, on which I stood. Then come two beautiful rows of white water, dashing into a pool a little way above the promontory; then there is a swirl of water round its corner into a pool below on its right, black as death and seemingly of great depth; then a rush through a very narrow outlet into another pool, from which the water clamours away down the glen. Such is the Rhaiadr y Wennol, or Swallow Fall; called so from the rapidity with which the waters rush and skip along.

On asking the woman on whose property the fall was, she informed me that it was on the property of the Gwedir family. The name of Gwedir brought to my mind the *History of the Gwedir Family,* a rare and curious book which I had read in my boyhood and which was written by the representative of that family, a certain Sir John Wynne, about the beginning of the seventeenth century. It gives an account of the fortunes of the family from its earliest rise : but more particularly after it had emigrated, in order to avoid bad neighbours, from a fair and fertile district into rugged Snowdonia, where it found anything but the repose it came in quest of. The book which is written in bold graphic English flings considerable light on the state of society in Wales, in the time of the Tudors, a truly deplorable state, as the book is full of accounts of feuds, petty but desperate skirmishes, and revengeful murders. To many of the domestic sagas, or histories of ancient Icelandic families, from the character of the events which it describes and also from the manner in which it describes them, the *History of the Gwedir Family*, by Sir John Wynne, bears a striking resemblance.

After giving the woman sixpence I left the fall, and
proceeded on my way. I presently crossed a bridge
under which ran the river of the fall, and was soon in a
wide valley on each side of which were lofty hills dotted
with wood, and at the top of which stood a mighty
mountain, bare and precipitous with two paps like those
of Pindus opposite Janina, but somewhat sharper.   It
was a region of fairy beauty and of wild grandeur.
Meeting an old bleared-eyed farmer I inquired the name
of the mountain and learned that it was called Moel
Siabod or Shabod.   Shortly after leaving him, I turned
from the road to inspect a monticle which appeared to
me to have something of the appearance of a burial
heap.   It stood in a green meadow by the river which
ran down the valley on the left.   Whether it was a
grave hill or a natural monticle, I will not say; but
standing in the fair meadow, the rivulet murmuring
beside it, and the old mountain looking down upon it,
I thought it looked a very meet resting-place for an old
Celtic king.

Turning round the northern side of the mighty Siabod
I soon reached the village of Capel Curig, standing in
a valley between two hills, the easternmost of which is
the aforesaid Moel Siabod.   Having walked now
twenty miles in a broiling day I thought it high time
to take some refreshment, and inquired the way to the
inn.   The inn, or rather the hotel, for it was a very
magnificent edifice, stood at the entrance of a pass
leading to Snowdon, on the southern side of the valley
in a totally different direction from the road leading to
Bangor, to which place I was bound.   There I dined in
a grand saloon amidst a great deal of fashionable company, who, probably conceiving from my heated and
dusty appearance that I was some poor fellow travelling
on foot from motives of economy, surveyed me with
looks of the most supercilious disdain, which, however,
neither deprived me of my appetite nor operated un-
comfortably on my feelings.

My dinner finished, I paid my bill and having
sauntered a little about the hotel garden, which is
situated on the border of a small lake and from which
through the vista of the pass Snowdon may be seen
towering in majesty at the distance of about six miles,

I started for Bangor, which is fourteen miles from Capel Curig.

The road to Bangor from Capel Curig is almost due west. An hour's walking brought me to a bleak moor, extending for a long way amidst wild sterile hills.

The first of a chain on the left was a huge lumpy hill with a precipice towards the road probably three hundred feet high. When I had come nearly parallel with the commencement of this precipice, I saw on the left-hand side of the road two children looking over a low wall behind which at a little distance stood a wretched hovel. On coming up I stopped and looked at them : they were a boy and a girl; the first about twelve, the latter a year or two younger; both wretchedly dressed and looking very sickly.

"Have you any English?" said I, addressing the boy in Welsh.

"Dim gair," said the boy; "not a word; there is no Saesneg near here."

"What is the name of this place?"

"The name of our house is Helyg."

"And what is the name of that hill?" said I, pointing to the hill of the precipice.

"Allt y Gôg—the high place of the cuckoo."

"Have you a father and mother?"

"We have."

"Are they in the house?"

"They have gone to Capel Curig."

"And they left you alone?"

"They did. With the cat and the trin-wire."

"Do your father and mother make wire-work?"

"They do. They live by making it."

"What is the wire-work for?"

"It is for hedges to fence the fields with."

"Do you help your father and mother?"

"We do; as far as we can."

"You both look unwell."

"We have lately had the cryd " (ague).

"Is there much cryd about here?"

"Plenty."

"Do you live well?"

"When we have bread we live well."

" If I give you a penny will you bring me some
water?"

" We will; whether you give us the penny or not.
Come, sister, let us go and fetch the gentleman
water."

They ran into the house and presently returned, the
girl bearing a pan of water. After I had drunk I gave
each of the children a penny, and received in return
from each a diolch or thanks.

" Can either of you read?"

" Neither one nor the other."

" Can your father and mother read?"

" My father cannot, my mother can a little."

" Are there any books in the house?"

" There are not."

" No Bible?"

" There is no book at all."

" Do you go to church?"

" We do not."

" To chapel?"

" In fine weather."

" Are you happy?"

" When there is bread in the house and no cryd we
are all happy."

" Farewell to you, children."

" Farewell to you, gentleman!" exclaimed both.

" I have learnt something," said I, " of Welsh
cottage life and feeling from that poor sickly child."

I had passed the first and second of the hills which
stood on the left, and a huge long mountain on the
right which confronted both when a young man came
down from a gulley on my left hand, and proceeded in
the same direction as myself. He was dressed in a
blue coat and corduroy trowsers and appeared to be
of a condition a little above that of a labourer. He
shook his head and scowled when I spoke to him in
English, but smiled on my speaking Welsh and said:
" Ah, you speak Cumraeg: I thought no Sais could
speak Cumraeg." I asked him if he was going far.

" About four miles," he replied.

" On the Bangor road?"

" Yes," said he; " down the Bangor road."

I learned that he was a carpenter, and that he had

been up the gully to see an acquaintance—perhaps a sweetheart. We passed a lake on our right which he told me was called Llyn Ogwen, and that it abounded with fish. He was very amusing and expressed great delight at having found an Englishman who could speak Welsh. "It will be a thing to talk of," said he, "for the rest of my life." He entered two or three cottages by the side of the road, and each time he came out I heard him say: "I am with a Sais, who can speak Cumraeg." At length we came to a gloomy-looking valley trending due north; down this valley the road ran having an enormous wall of rocks on its right and a precipitous hollow on the left, beyond which was a wall equally high as the other one. When we had proceeded some way down the road my guide said: "You shall now hear a wonderful echo," and shouting, "taw, taw," the rocks replied in a manner something like the baying of hounds. "Hark to the dogs!" exclaimed my companion. "This pass is called Nant yr ieuanc gwn, the pass of the young dogs, because when one shouts it answers with a noise resembling the crying of hounds."

The sun was setting when we came to a small village at the bottom of the pass. I asked my companion its name. "Ty yn y maes," he replied, adding as he stopped before a small cottage that he was going no farther, as he dwelt there.

"Is there a public-house here?" said I.

"There is," he replied, "you will find one a little farther up on the right hand."

"Come, and take some ale," said I.

"No," said he.

"Why not?" I demanded.

"I am a teetotaller," he replied.

"Indeed," said I, and having shaken him by the hand, thanked him for his company, and bidding him farewell, went on. He was the first person I had ever met of the fraternity to which he belonged, who did not endeavour to make a parade of his abstinence and self-denial.

After drinking some tolerably good ale in the public-house I again started. As I left the village a clock struck eight. The evening was delightfully cool; but it soon became nearly dark. I passed under high rocks, by houses and by groves, in which nightingales were singing, to listen to whose entrancing melody I more than once stopped. On coming to a town, lighted up and thronged with people, I asked one of a group of young fellows its name.

" Bethesda," he replied.

" A scriptural name," said I.

" Is it?" said he; " well, if its name is scriptural the manners of its people are by no means so."

A little way beyond the town a man came out of a cottage and walked beside me. He had a basket in his hand. I quickened my pace; but he was a tremendous walker, and kept up with me. On we went side by side for more than a mile without speaking a word. At length, putting out my legs in genuine Barclay fashion, I got before him about ten yards, then turning round laughed and spoke to him in English. He too laughed and spoke, but in Welsh. We now went on like brothers, conversing, but always walking at great speed. I learned from him that he was a market gardener living at Bangor, and that Bangor was three miles off. On the stars shining out we began to talk about them.

Pointing to Charles's wain I said, " A good star for travellers."

Whereupon pointing to the North star, he said :

" I forwyr da iawn—a good star for mariners."

We passed a large house on our left.

" Who lives there?" said I.

" Mr. Smith," he replied. " It is called Plas Newydd; milltir genom etto—we have yet another mile."

In ten minutes we were at Bangor. I asked him where the Albion Hotel was.

" I will show it you," said he, and so he did.

As we came under it I heard the voice of my wife, for she, standing on a balcony and distinguishing me by the lamplight, called out. I shook hands with the kind six-mile-an-hour market gardener, and going into the inn found my wife and daughter, who rejoiced to see me. We presently had tea.

CHAPTER XXVII

Bangor—Edmund Price—The Bridges—Bookselling—Future Pope
—Wild Irish—Southey.

BANGOR is seated on the spurs of certain high hills
near the Menai, a strait separating Mona or Anglesey
from Caernarvonshire. It was once a place of Druidical
worship, of which fact, even without the testimony of
history and tradition, the name which signifies " upper
circle " would be sufficient evidence. On the decay of
Druidism a town sprang up on the site and in the
neighbourhood of the " upper circle," in which in the
sixth century a convent or university was founded by
Deiniol, who eventually became Bishop of Bangor.
This Deiniol was the son of Deiniol Vawr, a zealous
Christian prince who founded the convent of Bangor
Is Coed, or Bangor beneath the wood, in Flintshire,
which was destroyed and its inmates almost to a man
put to the sword by Ethelbert a Saxon king, and his
barbarian followers at the instigation of the monk
Austin, who hated the brethren because they refused
to acknowledge the authority of the Pope, whose dele-
gate he was in Britain. There were in all three
Bangors; the one at Is Coed, another in Powis, and
this Caernarvonshire Bangor, which was generally
termed Bangor Vawr or Bangor the great. The two
first Bangors have fallen into utter decay, but Bangor
Vawr is still a bishop's see, boasts of a small but
venerable cathedral, and contains a population of above
eight thousand souls.

Two very remarkable men have at different periods
conferred a kind of lustre upon Bangor by residing in
it, Taliesin in the old, and Edmund Price in comparatively modern time. Both of them were poets. Taliesin
flourished about the end of the fifth century, and for the
sublimity of his verses was for many centuries called by
his countrymen the Bardic King. Amongst his pieces
is one generally termed " The Prophecy of Taliesin,"
which announced long before it happened the entire
subjugation of Britain by the Saxons, and which is

perhaps one of the most stirring pieces of poetry ever produced. Edmund Price flourished during the time of Elizabeth. He was archdeacon of Merionethshire, but occasionally resided at Bangor for the benefit of his health. Besides being one of the best Welsh poets of his age he was a man of extraordinary learning, possessing a thorough knowledge of no less than eight languages.

The greater part of his compositions, however clever and elegant, are, it must be confessed, such as do little credit to the pen of an ecclesiastic, being bitter poignant satires, which were the cause of much pain and misery to individuals; one of his works, however, is not only of a kind quite consistent with his sacred calling, but has been a source of considerable blessing. To him the Cambrian Church is indebted for the version of the Psalms, which for the last two centuries it has been in the habit of using. Previous to the version of the Archdeacon a translation of the Psalms had been made into Welsh by William Middleton, an officer in the naval service of Queen Elizabeth, in the four-and-twenty alliterative measures of the ancient bards. It was elegant and even faithful, but far beyond the comprehension of people in general, and consequently by no means fitted for the use of churches, though intended for that purpose by the author, a sincere Christian, though a warrior. Avoiding the error into which his predecessor had fallen, the Archdeacon made use of a measure intelligible to people of every degree, in which alliteration is not observed, and which is called by the Welsh y mesur cyffredin, or the common measure. His opinion of the four-and-twenty measures the Archdeacon has given to the world in four cowydd lines to the following effect :

"I've read the master-pieces great
Of languages no less than eight,
But ne'er have found a woof of song
So strict as that of Cambria's tongue."

After breakfast on the morning subsequent to my arrival, Henrietta and I roamed about the town, and then proceeded to view the bridges which lead over the strait to Anglesey. One, for common traffic, is a most beautiful suspension bridge completed in 1820, the

result of the mental and manual labours of the ingeni-
ous Telford; the other is a tubular railroad bridge, a
wonderful structure, no doubt, but anything but graceful. We remained for some time on the first bridge,
admiring the scenery, and were not a little delighted,
as we stood leaning over the principal arch, to see a
proud vessel pass beneath us at full sail.

Satiated with gazing we passed into Anglesey, and
making our way to the tubular bridge, which is to the
west of the suspension one, entered one of its passages
and returned to the mainland.

The air was exceedingly hot and sultry, and on
coming to a stone bench, beneath a shady wall, we both
sat down, panting, on one end of it; as we were resting
ourselves, a shabby-looking man with a bundle of books
came and seated himself at the other end, placing his
bundle beside him; then taking out from his pocket a
dirty red handkerchief, he wiped his face, which was
bathed in perspiration, and ejaculated: " By Jasus, it
is blazing hot!"

" Very hot, my friend," said I; " have you travelled
far to-day?"

" I have not, your hanner; I have been just walking
about the dirty town trying to sell my books."

" Have you been successful?"

" I have not, your hanner; only three pence have I
taken this blessed day."

" What do your books treat of?"

" Why that is more than I can tell your hanner;
my trade is to sell the books not to read them. Would
your hanner like to look at them?"

" O dear no," said I; " I have long been tired of
books; I have had enough of them."

" I dare say, your hanner; from the state of your
hanner's eyes I should say as much; they look so weak
—picking up learning has ruined your hanner's sight."

" May I ask," said I, " from what country you are?"

" Sure your hanner may; and it is a civil answer
you will get from Michael Sullivan. It is from ould
Ireland I am, from Castlebar in the county Mayo."

" And how came you into Wales?"

" From the hope of bettering my condition, your
hanner, and a foolish hope it was."

"You have not bettered your condition, then?"

"I have not, your hanner; for I suffer quite as much hunger and thirst as ever I did in ould Ireland."

"Did you sell books in Ireland?"

"I did nat, your hanner; I made buttons and clothes —that is I pieced them. I was several trades in ould Ireland, your hanner; but none of them answering, I came over here."

"Where you commenced bookselling?" said I.

"I did nat, your hanner. I first sold laces, and then I sold loocifers, and then something else; I have followed several trades in Wales, your hanner; at last I got into the bookselling trade, in which I now am."

"And it answers, I suppose, as badly as the others?"

"Just as badly, your hanner; divil a bit better."

"I suppose you never beg?"

"Your hanner may say that; I was always too proud to beg. It is begging I laves to the wife I have."

"Then you have a wife?"

"I have, your hanner; and a daughter, too; and a good wife and daughter they are. What would become of me without them I do not know."

"Have you been long in Wales?"

"Not very long, your hanner; only about twenty years."

"Do you travel much about?"

"All over North Wales, your hanner; to say nothing of the southern country."

"I suppose you speak Welsh?"

"Not a word, your hanner. The Welsh speak their language so fast, that divil a word could I ever contrive to pick up."

"Do you speak Irish?"

"I do, your hanner; that is when people spake to me in it."

I spoke to him in Irish; after a little discourse he said in English:

"I see your hanner is a Munster man. Ah! all the learned men comes from Munster. Father Toban comes from Munster."

"I have heard of him once or twice before," said I.

"I dare say your hanner has. Everyone has heard of Father Toban; the greatest scholar in the world, who they say stands a better chance of being made Pope, some day or other, than any saggart in Ireland."

" Will you take sixpence?"

" I will, your hanner; if your hanner offers it; but I never beg; I leave that kind of work to my wife and daughter, as I said before."

After giving him the sixpence, which he received with a lazy " thank your hanner," I got up, and followed by my daughter returned to the town.

Henrietta went to the inn, and I again strolled about the town. As I was standing in the middle of one of the busiest streets I suddenly heard a loud and dissonant gabbling, and glancing around beheld a number of wild-looking people, male and female. Wild looked the men, yet wilder the women. The men were very lightly clad, and were all barefooted and bareheaded; they carried stout sticks in their hands. The women were barefooted too, but had for the most part head-dresses; their garments consisted of blue cloaks and striped gingham gowns. All the females had common tin articles in their hands which they offered for sale with violent gestures to the people in the streets, as they walked along, occasionally darting into the shops, from which, however, they were almost invariably speedily ejected by the startled proprietors, with looks of disgust and almost horror. Two ragged, red-haired lads led a gaunt pony, drawing a creaking cart, stored with the same kind of articles of tin, which the women bore. Poorly clad, dusty and soiled as they were, they all walked with a free, independent, and almost graceful carriage.

" Are those people from Ireland?" said I to a decent-looking man, seemingly a mechanic, who stood near me, and was also looking at them, but with anything but admiration.

" I am sorry to say they are, sir," said the man, who from his accent was evidently an Irishman, " for they are a disgrace to their country."

I did not exactly think so. I thought that in many respects they were fine specimens of humanity.

" Every one of those wild fellows," said I to myself, " is worth a dozen of the poor mean-spirited book-tramper I have lately been discoursing with."

In the afternoon I again passed over into Anglesey, but this time not by the bridge but by the ferry on the north-east of Bangor, intending to go to Beaumaris, about two or three miles distant : an excellent road, on the left side of which is a high bank fringed with dwarf oaks, and on the right the Menai strait, leads to it. Beaumaris is at present a watering-place. On one side of it, close upon the sea stands the ruins of an immense castle, once a Norman stronghold, but built on the site of a palace belonging to the ancient kings of North Wales, and a favourite residence of the celebrated Owain Gwynedd, the father of the yet more celebrated Madoc, the original discoverer of America. I proceeded at once to the castle, and clambering to the top of one of the turrets, looked upon Beaumaris Bay, and the noble rocky coast of the mainland to the south-east beyond it, the most remarkable object of which is the gigantic Penman Mawr, which interpreted is " the great head-stone," the termination of a range of craggy hills descending from the Snowdon mountains.

" What a bay ! " said I, " for beauty it is superior to the far-famed one of Naples. A proper place for the keels to start from, which unguided by the compass found their way over the mighty and mysterious Western Ocean. "

I repeated all the Bardic lines I could remember connected with Madoc's expedition, and likewise many from the Madoc of Southey, not the least of Britain's four great latter poets, decidedly her best prose writer, and probably the purest and most noble character to which she has ever given birth ; and then, after a long, lingering look, descended from my altitude, and returned, not by the ferry, but by the suspension bridge to the mainland.

CHAPTER XXVIII

Robert Lleiaf—Prophetic Englyn—The Second Sight—Duncan
Campbell — Nial's Saga — Family of Nial — Gunnar — The
Avenger.

" Av i dir Môn, cr dwr Menai,
Tros y traeth, ond aros trai."

" I will go to the land of Mona, notwithstanding the water of
the Menai, across the sand, without waiting for the ebb."

So sang a bard about two hundred and forty years
ago, who styled himself Robert Lleiaf, or the least of
the Roberts. The meaning of the couplet has always
been considered to be and doubtless is, that a time
would come when a bridge would be built across the
Menai, over which one might pass with safety and
comfort, without waiting till the ebb was sufficiently
low to permit people to pass over the traeth, or sand,
which, from ages the most remote, had been used as
the means of communication between the mainland and
the Isle of Mona or Anglesey. Grounding their hopes
upon that couplet, people were continually expecting to
see a bridge across the Menai : more than two hundred
years, however, elapsed before the expectation was fulfilled by the mighty Telford flinging over the strait an
iron suspension bridge, which, for grace and beauty,
has perhaps no rival in Europe.

The couplet is a remarkable one. In the time of its
author there was nobody in Britain capable of building
a bridge, which could have stood against the tremendous
surges which occasionally vex the Menai; yet the
couplet gives intimation that a bridge over the Menai
there would be, which clearly argues a remarkable foresight in the author, a feeling that a time would at
length arrive when the power of science would be so
far advanced, that men would be able to bridge over
the terrible strait. The length of time which intervened
between the composition of the couplet and the fulfil-
ment of the promise, shows that a bridge over the
Menai was no pont y meibion, no children's bridge,
nor a work for common men. O, surely Lleiaf was a
man of great foresight !

A man of great foresight, but nothing more; he foretold a bridge over the Menai, when no one could have built one, a bridge over which people could pass, aye, and carts and horses; we will allow him the credit of foretelling such a bridge; and when Telford's bridge was flung over the Menai, Lleiaf's couplet was verified. But since Telford's another bridge has been built over the Menai, which enables things to pass which the bard certainly never dreamt of. He never hinted at a bridge over which thundering trains would dash, if required, at the rate of fifty miles an hour; he never hinted at steam travelling, or a railroad bridge, and the second bridge over the Menai is one.

That Lleiaf was a man of remarkable foresight cannot be denied, but there are no grounds which entitle him to be considered a possessor of the second sight. He foretold a bridge, but not a railroad bridge; had he foretold a railroad bridge, or hinted at the marvels of steam, his claim to the second sight would have been incontestable.

What a triumph for Wales; what a triumph for bardism, if Lleiaf had ever written an englyn, or couplet, in which not a bridge for common traffic, but a railroad bridge over the Menai was hinted at, and steam travelling distinctly foretold! Well, though Lleiaf did not write it, there exists in the Welsh language an englyn, almost as old as Lleiaf's time, in which steam travelling in Wales and Anglesey is foretold, and in which, though the railroad bridge over the Menai is not exactly mentioned, it may be considered to be included; so that Wales and bardism have equal reason to be proud. This is the englyn alluded to :—

> " Codais, ymolchais yn Môn, cyn naw awr
> Ciniewa 'n Nghaer Lleon,
> Pryd gosber yn y Werddon,
> Prydnawn wrth dan mawn yn Môn."

The above englyn was printed in the *Greal,* 1792, p. 316; the language shows it to be a production of about the middle of the seventeenth century. The following is nearly a literal translation :—

> " I got up in Mona as soon as 'twas light,
> At nine in old Chester my breakfast I took ;
> In Ireland I dined, and in Mona, ere night,
> By the turf fire sat, in my own ingle nook."

Now, as sure as the couplet by Robert Lleiaf foretells
that a bridge would eventually be built over the strait,
by which people would pass, and traffic be carried on,
so surely does the above englyn foreshadow the speed
by which people would travel by steam, a speed by
which distance is already all but annihilated. At present
it is easy enough to get up at dawn at Holyhead, the
point of Anglesey the most distant from Chester, and
to breakfast at that old town by nine; and though the
feat has never yet been accomplished, it would be quite
possible, provided proper preparations were made, to
start from Holyhead at daybreak, breakfast at Chester
at nine, or before, dine in Ireland at two, and get back
again to Holyhead ere the sun of the longest day has
set. And as surely as the couplet about the bridge
argues great foresight in the man that wrote it, so
surely does the englyn prove that its author must have
been possessed of the faculty of second sight, as nobody
without it could, in the middle of the seventeenth
century, when the powers of steam were unknown,
have written anything in which travelling by steam is
so distinctly alluded to.

Truly some old bard of the seventeenth century
must in a vision of the second sight have seen the
railroad bridge across the Menai, the Chester train
dashing across it at high railroad speed, and a figure
exactly like his own seated comfortably in a third-class
carriage.

And now a few words on the second sight; a few
calm, quiet words, in which there is not the slightest
wish to display either eccentricity or book-learning.

The second sight is a power of seeing events before
they happen, or of seeing events which are happening
far beyond the reach of the common sight, or between
which and the common sight barriers intervene, which
it cannot pierce. The number of those who possess this
gift or power is limited, and perhaps no person ever
possessed it in a perfect degree : some more frequently
see coming events, or what is happening at a distance,
than others; some see things dimly, others with great
distinctness. The events seen are sometimes of great
importance, sometimes highly nonsensical and trivial;
sometimes they relate to the person who sees them,

sometimes to other people. This is all that can be said with anything like certainty with respect to the nature of the second sight, a faculty for which there is no accounting, which, were it better developed, might be termed the sixth sense.

The second sight is confined to no particular country, and has at all times existed. Particular nations have obtained a celebrity for it for a time, which they have afterwards lost, the celebrity being transferred to other nations, who were previously not noted for the faculty. The Jews were at one time particularly celebrated for the possession of the second sight; they are no longer so. The power was at one time very common amongst the Icelanders and the inhabitants of the Hebrides, but it is so no longer. Many and extraordinary instances of the second sight have lately occurred in that part of England generally termed East Anglia, where in former times the power of the second sight seldom manifested itself.

There are various books in existence in which the second sight is treated of or mentioned. Amongst others there is one called Martin's *Visit to the Hebrides,* published in the year 1700, which is indeed the book from which most writers in English, who have treated of the second sight, have derived their information. The author gives various anecdotes of the second sight, which he had picked up during his visits to those remote islands, which until the publication of his tour were almost unknown to the world. It will not be amiss to observe here that the term second sight is of Lowland Scotch origin, and first made its appearance in print in Martin's book. The Gaelic term for the faculty is taibhsearachd, the literal meaning of which is what is connected with a spectral appearance, the root of the word being taibhse, a spectral appearance or vision.

Then there is the history of Duncan Campbell. The father of this person was a native of Shetland, who being shipwrecked on the coast of Swedish Lapland, and hospitably received by the natives, married a woman of the country, by whom he had Duncan, who was born deaf and dumb. On the death of his mother the child was removed by his father to Scotland, where he was educated and taught the use of the finger alphabet, by means of which people are enabled to hold discourse with each other, without moving the lips or tongue. The alphabet was originally invented in Scotland, and at the present day is much in use there, not only amongst dumb people, but many others, who employ it as a silent means of communication. Nothing is more usual than to see passengers in a common conveyance in Scotland discoursing with their fingers. Duncan at an early period gave indications of possessing the second sight. After various adventures he came to London, where for many years he practised as a fortune-teller, pretending to answer all questions, whether relating to the past or the future, by means of the second sight. There can be no doubt that this man was to a certain extent an impostor; no person exists having a thorough knowledge either of the past or future by means of the second sight, which only visits particular people by fits and starts, and which is quite independent of individual will; but it is equally certain that he disclosed things which no person could have been acquainted with without visitations of the second sight. His papers fell into the hands of Defoe, who wrought them up in his own peculiar manner, and gave them to the world under the title of the *Life of Mr. Duncan Campbell*, the deaf and dumb gentleman; with an appendix containing many anecdotes of the second sight from Martin's tour.

But by far the most remarkable book in existence, connected with the second sight, is one in the ancient Norse language entitled *Nial's Saga*.[1] It was written in Iceland about the year 1200, and contains the history of a certain Nial and his family, and likewise notices of various other people. This Nial was what was called a spámadr, that is, a spaeman or a person capable of foretelling events. He was originally a heathen—when, however, Christianity was introduced into Iceland, he

[1] One or two of the characters and incidents in this Saga are mentioned in the *Romany Rye*. London, 1857, vol. i. p. 240 ; vol. ii. p. 150.
A partial translation of the *Saga*, made by myself, has been many years in existence. It forms part of a mountain of unpublished translations from the Northern languages. In my younger days no London publisher, or indeed magazine editor, would look at anything from the Norse, Danish, etc.

was amongst the first to embrace it, and persuaded his
family and various people of his acquaintance to do the
same, declaring that a new faith was necessary, the old
religion of Odin, Thor and Frey being quite unsuited to
the times. The book is no romance, but a domestic
history compiled from tradition about two hundred
years after the events which it narrates had taken place.
Of its style, which is wonderfully terse, the following
translated account of Nial and his family will perhaps
convey some idea :—

" There was a man called Nial who was the son of
Thorgeir Gelling, the son of Thorolf. The mother of
Nial was called Asgerdr; she was the daughter of
Ar, the Silent, the Lord of a district in Norway. She
had come over to Iceland and settled down on land to
the west of Markarfliot, between Oldustein and Selia-
landsmul. Holtathorir was her son, father of Thorleif
Krak, from whom the Skogverjars are come, and likewise of Thorgrim the big and Skorargeir. Nial dwelt
at Bergthorshvâl in Landey, but had another house at
Thorolfell. Nial was very rich in property and handsome to look at, but had no beard. He was so great
a lawyer that it was impossible to find his equal; he was
very wise, and had the gift of foretelling events; he was
good at counsel, and of a good disposition, and whatever counsel he gave people was for their best; he was
gentle and humane, and got every man out of trouble
who came to him in his need. His wife was called
Bergthora; she was the daughter of Skarphethin. She
was a bold-spirited woman who feared nobody, and
was rather rough of temper. They had six children,
three daughters and three sons, all of whom will be
frequently mentioned in this saga."

In the history many instances are given of Nial's
skill in giving good advice and his power of seeing
events before they happened. Nial lived in Iceland
during most singular times, in which though there were
laws provided for every possible case, no man could
have redress for any injury unless he took it himself or
his friends took it for him, simply because there were
no ministers of justice supported by the State, author-
ized and empowered to carry the sentence of the law
into effect. For example, if a man were slain his death

would remain unpunished unless he had a son or a brother, or some other relation to slay the slayer, or to force him to pay "bod," that is, amends in money, to be determined by the position of the man who was slain. Provided the man who was slain had relations, his death was generally avenged, as it was considered the height of infamy in Iceland to permit one's relations to be murdered, without slaying their murderers, or obtaining bod from them. The right, however, permitted to relations of taking with their own hands the lives of those who had slain their friends, produced incalculable mischiefs; for if the original slayer had friends, they, in the event of his being slain in retaliation for what he had done, made it a point of honour to avenge his death, so that by the lex talionis feuds were perpetuated. Nial was a great benefactor to his countrymen, by arranging matters between people at variance, in which he was much helped by his knowledge of the law, and by giving wholesome advice to people in precarious situations, in which he was frequently helped by the power which he possessed of the second sight. On several occasions, he settled the disputes, in which his friend Gunnar was involved, a noble, generous character, and the champion of Iceland, but who had a host of foes, envious of his renown; and it was not his fault if Gunnar was eventually slain, for if the advice which he gave had been followed the champion would have died an old man; and if his own sons had followed his advice, and not been over fond of taking vengeance on people who had wronged them, they would have escaped a horrible death in which he himself was involved, as he had always foreseen he should be.

"Dost thou know by what death thou thyself will die?" said Gunnar to Nial, after the latter had been warning him that if he followed a certain course he would die by a violent death.

"I do," said Nial.

"What is it?" said Gunnar.

"What people would think the least probable," replied Nial.

He meant that he should die by fire. The kind generous Nial, who tried to get everybody out of difficulty, perished by fire. His sons by their violent conduct had incensed numerous people against them. The house in which they lived with their father was beset at night by an armed party, who, unable to break into it owing to the desperate resistance which they met with from the sons of Nial, Skarphethin, Helgi and Grimmr and a comrade of theirs called Kari,[1] set it in a blaze, in which perished Nial the lawyer and man of the second sight, his wife, Bergthora, and two of their sons, the third, Helgi, having been previously slain, and Kari, who was destined to be the avenger of the ill-fated family, having made his escape, after performing deeds of heroism, which for centuries after were the themes of song and tale in the ice-bound isle.

CHAPTER XXIX

Snowdon—Caernarvon—Maxen Wledig—Moel y Cynghorion—
The Wyddfa—Snow of Snowdon—Rare Plant.

On the third morning after our arrival at Bangor we set out for Snowdon.

Snowdon or Eryri is no single hill, but a mountainous region, the loftiest part of which, called Y Wyddfa, nearly four thousand feet above the level of the sea, is generally considered to be the highest point of Southern Britain. The name Snowdon was bestowed upon this region by the early English on account of its snowy appearance in winter; Eryri by the Britons, because in the old time it abounded with eagles, Eryri[2] in the ancient British language signifying an eyrie or breeding place of eagles.

Snowdon is interesting on various accounts. It is interesting for its picturesque beauty. Perhaps in the

---

[1] All these three names are very common in Norfolk, the population of which is of Norse origin. Skarphethin is at present pronounced Sharpin, Helgi Heely. Skarphethin, interpreted, is a keen pirate.

[2] Eryri likewise signifies an excrescence or scrofulous eruption. It is possible that many will be disposed to maintain that in the case of Snowdon the word is intended to express a rugged excrescence or eruption on the surface of the earth.

whole world there is no region more picturesquely beautiful than Snowdon, a region of mountains, lakes, cataracts, and groves, in which Nature shows herself in her most grand and beautiful forms.

It is interesting from its connection with history : it was to Snowdon that Vortigern retired from the fury of his own subjects, caused by the favour which he showed to the detested Saxons. It was there that he called to his counsels Merlin, said to be begotten on a hag by an incubus, but who was in reality the son of a Roman consul by a British woman. It was in Snowdon that he built the castle, which he fondly deemed would prove impregnable, but which his enemies destroyed by flinging wildfire over its walls; and it was in a wind-beaten valley of Snowdon, near the sea, that his dead body decked in green armour had a mound of earth and stones raised over it. It was on the heights of Snowdon that the brave but unfortunate Llywelin ap Griffith made his last stand for Cambrian independence; and it was to Snowdon that that very remarkable man, Owen Glendower, retired with his irregular bands before Harry the Fourth and his numerous and disciplined armies, soon, however, to emerge from its defiles and follow the foe, retreating less from the Welsh arrows from the crags, than from the cold, rain, and starvation of the Welsh hills.

But it is from its connection with romance that Snowdon derives its chief interest. Who when he thinks of Snowdon does not associate it with the heroes of romance, Arthur and his knights? whose fictitious adventures, the splendid dreams of Welsh and Breton minstrels, many of the scenes of which are the valleys and passes of Snowdon, are the origin of romance, before which what is classic has for more than half a century been waning, and is perhaps eventually destined to disappear. Yes, to romance Snowdon is indebted for its interest and consequently for its celebrity; but for romance Snowdon would assuredly not be what it at present is, one of the very celebrated hills of the world, and to the poets of modern Europe almost what Parnassus was to those of old.

To the Welsh, besides being the hill of the Awen or Muse, it has always been the hill of hills, the loftiest of all mountains, the one whose snow is the coldest, to climb to whose peak is the most difficult of all feats, and the one whose fall will be the most astounding catastrophe of the last day.

To view this mountain I and my little family set off in a calèche on the third morning after our arrival at Bangor.

Our first stage was to Caernarvon. As I subsequently made a journey to Caernarvon on foot, I shall say nothing about the road till I give an account of that expedition, save that it lies for the most part in the neighbourhood of the sea. We reached Caernarvon, which is distant ten miles from Bangor, about eleven o'clock, and put up at an inn to refresh ourselves and the horses. It is a beautiful little town situated on the southern side of the Menai Strait at nearly its western extremity. It is called Caernarvon, because it is opposite Mona or Anglesey : Caernarvon signifying the town or castle opposite Mona. Its principal feature is its grand old castle, fronting the north, and partly surrounded by the sea. This castle was built by Edward the First after the fall of his brave adversary Llewelyn, and in it was born his son Edward whom, when an infant, he induced the Welsh chieftains to accept as their prince without seeing, by saying that the person whom he proposed to be their sovereign was one who was not only born in Wales, but could not speak a word of the English language. The town of Caernarvon, however, existed long before Edward's time, and was probably originally a Roman station. According to Welsh tradition it was built by Maxen Wledig or Maxentius, in honour of his wife Ellen, who was born in the neighbourhood. Maxentius, who was a Briton by birth, and partly by origin, contested unsuccessfully the purple with Gratian and Valentinian, and to support his claim led over to the Continent an immense army of Britons, who never returned, but on the fall of their leader settled down in that part of Gaul generally termed Armorica, which means a maritime region, but which the Welsh call Llydaw, or Lithuania, which was the name, or something like the name, which the region bore when Maxen's army took possession of it, owing, doubtless, to its having been the quarters of a legion composed of barbarians from the country of Leth or Lithuania.

After staying about an hour at Caernarvon we started for Llanberis, a few miles to the east. Llanberis is a small village situated in a valley, and takes its name from Peris, a British saint of the sixth century, son of Helig ab Glanog. The valley extends from west to east, having the great mountain of Snowdon on its south, and a range of immense hills on its northern, side. We entered this valley by a pass called Nant y Glo or the ravine of the coal, and passing a lake on our left, on which I observed a solitary coracle, with a fisherman in it, were presently at the village. Here we got down at a small inn, and having engaged a young lad to serve as guide, I set out with Henrietta to ascend the hill, my wife remaining behind, not deeming herself sufficiently strong to encounter the fatigue of the expedition.

Pointing with my finger to the head of Snowdon towering a long way from us in the direction of the east, I said to Henrietta :—

" Dacw Eryri, yonder is Snowdon. Let us try to get to the top. The Welsh have a proverb : ' It is easy to say yonder is Snowdon; but not so easy to ascend it.' Therefore I would advise you to brace up your nerves and sinews for the attempt."

We then commenced the ascent, arm in arm, followed by the lad, I singing at the stretch of my voice a celebrated Welsh stanza, in which the proverb about Snowdon is given, embellished with a fine moral, and which may thus be rendered :—

> " Easy to say, ' Behold Eryri,'
> But difficult to reach its head ;
> Easy for him whose hopes are cheery
> To bid the wretch be comforted."

We were far from being the only visitors to the hill this day; groups of people, or single individuals, might be seen going up or descending the path as far as the eye could reach. The path was remarkably good, and for some way the ascent was anything but steep. On our left was the vale of Llanberis, and on our other side a broad hollow, or valley of Snowdon, beyond which were two huge hills forming part of the body of the grand mountain, the lowermost of which our guide told me was called Moel Elia, and the uppermost Moel y Cynghorion. On we went until we had passed both these hills, and come to the neighbourhood of a great wall of rocks constituting the upper region of Snowdon, and where the real difficulty of the ascent commences. Feeling now rather out of breath we sat down on a little knoll with our faces to the south, having a small lake near us, on our left hand, which lay dark and deep, just under the great wall.

Here we sat for some time resting and surveying the scene which presented itself to us, the principal object of which was the north-eastern side of the mighty Moel y Cynghorion, across the wide hollow or valley, which it overhangs in the shape of a sheer precipice some five hundred feet in depth. Struck by the name of Moel y Cynghorion, which in English signifies the hill of the counsellors, I inquired of our guide why the hill was so called, but as he could afford me no information on the point I presumed that it was either called the hill of the counsellors from the Druids having held high consultation on its top, in time of old, or from the unfortunate Llewelyn having consulted there with his chieftains, whilst his army lay encamped in the vale below.

Getting up we set about surmounting what remained of the ascent. The path was now winding and much more steep than it had hitherto been. I was at one time apprehensive that my gentle companion would be obliged to give over the attempt; the gallant girl, however, persevered, and in little more than twenty minutes from the time when we arose from our resting-place under the crags, we stood, safe and sound, though panting, upon the very top of Snowdon—the far-famed Wyddfa.

The Wyddfa is about thirty feet in diameter and is surrounded on three sides by a low wall. In the middle of it is a rude cabin, in which refreshments are sold, and in which a person resides throughout the year, though there are few or no visitors to the hill's top, except during the months of summer. Below on all sides are frightful precipices except on the side of the west. Towards the east it looks perpendicularly into the dyffrin or vale, nearly a mile below, from which to the gazer it is at all times an object of admiration, of wonder, and almost of fear.

There we stood on the Wyddfa, in a cold bracing atmosphere, though the day was almost stiflingly hot in the regions from which we had ascended. There we stood enjoying a scene inexpressibly grand, comprehending a considerable part of the mainland of Wales, the whole of Anglesey, a faint glimpse of part of Cumberland; the Irish Channel, and what might be either a misty creation or the shadowy outlines of the hills of Ireland. Peaks and pinnacles and huge moels stood up here and there, about us and below us, partly in glorious light, partly in deep shade. Manifold were the objects which we saw from the brow of Snowdon, but of all the objects which we saw, those which filled us with most delight and admiration, were numerous lakes and lagoons, which, like sheets of ice or polished silver, lay reflecting the rays of the sun in the deep valleys at his feet.

"Here," said I to Henrietta, "you are on the top crag of Snowdon, which the Welsh consider, and perhaps with justice to be the most remarkable crag in the world; which is mentioned in many of their old wild romantic tales, and some of the noblest of their poems, amongst others in the 'Day of Judgment,' by the illustrious Goronwy Owen, where it is brought forward in the following manner :

> ' Ail i'r ar ael Eryri,
> Cyfartal hoewal a hi.'

' The brow of Snowdon shall be levelled with the ground, and the eddying waters shall murmur round it.'

"You are now on the top crag of Snowdon, generally termed Y Wyddfa,[1] which means a conspicuous place or tumulus, and which is generally in winter covered with snow; about which snow there are in the Welsh language two curious englynion or stanzas consisting entirely of vowels with the exception of one consonant namely the letter R.

[1] It will not be amiss to observe that the original term is gwyddfa; but gwyddfa being a feminine noun or compound commencing with g, which is a mutable consonant, loses the initial letter before y the definite article—you say Gwyddfa a tumulus, but not y gwyddfa *the* tumulus.

" ' Oer yw'r Eira ar Eryri,--o'ryw
Ar awyr i rewi ;
Oer yw'r ia ar riw 'r ri,
A'r Eira oer yw 'Ryri.

" ' O Ri y'Ryri yw'r oera,—o'r âr,
Ar oror wir arwa ;
O'r awyr a yr Eira,
O'i ryw i roi rew a'r ia.

" ' Cold is the snow on Snowdon's brow,
It makes the air so chill ;
For cold, I trow, there is no snow
Like that of Snowdon's hill.

" ' A hill most chill is Snowdon's hill,
And wintry is his brow ;
From Snowdon's hill the breezes chill
Can freeze the very snow.' "

Such was the harangue which I uttered on the top
of Snowdon; to which Henrietta listened with attention; three or four English, who stood nigh, with
grinning scorn, and a Welsh gentleman with considerable interest. The latter coming forward shook me by
the hand exclaiming :
" Wyt ti Lydaueg ?"
" I am not a Llydauan," said I ; " I wish I was, or
anything but what I am, one of a nation amongst whom
any knowledge save what relates to money-making and
over-reaching is looked upon as a disgrace. I am
ashamed to say that I am an Englishman."
I then returned his shake of the hand ; and bidding
Henrietta and the guide follow me went into the cabin,
where Henrietta had some excellent coffee and myself
and the guide a bottle of tolerable ale ; very much
refreshed we set out on our return.
A little way from the top, on the right-hand side as
you descend, there is a very steep path running down
in a zigzag manner to the pass which leads to Capel
Curig. Up this path it is indeed a task of difficulty to
ascend to the Wyddfa, the one by which we mounted
being comparatively easy. On Henrietta's pointing
out to me a plant, which grew on a crag by the side
of this path some way down, I was about to descend
in order to procure it for her, when our guide springing
forward darted down the path with the agility of a
young goat, and in less than a minute returned with it

in his hand and presented it gracefully to the dear girl, who on examining it said it belonged to a species of which she had long been desirous of possessing a specimen. Nothing material occurred in our descent to Llanberis, where my wife was anxiously awaiting us. The ascent and descent occupied four hours. About ten o'clock at night we again found ourselves at Bangor.

CHAPTER XXX

Gronwy Owen—Struggles of Genius—The Stipend.

THE day after our expedition to Snowdon I and my family parted ; they returning by railroad to Chester and Llangollen whilst I took a trip into Anglesey to visit the birthplace of the great poet Goronwy Owen, whose works I had read with enthusiasm in my early years.

Goronwy or Gronwy Owen, was born in the year 1722, at a place called Llanfair Mathafarn Eithaf in Anglesey. He was the eldest of three children. His parents were peasants and so exceedingly poor that they were unable to send him to school. Even, how-ever, when an unlettered child he gave indications that he was visited by the awen or muse. At length the celebrated Lewis Morris chancing to be at Llanfair, became acquainted with the boy, and struck with his natural talents, determined that he should have all the benefit which education could bestow. He accordingly, at his own expense, sent him to school at Beaumaris, where he displayed a remarkable aptitude for the acqui-sition of learning. He subsequently sent him to Jesus College, Oxford, and supported him there whilst study-ing for the Church. Whilst at Jesus, Gronwy distin-guished himself as a Greek and Latin scholar, and gave such proofs of poetical talent in his native lan-guage, that he was looked upon by his countrymen of that Welsh college as the rising Bard of the age. After completing his collegiate course he returned to Wales, where he was ordained a minister of the Church in the year 1745. The next seven years of his life were a series of cruel disappointments and pecuniary embarrassments. The grand wish of his heart was to obtain a curacy and to settle down in Wales. Certainly a very reasonable wish. To say nothing of his being a great genius, he was eloquent, highly learned, modest, meek and of irreproachable morals, yet Gronwy Owen could obtain no Welsh curacy, nor could his friend Lewis Morris, though he exerted himself to the utmost, procure one for him. It is true that he was told that he might go to Llanfair, his native place, and officiate there at a time when the curacy happened to be vacant, and thither he went, glad at heart to get back amongst his old friends, who enthusiastically welcomed him; yet scarcely had he been there three weeks when he received notice from the Chaplain of the Bishop of Bangor that he must vacate Llanfair in order to make room for a Mr. John Ellis, a young clergyman of large independent fortune, who was wishing for a curacy under the Bishop of Bangor, Doctor Hutton—so poor Gronwy the eloquent, the learned, the meek was obliged to vacate the pulpit of his native place to make room for the rich young clergyman, who wished to be within dining distance of the palace of Bangor. Truly in this world the full shall be crammed, and those who have little, shall have the little which they have taken away from them. Unable to obtain employment in Wales, Gronwy sought for it in England, and after some time procured the curacy of Oswestry in Shropshire, where he married a respectable young woman, who eventually brought him two sons and a daughter.

From Oswestry he went to Donnington, near Shrewsbury, where under a certain Scotchman named Douglas, who was an absentee, and who died Bishop of Salisbury, he officiated as curate and master of a grammar school for a stipend—always grudgingly and contumeliously paid—of three-and-twenty pounds a year. From Donnington he removed to Walton in Cheshire, where he lost his daughter, who was carried off by a fever. His next removal was to Northolt, a pleasant village in the neighbourhood of London.

He held none of his curacies long, either losing them from the caprice of his principals, or being compelled to resign them from the parsimony which they practised towards him. In the year 1756 he was living in a garret in London vainly soliciting employment in his sacred calling, and undergoing with his family the greatest privations. At length his friend Lewis Morris, who had always assisted him to the utmost of his ability, procured him the mastership of a government school at New Brunswick in North America with a salary of three hundred pounds a year. Thither he went with his wife and family, and there he died sometime about the year 1780.

He was the last of the great poets of Cambria, and with the exception of Ab Gwilym, the greatest which she has produced. His poems which for a long time had circulated through Wales in manuscript were first printed in the year 1819. They are composed in the ancient Bardic measures, and were with one exception, namely an elegy on the death of his benefactor Lewis Morris, which was transmitted from the New World, written before he had attained the age of thirty-five. All his pieces are excellent, but his masterwork is decidedly the " Cywydd y Farn " or " Day of Judgment." This poem which is generally considered by the Welsh as the brightest ornament of their ancient language, was composed at Donnington, a small hamlet in Shropshire on the north-west spur of the Wrekin, at which place, as has been already said, Gronwy toiled as schoolmaster and ourale under Douglas the Scot, for a stipend of three-and-twenty pounds a year.

CHAPTER XXXI

Start for Anglesey—The Post Master—Asking Questions—
Mynydd Lydiart—Mr. Pritchard—Way to Llanfair.

WHEN I started from Bangor, to visit the birthplace of Gronwy Owen, I by no means saw my way clearly before me. I knew that he was born in Anglesey in a parish called Llanfair Mathafarn eithaf, that is St. Mary's of farther Mathafarn—but as to where this Mathafarn lay, north or south, near or far, I knew positively nothing. Passing through the northern suburb of Bangor I saw a small house in front of which was written " post-office " in white letters; before this house underneath a shrub in a little garden sat an old man reading. Thinking that from this person, whom I judged to be the post-master, I was as likely to obtain information with respect to the place of my destination as from any one, I stopped and taking off my hat for a moment, inquired whether he could tell me anything about the direction of a place called Llanfair Mathafarn eithaf. He did not seem to understand my question, for getting up he came towards me and asked what I wanted : I repeated what I had said, whereupon his face became animated.

"Llanfair Mathafarn eithaf !" said he. "Yes, I can tell you about it, and with good reason for it lies not far from the place where I was born."

The above was the substance of what he said, and nothing more, for he spoke in English somewhat broken.

"And how far is Llanfair from here?" said I.

"About ten miles," he replied.

"That's nothing," said I; "I was afraid it was much farther."

"Do you call ten miles nothing," said he, "in a burning day like this? I think you will be both tired and thirsty before you get to Llanfair, supposing you go there on foot. But what may your business be at Llanfair?" said he looking at me inquisitively. "It is a strange place to go to, unless you go to buy hogs or cattle."

"I go to buy neither hogs nor cattle," said I, "though I am somewhat of a judge of both; I go on a more important errand, namely to see the birth-place of the great Gronwy Owen."

"Are you any relation of Gronwy Owen?" said the old man, looking at me more inquisitively than before, through a large pair of spectacles, which he wore.

"None whatever," said I.

"Then why do you go to see his parish? It is a very poor one."

"From respect to his genius," said I; "I read his works long ago, and was delighted with them."

"Are you a Welshman?" said the old man.

"No," said I, "I am no Welshman."

"Can you speak Welsh?" said he, addressing me in that language.

"A little," said I; "but not so well as I can read it."

"Well," said the old man, "I have lived here a great many years, but never before did a Saxon call upon me, asking questions about Gronwy Owen, or his birth-place. Immortality to his memory! I owe much to him, for reading his writings taught me to be a poet!"

"Dear me!" said I, "are you a poet?"

"I trust I am," said he; "though the humblest of Ynys Fon."

A flash of proud fire, methought, illumined his features as he pronounced these last words.

"I am most happy to have met you," said I; "but tell me how am I to get to Llanfair?"

"You must go first," said he, "to Traeth Coch, which in Saxon is called the 'Red Sand.' In the village called the Pentraeth which lies above the sand, I was born; through the village and over the bridge you must pass, and after walking four miles due north you will find yourself in Llanfair eithaf, at the northern extremity of Mon. Farewell! That ever Saxon should ask me about Gronwy Owen, and his birth-place! I scarcely believe you to be a Saxon, but whether you be or not, I repeat farewell."

Coming to the Menai Bridge I asked the man who took the penny toll at the entrance, the way to Pentraeth Coch.

"You see that white house by the wood," said he, pointing some distance into Anglesey; "you must make towards it till you come to a place where there are four cross roads and then you must take the road to the right."

Passing over the bridge I made my way towards the house by the wood which stood on the hill till I came where the four roads met, when I turned to the right as directed.

The country through which I passed seemed tolerably well cultivated, the hedge-rows were very high, seeming to spring out of low stone walls. I met two or three gangs of reapers proceeding to their work with scythes in their hands.

In about half-an-hour I passed by a farm-house

partly surrounded with walnut trees. Still the same high hedges on both sides of the road : are these relics of the sacrificial groves of Mona? thought I to myself. Then I came to a wretched village through which I hurried at the rate of six miles an hour. I then saw a long lofty craggy hill on my right hand towards the east.

"What mountain is that?" said I to an urchin playing in the hot dust of the road.

"Mynydd Lidiart!" said the urchin, tossing up a handful of the hot dust into the air, part of which in descending fell into my eyes.

I shortly afterwards passed by a handsome lodge. I then saw groves, mountain Lidiart forming a noble background.

"Who owns this wood?" said I in Welsh to two men who were limbing a felled tree by the roadside.

"Lord Vivian," answered one, touching his hat.

"The gentleman is our countryman," said he to the other after I had passed.

I was now descending the side of a pretty valley, and soon found myself at Pentraeth Coch. The part of the Pentraeth where I now was consisted of a few houses and a church, or something which I judged to be a church, for there was no steeple; the houses and church stood about a little open spot or square, the church on the east, and on the west a neat little inn or public-house over the door of which was written " The White Horse. Hugh Pritchard." By this time I had verified in part the prediction of the old Welsh poet of the post-office. Though I was not arrived at Llanfair I was, if not tired, very thirsty, owing to the burning heat of the weather, so I determined to go in and have some ale. On entering the house I was greeted in English by Mr. Hugh Pritchard himself, a tall bulky man with a weather-beaten countenance, dressed in a brown jerkin and corduroy trowsers, with a broad low-crowned buff-coloured hat on his head, and what might be called half shoes and half high-lows on his feet. He had a short pipe in his mouth which when he greeted me he took out, but replaced as soon as the greeting was over, which consisted of " Good day, sir," delivered in a frank hearty tone. I looked Mr. Hugh Pritchard in the face and thought I had never seen a more honest countenance. On my telling Mr. Pritchard that I wanted a pint of ale a buxom damsel came forward and led me into a nice cool parlour on the right-hand side of the door and then went to fetch the ale.

Mr. Pritchard meanwhile went into a kind of tap-room, fronting the parlour, where I heard him talking in Welsh about pigs and cattle to some of his customers. I observed that he spoke with some hesitation; which circumstance I mention as rather curious, he being the only Welshman I have ever known who, when speaking his native language, appeared to be at a loss for words. The damsel presently brought me the ale, which I tasted and found excellent; she was going away when I asked her whether Mr. Pritchard was her father; on her replying in the affirmative I inquired whether she was born in that house.

" No!" said she; " I was born in Liverpool; my father was born in this house, which belonged to his fathers before him, but he left it at an early age and married my mother in Liverpool, who was an Anglesey woman, and so I was born in Liverpool."

" And what did you do in Liverpool?" said I.

" My mother kept a little shop," said the girl, " whilst my father followed various occupations."

" And how long have you been here?" said I.

" Since the death of my grandfather," said the girl, " which happened about a year ago. When he died my father came here and took possession of his birthright."

" You speak very good English," said I; " have you any Welsh?"

" O yes, plenty," said the girl; " we always speak Welsh together, but being born at Liverpool, I of course have plenty of English."

" And which language do you prefer?" said I.

" I think I like English best," said the girl, " it is the most useful language."

" Not in Anglesey," said I.

" Well," said the girl, " it is the most genteel."

" Gentility," said I, " will be the ruin of Welsh, as it has been of many other things—what have I to pay for the ale?"

" Threepence," said she.

I paid the money, and the girl went out. I finished my ale, and getting up made for the door; at the door I was met by Mr. Hugh Pritchard, who came out of the tap-room to thank me for my custom, and to bid me farewell. I asked him whether I should have any difficulty in finding the way to Llanfair.

" None whatever," said he; " you have only to pass over the bridge of the traeth, and to go due north for about four miles, and you will find yourself in Llanfair."

" What kind of place is it?" said I.

" A poor straggling village," said Mr. Pritchard.

" Shall I be able to obtain a lodging there for the night?" said I.

" Scarcely one such as you would like," said Hugh.

" And where had I best pass the night?" I demanded.

" We can accommodate you comfortably here," said Mr. Pritchard, " provided you have no objection to come back."

I told him that I should be only too happy, and forthwith departed, glad at heart that I had secured a comfortable lodging for the night.

CHAPTER XXXII

Leave Pentraeth—Tranquil Scene—the Knoll—The Miller and his Wife—Poetry of Gronwy—Kind Offer—Church of Llanfair— No English—Confusion of Ideas—Tŷ Gronwy—Notable Little Girl—The Sycamore Leaf—Home from California.

THE village of Pentraeth Coch occupies two sides of a romantic dell—that part of it which stands on the southern side, and which comprises the church and the little inn, is by far the prettiest, that which occupies the northern, is a poor assemblage of huts, a brook rolls at the bottom of the dell over which there is a little bridge: coming to the bridge I stopped, and looked over the side into the water running briskly below, an aged man who looked like a beggar, but who did not beg of me, stood by.

" To what place does this water run?" said I in English.

" I know no Saxon," said he in trembling accents.
I repeated my question in Welsh.

" To the sea," he said, " which is not far off ; indeed
it is so near, that when there are high tides the salt
water comes up to this bridge."

" You seem feeble?" said I.

" I am so," said he, " for I am old."

" How old are you?" said I.

" Sixteen after sixty," said the old man with a sigh;
" and I have nearly lost my sight and my hearing."

" Are you poor?" said I.

" Very," said the old man.

I gave him a trifle which he accepted with thanks.

" Why is this sand called the red sand?" said I.

" I cannot tell you," said the old man; " I wish I
could, for you have been kind to me."

Bidding him farewell I passed through the northern
part of the village to the top of the hill. I walked a
little way forward and then stopped, as I had done at
the bridge in the dale, and looked to the east, over a
low stone wall.

Before me lay the sea or rather the northern entrance
of the Menai Straits. To my right was mountain
Lidiart projecting some way into the sea, to my left,
that is to the north, was a high hill, with a few white
houses near its base, forming a small village, which a
woman who passed by knitting told me was called
Llan Peder Goch or the Church of Red Saint Peter.
Mountain Lidiart and the Northern Hill formed the
headlands of a beautiful bay into which the waters of
the traeth dell, from which I had come, were discharged. A sandbank, probably covered with the sea
at high tide, seemed to stretch from mountain Lidiart
a considerable way towards the northern hill. Mountain, bay, and sandbank were bathed in sunshine; the
water was perfectly calm; nothing was moving upon
it, nor upon the shore, and I thought I had never beheld
a more beautiful and tranquil scene.

I went on. The country which had hitherto been
very beautiful, abounding with yellow corn-fields, became sterile and rocky; there were stone walls, but no
hedges. I passed by a moor on my left, then a moory
hillock on my right; the way was broken and stony;

all traces of the good roads of Wales had disappeared; the habitations which I saw by the way were miserable hovels into and out of which large sows were stalking, attended by their farrows.

"Am I far from Llanfair?" said I to a child.

"You are in Llanfair, gentleman," said the child.

A desolate place was Llanfair. The sea in the neighbourhood to the south, limekilns with their stifling smoke not far from me. I sat down on a little green knoll on the right-hand side of the road; a small house was near me, and a desolate-looking mill at about a furlong's distance, to the south. Hogs came about me grunting and sniffing. I felt quite melancholy.

"Is this the neighbourhood of the birth-place of Gronwy Owen?" said I to myself. "No wonder that he was unfortunate through life, springing from such a region of wretchedness."

Wretched as the region seemed, however, I soon found there were kindly hearts close by me.

As I sat on the knoll I heard some one slightly cough very near me, and looking to the left saw a man dressed like a miller looking at me from the garden of the little house, which I have already mentioned.

I got up and gave him the sele of the day in English. He was a man about thirty, rather tall than otherwise, with a very prepossessing countenance. He shook his head at my English.

"What," said I, addressing him in the language of the country, "have you no English? Perhaps you have Welsh?"

"Plenty," said he, laughing; "there is no lack of Welsh amongst any of us here. Are you a Welshman?"

"No," said I, "an Englishman from the far east of Lloegr."

"And what brings you here?" said the man.

"A strange errand," I replied, "to look at the birth-place of a man who has long been dead."

"Do you come to seek for an inheritance?" said the man.

"No," said I. "Besides the man whose birth-place I came to see died poor, leaving nothing behind him but immortality."

"Who was he?" said the miller.

" Did you ever hear a sound of Gronwy Owen?"
said I.

" Frequently," said the miller; " I have frequently
heard a sound of him. He was born close by in a house
yonder," pointing to the south.

" O yes, gentleman," said a nice-looking woman,
who holding a little child by the hand was come to the
house-door, and was eagerly listening, " we have frequently heard speak of Gronwy Owen; there is much
talk of him in these parts."

" I am glad to hear it," said I, " for I half feared
that his name would not be known here."

" Pray, gentleman, walk in !" said the miller; " we
are going to have our afternoon's meal, and shall be
rejoiced if you will join us."

" Yes, do, gentleman," said the miller's wife, for
such the good woman was; " and many a welcome
shall you have."

I hesitated, and was about to excuse myself.

" Don't refuse, gentleman !" said both, " surely you
are not too proud to sit down with us?"

" I am afraid I shall only cause you trouble," said I.

" Dim blinder, no trouble," exclaimed both at once;
" pray do walk in !"

I entered the house, and the kitchen, parlour, or
whatever it was, a nice little room with a slate floor.
They made me sit down at a table by the window,
which was already laid for a meal.   There was a
clean cloth upon it, a tea-pot, cups and saucers, a large
plate of bread-and-butter, and a plate, on which were a
few very thin slices of brown, watery cheese.

My good friends took their seats, the wife poured
out tea for the stranger and her husband, helped us
both to bread-and-butter and the watery cheese, then
took care of herself.   Before, however, I could taste the
tea, the wife, seeming to recollect herself, started up,
and hurrying to a cupboard, produced a basin full of
snow-white lump sugar, and taking the spoon out of
my hand, placed two of the largest lumps in my cup,
though she helped neither her husband nor herself; the
sugar-basin being probably only kept for grand
occasions.

My eyes filled with tears; for in the whole course of

my life I had never experienced so much genuine hospitality. Honour to the miller of Mona and his wife; and honour to the kind hospitable Celts in general! How different is the reception of this despised race of the wandering stranger from that of ——. However, I am a Saxon myself, and the Saxons have no doubt their virtues; a pity that they should be all uncouth and ungracious ones!

I asked my kind host his name.

"John Jones," he replied, "Melinydd of Llanfair."

"Is the mill which you work your own property?" I inquired.

"No," he answered, "I rent it of a person who lives close by."

"And how happens it," said I, "that you speak no English?"

"How should it happen," said he, "that I should speak any? I have never been far from here; my wife who has lived at service at Liverpool can speak some."

"Can you read poetry?" said I.

"I can read the psalms and hymns, that they sing at our chapel," he replied.

"Then you are not of the Church?" said I.

"I am not," said the miller; "I am a Methodist."

"Can you read the poetry of Gronwy Owen?" said I.

"I cannot," said the miller, "that is with any comfort; his poetry is in the ancient Welsh measures, which make poetry so difficult, that few can understand it."

"I can understand poetry in those measures," said I.

"And how much time did you spend," said the miller, "before you could understand the poetry of the measures?"

"Three years," said I.

The miller laughed.

"I could not have afforded all that time," said he, "to study the songs of Gronwy. However, it is well that some people should have time to study them. He was a great poet as I have been told, and is the glory of our land—but he was unfortunate; I have read his life in Welsh and part of his letters; and in doing so have shed tears."

"Has his house any particular name?" said I.

" It is called sometimes Tŷ Gronwy," said the miller ;
" but more frequently Tafarn Goch."

" The Red Tavern?" said I. " How is it that so
many of your places are called Goch? there is Pentraeth
Goch ; there is Saint Pedair Goch, and here at Llanfair
is Tafarn Goch."

The miller laughed.

" It will take a wiser man than I," said he, " to
answer that question."

The repast over I rose up, gave my host thanks, and
said " I will now leave you, and hunt up things connected with Gronwy."

" And where will you find a lletty for night, gentleman?" said the miller's wife. " This is a poor place,
but if you will make use of our home you are welcome."

" I need not trouble you," said I, " I return this
night to Pentraeth Goch where I shall sleep."

" Well," said the miller, " whilst you are at Llanfair
I will accompany you about. Where shall we go to
first?"

" Where is the church?" said I. " I should like to
see the church where Gronwy worshipped God as a
boy."

" The church is at some distance," said the man ;
" it is past my mill, and as I want to go to the mill for
a moment, it will be perhaps well to go and see the
church, before we go to the house of Gronwy."

I shook the miller's wife by the hand, patted a little
yellow-haired girl of about two years old on the head
who during the whole time of the meal had sat on the
slate floor looking up into my face, and left the house
with honest Jones.

We directed our course to the mill, which lay some
way down a declivity towards the sea. Near the mill
was a comfortable-looking house, which my friend told
me belonged to the proprietor of the mill.

A rustic-looking man stood in the millyard, who he
said was the proprietor—the honest miller went into
the mill, and the rustic-looking proprietor greeted me
in Welsh, and asked me if I was come to buy hogs.

" No," said I ; " I am come to see the birth-place of
Gronwy Owen ;" he stared at me for a moment, then

seemed to muse, and at last walked away saying " Ah !
a great man."

The miller presently joined me, and we proceeded
farther down the hill. Our wȧy lay between stone
walls, and sometimes over them. The land was moory
and rocky, with nothing grand about it, and the miller
described it well when he said it was tîr gwael—mean
land. In about a quarter of an hour we came to the
churchyard into which we got, the gate being locked,
by clambering over the wall.

The church stands low down the descent, not far
distant from the sea. A little brook, called in the language of the country a frwd, washes its yard-wall on
the south. It is a small edifice with no spire, but to the
south-west there is a little stone erection rising from
the roof, in which hangs a bell—there is a small porch
looking to the south. With respect to its interior I
can say nothing, the door being locked. It is probably
like the outside, simple enough. It seemed to be about
two hundred and fifty years old, and to be kept in
tolerable repair. Simple as the edifice was, I looked
with great emotion upon it; and could I do else, when
I reflected that the greatest British poet of the last
century had worshipped God within it, with his poor
father and mother, when a boy?

I asked the miller whether he could point out to me
any tombs or grave-stones of Gronwy's family, but he
told me that he was not aware of any. On looking
about I found the name of Owen in the inscription on
the slate slab of a respectable-looking modern tomb, on
the north-east side of the church. The inscription was
as follows :

Er cof am Jane Owen
Gwraig Edward Owen,
Monachlog Llanfair Mathafarn eithaf,
A fu farw Chwefror 28 1842
Yn 51 Oed.

i.e. " To the memory of Jane Owen wife of Edward Owen, of
the monastery of St. Mary of farther Mathafarn, who died February 28, 1842, aged fifty-one."

Whether the Edward Owen mentioned here was any
relation to the great Gronwy, I had no opportunity
of learning. I asked the miller what was meant by the

monastery, and he told me that it was the name of a building to the north-east near the sea, which had once been a monastery, but had been converted into a farm-house, though it still retained its original name. " May all monasteries be converted into farm-houses," said I, " and may they still retain their original names in mockery of popery!"

Having seen all I could well see of the church and its precincts I departed with my kind guide. After we had retraced our steps some way, we came to some stepping-stones on the side of a wall, and the miller pointing to them said :

" The nearest way to the house of Gronwy will be over the llamfa."

I was now become ashamed of keeping the worthy fellow from his business and begged him to return to his mill. He refused to leave me, at first, but on my pressing him to do so, and on my telling him that I could find the way to the house of Gronwy very well by myself, he consented. We shook hands, the miller wished me luck, and betook himself to his mill, whilst I crossed the llamfa. I soon, however, repented having left the path by which I had come. I was presently in a maze of little fields with stone walls over which I had to clamber. At last I got into a lane with a stone wall on each side. A man came towards me and was about to pass me—his look was averted, and he was evidently one of those who have " no English." A Welshman of his description always averts his look when he sees a stranger who he thinks has " no Welsh," lest the stranger should ask him a question and he be obliged to confess that he has " no English."

" Is this the way to Llanfair?" said I to the man. The man made a kind of rush in order to get past me.

" Have you any Welsh?" I shouted as loud as I could bawl.

The man stopped, and turning a dark sullen countenance half upon me said, " Yes, I have Welsh."

" Which is the way to Llanfair?" said I.

" Llanfair, Llanfair?" said the man, " what do you mean?"

" I want to get there," said I.

" Are you not there already?" said the fellow stamping on the ground, " are you not in Llanfair?"

" Yes, but I want to get to the town."

" Town, town! Oh, I have no English," said the man; and off he started like a frightened bullock. The poor fellow was probably at first terrified at seeing an Englishman, then confused at hearing an Englishman speak Welsh, a language which the Welsh in general imagine no Englishman can speak, the tongue of an Englishman as they say not being long enough to pronounce Welsh; and lastly utterly deprived of what reasoning faculties he had still remaining by my asking him for the town of Llanfair, there being properly no town.

I went on and at last getting out of the lane, found myself upon the road, along which I had come about two hours before; the house of the miller was at some distance on my right. Near me were two or three houses and part of the skeleton of one, on which some men, in the dress of masons, seemed to be occupied. Going up to these men I said in Welsh to one, whom I judged to be the principal, and who was rather a tall fine-looking fellow:

" Have you heard a sound of Gronwy Owain?"

Here occurred another instance of the strange things people do when their ideas are confused. The man stood for a moment or two, as if transfixed, a trowel motionless in one of his hands, and a brick in the other; at last giving a kind of gasp, he answered in very tolerable Spanish:

" Si, señor! he oido."

" Is his house far from here?" said I in Welsh.

" No, señor!" said the man, " no esta muy lejos."

" I am a stranger here, friend, can anybody show me the way?"

"Si Señor! este mozo luego acompañara usted."

Then turning to a lad of about eighteen, also dressed as a mason, he said in Welsh:

" Show this gentleman instantly the way to Tafarn Goch."

The lad flinging a hod down, which he had on his shoulder, instantly set off, making me a motion with his head to follow him. I did so, wondering what the man could mean by speaking to me in Spanish. The lad walked by my side in silence for about two furlongs till we came to a range of trees, seemingly sycamores, behind which was a little garden, in which stood a long low house with three chimneys. The lad stopping flung open a gate which led into the garden, then crying to a child which he saw within : " Gad roi tro "—let the man take a turn; he was about to leave me, when I stopped him to put sixpence into his hand. He received the money with a gruff " Diolch!" and instantly set off at a quick pace. Passing the child who stared at me, I walked to the back part of the house, which seemed to be a long mud cottage. After examining the back part I went in front, where I saw an aged woman with several children, one of whom was the child I had first seen; she smiled and asked me what I wanted.

I said that I had come to see the house of Gronwy. She did not understand me, for shaking her head she said that she had no English, and was rather deaf. Raising my voice to a very high tone I said :

" Tŷ Gronwy !"

A gleam of intelligence flashed now in her eyes.

" Tŷ Gronwy," she said, " ah ! I understand. Come in, sir."

There were three doors to the house; she led me in by the midmost Into a common cottage room, with no other ceiling, seemingly, than the roof. She bade me sit down by the window by a little table, and asked me whether I would have a cup of milk and some bread-and-butter; I declined both, but said I should be thankful for a little water.

This she presently brought me in a teacup. I drank it, the children amounting to five standing a little way from me staring at me. I asked her if this was the house in which Gronwy was born. She said it was, but that it had been altered very much since his time— that three families had lived in it, but that she believed he was born about where we were now.

A man now coming in who lived at the next door, she said, I had better speak to him and tell him what I wanted to know, which he could then communicate to her, as she could understand his way of speaking much better than mine. Through the man I asked her

whether there was any one of the blood of Gronwy
Owen living in the house. She pointed to the children
and said they had all some of his blood. I asked in
what relationship they stood to Gronwy. She said she
could hardly tell, that tri priodas three marriages stood
between, and that the relationship was on the mother's
side. I gathered from her that the children had lost
their mother, that their name was Jones, and that their
father was her son. I asked if the house in which they
lived was their own; she said no, that it belonged to
a man who lived at some distance. I asked if the
children were poor.
"Very," said she.
I gave them each a trifle, and the poor old lady
thanked me with tears in her eyes.
I asked whether the children could read; she said
they all could, with the exception of the two youngest.
The eldest she said could read anything, whether Welsh
or English; she then took from the window-sill a book,
which she put into my hand, saying the child could read
it and understand it. I opened the book; it was an
English school book treating on all the sciences.
"Can you write?" said I to the child, a little stubby
girl of about eight, with a broad flat red face and grey
eyes, dressed in a chintz gown, a little bonnet on her
head, and looking the image of notableness.
The little maiden, who had never taken her eyes off
me for a moment during the whole time I had been in
the.room, at first made no answer; being, however, bid
by her grandmother to speak, she at length answered
in a soft voice, "Medraf, I can."
"Then write your name in this book," said I, taking
out a pocket-book and a pencil, "and write likewise
that you are related to Gronwy Owen—and be sure you
write in Welsh."
The little maiden very demurely took the book and
pencil, and placing the former on the table wrote as
follows:
"Ellen Jones yn perthyn o bell i gronow owen."
That is "Ellen Jones belonging from afar to Gronwy
Owen."
When I saw the name of Ellen I had no doubt that
the children were related to the illustrious Gronwy.

Ellen is a very uncommon Welsh name, but it seems to have been a family name of the Owens; it was borne by an infant daughter of the poet whom he tenderly loved, and who died whilst he was toiling at Walton in Cheshire,—

" Ellen, my darling,
Who liest in the churchyard of Walton,"

says poor Gronwy in one of the most affecting elegies ever written.

After a little farther conversation I bade the family farewell and left the house. After going down the road a hundred yards I turned back in order to ask permission to gather a leaf from one of the sycamores. Seeing the man who had helped me in my conversation with the old woman standing at the gate, I told him what I wanted, whereupon he instantly tore down a handful of leaves and gave them to me—thrusting them into my coat-pocket I thanked him kindly and departed.

Coming to the half-erected house, I again saw the man to whom I had addressed myself for information. I stopped, and speaking Spanish to him, asked how he had acquired the Spanish language.

" I have been in Chili, sir," said he in the same tongue, " and in California, and in those places I learned Spanish."

" What did you go to Chili for?" said I; " I need not ask you on what account you went to California."

" I went there as a mariner," said the man; " I sailed out of Liverpool for Chili."

" And how is it," said I, " that being a mariner and sailing in a Liverpool ship you do not speak English?"

" I speak English, señor," said the man, " perfectly well."

" Then how in the name of wonder," said I, speaking English, " came you to answer me in Spanish? I am an Englishman thorough bred."

" I can scarcely tell you how it was, sir," said the man scratching his head, " but I thought I would speak to you in Spanish."

" And why not English?" said I.

" Why, I heard you speaking Welsh," said the man, " and as for an Englishman speaking Welsh——"

" But why not answer me in Welsh?" said I.

" Why, I saw it was not your language, sir," said the man, " and as I had picked up some Spanish I thought it would be but fair to answer you in it."

" But how did you know that I could speak Spanish?" said I.

" I don't know indeed, sir," said the man; " but I looked at you, and something seemed to tell me that you could speak Spanish. I can't tell you how it was, sir," said he, looking me very innocently in the face, " but I was forced to speak Spanish to you. I was indeed !"

" The long and short of it was," said I, " that you took me for a foreigner, and thought that it would be but polite to answer me in a foreign language."

" I dare say it was so, sir," said the man. " I dare say it was just as you say."

" How did you fare in California?" said I.

" Very fairly indeed, sir," said the man. " I made some money there, and brought it home, and with part of it I am building this house."

" I am very happy to hear it," said I, " you are really a remarkable man—few return from California speaking Spanish as you do, and still fewer with money in their pockets."

The poor fellow looked pleased at what I said, more especially at that part of the sentence which touched upon his speaking Spanish well. Wishing him many years of health and happiness in the house he was building, I left him, and proceeded on my path towards Pentraeth Coch.

After walking some way, I turned round in order to take a last look of a place which had so much interest for me. The mill may be seen from a considerable distance; so may some of the scattered houses, and also the wood which surrounds the house of the illustrious Gronwy. Prosperity to Llanfair ! and may many a pilgrimage be made to it of the same character as my own.

CHAPTER XXXIII

Boxing Harry—Mr. Bos—Black Robin—Drovers—
Commercial Travellers.

I ARRIVED at the hostelry of Mr. Pritchard without meeting any adventure worthy of being marked down. I went into the little parlour, and, ringing the bell, was presently waited upon by Mrs. Pritchard, a nice matronly woman, whom I had not before seen, of whom I inquired what I could have for dinner.

"This is no great place for meat," said Mrs. Pritchard, "that is fresh meat, for sometimes a fortnight passes without anything being killed in the neighbourhood. I am afraid at present there is not a bit of fresh meat to be had. What we can get you for dinner I do not know, unless you are willing to make shift with bacon and eggs."

"I'll tell you what I'll do," said I, "I will have the bacon and eggs with tea and bread-and-butter, not forgetting a pint of ale—in a word, I will box Harry."

"I suppose you are a commercial gent," said Mrs. Pritchard.

"Why do you suppose me a commercial gent?" said I. "Do I look one?"

"Can't say you do much," said Mrs. Pritchard; "you have no rings on your fingers, nor a gilt chain at your waistcoat-pocket, but when you said 'box Harry,' I naturally took you to be one of the commercial gents, for when I was at Liverpool I was told that that was a word of theirs."

"I believe the word properly belongs to them," said I. "I am not one of them; but I learnt it from them, a great many years ago, when I was much amongst them. Those whose employers were in a small way of business, or allowed them insufficient salaries, frequently used to 'box Harry,' that is have a beef-steak, or mutton-chop, or perhaps bacon and eggs, as I am going to have, along with tea and ale instead of the regular dinner of a commercial gentleman, namely, fish, hot joint and fowl, pint of sherry, tart, ale and cheese, and bottle of old port, at the end of all."

Having made arrangements for "boxing Harry"

I went into the tap-room, from which I had heard the voice of Mr. Pritchard proceeding during the whole of my conversation with his wife. Here I found the worthy landlord seated with a single customer; both were smoking. The customer instantly arrested my attention. He was a man seemingly about forty years of age with a broad red face, with certain somethings, looking very much like incipient carbuncles, here and there upon it. His eyes were grey and looked rather as if they squinted; his mouth was very wide, and when it opened displayed a set of strong white, uneven teeth. He was dressed in a pepper-and-salt coat of the Newmarket cut, breeches of corduroy and brown top boots, and had on his head a broad, black, coarse, low-crowned hat. In his left hand he held a heavy white whale-bone whip with a brass head. I sat down on a bench nearly opposite to him and the landlord.

" Well," said Mr. Pritchard; " did you find your way to Llanfair?"

" Yes," said I.

" And did you execute the business satisfactorily which led you there?" said Mr. Pritchard.

" Perfectly," said I.

" Well, what did you give a stone for your live pork?" said his companion glancing up at me, and speaking in a gruff voice.

" I did not buy any live pork," said I; " do you take me for a pig-jobber?"

" Of course," said the man in pepper-and-salt; " who but a pig-jobber could have business at Llanfair?"

" Does Llanfair produce nothing but pigs?" said I.

" Nothing at all," said the man in the pepper-and-salt; " that is nothing worth mentioning. You wouldn't go there for runts, that is if you were in your right senses; if you were in want of runts you would have gone to my parish and have applied to me Mr. Bos; that is if you were in your senses. Wouldn't he, John Pritchard?"

Mr. Pritchard thus appealed to took the pipe out of his mouth, and with some hesitation said that he believed the gentleman neither went to Llanfair for pigs nor black cattle but upon some particular business.

" Well," said Mr. Bos, " it may be so, but I can't conceive how any person, either gentle or simple, could have any business in Anglesey save that business was pigs or cattle."

" The truth is," said I, " I went to Llanfair to see the birth-place of a great man—the cleverest Anglesey ever produced."

" Then you went wrong," said Mr. Bos, " you went to the wrong parish, you should have gone to Penmynnydd; the clebber man of Anglesey was born and buried at Penmynnydd; you may see his tomb in the church."

" You are alluding to Black Robin," said I, " who wrote the ode in praise of Anglesey—yes, he was a very clever young fellow, but excuse me, he was not half such a poet as Gronwy Owen."

" Black Robin," said Mr. Bos, " and Gronow Owen, who the Devil were they? I never heard of either. I wasn't talking of them, but of the clebberest man the world ever saw. Did you never hear of Owen Tiddir? If you didn't, where did you get your education?"

" I have heard of Owen Tudor," said I, " but never understood that he was particularly clever; handsome he undoubtedly was but clever——"

" How not clebber?" interrupted Mr. Bos. " If he wasn't clebber, who was clebber? Didn't he marry a great queen, and was not Harry the Eighth his great grandson?"

" Really," said I, " you know a great deal of history."

" I should hope I do," said Mr. Bos. " O, I wasn't at school at Blewmaris for six months for nothing; and I haven't been in Northampton, and in every town in England without learning something of history. With regard to history I may say that few——. Won't you drink?" said he, patronizingly, as he pushed a jug of ale which stood before him on a little table towards me.

Begging politely to be excused on the plea that I was just about to take tea, I asked him in what capacity he had travelled all over England.

" As a drover, to be sure," said Mr. Bos, " and I may say that there are not many in Anglesey better known in England than myself—at any rate I may say that there is not a public-house between here and Worcester at which I am not known."

"Pray excuse me," sad I, "but is not droving rather a low-lifed occupation?"

"Not half so much as pig-jobbing," said Bos, "and that that's your trade I am certain, or you would never have gone to Llanfair."

"I am no pig-jobber," said I, "and when I asked you that question about droving, I merely did so because one Ellis Wynn, in a book he wrote, gives the drovers a very bad character, and puts them in Hell for their mal-practices."

"O, he does," said Mr. Bos, "well the next time I meet him at Corwen I'll crack his head for saying so. Mal-practices—he had better look at his own, for he is a pig-jobber too. Written a book has he? then I suppose he has been left a legacy, and gone to school after middle-age, for when I last saw him, which is four years ago, he could neither read nor write."

I was about to tell Mr. Bos that the Ellis Wynn that I meant was no more a pig-jobber than myself, but a respectable clergyman, who had been dead considerably upwards of a hundred years, and that also, notwithstanding my respect for Mr. Bos's knowledge of history, I did not believe that Owen Tudor was buried at Penmynnydd, when I was prevented by the entrance of Mrs. Pritchard, who came to inform me that my repast was ready in the other room, whereupon I got up and went into the parlour to "box Harry."

Having despatched my bacon and eggs, tea and ale, I fell into deep meditation. My mind reverted to a long past period of my life, when I was to a certain extent mixed up with commercial travellers, and had plenty of opportunities of observing their habits, and the terms employed by them in conversation. I called up several individuals of the two classes into which they used to be divided, for commercial travellers in my time were divided into two classes, those who ate dinners and drank their bottle of port, and those who "boxed Harry." What glorious fellows the first seemed! What airs they gave themselves! What oaths they swore!

and what influence they had with hostlers and chambermaids! and what a sneaking-looking set the others
were! shabby in their apparel; no fine ferocity in their
countenances; no oaths in their mouths, except such
a trumpery apology for an oath as an occasional "confounded hard"; with little or no influence at inns,
scowled at by hostlers, and never smiled at by chambermaids—and then I remembered how often I had
bothered my head in vain to account for the origin of
the term "box Harry," and how often I had in vain
applied both to those who did box and to those who
did not "box Harry," for a clear and satisfactory
elucidation of the expression—and at last found myself
again bothering my head as of old in a vain attempt
to account for the origin of the term "boxing Harry."

CHAPTER XXXIV

Northampton—Horse-Breaking—Snoring.

TIRED at length with my vain efforts to account for
the term which in my time was so much in vogue
amongst commercial gentlemen I left the little parlour,
and repaired to the common room. Mr. Pritchard and
Mr. Bos were still there smoking and drinking, but
there was now a candle on the table before them, for
night was fast coming on. Mr. Bos was giving an
account of his travels in England, sometimes in Welsh,
sometimes in English, to which Mr. Pritchard was
listening with the greatest attention, occasionally
putting in a "see there now," and "what a fine thing
it is to have gone about." After some time Mr.
Bos exclaimed:

"I think, upon the whole, of all the places I have
seen in England I like Northampton best."

"I suppose," said I, "you found the men of Northampton good-tempered, jovial fellows?"

"Can't say I did," said Mr. Bos; "they are all
shoemakers, and of course quarrelsome and contra-
dictory, for where was there ever a shoemaker who
was not conceited and easily riled? No, I have little to

say in favour of Northampton, as far as the men are concerned. It's not the men but the women that make me speak in praise of Northampton. The men are all ill-tempered, but the women quite the contrary. I never saw such a place for merched anladd as Northampton. I was a great favourite with them, and could tell you such tales."

And then Mr. Bos putting his hat rather on one side of his head told us two or three tales of his adventures with the merched anladd of Northampton, which brought powerfully to mind part of what Ellis Wynn had said with respect to the practices of drovers in his day, detestation for which had induced him to put the whole tribe into Hell.

All of a sudden I heard a galloping down the road, and presently a mighty plunging, seemingly of a horse, before the door of the inn. I rushed out followed by my companions, and lo, on the open space before the inn was a fine young horse, rearing and kicking, with a young man on his back. The horse had neither bridle nor saddle, and the young fellow merely rode him with a rope, passed about his head—presently the horse became tolerably quiet, and his rider jumping off led him into the stable, where he made him fast to the rack and then came and joined us, whereupon we all went into the room from which I and the others had come on hearing the noise of the struggle.

" How came you on the colt's back, Jenkins?" said Mr. Pritchard, after we had all sat down and Jenkins had called for some cwrw. " I did not know that he was broke in."

" I am breaking him in myself," said Jenkins, speaking Welsh. " I began with him to-night."

" Do you mean to say," said I, " that you have begun breaking him in by mounting his back?"

" I do," said the other.

" Then depend upon it," said I, " that it will not be long before he will either break his neck or knees or he will break your neck or crown. You are not going the right way to work."

" O, myn Diawl!" said Jenkins, " I know better. In a day or two I shall have made him quite tame, and have got him into excellent paces, and shall have saved the money I must have paid away, had I put him into a jockey's hands."

Time passed, night came on, and other guests came in. There was much talking of first-rate Welsh and very indifferent English, Mr. Bos being the principal speaker in both languages; his discourse was chiefly on the comparative merits of Anglesey runts and Scotch bullocks, and those of the merched anladd of Northampton and the lasses of Wrexham. He preferred his own country runts to the Scotch kine, but said upon the whole, though a Welshman, he must give a preference to the merched of Northampton over those of Wrexham, for free-and-easy demeanour, notwithstanding that in that point which he said was the most desirable point in females, the lasses of Wrexham were generally considered out-and-outers.

Fond as I am of listening to public-house conversation, from which I generally contrive to extract both amusement and edification, I became rather tired of this, and getting up, strolled about the little village by moonlight till I felt disposed to retire to rest, when returning to the inn, I begged to be shown the room in which I was to sleep. Mrs. Pritchard forthwith taking a candle conducted me to a small room upstairs. There were two beds in it. The good lady pointed to one, next the window, in which there were nice clean sheets, told me that was the one which I was to occupy, and bidding me good-night, and leaving the candle, departed. Putting out the light I got into bed, but instantly found that the bed was not long enough by at least a foot. "I shall pass an uncomfortable night," said I, "for I never yet could sleep comfortably in a bed too short. However, as I am on my travels, I must endeavour to accommodate myself to circumstances." So I endeavoured to compose myself to sleep; before, however, I could succeed, I heard the sound of stumping steps coming upstairs, and perceived a beam of light through the crevices of the door, and in a moment more the door opened and in came two loutish farming lads whom I had observed below, one of them bearing a rushlight stuck in an old blacking-bottle. Without saying a word they flung off part of their clothes, and one of them having blown out the rushlight, they both tumbled into bed, and in a moment were snoring most sonorously. "I am in a short bed," said I, "and have snorers close by me; I fear I shall have a sorry night of it." I determined, however, to adhere to my resolution of making the best of circumstances, and lay perfectly quiet, listening to the snorings as they rose and fell; at last they became more gentle and I fell asleep, notwithstanding my feet were projecting some way from the bed. I might have lain ten minutes or a quarter of an hour when I suddenly started up in the bed broad awake. There was a great noise below the window of plunging and struggling interspersed with Welsh oaths. Then there was a sound as if of a heavy fall, and presently a groan. "I shouldn't wonder," said I, "if that fellow with the horse has verified my words, and has either broken his horse's neck or his own. However, if he has, he has no one to blame but himself. I gave him fair warning, and shall give myself no further trouble about the matter, but go to sleep," and so I did.

CHAPTER XXXV

Brilliant Morning—Travelling with Edification—A Good Clergyman—Gybi.

I AWOKE about six o'clock in the morning, having passed the night much better than I anticipated. The sun was shining bright and gloriously into the apartment. On looking into the other bed I found that my chums, the young farm-labourers, had deserted it. They were probably already in the field busy at labour. After lying a little time longer I arose, dressed myself and went down. I found my friend honest Pritchard smoking his morning pipe at the front door, and after giving him the sele of the day, I inquired of him the cause of the disturbance beneath my window the night before, and learned that the man of the horse had been thrown by the animal off its back, that the horse almost immediately after had slipped down, and both had been led home very much hurt. We then talked about farming and the crops, and at length got into a discourse about Liverpool. I asked him how he liked that mighty seaport; he said very well, but that he did not know much about it—for though he had a house there where his family had resided, he had not lived much at Liverpool himself his absences from that place having been many and long.

"Have you travelled then much about England?" said I.

"No," he replied. "When I have travelled it has chiefly been across the sea to foreign places."

"But what foreign places have you visited?" said I.

"I have visited," said Pritchard, "Constantinople, Alexandria, and some other cities in the south latitudes."

"Dear me," said I, "you have seen some of the most celebrated places in the world—and yet you were silent, and said nothing about your travels whilst that fellow Bos was pluming himself at having been at such places as Northampton and Worcester, the haunts of shoemakers and pig-jobbers."

"Ah," said Pritchard, "but Mr. Bos has travelled with edification; it is a fine thing to have travelled when one has done so with edification, but I have not. There is a vast deal of difference between me and him —he is considered the 'cutest man in these parts, and is much looked up to."

"You are really," said I, "the most modest person I have ever known and the least addicted to envy. Let me see whether you have travelled without edification."

I then questioned him about the places which he had mentioned, and found he knew a great deal about them, amongst other things he described Cleopatra's needle, and the At Maidan at Constantinople with surprising exactness.

"You put me out," said I; "you consider yourself inferior to that droving fellow Bos and to have travelled without edification, whereas you know a thousand times more than he, and indeed much more than many a person who makes his five hundred a year by going about lecturing on foreign places, but as I am no flatterer I will tell you that you have a fault which will always prevent your rising in this world, you have modesty; those who have modesty shall have no advancement, whilst those who can blow their own horn lustily shall be made governors. But allow me to ask you in what capacity you went abroad?''

" As engineer to various steamships,'' said Pritchard.

" A director of the power of steam,'' said I, '' and an explorer of the wonders of Iscander's city willing to hold the candle to Mr. Bos. I will tell you what, you are too good for this world, let us hope you will have your reward in the next.''

I breakfasted and asked for my bill; the bill amounted to little or nothing—half-a-crown I think for tea-dinner, sundry jugs of ale, bed and breakfast. I defrayed it, and then inquired whether it would be possible for me to see the inside of the church.

" O yes,'' said Pritchard. " I can let you in, for I am churchwarden and have the key.''

The church was a little edifice of some antiquity, with a little wing and without a spire; it was situated amidst a grove of trees. As we stood with our hats off in the sacred edifice, I asked Pritchard if there were many Methodists in those parts.

" Not so many as there were,'' said Pritchard, " they are rapidly decreasing, and indeed Dissenters in general. The cause of their decrease is that a good clergyman has lately come here, who visits the sick and preaches Christ, and in fact does his duty. If all our clergymen were like him there would not be many Dissenters in Ynis Fon.''

Outside the church, in the wall, I observed a tablet with the following inscription in English:

Here lieth interred the body of Ann, wife of Robert Paston, who deceased the sixth day of October, Anno Domini

1671.

R. P. A.

" You seem struck with that writing?'' said Pritchard, observing that I stood motionless, staring at the tablet.

" The name of Paston,'' said I, " struck me; it is the name of a village in my own native district, from which an old family, now almost extinct, derived its name. How came a Paston into Ynis Fon? Are there any people bearing that name at present in these parts?"

" Not that I am aware," said Pritchard.

" I wonder who his wife Ann was?" said I, "from the style of that tablet she must have been a considerable person."

" Perhaps she was the daughter of the Lewis family of Llan Dyfnant," said Pritchard; "that's an old family and a rich one. Perhaps he came from a distance and saw and married a daughter of the Lewis of Dyfnant—more than one stranger has done so. Lord Vivian came from a distance and saw and married a daughter of the rich Lewis of Dyfnant."

I shook honest Pritchard by the hand, thanked him for his kindness and wished him farewell, whereupon he gave mine a hearty squeeze, thanking me for my custom.

" Which is my way," said I, "to Pen Caer Gybi?"

" You must go about a mile on the Bangor road, and then turning to the right pass through Penmynnydd, but what takes you to Holyhead?"

" I wish to see," said I, "the place where Cybi the tawny saint preached and worshipped. He was called tawny because from his frequent walks in the blaze of the sun his face had become much sun-burnt. This is a furiously hot day, and perhaps by the time I get to Holyhead, I may be so sun-burnt as to be able to pass for Cybi himself."

CHAPTER XXXVI

Moelfre—Owain Gwynedd—Church of Penmynnydd—The Rose of Mona.

LEAVING Pentraeth Coch I retraced my way along the Bangor road till I came to the turning on the right. Here I diverged from the aforesaid road, and proceeded along one which led nearly due west; after travelling about a mile I stopped, on the top of a little hill; cornfields were on either side, and in one an aged man was reaping close to the road; I looked south, west, north and east; to the south was the Snowdon range far away, with the Wyddfa just discernible; to the west and north was nothing very remarkable, but to the east or rather north-east, was mountain Lidiart and the tall hill confronting it across the bay.

"Can you tell me," said I to the old reaper, "the name of that bald hill, which looks towards Lidiart?"

"We call that hill Moelfre," said the old man desisting from his labour, and touching his hat.

"Dear me," said I; "Moelfre, Moelfre!"

"Is there anything wonderful in the name, sir?" said the old man, smiling.

"There is nothing wonderful in the name," said I, "which merely means the bald hill, but it brings wonderful recollections to my mind. I little thought when I was looking from the road near Pentraeth Coch yesterday on that hill, and the bay and strand below it, and admiring the tranquillity which reigned over all, that I was gazing upon the scene of one of the most tremendous conflicts recorded in history or poetry."

"Dear me," said the old reaper; "and whom may it have been between? the French and English, I suppose."

"No," said I; "it was fought between one of your Welsh kings, the great Owain Gwynedd, and certain northern and Irish enemies of his."

"Only think," said the old man, "and it was a fierce battle, sir?"

"It was, indeed," said I; "according to the words of a poet, who described it, the Menai could not ebb on account of the torrent of blood which flowed into it, slaughter was heaped upon slaughter, shout followed shout, and around Moelfre a thousand war flags waved."

"Well, sir," said the old man, "I never before heard anything about it, indeed I don't trouble my head with histories, unless they be Bible histories."

"Are you a Churchman?" said I.

"No," said the old man, shortly; "I am a Methodist."

"I belong to the Church," said I.

"So I should have guessed, sir, by your being so

well acquainted with pennillion and histories. Ah, the Church. . . ."

" This is dreadfully hot weather," said I, "and I should like to offer you sixpence for ale, but as I am a Churchman I suppose you would not accept it from my hands."

" The Lord forbid, sir," said the old man, " that I should be so uncharitable ! If your honour chooses to give me sixpence, I will receive it willingly. Thank your honour ! Well, I have often said there is a great deal of good in the Church of England."

I once more looked at the hill which overlooked the scene of Owen Gwynedd's triumph over the united forces of the Irish Lochlanders and Normans, and then after inquiring of the old man whether I was in the right direction for Penmynnydd, and finding that I was, I set off at a great pace, singing occasionally snatches of Black Robin's ode in praise of Anglesey, amongst others the following stanza :—

" Bread of the wholesomest is found
In my mother-land of Anglesey ;
Friendly bounteous men abound
In Penmynnydd of Anglesey."

I reached Penmynnydd, a small village consisting of a few white houses and a mill. The meaning of Penmynnydd is literally the top of a hill. The village does not stand on a hill, but the church, which is at some distance, stands on one, or rather on a hillock. And it is probable from the circumstance of the church standing on a hillock, that the parish derives its name. Towards the church, after a slight glance at the village, I proceeded with hasty steps, and was soon at the foot of the hillock. A house, that of the clergyman, stands near the church, on the top of the hill. I opened a gate, and entered a lane which seemed to lead up to the church.

As I was passing some low buildings, probably offices pertaining to the house, a head was thrust from a doorway, which stared at me. It was a strange hirsute head, and probably looked more strange and hirsute than it naturally was, owing to its having a hairy cap upon it.

"Good day," said I.

"Good days, sar," said the head, and in a moment more a man of middle stature, about fifty, in hairy cap, shirt-sleeves, and green apron round his waist, stood before me. He looked the beau-ideal of a servant of all work.

"Can I see the church?" said I.

"Ah, you want to see the church," said honest Scrub. "Yes sar! you shall see the church. You go up road there past church—come to house, knock at door—say what you want—and nice little girl show you church. Ah, you quite right to come and see church—fine tomb there and clebber man sleeping in it with his wife, clebber man that—Owen Tiddir; married great queen—dyn clebber iawn."

Following the suggestions of the man of the hairy cap, I went round the church and knocked at the door of the house, a handsome parsonage. A nice little servant-girl presently made her appearance at the door, of whom I inquired whether I could see the church.

"Certainly, sir," said she; "I will go for the key and accompany you."

She fetched the key and·away we went to the church. It is a venerable chapel-like edifice, with a belfry towards the west; the roof, sinking by two gradations, is lower at the eastern or altar end than at the other. The girl, unlocking the door, ushered me into the interior.

"Which is the tomb of Tudor?" said I to the pretty damsel.

"There it is, sir," said she, pointing to the north side of the church; "there is the tomb of Owen Tudor."

Beneath a low-roofed arch lay sculptured in stone, on an altar tomb, the figures of a man and woman; that of the man in armour; that of the woman in graceful drapery. The male figure lay next the wall.

"And you think," said I to the girl, "that yonder figure is that of Owen Tudor?"

"Yes, sir," said the girl; "yon figure is that of Owen Tudor; the other is that of his wife, the great queen; both their bodies rest below."

I forbore to say that the figures were not those of

Owen Tudor and the great queen, his wife; and I forbore to say that their bodies did not rest in that church,
nor anywhere in the neighbourhood, for I was unwilling
to dispel a pleasing delusion. The tomb is doubtless a
tomb of one of the Tudor race, and of a gentle partner
of his, but not of the Rose of Mona and Catherine of
France.   Her bones rest in some corner of West-
minster's noble abbey; his moulder amongst those of
thousands of others, Yorkists and Lancastrians, under
the surface of the plain, where Mortimer's cross once
stood, that plain on the eastern side of which meanders
the murmuring Lug; that noble plain, where one of
the hardest battles which ever blooded English soil was
fought; where beautiful young Edward gained a crown,
and old Owen lost a head, which when young had been
the most beautiful of heads, which had gained for him
the appellation of the Rose of Anglesey, and which
had captivated the glances of the fair daughter of
France, the widow of Monmouth's Harry, the immortal
victor of Agincourt.

Nevertheless, long did I stare at that tomb which,
though not that of the Rose of Mona and his queen,
is certainly the tomb of some mighty one of the mighty
race of Theodore—then saying something in Welsh to
the pretty damsel at which she started, and putting
something into her hand, at which she curtseyed, I
hurried out of the church.

CHAPTER XXXVII

Mental Excitation—Land of Poets—The Man in Grey—Drinking
Healths—The Greatest Prydydd—Envy—Welshmen not Hogs
—Gentlemanly Feeling—What Pursuit?—Tell him to Walk
Up—Editor of the *Times*—Careful Wife—Departure.

I REGAINED the high road by a short cut, which I discovered across a field. I proceeded rapidly along for
some time. My mind was very much excited: I was
in the birth-place of the mighty Tudors—I had just seen
the tomb of one of them; I was also in the land of the
bard; a country which had produced Gwalchmai who
sang the triumphs of Owain, and him who had sung

the Cowydd of Judgment, Gronwy Owen. So no wonder I was excited. On I went reciting bardic snatches
connected with Anglesey. At length I began repeating
Black Robin's ode in praise of the island, or rather
my own translation of it, executed more than thirty
years before, which amongst others, contains the following lines :—

> " Twelve sober men the muses woo,
>   Twelve sober men in Anglesey,
>   Dwelling at home, like patriots true,
>   In reverence for Anglesey."

" Oh," said I, after I had recited that stanza, " what
would I not give to see one of those sober patriotic
bards, or at least one of their legitimate successors,
for by this time no doubt, the sober poets, mentioned
by Black Robin, are dead. That they left legitimate
successors who can doubt? for Anglesey is never to be
without bards. Have we not the words, not of Robin
the Black, but Huw the Red to that effect?

> " ' Brodir, gnawd ynddi prydydd ;
>   Heb ganu ni bu ni bydd.'

" That is : a hospitable country, in which a poet is a
thing of course. It has never been and will never be
without song."

Here I became silent, and presently arrived at the
side of a little dell or ravine, down which the road led
from east to west. The northern and southern sides
of this dell were precipitous. Beneath the southern one
stood a small cottage. Just as I began to descend the
eastern side, two men began to descend the opposite
one, and it so happened that we met at the bottom of
the dingle, just before the house, which bore a sign,
and over the door of which was an inscription to the
effect that ale was sold within. They saluted me ; I
returned their salutation, and then we all three stood
still looking at one another. One of the men was
rather a tall figure, about forty, dressed in grey, or
pepper-and-salt, with a cap of some kind on his head,
his face was long and rather good-looking, though
slightly pock-broken. There was a peculiar gravity
upon it. The other person was somewhat about sixty—

he was much shorter than his companion, and much worse dressed—he wore a hat that had several holes in it, a dusty, rusty black coat, much too large for him; ragged yellow velveteen breeches, indifferent fustian gaiters, and shoes, cobbled here and there, one of which had rather an ugly bulge by the side near the toes. His mouth was exceedingly wide, and his nose remarkably long; its extremity of a deep purple; upon his features was a half-simple smile or leer; in his hand was a long stick. After we had all taken a full view of one another I said in Welsh, addressing myself to the man in grey, " Pray may I take the liberty of asking the name of this place?"

" I believe you are an Englishman, sir," said the man in grey, speaking English, " I will therefore take the liberty of answering your question in the English tongue. The name of this place is Dyffryn Gaint."

" Thank you," said I; " you are quite right with regard to my being an Englishman; perhaps you are one yourself?"

" Sir," said the man in grey, " I have not the honour to be so. I am a native of the small island in which we are."

" Small," said I, " but famous, particularly for producing illustrious men."

" That's very true indeed, sir," said the man in grey, drawing himself up; " it is particularly famous for producing illustrious men."

" There was Owen Tudor?" said I.

" Very true," said the man in grey, " his tomb is in the church a little way from hence."

" Then," said I, " there was Gronwy Owen, one of the greatest bards that ever lived. Out of reverence to his genius I went yesterday to see the place of his birth."

" Sir," said the man in grey, " I should be sorry to leave you without enjoying your conversation at some length. In yonder house they sell good ale, perhaps you will not be offended if I ask you to drink some with me and my friend?"

" You are very kind," said I, " I am fond of good ale, and fonder still of good company—suppose we go in?"

We went into the cottage, which was kept by a man and his wife, both of whom seemed to be perfectly well acquainted with my two new friends. We sat down on stools, by a clean white table in a little apartment with a clay floor—notwithstanding the heat of the weather, the little room was very cool and pleasant owing to the cottage being much protected from the sun by its situation. The man in grey called for a jug of ale, which was presently placed before us along with three glasses. The man in grey, having filled the glasses from the jug which might contain three pints, handed one to me, another to his companion, and then taking the third drank to my health. I drank to his, and that of his companion; the latter, after nodding to us both, emptied his at a draught, and then with a kind of half-fatuous leer, exclaimed "Da iawn, very good."

The ale, though not very good, was cool and neither sour nor bitter; we then sat for a moment or two in silence, my companions on one side of the table, and I on the other. After a little time the man in grey looking at me said:

"Travelling I suppose in Anglesey for pleasure?"

"To a certain extent," said I; "but my chief object in visiting Anglesey was to view the birth-place of Gronwy Owen; I saw it yesterday and am now going to Holyhead chiefly with a view to see the country."

"And how came you, an Englishman, to know anything of Gronwy Owen?"

"I studied Welsh literature when young," said I, "and was much struck with the verses of Gronwy: he was one of the great bards of Wales, and certainly the most illustrious genius that Anglesey ever produced."

"A great genius I admit," said the man in grey, "but pardon me, not exactly the greatest Ynis Fon has produced. The race of the bards is not quite extinct in the island, sir, I could name one or two—however, I leave others to do so—but I assure you the race of bards is not quite extinct here."

"I am delighted to hear you say so," said I, "and make no doubt that you speak correctly, for the Red Bard has said that Mona is never to be without a poet —but where am I to find one? Just before I saw you

I was wishing to see a poet; I would willingly give a quart of ale to see a genuine Anglesey poet."

"You would, sir, would you?" said the man in grey, lifting his head on high, and curling his upper lip.

"I would, indeed," said I, "my greatest desire at present is to see an Anglesey poet, but where am I to find one?"

"Where is he to find one?" said he of the tattered hat; "where's the gwr boneddig to find a prydydd? No occasion to go far, he, he, he."

"Well," said I, "but where is he?"

"Where is he? why there," said he pointing to the man in grey—"the greatest prydydd in tîr Fon or the whole world."

"Tut, tut, hold your tongue," said the man in grey.

"Hold my tongue, myn Diawl, not I—I speak the truth," then filling his glass he emptied it exclaiming, "I'll not hold my tongue. The greatest prydydd in the whole world."

"Then I have the honour to be seated with a bard of Anglesey?" said I, addressing the man in grey.

"Tut, tut," said he of the grey suit.

"The greatest prydydd in the whole world," iterated he of the bulged shoe, with a slight hiccup, as he again filled his glass.

"Then," said I, "I am truly fortunate."

"Sir," said the man in grey, "I had no intention of discovering myself, but as my friend here has betrayed my secret, I confess that I am a bard of Anglesey—my friend is an excellent individual but indiscreet, highly indiscreet, as I have frequently told him," and here he looked most benignantly reproachful at him of the tattered hat.

"The greatest prydydd," said the latter, "the greatest prydydd that——" and leaving his sentence incomplete he drank off the ale which he had poured into his glass.

"Well," said I, "I cannot sufficiently congratulate myself, for having met an Anglesey bard—no doubt a graduate one. Anglesey was always famous for graduate bards, for what says Black Robin?

"'Though Arvon graduate bards can boast,
Yet more canst thou, O Anglesey.'"

" I suppose by graduate bard you mean one who has gained the chair at an eisteddfod?" said the man in grey. " No, I have never gained the silver chair—I have never had an opportunity. I have been kept out of the eisteddfodau. There is such a thing as envy, sir— but there is one comfort, that envy will not always prevail."

" No," said I; " envy will not always prevail— envious scoundrels may chuckle for a time at the seemingly complete success of the dastardly arts to which they have recourse, in order to crush merit—but Providence is not asleep. All of a sudden they see their supposed victim on a pinnacle far above their reach. Then there is weeping, and gnashing of teeth with a vengeance, and the long melancholy howl. O, there is nothing in this world which gives one so perfect an idea of retribution as the long melancholy howl of the disappointed envious scoundrel when he sees his supposed victim smiling on an altitude far above his reach."

" Sir," said the man in grey, " I am delighted to hear you. Give me your hand, your honourable hand. Sir, you have now felt the hand-grasp of a Welshman, to say nothing of an Anglesey bard, and I have felt that of a Briton, perhaps a bard, a brother, sir? O, when I first saw your face out there in the dyffryn, I at once recognised in it that of a kindred spirit, and I felt compelled to ask you to drink. Drink sir! but how is this? the jug is empty—how is this?—O, I see—my friend, sir, though an excellent individual, is indiscreet, sir—very indiscreet. Landlord, bring this moment another jug of ale."

" The greatest prydydd," stuttered he of the bulged shoe—" the greatest prydydd—Oh——"

" Tut, tut," said the man in grey.

" I speak the truth and care for no one," said he of the tattered hat. " I say the greatest prydydd. If any one wishes to gainsay me let him show his face, and Myn Diawl——"

The landlord brought the ale, placed it on the table, and then stood as if waiting for something.

" I suppose you are waiting to be paid," said I; " what is your demand?"

" Sixpence for this jug, and sixpence for the other,"
said the landlord.

I took out a shilling and said : " It is but right that
I should pay half of the reckoning, and as the whole
affair is merely a shilling matter I should feel obliged
in being permitted to pay the whole, so, landlord, take
the shilling and remember you are paid." I then delivered the shilling to the landlord, but had no sooner
done so than the man in grey, starting up in violent
agitation, wrested the money from the other, and flung
it down on the table before me saying :—

" No, no, that will never do. I invited you in here
to drink, and now you would pay for the liquor which
I ordered. You English are free with your money, but
you are sometimes free with it at the expense of
people's feelings. I am a Welshman, and I know
Englishmen consider all Welshmen hogs. But we are
not hogs, mind you ! for we have little feelings which
hogs have not. Moreover, I would have you know that
we have money, though perhaps not so much as the
Saxon." Then putting his hand into his pocket he
pulled out a shilling, and giving it to the landlord said
in Welsh : " Now thou art paid, and mayst go thy
ways till thou art again called for. I do not know why
thou didst stay after thou hadst put down the ale.
Thou didst know enough of me to know that thou didst
run no risk of not being paid."

" But," said I, after the landlord had departed, " I
must insist on being my share. Did you not hear me
say that I would give a quart of ale to see a poet?"

" A poet's face," said the man in grey, " should be
common to all, even like that of the sun. He is no
true poet, who would keep his face from the world."

" But," said I, " the sun frequently hides his head
from the world, behind a cloud."

" Not so," said the man in grey. " The sun does
not hide his face, it is the cloud that hides it. The sun
is always glad enough to be seen, and so is the poet.
If both are occasionally hid, trust me it is no fault of
theirs. Bear that in mind ; and now pray take up your
money."

" The man is a gentleman," thought I to myself,
" whether poet or not ; but I really believe him to be a

poet; were he not he could hardly talk in the manner I have just heard him."

The man in grey now filled my glass, his own and that of his companion. The latter emptied his in a minute, not forgetting first to say " the best prydydd in all the world !" The man in grey was also not slow to empty his own. The jug now passed rapidly between my two friends, for the poet seemed determined to have his full share of the beverage. I allowed the ale in my glass to remain untasted, and began to talk about the bards, and to quote from their works. I soon found that the man in grey knew quite as much of the old bards and their works as myself. In one instance he convicted me of a mistake.

I had quoted those remarkable lines in which an old bard, doubtless seeing the Menai Bridge by means of second sight, says :—" I will pass to the land of Mona notwithstanding the waters of Menai, without waiting for the ebb "—and was feeling not a little proud of my erudition when the man in grey, after looking at me for a moment fixedly, asked me the name of the bard who composed them—" Sion Tudor," I replied.

" There you are wrong," said the man in grey; " his name was not Sion Tudor, but Robert Vychan, in English, Little Bob. Sion Tudor wrote an englyn on the Skerries whirlpool in the Menai; but it was Little Bob who wrote the stanza in which the future bridge over the Menai is hinted at."

" You are right," said I, " you are right. Well, I am glad that all song and learning are not dead in Ynis Fon."

" Dead," said the man in grey, whose features began to be rather flushed, " they are neither dead, nor ever will be. There are plenty of poets in Anglesey—why, I can mention twelve, and amongst them, and not the least—pooh, what was I going to say?—twelve there are, genuine Anglesey poets, born there, and living there for the love they bear their native land. When I say they all live in Anglesey, perhaps I am not quite accurate, for one of the dozen does not exactly live in Anglesey, but just over the bridge. He is an elderly man, but his awen, I assure you, is as young and vigorous as ever."

" I shouldn't be at all surprised," said I, " if he was a certain ancient gentleman, from whom I obtained information yesterday, with respect to the birth-place of Gronwy Owen."

" Very likely," said the man in grey; " well, if you have seen him consider yourself fortunate, for he is a genuine bard, and a genuine son of Anglesey, notwithstanding he lives across the water."

" If he is the person I allude to," said I, " I am doubly fortunate, for I have seen two bards of Anglesey."

" Sir," said the man in grey, " I consider myself quite as fortunate in having met such a Saxon as yourself, as it is possible for you to do, in having seen two bards of Ynis Fon."

" I suppose you follow some pursuit besides bardism?" said I; " I suppose you farm?"

" I do not farm," said the man in grey, " I keep an inn."

" Keep an inn?" said I.

" Yes," said the man in grey. " The ⸺ Arms at L⸺."

" Sure," said I, " inn-keeping and bardism aie not very cognate pursuits?"

" You are wrong," said the man in grey, " I believe the awen, or inspiration, is quite as much at home in the bar as in the barn, perhaps more. It is that belief which makes me tolerably satisfied with my position, and prevents me from asking Sir Richard to give me a farm instead of an inn."

" I suppose," said I, " that Sir Richard is your landlord?"

" He is," said the man in grey, " and a right noble landlord too."

" I suppose," said I, " that he is right proud of his tenant?"

" He is," said the man in grey, " and I am proud of my landlord, and will here drink his health. I have often said that if I were not what I am, I should wish to be Sir Richard."

" You consider yourself his superior?" said I.

" Of course," said the man in grey—" a baronet is a baronet; but a bard is a bard you know—I never forget what I am, and the respect due to my sublime calling. About a month ago I was seated in an upper apartment, in a fit of rapture; there was a pen in my hand, and paper before me on the table, and likewise a jug of good ale, for I always find that the awen is most prodigal of her favours, when a jug of good ale is before me. All of a sudden my wife came running up, and told me that Sir Richard was below, and wanted to speak to me. 'Tell him to walk up,' said I. 'Are you mad?' said my wife. 'Don't you know who Sir Richard is?' 'I do,' said I, 'a baronet is a baronet, but a bard is a bard. Tell him to walk up.' Well, my wife went and told Sir Richard that I was writing, and could not come down, and that she hoped he would not object to walk up. 'Certainly not; certainly not,' said Sir Richard. 'I shall be only too happy to ascend to a genius on his hill. You may be proud of such a husband, Mrs. W.' And here it will be as well to tell you that my name is W——, J. W. of ——. Sir Richard then came up, and I received him with gravity and politeness. I did not rise, of course, for I never forget myself a moment, but I told him to sit down, and added that after I had finished the pennill I was engaged upon, I would speak to him. Well, Sir Richard smiled and sat down, and begged me not to hurry myself, for that he could wait. So I finished the pennill, deliberately, mind you, for I did not forget who I was, and then turning to Sir Richard entered upon business with him.''

'' I suppose Sir Richard is a very good-tempered man?'' said I.

'' I don't know,'' said the man in grey. '' I have seen Sir Richard in a devil of a passion, but never with me—no, no! Trust Sir Richard for not riding the high horse with me—a baronet is a baronet, but a bard is a bard; and that Sir Richard knows.''

'' The greatest prydydd,'' said the man of the tattered hat, emptying the last contents of the jug into his glass, '' the greatest prydydd that——''

'' Well,'' said I, '' you appear to enjoy very great consideration, and yet you were talking just now of being ill-used.''

'' So I have been,'' said the man in grey, '' I have

been kept out of the eisteddfodau—and then—what do you think? That fellow the editor of the *Times*——"

" O," said I, " if you have anything to do with the editor of the *Times* you may, of course, expect nothing but shabby treatment, but what business could you have with him?"

" Why I sent him some pennillion for insertion, and he did not insert them."

" Were they in Welsh or English?"

" In Welsh, of course."

" Well, then the man had some excuse for disregarding them—because you know the *Times* is written in English."

" O, you mean the London *Times*," said the man in grey. " Pooh! I did not allude to that trumpery journal, but the Liverpool *Times*, the Amserau. I sent some pennillion to the editor for insertion and he did not insert them. Peth a clwir cenfigen yn Saesneg?"

" We call cenfigen in English envy," said I; " but as I told you before, envy will not always prevail."

" You cannot imagine how pleased I am with your company," said the man in grey. " Landlord, landlord!"

" The greatest prydydd," said the man of the tattered hat, " the greatest prydydd."

" Pray don't order any more on my account," said I, " as you see my glass is still full. I am about to start for Caer Gybi. Pray where are you bound for?"

" For Bangor," said the man in grey. " I am going to the market."

" Then I would advise you to lose no time," said I, " or you will infallibly be too late; it must now be one o'clock."

" There is no market to-day," said the man in grey, " the market is to-morrow, which is Saturday. I like to take things leisurely, on which account, when I go to market, I generally set out the day before, in order that I may enjoy myself upon the road. I feel myself so happy here that I shall not stir till the evening. Now pray stay with me and my friend till then."

" I cannot," said I, " if I stay longer here I shall never reach Caer Gybi to-night. But allow me to ask

whether your business at L—— will not suffer by your
spending so much time on the road to market?"

"My wife takes care of the business whilst I am
away," said the man in grey, "so it won't suffer much.
Indeed it is she who chiefly conducts the business of
the inn. I spend a good deal of time from home, for
besides being a bard and innkeeper, I must tell you
I am a horse-dealer and a jobber, and if I go to Bangor
it is in the hope of purchasing a horse or pig worth the
money."

"And is your friend going to market too?" said I.

"My friend goes with me to assist me and bear me
company. If I buy a pig he will help me to drive it
home; if a horse, he will get up upon its back behind
me. I might perhaps do without him, but I enjoy his
company highly. He is sometimes rather indiscreet,
but I do assure you he is exceedingly clever."

"The greatest prydydd," said the man of the bulged
shoe, "the greatest prydydd in the world."

"O, I have no doubt of his cleverness," said I,
"from what I have observed of him. Now before I go
allow me to pay for your next jug of ale."

"I will do no such thing," said the man in grey.
"No farthing do you pay here for me or my friend
either. But I will tell you what you may do. I am, as
I have told you, an innkeeper as well as a bard. By the
time you get to L—— you will be hot and hungry and
in need of refreshment, and if you think proper to
patronize my house, the —— Arms by taking your
chop and pint there, you will oblige me. Landlord,
some more ale."

"The greatest prydydd," said he of the bulged shoe,
"the greatest prydydd——"

"I will most certainly patronize your house," said
I to the man in grey, and shaking him heartily by the
hand I departed.

CHAPTER XXXVIII

Inn at L——The Handmaid—The Decanter—Religious Gentleman
—Truly Distressing—Sententiousness—Way to Pay Bills.

I PROCEEDED on my way in high spirits indeed, having
now seen not only the tomb of the Tudors, but one of
those sober poets for which Anglesey has always been
so famous. The country was pretty, with here and there
a hill, a harvest-field, a clump of trees or a grove. I
soon reached L——, a small but neat town. "Where
is the —— Arms?" said I to a man whom I met.

"Yonder, sir, yonder," said he, pointing to a magnificent structure on the left.

I went in and found myself in a spacious hall. A
good-looking young woman in a white dress, with a
profusion of pink ribbons confronted me with a curtsey.
"A pint and a chop!" I exclaimed, with a flourish of
my hand and at the top of my voice. The damsel gave
a kind of start, and then, with something like a toss of
the head, led the way into a very large room, on the
left, in which were many tables, covered with snowy-
white cloths, on which were plates, knives and forks,
the latter seemingly of silver, tumblers, and wine-
glasses.

"I think you asked for a pint and a chop, sir?" said
the damsel, motioning me to sit down at one of the
tables.

"I did," said I, as I sat down, "let them be brought
with all convenient speed, for I am in something of a
hurry."

"Very well, sir," said the damsel, and then with
another kind of toss of the head, she went away, not
forgetting to turn half round, to take a furtive glance at
me, before she went out of the door.

"Well," said I, as I looked at the tables, with their
snowy-white cloths, tumblers, wine-glasses and what
not, and at the walls of the room glittering with
mirrors, "surely a poet never kept so magnificent an
inn before; there must be something in this fellow
besides the awen, or his house would never exhibit
such marks of prosperity, and good taste—there must

be something in this fellow; though he pretends to be a wild erratic son of Parnassus, he must have an eye to the main chance, a genius for turning the penny, or rather the sovereign, for the accommodation here is no penny accommodation, as I shall probably find. Perhaps, however, like myself, he has an exceedingly clever wife who whilst he is making verses, or running about the country swigging ale with people in bulged shoes, or buying pigs or glandered horses, looks after matters at home, drives a swinging trade, and keeps not only herself, but him respectable—but even in that event he must have a good deal of common sense in him, even like myself, who always allow my wife to buy and sell, carry money to the bank, draw cheques, inspect and pay tradesmen's bills, and transact all my real business, whilst I myself pore over old books, walk about shires, discoursing with gypsies, under hedge-rows, or with sober bards—in hedge alehouses." I continued musing in this manner until the handmaid made her appearance with a tray, on which were covers and a decanter, which she placed before me. "What is that?" said I, pointing to a decanter.

"Only a pint of sherry, sir," said she of the white dress and ribbons.

"Dear me," said I, "I ordered no sherry, I wanted some ale—a pint of ale."

"You called for a pint, sir," said the handmaid, "but you mentioned no ale, and I naturally supposed that a gentleman of your appearance"—here she glanced at my dusty coat—"and speaking in the tone you did, would not condescend to drink ale with his chop; however, as it seems I have been mistaken, I can take away the sherry and bring you the ale."

"Well, well," said I, "you can let the sherry remain; I do not like sherry, and am very fond of ale, but you can let the wine remain; upon the whole I am glad you brought it. Indeed, I merely came to do a good turn to the master of the house."

"Thank you, sir," said the handmaid.

"Are you his daughter?" said I.

"O no, sir," said the handmaid reverently; "only his waiter."

"You may be proud to wait on him," said I.

" I am, sir," said the handmaid, casting down her eyes.

" I suppose he is much respected in the neighbourhood?" said I.

" Very much so, sir," said the damsel, " especially amidst the connection."

" The connection," said I. " Ah I see, he has extensive consanguinity, most Welsh have. But," I continued, " there is such a thing as envy in the world, and there are a great many malicious people in the world, who speak against him."

" A great many, sir, but we take what they say from whence it comes."

" You do quite right," said I. " Has your master written any poetry lately?"

" Sir !" said the damsel, staring at me.

" Any poetry," said I, " any pennillion?"

" No, sir," said the damsel; " my master is a respectable man, and would scorn to do anything of the kind."

" Why," said I, " is not your master a bard as well as an innkeeper?"

" My master, sir, is an innkeeper," said the damsel, " but as for the other, I don't know what you mean."

" A bard," said I, " is a prydydd, a person who makes verses—pennillion; does not your master make them?"

" My master make them? No, sir; my master is a religious gentleman, and would scorn to make such profane stuff."

" Well," said I, " he told me he did within the last two hours. I met him at Dyffryn Gaint, along with another man, and he took me into the public-house, where we had a deal of discourse."

" You met my master at Dyffryn Gaint?" said the damsel.

" Yes," said I, " and he treated me with ale, told me that he was a poet, and that he was going to Bangor to buy a horse or a pig."

" I don't see how that could be, sir," said the damsel; " my master is at present in the house, rather unwell, and has not been out for the last three days. There must be some mistake."

" Mistake," said I. " Isn't this the —— Arms?"

" Yes, sir, it is."

" And isn't your master's name W——?"

" No, sir, my master's name is H——, and a more respectable man——"

" Well," said I, interrupting her, " all I can say is that I met a man in Dyffryn Gaint, who treated me with ale, told me that his name was W——, that he was a prydydd and kept the —— Arms at L——."

" Well," said the damsel, " now I remember there is a person of that name in L——, and he also keeps a house which he calls the —— Arms, but it is only a public-house."

" But," said I, " is he not a prydydd, an illustrious poet; does he not write pennillion which everybody admires?"

" Well," said the damsel, " I believe he does write things which he calls pennillion, but everybody laughs at them."

" Come, come," said I, " I will not hear the productions of a man who treated me with ale spoken of with disrespect. I am afraid that you are one of his envious maligners, of which he gave me to understand that he had a great many."

" Envious, sir! not I indeed; and if I were disposed to be envious of anybody it would not be of him; O dear, why he is——"

" A bard of Anglesey," said I, interrupting her, " such a person as Gronwy Owen describes in the following lines, which by the bye were written upon himself :—

> " ' Where'er he goes he's sure to find
> Respectful looks and greetings kind.'

" I tell you that it was out of respect to that man that I came to this house. Had I not thought that he kept it, I should not have entered it and called for a pint and chop. How distressing! how truly distressing!"

" Well, sir," said the damsel, " if there is anything distressing you have only to thank your acquaintance who chooses to call his mughouse by the name of a respectable hotel, for I would have you know that this is an hotel, and kept by a respectable and religious man, and not kept by——. However, I scorn to say more, especially as I might be misinterpreted. Sir, there's your pint and chop, and if you wish for anything else you can ring. Envious, indeed, of such. Marry come up!'' and with a toss of her head, higher than any she had hitherto given, she bounced out of the room.

Here was a pretty affair! I had entered the house and ordered the chop and pint in the belief that by so doing I was patronising the poet, and lo, I was not in the poet's house, and my order would benefit a person for whom, however respectable and religious, I cared not one rush. Moreover, the pint which I had ordered appeared in the guise not of ale, which I am fond of, but of sherry, for which I have always entertained a sovereign contempt, as a silly, sickly compound, the use of which will transform a nation, however bold and warlike by nature, into a race of sketchers, scribblers, and punsters, in fact into what Englishmen are at the present day. But who was to blame? Why, who but the poet and myself? The poet ought to have told me that there were two houses in L—— bearing the sign of the —— Arms, and that I must fight shy of the hotel and steer for the pot-house, and when I gave the order I certainly ought to have been a little more explicit; when I said a pint, I ought to have added—of ale. Sententiousness is a fine thing sometimes, but not always. By being sententious here, I got sherry, which I dislike, instead of ale which I like, and should have to pay more for what was disagreeable than I should have had to pay for what was agreeable. Yet I had merely echoed the poet's words in calling for a pint and chop, so after all the poet was to blame for both mistakes. But perhaps he meant that I should drink sherry at his house, and when he advised me to call for a pint, he meant a pint of sherry. But the maid had said he kept a pot-house, and no pot-houses have wine-licences; but the maid after all might be an envious baggage, and no better than she should be. But what was now to be done? Why, clearly make the best of the matter, eat the chop and leave the sherry. So I commenced eating the chop, which was by this time nearly cold.

After eating a few morsels I looked at the sherry; " I may as well take a glass," said I. So with a wry face I poured myself out a glass.

" What detestable stuff !" said I, after I had drunk it. " However, as I shall have to pay for it I may as well go through with it." So I poured myself out another glass, and by the time I had finished the chop I had finished the sherry also.

And now what was I to do next? Why, my best advice seemed to be to pay my bill and depart. But I had promised the poet to patronise his house, and had by mistake ordered and despatched a pint and chop in a house which was not the poet's. Should I now go to his house and order a pint and chop there? Decidedly not ! I had patronised a house which I believed to be the poet's ; if I patronised the wrong one, the fault was his, not mine—he should have been more explicit. I had performed my promise, at least in intention.

Perfectly satisfied with the conclusion I had come to, I rang the bell. " The bill?" said I to the handmaid.

" Here it is !" said she, placing a strip of paper in my hand.

I looked at the bill, and, whether moderate or immoderate, paid it with a smiling countenance, commended the entertainment highly, and gave the damsel something handsome for her trouble in waiting on me.

Reader, please to bear in mind that as all bills must be paid, it is much more comfortable to pay them with a smile than with a frown, and that it is much better by giving sixpence, or a shilling to a poor servant, which you will never miss at the year's end, to be followed from the door of an inn by good wishes, than by giving nothing to be pursued by cutting silence, or the yet more cutting Hm !

" Sir," said the good-looking, well-ribboned damsel, " I wish you a pleasant journey, and whenever you please again to honour our establishment with your presence, both my master and myself shall be infinitely obliged to you."

CHAPTER XXXIX

Oats and Methodism—The Little Girl—Tŷ Gwyn—Bird of the Roof —Purest English—Railroads—Inconsistency—The Boots.

It might be about four in the afternoon when I left L—— bound for Pen Caer Gybi, or Holy Head, seventeen miles distant. I reached the top of the hill on the west of the little town, and then walked briskly forward. The country looked poor and mean—on my right was a field of oats, on my left a Methodist chapel—oats and Methodism! what better symbols of poverty and meanness?

I went onward a long way; the weather was broiling hot, and I felt thirsty. On the top of a long ascent stood a house by the roadside. I went to the door and knocked—no answer—" Oes neb yn y tŷ?" said I.

" Oes !" said an infantine voice.

I opened the door, and saw a little girl. " Have you any water?" said I.

" No," said the child; " but I have this," and she brought me some butter-milk in a basin. I just tasted it, gave the child a penny and blessed her.

" Oes genoch tad?"

" No," said she; " but I have a mam." Tad im mam; blessed sounds; in all languages expressing the same blessed things.

After walking for some hours I saw a tall blue hill in the far distance before me. " What is the name of that hill?" said I to a woman whom I met.

" Pen Caer Gybi," she replied.

Soon after I came to a village near to a rocky gulley. On inquiring the name of the village, I was told it was Llan yr Afon, or the church of the river. I passed on; the country was neither grand nor pretty—it exhibited a kind of wildness, however, which did not fail to interest me—there were stones, rocks, and furze in abundance. Turning round the corner of a hill, I observed through the mists of evening, which began to gather about me, what seemed to be rather a genteel house on the road-side, on my left, and a little way

behind it a strange kind of monticle, on which I thought
I observed tall upright stones. Quickening my pace, I
soon came parallel with the house, which, as I drew
nigh, ceased to look like a genteel house, and exhibited
an appearance of great desolation. It was a white, or
rather grey structure of some antiquity. It was evidently used as a farm-house, for there was a yard
adjoining to it, in which were stacks and agricultural
implements. Observing two men in the yard, I went
in. They were respectable, farming-looking men, between forty and fifty; one had on a coat and hat, the
other a cap and jacket. " Good evening," I said in
Welsh.

" Good evening," they replied in the same language,
looking inquiringly at me.

" What is the name of this place?" said I.

" It is called Tŷ gwyn," said the man of the hat.

" On account of its colour, I suppose?" said I.

" Just so," said the man of the hat.

" It looks old," said I.

" And it is old," he replied. " In the time of the
Papists it was one of their chapels."

" Does it belong to you?" I demanded.

" O no, it belongs to one Mr. Sparrow from Liverpool. I am his bailiff, and this man is a carpenter who
is here doing a job for him."

Here ensued a pause, which was broken by the man
of the hat saying in English to the man of the cap—

" Who can this strange fellow be? he has not a word
of English, and though he speaks Welsh, his Welsh
sounds very different from ours. Who can he be?"

" I am sure I don't know," said the other.

" I know who he is," said the first; " he comes from
Llydaw, or Armorica, which was peopled from Britain
estalom, and where I am told the real old Welsh
language is still spoken."

" I think I heard you mention the word Llydaw?"
said I to the man of the hat.

" Ah," said the man of the hat, speaking Welsh, " I
was right after all; oh, I could have sworn you were
Llydaweg. Well, how are the descendants of the
ancient Britons getting on in Llydaw?"

" They were getting on tolerably well," said I,

" when I last saw them, though all things do not go exactly as they could wish."

" Of course not," said he of the hat. " We too have much to complain of here; the lands are almost entirely taken possession of by Saxons, wherever you go you will find them settled, and a Saxon bird of the roof must build its nest in Gwyn dŷ."

" You call a sparrow in your Welsh a bird of the roof, do you not?" said I.

" We do," said he of the hat. " You speak Welsh very well, considering you were not born in Wales. It is really surprising that the men of Llydaw should speak the iaith so pure as they do."

" The Welsh, when they went over there," said I, " took effectual means that their descendants should speak good Welsh, if all tales be true."

" What means?" said he of the hat.

" Why," said I, " after conquering the country they put all the men to death, and married the women, but before a child was born they cut out all the women's tongues, so that the only language the children heard when they were born was pure Cumraeg. What do you think of that?"

" Why, that it was a cute trick," said he of the hat.

" A more clever trick I never heard," said he of the cap.

" Have you any memorials in the neighbourhood of the old Welsh?" said I.

" What do you mean?" said the man of the hat.

" Any altars of the Druids?" said I; " any stone tables?"

" None," said the man of the hat.

" What may those stones be?" said I, pointing to the stones which had struck my attention.

" Mere common rocks," said the man.

" May I go and examine them?" said I.

" O yes," said he of the hat, " and we will go with you."

We went to the stones, which were indeed common rocks, and which, when I reached them, presented quite a different appearance from that which they presented to my eye when I viewed them from afar.

"Are there many altars of the Druids in Llydaw?" said the man of the hat.

"Plenty," said I; "but those altars are older than the time of the Welsh colonists, and were erected by the old Gauls."

"Well," said the man of the cap, "I am glad to have seen a man of Llydaw."

, "Whom do you call a man of Llydaw?" said I.

"Whom but yourself?" said he of the hat.

"I am not a man of Llydaw," said I in English, "but of Norfolk, where the people eat the best dumplings in the world, and speak the purest English. Now a thousand thanks for your civility. I would have some more chat with you, but night is coming on, and I am bound to Holyhead."

Then leaving the men staring after me, I bent my steps towards Holyhead.

I passed by a place called Llan something, standing lonely on its hill. The country around looked sad and desolate. It is true night had come on when I saw it.

On I hurried. The voices of children sounded sweetly at a distance across the wild champaign on my left.

It grew darker and darker. On I hurried along the road; at last I came to lone, lordly groves. On my right was an open gate and a lodge. I went up to the lodge. The door was open, and in a little room I beheld a nice-looking old lady sitting by a table, on which stood a lighted candle, with her eyes fixed on a large book.

"Excuse me," said I; "but who owns this property?"

The old lady looked up from her book, which appeared to be a Bible, without the slightest surprise, though I certainly came upon her unawares, and answered:

"Mr. John Wynn."

I shortly passed through a large village, or rather town, the name of which I did not learn. I then went on for a mile or two, and saw a red light at some distance. The road led nearly up to it, and then diverged towards the north. Leaving the road, I made towards the light by a lane, and soon came to a railroad station.

"You won't have long to wait, sir," said a man—
"the train to Holyhead will be here presently."

"How far is it to Holyhead?" said I.

"Two miles, sir, and the fare is only sixpence."

"I despise railroads," said I, "and those who travel by them," and without waiting for an answer returned to the road. Presently I heard the train—it stopped for a minute at the station, and then continuing its course, passed me on my left hand, voiding fierce sparks, and making a terrible noise—the road was a melancholy one; my footsteps sounded hollow upon it. I seemed to be its only traveller—a wall extended for a long, long way on my left. At length I came to a turnpike. I felt desolate, and wished to speak to somebody. I tapped at the window, at which there was a light; a woman opened it. "How far to Holyhead?" said I in English.

"Dim Saesneg," said the woman.

I repeated my question in Welsh.

"Two miles," said she.

"Still two miles to Holyhead by the road," thought I. "Nos da," said I to the woman, and sped along. At length I saw water on my right, seemingly a kind of bay, and presently a melancholy ship. I doubled my pace, which was before tolerably quick, and soon saw a noble-looking edifice on my left, brilliantly lighted up. "What a capital inn that would make," said I, looking at it wistfully, as I passed it. Presently I found myself in the midst of a poor, dull, ill-lighted town.

"Where is the inn?" said I to a man.

"The inn, sir? you have passed it. The inn is yonder," he continued, pointing towards the noble-looking edifice.

"What, is that the inn?" said I.

"Yes, sir, the railroad hotel—and a first-rate hotel it is."

"And are there no other inns?"

"Yes; but they are all poor places. No gent puts up at them—all the gents by the railroad put up at the railroad hotel."

What was I to do? after turning up my nose at the railroad, was I to put up at its hotel? Surely to do so would be hardly acting with consistency. "Ought I not rather to go to some public-house, frequented by captains of fishing-smacks, and be put in a bed a foot too short for me," said I, as I reflected on my last night's couch at Mr. Pritchard's. "No, that won't do—I shall go to the hotel; I have money in my pocket, and a person with money in his pocket has surely a right to be inconsistent if he pleases."

So I turned back and entered the railway hotel with lofty port and with sounding step, for I had twelve sovereigns in my pocket, besides a half one, and some loose silver, and feared not to encounter the gaze of any waiter or landlord in the land. "Send boots!" I roared to the waiter, as I flung myself down in an arm-chair in a magnificent coffee-room. "What the deuce are you staring at? send boots, can't you, and ask what I can have for dinner."

"Yes, sir," said the waiter, and with a low bow departed.

"These boots are rather dusty," said the boots, a grey-haired, venerable-looking man, after he had taken off my thick, solid, square-toed boots. "I suppose you came walking from the railroad?"

"Confound the railroad!" said I: "I came walking from Bangor. I would have you know that I have money in my pocket, and can afford to walk. I am fond of the beauties of nature; now it is impossible to see much of the beauties of nature unless you walk. I am likewise fond of poetry, and take especial delight in inspecting the birth-places and haunts of poets. It is because I am fond of poetry, poets and their haunts, that I am come to Anglesey. Anglesey does not abound in the beauties of nature, but there never was such a place for poets; you meet a poet, or the birth-place of a poet, everywhere."

"Did your honour ever hear of Gronwy Owen?" said the old man.

"I have," I replied, "and yesterday I visited his birth-place; so you have heard of Gronwy Owen?"

"Heard of him, your honour; yes, and read his works. That 'Cowydd y Farn' of his is a wonderful poem."

"You say right," said I; "the 'Cowydd of Judg-

ment ' contains some of the finest things ever written—
that description of the toppling down of the top crag
of Snowdon, at the day of Judgment, beats anything
in Homer."

"Then there was Lewis Morris, your honour," said
the old man, "who gave Gronwy his education and
wrote ' The Lasses of Meirion '—and——"

"And ' The Cowydd to the Snail,' " said I, interrupting him—" a wonderful man he was."

" I am rejoiced to see your honour in our house,"
said boots; " I never saw an English gentleman before
who knew so much about Welsh poetry, nor a Welsh
one either. Ah, if your honour is fond of poets and
their places you did right to come to Anglesey—and
your honour was right in saying that you can't stir a
step without meeting one; you have an example of the
truth of that in me—for to tell your honour the truth,
I am a poet myself, and no bad one either."

Then tucking the dusty boots under his arm, the old
man, with a low congee, and a "Good-night, your
honour!" shuffled out of the room.

CHAPTER XL

Caer Gybi—Lewis Morris— Noble Character.

I DINED, or rather supped, well at the Railroad Inn——
I beg its pardon, Hotel, for the word Inn at the present
day is decidedly vulgar. I likewise slept well; how
could I do otherwise, passing the night, as I did, in an
excellent bed in a large, cool, quiet room? I arose
rather late, went down to the coffee-room and took
my breakfast leisurely, after which I paid my bill and
strolled forth to observe the wonders of the place.

Caer Gybi, or Cybi's town, is situated on the southern
side of a bay on the north-western side of Anglesey.
Close to it, on the south-west, is a very high headland,
called in Welsh Pen Caer Gybi, or the head of Cybi's
city, and in English Holyhead. On the north, across
the bay, is another mountain of equal altitude, which,
if I am not mistaken, bears in Welsh the name of
Mynydd Llanfair, or Saint Mary's Mount. It is called

Cybi's town from one Cybi, who, about the year 500, built a college here, to which youths, noble and ignoble, resorted from far and near. He was a native of Dyfed, or Pembrokeshire, and was a friend, and for a long time a fellow-labourer, of Saint David. Besides being learned, according to the standard of the time, he was a great walker, and from bronzing his countenance by frequent walking in the sun, was generally called Cybi Velin, which means tawny, or yellow Cybi.

So much for Cybi, and his town! And now something about one whose memory haunted me much more than that of Cybi during my stay at Holyhead.

Lewis Morris was born at a place called Tref y Beirdd, in Anglesey, in the year 1700. Anglesey, or Mona, has given birth to many illustrious men, but few, upon the whole, entitled to more honourable mention than himself. From a humble situation in life, for he served an apprenticeship to a cooper at Holyhead, he raised himself by his industry and talents to affluence and distinction, became a landed proprietor in the county of Cardigan, and inspector of the royal domains and mines in Wales. Perhaps a man more generally accomplished never existed; he was a first-rate mechanic, an expert navigator, a great musician, both in theory and practice, and a poet of singular excellence. Of him it was said, and with truth, that he could build a ship and sail it, frame a harp and make it speak, write an ode and set it to music. Yet that saying, eulogistic as it is, is far from expressing all the vast powers and acquirements of Lewis Morris. Though self-taught, he was confessedly the best Welsh scholar of his age, and was well-versed in those cognate dialects of the Welsh—the Cornish, Armoric, Highland Gaelic and Irish. He was likewise well acquainted with Hebrew, Greek and Latin, had studied Anglo-Saxon with some success, and was a writer of bold and vigorous English. He was besides a good general antiquary, and for knowledge of ancient Welsh customs, traditions and superstitions had no equal. Yet all has not been said which can be uttered in his praise: he had qualities of mind which entitled him to higher esteem than any accomplishment connected with intellect or skill. Amongst these were his noble generosity and sacrifice of self for the benefit of others. Weeks and months he was in the habit of devoting to the superintendence of the affairs of the widow and the fatherless : one of his principal delights was to assist merit, to bring it before the world, and to procure for it its proper estimation : it was he who first discovered the tuneful genius of blind Parry; it was he who first put the harp into his hand; it was he who first gave him scientific instruction; it was he who cheered him with encouragement, and assisted him with gold. It was he who instructed the celebrated Evan Evans in the ancient language of Wales, enabling that talented but eccentric individual to read the pages of the red book of Hergest as easily as those of the Welsh Bible; it was he who corrected his verses with matchless skill, refining and polishing them till they became well worthy of being read by posterity; it was he who gave him advice, which, had it been followed, would have made the Prydydd Hir, as he called himself, one of the most illustrious Welshmen of the last century; and it was he who first told his countrymen that there was a youth of Anglesey whose genius, if properly encouraged, promised fair to rival that of Milton : one of the most eloquent letters ever written is one by him, in which he descants upon the beauties of certain poems of Gronwy Owen, the latent genius of whose early boyhood he had observed, whom he had clothed, educated, and assisted up to the period when he was ordained a minister of the Church, and whom he finally rescued from a state bordering on starvation in London, procuring for him an honourable appointment in the New World. Immortality to Lewis Morris ! But immortality he has won, even as his illustrious pupil has said, who in his elegy upon his bene-factor, written in America, in the four-and-twenty measures, at a time when Gronwy had not heard the Welsh language spoken for more than twenty years, has words to the following effect :—

" As long as Bardic lore shall last, science and learning be cherished, the language and blood of the Britons undefiled, song be heard on Parnassus, heaven and earth be in existence, foam be on the surge, and water in the river, the name of Lewis of Mon shall be held in grateful remembrance."

CHAPTER XLI

The Pier—Irish Reapers—Wild Irish Face—Father Toban—The Herd of Swine—Latin Blessing.

THE day was as hot as the preceding one. I walked slowly towards the west, and presently found myself upon a pier, or breakwater, at the mouth of the harbour. A large steamer lay at a little distance within the pier. There were fishing boats on both sides, the greater number on the outer side, which lies towards the hill of Holyhead. On the shady side of the break-water, under the wall, were two or three dozen of Irish reapers; some were lying asleep, others in parties of two or three were seated with their backs against the wall, and were talking Irish; these last all appeared to be well-made, middle-sized young fellows, with rather a ruffianly look; they stared at me as I passed. The whole party had shillealahs either in their hands or by their sides. I went to the extremity of the pier, where was a little light-house, and then turned back. As I again drew near the Irish, I heard a hubbub, and observed a great commotion amongst them. All, whether those whom I had seen sitting, or those whom I had seen reclining, had got, or were getting, on their legs. As I passed them they were all standing up, and their eyes were fixed upon me with a strange kind of expression, partly of wonder, methought, partly of respect. "Yes, 'tis he, sure enough," I heard, one whisper. On I went, and at about thirty yards from the last I stopped, turned round, and leaned against the wall. All the Irish were looking at me—presently they formed into knots, and began to discourse very eagerly in Irish, though in an under tone. At length I observed a fellow going from one knot to the other, exchanging a few words with each. After he had held communication with all, he nodded his head, and came towards me with a quick step; the rest stood silent and motion-less, with their eyes turned in the direction in which I was, and in which he was advancing. He stopped within a yard of me, and took off his hat. He was an athletic fellow of about twenty-eight, dressed in brown frieze. His features were swarthy, and his eyes black; in every lineament of his countenance was a jumble of savagery and roguishness. I never saw a more genuine wild Irish face—there he stood, looking at me full in the face, his hat in one hand, and his shillealah in the other.

"Well, what do you want?" said I, after we had stared at each other about half a minute.

"Sure, I'm just come on the part of the boys and myself to beg a bit of a favour of your reverence."

"Reverence," said I, "what do you mean by styling me reverence?"

"Och sure, because to be styled your reverence is the right of your reverence."

"Pray, what do you take me for?"

"Och sure, we knows your reverence very well."

"Well, who am I?"

"Och, why Father Toban, to be sure."

"And who knows me to be Father Toban?"

"Och, a boy here knows your reverence to be Father Toban."

"Where is that boy?"

"Here he stands, your reverence."

"Are you that boy?"

"I am, your reverence."

"And you told the rest that I was Father Toban?"

"I did, your reverence."

"And you know me to be Father Toban?"

"I do, your reverence."

"How do you know me to be Father Toban?"

"Och, why because many's the good time that I have heard your reverence, Father Toban, say mass."

"And what is it you want me to do?"

"Why, see here, your reverence, we are going to embark in the dirty steamer yonder for ould Ireland, which starts as soon as the tide serves, and we want your reverence to bless us before we goes."

"You want me to bless you?"

"We do, your reverence; we want you to spit out a little bit of a blessing upon us before we goes on board."

"And what good would my blessing do you?"

"All kinds of good, your reverence; it would prevent the dirty steamer from catching fire, your reverence, or from going down, your reverence, or from running against the blackguard Hill of Howth in the mist, provided there should be one.''

"And suppose I were to tell you that I am not Father Toban?''

"Och, your reverence will never think of doing that.''

"Would you believe me if I did?''

"We would not, your reverence.''

"If I were to swear that I am not Father Toban?''

"We would not, your reverence.''

"On the evangiles?''

"We would not, your reverence.''

"On the Cross?''

"We would not, your reverence.''

"And suppose I were to refuse to give you a blessing?''

"Och, your reverence will never refuse to bless the poor boys.''

"But suppose I were to refuse?''

"Why, in such a case, which by the bye is altogether impossible, we should just make bould to give your reverence a good bating.''

"You would break my head?''

"We would, your reverence.''

"Kill me?''

"We would, your reverence.''

"You would really put me to death?''

"We would not, your reverence.''

"And what's the difference between killing and putting to death?''

"Och, sure there's all the difference in the world. Killing manes only a good big bating, such as every Irishman is used to, and which your reverence would get over long before matins, whereas putting your reverence to death would prevent your reverence from saying mass for ever and a day.''

"And you are determined on having a blessing?''

"We are, your reverence.''

"By hook or by crook?''

"By hook or by crook, your reverence.''

"Before I bless you, will you answer me a question or two?''

" I will, your reverence."

" Are you not a set of great big blackguards?"

" We are, your reverence."

" Without one good quality?"

" We are, your reverence."

" Would it not be quite right to saddle and bridle you all, and ride you violently down Holyhead or the Giant's Causeway into the waters, causing you to perish there, like the herd of swine of old?"

" It would, your reverence."

" And knowing and confessing all this, you have the cheek to come and ask me for a blessing?"

" We have, your reverence."

" Well, how shall I give the blessing?"

" Och, sure your reverence knows very well how to give it."

" Shall I give it in Irish?"

" Och, no, your reverence—a blessing in Irish is no blessing at all."

" In English?"

" Och, murder, no, your reverence, God preserve us all from an English blessing."

" In Latin?"

" Yes, sure, your reverence; in what else should you bless us but in holy Latin?"

" Well, then, prepare yourselves."

" We will, your reverence—stay one moment whilst I whisper to the boys that your reverence is about to bestow your blessing upon us."

Then turning to the rest, who all this time had kept their eyes fixed intently upon us, he bellowed with the voice of a bull :

" Down on your marrow bones, ye sinners, for his reverence Toban is about to bless us all in holy Latin."

He then flung himself on his knees on the pier, and all his countrymen, baring their heads, followed his example—yes, there knelt thirty bare-headed Eirionaich on the pier of Caer Gybi, beneath the broiling sun. I gave them the best Latin blessing I could remember out of two or three which I had got by memory out of an old Popish book of devotion, which I bought in my boyhood at a stall. Then turning to the deputy, I said, " Well, now are you satisfied?"

" Sure, I have a right to be satisfied, your reverence;
and so have we all—sure, we can now all go on board
the dirty steamer, without fear of fire or water, or the
blackguard Hill of Howth either."

" Then get up, and tell the rest to get up, and please
to know, and let the rest know, that I do not choose
to receive farther trouble, either by word or look, from
any of ye, as long as I remain here."

" Your reverence shall be obeyed in all things," said
the fellow, getting up. Then walking away to his companions, he cried, " Get up, boys, and plase to know
that his reverence Toban is not to be farther troubled
by being looked at or spoken to by any one of us, as
long as he remains upon this dirty pier."

" Divil a bit farther trouble shall he have from us!"
exclaimed many a voice, as the rest of the party arose
from their knees.

In half-a-minute they disposed themselves in much
the same manner as that in which they were when I
first saw them : some flung themselves again to sleep
under the wall, some seated themselves with their
backs against it, and laughed and chatted, but without
taking any notice of me; those who sat and chatted
took, or appeared to take, as little notice as those who
lay and slept, of his reverence Father Toban.

CHAPTER XLII

Gage of Suffolk—Fellow in a Turban—Town of Holyhead—
Father Boots—An Expedition—Holyhead and Finisterræ—
Gryffith ab Cynan—The Fairies' Well.

LEAVING the pier, I turned up a street to the south, and
was not long before I arrived at a kind of market-place,
where were carts and stalls, and on the ground, on
cloths, apples and plums, and abundance of greengages
—the latter, when good, decidedly the finest fruit in
the world; a fruit, for the introduction of which into
England, the English have to thank one Gage, of an
ancient Suffolk family, at present extinct, after whose
name the fruit derives the latter part of its appellation.
Strolling about the market-place, I came in contact

with a fellow dressed in a turban and dirty blue linen
robes and trowsers. He bore a bundle of papers in his
hand, one of which he offered to me. I asked him who
he was.

" Arap," he replied.

He had a dark, cunning, roguish countenance, with
small eyes, and had all the appearance of a Jew. I
spoke to him in what Arabic I could command on a
sudden, and he jabbered to me in a corrupt dialect,
giving me a confused account of a captivity which he
had undergone amidst savage Mahometans. At last
I asked him what religion he was of.

" The Christian," he replied.

" Have you ever been of the Jewish?" said I.

He returned no answer save by a grin.

I took the paper, gave him a penny, and then walked
away. The paper contained an account in English of
how the bearer, the son of Christian parents, had been
carried into captivity by two Mahometan merchants,
father and son, from whom he had escaped with the
greatest difficulty.

" Pretty fools," said I, " must any people have been
who ever stole you; but O what fools if they wished
to keep you after they had got you!"

The paper was stuffed with religious and anti-slavery
cant, and merely wanted a little of the teetotal nonsense
to be a perfect specimen of humbug.

I strolled forward, encountering more carts and
more heaps of greengages; presently I turned to the
right by a street, which led some way up the hill. The
houses were tolerably large and all white. The town,
with its white houses placed by the seaside, on the
skirt of a mountain, beneath a blue sky and a broiling
sun, put me something in mind of a Moorish piratical
town, in which I had once been. Becoming soon tired
of walking about, without any particular aim, in so
great a heat, I determined to return to the inn, call for
ale, and deliberate on what I had best next do. So I
returned and called for ale. The ale which was brought
was not ale which I am particularly fond of. The ale
which I am fond of is ale about nine or ten months old,
somewhat hard, tasting well of the malt and little of the
hop—ale such as farmers, and noblemen too, of the

good old time, when farmers' daughters did not play on
pianos and noblemen did not sell their game, were in
the habit of offering to both high and low, and drinking
themselves. The ale which was brought me was thin,
washy stuff, which though it did not taste much of hop,
tasted still less of malt, made and sold by one Allsopp,
who I am told calls himself a squire and a gentleman—
as he certainly may be with quite as much right as
many a lord calls himself a nobleman and a gentleman;
for surely it is not a fraction more trumpery to make
and sell ale than to fatten and sell game. The ale of
the Saxon squire, for Allsopp is decidedly an old Saxon
name, however unakin to the practice of old Saxon
squires the selling of ale may be, was drinkable, for it
was fresh, and the day, as I have said before, exceedingly hot; so I took frequent draughts out of the
shining metal tankard in which it was brought,
deliberating both whilst drinking, and in the intervals
of drinking, on what I had next best do. I had some
thoughts of crossing to the northern side of the bay,
then, bearing to the north-east, wend my way to
Amlwch, follow the windings of the sea-shore to
Mathafarn eithaf and Pentraeth Coch, and then return
to Bangor, after which I could boast that I had walked
round the whole of Anglesey, and indeed trodden no
inconsiderable part of the way twice. Before coming,
however, to any resolution I determined to ask the
advice of my friend the boots on the subject. So I
finished my ale, and sent word by the waiter that I
wished to speak to him; he came forthwith, and after
communicating my deliberations to him in a few words
I craved his counsel. The old man, after rubbing his
right forefinger behind his right ear for about a quarter
of a minute, inquired if I meant to return to Bangor,
and on my telling him that it would be necessary for
me to do so, as I intended to walk back to Llangollen
by Caernarvon and Beth Gelert, strongly advised me to
return to Bangor by the railroad train, which would
start at seven in the evening, and would convey me
thither in an hour and a half. I told him that I hated
railroads, and received for answer that he had no
particular liking for them himself, but that he occasionally made use of them on a pinch, and supposed

that I likewise did the same. I then observed that if I followed his advice I should not see the north side of the island nor its principal town Amlwch, and received for answer that if I never did, the loss would not be great. That as for Amlwch, it was a poor poverty-stricken place; the inn a shabby affair, the master a very so-so individual, and the boots a fellow without either wit or literature. That upon the whole he thought I might be satisfied with what I had seen already, for after having visited Owen Tudor's tomb, Caer Gybi and his hotel, I had in fact seen the cream of Mona. I then said that I had one objection to make, which was that I really did not know how to employ the time till seven o'clock, for that I had seen all about the town.

"But has your honour ascended the Head?" demanded Father Boots.

"No," said I, "I have not."

"Then," said he, "I will soon find your honour ways and means to spend the time agreeably till the starting of the train. Your honour shall ascend the head under the guidance of my nephew, a nice intelligent lad, your honour, and always glad to earn a shilling or two. By the time your honour has seen all the wonders of the Head and returned, it will be five o'clock. Your honour can then dine, and after dinner trifle away the minutes over your wine or brandy-and-water till seven, when your honour can step into a first-class for Bangor."

I was struck with the happy manner in which he had removed the difficulty in question, and informed him that I was determined to follow his advice. He hurried away, and presently returned with his nephew, to whom I offered half-a-crown provided he would show me all about Pen Caer Gyby. He accepted my offer with evident satisfaction, and we lost no time in setting out upon our expedition.

We had to pass over a great deal of broken ground, sometimes ascending, sometimes descending, before we found ourselves upon the side of what may actually be called the headland. Shaping our course westward we came to the vicinity of a lighthouse standing on the verge of a precipice, the foot of which was washed by the sea.

Leaving the lighthouse on our right we followed a steep winding path which at last brought us to the top of the pen or summit, rising according to the judgment which I formed about six hundred feet from the surface of the sea. Here was a level spot some twenty yards across, in the middle of which stood a heap of stones or cairn. I asked the lad whether this cairn bore a name and received for answer that it was generally called Bar-cluder y Cawr Glâs, words which seem to signify the top heap of the Grey Giant.

"Some king, giant, or man of old renown lies buried beneath this cairn," said I. "Whoever he may be I trust he will excuse me for mounting it, seeing that I do so with no disrespectful spirit." I then mounted the cairn, exclaiming :

> "Who lies 'neath the cairn on the headland hoar,
> His hand yet holding his broad claymore,
> Is it Beli, the son of Benlli Gawr?"

There stood I on the cairn of the Grey Giant, looking around me. The prospect, on every side, was noble : the blue interminable sea to the west and north; the whole stretch of Mona to the east; and far away to the south the mountainous region of Eryri, comprising some of the most romantic hills in the world. In some respects this Pen Santaidd, this holy headland, reminded me of Finisterræ, the Gallegan promontory which I had ascended some seventeen years before, whilst engaged in battling the Pope with the sword of the gospel in his favourite territory. Both are bold, bluff headlands looking to the west, both have huge rocks in their vicinity, rising from the bosom of the brine. For a time, as I stood on the cairn, I almost imagined myself on the Gallegan hill; much the same scenery presented itself as there, and a sun equally fierce struck upon my head as that which assailed it on the Gallegan hill. For a time all my thoughts were of Spain. It was not long, however, before I bethought me that my lot was now in a different region, that I had done with Spain for ever, after doing for her all that lay in the power of a lone man, who had never in this world anything to depend upon, but God and his own slight strength. Yes, I had done with Spain, and was now in Wales; and, after a slight sigh, my thoughts became all intensely Welsh. I thought on the old times when Mona was the grand seat of Druidical superstition, when adoration was paid to Dwy Fawr, and Dwy Fach, the sole survivors of the apocryphal Deluge; to Hu the Mighty and his plough; to Ceridwen and her cauldron; to András the Horrible; to Wyn ab Nudd, Lord of Unknown, and to Beli, Emperor of the Sun. I thought on the times when the Beal fire blazed on this height, on the neighbouring promontory, on the cope-stone of Eryri, and on every high hill throughout Britain on the eve of the first of May. I thought on the day when the bands of Suetonius crossed the Menai strait in their broad-bottomed boats, fell upon the Druids and their followers, who with wild looks and brandished torches lined the shore, slew hundreds with merciless butchery upon the plains, and pursued the remainder to the remotest fastnesses of the isle. I figured to myself long-bearded men with white vest-ments toiling up the rocks, followed by fierce warriors with glittering helms and short broad two-edged swords; I thought I heard groans, cries of rage, and the dull, awful sound of bodies precipitated down rocks. Then as I looked towards the sea I thought I saw the fleet of Gryffith Ab Cynan steering from Ireland to Aber Menai, Gryffith the son of a fugitive king, born in Ireland in the Commot of Columbcille, Gryffith the frequently baffled, the often victorious; once a manacled prisoner sweating in the sun, in the market-place of Chester, eventually king of North Wales; Gryffith, who " though he loved well the trumpet's clang loved the sound of the harp better;" who led on his warriors to twenty-four battles, and presided over the composi-tion of the twenty-four measures of the Cambrian song. Then I thought—— But I should tire the reader were I to detail all the intensely Welsh thoughts, which crowded into my head as I stood on the Cairn of the Grey Giant.

Satiated with looking about and thinking, I sprang from the cairn and rejoined my guide. We now de-scended the eastern side of the hill till we came to a singular-looking stone, which had much the appearance of a Druid's stone. I inquired of my guide whether there was any tale connected with this stone.

" None," he replied; " but I have heard people say that it was a strange stone and on that account I brought you to look at it."

A little farther down he showed me part of a ruined wall.

" What name does this bear?" said I.

" Clawdd yr Afalon," he replied. " The dyke of the orchard."

" A strange place for an orchard," I replied. " If there was ever an orchard on this bleak hill, the apples must have been very sour."

Over rocks and stones we descended till we found ourselves on a road, not very far from the shore, on the south-east side of the hill.

" I am very thirsty," said I, as I wiped the perspiration from my face; " how I should like now to drink my fill of cool spring water."

" If your honour is inclined for water," said my guide, " I can take you to the finest spring in all Wales."

" Pray do so," said I, " for I really am dying of thirst."

" It is on our way to the town," said the lad, " and is scarcely a hundred yards off."

He then led me to the fountain. It was a little well under a stone wall, on the left side of the way. It might be about two feet deep, was fenced with rude stones, and had a bottom of sand.

" There," said the lad, " is the fountain. It is called the Fairies' well, and contains the best water in Wales."

I lay down and drank. O, what water was that of the Fairies' well! I drank and drank and thought I could never drink enough of that delicious water; the lad all the time saying that I need not be afraid to drink, as the water of the Fairies' well had never done harm to anybody. At length I got up, and standing by the fountain repeated the lines of a bard on a spring, not of a Welsh but a Gaelic bard, which are perhaps the finest lines ever composed on the theme. Yet Mac-Intyre, for such was his name, was like myself an admirer of good ale, to say nothing of whiskey, and loved to indulge in it at a proper time and place. But there is a time and place for everything, and sometimes the warmest admirer of ale would prefer the lymph of the hill-side fountain to the choicest ale that ever foamed in tankard from the cellars of Holkham. Here are the lines, most faithfully rendered :

> " The wild wine of nature,
> Honey-like in its taste,
> The genial, fair, thin element
> Filtering through the sands,
> Which is sweeter than cinnamon,
> And is well-known to us hunters.
> O, that eternal, healing draught,
> Which comes from under the earth,
> Which contains abundance of good
> And costs no money !"

Returning to the hotel I satisfied my guide and dined. After dinner I trifled agreeably with my brandy-and-water till it was near seven o'clock when I paid my bill, thought of the waiter and did not forget Father Boots. I then took my departure, receiving and returning bows, and walking to the station got into a first-class carriage and soon found myself at Bangor.

CHAPTER XLIII

The Inn at Bangor—Port Dyn Norwig—Sea Serpent—Thoroughly Welsh Place—Blessing of Health.

I WENT to the same inn at Bangor at which I had been before. It was Saturday night and the house was thronged with people, who had arrived by train from Manchester and Liverpool, with the intention of passing the Sunday in the Welsh town. I took tea in an immense dining or ball-room, which was, however, so crowded with guests that its walls literally sweated. Amidst the multitude I felt quite solitary—my beloved ones had departed for Llangollen, and there was no one with whom I could exchange a thought or a word of kindness. I addressed several individuals, and in every instance repented; from some I got no answers, from others what was worse than no answers at all—in every countenance near me suspicion, brutality, or conceit, was most legibly imprinted—I was not amongst Welsh, but the scum of manufacturing England.

Every bed in the house was engaged—the people of the house, however, provided me a bed at a place which they called the cottage, on the side of a hill in the outskirts of the town. There I passed the night comfortably enough. At about eight in the morning I arose, returned to the inn, breakfasted, and departed for Bethgelert by way of Caernarvon.

It was Sunday, and I had originally intended to pass the day at Bangor, and to attend divine service twice at the cathedral, but I found myself so very uncomfortable, owing to the crowd of interlopers, that I determined to proceed on my journey without delay; making up my mind, however, to enter the first church I should meet in which service was being performed; for it is really not good to travel on the Sunday without going into a place of worship.

The day was sunny and fiercely hot, as all the days had lately been. In about an hour I arrived at Port Dyn Norwig: it stood on the right side of the road. The name of this place, which I had heard from the coachman who drove my family and me to Caernarvon and Llanberis a few days before, had excited my curiosity in respect to it, as it signifies the Port of the Norway man, so I now turned aside to examine it. "No doubt," said I to myself, "the place derives its name from the piratical Danes and Norse having resorted to it in the old time." Port Dyn Norwig seems to consist of a creek, a staithe, and about a hundred houses : a few small vessels were lying at the staithe. I stood about ten minutes upon it staring about, and then feeling rather oppressed by the heat of the sun, I bent my way to a small house which bore a sign, and from which a loud noise of voices proceeded. "Have you good ale?" said I in English to a good-looking buxom dame, of about forty, whom I saw in the passage.

She looked at me but returned no answer.

"Oes genoch cwrw da?" said I.

"Oes!" she replied with a smile, and opening the door of a room on the left-hand bade me walk in.

I entered the room; six or seven men, seemingly

sea-faring people, were seated drinking and talking vociferously in Welsh. Their conversation was about the sea-serpent; some believed in the existence of such a thing, others did not—after a little time one said, " Let us ask this gentleman for his opinion."

" And what would be the use of asking him?" said another, " we have only Cumraeg, and he has only Saesneg."

" I have a little broken Cumraeg, at the service of this good company," said I. " With respect to the snake of the sea I beg leave to say that I believe in the existence of such a creature; and am surprised that any people in these parts should not believe in it; why, the sea-serpent has been seen in these parts."

" When was that, Gwr Bonneddig?" said one of the company.

" About fifty years ago," said I. " Once in October, in the year 1805, as a small vessel of the Traeth was upon the Menai, sailing very slowly, the weather being very calm, the people on board saw a strange creature like an immense worm swimming after them. It soon overtook them, climbed on board through the tiller-hole, and coiled itself on the deck under the mast—the people at first were dreadfully frightened, but taking courage they attacked it with an oar and drove it overboard; it followed the vessel for some time but a breeze springing up they lost sight of it."

" And how did you learn this?" said the last who had addressed me.

" I read the story," said I, " in a pure Welsh book called the *Greal*."

" I now remember hearing the same thing," said an old man, " when I was a boy; it had slipped out of my memory, but now I remember all about it. The ship was called the *Robert Ellis*. Are you of these parts, gentleman?"

" No," said I, " I am not of these parts."

" Then you are of South Wales—indeed your Welsh is very different from ours."

" I am not of South Wales," said I, " I am the seed not of the sea-snake but of the coiling serpent, for so one of the old Welsh poets called the Saxons."

" But how did you learn Welsh?" said the old man.

"I learned it by the grammar," said I, "a long time ago."

"Ah, you learnt it by the grammar," said the old man; "that accounts for your Welsh being different from ours. We did not learn our Welsh by the grammar—your Welsh is different from ours, and of course better, being the Welsh of the grammar. Ah, it is a fine thing to be a grammarian."

"Yes, it is a fine thing to be a grammarian," cried the rest of the company, and I observed that everybody now regarded me with a kind of respect.

A jug of ale which the hostess had brought me had been standing before me some time. I now tasted it and found it very good. Whilst dispatching it, I asked various questions about the old Danes, the reason why the place was called the port of the Norwegian, and about its trade. The good folks knew nothing about the old Danes, and as little as to the reason of its being called the port of the Norwegian—but they said that besides that name it bore that of Melin Heli, or the mill of the salt pool, and that slates were exported from thence, which came from quarries close by.

Having finished my ale I bade the company adieu and quitted Port Dyn Norwig, one of the most thoroughly Welsh places I had seen, for during the whole time I was in it, I heard no words of English uttered, except the two or three spoken by myself. In about an hour I reached Caernarvon.

The road from Bangor to Caernarvon is very good and the scenery interesting—fine hills border it on the left, or south-east, and on the right at some distance is the Menai with Anglesey beyond it. Not far from Caernarvon a sandbank commences, extending for miles up the Menai, towards Bangor, and dividing the strait into two.

I went to the Castle Inn which fronts the square or market-place, and being shown into a room ordered some brandy-and-water, and sat down. Two young men were seated in the room. I spoke to them and received civil answers, at which I was rather astonished, as I found by the tone of their voices that they were English. The air of one was far superior to that of the other, and with him I was soon in conversation.

In the course of discourse he informed me that being a martyr to ill-health he had come from London to Wales, hoping that change of air, and exercise on the Welsh hills, would afford him relief, and that his friend had been kind enough to accompany him. That he had been about three weeks in Wales, had taken all the exercise that he could, but that he was still very unwell, slept little and had no appetite. I told him not to be discouraged, but to proceed in the course which he had adopted till the end of the summer, by which time I thought it very probable that he would be restored to his health, as he was still young. At these words of mine a beam of hope brightened his countenance, and he said he had no other wish than to regain his health, and that if he did he should be the happiest of men. The intense wish of the poor young man for health caused me to think how insensible I had hitherto been to the possession of the greatest of all terrestrial blessings. I had always had the health of an elephant, but I never remember to have been sensible to the magnitude of the blessing or in the slightest degree grateful to the God who gave it. I shuddered to think how I should feel if suddenly deprived of my health. Far worse, no doubt, than that poor invalid. He was young, and in youth there is hope— but I was no longer young. At last, however, I thought that if God took away my health He might so far alter my mind that I might be happy even without health, or the prospect of it; and that reflection made me quite comfortable.

CHAPTER XLIV

National School—The Young Preacher—Pont Bettws—Spanish Words—Two Tongues, Two Faces—The Elephant's Snout—Llyn Cwellyn—The Snowdon Ranger—My House—Castell y Cidwm—Descent to Bethgelert.

IT might be about three o'clock in the afternoon when I left Caernarvon for Bethgelert, distant about thirteen miles. I journeyed through a beautiful country of hill and dale, woods and meadows, the whole gilded by abundance of sunshine. After walking about an hour

without intermission I reached a village, and asked a
man the name of it.

" Llan—— something," he replied.

As he was standing before a long building, through
the open door of which a sound proceeded like that of
preaching, I asked him what place it was, and what
was going on in it, and received for answer that it was
the National School, and that there was a clergyman
preaching in it. I then asked if the clergyman was of
the Church, and on learning that he was, I forthwith
entered the building, where in one end of a long room
I saw a young man in a white surplice preaching from
a desk to about thirty or forty people, who were seated
on benches before him. I sat down and listened. The
young man preached with great zeal and fluency. The
sermon was a very seasonable one, being about the
harvest, and in it things temporal and spiritual were
very happily blended. The part of the sermon which
I heard—I regretted that I did not hear the whole—
lasted about five-and-twenty minutes : a hymn followed,
and then the congregation broke up. I inquired the name
of the young man who preached, and was told that it
was Edwards, and that he came from Caernarvon.
The name of the incumbent of the parish was Thomas.

Leaving the village of the harvest sermon, I proceeded on my way, which lay to the south-east. I was
now drawing nigh to the mountainous district of Eryri
—a noble hill called Mount Eilio appeared before me
to the north; an immense mountain called Pen Drws
Coed lay over against it on the south, just like a
couchant elephant, with its head lower than the top of
its back. After a time, I entered a most beautiful sunny
valley, and presently came to a bridge over a pleasant
stream running in the direction of the south. As I
stood upon that bridge, I almost fancied myself in
paradise; everything looked so beautiful or grand—
green, sunny meadows lay all around me, intersected
by the brook, the waters of which ran with tinkling
laughter over a shingley bottom. Noble Eilio to the
north; enormous Pen Drws Coed to the south; a tall
mountain far beyond them to the east. " I never was in
such a lovely spot !" I cried to myself in a perfect
rapture. " O, how glad I should be to learn the name

of this bridge, standing on which I have had 'heaven opened to me,' as my old friends the Spaniards used to say.'' Scarcely had I said these words, when I observed a man and a woman coming towards the bridge from the direction in which I was bound. I hastened to meet them, in the hope of obtaining information; they were both rather young, and were probably a couple of sweethearts taking a walk, or returning from meeting. The woman was a few steps in advance of the man; seeing that I was about to address her, she averted her head and quickened her steps, and before I had completed the question, which I put to her in Welsh, she had bolted past me screaming, "Ah Dim Saesneg," and was several yards distant.

I then addressed myself to the man, who had stopped, asking him the name of the bridge.

"Pont Bettws," he replied.

"And what may be the name of the river?" said I.

"Afon—— something," said he.

And on my thanking him, he went forward to the woman, who was waiting for him by the bridge.

"Is that man Welsh or English?" I heard her say when he had rejoined her.

"I don't know," said the man—"he was civil enough; why were you such a fool?"

"O, I thought he would speak to me in English," said the woman, "and the thought of that horrid English puts me into such a flutter; you know I can't speak a word of it."

They proceeded on their way, and I proceeded on mine, and presently coming to a little inn on the left side of the way, at the entrance of a village, I went in.

A respectable-looking man and woman were seated at tea at a table in a nice clean kitchen. I sat down on a chair near the table, and called for ale—the ale was brought me in a jug—I drank some, put the jug on the table, and began to discourse with the people in Welsh—a handsome dog was seated on the ground; suddenly it laid one of its paws on its master's knee.

"Down, Perro," said he.

"Perro!" said I; "why do you call the dog Perro?"

"We call him Perro," said the man, "because his name is Perro."

" But how came you to give him that name?"
said I.

" We did not give it to him," said the man—" he
bore that name when he came into our hands; a farmer
gave him to us when he was very young, and told us
his name was Perro."

" And how came the farmer to call him Perro?"
said I.

" I don't know," said the man—" why do you ask?"

" Perro," said I, " is a Spanish word, and signifies
a dog in general. I am rather surprised that a dog in
the mountains of Wales should be called by the
Spanish word for dog." I fell into a fit of musing.
" How Spanish words are diffused! Wherever you go
you will find some Spanish word or other in use. I have
heard Spanish words used by Russian mujiks, and
Turkish fig-gatherers—I have this day heard a Spanish
word in the mountains of Wales, and I have no doubt
that were I to go to Iceland I should find Spanish
words used there. How can I doubt it? when I reflect
that more than six hundred years ago, one of the
words to denote a bad woman was Spanish. In the
oldest of Icelandic domestic sagas, Skarphedin, the son
of Nial the seer, called Hallgerdr, widow of Gunnar,
a puta—and that word so maddened Hallgerdr, that she
never rested till she had brought about his destruction.
Now, why this preference everywhere for Spanish
words, over those of every other language? I never
heard French words or German words used by Russian
mujiks and Turkish fig-gatherers. I question whether
I should find any in Iceland forming part of the ver-
nacular. I certainly never found a French or even a
German word in an old Icelandic saga. Why this par-
tiality everywhere for Spanish words? the question is
puzzling; at any rate it puts me out——"

" Yes, it puts me out!" I exclaimed aloud, striking
my fist on the table with a vehemence which caused
the good folks to start half up from their seats—before
they could say anything, however, a vehicle drove up
to the door, and a man, getting out, came into the
room. He had a glazed hat on his head, and was
dressed something like the guard of a mail. He touched
his hat to me, and called for a glass of whiskey. I gave

him the sele of the evening, and entered into conversation with him in English. In the course of discourse I learned that he was the postman, and was going his rounds in his cart—he was more than respectful to me, he was fawning and sycophantic. The whiskey was brought, and he stood with the glass in his hand. Suddenly he began speaking Welsh to the people; before, however, he had uttered two sentences, the woman lifted her hands with an alarmed air, crying " Hush ! he understands." The fellow was turning me to ridicule. I flung my head back, closed my eyes, opened my mouth, and laughed aloud. The fellow stood aghast; his hand trembled, and he spilt the greater part of the whiskey upon the ground. At the end of about half-a-minute I got up, asked what I had to pay, and on being told two pence, I put down the money. Then going up to the man, I put my right fore-finger very near to his nose, and said, " Dwy o iaith dwy o wyneb; two languages, two faces, friend !" Then after leering at him for a moment, I wished the people of the house good evening, and departed.

Walking rapidly on towards the east, I soon drew near the termination of the valley. The valley terminates in a deep gorge, or pass, between Mount Eilio —which, by the bye, is part of the chine of Snowdon— and Pen Drws Coed. The latter, that couchant elephant with its head turned to the north-east, seems as if it wished to bar the pass with its trunk; by its trunk I mean a kind of jaggy ridge which descends down to the road. I entered the gorge, passing near a little waterfall which with much noise runs down the precipitous side of Mount Eilio—presently I came to a little mill by the side of a brook running towards the east. I asked the miller-woman, who was standing near the mill, with her head turned towards the setting sun, the name of the mill and the stream. " The mill is called the mill of the river of Lake Cwellyn," said she, " and the river is called the river of Lake Cwellyn."

" And who owns the land?" said I.

" Sir Richard," said she. " I Sir Richard yw yn perthyn y tîr. Mr. Williams, however, possesses some part of Mount Eilio."

" And who is Mr. Williams?" said I.

"Who is Mr. Williams?" said the miller's wife.
"Ho, ho! what a stranger you must be to ask me
who is Mr. Williams."

I smiled and passed on. The mill was below the
level of the road, and its wheel was turned by the
water of a little conduit supplied by the brook at some
distance above the mill. I had observed similar conduits
employed for similar purposes in Cornwall. A little
below the mill was a weir, and a little below the weir
the river ran frothing past the extreme end of the
elephant's snout. Following the course of the river, I
at last emerged with it from the pass into a valley
surrounded by enormous mountains. Extending along
it from west to east, and occupying its entire southern
part, lay an oblong piece of water, into which the
streamlet of the pass discharged itself. This was one
of the many beautiful lakes, which a few days before
I had seen from the Wyddfa. As for the Wyddfa, I
now beheld it high above me in the north-east, looking
very grand indeed, shining like a silver helmet whilst
catching the glories of the setting sun.

I proceeded slowly along the road, the lake below
me on my right hand, whilst the shelvy side of Snowdon
rose above me on the left. The evening was calm and
still, and no noise came upon my ear save the sound of
a cascade falling into the lake from a black mountain,
which frowned above it on the south, and cast a gloomy
shadow far over it.

This cataract was in the neighbourhood of a singular-
looking rock, projecting above the lake from the mountain's side. I wandered a considerable way without
meeting or seeing a single human being. At last, when
I had nearly gained the eastern end of the valley, I
saw two men seated on the side of the hill, on the verge
of the road, in the vicinity of a house which stood a
little way up the hill. The lake here was much wider
than I had hitherto seen it, for the huge mountain on
the south had terminated, and the lake expanded considerably in that quarter, having instead of the black
mountain a beautiful hill beyond it.

I quickened my steps, and soon came up to the two
individuals. One was an elderly man, dressed in a
smock frock, and with a hairy cap on his head. The

other was much younger, wore a hat, and was dressed in a coarse suit of blue, nearly new, and doubtless his Sunday's best. He was smoking a pipe. I greeted them in English, and sat down near them. They responded in the same language, the younger man with considerable civility and briskness, the other in a tone of voice denoting some reserve.

"May I ask the name of this lake?" said I, addressing myself to the young man, who sat between me and the elderly one.

"Its name is Llyn Cwellyn, sir," said he, taking the pipe out of his mouth. "And a fine lake it is."

"Plenty of fish in it?" I demanded.

"Plenty, sir; plenty of trout and pike and char."

"Is it deep?" said I.

"Near the shore it is shallow, sir, but in the middle and near the other side it is deep, so deep that no one knows how deep it is."

"What is the name," said I, "of the great black mountain there on the other side?"

"It is called Mynydd Mawr, or the Great Mountain. Yonder rock, which bulks out from it, down the lake yonder, and which you passed as you came along, is called Castell Cidwm, which means Wolf's rock or castle."

"Did a wolf ever live there?" I demanded.

"Perhaps so," said the man, "for I have heard say that there were wolves of old in Wales."

"And what is the name of the beautiful hill yonder, before us across the water?"

"That, sir, is called Cairn Drws y Coed," said the man.

"The stone heap of the gate of the wood," said I.

"Are you Welsh, sir?" said the man.

"No," said I, "but I know something of the language of Wales. I suppose you live in that house?"

"Not exactly, sir; my father-in-law here lives in that house, and my wife with him. I am a miner, and spend six days in the week at my mine, but every Sunday I come here, and pass the day with my wife and him."

"And what profession does he follow?" said I; "is he a fisherman?"

"Fisherman!" said the elderly man contemptuously, "not I. I am the Snowdon Ranger."

"And what is that?" said I.

The elderly man tossed his head proudly, and made no reply.

"A ranger means a guide, sir," said the younger man—"my father-in-law is generally termed the Snowdon Ranger because he is a tip-top guide, and he has named the house after him the Snowdon Ranger. He entertains gentlemen in it who put themselves under his guidance in order to ascend Snowdon and to see the country."

"There is some difference in your professions," said I; "he deals in heights, you in depths; both, however, are break-necky trades."

"I run more risk from gunpowder than anything else," said the younger man. "I am a slate-miner, and am continually blasting. I have, however, had my falls. Are you going far to-night, sir?"

"I am going to Bethgelert," said I.

"A good six miles, sir, from here. Do you come from Caernarvon?"

"Farther than that," said I. "I come from Bangor."

"To-day, sir, and walking?"

"To-day, and walking."

"You must be rather tired, sir; you came along the valley very slowly."

"I am not in the slightest degree tired," said I; "when I start from here, I shall put on my best pace, and soon get to Bethgelert."

"Anybody can get along over level ground," said the old man, laconically.

"Not with equal swiftness," said I. "I do assure you, friend, to be able to move at a good swinging pace over level ground is something not to be sneezed at. Not," said I, lifting up my voice, "that I would for a moment compare walking on the level ground to mountain ranging, pacing along the road to springing up crags like a mountain goat, or assert that even Powell himself, the first of all road walkers, was entitled to so bright a wreath of fame as the Snowdon Ranger."

" Won't you walk in, sir?" said the elderly man.

" No, I thank you," said I; " I prefer sitting out here, gazing on the lake and the noble mountains."

" I wish you would, sir," said the elderly man, " and take a glass of something; I will charge you nothing."

" Thank you," said I—" I am in want of nothing, and shall presently start. Do many people ascend Snowdon from your house?"

" Not so many as I could wish," said the ranger; " people in general prefer ascending Snowdon from that trumpery place Bethgelert; but those who do are fools—begging your honour's pardon. The place to ascend Snowdon from is my house. The way from my house up Snowdon is wonderful for the romantic scenery which it affords; that from Bethgelert can't be named in the same day with it for scenery; moreover, from my house you may have the best guide in Wales; whereas the guides of Bethgelert—but I say nothing. If your honour is bound for the Wyddfa, as I suppose you are, you had better start from my house to-morrow under my guidance."

" I have already been up the Wyddfa from Llanberis," said I, " and am now going through Bethgelert to Llangollen, where my family are; were I going up Snowdon again, I should most certainly start from your house under your guidance, and were I not in a hurry at present, I would certainly take up my quarters here for a week, and every day make excursions with you into the recesses of Eryri. I suppose you are acquainted with all the secrets of the hills?"

" Trust the old ranger for that, your honour. I would show your honour the black lake in the frightful hollow, in which the fishes have monstrous heads and little bodies, the lake on which neither swan, duck nor any kind of wildfowl was ever seen to light. Then I would show your honour the fountain of the hopping creatures, where, where——"

" Were you ever at that Wolf's crag, that Castell y Cidwm?" said I.

" Can't say I ever was, your honour. You see it lies so close by, just across the lake, that——"

" You thought you could see it any day, and so never

went," said I. "Can you tell me whether there are any ruins upon it?"

"I can't, your honour."

"I shouldn't wonder," said I, "if in old times it was the stronghold of some robber-chieftain; cidwm in the old Welsh is frequently applied to a ferocious man. Castell Cidwm, I should think, rather ought to be translated the robber's castle, than the wolf's rock. If I ever come into these parts again, you and I will visit it together, and see what kind of a place it is. Now farewell! It is getting late." I then departed.

"What a nice gentleman!" said the younger man, when I was a few yards distant.

"I never saw a nicer gentleman," said the old ranger.

I sped along, Snowdon on my left, the lake on my right, and the tip of a mountain peak right before me in the east. After a little time I looked back; what a scene! The silver lake and the shadowy mountain over its southern side looking now, methought, very much like Gibraltar. I lingered and lingered, gazing and gazing, and at last only by an effort tore myself away. The evening had now become delightfully cool in this land of wonders. On I sped, passing by two noisy brooks coming from Snowdon to pay tribute to the lake. And now I had left the lake and the valley behind, and was ascending a hill. As I gained its summit, up rose the moon to cheer my way. In a little time, a wild stony gorge confronted me, a stream ran down the gorge with hollow roar, a bridge lay across it. I asked a figure whom I saw standing by the bridge the place's name. "Rhyd du"—the black ford—I crossed the bridge. The voice of the Methodist was yelling from a little chapel on my left. I went to the door and listened: "When the sinner takes hold of God, God takes hold of the sinner." The voice was frightfully hoarse. I passed on; night fell fast around me, and the mountain to the south-east, towards which I was tending, looked blackly grand. And now I came to a milestone, on which I read with difficulty: "Three miles to Bethgelert." The way for some time had been upward, but now it was downward. I reached a torrent, which, coming from the north-west, rushed under a bridge, over which I passed. The torrent attended me on my right hand the whole way to Bethgelert. The descent now became very rapid. I passed a pine wood on my left, and proceeded for more than two miles at a tremendous rate. I then came to a wood —this wood was just above Bethgelert—proceeding in the direction of a black mountain, I found myself amongst houses, at the bottom of a valley. I passed over a bridge, and inquiring of some people, whom I met, the way to the inn, was shown an edifice brilliantly lighted up, which I entered.

CHAPTER XLV

Inn at Bethgelert—Delectable Company—Lieutenant P——.

THE inn, or hotel, at Bethgelert, was a large and commodious building, and was anything but thronged with company; what company, however, there was, was disagreeable enough, perhaps more so than that in which I had been the preceding evening, which was composed of the scum of Manchester and Liverpool; the company amongst which I now was consisted of some seven or eight individuals, two of them were military puppies, one a tallish fellow, who, though evidently upwards of thirty, affected the airs of a languishing girl, and would fain have made people believe that he was dying of ennui and lassitude. The other was a short spuddy fellow, with a broad, ugly face, and with spectacles on his nose, who talked very consequentially about "the service" and all that, but whose tone of voice was coarse, and his manner that of an under-bred person; then there was an old fellow about sixty-five, a civilian, with a red, carbuncled face; he was father of the spuddy military puppy, on whom he occasionally cast eyes of pride and almost adoration, and whose sayings he much applauded, especially certain double entendres, to call them by no harsher term, directed to a fat girl, weighing some fifteen stone, who officiated in the coffee-room as waiter. Then there was a creature to do justice to whose appearance would require the pencil of a Hogarth. He was about five feet three inches and a quarter high, and might have weighed, always provided a stone weight had been attached to him, about half as much as the fat girl. His countenance was cadaverous, and was eternally agitated by something between a grin and a simper. He was dressed in a style of superfine gentility, and his skeleton fingers were bedizened with tawdry rings. His conversation was chiefly about his bile and his secretions, the efficacy of licorice in producing a certain effect, and the expediency of changing one's linen at least three times a day; though had he changed his six I should have said that the purification of the last shirt would have been no sinecure to the laundress. His accent was decidedly Scotch : he spoke familiarly of Scott, and one or two other Scotch worthies, and more than once insinuated that he was a member of Parliament. With respect to the rest of the company I say nothing, and for the very sufficient reason that, unlike the above described batch, they did not seem disposed to be impertinent towards me.

Eager to get out of such society, I retired early to bed. As I left the room the diminutive Scotch individual was describing to the old simpleton, who, on the ground of the other's being a " member," was listening to him with extreme attention, how he was labouring under an excess of bile, owing to his having left his licorice somewhere or other. I passed a quiet night, and in the morning breakfasted, paid my bill, and departed. As I went out of the coffee-room, the spuddy, broad-faced military puppy with spectacles was vociferating to the languishing military puppy, and to his old simpleton of a father, who was listening to him with his usual look of undisguised admiration, about the absolute necessity of kicking Lieutenant P—— out of the army for having disgraced " the service." Poor P——, whose only crime was trying to defend himself with fist and candlestick from the manual attacks of his brutal messmates.

CHAPTER XLVI

The Valley of Gelert—Legend of the Dog—Magnificent Scenery—
The Knicht—Goats in Wales—The Frightful Crag—Temperance House—Smile and Curtsey.

BETHGELERT is situated in a valley surrounded by huge
hills, the most remarkable of which are Moel Hebog
and Cerrig Llan; the former fences it on the south, and
the latter, which is quite black and nearly perpendicular,
on the east. A small stream rushes through the valley,
and sallies forth by a pass at its south-eastern end.
The valley is said by some to derive its name of Bedd-
gelert, which signifies the grave of Celert, from being
the burial-place of Celert, a British saint of the sixth
century, to whom Llangeler in Carmarthenshire is
believed to have been consecrated; but the popular and
most universally received tradition is that it has its
name from being the resting-place of a faithful dog
called Celert, or Gelert, killed by his master, the warlike and celebrated Llewelyn ab Jorweith, from an
unlucky misapprehension. Though the legend is known
to most people, I shall take the liberty of relating it.
Llywelyn, during his contests with the English, had
encamped with a few followers in the valley, and one
day departed with his men on an expedition, leaving his
infant son in a cradle in his tent, under the care of his
hound Gelert, after giving the child its fill of goat's
milk. Whilst he was absent, a wolf from the neighbouring mountains, in quest of prey, found its way
into the tent, and was about to devour the child, when
the watchful dog interfered, and after a desperate conflict, in which the tent was torn down, succeeded in
destroying the monster. Llywelyn, returning at evening, found the tent on the ground, and the dog, covered
with blood, sitting beside it. Imagining that the blood
with which Gelert was besmeared was that of his own
son, devoured by the animal to whose care he had con-
fided him, Llewelyn, in a paroxysm of natural indignation, forthwith transfixed the faithful creature with his
spear. Scarcely, however, had he done so, when his
ears were startled by the cry of a child from beneath

the fallen tent, and hastily removing the canvas, he found the child in its cradle quite uninjured, and the body of an enormous wolf, frightfully torn and mangled, lying near. His breast was now filled with conflicting emotions; joy for the preservation of his son, and grief for the fate of his dog, to whom he forthwith hastened. The poor animal was not quite dead, but presently expired, in the act of licking its master's hand. Llywelyn mourned over him as over a brother, buried him with funeral honours in the valley, and erected a tomb over him as over a hero. From that time the valley was called Bethgelert.

Such is the legend, which, whether true or fictitious, is singularly beautiful and affecting.

The tomb, or what is said to be the tomb, of Gelert, stands in a beautiful meadow just below the precipitous side of Cerrig Llan; it consists of a large slab lying on its side, and two upright stones. It is shaded by a weeping willow, and is surrounded by a hexagonal paling. Who is there acquainted with the legend, whether he believes that the dog lies beneath those stones or not, can visit them without exclaiming, with a sigh, " Poor Gelert !"

After wandering about the valley for some time, and seeing a few of its wonders, I inquired my way for Festiniog, and set off for that place. The way to it is through the pass at the south-east end of the valley. Arrived at the entrance of the pass, I turned round to look at the scenery I was leaving behind me; the view which presented itself to my eyes was very grand and beautiful. Before me lay the meadow of Gelert, with the river flowing through it towards the pass. Beyond the meadow the Snowdon range; on the right the mighty Cerrig Llan; on the left the equally mighty, but not quite so precipitous, Hebog. Truly, the valley of Gelert is a wondrous valley—rivalling for grandeur and beauty any vale either in the Alps or Pyrenees. After a long and earnest view, I turned round again, and proceeded on my way.

Presently I came to a bridge bestriding the stream, which a man told me was called Pont Aber Glâs Lyn, or the bridge of the debouchement of the grey lake. I soon emerged from the pass, and after proceeding some way, stopped again to admire the scenery. To the west was the Wyddfa; full north was a stupendous range of rocks; behind them a conical peak, seemingly rivalling the Wyddfa itself in altitude; between the rocks and the road, where I stood, was beautiful forest scenery. I again went on, going round the side of a hill by a gentle ascent. After a little time I again stopped to look about me. There was the rich forest scenery to the north, behind it were the rocks, and behind the rocks rose the wonderful conical hill impaling heaven; confronting it to the south-east was a huge lumpish hill. As I stood looking about me, I saw a man coming across a field which sloped down to the road from a small house. He presently reached me, stopped and smiled. A more open countenance than his I never saw in all the days of my life.

" Dydd dachwi, sir," said the man of the open countenance, " the weather is very showy."

" Very showy, indeed," said I; " I was just now wishing for somebody, of whom I might ask a question or two."

" Perhaps I can answer those questions, sir?"

" Perhaps you can. What is the name of that wonderful peak sticking up behind the rocks to the north?"

" Many people have asked that question, sir, and I have given them the answer which I now give you. It is called the ' Knicht,' sir; and a wondrous hill it is."

" And what is the name of yonder hill opposite to it, to the south, rising like one big lump?"

" I do not know the name of that hill, sir, farther than that I have heard it called the Great Hill."

" And a very good name for it," said I; " do you live in that house?"

" I do, sir, when I am at home."

" And what occupation do you follow?"

" I am a farmer, though a small one."

" Is your farm your own?"

" It is not, sir; I am not so far rich."

" Who is your landlord?"

" Mr. Blicklin, sir. He is my landlord."

" Is he a good landlord?"

" Very good, sir; no one can wish for a better landlord."

"Has he a wife?"

"In truth, sir, he has; and a very good wife she is."

"Has he children?"

"Plenty, sir; and very fine children they are."

"Is he Welsh?"

"He is, sir! Cumro pur iawn."

"Farewell," said I; "I shall never forget you; you are the first tenant I ever heard speak well of his landlord, or any one connected with him."

"Then you have not spoken to the other tenants of Mr. Blicklin, sir. Every tenant of Mr. Blicklin would say the same of him as I have said, and of his wife and his children too. Good day, sir!"

I wended on my way; the sun was very powerful; saw cattle in a pool on my right, maddened with heat and flies, splashing and fighting. Presently I found myself with extensive meadows on my right, and a wall of rocks on my left, on a lofty bank below which I saw goats feeding; beautiful creatures they were, white and black, with long, silky hair, and long, upright horns. They were of large size, and very different in appearance from the common race. These were the first goats which I had seen in Wales; for Wales is not at present the land of goats, whatever it may have been.

I passed under a crag, exceedingly lofty, and of very frightful appearance. It hung menacingly over the road. With this crag the wall of rocks terminated; beyond it lay an extensive strath, meadow, or marsh, bounded on the east by a lofty hill. The road lay across the marsh. I went forward, crossed a bridge over a beautiful streamlet, and soon arrived at the foot of the hill. The road now took a turn to the right, that is, to the south, and seemed to lead round the hill. Just at the turn of the road stood a small, neat cottage. There was a board over the door with an inscription. I drew nigh and looked at it, expecting that it would tell me that good ale was sold within, and read "Tea made here, the draught which cheers but not inebriates." I was before what is generally termed a temperance house.

"The bill of fare does not tempt you, sir," said a woman, who made her appearance at the door, just as I was about to turn away with an exceedingly wry face.

" It does not," said I, " and you ought to be ashamed
of yourself to have nothing better to offer a traveller
than a cup of tea. I am faint; and I want good ale to
give me heart, not wishy-washy tea to take away the
little strength I have."

" What would you have me do, sir? Glad should
I be to have a cup of ale to offer you, but the magistrates, when I applied to them for a license, refused
me one; so I am compelled to make a cup of tea in
order to get a crust of bread. And if you choose to
step in, I will make you a cup of tea, not wishy-washy,
I assure you, but as good as ever was brewed."

" I had tea for my breakfast at Bethgelert," said
I, " and want no more till to-morrow morning. What's
the name of that strange-looking crag across the
valley?"

" We call it Craig yr hyll ddrem, sir; which
means—— I don't know what it means in English."

" Does it mean the Crag of the frightful look?"

" It does, sir," said the woman; " ah, I see you
understand Welsh. Sometimes it is called Allt Tracth."

" The high place of the sandy channel," said I.
" Did the sea ever come up here?"

" I can't say, sir; perhaps it did; who knows?'

" I shouldn't wonder," said I, " if there was once an
arm of the sea between that crag and this hill. Thank
you! Farewell!"

" Then you won't walk in, sir?"

" Not to drink tea," said I; " tea is a good thing at
a proper time, but were I to drink it now it would make
me ill."

" Pray, sir, walk in," said the woman, " and perhaps
I can accommodate you."

" Then you have ale?" said I.

" No, sir; not a drop; but perhaps I can set something before you which you will like as well."

" That I question," said I; " however, I will walk
in."

The woman conducted me into a nice little parlour,
and, leaving me, presently returned with a bottle and
tumbler on a tray.

" Here, sir," said she, " is something which, though
not ale, I hope you will be able to drink."

" What is it?" said I.

" It is——, sir; and better never was drunk."

I tasted it; it was terribly strong. Those who wish for either whiskey or brandy far above proof should always go to a temperance house.

I told the woman to bring me some water, and she brought me a jug of water cold from the spring. With a little of the contents of the bottle, and a deal of the contents of the jug, I made myself a beverage tolerable enough; a poor substitute, however, to a genuine Englishman for his proper drink, the liquor which, according to the Edda, is called by men ale, and by the gods, beer.

I asked the woman whether she could read; she told me that she could, both Welsh and English; she likewise informed me that she had several books in both languages. I begged her to show me some, whereupon she brought me some half-dozen, and placing them on the table, left me to myself. Amongst the books was a volume of poems in Welsh, written by Robert Williams of Betws Fawr, styled in poetic language, Gwilym Du O Eifion. The poems were chiefly on religious subjects. The following lines, which I copied from " Pethau a wnaed mewn Gardd," or things written in a garden, appeared to me singularly beautiful :—

> " Mewn gardd y cafodd dyn ei dwyllo;
> Mewn gardd y rhoed oddewid iddo;
> Mewn gardd bradychwyd Iesu hawddgar;
> Mewn gardd amdowyd ef mewn daeär."

> " In a garden the first of our race was deceived;
> In a garden the promise of grace he received;
> In a garden was Jesus betray'd to His doom;
> In a garden His body was laid in the tomb."

Having finished my glass of " summut " and my translation, I called to the woman and asked her what I had to pay.

" Nothing," said she; " if you had had a cup of tea I should have charged sixpence."

" You make no charge," said I, " for what I have had."

" Nothing, sir; nothing."

" But suppose," said I, " I were to give you something by way of present, would you——" and here I stopped.

The woman smiled.

" Would you fling it in my face?" said I.

" O dear, no, sir," said the woman, smiling more than before.

I gave her something—it was not a sixpence—at which she not only smiled, but curtseyed; then bidding her farewell I went out of the door.

I was about to take the broad road, which led round the hill, when she inquired of me where I was going, and on my telling her to Festiniog, she advised me to go by a by-road behind the house, which led over the hill.

" If you do, sir," said she, " you will see some of the finest prospects in Wales, get into the high road again, and save a mile and a half of way."

I told the temperance woman I would follow her advice, whereupon she led me behind the house, pointed to a rugged path, which with a considerable ascent seemed to lead towards the north, and after giving certain directions, not very intelligible, returned to her temperance temple.

CHAPTER XLVII

Spanish Proverb—The Short Cut—Predestination—Rhys Goch—
Old Crusty—Undercharging—The Cavalier.

THE Spaniards have a proverb : " No hay atajo sin trabajo," there is no short cut without a deal of labour. This proverb is very true, as I know by my own experience, for I never took a short cut in my life, and I have taken many in my wanderings, without falling down, getting into a slough, or losing my way. On the present occasion I lost my way, and wandered about for nearly two hours amidst rocks, thickets, and precipices, without being able to find it. The temperance woman, however, spoke nothing but the truth, when she said I should see some fine scenery. From a rock I obtained a wonderful view of the Wyddfa towering in sublime grandeur in the west, and of the beautiful, but spectral, Knicht shooting up high in the north; and from the top of a bare hill I obtained a prospect to the south, noble indeed—waters, forests, hoary mountains, and in the far distance the sea. But all these fine prospects were a poor compensation for what I underwent: I was scorched by the sun, which was insufferably hot, and my feet were bleeding from the sharp points of the rocks, which cut through my boots like razors. At length, coming to a stone wall, I flung myself down under it, and almost thought that I should give up the ghost. After some time, however, I recovered, and, getting up, tried to find my way out of the anialwch. Sheer good fortune caused me to stumble upon a path, by following which I came to a lone farm-house, where a good-natured woman gave me certain directions, by means of which I at last got out of the hot, stony wilderness—for such it was—upon a smooth, royal road.

"Trust me again taking any short cuts," said I, "after the specimen I have just had." This, however, I had frequently said before, and have said since after taking short cuts—and probably shall often say again before I come to my great journey's end.

I turned to the east, which I knew to be my proper direction, and being now on smooth ground, put my legs to their best speed. The road by a rapid descent conducted me to a beautiful valley, with a small town at its southern end. I soon reached the town, and on inquiring its name, found I was in Tan y Bwlch, which interpreted signifieth " Below the Pass." Feeling much exhausted, I entered the Grapes Inn.

On my calling for brandy-and-water, I was shown into a handsome parlour. The brandy-and-water soon restored the vigour which I had lost in the wilderness. In the parlour was a serious-looking gentleman, with a glass of something before him. With him, as I sipped my brandy-and-water, I got into discourse. The discourse soon took a religious turn, and terminated in a dispute. He told me he believed in Divine predestination; I told him I did not, but that I believed in divine prescience. He asked me whether I hoped to be saved; I told him I did, and asked him whether he hoped to be saved. He told me he did not, and as he said so, he

tapped with a silver tea-spoon on the rim of his glass.
I said that he seemed to take very coolly the prospect
of damnation; he replied that it was of no use taking
what was inevitable otherwise than coolly. I asked
him on what ground he imagined he should be lost;
he replied on the ground of being predestined to be
lost. I asked him how he knew he was predestined to
be lost; whereupon he asked me how I knew I was to
be saved; I told him I did not know I was to be saved,
but trusted I should be so by belief in Christ, who
came into the world to save sinners, and that if he
believed in Christ he might be as easily saved as myself,
or any other sinner who believed in Him. Our dispute
continued a considerable time longer; at last, finding
him silent, and having finished my brandy-and-water,
I got up, rang the bell, paid for what I had had, and
left him looking very miserable, perhaps at finding that
he was not quite so certain of eternal damnation as he
had hitherto supposed. There can be no doubt that the
idea of damnation is anything but disagreeable to some
people; it gives them a kind of gloomy consequence in
their own eyes. We must be something particular,
they think, or God would hardly think it worth His
while to torment us for ever.

I inquired the way to Festiniog, and finding that I
had passed by it on my way to the town, I went back,
and, as directed, turned to the east up a wide pass,
down which flowed a river. I soon found myself in
another and very noble valley intersected by the river,
which was fed by numerous streams rolling down the
sides of the hills. The road which I followed in the
direction of the east, lay on the southern side of the
valley, and led upward by a steep ascent. On I went,
a mighty hill close on my right. My mind was full of
enthusiastic fancies; I was approaching Festiniog, the
birthplace of Rhys Goch, who styled himself Rhys Goch
of Eryri, or Red Rhys of Snowdon, a celebrated bard,
and a partisan of Owen Glendower, who lived to an
immense age, and who, as I had read, was in the habit
of composing his pieces seated on a stone which formed
part of a Druidical circle, for which reason the stone
was called the chair of Rhys Goch; yes, my mind was
full of enthusiastic fancies, all connected with this Rhys

Goch, and as I went along slowly I repeated stanzas of furious war songs of his, exciting his countrymen to exterminate the English, and likewise snatches of an abusive ode composed by him against a fox who had run away with his favourite peacock, a piece so abounding with hard words, that it was termed the Drunkard's chokepear, as no drunkard was ever able to recite it, and ever and anon I wished I could come in contact with some native of the region, with whom I could talk about Rhys Goch, and who could tell me whereabouts stood his chair.

Strolling along in this manner, I was overtaken by an old fellow with a stick in his hand, walking very briskly. He had a crusty, and rather conceited look. I spoke to him in Welsh, and he answered in English, saying that I need not trouble myself by speaking Welsh, as he had plenty of English, and of the very best. We were from first to last at cross purposes. I asked him about Rhys Goch and his chair. He told me that he knew nothing of either, and began to talk of Her Majesty's ministers, and the fine sights of London. I asked him the name of a stream which, descending a gorge on our right, ran down the side of a valley, to join the river at its bottom. He told me that he did not know, and asked me the name of the Queen's eldest daughter. I told him I did not know, and remarked that it was very odd that he could not tell me the name of a stream in his own vale. He replied that it was not a bit more odd than that I could not tell him the name of the eldest daughter of the Queen of England; I told him that when I was in Wales I wanted to talk about Welsh matters, and he told me that when he was with English he wanted to talk about English matters. I returned to the subject of Rhys Goch and his chair, and he returned to the subject of Her Majesty's ministers, and the fine folks of London. I told him that I cared not a straw about Her Majesty's ministers and the fine folks of London, and he replied that he cared not a straw for Rhys Goch, his chair, or old women's stories of any kind.

Regularly incensed against the old fellow, I told him he was a bad Welshman, and he retorted by saying I was a bad Englishman. I said he appeared to know next to nothing. He retorted by saying I knew less than nothing, and, almost inarticulate with passion, added that he scorned to walk in such illiterate company, and suiting the action to the word, sprang up a steep and rocky footpath on the right, probably a short cut to his domicile, and was out of sight in a twinkling. We were both wrong; I most so. He was crusty and conceited, but I ought to have humoured him, and then I might have got out of him anything he knew, always supposing that he knew anything.

About an hour's walk from Tan y Bwlch brought me to Festiniog, which is situated on the top of a lofty hill looking down from the south-east, on the valley which I have described, and which, as I know not its name, I shall style the Valley of the numerous streams. I went to the inn, a large old-fashioned house, standing near the church; the mistress of it was a queer-looking old woman, antiquated in her dress, and rather blunt in her manner. Of her, after ordering dinner, I made inquiries respecting the chair of Rhys Goch, but she said that she had never heard of such a thing; and after glancing at me askew for a moment, with a curiously formed left eye which she had, went away muttering chair, chair, leaving me in a large and rather dreary parlour, to which she had shown me. I felt very fatigued, rather I believe from that unlucky short cut than from the length of the way, for I had not come more than eighteen miles. Drawing a chair towards a table, I sat down, and placing my elbows upon the board, I leaned my face upon my upturned hands, and presently fell into a sweet sleep, from which I awoke exceedingly refreshed, just as a maid opened the room door to lay the cloth.

After dinner I got up, went out, and strolled about the place. It was small, and presented nothing very remarkable. Tired of strolling, I went and leaned my back against the wall of the churchyard, and enjoyed the cool of the evening, for evening, with its coolness and shadows, had now come on.

As I leaned against the wall, an elderly man came up and entered into discourse with me. He told me he was a barber by profession, had travelled all over Wales, and had seen London. I asked him about the chair of Rhys Goch. He told me that he had heard of some such chair a long time ago, but could give me no information as to where it stood. I know not how it happened that he came to speak about my landlady, but speak about her he did. He said that she was a good kind of woman, but totally unqualified for business, as she knew not how to charge. On my observing that that was a piece of ignorance with which few landladies, or landlords either, were taxable, he said that, however other publicans might overcharge, undercharging was her foible, and that she had brought herself very low in the world by it—that to his certain knowledge she might have been worth thousands instead of the trifle which she was possessed of, and that she was particularly notorious for undercharging the English, a thing never before dreamt of in Wales. I told him that I was very glad that I had come under the roof of such a landlady; the old barber, however, said that she was setting a bad example, that such goings on could not last long, that he knew how things would end, and finally working himself up into a regular tiff, left me abruptly without wishing me good night.

I returned to the inn, and called for lights; the lights were placed upon the table in the old-fashioned parlour, and I was left to myself. I walked up and down the room some time, at length, seeing some old books lying in a corner, I laid hold of them, carried them to the table, sat down, and began to inspect them; they were the three volumes of Scott's " Cavalier "—I had seen this work when a youth, and thought it a tiresome, trashy publication. Looking over it now, when I was grown old, I thought so still, but I now detected in it what from want of knowledge I had not detected in my early years, what the highest genius, had it been manifested in every page, could not have compensated for—base, fulsome adulation of the worthless great, and most unprincipled libelling of the truly noble ones of the earth, because they, the sons of peasants and handycraftsmen, stood up for the rights of outraged humanity, and proclaimed that it is worth makes the man, and not embroidered clothing. The heartless, unprincipled son of the tyrant was transformed, in that worthless book, into a slightly dissipated, it is true, but

upon the whole brave, generous, and amiable being;
and Harrison, the English Regulus, honest, brave, un-
flinching Harrison, into a pseudo-fanatic, a mixture of
the rogue and fool, Harrison probably the man of the
most ·noble and courageous heart that England ever
produced; who, when all was lost, scorned to flee, like
the second Charles from Worcester, but braved infamous judges and the gallows; who, when reproached
on his mock trial with complicity in the death of the
king, gave the noble answer that " It was a thing not
done in a corner," and when in the cart on the way to
Tyburn, on being asked jeeringly by a lord's bastard
in the crowd, "Where is the good old cause now?"
thrice struck his strong fist on the breast which contained his courageous heart, exclaiming, " Here, here,
here!" Yet for that " Cavalier," that trumpery publication, the booksellers of England, on its first appearance,
gave an order to the amount of six thousand pounds.
But they were wise in their generation; they knew that
the book would please the base, slavish taste of the age,
a taste which the author of the work had had no slight
share in forming.

Tired after a while with turning over the pages of
the trashy " Cavalier," I returned the volumes to their
place in the corner, blew out one candle, and taking the
other in my hand marched off to bed.

CHAPTER XLVIII

The Bill—The Two Mountains—Sheet of Water—The Afanc-
Crocodile—The Afanc-Beaver—Tai Hirion—Kind Woman—
Arenig Vawr—The Beam and Mote—Bala.

AFTER breakfasting I demanded my bill. I was curious
to see how little the amount would be, for after what I
had heard from the old barber the preceding evening
about the utter ignorance of the landlady in making a
charge, I naturally expected that I should have next to
nothing to pay. When it was brought, however, and
the landlady brought it herself, I could scarcely believe
my eyes. Whether the worthy woman had lately come
to a perception of the folly of undercharging, and had

determined to adopt a different system; whether it was that, seeing me the only guest in the house, she had determined to charge for my entertainment what she usually charged for that of two or three—strange, by the bye, that I should be the only guest in a house notorious for undercharging—I know not, but certain it is the amount of the bill was far, far from the next to nothing which the old barber had led me to suppose I should have to pay, who, perhaps, after all had very extravagant ideas with respect to making out a bill for a Saxon. It was, however, not a very unconscionable bill, and merely amounted to a trifle more than I had paid at Bethgelert for somewhat better entertainment.

Having paid the bill without demur, and bidden the landlady farewell, who displayed the same kind of indifferent bluntness which she had manifested the day before, I set off in the direction of the east, intending that my next stage should be Bala. Passing through a toll-gate I found myself in a kind of suburb consisting of a few cottages. Struck with the neighbouring scenery, I stopped to observe it. A mighty mountain rises in the north almost abreast of Festiniog; another towards the east divided into two of unequal size. Seeing a woman of an interesting countenance seated at the door of a cottage, I pointed to the hill towards the north, and speaking the Welsh language, inquired its name.

"That hill, sir," said she, "is called Moel Wyn."

Now Moel Wyn signifies the white, bare hill.

"And how do you call those two hills towards the east?"

"We call one, sir, Mynydd Mawr, the other Mynydd Bach."

Now Mynydd Mawr signifies the great mountain, and Mynydd Bach the little one.

"Do any people live in those hills?"

"The men who work the quarries, sir, live in those hills. They and their wives and their children. No other people."

"Have you any English?"

"I have not, sir. No people who live on this side the talcot (tollgate) for a long way have any English."

I proceeded on my journey. The country for some

way eastward of Festiniog is very wild and barren, consisting of huge hills without trees or verdure. About three miles' distance, however, there is a beautiful valley, which you look down upon from the southern side of the road, after having surmounted a very steep ascent. This valley is fresh and green, and the lower parts of the hills on its farther side are, here and there, adorned with groves. At the eastern end is a deep, dark gorge, or ravine, down which tumbles a brook in a succession of small cascades. The ravine is close by the road. The brook, after disappearing for a time, shows itself again far down in the valley, and is doubtless one of the tributaries of the Tan y Bwlch river, perhaps the very same brook the name of which I could not learn the preceding day in the vale.

As I was gazing on the prospect, an old man driving a peat cart came from the direction in which I was going. I asked him the name of the ravine, and he told me it was Ceunant Coomb, or hollow-dingle coomb. I asked the name of the brook, and he told me that it was called the brook of the hollow-dingle coomb, adding that it ran under Pont Newydd, though where that was I knew not. Whilst he was talking with me he stood uncovered. Yes, the old peat driver stood with his hat in his hand whilst answering the questions of the poor, dusty foot-traveller. What a fine thing to be an Englishman in Wales!

In about an hour I came to a wild moor; the moor extended for miles and miles. It was bounded on the east and south by immense hills and moels. On I walked at a round pace, the sun scorching me sore, along a dusty, hilly road, now up, now down. Nothing could be conceived more cheerless than the scenery around. The ground on each side of the road was mossy and rushy—no houses—instead of them were peat stacks, here and there, standing in their blackness. Nothing living to be seen except a few miserable sheep picking the wretched herbage, or lying panting on the shady side of the peat clumps. At length I saw something which appeared to be a sheet of water at the bottom of a low ground on my right. It looked far off—" Shall I go and see what it is?" thought I to myself. " No," thought I. " It is too far off "—so on

I walked till I lost sight of it, when I repented and thought I would go and see what it was. So I dashed down the moory slope on my right, and presently saw the object again—and now I saw that it was water. I sped towards it through gorse and heather, occasionally leaping a deep drain. At last I reached it. It was a small lake. Wearied and panting, I flung myself on its bank, and gazed upon it.

There lay the lake in the low bottom, surrounded by the heathery hillocks; there it lay quite still, the hot sun reflected upon its surface, which shone like a polished blue shield. Near the shore it was shallow, at least near that shore upon which I lay. But farther on, my eye, practised in deciding upon the depths of waters, saw reason to suppose that its depth was very great. As I gazed upon it my mind indulged in strange musings. I thought of the afanc, a creature which some have supposed to be the harmless and industrious beaver, others the frightful and destructive crocodile. I wondered whether the afanc was the crocodile or the beaver, and speedily had no doubt that the name was originally applied to the crocodile.

"O, who can doubt," thought I, "that the word was originally intended for something monstrous and horrible? Is there not something horrible in the look and sound of the word afanc, something connected with the opening and shutting of immense jaws, and the swallowing of writhing prey? Is not the word a fitting brother of the Arabic timsah, denoting the dread horny lizard of the waters? Moreover, have we not the voice of tradition that the afanc was something monstrous? Does it not say that Hu the Mighty, the inventor of husbandry, who brought the Cumry from the summer-country, drew the old afanc out of the lake of lakes with his four gigantic oxen? Would he have had recourse to them to draw out the little harmless beaver? O, surely not. Yet have I no doubt that, when the crocodile had disappeared from the lands where the Cumric language was spoken, the name afanc was applied to the beaver, probably his successor in the pool; the beaver now called in Cumric Llostlydan, or the broad-tailed, for tradition's voice is strong that the beaver has at one time been called the afanc." Then I won-

dered whether the pool before me had been the haunt
of the afanc, considered both as crocodile and beaver.
I saw no reason to suppose that it had not. "If crocodiles," thought I, "ever existed in Britain, and who
shall say that they have not? seeing that their remains
have been discovered, why should they not have
haunted this pool? If beavers ever existed in Britain,
and do not tradition and Giraldus say that they have?
why should they not have existed in this pool?

"At a time almost inconceivably remote, when the
hills around were covered with woods, through which
the elk and the bison and the wild cow strolled, when
men were rare throughout the lands, and unlike in
most things to the present race—at such a period—and
such a period there has been—I can easily conceive that
the afanc-crocodile haunted this pool, and that when the
elk or bison or wild cow came to drink of its waters,
the grim beast would occasionally rush forth, and seizing his bellowing victim, would return with it to the
deeps before me to luxuriate at his ease upon its flesh.
And at a time less remote, when the crocodile was no
more, and though the woods still covered the hills, and
wild cattle strolled about, men were more numerous
than before, and less unlike the present race, I can
easily conceive this lake to have been the haunt of the
afanc-beaver, that he here built cunningly his house of
trees and clay, and that to this lake the native would
come with his net and his spear to hunt the animal for
his precious fur. Probably if the depths of that pool
were searched, relics of the crocodile and the beaver
might be found, along with other strange things connected with the periods in which they respectively lived.
Happy were I if for a brief space I could become a
Cingalese, that I might swim out far into that pool,
dive down into its deepest part, and endeavour to discover any strange things which beneath its surface may
lie." Much in this guise rolled my thoughts as I lay
stretched on the margin of the lake.

Satiated with musing, I at last got up, and endeavoured to regain the road. I found it at last, though
not without considerable difficulty. I passed over
moors, black and barren, along a dusty road till I came
to a valley; I was now almost choked with dust and

thirst, and longed for nothing in the world so much as for water; suddenly I heard its blessed sound, and perceived a rivulet on my left hand. It was crossed by two bridges, one immensely old and terribly dilapidated, the other old enough, but in better repair—went and drank under the oldest bridge of the two. The water tasted of the peat of the moors, nevertheless I drank greedily of it, for one must not be over-delicate upon the moors.

Refreshed with my draught, I proceeded briskly on my way, and in a little time saw a range of white buildings, diverging from the road on the right hand, the gable of the first abutting upon it. A kind of farmyard was before them. A respectable-looking woman was standing in the yard. I went up to her and inquired the name of the place.

"These houses, sir," said she, "are called Tai Hirion Mignaint. Look over that door and you will see T. H., which letters stand for Tai Hirion. Mignaint is the name of the place where they stand."

I looked, and upon a stone which formed the lintel of the middlemost door I read T. H. 1630.

The words Tai Hirion, it will be as well to say, signify the long houses.

I looked long and steadfastly at the inscription, my mind full of thoughts of the past.

"Many a year has rolled by since these houses were built," said I, as I sat down on a stepping-stone.

"Many, indeed, sir," said the woman, "and many a strange thing has happened."

"Did you ever hear of one Oliver Cromwell?" said I.

"O yes, sir, and of King Charles too. The men of both have been in this yard and have baited their horses; aye, and have mounted their horses from the stone on which you sit."

"I suppose they were hardly here together?" said I.

"No, no, sir," said the woman, "they were bloody enemies, and could never set their horses together."

"Are these long houses," said I, "inhabited by different families?"

"Only by one, sir; they make now one farm-house."

"Are you the mistress of it?" said I.

" I am, sir, and my husband is the master. Can I bring you anything, sir?"

" Some water," said I, " for I am thirsty, though I drank under the old bridge."

The good woman brought me a basin of delicious milk and water.

" What are the names of the two bridges," said I, " a little way from here?"

" They are called, sir, the old and new bridge of Tai Hirion; at least we call them so."

" And what do you call the ffrwd that runs beneath them?"

" I believe, sir, it is called the river Twerin."

" Do you know a lake far up there amidst the moors?"

" I have seen it, sir; they call it Llyn Twerin."

" Does the river Twerin flow from it?"

" I believe it does, sir; but I do not know."

" Is the lake deep?"

" I have heard that it is very deep, sir; so much so, that nobody knows its depth."

" Are there fish in it?"

" Digon, sir, digon iawn, and some very large. I once saw a Pen-hwyad from that lake which weighed fifty pounds."

After a little farther conversation I got up, and, thanking the kind woman, departed. I soon left the moors behind me, and continued walking till I came to a few houses on the margin of a meadow or fen in a valley, through which the way trended to the east. They were almost overshadowed by an enormous mountain, which rose beyond the fen on the south. Seeing a house which bore a sign, and at the door of which a horse stood tied, I went in, and a woman coming to meet me in a kind of passage, I asked her if I could have some ale.

" Of the best, sir," she replied, and conducted me down the passage into a neat room, partly kitchen, partly parlour, the window of which looked out upon the fen. A rustic-looking man sat smoking at a table, with a jug of ale before him. I sat down near him, and the good woman brought me a similar jug of ale, which on tasting I found excellent. My spirits, which had been for some time very flagging, presently revived, and I entered into conversation with my companion at the table. From him I learned that he was a farmer of the neighbourhood, that the horse tied before the door belonged to him, that the present times were very bad for the producers of grain, with very slight likelihood of improvement; that the place at which we were was called Rhyd y fen, or the ford across the fen; that it was just half-way between Festiniog and Bala, that the clergyman of the parish was called Mr. Pughe, a good kind of man, but very purblind in a spiritual sense; and finally that there was no safe religion in the world, save that of the Calvinistic Methodists, to which my companion belonged.

Having finished my ale, I paid for it, and leaving the Calvinistic farmer still smoking, I departed from Rhyd y fen. On I went along the valley, the enormous hill on my right, a moel of about half its height on my left, and a tall hill bounding the prospect in the east, the direction in which I was going. After a little time, meeting two women, I asked them the name of the mountain to the south.

" Arenig Vawr," they replied, or something like it.

Presently meeting four men, I put the same question to the foremost, a stout, burly, intelligent-looking fellow, of about fifty. He gave me the same name as the women. I asked if anybody lived upon it.

" No," said he, " too cold for man."

" Fox?" said I.

" No ! too cold for fox."

" Crow?" said I.

" No; too cold for crow; crow would be starved upon it." He then looked me in the face, expecting probably that I should smile.

I, however, looked at him with all the gravity of a judge, whereupon he also observed the gravity of a judge, and we continued looking at each other with all the gravity of judges till we both simultaneously turned away, he followed by his companions going his path, and I going mine.

I subsequently remembered that Arenig is mentioned in a Welsh poem, though in anything but a flattering and advantageous manner. The writer calls it Arenig ddiffaith, or barren Arenig, and says that it intercepts from him the view of his native land. Arenig is certainly barren enough, for there is neither tree nor shrub upon it, but there is something majestic in its huge bulk. Of all the hills which I saw in Wales, none made a greater impression upon me.

Towards evening I arrived at a very small and pretty village, in the middle of which was a toll-gate—seeing an old woman seated at the door of the gate-house, I asked her the name of the village. "I have no Saesneg!" she screamed out.

"I have plenty of Cumraeg," said I, and repeated my question. Whereupon she told me that it was called Tref y Talcot—the village of the toll-gate. That it was a very nice village, and that she was born there. She then pointed to two young women who were walking towards the gate at a very slow pace, and told me they were English. "I do not know them," said I. The old lady, who was somewhat deaf, thinking that I said I did not know English, leered at me complacently, and said that in that case I was like herself, for she did not speak a word of English, adding that a body should not be considered a fool for not speaking English. She then said that the young women had been taking a walk together, and that they were much in each other's company for the sake of conversation, and no wonder, as the poor simpletons could not speak a word of Welsh. I thought of the beam and mote mentioned in Scripture, and then cast a glance of compassion on the two poor young women. For a moment I fancied myself in the times of Owen Glendower, and that I saw two females, whom his marauders had carried off from Cheshire or Shropshire to toil and slave in the Welshery, walking together after the labours of the day were done, and bemoaning their misfortunes in their own homely English.

Shortly after leaving the village of the toll-gate I came to a beautiful valley. On my right hand was a river, the farther bank of which was fringed with trees; on my left was a gentle ascent, the lower part of which was covered with rich grass, and the upper with yellow, luxuriant corn; a little farther on was a green grove, behind which rose up a moel. A more bewitching scene

I never beheld. Ceres and Pan seemed in this place to have met to hold their bridal. The sun now descending shone nobly upon the whole. After staying for some time to gaze, I proceeded, and soon met several carts, from the driver of one of which I learned that I was yet three miles from Bala. I continued my way and came to a bridge, a little way beyond which I overtook two men, one of whom, an old fellow, held a very long whip in his hand, and the other, a much younger man with a cap on his head, led a horse. When I came up the old fellow took off his hat to me, and I forthwith entered into conversation with him. I soon gathered from him that he was a horse-dealer from Bala, and that he had been out on the road with his servant to break a horse. I astonished the old man with my knowledge of Welsh and horses, and learned from him, for conceiving I was one of the right sort, he was very communicative, two or three curious particulars connected with the Welsh mode of breaking horses. Discourse shortened the way to both of us, and we were soon in Bala. In the middle of the town he pointed to a large old-fashioned house on the right hand, at the bottom of a little square, and said, " Your honour was just asking me about an inn. That is the best inn in Wales, and if your honour is as good a judge of an inn as of a horse, I think you will say so when you leave it. Prydnawn da 'chwi!''

CHAPTER XLIX

Tom Jenkins—Ale of Bala—Sober Moments—Local Prejudices— The States—Unprejudiced Man—Welsh Pensilvanian Settlers —Drapery Line—Evening Saunter.

Scarcely had I entered the door of the inn when a man presented himself to me with a low bow. He was about fifty years of age, somewhat above the middle size, and had grizzly hair, and a dark, freckled countenance, in which methought I saw a considerable dash of humour. He wore brown clothes, had no hat on his head, and held a napkin in his hand. " Are you the master of this hotel?'' said I.

" No, your honour,'' he replied, " I am only the

waiter, but I officiate for my master in all things; my master has great confidence in me, sir."

"And I have no doubt," said I, "that he could not place his confidence in any one more worthy."

With a bow yet lower than the preceding one the waiter replied with a smirk and a grimace, "Thank, your honour, for your good opinion. I assure your honour that I am deeply obliged."

His air, manner, and even accent, were so like those of a Frenchman, that I could not forbear asking him whether he was one.

He shook his head and replied, "No, your honour, no, I am not a Frenchman, but a native of this poor country, Tom Jenkins by name."

"Well," said I, "you really look and speak like a Frenchman, but no wonder; the Welsh and French are much of the same blood. Please now to show me into the parlour."

He opened the door of a large apartment, placed a chair by a table which stood in the middle, and then with another bow requested to know my farther pleasure. After ordering dinner I said that, as I was thirsty, I should like to have some ale forthwith.

"Ale you shall have, your honour," said Tom, "and some of the best ale that can be drunk. This house is famous for ale."

"I suppose you get your ale from Llangollen," said I, "which is celebrated for its ale over Wales."

"Get our ale from Llangollen?" said Tom, with a sneer of contempt, "no, nor anything else. As for the ale, it was brewed in this house by your honour's humble servant."

"Oh," said I, "if you brewed it, it must of course be good. Pray bring me some immediately, for I am anxious to drink ale of your brewing."

"Your honour shall be obeyed," said Tom, and disappearing, returned in a twinkling with a tray, on which stood a jug filled with liquor, and a glass. He forthwith filled the glass, and pointing to its contents, said—

"There, your honour, did you ever see such ale? Observe its colour! Does it not look for all the world as pale and delicate as cowslip wine?"

" I wish it may not taste like cowslip wine," said I ;
" to tell you the truth, I am no particular admirer of ale
that looks pale and delicate; for I always think there
is no strength in it."

" Taste it, your honour," said Tom, " and tell me if
you ever tasted such ale."

I tasted it, and then took a copious draught. The
ale was indeed admirable, equal to the best that I had
ever before drunk—rich and mellow, with scarcely any
smack of the hop in it, and though so pale and delicate
to the eye, nearly as strong as brandy. I commended
it highly to the worthy Jenkins, who exultingly exclaimed—

" That Llangollen ale indeed ! no, no ! ale like that,
your honour, was never brewed in that trumpery hole
Llangollen."

" You seem to have a very low opinion of Llangollen?" said I.

" How can I have anything but a low opinion of it,
your honour? A trumpery hole it is, and ever will
remain so."

" Many people of the first quality go to visit it,"
said I.

" That is because it lies so handy for England, your
honour. If it did not, nobody would go to see it.
What is there to see in Llangollen?"

" There is not much to see in the town, I admit,"
said I, " but the scenery about it is beautiful; what
mountains !"

" Mountains, your honour, mountains ! well, we have
mountains too, and as beautiful as those of Llangollen.
Then we have our lake, our Llyn Tegid, the lake of
beauty. Show me anything like that near Llangollen !"

" Then," said I, " there is your mound, your Tomen
Bala. The Llangollen people can show nothing like
that."

Tom Jenkins looked at me for a moment with some
surprise, and then said : " I see you have been here
before, sir."

" No," said I, " never, but I have read about the
Tomen Bala in books, both Welsh and English."

" You have, sir?" said Tom. " Well, I am rejoiced
to see so book-learned a gentleman in our house. The

Tomen Bala has puzzled many a head. What do the books which mention it say about it, your honour?"

"Very little," said I, "beyond mentioning it; what do the people here say of it?"

"All kinds of strange things, your honour."

"Do they say who built it?"

"Some say the Tylwyth Teg built it, others that it was cast up over a dead king by his people. The truth is, nobody here knows who built it, or anything about it, save that it is a wonder. Ah, those people of Llangollen can show nothing like it."

"Come," said I, "you must not be so hard upon the people of Llangollen. They appear to me, upon the whole, to be an eminently respectable body."

The Celtic waiter gave a genuine French shrug. "Excuse me, your honour, for being of a different opinion. They are all drunkards."

"I have occasionally seen drunken people at Llangollen," said I, "but I have likewise seen a great many sober."

"That is, your honour, you have seen them in their sober moments; but if you had watched, your honour, if you had kept your eye on them, you would have seen them reeling too."

"That I can hardly believe," said I.

"Your honour can't! but I can who know them. They are all drunkards, and nobody can live among them without being a drunkard. There was my nephew——"

"What of him?" said I.

"Why, he went to Llangollen, your honour, and died of a drunken fever in less than a month."

"Well, but might he not have died of the same, if he had remained at home?"

"No, your honour, no! he lived here many a year, and never died of a drunken fever; he was rather fond of liquor, it is true, but he never died at Bala of a drunken fever; but when he went to Llangollen he did. Now, your honour, if there is not something more drunken about Llangollen than about Bala, why did my nephew die at Llangollen of a drunken fever?"

"Really," said I, "you are such a close reasoner, that I do not like to dispute with you. One observation, however, I wish to make: I have lived at Llangollen without, I hope, becoming a drunkard."

"Oh, your honour is out of the question," said the Celtic waiter, with a strange grimace. "Your honour is an Englishman, an English gentleman, and of course could live all the days of your life at Llangollen without being a drunkard, he he! Who ever heard of an Englishman, especially an English gentleman, being a drunkard, he he he! And now, your honour, pray excuse me, for I must go and see that your honour's dinner is being got ready in a suitable manner."

Thereupon he left me, with a bow yet lower than any I had previously seen him make. If his manners put me in mind of those of a Frenchman, his local prejudices brought powerfully to my recollection those of a Spaniard. Tom Jenkins swears by Bala and abuses Llangollen, and calls its people drunkards, just as a Spaniard exalts his own village, and vituperates the next and its inhabitants, whom, though he will not call them drunkards, unless, indeed, he happens to be a Gallegan, he will not hesitate to term "una caterva de pillos y embusteros."

The dinner when it appeared was excellent, and consisted of many more articles than I had ordered. After dinner, as I sat "trifling" with my cold brandy-and-water, an individual entered—a short, thick, dumpy man about thirty, with brown clothes and a broad hat, and holding in his hand a large leather bag. He gave me a familiar nod, and passing by the table, at which I sat, to one near the window, he flung the bag upon it, and seating himself in the chair with his profile towards me, he untied the bag, from which he poured a large quantity of sovereigns upon the table, and fell to counting them. After counting them three times, he placed them again in the bag, which he tied up; then taking a small book, seemingly an account-book, out of his pocket, he wrote something in it with a pencil; then putting it in his pocket, he took the bag, and unlocking a beaufet which stood at some distance behind him against the wall, he put the bag into a drawer; then again locking the beaufet, he sat down in the chair, then tilting the chair back upon its hind legs, he kept swaying himself backwards and forwards upon it, his toes sometimes upon the ground, sometimes mounting until they tapped against the nether side of the table, surveying me all the time with a queer kind of a side glance, and occasionally ejecting saliva upon the carpet in the direction of the place where I sat.

" Fine weather, sir," said I at last, rather tired of being skewed and spit at in this manner.

" Why yaas," said the figure; " the day is tolerably fine, but I have seen a finer."

" Well, I don't remember to have seen one," said I; " it is as fine a day as I have seen during the present season, and finer weather than I have seen during this season I do not think I ever saw before."

" The weather is fine enough for Britain," said the figure, " but there are other countries besides Britain."

" Why," said I, " there's the States, 'tis true."

" Ever been in the States, Mr.?" said the figure quickly.

" Have I ever been in the States," said I, " have I ever been in the States?"

" Perhaps you are of the States, Mr.; I thought so from the first."

" The States are fine countries," said I.

" I guess they are, Mr."

" It would be no easy matter to whip the States."

" So I should guess, Mr."

" That is single-handed," said I.

" Single-handed, no, nor double-handed either. Let England and France and the State which they are now trying to whip without being able to do it, that's Russia, all unite in a union to whip the Union, and if instead of whipping the States they don't get a whipping themselves, call me a braying jackass——"

" I see, Mr.," said I, " that you are a sensible man, because you speak very much my own opinion. However, as I am an unprejudiced person, like yourself, I wish to do justice to other countries—the States are fine countries—but there are other fine countries in the world. I say nothing of England; catch me saying anything good of England; but I call Wales a fine country: gainsay it who may, I call Wales a fine country."

" So it is, Mr."

"I'll go farther," said I; "I wish to do justice to everything : I call the Welsh a fine language."

"So it is, Mr. Ah, I see you are an unprejudiced man. You don't understand Welsh, I guess."

"I don't understand Welsh," said I; "I don't understand Welsh. That's what I call a good one."

"Medrwch siarad Cumraeg?" said the short figure, spitting upon the carpet.

"Medraf," said I.

"You can, Mr. ! Well, if that don't whip the Union. But I see : you were born in the States of Welsh parents."

"No harm in being born in the States of Welsh parents," said I.

"None at all, Mr. ; I was myself, and the first language I learnt to speak was Welsh. Did your people come from Bala, Mr. ?"

"Why no ! Did yourn?"

"Why yaas—at least from the neighbourhood. What State do you come from? Virginny?"

"Why no !"

"Perhaps Pensilvany country?"

"Pensilvany is a fine state," said I.

"So it is, Mr. O, that is your state, is it? I come from Varmont."

"You do, do you? Well, Varmont is not a bad state, but not equal to Pensilvany, and I'll tell you two reasons why; first, it has not been so long settled, and second, there is not so much Welsh blood in it as there is in Pensilvany."

"Is there much Welsh blood in Pensilvany, then?"

"Plenty, Mr., plenty. Welsh flocked over to Pensilvany even as far back as the time of William Penn, who, as you know, Mr., was the first founder of the Pensilvany State. And that puts me in mind that there is a curious account extant of the adventures of one of the old Welsh settlers in Pensilvania. It is to be found in a letter in an old Welsh book. The letter is dated 1705, and is from one Huw Jones, born of Welsh parents in Pensilvany country to a cousin of his of the same name, residing in the neighbourhood of this very town of Bala in Merionethshire where you and I, Mr., now are. It is in answer to certain inquiries made by the cousin, and is written in pure old Welsh language. It gives an account of how the writer's father left this neighbourhood to go to Pensilvania; how he embarked on board the ship *William Pen;* how he was thirty weeks on the voyage from the Thames to the Delaware. Only think, Mr., of a ship now-a-days being thirty weeks on the passage from the Thames to the Delaware river; how he learnt the English language on the voyage; how he and his companions nearly perished with hunger in the wild wood after they landed; how Pensilvania city was built; how he became a farmer and married a Welsh woman, the widow of a Welshman from shire Denbigh, by whom he had the writer and several other children; how the father used to talk to his children about his native region, and the places round about Bala, and fill their breasts with longing for the land of their fathers; and finally how the old man died, leaving his children and their mother in prosperous circumstances. It is a wonderful letter, Mr., all written in the pure old Welsh language."

" I say, Mr., you are a cute one, and know a thing or two. I suppose Welsh was the first language you learnt, like myself?"

" No, it wasn't—I like to speak the truth—never took to either speaking or reading the Welsh language till I was past sixteen."

" 'Stonishing! but see the force of blood at last. In any line of business?"

" No, Mr., can't say I am."

" Have money in your pocket, and travel for pleasure. Come to see father's land."

" Come to see old Wales. And what brings you here, Hiraeth?"

" That's longing. No, not exactly. Came over to England to see what I could do. Got in with house at Liverpool in the drapery business. Travel for it hereabouts, having connections and speaking the language. Do branch business here for a banking-house besides. Manage to get on smartly."

" You look a smart un. But don't you find it sometimes hard to compete with English travellers in the drapery line?"

" I guess not. English travellers! set of nat'rals.

Don't know the language and nothing else. Could whip a dozen any day. Regularly flummox them."

" You do, Mr.? Ah, I see you're a cute un. Glad to have met you."

" I say, Mr., you have not told me from what county your forefathers were."

" From Norfolk and Cornwall counties."

" Didn't know there were such counties in Wales."

" But there are in England."

" Why, you told me you were of Welsh parents."

" No, I didn't. You told yourself so."

" But how did you come to know Welsh?"

" Why, that's my bit of a secret."

" But you are of the United States?"

" Never knew that before."

" Mr., you flummox me."

" Just as you do the English drapery travellers. Ah, you're a cute un—but do you think it altogether a cute trick to stow all those sovereigns in that drawer?"

" Who should take them out, Mr.?"

" Who should take them out? Why, any of the swell mob, that should chance to be in the house, might unlock the drawer with their flash keys as soon as your back is turned, and take out all the coin."

" But there are none of the swell mob here."

" How do you know that?" said I; " the swell mob travel wide about—how do you know that I am not one of them?"

" The swell mob don't speak Welsh, I guess."

" Don't be too sure of that," said I—" the swell coves spare no expense for their education—so that they may be able to play parts according to circumstances. I strongly advise you, Mr., to put that bag somewhere else, lest something should happen to it."

" Well, Mr., I'll take your advice. These are my quarters, and I was merely going to keep the money here for convenience' sake. The money belongs to the bank, so it is but right to stow it away in the bank safe. I certainly should be loth to leave it here with you in the room, after what you have said." He then got up, unlocked the drawer, took out the bag, and with a " good night, Mr.," left the room.

I " trifled " over my brandy-and-water till I finished

it, and then walked forth to look at the town. I turned up a street, which led to the east, and soon found myself beside the lake at the north-west extremity of which Bala stands. It appeared a very noble sheet of water, stretching from north to south for several miles. As, however, night was fast coming on, I did not see it to its full advantage. After gazing upon it for a few minutes, I sauntered back to the square, or market-place, and leaning my back against a wall, listened to the conversation of two or three groups of people who were standing near, my motive for doing so being a desire to know what kind of Welsh they spoke. Their language, as far as I heard it, differed in scarcely any respect from that of Llangollen. I, however, heard very little of it, for I had scarcely kept my station a minute when the good folks became uneasy, cast side-glances at me, first dropped their conversation to whispers, next held their tongues altogether, and finally moved off, some going to their homes, others moving to a distance, and then grouping together— even certain ragged boys who were playing and chattering near me became uneasy, first stood still, then stared at me, and then took themselves off and played and chattered at a distance. Now what was the cause of all this? Why, suspicion of the Saxon. The Welsh are afraid lest an Englishman should understand their language, and, by hearing their conversation, become acquainted with their private affairs; or, by listening to it, pick up their language, which they have no mind that he should know—and their very children sympathise with them. All conquered people are suspicious of their conquerors. The English have forgot that they ever conquered the Welsh, but some ages will elapse before the Welsh forget that the English have conquered them.

CHAPTER L

The Breakfast—The Tomen Bala—El Punto de la Vana.

I SLEPT soundly that night, as well I might, my bed being good and my body weary. I arose about nine, dressed and went down to the parlour, which was vacant. I rang the bell, and on Tom Jenkins making his appearance, I ordered breakfast, and then asked for the Welsh American, and learned that he had breakfasted very early, and had set out in a gig on a journey to some distance. In about twenty minutes after I had ordered it, my breakfast made its appearance. A noble breakfast it was; such, indeed, as I might have read of, but had never before seen. There was tea and coffee, a goodly white loaf and butter; there were a couple of eggs and two mutton chops. There was broiled and pickled salmon—there was fried trout—there were also potted trout and potted shrimps. Mercy upon me ! I had never previously seen such a breakfast set before me, nor, indeed, have I subsequently. Yes, I have subsequently, and at that very house, when I visited it some months after.

After breakfast I called for the bill. I forget the exact amount of the bill, but remember that it was very moderate. I paid it, and gave the noble Thomas a shilling, which he received with a bow and truly French smile—that is, a grimace. When I departed the landlord and landlady, highly respectable-looking elderly people, were standing at the door, one on each side, and dismissed me with suitable honour, he with a low bow, she with a profound curtsey.

Having seen little of the town on the preceding evening, I determined before setting out for Llangollen to become better acquainted with it, and accordingly took another stroll about it.

Bala is a town containing three or four thousand inhabitants, situated near the northern end of an oblong valley, at least two-thirds of which are occupied by Llyn Tegid. It has two long streets, extending from north to south, a few narrow cross ones, an ancient

church, partly overgrown with ivy, with a very pointed
steeple, and a town-hall of some antiquity, in which
Welsh interludes used to be performed. After gratifying my curiosity with respect to the town, I visited the
mound—the wondrous Tomen Bala.

The Tomen Bala stands at the northern end of the
town. It is apparently formed of clay, is steep and of
difficult ascent. In height it is about thirty feet, and in
diameter at the top about fifty. On the top grows a
gwern, or alder-tree, about a foot thick, its bark terribly scotched with letters and uncouth characters,
carved by the idlers of the town, who are fond of re-
sorting to the top of the mound in fine weather, and
lying down on the grass which covers it. The Tomen
is about the same size as Glendower's Mount on the
Dee, which it much resembles in shape. Both belong
to that brotherhood of artificial mounds of unknown
antiquity, found scattered, here and there, throughout
Europe and the greater part of Asia, the most remarkable specimen of which is, perhaps, that which stands
on the right side of the way from Adrianople to Stam-
boul, and which is called by the Turks Mourad Tepehsi,
or the tomb of Mourad. Which mounds seem to have
been originally intended as places of sepulture, but in
many instances were afterwards used as strongholds,
bonhills or beacon-heights, or as places on which
adoration was paid to the host of heaven.

From the Tomen there is a noble view of the Bala
valley, the Lake of Beauty up to its southern extremity,
and the neighbouring and distant mountains. Of Bala,
its lake, and Tomen, I shall have something to say on
a future occasion.

Leaving Bala, I passed through the village of Llanfair, and found myself by the Dee, whose course I
followed for some way. Coming to the northern extremity of the Bala valley, I entered a pass tending
due north. Here the road slightly diverged from the
river. I sped along, delighted with the beauty of the
scenery. On my left was a high bank covered with
trees, on my right a grove, through openings in which
I occasionally caught glimpses of the river, over whose
farther side towered noble hills. An hour's walking
brought me into a comparatively open country, fruitful

and charming. At about one o'clock I reached a large village, the name of which, like those of most Welsh villages, began with Llan. There I refreshed myself for an hour or two in an old-fashioned inn, and then resumed my journey.

I passed through Corwen; again visited Glendower's monticle upon the Dee, and reached Llangollen shortly after sunset, where I found my beloved two well and glad to see me.

That night, after tea, Henrietta played on the guitar the old muleteer tune of " El Punto de la Vana," or the main point at the Havanna, whilst I sang the words :—

> " Never trust the sample when you go your cloth to buy :
> The woman's most deceitful that's dressed most daintily,
> The lasses of Havanna ride to mass in coaches yellow,
> But ere they go they ask if the priest's a handsome fellow.
> The lasses of Havanna as mulberries are dark,
> And try to make them fairer by taking Jesuit's bark."

CHAPTER LI

The Ladies of Llangollen—Sir Alured—Eisteddfodau— " Pleasure and Care."

SHORTLY after my return I paid a visit to my friends at the vicarage, who were rejoiced to see me back, and were much entertained with the account I gave of my travels. I next went to visit the old church clerk of whom I had so much to say on a former occasion. After having told him some particulars of my expedition, to all of which he listened with great attention, especially to that part which related to the church of Penmynydd and the tomb of the Tudors, I got him to talk about the ladies of Llangollen, of whom I knew very little save what I had heard from general report. I found he remembered their first coming to Llangollen, their living in lodgings, their purchasing the ground called Pen y maes, and their erecting upon it the mansion to which the name of Plas Newydd was given. He said they were very eccentric, but good and kind, and had always shown most particular favour to himself; that both were highly connected, especially Lady Eleanor

Butler, who was connected by blood with the great
Duke of Ormond, who commanded the armies of
Charles in Ireland in the time of the great rebellion,
and also with the Duke of Ormond who succeeded
Marlborough in the command of the armies in the Low
Countries in the time of Queen Anne, and who fled to
France shortly after the accession of George the First
to the throne, on account of being implicated in the
treason of Harley and Bolingbroke; and that her ladyship was particularly fond of talking of both those
dukes, and relating anecdotes concerning them. He
said that the ladies were in the habit of receiving the
very first people in Britain, " amongst whom," said the
old church clerk, " was an ancient gentleman of most
engaging appearance and captivating manners, called
Sir Alured C——. He was in the army, and in his
youth, owing to the beauty of his person, was called
' the handsome captain.' It was said that one of the
royal princesses was desperately in love with him, and
that on that account George the Third insisted on his
going to India. Whether or not there was truth in the
report, to India he went, where he served with distinction for a great many years. On his return, which
was not till he was upwards of eighty, he was received
with great favour by William the Fourth, who amongst
other things made him a field-marshal. As often as
October came round did this interesting and venerable
gentleman make his appearance at Llangollen to pay
his respects to the ladies, especially.to Lady Eleanor,
whom he had known at Court as far back, they say, as
the American war. It was rumoured at Llangollen
that Lady Eleanor's death was a grievous blow to Sir
Alured, and that he would never be seen there again.
However, when October came round he made his appearance at the vicarage, where he had always been in
the habit of taking up his quarters, and called on and
dined with Miss Ponsonby at Plas Newydd, but it was
observed that he was not so gay as he had formerly
been. In the evening, on his taking leave of Miss
Ponsonby, she said that he had used her ill. Sir
Alured coloured, and asked her what she meant, adding
that he had not to his knowledge used any person ill
in the course of his life. ' But I say you have used me

ill, very ill,' said Miss Ponsonby, raising her voice, and the words 'very ill' she repeated several times. At last the old soldier, waxing rather warm, demanded an explanation. 'I'll give it you,' said Miss Ponsonby; 'were you not going away after having only kissed my hand?' 'O,' said the general, 'if that is my offence, I will soon make you reparation,' and instantly gave her a hearty smack on the lips, which ceremony he never forgot to repeat after dining with her on subsequent occasions.''

We got on the subject of bards, and I mentioned to him Gruffydd Hiraethog, the old poet buried in the chancel of Llangollen church. The old clerk was not aware that he was buried there, and said that though he had heard of him, he knew little or nothing about him.

" Where was he born?'' said he.

" In Denbighshire,'' I replied, " near the mountain Hiraethog, from which circumstance he called himself in poetry Gruffydd Hiraethog.''

" When did he flourish?''

" About the middle of the sixteenth century.''

" What did he write?''

" A great many didactic pieces,'' said I; " in one of which is a famous couplet to this effect :

> ' He who satire loves to sing
> On himself will satire bring.' ''

" Did you ever hear of William Lleyn?'' said the old gentleman.

" Yes,'' said I; " he was a pupil of Hiraethog, and wrote an elegy on his death, in which he alludes to Gruffydd's skill in an old Welsh metre, called the Cross Consonancy, in the following manner :

> ' In Eden's grove from Adam's mouth
> Upsprang a muse of noble growth ;
> So from thy grave, O poet wise,
> Cross Consonancy's boughs shall rise.' ''

" Really,'' said the old clerk, " you seem to know something about Welsh poetry. But what is meant by a muse springing up from Adam's mouth in Eden?''

" Why, I suppose,'' said I, " that Adam invented poetry.''

I made inquiries of him about the eisteddfodau, or sessions of bards, and expressed a wish to be present at one of them. He said that they were very interesting; that bards met at particular periods and recited poems on various subjects which had been given out beforehand, and that prizes were allotted to those whose compositions were deemed the best by the judges. He said that he had himself won the prize for the best englyn on a particular subject at an eisteddfod at which Sir Watkin Williams Wynn presided, and at which Heber, afterwards Bishop of Calcutta, was present, who appeared to understand Welsh well, and who took much interest in the proceedings of the meeting.

Our discourse turning on the latter Welsh poets, I asked him if he had been acquainted with Jonathan Hughes, who, the reader will remember, was the person whose grandson I met, and in whose arm-chair I sat at Tŷ yn y pistyll, shortly after my coming to Llangollen. He said that he had been well acquainted with him, and had helped to carry him to the grave, adding, that he was something of a poet, but that he had always considered his forte lay in strong good sense rather than poetry. I mentioned Thomas Edwards, whose picture I had seen in Valle Crucis Abbey. He said that he knew him tolerably well, and that the last time he saw him was when he, Edwards, was about seventy years of age, when he sent him in a cart to the house of a great gentleman near the aqueduct, where he was going to stay on a visit. That Tom was about five feet eight inches high, lusty and very strongly built; that he had something the matter with his right eye; that he was very satirical and very clever; that his wife was a very clever woman and satirical; his two daughters both clever and satirical, and his servant-maid remarkably satirical and clever, and that it was impossible to live with Twm O'r Nant without learning to be clever and satirical; that he always appeared to be occupied with something, and that he had heard him say there was something in him that would never let him be idle; that he would walk fifteen miles to a place where he was to play an interlude, and that as soon as he got there he would begin playing it at once, however tired he might be. The old gentleman concluded by saying that he had never read the works of Twm O'r Nant, but that he had heard that his best piece was the interlude called " Pleasure and Care."

CHAPTER LII

The Treachery of the Long Knives—The North Briton—The Wounded Butcher—The Prisoner.

ON the tenth of September our little town was flung into some confusion by one butcher having attempted to cut the throat of another. The delinquent was a Welshman, who it was said had for some time past been somewhat out of his mind; the other party was an Englishman, who escaped without further injury than a deep gash in the cheek. The Welshman might be mad, but it appeared to me that there was some method in his madness. He tried to cut the throat of a butcher; didn't this look like wishing to put a rival out of the way? and that butcher an Englishman; didn't this look like wishing to pay back upon the Saxon what the Welsh call bradwriaeth y cyllyll hirion, the treachery of the long knives? So reasoned I to myself. But here perhaps the reader will ask what is meant by " the treachery of the long knives?" whether he does or not I will tell him.

Hengist, wishing to become paramount in Southern Britain, thought that the easiest way to accomplish his wish would be by destroying the South British chieftains. Not believing that he should be able to make away with them by open force, he determined to see what he could do by treachery. Accordingly he invited the chieftains to a banquet, to be held near Stonehenge, or the Hanging Stones, on Salisbury Plain. The unsuspecting chieftains accepted the invitation, and on the appointed day repaired to the banquet, which was held in a huge tent. Hengist received them with a smiling countenance, and every appearance of hospitality, and caused them to sit down to table, placing by the side of every Briton one of his own people. The banquet commenced, and all seemingly was mirth and hilarity. Now Hengist had commanded his people that, when he should get up and cry " nemet eoure saxes," that is, take your knives, each Saxon should draw his long sax, or knife, which he wore at his side, and should plunge it into the throat of his neighbour. The banquet went on, and in the midst of it, when the un-suspecting Britons were revelling on the good cheer which had been provided for them, and half-drunken with the mead and beer which flowed in torrents, uprose Hengist, and with a voice of thunder uttered the fatal words, " nemet eoure saxes;" the cry was obeyed, each Saxon grasped his knife, and struck with it at the throat of his defenceless neighbour. Almost every blow took effect; only three British chieftains escaping from the banquet of blood. This infernal carnage the Welsh have appropriately denominated the treachery of the long knives. It will be as well to observe that the Saxons derived their name from the saxes, or long knives, which they wore at their sides, and at the use of which they were terribly proficient.

Two or three days after the attempt at murder at Llangollen, hearing that the Welsh butcher was about to be brought before the magistrates, I determined to make an effort to be present at the examination. Ac-cordingly I went to the police station and inquired of the superintendent whether I could be permitted to attend. He was a North Briton, as I have stated some-where before, and I had scraped acquaintance with him, and had got somewhat into his good graces by praising Dumfries, his native place, and descanting to him upon the beauties of the poetry of his celebrated countryman, my old friend, Allan Cunningham, some of whose works he had perused, and with whom, as he said, he had once the honour of shaking hands. In reply to my question he told me that it was doubtful whether any examination would take place, as the wounded man was in a very weak state, but that if I would return in half-an-hour he would let me know. I went away, and at the end of the half-hour returned, when he told me that there would be no public examination, owing to the extreme debility of the wounded man, but that one of the magis-trates was about to proceed to his house and take his deposition in the presence of the criminal, and also of the witnesses of the deed, and that if I pleased I might go along with him, and he had no doubt that the magistrate would have no objection to my being present. We set out together; as we were going along I questioned him about the state of the country, and gathered from him that there was occasionally a good deal of crime in Wales.

" Are the Welsh a clannish people?" I demanded.

" Very," said he.

" As clannish as the Highlanders?" said I.

" Yes," said he, " and a good deal more."

We came to the house of the wounded butcher, which was some way out of the town in the north-western suburb. The magistrate was in the lower apartment with the clerk, one or two officials, and the surgeon of the town. He was a gentleman of about two or three-and-forty, with a military air and large moustaches, for besides being a justice of the peace, and a landed proprietor, he was an officer in the army. He made me a polite bow when I entered, and I requested of him permission to be present at the examination. He hesitated a moment, and then asking me my motive for wishing to be present at it.

" Merely curiosity," said I.

He then observed that, as the examination would be a private one, my being permitted or not was quite optional.

" I am aware of that," said I, " and if you think my remaining is objectionable, I will forthwith retire." He looked at the clerk, who said there could be no objection to my staying, and turning round to his superior, said something to him which I did not hear, whereupon the magistrate again bowed, and said that he should be very happy to grant my request.

We went upstairs, and found the wounded man in bed, with a bandage round his forehead, and his wife sitting by his bedside. The magistrate and his officials took their seats, and I was accommodated with a chair. Presently the prisoner was introduced under the charge of a policeman. He was a fellow somewhat above thirty, of the middle size, and wore a dirty white frock coat; his right arm was partly confined by a manacle—a young girl was sworn, who deposed that she saw the prisoner run after the other with something in his hand. The wounded man was then asked whether he thought he was able to make a deposition; he replied in a very feeble tone that he thought he was, and after being sworn, deposed that on the preceding Saturday, as he was going to his stall, the prisoner came up to him and asked whether he had ever done him any injury? he said no. "I then," said he, "observed the prisoner's countenance undergo a change, and saw him put his hand to his waistcoat pocket and pull out a knife. I straight became frightened, and ran away as fast as I could; the prisoner followed, and overtaking me, stabbed me in the face. I ran into the yard of a public-house, and into the shop of an acquaintance, where I fell down, the blood spouting out of my wound." Such was the deposition of the wounded butcher. He was then asked whether there had been any quarrel between him and the prisoner? He said there had been no quarrel, but that he had refused to drink with the prisoner when he requested him, which he had done very frequently, and had more than once told him that he did not wish for his acquaintance. The prisoner, on being asked, after the usual caution, whether he had anything to say, said that he merely wished to mark the man, but not to kill him. The surgeon of the place deposed to the nature of the wound, and on being asked his opinion with respect to the state of the prisoner's mind, said that he believed that he might be labouring under a delusion. After the prisoner's bloody weapon and coat had been produced, he was committed.

It was generally said that the prisoner was disordered in his mind; I held my tongue, but judging from his look and manner, I saw no reason to suppose that he was any more out of his senses than I myself, or any person present, and I had no doubt that what induced him to commit the act was rage at being looked down upon by a quondam acquaintance, who was rising a little in the world, exacerbated by the reflection that the disdainful quondam acquaintance was one of the Saxon race, against which every Welshman entertains a grudge more or less virulent, which, though of course very unchristianlike, is really, brother Englishman, after the affair of the long knives, and two or three other actions of a somewhat similar character, of our noble Anglo-Saxon progenitors, with which all Welshmen are perfectly well acquainted, not very much to be wondered at.

CHAPTER LIII

The Dylluan—The Oldest Creatures.

MUCH rain fell about the middle of the month; in the intervals of the showers I occasionally walked by the banks of the river, which speedily became much swollen; it was quite terrible both to the sight and ear near the "Robber's Leap;" there were breakers above the higher stones at least five feet high, and a roar around almost sufficient "to scare a hundred men." The pool of Catherine Lingo was strangely altered; it was no longer the quiet pool which it was in summer, verifying the words of the old Welsh poet that the deepest pool of the river is always the stillest in the summer and of the softest sound, but a howling turbid gulf, in which branches of trees, dead animals, and rubbish were whirling about in the wildest confusion. The nights were generally less rainy than the days, and sometimes by the pallid glimmer of the moon I would take a stroll along some favourite path or road. One night, as I was wandering slowly along the path leading through the groves of Pen y Coed, I was startled by an un-earthly cry—it was the shout of the dylluan, or owl, as it flitted over the tops of the trees on its nocturnal business.

Oh, that cry of the dylluan! what a strange, wild cry it is; how unlike any other sound in nature! a cry which no combination of letters can give the slightest idea of. What resemblance does Shakespear's to-whit-to-whoo bear to the cry of the owl? none whatever; those who hear it for the first time never know what it is, however accustomed to talk of the cry of the owl and to-whit-to-whoo. A man might be wandering through a wood with Shakespear's owl-chorus in his mouth, but were he then to hear for the first time the real shout of the owl, he would assuredly stop short and wonder whence that unearthly cry could proceed.

Yet no doubt that strange cry is a fitting cry for the owl, the strangest in its habits and look of all birds, the bird of whom by all nations the strangest tales are told. Oh, what strange tales are told of the owl, especially in connection with its long-lifedness; but of all the strange, wild tales connected with the age of the owl, strangest of all is the old Welsh tale. When I heard the owl's cry in the groves of Pen y Coed, that tale rushed into my mind. I had heard it from the singular groom, who had taught me to gabble Welsh in my boyhood, and had subsequently read it in an old tattered Welsh story-book, which by chance fell into my hands. The reader will perhaps be obliged by my relating it.

"The eagle of the alder grove, after being long married, and having had many children by his mate, lost her by death, and became a widower. After some time he took it into his head to marry the owl of the Cowlyd Coomb; but fearing he should have issue by her, and by that means sully his lineage, he went first of all to the oldest creatures in the world, in order to obtain information about her age. First he went to the stag of Ferny-side brae, whom he found sitting by the old stump of an oak, and inquired the age of the owl. The stag said : ' I have seen this oak an acorn which is now lying on the ground without either leaves or bark : nothing in the world wore it up but my rubbing myself against it once a day when I got up, so I have seen a vast number of years, but I assure you that I have never seen the owl older or younger than she is to-day. However, there is one older than myself, and that is the salmon-trout of Glyn Llifon.' To him went the eagle, and asked him the age of the owl, and got for answer : ' I have a year over my head for every gem on my skin, and for every egg in my roe, yet have I always seen the owl look the same; but there is one older than myself, and that is the ousel of Cilgwry.' Away went the eagle to Cilgwry, and found the ousel standing upon a little rock, and asked him the age of the owl. Quoth the ousel : ' You see that the rock below me is not larger than a man can carry in one of his hands : I have seen it so large that it would have taken a hundred oxen to drag it, and it has never been worn save by my drying my beak upon it once every night, and by my striking the tip of my wing against it in rising in the morning, yet never have I known the owl older or younger than she is to-day. However, there is one older than I, and that is the toad of Cors Fochnod; and unless he knows her age no one knows it.' To him went the eagle, and asked the age of the owl, and the toad replied : ' I have never eaten anything save what I have sucked from the earth, and have never eaten half my fill in all the days of my life; but do you see those two great hills beside the cross? I have seen the place where they stand level ground, and nothing produced those heaps save what I discharged from my body, who have ever eaten so very little—yet never have I known the owl anything else but an old hag who cried Too-hoo-hoo, and scared children with her voice, even as she does at present.' So the eagle of Gwernabwy, the stag of Ferny-side brae, the salmon-trout of Glyn Llifon, the ousel of Cilgwry, the toad of Cors Fochnod, and the owl of Coomb Cowlyd, are the oldest creatures in the world, the oldest of them all being the owl.''

CHAPTER LIV

Chirk—The Middleton Family—Castell y Waen—The Park—The Court Yard—The Young Housekeeper—The Portraits—Melin y Castell—Humble Meal—Fine Chests for the Dead—Hales and Hercules.

THE weather having become fine, myself and family determined to go and see Chirk Castle, a mansion ancient and beautiful, and abounding with all kinds of agreeable and romantic associations. It was founded about the beginning of the fifteenth century by a St. John, Lord of Bletsa, from a descendant of whom it was purchased in the year 1615 by Sir Thomas Middleton, the scion of an ancient Welsh family who, following commerce, acquired a vast fortune, and was Lord Mayor of London. In the time of the great civil war it hoisted the banner of the king, and under Sir Thomas, the son of the Lord Mayor, made a brave defence against Lambert, the Parliamentary General, though eventually compelled to surrender. It was held successively by four Sir Thomas Middletons, and if it acquired a warlike celebrity under the second, it obtained a peculiarly hospitable one under the fourth, whose daughter, the fruit of a second marriage, became Countess of Warwick, and eventually the wife of the poet and moralist, Addison. In his time the hospitality of Chirk became the theme of many a bard, particularly of Huw Morris, who, in one of his songs, has gone so far as to say that were the hill of Cefn Uchaf turned into beef and bread, and the rill Ceiriog into beer or wine, they would be consumed in half a year by the hospitality of Chirk. Though no longer in the hands of one of the name of Middleton, Chirk Castle is still possessed by one of the blood, the mother of the present proprietor being the eldest of three sisters, lineal descendants of the Lord Mayor, between whom, in default of an heir male, the wide possessions of the Middleton family were divided. This gentleman, who bears the name of Biddulph, is Lord Lieutenant of the county of Denbigh, and notwithstanding his war-breathing name, which is Gothic, and signifies Wolf of Battle, is a person of highly amiable disposition, and one who takes great interest in the propagation of the Gospel of peace and love.

To view this place which, though in English called Chirk Castle, is styled in Welsh Caetell y Waen, or the Castle of the Meadow, we started on foot about ten o'clock of a fine bright morning, attended by John Jones. There are two roads from Llangollen to Chirk, one the low or post road, and the other leading over the Berwyn. We chose the latter. We passed by the Yew cottage, which I have described on a former occasion, and began to ascend the mountain, making towards its north-eastern corner. The road at first was easy enough, but higher up became very steep, and somewhat appalling, being cut out of the side of the hill which shelves precipitously down towards the valley of the Dee. Near the top of the mountain were three lofty beech trees, growing on the very verge of the precipice. Here the road for about twenty yards is fenced on its dangerous side by a wall, parts of which are built between the stems of the trees. Just beyond the wall a truly noble prospect presented itself to our eyes. To the north were bold hills, their sides and skirts adorned with numerous woods and white farmhouses; a thousand feet below us was the Dee, and its wondrous Pont y Cysultau. John Jones said that if certain mists did not intervene we might descry " the sea of Liverpool;" and perhaps the only thing wanting to make the prospect complete was that sea of Liverpool. We were, however, quite satisfied with what we saw, and turning round the corner of the hill, reached its top, where for a considerable distance there is level ground, and where, though at a great altitude, we found ourselves in a fair and fertile region, and amidst a scene of busy rural life. We saw fields and inclosures, and here and there corn-stacks, some made, and others not yet completed, about which people were employed, and waggons and horses moving. Passing over the top of the hill, we began to descend the southern side, which was far less steep than the one we had lately surmounted. After a little way the road descended through a wood, which John Jones told us was the beginning of the " Park of Biddulph."

" There is plenty of game in this wood," said he; " pheasant cocks and pheasant hens, to say nothing of hares and coneys; and in the midst of it there is a space sown with a particular kind of corn for the support of the pheasant hens and pheasant cocks, which in the shooting-season afford pleasant sport for Biddulph and his friends."

Near the foot of the descent, just where the road made a turn to the east, we passed by a building which stood amidst trees, with a pond and barns near it.

" This," said John Jones, " is the house where the bailiff lives, who farms and buys and sells for Biddulph, and fattens the beeves and swine, and the geese, ducks, and other poultry which Biddulph consumes at his table."

The scenery was now very lovely, consisting of a mixture of hill and dale, open space and forest, in fact the best kind of park scenery. We caught a glimpse of a lake, in which John Jones said there were generally plenty of swans, and presently saw the castle, which stands on a green grassy slope, from which it derives its Welsh name of Castell y Waen; gwaen in the Cumrian language signifying a meadow or unenclosed place. It fronts the west, the direction from which we were coming; on each side it shows five towers, of which the middlemost, which protrudes beyond the rest, and at the bottom of which is the grand gate, is by far the bulkiest. A noble edifice it looked, and to my eye bore no slight resemblance to Windsor Castle.

Seeing a kind of ranger, we inquired of him what it was necessary for us to do, and by his direction proceeded to the southern side of the castle, and rung the bell at a small gate. The southern side had a far more antique appearance than the western; huge towers, with small windows, and partly covered with ivy, frowned down upon us. A servant making his appearance, I inquired whether we could see the house; he said we could, and that the housekeeper would show it to us in a little time, but that at present she was engaged. We entered a large quadrangular court; on the left hand side was a door and staircase leading into the interior of the building, and farther on was a gateway, which was no doubt the principal entrance from the park. On the eastern side of the spacious court was a kennel, chained to which was an enormous dog, partly of the bloodhound, partly of the mastiff species, who occasionally uttered a deep magnificent bay. As the sun was hot we took refuge from it under the gateway, the gate of which, at the farther end, towards the park, was closed. Here my wife and daughter sat down on a small brass cannon, seemingly a six-pounder, which stood on a very dilapidated carriage; from the appearance of the gun, which was of an ancient form and very much battered, and that of the carriage, I had little doubt that both had been in the castle at the time of the siege. As my two loved ones sat I walked up and down, recalling to my mind all I had heard and read in connection with this castle. I thought of its gallant defence against the men of Oliver; I thought of its roaring hospitality in the time of the fourth Sir Thomas; and I thought of the many beauties who had been born in its chambers, had danced in its halls, had tripped across its court, and had subsequently given heirs to illustrious families.

At last we were told that the housekeeper was waiting for us. The housekeeper, who was a genteel, good-looking young woman, welcomed us at the door which led into the interior of the house. After we had written our names, she showed us into a large room or hall on the right-hand side on the ground floor, where were some helmets and ancient halberts, and also some pictures of great personages. The floor was of oak, and so polished and slippery that walking upon it was attended with some danger. Wishing that John Jones, our faithful attendant, who remained timidly at the doorway, should participate with us in the wonderful sights we were about to see, I inquired of the house-keeper whether he might come with us. She replied with a smile that it was not the custom to admit guides into the apartments, but that he might come provided he chose to take off his shoes; adding, that the reason she wished him to take off his shoes was, an appre-hension that if he kept them on he would injure the floors with their rough nails. She then went to John Jones and told him in English that he might attend us provided he took off his shoes; poor John, however, only smiled, and said, " Dim Saesneg !"

" You must speak to him in your native language," said I, " provided you wish him to understand you— he has no English."

" I am speaking to him in my native language," said the young housekeeper, with another smile; " and if he has no English, I have no Welsh."

" Then you are English?" said I.

" Yes," she replied, " a native of London."

" Dear me," said I. " Well, it's no bad thing to be English after all; and as for not speaking Welsh, there are many in Wales who would be glad to have much less Welsh than they have." I then told John Jones the condition on which he might attend us, whereupon he took off his shoes with great glee and attended us, holding them in his hand.

We presently went upstairs to what the housekeeper told us was the principal drawing-room, and a noble room it was, hung round with the portraits of kings and queens and the mighty of the earth. Here, on canvas, was noble Mary the wife of William of Orange,

and her consort by her side, whose part like a true
wife she always took. Here was wretched Mary of
Scotland, the murderess of her own lord. Here were
the two Charleses, and both the Dukes of Ormond—
the great Duke who fought stoutly in Ireland against
Papist and Roundhead; and the Pretender's Duke who
tried to stab his native land, and died a foreign colonel.
And here, amongst other daughters of the house, was
the very proud daughter of the house, the Warwick
Dowager who married the Spectator, and led him the
life of a dog. She looked haughty and cold, and not
particularly handsome; but I could not help gazing with
a certain degree of interest and respect on the countenance of the vixen, who served out the gentility wor-
shipper in such prime style. Many were the rooms
which we entered, of which I shall say nothing, save
that they were noble in size, and rich in objects of
interest. At last we came to what was called the
picture gallery. It was a long panelled room, extending
nearly the whole length of the northern side. The first
thing which struck us on entering was the huge skin
of a lion stretched out upon the floor; the head, however, which was towards the door, was stuffed, and
with its monstrous teeth looked so formidable and
lifelike that we were almost afraid to touch it. Against
every panel was a portrait; amongst others was that
of Sir Thomas Middleton, the stout governor of the
castle during the time of the siege. Near to it was the
portrait of his rib, Dame Middleton. Farther down
on the same side were two portraits of Nell Gwynn;
the one painted when she was a girl, the other when
she had attained a more mature age. They were both
by Lely, the Apelles of the Court of wanton Charles.
On the other side was one of the Duke of Gloucester,
the son of Queen Anne, who, had he lived, would have
kept the Georges from the throne. In this gallery, on
the southern side, was a cabinet of ebony and silver,
presented by Charles the Second to the brave warrior
Sir Thomas, and which, according to tradition, cost
seven thousand pounds. This room, which was perhaps
the most magnificent in the castle, was the last we
visited. The candle of God whilst we wandered through
these magnificent halls was flaming in the firmament,

and its rays penetrating through the long, narrow windows, showed them off, and all the gorgeous things which they contained, to great advantage. When we left the castle we all said, not excepting John Jones, that we had never seen in our lives anything more princely and delightful than the interior.

After a little time my wife and daughter, complaining of being rather faint, I asked John Jones whether there was an inn in the neighbourhood where some refreshment could be procured. He said there was, and that he would conduct us to it. We directed our course towards the east, rousing successively, and setting a-scampering, three large herds of deer—the common ones were yellow and of no particular size—but at the head of each herd we observed a big old black fellow with immense antlers; one of these was particularly large, indeed as huge as a bull. We soon came to the verge of a steep descent, down which we went, not without some risk of falling. At last we came to a gate; it was locked; however, on John Jones shouting, an elderly man, with his right hand bandaged, came and opened it. I asked him what was the matter with his hand, and he told me that he had lately lost three fingers, whilst working at a saw-mill up at the castle. On my inquiring about the inn, he said he was the master of it, and led the way to a long, neat, low house nearly opposite to a little bridge over a brook, which ran down the valley towards the north. I ordered some ale and bread-and-butter, and whilst our repast was being got ready, John Jones and I went to the bridge.

"This bridge, sir," said John, "is called Pont y Velin Castell, the bridge of the Castle Mill; the inn was formerly the mill of the castle, and is still called Melin y Castell. As soon as you are over the bridge you are in shire Amwythig, which the Saxons call Shropshire. A little way up on yon hill is Clawdd Offa, or Offa's dyke, built of old by the Brenin Offa in order to keep us poor Welsh within our bounds."

As we stood on the bridge, I inquired of Jones the name of the brook which was running merrily beneath it.

"The Ceiriog, sir," said John; "the same river that we saw at Pont y Meibion."

" The river," said I, " which Huw Morris loved so
well, whose praises he has sung, and which he has introduced along with Cefn Uchaf in a stanza in which
he describes the hospitality of Chirk Castle in his day,
and which runs thus :

> ' Pe byddai 'r Cefn Ucha,
> Yn gig ac yn fara,
> A Cheiriog fawr yma'n fir aml bob tro,
> Rhy ryfedd fae iddyn'
> Barhâu hanner blwyddyn,
> I wyr bob yn gan-nyn ar ginio.' "

" A good penill that, sir," said John Jones. " Pity
that the halls of great people no longer flow with rivers
of beer, nor have mountains of bread and beef for all
comers."

" No pity at all," said I ; " things are better as they
are. Those mountains of bread and beef, and those
rivers of ale merely encouraged vassalage, fawning and
idleness; better to pay for one's dinner proudly and in-
dependently at one's inn, than to go and cringe for it
at a great man's table."

We crossed the bridge, walked a little way up the
hill, which was beautifully wooded, and then retraced
our steps to the little inn, where I found my wife and
daughter waiting for us, and very hungry. We sat
down, John Jones with us, and proceeded to despatch
our bread-and-butter and ale. The bread-and-butter
were good enough, but the ale poorish. O, for an Act
of Parliament to force people to brew good ale ! After
finishing our humble meal we got up, and having paid
our reckoning, went back into the park, the gate of
which the landlord again unlocked for us.

We strolled towards the north along the base of the
hill. The imagination of man can scarcely conceive a
scene more beautiful than the one which we were now
enjoying. Huge oaks studded the lower side of the
hill, towards the top was a belt of forest, above which
rose the eastern walls of the castle; the whole forest,
castle, and the green bosom of the hill glorified by the
lustre of the sun. As we proceeded we again roused the
deer, and again saw the three old black fellows, evidently the patriarchs of the herds, with their white,
enormous horns; with these ancient gentlefolks I very

much wished to make acquaintance, and tried to get near them, but no! they would suffer no such thing; off they glided, their white antlers, like the barked top boughs of old pollards, glancing in the sunshine, the smaller dappled creatures following them bounding and frisking. We had again got very near the castle, when John Jones told me that if we would follow him, he would show us something very remarkable: I asked him what it was.

"Llun Cawr," he replied. "The figure of a giant."

"What giant?" said I.

But on this point he could give me no information. I told my wife and daughter what he had said, and finding that they wished to see the figure, I bade John Jones lead us to it. He led us down an avenue just below the eastern side of the castle; noble oaks and other trees composed it, some of them probably near a hundred feet high; John Jones observing me looking at them with admiration, said:

"They would make fine chests for the dead, sir."

What an observation! how calculated, amidst the most bounding joy and bliss, to remind man of his doom! A moment before I had felt quite happy, but now I felt sad and mournful. I looked at my wife and daughter, who were gazing admiringly on the beauteous scenes around them, and remembered that, in a few short years at most, we should all three be laid in the cold, narrow house formed of four elm or oaken boards, our only garment the flannel shroud, the cold, damp earth above us instead of the bright, glorious sky. O, how sad and mournful I became! I soon comforted myself, however, by reflecting that such is the will of Heaven, and that Heaven is good.

After we had descended the avenue some way, John Jones began to look about him, and getting on the bank on the left side, disappeared. We went on, and in a little time saw him again beckoning to us some way farther down, but still on the bank. When we drew nigh to him, he bade us get on the bank; we did so, and followed him some way amidst furze and lyng. All of a sudden he exclaimed, "There it is!" We looked, and saw a large figure standing on a pedestal. On going up to it we found it to be a Hercules leaning

on his club,—indeed a copy of the Farnese Hercules, as
we gathered from an inscription in Latin partly defaced.
We felt rather disappointed, as we expected that it
would have turned out to be the figure of some huge
Welsh champion of old. We, however, said nothing to
our guide. John Jones, in order that we might properly
appreciate the size of the statue by contrasting it with
his own body, got upon the pedestal and stood up beside
the figure, to the elbow of which his head little more
than reached.

I told him that in my country, the eastern part of
Lloegr, I had seen a man quite as tall as the statue.

"Indeed, sir," said he; "who is it?"

"Hales, the Norfolk giant," I replied, "who has a
sister seven inches shorter than himself, who is yet
seven inches taller than any man in the county when her
brother is out of it."

When John Jones got down he asked me who the
man was whom the statue was intended to represent.

"Erchwl," I replied, "a mighty man of old, who
with his club cleared the country of thieves, serpents,
and monsters."

I now proposed that we should return to Llangollen,
whereupon we retraced our steps, and had nearly
reached the farm-house of the castle, when John Jones
said that we had better return by the low road, by doing
which we should see the castle-lodge, and also its gate,
which was considered one of the wonders of Wales.
We followed his advice, and passing by the front of the
castle northwards, soon came to the lodge. The lodge
had nothing remarkable in its appearance, but the gate,
which was of iron, was truly magnificent.

On the top were two figures of wolves, which John
Jones supposed to be those of foxes. The wolf of Chirk
is not intended to be expressive of the northern name of
its proprietor, but is the armorial bearing of his family
by the maternal side, and originated in one Ryred, surnamed Blaidd, or Wolf, from his ferocity in war; from
whom the family, which only assumed the name of
Middleton in the beginning of the thirteenth century,
on the occasion of its representative marrying a rich
Shropshire heiress of that name, traces descent.

The wolf of Chirk is a Cambrian, not a Gothic wolf, and though "a wolf of battle," is the wolf not of Biddulph, but of Ryred.

CHAPTER LV

A Visitor—Apprenticeship to the Law—Croch Daranau Lope de Vega—No life like the Traveller's.

ONE morning as I sat alone a gentleman was announced. On his entrance I recognised in him the magistrate's clerk, owing to whose good word, as it appeared to me, I had been permitted to remain during the examination into the affair of the wounded butcher. He was a stout, strong-made man, somewhat under the middle height, with a ruddy face, and very clear, grey eyes. I handed him a chair, which he took, and said that his name was R——, and that he had taken the liberty of calling, as he had a great desire to be acquainted with me. On my asking him his reason for that desire, he told me that it proceeded from his having read a book of mine about Spain, which had much interested him.

"Good," said I, "you can't give an author a better reason for coming to see him than being pleased with his book. I assure you that you are most welcome."

After a little general discourse, I said that I presumed he was in the law.

"Yes," said he, "I am a member of that much-abused profession."

"And unjustly abused," said I; "it is a profession which abounds with honourable men, and in which I believe there are fewer scamps than in any other. The most honourable men I have ever known have been lawyers; they were men whose word was their bond, and who would have preferred ruin to breaking it. There was my old master, in particular, who would have died sooner than broken his word. God bless him! I think I see him now, with his bald, shining pate, and his finger on an open page of *Preston's Conveyancing.*"

" Sure you are not a limb of the law?" said Mr. R——.

" No," said I, " but I might be, for I served an apprenticeship to it."

" I am glad to hear it," said Mr. R——, shaking me by the hand. " Take my advice, come and settle at Llangollen, and be my partner."

" If I did," said I, " I am afraid that our partnership would be of short duration ; you would find me too eccentric and flighty for the law. Have you a good practice?" I demanded after a pause.

" I have no reason to complain of it," said he, with a contented air.

" I suppose you are married?" said I.

" O yes," said he, " I have both a wife and family."

" A native of Llangollen?" said I.

" No," said he; " I was born at Llan Silin, a place some way off across the Berwyn."

" Llan Silin?" said I; " I have a great desire to visit it some day or other."

" Why so?" said he; " it offers nothing interesting."

" I beg your pardon," said I; " unless I am much mistaken, the tomb of the great poet Huw Morris is in Llan Silin churchyard."

" Is it possible that you have ever heard of Huw Morris?"

" O yes," said I; " and I have not only heard of him, but am acquainted with his writings; I read them when a boy."

" How very extraordinary," said he; " well, you are quite right about his tomb; when a boy I have played dozens of times on the flat stone with my school-fellows."

We talked of Welsh poetry; he said he had not dipped much into it, owing to its difficulty; that he was master of the colloquial language of Wales, but understood very little of the language of Welsh poetry, which was a widely different thing. I asked him whether he had seen Owen Pugh's translation of *Paradise Lost*. He said he had, but could only partially understand it, adding, however, that those parts which he could make out appeared to him to be admirably executed, that amongst these there was one which had particularly struck him, namely:

> " Ar eu col o rygnu croch
> Daranau."

The rendering of Milton's

> " And on their hinges grate
> Harsh thunder,"

which, grand as it was, was certainly equalled by the Welsh version, and perhaps surpassed, for that he was disposed to think that there was something more terrible in "croch daranau" than in "harsh thunder."

" I am disposed to think so too," said I. " Now can you tell me where Owen Pugh is buried?"

" I cannot," said he; " but I suppose you can tell me; you, who know the burying-place of Huw Morris, are probably acquainted with the burying-place of Owen Pugh."

" No," said I, " I am not. Unlike Huw Morris, Owen Pugh has never had his history written, though perhaps quite as interesting a history might be made out of the life of the quiet student as out of that of the popular poet. As soon as ever I learn where his grave is, I shall assuredly make a pilgrimage to it." Mr. R—— then asked me a good many questions about Spain, and a certain singular race of people about whom I have written a good deal. Before going away he told me that a friend of his, of the name of J——, would call upon me, provided he thought I should not consider his doing so an intrusion. " Let him come by all means," said I; " I shall never look upon a visit from a friend of yours in the light of an intrusion."

In a few days came his friend, a fine, tall, athletic man of about forty. " You are no Welshman," said I, as I looked at him.

" No," said he, " I am a native of Lincolnshire, but I have resided in Llangollen for thirteen years."

" In what capacity?" said I.

" In the wine-trade," said he.

" Instead of coming to Llangollen," said I, " and entering into the wine-trade, you should have gone to London, and enlisted into the life-guards."

" Well," said he, with a smile, " I had once or twice
thought of doing so. However, fate brought me to
Llangollen, and I am not sorry that she did, for I have
done very well here."

I soon found out that he was a well-read and indeed
highly accomplished man. Like his friend R——, Mr.
J—— asked me a great many questions about Spain.
By degrees we got on the subject of Spanish literature.
I said that the literature of Spain was a first-rate
literature, but that it was not very extensive. He asked
me whether I did not think that Lope de Vega was
much overrated."

" Not a bit," said I; " Lope de Vega was one of the
greatest geniuses that ever lived. He was not only a
great dramatist and lyric poet, but a prose writer of
marvellous ability, as he proved by several admirable
tales, amongst which is the best ghost story in the
world."

Another remarkable person whom I got acquainted
with about this time, was A——, the innkeeper, who
lived a little way down the road, of whom John Jones
had spoken so highly, saying, amongst other things,
that he was the clebberest man in Llangollen. One day
as I was looking in at his gate, he came forth, took off
his hat, and asked me to do him the honour to come in
and look at his grounds. I complied, and as he showed
me about he told me his history, in nearly the following
words :—

" I am a Devonian by birth. For many years I
served a travelling gentleman, whom I accompanied in
all his wanderings. I have been five times across the
Alps, and in every capital of Europe. My master at
length dying, left me in his will something handsome,
whereupon I determined to be a servant no longer, but
married, and came to Llangollen, which I had visited
long before with my master, and had been much pleased
with. After a little time, these premises becoming
vacant, I took them, and set up in the public line, more
to have something to do, than for the sake of gain,
about which, indeed, I need not trouble myself much;
my poor dear master, as I said before, having done
very handsomely by me at his death. Here I have
lived for several years, receiving strangers, and improv-

ing my houses and grounds. I am tolerably comfortable, but confess I sometimes look back to my former roving life rather wistfully, for there is no life so merry as the traveller's.''

He was about the middle age, and somewhat under the middle size. I had a good deal of conversation with him, and was much struck with his frank, straightforward manner. He enjoyed a high character at Llangollen for probity, and likewise for cleverness, being reckoned an excellent gardener, and an almost unequalled cook. His master, the travelling gentleman, might well leave him a handsome remembrance in his will, for he had not only been an excellent and trusty servant to him, but had once saved his life at the hazard of his own, amongst the frightful precipices of the Alps. Such retired gentlemen's servants, or such publicans either, as honest A——, are not every day to be found. His grounds, principally laid out by his own hands, exhibited an infinity of taste, and his house, into which I looked, was a perfect picture of neatness. Any tourist visiting Llangollen for a short period could do no better than take up his abode at the hostelry of honest A——.

CHAPTER LVI

Ringing of Bells—Battle of Alma—The Brown Jug—Ale of Llangollen—Reverses.

On the third of October—I think that was the date— as my family and myself, attended by trusty John Jones, were returning on foot from visiting a park not far from Rhiwabon, we heard, when about a mile from Llangollen, a sudden ringing of the bells of the place, and a loud shouting. Presently we observed a postman hurrying in a cart from the direction of the town. '' Peth yw y matter?'' said John Jones. '' Y matter, y matter!'' said the postman, in a tone of exultation. '' Sebastopol wedi cymmeryd Hurrah!''

'' What does he say?'' said my wife anxiously to me.

'' Why, that Sebastopol is taken,'' said I.

"Then you have been mistaken," said my wife, smiling, "for you always said that the place would either not be taken at all, or would cost the allies to take it a deal of time, and an immense quantity of blood and treasure, and here it is taken at once, for the allies only landed the other day. Well, thank God, you have been mistaken!"

"Thank God, indeed," said I, "always supposing that I have been mistaken—but I hardly think, from what I have known of the Russians, that they would let their town—however, let us hope that they have let it be taken, Hurrah!"

We reached our dwelling. My wife and daughter went in. John Jones betook himself to his cottage, and I went into the town, in which there was a great excitement; a wild running troop of boys was shouting "Sebastopol wedi cymmeryd Hurrah! Hurrah!" Old Mr. Jones was standing bareheaded at his door. "Ah," said the old gentleman, "I am glad to see you. Let us congratulate each other," he added, shaking me by the hand. "Sebastopol taken, and in so short a time. How fortunate!"

"Fortunate indeed," said I, returning his hearty shake; "I only hope it may be true."

"O, there can be no doubt of its being true," said the old gentleman. "The accounts are most positive. Come in, and I will tell you all the circumstances." I followed him into his little back parlour, where we both sat down.

"Now," said the old church-clerk, "I will tell you all about it. The allies landed about twenty miles from Sebastopol, and proceeded to march against it. When nearly half way, they found the Russians posted on a hill. Their position was naturally very strong, and they had made it more so by means of redoubts and trenches. However, the allies, undismayed, attacked the enemy, and after a desperate resistance, drove them over the hill, and following fast at their heels, entered the town pell-mell with them, taking it and all that remained alive of the Russian army. And what do you think? The Welsh highly distinguished themselves. The Welsh fusileers were the first to mount the hill. They suffered horribly—indeed, almost the whole regiment was cut to

pieces; but what of that? they showed that the courage
of the Ancient Britons still survives in their descendants.
And now I intend to stand beverage. I assure you I
do. No words! I insist upon it. I have heard you
say you are fond of good ale, and I intend to fetch you
a pint of such ale as I am sure you never drank in your
life." Thereupon he hurried out of the room, and
through the shop into the street.

"Well," said I, when I was by myself, "if this news
does not regularly surprise me! I can easily conceive
that the Russians would be beaten in a pitched battle by
the English and French—but that they should have
been so quickly followed up by the allies as not to be
able to shut their gates and man their walls is to me
inconceivable. Why, the Russians retreat like the wind,
and have a thousand ruses at command, in order to
retard an enemy. So at least I thought, but it is plain
that I know nothing about them, nor indeed much of
my own countrymen; I should never have thought that
English soldiers could have marched fast enough to
overtake Russians, more especially with such a being to
command them, as ——, whom I, and indeed almost
every one else, have always considered a dead weight
on the English service. I suppose, however, that both
they and their commander were spurred on by the
active French."

Presently the old church clerk made his appearance,
with a glass in one hand, and a brown jug of ale in the
other.

"Here," said he, filling the glass, "is some of the
real Llangollen ale; I got it from the little inn, the
Eagle, over the way, which was always celebrated
for its ale. They stared at me when I went in and asked
for a pint of ale, as they knew that for twenty years
I have drunk no liquor whatever, owing to the state
of my stomach, which will not allow me to drink anything stronger than water and tea. I told them, however, it was for a gentleman, a friend of mine, whom I
wished to treat in honour of the fall of Sebastopol."

I would fain have excused myself, but the old gentleman insisted on my drinking.

"Well," said I, taking the glass, "thank God that
our gloomy forebodings are not likely to be realised.

Oes y byd i'r glôd Frythoneg! May Britain's glory
last as long as the world!"

Then, looking for a moment at the ale, which was
of a dark-brown colour, I put the glass to my lips, and
drank.

"Ah," said the old church clerk, "I see you like it,
for you have emptied the glass at a draught."

"It is good ale," said I.

"Good," said the old gentleman rather hastily,
"good; did you ever taste any so good in your life?"

"Why, as to that," said I, "I hardly know what
to say; I have drunk some very good ale in my day.
However, I'll trouble you for another glass."

"O ho, you will," said the old gentleman; "that's
enough; if you did not think it first-rate you would not
ask for more. This," said he, as he filled the glass
again, "is genuine malt and hop liquor, brewed in a
way only known, they say, to some few people in this
place. You must, however, take care how much you
take of it. Only a few glasses will make you dispute
with your friends, and a few more quarrel with them.
Strange things are said of what Llangollen ale made
people do of yore; and I remember that when I was
young and could drink ale, two or three glasses of the
Llangollen juice of the barleycorn would make me—
however, those times are gone by."

"Has Llangollen ale," said I, after tasting the second
glass, "ever been sung in Welsh? is there no englyn
upon it?"

"No," said the old church clerk, "at any rate, that
I am aware."

"Well," said I, "I can't sing its praises in a Welsh
englyn, but I think I can contrive to do so in an English
quatrain, with the help of what you have told me.
What do you think of this?—

"'Llangollen's brown ale is with malt and hop rife;
'Tis good; but don't quaff it from evening till dawn;
For too much of that ale will incline you to strife;
Too much of that ale has caused knives to be drawn.'"

"That's not so bad," said the old church clerk,
"but I think some of our bards could have produced
something better—that is, in Welsh; for example,

old——. What's the name of the old bard who wrote so many englynion on ale?"

" Sion Tudor," said I; " O yes; but he was a great poet. Ah, he has written some wonderful englynion on ale; but you will please to bear in mind that all his englynion are upon bad ale, and it is easier to turn to ridicule what is bad than to do anything like justice to what is good."

O, great was the rejoicing for a few days at Llangollen for the reported triumph; and the share of the Welsh in that triumph reconciled for a time the descendants of the Ancient Britons to the seed of the coiling serpent. " Welsh and Saxons together will conquer the world!" shouted brats as they stood barefooted in the kennel. In a little time, however, news not quite so cheering arrived. There had been a battle fought, it is true, in which the Russians had been beaten, and the little Welsh had very much distinguished themselves, but no Sebastopol had been taken. The Russians had retreated to their town, which, till then almost defenceless on the land side, they had, following their old maxim of " never despair," rendered almost impregnable in a few days, whilst the allies, chiefly owing to the supineness of the British commander, were loitering on the field of battle. In a word, all had happened which the writer, from his knowledge of the Russians and his own countrymen, had conceived likely to happen from the beginning. Then came the news of the commencement of a seemingly interminable siege, and of disasters and disgraces on the part of the British; there was no more shouting at Llangollen in connection with the Crimean expedition. But the subject is a disagreeable one, and the writer will dismiss it after a few brief words.

It was quite right and consistent with the justice of God that the British arms should be subjected to disaster and ignominy about that period. A deed of infamous injustice and cruelty had been perpetrated, and the perpetrators, instead of being punished, had received applause and promotion; so if the British expedition to Sebastopol was a disastrous and ignominious one, who can wonder? Was it likely that the groans of poor Parry would be unheard from the corner to which he had retired to hide his head by "the Ancient of days," who sits above the cloud, and from thence sends judgments?

CHAPTER LVII

The Newspaper—A New Walk—Pentré y Dwr—Oatmeal and Barley-meal—The Man on Horseback—Heavy News.

"Dear me," said I to my wife, as I sat by the fire one Saturday morning, looking at a newspaper which had been sent to us from our own district, "what is this? Why, the death of our old friend Dr. ——. He died last Tuesday week, after a short illness, for he preached in his church at —— the previous Sunday."

"Poor man!" said my wife. "How sorry I am to hear of his death! However, he died in the fulness of years, after a long and exemplary life. He was an excellent man and good Christian shepherd. I knew him well; you, I think, only saw him once."

"But I shall never forget him," said I, "nor how animated his features became when I talked to him about Wales, for he, you know, was a Welshman. I forgot to ask what part of Wales he came from. I suppose I shall never know now."

Feeling indisposed either for writing or reading, I determined to take a walk to Pentré y Dwr, a village in the north-west part of the valley, which I had not yet visited. I purposed going by a path under the Eglwysig crags, which I had heard led thither, and to return by the monastery. I set out. The day was dull and gloomy. Crossing the canal, I pursued my course by romantic lanes, till I found myself under the crags. The rocky ridge here turns away to the north, having previously run from the east to the west.

After proceeding nearly a mile amidst very beautiful scenery, I came to a farm-yard, where I saw several men engaged in repairing a building. This farm-yard was in a very sequestered situation; a hill overhung it on the west, half-way up whose side stood a farm-house, to which it probably pertained. On the north-west was a most romantic hill covered with wood to the

very top. A wild valley led, I knew not whither, to the
north between crags and the wood-covered hill. Going
up to a man of respectable appearance, who seemed
to be superintending the others, I asked him in English
the way to Pentré y Dwr. He replied that I must
follow the path up the hill towards the house, behind
which I should find a road which would lead me
through the wood to Pentré Dwr. As he spoke very
good English, I asked where he had learnt it.

"Chiefly in South Wales," said he, "where they
speak less Welsh than here."

I gathered from him that he lived in the house on
the hill, and was a farmer. I asked him to what place
the road up the valley to the north led.

"We generally go by that road to Wrexham," he
replied; "it is a short but a wild road through the
hills."

After a little discourse on the times, which he told
me were not quite so bad for farmers as they had been,
I bade him farewell.

Mounting the hill, I passed round the house, as the
farmer had directed me, and turned to the west along
a path on the side of the mountain. A deep valley was
on my left, and on my right above me a thick wood,
principally of oak. About a mile farther on the path
winded down a descent, at the bottom of which I saw
a brook and a number of cottages beyond it.

I passed over the brook by means of a long slab laid
across, and reached the cottages. I was now, as I
supposed, in Pentré y Dwr, and a pentré y dwr most
truly it looked, for those Welsh words signify in English
the village of the water, and the brook here ran through
the village, in every room of which its pretty murmuring sound must have been audible. I looked about me
in the hope of seeing somebody of whom I could ask
a question or two, but seeing no one, I turned to the
south, intending to regain Llangollen by the way of
the monastery. Coming to a cottage, I saw a woman,
to all appearance very old, standing by the door, and
asked her in Welsh where I was.

"In Pentré Dwr," said she. "This house and those
yonder," pointing to the cottages past which I had
come, "are Pentré y Dwr. There is, however, another

Pentré Dwr up the glen yonder," said she, pointing towards the north—" which is called Pentré Dwr uchaf (the upper)—this is called Pentré Dwr isaf (the lower)."

" Is it called Pentré Dwr," said I, " because of the water of the brook?"

" Likely enough," said she, " but I never thought of the matter before."

She was blear-eyed, and her skin, which seemed drawn tight over her forehead and cheek-bones, was of the colour of parchment. I asked her how old she was.

" Fifteen after three twenties," she replied; meaning that she was seventy-five.

From her appearance, I should almost have guessed that she had been fifteen after four twenties. I, however, did not tell her so, for I am always cautious not to hurt the feelings of anybody, especially of the aged.

Continuing my way, I soon overtook a man driving five or six very large hogs. One of these, which was muzzled, was of a truly immense size, and walked with considerable difficulty, on account of its fatness. I walked for some time by the side of the noble porker, admiring it. At length a man rode up on horseback from the way we had come; he said something to the driver of the hogs, who instantly unmuzzled the immense creature, who gave a loud grunt on finding his snout and mouth free. From the conversation which ensued between the two men, I found that the driver was the servant, and the other the master.

" Those hogs are too fat to drive along the road," said I at last to the latter.

" We brought them in a cart as far as the Pentré Dwr," said the man on horseback, " but as they did not like the jolting we took them out."

" And where are you taking them to?" said I.

" To Llangollen," said the man, " for the fair on Monday."

" What does that big fellow weigh?" said I, pointing to the largest hog.

" He'll weigh about eighteen score," said the man.

" What do you mean by eighteen score?" said I.

" Eighteen score of pounds," said the man.

" And how much do you expect to get for him?"

" Eight pounds; I shan't take less."

" And who will buy him?" said I.

" Some gent from Wolverhampton or about there," said the man; "there will be plenty of gents from Wolverhampton at the fair."

" And what do you fatten your hogs upon?" said I.

" Oatmeal," said the man.

" And why not on barley-meal?"

" Oatmeal is the best," said the man; "the gents from Wolverhampton prefer them fattened on oatmeal."

" Do the gents of Wolverhampton," said I, "eat the hogs?"

" They do not," said the man; "they buy them to sell again; and they like hogs fed on oatmeal best, because they are the fattest."

" But the pork is not the best," said I; "all hog-flesh raised on oatmeal is bitter and wiry; because, do you see——"

" I see you are in the trade," said the man, "and understand a thing or two."

" I understand a thing or two," said I, "but I am not in the trade. Do you come from far?"

" From Llandeglo," said the man.

" Are you a hog-merchant?" said I.

" Yes," said he, "and a horse-dealer, and a farmer, though rather a small one."

" I suppose, as you are a horse-dealer," said I, "you travel much about?"

" Yes," said the man, "I have travelled a good deal about Wales and England."

" Have you been in Ynys Fon?" said I.

" I see you are a Welshman," said the man.

" No," said I, "but I know a little Welsh."

" Ynys Fon," said the man. "Yes, I have been in Anglesey more times than I can tell."

" Do you know Hugh Pritchard," said I, "who lives at Pentraeth Coch?"

" I know him well," said the man, "and an honest fellow he is."

" And Mr. Bos?" said I.

" What Bos?" said he. "Do you mean a lusty, red-faced man in top-boots and grey coat?"

" That's he," said I.

" He's a clever one," said the man. " I suppose by your knowing these people you are a drover or a horse-dealer. Yes," said he, turning half-round in his saddle and looking at me, " you are a horse-dealer. I remember you well now, and once sold a horse to you at Chelmsford."

" I am no horse-dealer," said I, " nor did I ever buy a horse at Chelmsford. I see you have been about England. Have you ever been in Norfolk or Suffolk?"

" No," said the man, " but I know something of Suffolk. I have an uncle there."

" Whereabouts in Suffolk?" said I.

" At a place called ——," said the man.

" In what line of business?" said I.

" In none at all; he is a clergyman."

" Shall I tell you his name?" said I.

" It is not likely you should know his name," said the man.

" Nevertheless," said I, " I will tell it you—his name was ——."

" Well," said the man, " sure enough that is his name."

" It was his name," said I, " but I am sorry to tell you he is no more. To-day is Saturday. He died last Tuesday week, and was probably buried last Monday. An excellent man was Dr. H. O. A credit to his country and to his order."

The man was silent for some time, and then said with a softer voice, and a very different manner from that he had used before, " I never saw him but once, and that was more than twenty years ago—but I have heard say that he was an excellent man— I see, sir, that you are a clergyman."

" I am no clergyman," said I, " but I knew your uncle and prized him. What was his native place?"

" Corwen," said the man; then taking out his hand-kerchief, he wiped his eyes, and said with a faltering voice, " This will be heavy news there."

We were now past the monastery, and bidding fare-well, I descended to the canal, and returned home by its bank, whilst the Welsh drover, the nephew of the learned, eloquent and exemplary Welsh doctor, pursued

with his servant and animals his way by the high road
to Llangollen.

Many sons of Welsh yeomen brought up to the
Church have become ornaments of it in distant Saxon
land, but few—very few—have by learning, eloquence
and Christian virtues, reflected so much lustre upon it
as Hugh O—— of Corwen.

CHAPTER LVIII

Sunday Night—Sleep, Sin, and Old Age—The Dream—Lanikin
Figure—A Literary Purchase.

THE Sunday morning was a gloomy one. I attended
service at church with my family. The service was in
English, and the younger Mr. E—— preached. The
text I have forgotten, but I remember perfectly well
that the sermon was scriptural and elegant. When we
came out the rain was falling in torrents. Neither I
nor my family went to church in the afternoon. I, however, attended the evening service, which is always in
Welsh. The elder Mr. E—— preached. Text, 2 Cor.
x. 5. The sermon was an admirable one, admonitory,
pathetic and highly eloquent; I went home very much
edified, and edified my wife and Henrietta, by repeating
to them in English the greater part of the discourse
which I had been listening to in Welsh. After supper,
in which I did not join, for I never take supper, provided I have taken dinner, they went to bed, whilst I
remained seated before the fire, with my back near the
table, and my eyes fixed upon the embers, which were
rapidly expiring, and in this posture sleep surprised
me. Amongst the proverbial sayings of the Welsh,
which are chiefly preserved in the shape of triads, is the
following one : " Three things come unawares upon a
man—sleep, sin, and old age." This saying holds sometimes good with respect to sleep and old age, but never
with respect to sin. Sin does not come unawares upon a
man ; God is just, and would never punish a man as
He always does for being overcome by sin, if sin were
able to take him unawares ; and neither sleep nor old
age always come unawares upon a man. People fre-

quently feel themselves going to sleep, and feel old age
stealing upon them; though there can be no doubt that
sleep and old age sometimes come unawares—old age
came unawares upon me; it was only the other day
that I was aware that I was old, though I had long been
old, and sleep came unawares upon me in that chair
in which I had sat down without the slightest thought
of sleeping. And there as I sat I had a dream—what
did I dream about? the sermon, musing upon which I
had been overcome by sleep? not a bit! I dreamt
about a widely different matter. Methought I was in
Llangollen fair, in the place where the pigs were sold,
in the midst of Welsh drovers, immense hogs and immense men, whom I took to be the gents of Wolverhampton. What huge fellows they were! almost as
huge as the hogs for which they higgled; the generality
of them dressed in brown sporting coats, drab breeches,
yellow-topped boots, splashed all over with mud, and
with low-crowned, broad-brimmed hats. One enormous
fellow particularly caught my notice. I guessed he
must have weighed at least eleven score, he had a
half-ruddy, half-tallowy face, brown hair, and rather
thin whiskers. He was higgling with the proprietor of
an immense hog, and as he higgled he wheezed as if he
had a difficulty of respiration, and frequently wiped off,
with a dirty-white pocket-handkerchief, drops of perspiration which stood upon his face. At last methought
he bought the hog for nine pounds, and had no sooner
concluded his bargain than, turning round to me, who
was standing close by staring at him, he slapped me on
the shoulder with a hand of immense weight, crying
with a half-piping, half-wheezing voice, " Coom, neighbour, coom, I and thou have often dealt; gi' me noo a
poond for my bargain, and it shall be all thy own." I
felt in a great rage at his unceremonious behaviour,
and owing to the flutter of my spirits whilst I was
thinking whether or not I should try and knock him
down, I awoke, and found the fire nearly out, and the
ecclesiastical cat seated on my shoulders. The creature
had not been turned out, as ought to have been, before
my wife and daughter retired, and feeling cold, had got
upon the table, and thence had sprung upon my back
for the sake of the warmth which it knew was to be

found there; and no doubt the springing on my shoulders by the ecclesiastical cat was what I took in my dream to be the slap on my shoulders by the Wolverhampton gent.

The day of the fair was dull and gloomy, an exact counterpart of the previous Saturday. Owing to some cause, I did not go into the fair till past one o'clock, and then, seeing neither immense hogs nor immense men, I concluded that the gents of Wolverhampton had been there, and after purchasing the larger porkers, had departed with their bargains to their native district. After sauntering about a little time, I returned home. After dinner I went again into the fair along with my wife; the stock business had long been over, but I observed more stalls than in the morning, and a far greater throng, for the country people for miles round had poured into the little town. By a stall, on which were some poor legs and shoulders of mutton, I perceived the English butcher, whom the Welsh one had attempted to slaughter. I recognised him by a patch which he wore on his cheek. My wife and I went up and inquired how he was. He said that he still felt poorly, but that he hoped he should get round. I asked him if he remembered me; and received for answer that he remembered having seen me when the examination took place into " his matter." I then inquired what had become of his antagonist, and was told that he was in prison awaiting his trial. I gathered from him that he was a native of the Southdown country, and a shepherd by profession; that he had been engaged by the squire of Porkington in Shropshire to look after his sheep, and that he had lived there a year or two, but becoming tired of his situation, he had come to Llangollen, where he had married a Welshwoman, and set up as a butcher. We told him that, as he was our countryman, we should be happy to deal with him sometimes; he, however, received the information with perfect apathy, never so much as saying, " Thank you." He was a tall, lanikin figure, with a pair of large, lack-lustre staring eyes, and upon the whole appeared to be good for very little. Leaving him, we went some way up the principal street; presently my wife turned into a shop, and I, observing a little bookstall, went up to it, and began to

inspect the books. They were chiefly in Welsh. Seeing
a kind of chap book, which bore on its title-page the
name of Twm O'r Nant, I took it up. It was called
Y Llwyn Celyn, or the Holly Grove, and contained the
life and one of the interludes of Tom O' the Dingle,
or Thomas Edwards. It purported to be the first of
four numbers, each of which, amongst other things,
was to contain one of his interludes. The price of the
number was one shilling. I questioned the man of the
stall about the other numbers, but found that this was
the only one which he possessed. ·Eager, however, to
read an interlude of the celebrated Tom, I purchased it,
and turned away from the stall. Scarcely had I done
so, when I saw a wild-looking woman, with two wild
children, looking at me. The woman curtseyed to me,
and I thought I recognised the elder of the two Irish
females whom I had seen in the tent on the green
meadow near Chester. I was going to address her, but
just then my wife called to me from the shop, and I
went to her, and when I returned to look for the woman
she and her children had disappeared, and though I
searched about for her, I could not see her, for which
I was sorry, as I wished very much to have some conversation with her about the ways of the Irish wan-
derers. I was thinking of going to look for her up
" Paddy's dingle," but my wife, meeting me, begged
me to go home with her, as it was getting late. So I
went home with my better half, bearing my late literary
acquisition in my hand.

That night I sat up very late reading the life of Twm
O'r Nant, written by himself in choice Welsh, and his
interlude, which was styled " Cyfoeth a Thylody; or,
Riches and Poverty." The life I had read in my boyhood in an old Welsh magazine, and I now read it
again with great zest, and no wonder, as it is probably
the most remarkable autobiography ever penned. The
interlude I had never seen before, nor indeed any of the
dramatic pieces of Twm O'r Nant, though I had frequently wished to procure some of them—so I read the
present one with great eagerness. Of the life I shall
give some account, and also some extracts from it,
which will enable the reader to judge of Tom's personal
character, and also an abstract of the interlude, from

which the reader may form a tolerably correct idea
of the poetical powers of him whom his countrymen
delight to call " the Welsh Shakespear."

CHAPTER LIX

History of Twm O'r Nant—Eagerness for Learning—The First
Interlude—The Cruel Fighter—Raising Wood—The Luckless
Hour—Turnpike-Keeping—Death in the Snow—Tom's Great
Feat—The Muse a Friend—Strength in Old Age—Resurrection
of the Dead.

" I AM the first-born of my parents,"—says Thomas
Edwards. " They were poor people, and very ignorant.
I was brought into the world in a place called Lower
Pen Parchell, on land which once belonged to the celebrated Iolo Goch. My parents afterwards removed to
the Nant (or dingle) near Nantglyn, situated in a place
called Coom Pernant. The Nant was the middlemost of
three homesteads, which are in the Coom, and are
called the Upper, Middle, and Lower Nant; and it so
happened that in the Upper Nant there were people who
had a boy of about the same age as myself, and for-
asmuch as they were better to do in the world than my
parents, they having only two children, whilst mine
had ten, I was called Tom of the Dingle, whilst he was
denominated Thomas Williams."

After giving some anecdotes of his childhood, he
goes on thus :—" Time passed on till I was about eight
years old, and then in the summer I was lucky enough
to be sent to school for three weeks; and as soon as I
had learnt to spell and read a few words, I conceived a
mighty desire to learn to write; so I went in quest of
elderberries to make me ink, and my first essay in
writing was trying to copy on the sides of the leaves of
books the letters of the words I read. It happened,
however, that a shop in the village caught fire, and the
greater part of it was burnt, only a few trifles being
saved, and amongst the scorched articles my mother
got for a penny a number of sheets of paper burnt at
the edges, and sewed them together to serve as copy-
books for me. Without loss of time I went to the

smith of Waendwysog, who wrote for me the letters
on the upper part of the leaves; and careful enough
was I to fill the whole paper with scrawlings, which
looked for all the world like crows' feet. I went on
getting paper and ink, and something to copy, now
from this person, and now from that, until I learned
to read Welsh and to write it at the same time."

He copied out a great many carols and songs, and
the neighbours, observing his fondness for learning,
persuaded his father to allow him to go to the village
school to learn English. At the end of three weeks,
however, his father, considering that he was losing his
time, would allow him to go no longer, but took him
into the fields, in order that the boy might assist him
in his labour. Nevertheless, Tom would not give up
his literary pursuits, but continued scribbling, and copying out songs and carols. When he was about ten he
formed an acquaintance with an old man, chapel-reader
in Pentré y Foelas, who had a great many old books in
his possession, which he allowed Tom to read; he then
had the honour of becoming amanuensis to a poet.

"I became very intimate," says he, "with a man
who was a poet; he could neither read nor write, but
he was a poet by nature, having a muse wonderfully
glib at making triplets and quartets. He was nick-
named Tum Tai of the Moor. He made an englyn for
me to put in a book, in which I was inserting all the
verses I could collect:

> "'Tom Evan's the lad for hunting up songs,
> Tom Evan to whom the best learning belongs;
> Betwixt his two pasteboards he verses has got,
> Sufficient to fill the whole country, I wot.'

"I was in the habit of writing my name Tom, or
Thomas Evans, before I went to school for a fortnight
in order to learn English; but then I altered it into
Thomas Edwards, for Evan Edwards was the name of
my father, and I should have been making myself a
bastard had I continued calling myself by my first
name. However, I had the honour of being secretary
to the old poet. When he had made a song, he would
keep it in his memory till I came to him. Sometimes
after the old man had repeated his composition to me,

I would begin to dispute with him, asking whether the thing would not be better another way, and he could hardly keep from flying into a passion with me for putting his work to the torture."

It was then the custom for young lads to go about playing what were called interludes, namely, dramatic pieces on religious or moral subjects, written by rustic poets. Shortly after Tom had attained the age of twelve he went about with certain lads of Nantglyn playing these pieces, generally acting the part of a girl, because, as he says, he had the best voice. About this time he wrote an interlude himself, founded on "John Bunyan's Spiritual Courtship," which was, however, stolen from him by a young fellow from Anglesey, along with the greater part of the poems and pieces which he had copied. This affair at first very much disheartened Tom; plucking up his spirits, however, he went on composing, and soon acquired amongst his neighbours the title of " the poet," to the great mortification of his parents, who were anxious to see him become an industrious husbandman.

" Before I was quite fourteen," says he, " I had made another interlude; but when my father and mother heard about it, they did all they could to induce me to destroy it. However, I would not burn it, but gave it to Hugh of Llangwin, a celebrated poet of the time, who took it to Llandyrnog, where he sold it for ten shillings to the lads of the place, who performed it the following summer; but I never got anything for my labour, save a sup of ale from the players when I met them. This at the heel of other things would have induced me to give up poetry, had it been in the power of anything to do so. I made two interludes," he continues, " one for the people of Llanbedr, in the Vale of Clwyd, and the other for the lads of Llanarmon in Yale, one on the subject of Naaman's leprosy, and the other about hypocrisy, which was a refashionment of the work of Richard Parry of Ddiserth. When I was young I had such a rage, or madness, for poetising, that I would make a song on almost anything I saw— and it was a mercy that many did not kill me, or break my bones, on account of my evil tongue. My parents often told me I should have some mischief done me if I went on in the way in which I was going. Once on a time, being with some companions as bad as myself, I happened to use some very free language in a place where three lovers were with a young lass of my neighbourhood, who lived at a place called Ty Celyn, with whom they kept company. I said in discourse that they were the cocks of Ty Celyn. The girl heard me, and conceived a spite against me on account of my scurrilous language. She had a brother, who was a cruel fighter; he took the part of his sister, and determined to chastise me. One Sunday evening he shouted to me as I was coming from Nantgyln—our ways were the same till we got nearly home—he had determined to give me a thrashing, and he had with him a piece of oak stick just suited for the purpose. After we had taunted each other for some time, as we went along, he flung his stick on the ground, and stripped himself stark naked. I took off my hat and my neckcloth, and took his stick in my hand; whereupon, running to the hedge, he took a stake, and straight we set to like two furies. After fighting for some time, our sticks were shivered to pieces and quite short; sometimes we were upon the ground, but did not give up fighting on that acount. Many people came up and would fain have parted us, but we would by no means let them. At last we agreed to go and pull fresh stakes, and then we went at it again, until he could no longer stand. The marks of this battle are upon him and me to this day. At last, covered with a gore of blood, he was dragged home by his neighbours. He was in a dreadful condition, and many thought he would die. On the morrow there came an alarm that he was dead, whereupon I escaped across the mountain to Pentré y Foelas, to the old man Sion Dafydd, to read his old books.''

After staying there a little time, and getting his wounds tended by an old woman, he departed, and skulked about in various places, doing now and then a little work, until, hearing his adversary was recovering, he returned to his home. He went on writing and performing interludes till he fell in love with a young woman rather religiously inclined, whom he married in the year 1763, when he was in his twenty-fourth year.

The young couple settled down on a little place near the town of Denbigh, called Ale Fowlio. They kept three cows and four horses. The wife superintended the cows, and Tom with his horses carried wood from Gwenynos to Ruddlan, and soon excelled all other carters "in loading, and in everything connected with the management of wood." Tom, in the pride of his heart, must needs be helping his fellow-carriers, whilst labouring with them in the forests, till his wife told him he was a fool for his pains, and advised him to go and load in the afternoon, when nobody would be about, offering to go and help him. He listened to her advice, and took her with him.

"The dear creature," says he, "assisted me for some time, but as she was with child, and on that account not exactly fit to turn the roll of the crane with levers of iron, I formed the plan of hooking the horses to the rope, in order to raise up the wood which was to be loaded, and by long teaching the horses to pull and to stop, I contrived to make loading a much easier task, both to my wife and myself. Now this was the first hooking of horses to the rope of the crane which was ever done either in Wales or England. Subsequently I had plenty of leisure and rest, instead of toiling amidst other carriers."

Leaving Ale Fowlio, he took up his abode nearer to Denbigh, and continued carrying wood. Several of his horses died, and he was soon in difficulties, and was glad to accept an invitation from certain miners of the county of Flint to go and play them an interlude. As he was playing them one called "A Vision of the Course of the World," which he had written for the occasion, and which was founded on, and named after, the first part of the work of Master Ellis Wyn, he was arrested at the suit of one Mostyn of Calcoed. He, however, got bail, and partly by carrying, and partly by playing interludes, soon raised enough money to pay his debt. He then made another interlude, called "Riches and Poverty," by which he gained a great deal of money. He then wrote two others, one called "The Three Associates of Man, namely the World, Nature, and Conscience;" the other entitled "The King, the Justice, the Bishop and the Husbandman,"

both of which he and certain of his companions acted
with great success. After he had made all that he could
by acting these pieces, he printed them. When printed,
they had a considerable sale, and Tom was soon able
to set up again as a carter. He went on carting and
carrying for upwards of twelve years, at the end of
which time he was worth, with one thing and the other,
upwards of three hundred pounds, which was considered a very considerable property about ninety years
ago in Wales. He then, in a luckless hour, " when,"
to use his own words, " he was at leisure at home,
like King David on the top of his house," mixed himself
up with the concerns of an uncle of his, a brother of
his father. He first became bail for him, and subsequently made himself answerable for the amount of a
bill, due by his uncle to a lawyer. His becoming
answerable for the bill nearly proved the utter ruin of
our hero. His uncle failed, and left him to pay it.
The lawyer took out a writ against him. It would
have been well for Tom if he had paid the money at
once, but he went on dallying and compromising with
the lawyer, till he became terribly involved in his web.
To increase his difficulties, work became slack; so at
last he packed his things upon his carts, and with his
family, consisting of his wife and three daughters, fled
into Montgomeryshire. The lawyer, however, soon got
information of his whereabout, and threatened to arrest
him. Tom, after trying in vain to arrange matters with
him, fled into South Wales, to Carmarthenshire, where
he carried wood for a timber-merchant, and kept a
turnpike gate, which belonged to the same individual.
But the " old cancer " still followed him, and his horses
were seized for the debt. His neighbours, however,
assisted him, and bought the horses in at a low price
when they were put up for sale, and restored them to
him, for what they had given. Even then the matter
was not satisfactorily settled, for, years afterwards,
on the decease of Tom's father, the lawyer seized upon
the property, which by law descended to Tom O'r
Nant, and turned his poor old mother out upon the
cold mountain side.

Many strange adventures occurred to Tom in South
Wales, but those which befell him whilst officiating

as a turnpike-keeper were certainly the most extraordinary. If what he says be true, as of course it is—for who shall presume to doubt Tom O' the Dingle's veracity?—whosoever fills the office of turnpike-keeper in Wild Wales should be a person of very considerable nerve.

"We were in the habit of seeing," says Tom, "plenty of passengers going through the gate without paying toll; I mean such things as are called phantoms, or illusions—sometimes there were hearses and mourning coaches, sometimes funeral processions on foot, the whole to be seen as distinctly as anything could be seen, especially at night-time. I saw myself on a certain night a hearse go through the gate whilst it was shut; I saw the horses and the harness, the postilion, and the coachman, and the tufts of hair such as are seen on the tops of hearses, and I saw the wheels scattering the stones in the road, just as other wheels would have done. Then I saw a funeral of the same character, for all the world like a real funeral; there was the bier and the black drapery. I have seen more than one. If a young man was to be buried there would be a white sheet, or something that looked like one—and sometimes I have seen a flaring candle going past.

"Once a traveller passing through the gate called out to me: 'Look! yonder is a corpse candle coming through the fields beside the highway.' So we paid attention to it as it moved, making apparently towards the church from the other side. Sometimes it would be quite near the road, another time some way into the fields. And sure enough after the lapse of a little time a body was brought by exactly the same route by which the candle had come, owing to the proper road being blocked up with snow.

"Another time there happened a great wonder connected with an old man of Carmarthen, who was in the habit of carrying fish to Brecon, Menny, and Monmouth, and returning with the poorer kind of Gloucester cheese: my people knew he was on the road, and had made ready for him, the weather being dreadful, wind blowing and snow drifting. Well! in the middle of the night my daughters heard the voice of the old man at the gate, and their mother called to them to open it

quick, and invite the old man to come in to the fire!
One of the girls got up forthwith, but when she went
out there was nobody to be seen. On the morrow, lo,
and behold! the body of the old man was brought past
on a couch, he having perished in the snow on the
mountain of Tre'r Castell. Now this is the truth of the
matter.''

Many wonderful feats did Tom perform connected
with loading and carrying, which acquired for him the
reputation of being the best wood carter of the south.
His dexterity at moving huge bodies was probably
never equalled. Robinson Crusoe was not half so
handy. Only see how he moved a ship into the water,
which a multitude of people were unable to do.

"After keeping the gate for two or three years,''
says he, "I took the lease of a piece of ground in
Llandeilo Fawr, and built a house upon it, which I got
licensed as a tavern for my daughters to keep. I myself
went on carrying wood as usual. Now it happened
that my employer, the merchant at Abermarlais, had
built a small ship, of about thirty or forty tons, in the
wood, about a mile and a quarter from the river Towy,
which is capable of floating small vessels as far as
Carmarthen. He had resolved that the people should
draw it to the river by way of sport, and had caused
proclamation to be made in four parish churches, that
on such a day a ship would be launched at Abermarlais,
and that food and drink would be given to any one
who would come and lend a hand at the work. Four
hogsheads of ale were broached, a great oven full of
bread was baked, plenty of cheese and butter bought,
and meat cooked for the more respectable people. The
ship was provided with four wheels, or rather four
great rolling stocks, fenced about with iron, with great
big axle-trees in them, well greased against the appointed day. I had been loading in the wood that day,
and sending the team forward, I went to see the business—and a pretty piece of business it turned out. All
the food was eaten, the drink swallowed to the last
drop, the ship drawn about three roods, and then left
in a deep ditch. By this time night was coming on, and
the multitude went away, some drunk, some hungry
for want of food, but the greater part laughing as if

they would split their sides. The merchant cried like a child, bitterly lamenting his folly, and told me that he should have to take the ship to pieces before he could ever get it out of the ditch.

" I told him that I could take it to the river, provided I could but get three or four men to help me; whereupon he said that if I could but get the vessel to the water, he would give me anything I asked, and earnestly begged me to come the next morning, if possible. I did come, with the lad and four horses. I went before the team, and set the men to work to break a hole through a great old wall, which stood as it were before the ship. We then laid a piece of timber across the hole from which was a chain, to which the tackle—that is, the rope and pulleys—was hooked. We then hooked one end of the rope to the ship, and set the horses to pull at the other. The ship came out of the hole prosperously enough, and then we had to hook the tackle to a tree, which was growing near, and by this means we got the ship forward; but when we came to soft ground we were obliged to put planks under the wheels to prevent their sinking under the immense weight; when we came to the end of the foremost planks, we put the hinder ones before, and so on; when there was no tree at hand to which we could hook the tackle, we were obliged to drive a post down to hook it to. So from tree to post it got down to the river in a few days. I was promised noble wages by the merchant, but I never got anything from him but promises and praises. Some people came to look at us, and gave us money to get ale, and that was all."

The merchant subsequently turned out a very great knave, cheating Tom on various occasions, and finally broke, very much in his debt. Tom was obliged to sell off everything, and left South Wales without horses or waggon; his old friend the Muse, however, stood him in good stead.

" Before I left," says he, " I went to Brecon, and printed the ' Interlude of the King, the Justice, the Bishop, and the Husbandman,' and got an old acquaintance of mine to play it with me, and help me to sell the books. I likewise busied myself in getting subscribers to a book of songs called the ' Garden of Minstrelsy.'

It was printed at Trefecca. The expense attending the printing amounted to fifty-two pounds, but I was fortunate enough to dispose of two thousand copies. I subsequently composed an interlude called 'Pleasure and Care,' and printed it; and after that I made an interlude called the 'Three Powerful Ones of the World: Poverty, Love, and Death.'"

The poet's daughters were not successful in the tavern speculation at Llandeilo, and followed their father into North Wales. The second he apprenticed to a milliner, the other two lived with him till the day of his death. He settled at Denbigh in a small house, which he was enabled to furnish by means of two or three small sums which he recovered for work done a long time before. Shortly after his return, his father died, and the lawyer seized the little property "for the old curse," and turned Tom's mother out.

After his return from the South, Tom went about for some time playing interludes, and then turned his hand to many things. He learnt the trade of stonemason, took jobs, and kept workmen. He then went amongst certain bricklayers, and induced them to teach him their craft; "and shortly," as he says, "became a very lion at bricklaying. For the last four or five years," says he, towards the conclusion of his history, "my work has been to put up iron ovens, and likewise furnaces of all kinds, also grates, stoves and boilers, and not unfrequently I have practised as a smoke doctor."

The following feats of strength he performed after his return from South Wales, when he was probably about sixty years of age :—

"About a year after my return from the South," says he, "I met with an old carrier of wood, who had many a time worked along with me. He and I were at the Hand at Ruthyn, along with various others, and in the course of discourse my friend said to me : 'Tom, thou art much weaker than thou wast when we carted wood together.' I answered that in my opinion I was not a bit weaker than I was then. Now it happened that at the moment we were talking there were some sacks of wheat in the hall, which were going to Chester by the carrier's waggon. They might hold about three bushels each, and I said that if I could get three of the sacks upon the table, and had them tied together, I would carry them into the street and back again; and so I did; many who were present tried to do the same thing, but all failed.

"Another time when I was at Chester I lifted a barrel of porter from the street to the hinder part of the waggon, solely by strength of back and arms."

He was once run over by a loaded waggon, but, strange to say, escaped without the slightest injury.

Towards the close of his life he had strong religious convictions, and felt a loathing for the sins which he had committed. "On their account," says he, in the concluding page of his biography, "there is a strong necessity for me to consider my ways, and to inquire about a Saviour, since it is utterly impossible for me to save myself without obtaining knowledge of the merits of the Mediator, in which I hope I shall terminate my short time on earth in the peace of God enduring unto all eternity."

He died in the year 1810, at the age of 71, shortly after the death of his wife, who seems to have been a faithful, loving partner. By her side he was buried in the earth of the graveyard of the White Church, near Denbigh. There can be little doubt that the souls of both will be accepted on the great day when, as Gronwy Owen says :—

"Like corn from the belly of the ploughed field, in a thick crop, those buried in the earth shall arise, and the sea shall cast forth a thousand myriads of dead above the deep billowy way."

CHAPTER LX

Mystery Plays—The Two Prime Opponents—Analysis of Interlude —" Riches and Poverty "—Tom's Grand Qualities.

IN the preceding chapter I have given an abstract of the life of Tom O' the Dingle; I will now give an analysis of his interlude; first, however, a few words on interludes in general. It is difficult to say, with anything like certainty, what is the meaning of the word interlude. It may mean, as Warton supposes in his history

of English Poetry, a short play performed between the
courses of a banquet, or festival; or it may mean the
playing of something by two or more parties, the inter-
change of playing or acting which occurs when two or
more people act. It was about the middle of the fifteenth
century that dramatic pieces began in England to be
called Interludes; for some time previous they had been
styled Moralities; but the earliest name by which they
were known was Mysteries. The first Mysteries composed in England were by one Ranald, or Ranulf, a
monk of Chester, who flourished about 1322, whose
verses are mentioned rather irreverently in one of the
visions of Piers Plowman, who puts them in the same
rank as the ballads about Robin Hood and Maid
Marion, making Sloth say:

" I cannot perfitly my Paternoster as the priest it singeth,
  But I can rhymes of Robin Hood and Ranald of Chester."

Long, however, before the time of this Ranald, Mysteries had been composed and represented both in Italy
and France. The Mysteries were very rude compositions; little more, as Warton says, than literal repre-
sentations of portions of Scripture. They derived their
name of Mysteries from being generally founded on the
more mysterious parts of Holy Writ—for example, the
Incarnation, the Atonement and the Resurrection. The
Moralities displayed something more of art and in-
vention than the Mysteries; in them virtues, vices and
qualities were personified, and something like a plot
was frequently to be discovered. They were termed
Moralities because each had its moral, which was
spoken at the end of the piece by a person called the
Doctor.[1] Much that has been said about the moralities
holds good with respect to the interludes. Indeed, for
some time dramatic pieces were called moralities and
interludes indifferently. In both there is a mixture of
allegory and reality. The latter interludes, however,
display more of everyday life than was ever observable
in the moralities, and more closely approximate to
modern plays. Several writers of genius have written
interludes, amongst whom are the English Skelton and

[1] *Essay on the Origin of the English Stage,* by Bishop Percy.
London, 1793.

the Scottish Lindsay, the latter of whom wrote eight pieces of that kind, the most celebrated of which is called "The Puir Man and the Pardonar." Both of these writers flourished about the same period, and made use of the interlude as a means of satirising the vices of the popish clergy. In the time of Charles the First the interlude went much out of fashion in England; in fact, the play, or regular drama, had superseded it. In Wales, however, it continued to the beginning of the present century, when it yielded to the influence of Methodism. Of all Welsh interlude composers, Twm O'r Nant, or Tom of the Dingle, was the most famous. Here follows the promised analysis of his "Riches and Poverty."

The entire title of the interlude is to this effect. The two prime opponents Riches and Poverty. A brief exposition of their contrary effects on the world; with short and appropriate explanations of their quality and substance, according to the rule of the four elements, Water, Fire, Earth, and Air.

First of all enter Fool, Sir Jemant Wamal, who in rather a foolish speech tells the audience that they are about to hear a piece composed by Tom the poet. Then appears Captain Riches, who makes a long speech about his influence in the world, and the general contempt in which Poverty is held; he is, however, presently checked by the Fool, who tells him some home truths, and asks him, among other questions, whether Solomon did not say that it is not meet to despise a poor man, who conducts himself rationally. Then appears Howel Tightbelly, the miser, who in capital verse, with very considerable glee and exultation, gives an account of his manifold rascalities. Then comes his wife, Esther Steady, home from the market, between whom and her husband there is a pithy dialogue. Captain Riches and Captain Poverty then meet, without rancour, however, and have a long discourse about the providence of God, whose agents they own themselves to be. Enter then an old worthless scoundrel called Diogyn Trwstan, or Luckless Lazybones, who is upon the parish, and who, in a very entertaining account of his life, confesses that he was never good for anything, but was a liar and an idler from his infancy.

Enter again the Miser along with poor Lowry, who asks the Miser for meal, and other articles, but gets nothing but threatening language. There is then a very edifying dialogue between Mr. Contemplation and Mr. Truth, who, when they retire, are succeeded on the stage by the Miser and John the Tavern-keeper. The publican owes the Miser money, and begs that he will be merciful to him. The Miser, however, swears that he will be satisfied with nothing but bond and judgment on his effects. The publican very humbly says that he will go to a friend of his, in order to get the bond made out; almost instantly comes the Fool, who reads an inventory of the publican's effects. The Miser then sings for very gladness, because everything in the world has hitherto gone well with him; turning round, however, what is his horror and astonishment to behold Mr. Death, close by him. Death hauls the Miser away, and then appears the Fool to moralise and dismiss the audience.

The appropriate explanations mentioned in the title are given in various songs which the various characters sing after describing themselves, or after dialogues with each other. The announcement that the whole exposition, etc., will be after the rule of the four elements, is rather startling; the dialogue, however, between Captain Riches and Captain Poverty shows that Tom was equal to his subject, and promised nothing that he could not perform.

Enter CAPTAIN POVERTY.

O Riches, thy figure is charming and bright,
And to speak in thy praise all the world doth delight,
But I'm a poor fellow all tatter'd and torn,
Whom all the world treateth with insult and scorn.

RICHES.

However mistaken the judgment may be
Of the world which is never from ignorance free,
The parts we must play, which to us are assign'd,
According as God has enlighten'd our mind.

Of elements four did our Master create,
The earth and all in it with skill the most great;
Need I the world's four materials declare—
Are they not water, fire, earth, and air?

Too wise was the mighty Creator to frame
A world from one element, water or flame ;
The one is full moist and the other full hot,
And a world made of either were useless, I wot.

And if it had all of mere earth been compos'd,
And no water nor fire been within it enclos'd,
It could ne'er have produc'd for a huge multitude
Of all kinds of living things suitable food

And if God what was wanted had not fully known,
But created the world of these three things alone,
How would any creature the heaven beneath,
Without the blest air have been able to breathe?

Thus all things created, the God of all grace,
Of four prime materials, each good in its place.
The work of His hands, when completed, He view'd,
And saw and pronounc'd that 'twas seemly and good.

POVERTY.

In the marvellous things, which to me thou hast told
The wisdom of God I most clearly behold,
And did He not also make man of the same
Materials He us'd when the world He did frame?

RICHES.

Creation is all, as the sages agree,
Of the elements four in man's body that be ;
Water's the blood, and fire is the nature
Which prompts generation in every creature.

The earth is the flesh which with beauty is rife,
The air is the breath, without which is no life ;
So man must be always accounted the same
As the substances four which exist in his frame.

And as in their creation distinction there's none
'Twixt man and the world, so the Infinite One
Unto man a clear wisdom did bounteously give
The nature of everything to perceive.

POVERTY.

But one thing to me passing strange doth appear :
Since the wisdom of man is so bright and so clear,
How comes there such jarring and warring to be
In the world betwixt Riches and Poverty?

RICHES.

That point we'll discuss without passion or fear
With the aim of instructing the listeners here ;
And haply some few who instruction require
May profit derive like the bee from the briar.

Man as thou knowest, in his generation
Is a type of the world and of all the creation;
Difference there's none in the manner of birth
'Twixt the lowliest hinds and the lords of the earth.

The world which the same thing as man we account
In one place is sea, in another is mount;
A part of it rock, and a part of it dale—
God's wisdom has made every place to avail.

There exist precious treasures of every kind
Profoundly in earth's quiet bosom enshrin'd;
There's searching about them, and ever has been,
And by some they are found, and by some never seen.

With wonderful wisdom the Lord God on high
Has contriv'd the two lights which exist in the sky;
The sun's hot as fire, and its ray bright as gold,
But the moon's ever pale, and by nature is cold.

The sun, which resembles a huge world of fire,
Would burn up full quickly creation entire
Save the moon with its temp'rament cool did assuage
Of its brighter companion the fury and rage.

Now I beg you the sun and the moon to behold,
The one that's so bright, and the other so cold,
And say if two things in creation there be
Better emblems of Riches and Poverty.

POVERTY.

In manner most brief, yet convincing and clear,
You have told the whole truth to my wond'ring ear,
And I see that 'twas God, who in all things is fair,
Has assign'd us the forms, in this world which we bear.

In the sight of the world doth the wealthy man seem
Like the sun which doth warm everything with its beam;
Whilst the poor needy wight with his pitiable case
Resembles the moon which doth chill with its face.

RICHES.

You know that full oft, in their course as they run,
An eclipse cometh over the moon or the sun;
Certain hills of the earth with their summits of pride
The face of the one from the other do hide.

The sun doth uplift his magnificent head,
And illumines the moon, which were otherwise dead,
Even as Wealth from its station on high,
Giveth work and provision to Poverty.

POVERTY.

I know, and the thought mighty sorrow instils,
The sins of the world are the terrible hills

An eclipse which do cause, or a dread obscuration,
To one or another in every vocation.

RICHES.

It is true that God gives unto each from his birth
Some task to perform whilst he wends upon earth,
But He gives correspondent wisdom and force
To the weight of the task, and the length of the course.

[Exit.

POVERTY.

I hope there are some, who 'twixt me and the youth
Have heard this discourse, whose sole aim is the truth,
Will see and acknowledge, as homeward they plod,
Each thing is arrang'd by the wisdom of God.

There can be no doubt that Tom was a poet, or he could never have treated the hackneyed subjects of Riches and Poverty in a manner so original, and at the same time so masterly, as he has done in the interlude above analysed; I cannot, however, help thinking that he was greater as a man than a poet, and that his fame depends more on the cleverness, courage and energy, which it is evident by his biography that he possessed, than on his interludes. A time will come when his interludes will cease to be read, but his making ink out of elderberries, his battle with the "cruel fighter," his teaching his horses to turn the crane, and his getting the ship to the water, will be talked of in Wales till the peak of Snowdon shall fall down.

CHAPTER LXI

Set out for Wrexham—Craig y Forwyn—Uncertainty—The Collier
—Cadogan Hall—Methodistical Volume.

HAVING learnt from a newspaper that a Welsh book on Welsh Methodism had been just published at Wrexham, I determined to walk to that place and purchase it. I could easily have procured the work through a bookseller at Llangollen, but I wished to explore the hill-road which led to Wrexham, what the farmer under the Eglwysig rocks had said of its wildness having excited my curiosity, which the procuring of the book afforded me a plausible excuse for gratifying. If one wants to

take any particular walk, it is always well to have some
business, however trifling, to transact at the end of it;
so having determined to go to Wrexham by the mountain road, I set out on the Saturday next after the one
on which I had met the farmer who had told me of it.

The day was gloomy, with some tendency to rain.
I passed under the hill of Dinas Bran. About a furlong
from its western base I turned round and surveyed it—
and perhaps the best view of the noble mountain is to
be obtained from the place where I turned round. How
grand, though sad, from there it looked, that grey
morning, with its fine ruin on its brow, above which
a little cloud hovered! It put me in mind of some old
king, unfortunate and melancholy, but a king still, with
the look of a king, and the ancestral crown still on his
furrowed forehead. I proceeded on my way, all was
wild and solitary, and the yellow leaves were falling
from the trees of the groves. I passed by the farm-
yard, where I had held discourse with the farmer on the
preceding Saturday, and soon entered the glen, the appearance of which had so much attracted my curiosity.
A torrent, rushing down from the north, was on my
right. It soon began to drizzle, and mist so filled the
glen that I could only distinguish objects a short way
before me, and on either side. I wandered on a considerable way, crossing the torrent several times by
rustic bridges. I passed two lone farm-houses, and at
last saw another on my left hand—the mist had now
cleared up, but it still slightly rained—the scenery was
wild to a degree—a little way before me was a tremendous pass, near it an enormous crag, of a strange
form, rising to the very heavens, the upper part of it of
a dull white colour. Seeing a respectable-looking man
near the house, I went up to him. "Am I in the
right way to Wrexham?" said I, addressing him in
English.

"You can get to Wrexham this way, sir," he replied.

"Can you tell me the name of that crag?" said I,
pointing to the large one.

"That crag, sir, is called Craig y Forwyn."

"The maiden's crag," said I; "why is it called so?"

"I do not know, sir; some people say that it is called
so because its head is like that of a woman, others

because a young girl in love leaped from the top of it and was killed."

"And what is the name of this house?" said I.

"This house, sir, is called Plas Uchaf."

"Is it called Plas Uchaf," said I, "because it is the highest house in the valley?"

"It is, sir; it is the highest of three homesteads; the next below it is Plas Canol—and the one below that Plas Isaf."

"Middle place and lower place," said I. "It is very odd that I know in England three people who derive their names from places so situated. One is Houghton, another Middleton, and the third Lowdon; in modern English, Hightown, Middletown, and Lowtown."

"You appear to be a person of great intelligence, sir."

"No, I am not—but I am rather fond of analysing words, particularly the names of persons and places. Is the road to Wrexham hard to find?"

"Not very, sir; that is, in the day-time. Do you live at Wrexham?"

"No," I replied, "I am stopping at Llangollen."

"But you won't return there to-night?"

"O yes, I shall!"

"By this road?"

"No, by the common road. This is not a road to travel by night."

"Nor is the common road, sir, for a respectable person on foot; that is, on a Saturday night. You will perhaps meet drunken colliers, who may knock you down."

"I will take my chance for that," said I, and bade him farewell. I entered the pass, passing under the strange-looking crag. After I had walked about half-a-mile the pass widened considerably, and a little way farther on debouched on some wild, moory ground. Here the road became very indistinct. At length I stopped in a state of uncertainty. A well-defined path presented itself, leading to the east, whilst northward before me there seemed scarcely any path at all. After some hesitation I turned to the east by the well-defined path, and by so doing went wrong, as I soon found.

I mounted the side of a brown hill covered with moss-

like grass, and here and there heather. By the time
I arrived at the top of the hill the sun shone out, and
I saw Rhiwabon and Cefn Mawr before me in the
distance. " I am going wrong," said I ; " I should have
kept on due north. However, I will not go back, but
will steeplechase it across the country to Wrexham,
which must be towards the north-east." So turning
aside from the path, I dashed across the hills in that
direction ; sometimes the heather was up to my knees,
and sometimes I was up to the knees in quags. At
length I came to a deep ravine, which I descended ; at
the bottom was a quagmire, which, however, I contrived to cross by means of certain stepping-stones,
and came to a cart-path up a heathery hill, which I
followed. I soon reached the top of the hill, and the
path still continuing, I followed it till I saw some small
grimy-looking huts, which I supposed were those of
colliers. At the door of the first I saw a girl. I
spoke to her in Welsh, and found she had little or
none. I passed on, and seeing the door of a cabin open,
I looked in—and saw no adult person, but several grimy
but chubby children. I spoke to them in English, and
found they could only speak Welsh. Presently I observed a robust woman advancing towards me ; she
was barefooted, and bore on her head an immense
lump of coal. I spoke to her in Welsh, and found she
could only speak English. " Truly," said I to myself,
" I am on the borders. What a mixture of races and
languages !" The next person I met was a man in a
collier's dress ; he was a stout-built fellow of the middle
age, with a coal-dusty, surly countenance. I asked him
in Welsh if I was in the right direction for Wrexham,
he answered in a surly manner in English that I was.
I again spoke to him in Welsh, making some indifferent
observation on the weather, and he answered in English
yet more gruffly than before. For the third time I
spoke to him in Welsh, whereupon, looking at me with
a grin of savage contempt, and showing a set of teeth
like those of a mastiff, he said, " How's this? why,
you haven't a word of English ! A pretty fellow, you,
with a long coat on your back, and no English on your
tongue ; an't you ashamed of yourself? Why, here am
I in a short coat, yet I'd have you to know that I can

speak English as well as Welsh, aye, and a good deal better." "All people are not equally clebber," said I, still speaking Welsh. "Clebber," said he, "clebber! what is clebber? why can't you say clever? Why, I never saw such a low, illiterate fellow in my life;" and with these words he turned away, with every mark of disdain, and entered a cottage near at hand.

"Here I have had," said I to myself, as I proceeded on my way, "to pay for the over-praise which I lately received. The farmer on the other side of the mountain called me a person of great intelligence, which I never pretended to be, and now this collier calls me a low, illiterate fellow, which I really don't think I am. There is certainly a Nemesis mixed up with the affairs of this world; every good thing which you get, beyond what is strictly your due, is sure to be required from you with a vengeance. A little over-praise by a great deal of under-rating—a gleam of good fortune by a night of misery."

I now saw Wrexham Church at about the distance of three miles, and presently entered a lane which led gently down from the hills, which were the same heights I had seen on my right hand, some months previously, on my way from Wrexham to Rhiwabon. The scenery now became very pretty—hedge-rows were on either side, a luxuriance of trees, and plenty of green fields. I reached the bottom of the lane, beyond which I saw a strange-looking house upon a slope on the right hand. It was very large, ruinous, and seemingly deserted. A little beyond it was a farm-house, connected with which was a long row of farming buildings along the roadside. Seeing a woman seated knitting at the door of a little cottage, I asked her in English the name of the old ruinous house.

"Cadogan Hall, sir," she replied.

"And whom does it belong to?" said I.

"I don't know exactly," replied the woman, "but Mr. Morris at the farm holds it, and stows his things in it."

"Can you tell me anything about it?" said I.

"Nothing farther," said the woman, "than that it is said to be haunted, and to have been a barrack many years ago."

" Can you speak Welsh?" said I.

" No," said the woman; " I are Welsh, but have no Welsh language."

Leaving the woman, I put on my best speed, and in about half-an-hour reached Wrexham.

The first thing I did on my arrival was to go to the bookshop and purchase the Welsh methodistic book. It cost me seven shillings, and was a thick, bulky octavo, with a cut-and-come-again expression about it, which was anything but disagreeable to me, for I hate your flimsy publications. The evening was now beginning to set in, and feeling somewhat hungry, I hurried off to the Wynstay Arms, through streets crowded with market people. On arriving at the inn, I entered the grand room and ordered dinner. The waiters, observing me splashed with mud from head to foot, looked at me dubiously; seeing, however, the respectable-looking volume which I bore in my hand—none of your railroad stuff—they became more assured, and I presently heard one say to the other, " It's all right—that's Mr. So-and-so, the great Baptist preacher. He has been preaching amongst the hills—don't you see his Bible?"

Seating myself at a table, I inspected the volume. And here, perhaps, the reader expects that I shall regale him with an analysis of the methodistical volume at least as long as that of the life of Tom O' the Dingle. In that case, however, he will be disappointed; all that I shall at present say of it is, that it contained a history of Methodism in Wales, with the lives of the principal Welsh Methodists. That it was fraught with curious and original matter, was written in a straightforward, methodical style, and that I have no doubt it will some day or other be extensively known and highly prized.

After dinner I called for half a pint of wine. Whilst I was trifling over it, a commercial traveller entered into conversation with me. After some time he asked me if I was going further that night.

" To Llangollen," said I.

" By the ten o'clock train?" said he.

" No," I replied, " I am going on foot."

" On foot!" said he; " I would not go on foot there this night for fifty pounds."

" Why not?" said I.

"For fear of being knocked down by the colliers, who will be all out and drunk."

"If not more than two attack me," said I, "I shan't much mind. With this book I am sure I can knock down one, and I think I can find play for the other with my fists."

The commercial traveller looked at me. "A strange kind of Baptist minister," I thought I heard him say.

CHAPTER LXII

Rhiwabon Road—The Public-house Keeper—No Welsh—The Wrong Road—The Good Wife.

I PAID my reckoning and started. The night was now rapidly closing in. I passed the toll-gate, and hurried along the Rhiwabon road, overtaking companies of Welsh going home, amongst whom were many individuals, whom, from their thick and confused speech, as well as from their staggering gait, I judged to be intoxicated. As I passed a red public-house on my right hand, at the door of which stood several carts, a scream of Welsh issued from it.

"Let any Saxon," said I, "who is fond of fighting, and wishes for a bloody nose, go in there."

Coming to the small village about a mile from Rhiwabon, I felt thirsty, and seeing a public-house, in which all seemed to be quiet, I went in. A thick-set man, with a pipe in his mouth, sat in the tap-room, and also a woman.

"Where is the landlord?" said I.

"I am the landlord," said the man huskily. "What do you want?"

"A pint of ale," said I.

The man got up, and, with his pipe in his mouth, went staggering out of the room. In about a minute he returned, holding a mug in his hand, which he put down on a table before me, spilling no slight quantity of the liquor as he did so. I put down three-pence on the table. He took the money up slowly, piece by piece, looked at it, and appeared to consider; then taking the pipe out of his mouth, he dashed it to seven pieces against the table, then staggered out of the room into the passage, and from thence apparently out of the house. I tasted the ale, which was very good; then turning to the woman, who seemed about three-and-twenty, and was rather good-looking, I spoke to her in Welsh.

"I have no Welsh, sir," said she.

"How is that?" said I; "this village is, I think, in the Welshery."

"It is," said she; "but I am from Shropshire."

"Are you the mistress of the house?" said I.

"No," said she, "I am married to a collier;" then getting up, she said, "I must go and see after my husband."

"Won't you take a glass of ale first?" said I, offering to fill a glass which stood on the table.

"No," said she; "I am the worst in the world for a glass of ale;" and without saying anything more she departed.

"I wonder whether your husband is anything like you with respect to a glass of ale?" said I to myself; then finishing my ale, I got up and left the house, which, when I departed, appeared to be entirely deserted.

It was now quite night, and it would have been pitchy-dark but for the glare of the forges. There was an immense glare to the south-west, which I conceived proceeded from those of Cefn Mawr. It lighted up the south-western sky; then there were two other glares nearer to me, seemingly divided by a lump of something, perhaps a grove of trees.

Walking very fast, I soon overtook a man. I knew him at once by his staggering gait.

"Ah, landlord!" said I; "whither bound?"

"To Rhiwabon," said he, huskily, "for a pint."

"Is the ale so good at Rhiwabon," said I, "that you leave home for it?"

"No," said he, rather shortly, "there's not a glass of good ale in Rhiwabon."

"Then why do you go thither?" said I.

"Because a pint of bad liquor abroad is better than a quart of good at home," said the landlord, reeling against the hedge.

"There are many in a higher station than you who

act upon that principle," thought I to myself as I passed on.

I soon reached Rhiwabon. There was a prodigious noise in the public-houses as I passed through it. " Colliers carousing," said I. " Well, I shall not go amongst them to preach temperance, though perhaps in strict duty I ought." At the end of the town, instead of taking the road on the left side of the church, I took that on the right. It was not till I had proceeded nearly a mile that I began to be apprehensive that I had mistaken the way. Hearing some people coming towards me on the road, I waited till they came up ; they proved to be a man and a woman. On my inquiring whether I was right for Llangollen, the former told me that I was not, and in order to get there it was necessary that I should return to Rhiwabon. I instantly turned round. About half-way back I met a man who asked me in English where I was hurrying to. I said to Rhiwabon, in order to get to Llangollen. " Well, then," said he, " you need not return to Rhiwabon—yonder is a short cut across the fields," and he pointed to a gate. I thanked him, and said I would go by it ; before leaving him, I asked to what place the road led which I had been following.

" To Pentre Castren," he replied. I struck across the fields, and should probably have tumbled half-a-dozen times over pales and the like, but for the light of the Cefn furnaces before me, which cast their red glow upon my path. I debouched upon the Llangollen road near to the tramway leading to the collieries. Two enormous sheets of flame shot up high into the air from ovens, illumining two spectral chimneys as high as steeples, also smoky buildings, and grimy figures moving about. There was a clanging of engines, a noise of shovels and a falling of coals truly horrible. The glare was so great that I could distinctly see the minutest lines upon my hand. Advancing along the tramway, I obtained a nearer view of the hellish buildings, the chimneys and the demoniac figures. It was just such a scene as one of those described by Ellis Wynn in his Vision of Hell. Feeling my eyes scorching, I turned away, and proceeded towards Llangollen, sometimes on the muddy road, sometimes on the dangerous causeway. For three miles at least I met nobody. Near Llangollen, as I was walking on the causeway, three men came swiftly towards me. I kept the hedge, which was my right; the two first brushed roughly past me, the third came full upon me, and was tumbled into the road. There was a laugh from the two first, and a loud curse from the last as he sprawled in the mire. I merely said " Nos Da'ki," and passed on, and in about a quarter of an hour reached home, where I found my wife awaiting me alone, Henrietta having gone to bed, being slightly indisposed. My wife received me with a cheerful smile. I looked at her, and the good wife of the Triad came to my mind.

" She is modest, void of deceit, and obedient.

" Pure of conscience, gracious of tongue, and true to her husband.

" Her heart not proud, her manners affable, and her bosom full of compassion for the poor.

" Labouring to be tidy, skilful of hand, and fond of praying to God.

" Her conversation amiable, her dress decent, and her house orderly.

" Quick of hand, quick of eye, and quick of understanding.

" Her person shapely, her manners agreeable, and her heart innocent.

" Her face benignant, her head intelligent, and provident.

" Neighbourly, gentle, and of a liberal way of thinking.

" Able in directing, providing what is wanting, and a good mother to her children.

" Loving her husband, loving peace, and loving God.

" Happy the man," adds the Triad, " who possesses such a wife." Very true, O Triad, always provided he is in some degree worthy of her; but many a man leaves an innocent wife at home for an impure Jezebel abroad, even as many a one prefers a pint of hog's wash abroad to a tankard of generous liquor at home.

CHAPTER LXIII

Preparations for Departure—Cat provided for—A Pleasant Party—
Last Night at Llangollen.

I WAS awakened early on the Sunday morning by the howling of wind. There was a considerable storm throughout the day, but unaccompanied by rain. I went to church both in the morning and the evening. The next day there was a great deal of rain. It was now the latter end of October; winter was coming on, and my wife and daughter were anxious to return home. After some consultation, it was agreed that they should depart for London, and that I should join them there after making a pedestrian tour in South Wales.

I should have been loth to quit Wales without visiting the Deheubarth, or Southern Region, a land differing widely, as I had heard, both in language and customs from Gwynedd, or the Northern—a land which had given birth to the illustrious Ab Gwilym, and where the great Ryce family had flourished, which very much distinguished itself in the Wars of the Roses—a member of which, Ryce ap Thomas, placed Henry the Seventh on the throne of Britain—a family of royal extraction, and which, after the death of Roderic the Great, for a long time enjoyed the sovereignty of the south.

We set about making the necessary preparations for our respective journeys. Those for mine were soon made. I bought a small leather satchel with a lock and key, in which I placed a white linen shirt, a pair of worsted stockings, a razor and a prayer-book. Along with it I bought a leather strap with which to sling it over my shoulder; I got my boots new soled, my umbrella, which was rather dilapidated, mended; put twenty sovereigns into my purse, and then said I am all right for the Deheubarth.

As my wife and daughter required much more time in making preparations for their journey than I for mine, and as I should only be in their way whilst they were employed, it was determined that I should depart on my expedition on Thursday, and that they should remain at Llangollen till the Saturday.

We were at first in some perplexity with respect to the disposal of the ecclesiastical cat; it would, of course, not do to leave it in the garden, to the tender mercies of the Calvinistic Methodists of the neighbourhood, more especially those of the flannel manufactory, and my wife and daughter could hardly carry it with them. At length we thought of applying to a young woman of sound Church principles, who was lately married, and lived over the water on the way to the railroad station, with whom we were slightly acquainted, to take charge of the animal; and she, on the first intimation of our wish, willingly acceded to it. So with her poor puss was left, along with a trifle for its milk-money, and with her, as we subsequently learned, it continued in peace and comfort, till one morning it sprang suddenly from the hearth into the air, gave a miew and died. So much for the ecclesiastical cat!

The morning of Tuesday was rather fine, and Mr. Ebenezer E——, who had heard of our intended departure, came to invite us to spend the evening at the vicarage. His father had left Llangollen the day before for Chester, where he expected to be detained some days. I told him we should be most happy to come. He then asked me to take a walk. I agreed with pleasure, and we set out, intending to go to Llansilio, at the western end of the valley, and look at the church. The church was an ancient building. It had no spire, but had the little erection on its roof, so usual to Welsh churches, for holding a bell.

In the churchyard is a tomb, in which an old squire of the name of Jones was buried about the middle of the last century. There is a tradition about this squire and tomb, to the following effect. After the squire's death there was a lawsuit about his property, in consequence of no will having been found. It was said that his will had been buried with him in the tomb, which after some time was opened, but with what success the tradition sayeth not.

In the evening we went to the vicarage. Besides the family and ourselves, there was Mr. R——, and one or two more. We had a very pleasant party; and as most of those present wished to hear something connected with Spain, I talked much about that country, sang songs of Germania, and related in an abridged form Lope de Vega's ghost story, which is decidedly the best ghost story in the world.

In the afternoon of Wednesday I went and took leave of certain friends in the town; amongst others of old Mr. Jones. On my telling him that I was about to leave Llangollen, he expressed considerable regret, but said that it was natural for me to wish to return to my native country. I told him that before returning to England I intended to make a pedestrian tour in South Wales. He said that he should die without seeing the south; that he had had several opportunities of visiting it when he was young, which he had neglected, and that he was now too old to wander far from home. He then asked me which road I intended to take. I told him that I intended to strike across the Berwyn to Llan Rhyadr, then visit Sycharth, once the seat of Owen Glendower, lying to the east of Llan Rhyadr, then return to that place, and after seeing the celebrated cataract, cross the mountains to Bala—whence I should proceed due south. I then asked him whether he had ever seen Sycharth and the Rhyadr; he told me that he had never visited Sycharth, but had seen the Rhyadr more than once. He then smiled, and said that there was a ludicrous anecdote connected with the Rhyadr, which he would relate to me. " A traveller once went to see the Rhyadr, and whilst gazing at it a calf, which had fallen into the stream above whilst grazing upon the rocks, came tumbling down the cataract. ' Wonderful!' said the traveller, and going away, reported that it was not only a fall of water, but of calves, and was very much disappointed, on visiting the waterfall on another occasion, to see no calf come tumbling down." I took leave of the kind old gentleman with regret, never expecting to see him again, as he was in his eighty-fourth year—he was a truly excellent character, and might be ranked amongst the venerable ornaments of his native place.

About half-past eight o'clock at night John Jones came to bid me farewell. I bade him sit down, and sent for a pint of ale to regale him with. Notwithstanding

the ale, he was very melancholy at the thought that
I was about to leave Llangollen, probably never to
return.   To enliven him I gave him an account of my
late expedition to Wrexham, which made him smile
more than once.   When I had concluded, he asked me
whether I knew the meaning of the word Wrexham;
I told him I believed I did, and gave him the derivation
which the reader will find in an early chapter of this
work.   He told me that with all due submission he
thought he could give me a better, which he had heard
from a very clever man, gwr deallus iawn, who lived
about two miles from Llangollen, on the Corwen road.
In the old time a man of the name of Sam kept a
gwestfa, or inn, at the place where Wrexham now
stands; when he died he left it to his wife, who kept
it after him, on which account the house was first
called Tŷ wraig Sam, the house of Sam's wife, and
then for shortness Wraig Sam, and a town arising
about it by degrees, the town, too, was called Wraig
Sam, which the Saxons corrupted into Wrexham.

I was much diverted with this Welsh derivation of
Wrexham, which I did not attempt to controvert.
After we had had some further discourse, John Jones
got up, shook me by the hand, gave a sigh, wished
me a " taith hyfryd," and departed.   Thus terminated
my last day at Llangollen.

CHAPTER LXIV

Departure for South Wales—Tregeiriog—Pleasing Scene—Trying
    to Read—Garmon and Lupus—The Cracked Voice—Effect of
    a Compliment—Llan Rhyadr.

THE morning of the 21st of October was fine and cold;
there was a rime frost on the ground.   At about eleven
o'clock I started on my journey for South Wales, intending that my first stage should be Llan Rhyadr.
My wife and daughter accompanied me as far as Plas
Newydd.   As we passed through the town I shook
hands with honest A——, whom I saw standing at the
door of a shop, with a kind of Spanish hat on his
head, and also with my venerable friend old Mr. Jones,

whom I encountered close beside his own domicile. At
the Plas Newydd I took an affectionate farewell of my
two loved ones, and proceeded to ascend the Berwyn.
Near the top I turned round to take a final look at the
spot where I had lately passed many a happy hour.
There lay Llangollen far below me, with its chimneys
placidly smoking, its pretty church rising in its centre,
its blue river dividing it into two nearly equal parts,
and the mighty hill of Brennus, overhanging it from
the north. I sighed, and repeating Einion Du's verse

> " Tangnefedd i Llangollen ! "

turned away.

I went over the top of the hill, and then began to
descend its southern side, obtaining a distant view of
the plains of Shropshire on the east. I soon reached the
bottom of the hill, passed through Llansanfraid, and
threading the vale of the Ceiriog, at length found myself
at Pont y Meibion, in front of the house of Huw
Morris, or rather of that which is built on the site of
the dwelling of the poet. I stopped, and remained
before the house, thinking of the mighty Huw, till the
door opened, and out came the dark-featured man, the
poet's descendant, whom I saw when visiting the place
in company with honest John Jones—he had now a
spade in his hand, and was doubtless going to his
labour. As I knew him to be of a rather sullen, un-
social disposition, I said nothing to him, but proceeded
on my way. As I advanced the valley widened, the hills
on the west receding to some distance from the river.
Came to Tregeiriog, a small village, which takes its
name from the brook; Tregeiriog signifying the hamlet
or village on the Ceiriog. Seeing a bridge which
crossed the rivulet at a slight distance from the road,
a little beyond the village, I turned aside to look at it.
The proper course of the Ceiriog is from south to
north; where it is crossed by the bridge, however, it
runs from west to east, returning to its usual course,
a little way below the bridge. The bridge was small,
and presented nothing remarkable in itself : I obtained,
however, as I looked over its parapet towards the west,
a view of a scene, not of wild grandeur, but of something which I like better, which richly compensated

me for the slight trouble I had taken in stepping aside
to visit the little bridge. About a hundred yards distant
was a small watermill, built over the rivulet, the wheel
going slowly, slowly round; large quantities of pigs,
the generality of them brindled, were either browsing
on the banks, or lying close to the sides, half immersed
in the water; one immense white hog, the monarch
seemingly of the herd, was standing in the middle of
the current. Such was the scene which I saw from the
bridge, a scene of quiet rural life well suited to the
brushes of two or three of the old Dutch painters, or
to those of men scarcely inferior to them in their own
style—Gainsborough, Moreland, and Crome. My mind
for the last half-hour had been in a highly-excited
state; I had been repeating verses of old Huw Morris,
brought to my recollection by the sight of his dwelling-
place; they were ranting roaring verses, against the
Roundheads. I admired the vigour, but disliked the
principles which they displayed; and admiration on the
one hand, and disapproval on the other, bred a commotion in my mind like that raised on the sea when tide
runs one way and wind blows another. The quiet scene
from the bridge, however, produced a sedative effect
on my mind, and when I resumed my journey I had forgotten Huw, his verses, and all about Roundheads
and Cavaliers.

I reached Llanarmon, another small village, situated
in a valley, through which the Ceiriog, or a river very
similar to it, flows. It is half-way between Llangollen
and Llan Rhyadr, being ten miles from each. I went
to a small inn, or public-house, sat down, and called for
ale. A waggoner was seated at a large table with a
newspaper before him on which he was intently
staring.

" What news?" said I in English.

" I wish I could tell you," said he in very broken
English; " but I cannot read."

" Then why are you looking at the paper?" said I.

" Because," said he, " by looking at the letters I
hope in time to make them out."

" You may look at them," said I, " for fifty years
without being able to make out one. You should go to
an evening school."

"I am too old," said he, "to do so now; if I did the children would laugh at me."

"Never mind their laughing at you," said I, "provided you learn to read; let them laugh who win!"

"You give good advice, mester," said he; "I think I shall follow it."

"Let me look at the paper," said I.

He handed it to me. It was a Welsh paper, and full of dismal accounts from the seat of war.

"What news, mester?" said the waggoner.

"Nothing but bad," said I; "the Russians are beating us and the French too."

"If the Rusiaid beat us," said the waggoner, "it is because the Francod are with us. We should have gone alone."

"Perhaps you are right," said I; "at any rate, we could not have fared worse than we are faring now."

I presently paid for what I had had, inquired the way to Llan Rhyadr, and departed.

The village of Llanarmon takes its name from its church, which is dedicated to Garmon, an Armorican bishop, who, with another called Lupus, came over into Britain in order to preach against the heresy of Pelagius. He and his colleague resided for some time in Flintshire, and whilst there enabled, in a remarkable manner, the Britons to achieve a victory over those mysterious people the Picts, who were ravaging the country far and wide. Hearing that the enemy were advancing towards Mold, the two bishops gathered together a number of the Britons, and placed them in ambush in a dark valley, through which it was necessary for the Picts to pass in order to reach Mold, strictly enjoining them to remain quiet till all their enemies should have entered the valley, and then do whatever they should see them, the two bishops, do. The Picts arrived, and when they were about half-way through the valley, the two bishops stepped forward from a thicket, and began crying aloud, "Alleluia!" The Britons followed their example, and the wooded valley resounded with cries of "Alleluia! alleluia!" The shouts and the unexpected appearance of thousands of men caused such terror to the Picts, that they took to flight in the greatest confusion, hundreds were trampled to death by their companions, and not a few were drowned in the river Alan [1] which runs through the valley.

There are several churches dedicated to Garmon in Wales, but whether there are any dedicated to Lupus I am unable to say.

After leaving Llanarmon I found myself amongst lumpy hills, through which the road led in the direction of the south. Arriving where several roads met, I followed one, and became bewildered amidst hills and ravines. At last I saw a small house close by a nant, or dingle, and turned towards it for the purpose of inquiring my way. On my knocking at the door, a woman made her appearance, of whom I asked in Welsh whether I was in the road to Llan Rhyadr. She said that I was out of it, but that if I went towards the south I should see a path on my left which would bring me to it. I asked her how far it was to Llan Rhyadr.

"Four long miles," she replied.

"And what is the name of the place where we are now?" said I.

"Cae Hir" (the long inclosure), said she.

"Are you alone in the house?" said I.

"Quite alone," said she; "but my husband and people will soon be home from the field, for it is getting dusk."

"Have you any Saxon?" said I.

"Not a word," said she, "have I of the iaith dieithr, nor has my husband, nor any one of my people."

I bade her farewell, and soon reached the road, which led south and north. As I was bound for the south, I strode forward briskly in that direction. The road was between romantic hills; heard Welsh songs proceeding from the hill fields on my right, and the murmur of a brook rushing down a deep nant on my left. I went on till I came to a collection of houses which an old woman, with a cracked voice and a small tin milk-pail, whom I assisted in getting over a stile into the road, told me was called Pen Strit—probably the head of the street. She spoke English, and on my

---

[1] The above account is chiefly taken from the curious Welsh book called "Drych y prif Oesoedd."

asking her how she had learnt the English tongue, she told me that she had learnt it of her mother, who was an English woman. She said that I was two miles from Llan Rhyadr, and that I must go straight forward. I did so, till I reached a place where the road branched into two, one bearing somewhat to the left, and the other to the right. After standing a minute in perplexity I took the right-hand road, but soon guessed that I had taken the wrong one, as the road dwindled into a mere footpath. Hearing some one walking on the other side of the hedge, I inquired in Welsh whether I was going right for Llan Rhyadr, and was answered by a voice in English, apparently that of a woman, that I was not, and that I must go back. I did so, and presently a woman came through a gate to me.

"Are you the person," said I, "who just now answered me in English after I had spoken in Welsh?"

"In truth I am," said she, with a half laugh.

"And how came you to answer me in English, after I had spoken to you in Welsh?"

"Because," said she, "it was easy enough to know by your voice that you were an Englishman."

"You speak English remarkably well," said I.

"And so do you Welsh," said the woman; "I had no idea that it was possible for any Englishman to speak Welsh half so well."

"I wonder," thought I to myself, "what you would have answered if I had said that you speak English execrably." By her own account, she could read both Welsh and English. She walked by my side to the turn, and then up the left-hand road, which she said was the way to Llan Rhyadr. Coming to a cottage, she bade me good-night, and went in. The road was horribly miry; presently, as I was staggering through a slough, just after I had passed a little cottage, I heard a cracked voice crying, "I suppose you lost your way?" I recognised it as that of the old woman whom I had helped over the stile. She was now standing behind a little gate, which opened into a garden before the cottage. The figure of a man was standing near her. I told her that she was quite right in her supposition.

" Ah," said she, " you should have gone straight forward."

" If I had gone straight forward," said I, " I must have gone over a hedge, at the corner of a field which separated two roads; instead of bidding me go straight forward, you should have told me to follow the left-hand road."

" Well," said she, " be sure you keep straight forward now."

I asked her who the man was standing near her.

" It is my husband," said she.

" Has he much English?" said I.

" None at all," said she, " for his mother was not English, like mine." I bade her good-night, and went forward. Presently I came to a meeting of roads, and to go straight forward it was necessary to pass through a quagmire; remembering, however, the words of my friend the beldame, I went straight forward, though in so doing I was sloughed up to the knees. In a little time I came to a rapid descent, and at the bottom of it to a bridge. It was now very dark; only the corner of the moon was casting a faint light. After crossing the bridge I had one or two ascents and descents. At last I saw lights before me, which proved to be those of Llan Rhyadr. I soon found myself in a dirty little street, and, inquiring for the inn, was kindly shown by a man to one which he said was the best, and which was called the Wynstay Arms.

CHAPTER LXV

Inn at Llan Rhyadr—A Low Englishman—Enquiries—The Cook —A Precious Couple.

THE inn seemed very large, but did not look very cheer-ful. No other guest than myself seemed to be in it, except in the kitchen, where I heard a fellow talking English, and occasionally yelling an English song; the master and mistress of the house were civil, and lighted me a fire in what was called the Commercial Room, and putting plenty of coals in the grate, soon made the apartment warm and comfortable. I ordered dinner, or rather supper, which in about half-an-hour was brought in by the woman. The supper, whether good or bad, I despatched with the appetite of one who had walked twenty miles over hill and dale.

Occasionally I heard a dreadful noise in the kitchen, and the woman told me that the fellow there was making himself exceedingly disagreeable, chiefly, she believed, because she had refused to let him sleep in the house—she said that he was a low fellow, that went about the country with fish, and that he was the more ready to insult her as the master of the house was now gone out. I asked if he was an Englishman. "Yes," said she, "a low Englishman."

"Then he must be low indeed," said I. "A low Englishman is the lowest of the low." After a little time I heard no more noise, and was told that the fellow was gone away. I had a little whisky and water, and then went to bed, sleeping in a tolerable chamber, but rather cold. There was much rain during the night, and also wind; windows rattled, and I occasionally heard the noise of falling tiles.

I arose about eight. Notwithstanding the night had been so tempestuous, the morning was sunshiny and beautiful. Having ordered breakfast, I walked out in order to have a look at the town. Llan Rhyadr is a small place, having nothing remarkable in it save an ancient church, and a strange little antique market-house, standing on pillars. It is situated at the western end of an extensive valley, and at the entrance of a glen. A brook, or rivulet, runs through it, which comes down the glen from the celebrated cataract, which is about four miles distant to the west. Two lofty mountains form the entrance of the glen, and tower above the town, one on the south and the other on the north. Their names, if they have any, I did not learn.

After strolling about the little place for about a quarter of an hour, staring at the things and the people, and being stared at by the latter, I returned to my inn, a structure built in the modern Gothic style, and which stands nearly opposite to the churchyard. Whilst breakfasting, I asked the landlady, who was bustling about the room, whether she had ever heard of Owen Glendower.

"In truth, sir, I have. He was a great gentleman who lived a long time ago, and, and——"

"Gave the English a great deal of trouble," said I.

"Just so, sir; at least, I dare say it is so, as you say it."

"And do you know where he lived?"

"I do not, sir; I suppose a great way off, somewhere in the south."

"Do you mean South Wales?"

"In truth, sir, I do."

"There you are mistaken," said I; "and also in supposing he lived a great way off. He lived in North Wales, and not far from this place."

"In truth, sir, you know more about him than I."

"Did you ever hear of a place called Sycharth?"

"Sycharth! Sycharth! I never did, sir."

"It is the place where Glendower lived, and it is not far off. I want to go there, but do not know the way."

"Sycharth! Sycharth!" said the landlady musingly; "I wonder if it is the place we call Sychnant."

"Is there such a place?"

"Yes, sure; about six miles from here, near Llangedwin."

"What kind of place is it?"

"In truth, sir, I do not know, for I was never there. My cook, however, in the kitchen, knows all about it, for she comes from there."

"Can I see her?"

"Yes, sure; I will go at once and fetch her."

She then left the room, and presently returned with the cook, a short, thick girl, with blue, staring eyes.

"Here she is, sir," said the landlady, "but she has no English."

"All the better," said I. "So you come from a place called Sychnant?" said I to the cook in Welsh.

"In truth, sir, I do," said the cook.

"Did you ever hear of a gwr boneddig called Owen Glendower?"

"Often, sir, often; he lived in our place."

"He lived in a place called Sycharth?" said I.

"Well, sir, and we of the place call it Sycharth as often as Sychnant; nay, oftener."

" Is his house standing?"

" It is not; but the hill on which it stood is still standing."

" Is it a high hill?"

" It is not; it is a small, light hill."

" A light hill!" said I to myself. " Old Iolo Goch, Owen Glendower's bard, said the chieftain dwelt in a house on a light hill."

> " There dwells the chief we all extol
> In timber house on lightsome knoll."

" Is there a little river near it," said I to the cook— " a ffrwd?"

" There is; it runs just under the hill."

" Is there a mill upon the ffrwd?"

" There is not; that is, now,—but there was in the old time; a factory of woollen stands now where the mill once stood."

> " A mill, a rushing brook upon,
> And pigeon tower fram'd of stone."

" So says Iolo Goch," said I to myself, " in his description of Sycharth; I am on the right road."

I asked the cook to whom the property of Sycharth belonged, and was told of course to Sir Watkin, who appears to be the Marquis of Carabas of Denbighshire. After a few more questions I thanked her and told her she might go. I then finished my breakfast, paid my bill, and, after telling the landlady that I should return at night, started for Llangedwin and Sycharth.

A broad and excellent road led along the valley in the direction in which I was proceeding.

The valley was beautiful, and dotted with various farm-houses, and the land appeared to be in as high a state of cultivation as the soil of my own Norfolk— that county so deservedly celebrated for its agriculture. The eastern side is bounded by lofty hills, and towards the north the vale is crossed by three rugged elevations, the middlemost of which, called, as an old man told me, Bryn Dinas, terminates to the west in an exceedingly high and picturesque crag.

After an hour's walking I overtook two people, a man and a woman laden with baskets, which hung

around them on every side. The man was a young
fellow of about eight-and-twenty, with a round face,
fair flaxen hair, and rings in his ears; the female was
a blooming buxom lass of about eighteen. After giving
them the sele of the day, I asked them if they were
English.

"Aye, aye, master," said the man; "we are
English."

"Where do you come from?" said I.

"From Wrexham," said the man.

"I thought Wrexham was in Wales," said I.

"If it be," said the man, "the people are not
Welsh; a man is not a horse because he happens to be
born in a stable."

"Is that young woman your wife?" said I.

"Yes," said he, "after a fashion"—and then he
leered at the lass, and she leered at him.

"Do you attend any place of worship?" said I.

"A great many, master!"

"What place do you chiefly attend?" said I.

"The Chequers, master!"

"Do they preach the best sermons there?" said I.

"No, master! but they sells the best ale there."

"Do you worship ale?" said I.

"Yes, master; I worships ale."

"Anything else?" said I.

"Yes, master! I and my mort worships something
besides good ale; don't we, Sue?" and then he leered
at the mort, who leered at him, and both made odd
motions backwards and forwards, causing the baskets
which hung around them to creak and rustle, and uttering loud shouts of laughter, which roused the echoes of
the neighbouring hills.

"Genuine descendants, no doubt," said I to myself
as I walked briskly on, "of certain of the old heathen
Saxons who followed Rag into Wales, and settled down
about the house which he built. Really, if these two are
a fair specimen of the Wrexham population, my friend
the Scotch policeman was not much out when he said
that the people of Wrexham were the worst people in
Wales."

CHAPTER LXVI

Sycharth—The kindly Welcome—Happy Couple—Sycharth—
Recalling the Dead—Ode to Sycharth.

I WAS now at the northern extremity of the valley near
a great house, past which the road led in the direction
of the north-east. Seeing a man employed in breaking
stones, I inquired the way to Sychnant.

" You must turn to the left," said he, " before you
come to yon great house, follow the path which you will
find behind it, and you will soon be in Sychnant."

" And to whom does the great house belong?"

" To whom? why, to Sir Watkin."

" Does he reside there?"

" Not often. He has plenty of other houses, but he
sometimes comes there to hunt."

" What is the place's name?"

" Llan Gedwin."

I turned to the left, as the labourer had directed me
The path led upward behind the great house, round a
hill thickly planted with trees. Following it, I at length
found myself on a broad road on the top extending
east and west, and having on the north and south
beautiful wooded hills. I followed the road, which
presently began to descend. On reaching level ground
I overtook a man in a waggoner's frock, of whom I
inquired the way to Sycharth. He pointed westward
down the vale to what appeared to be a collection of
houses, near a singular-looking monticle, and said,
" That is Sycharth."

We walked together till we came to a road which
branched off on the right to a little bridge.

" That is your way," said he, and pointing to a large
building beyond the bridge, towering up above a number of cottages, he said, " that is the factory of
Sycharth;" he then left me, following the high road,
whilst I proceeded towards the bridge, which I crossed,
and coming to the cottages, entered one on the right-
hand, of a remarkably neat appearance.

In a comfortable kitchen, by a hearth on which
blazed a cheerful billet, sat a man and woman. Both

arose when I entered; the man was tall, about fifty
years of age, and athletically built; he was dressed in a
white coat, corduroy breeches, shoes, and grey worsted
stockings. The woman seemed many years older than
the man; she was tall also, and strongly built, and
dressed in the ancient Welsh female costume, namely,
a kind of round half-Spanish hat, long blue woollen
kirtle, or gown, a crimson petticoat, and white apron,
and broad, stout shoes with buckles.

"Welcome, stranger," said the man, after looking
me a moment or two full in the face.

"Croesaw, dyn dieithr—welcome, foreign man,"
said the woman, surveying me with a look of great
curiosity.

"Won't you sit down?" said the man, handing me
a chair.

I sat down, and the man and woman resumed their
seats.

"I suppose you come on business connected with the
factory?" said the man.

"No," said I, "my business is connected with Owen
Glendower."

"With Owen Glendower?" said the man, staring.

"Yes," said I; "I came to see his place."

"You will not see much of his house now," said the
man—"it is down; only a few bricks remain."

"But I shall see the place where his house stood,"
said I; "which is all I expected to see."

"Yes; you can see that."

"What does the dyn dieithr say?" said the woman
in Welsh, with an inquiring look.

"That he is come to see the place of Owen
Glendower."

"Ah!" said the woman with a smile.

"Is that good lady your wife?" said I.

"She is."

"She looks much older than yourself."

"And no wonder. She is twenty-one years older."

"How old are you?"

"Fifty-three."

"Dear me," said I, "what a difference in your ages!
How came you to marry?"

"She was a widow, and I had lost my wife. We

were lone in the world, so we thought we would marry."

" Do you live happily together?"

" Very."

" Then you did quite right to marry. What is your name?"

" David Robert."

" And that of your wife?"

" Gwen Robert."

" Does she speak English?"

" She speaks some, but not much."

" Is the place where Owen lived far from here?"

" It is not. It is the round hill a little way above the factory."

" Is the path to it easy to find?"

" I will go with you," said the man. " I work at the factory, but I need not go there for an hour at least."

He put on his hat, and bidding me follow him, went out. He led me over a gush of water which, passing under the factory, turns the wheel; thence over a field or two towards a house at the foot of the mountain, where he said the steward of Sir Watkin lived, of whom it would be as well to apply for permission to ascend the hill, as it was Sir Watkin's ground. The steward was not at home; his wife was, however, and she, when we told her we wished to go to the top of Owain Glendower's Hill, gave us permission with a smile. We thanked her, and proceeded to mount the hill, or monticle, once the residence of the great Welsh chieftain, whom his own deeds and the pen of Shakespear have rendered immortal.

Owen Glendower's hill, or mount, at Sycharth, unlike the one bearing his name on the banks of the Dee, is not an artificial hill, but the work of nature, save and except that to a certain extent it has been modified by the hand of man. It is somewhat conical, and consists of two steps, or gradations, where two fosses scooped out of the hill go round it, one above the other, the lower one embracing considerably the most space. Both these fosses are about six feet deep, and at one time doubtless were bricked, as stout, large, red bricks are yet to be seen, here and there, in their sides. The

top of the mount is just twenty-five feet across. When
I visited it, it was covered with grass, but had once
been subjected to the plough, as various furrows indicated. The monticle stands not far from the western
extremity of the valley, nearly midway between two
hills which confront each other north and south, the
one to the south being the hill which I had descended,
and the other a beautiful wooded height which is called
in the parlance of the country Llwyn Sycharth, or the
grove of Sycharth, from which comes the little gush of
water which I had crossed, and which now turns the
wheel of the factory, and once turned that of Owen
Glendower's mill, and filled his two moats; part of the
water, by some mechanical means, having been forced
up the eminence. On the top of this hill, or monticle,
in a timber house, dwelt the great Welshman, Owen
Glendower, with his wife, a comely, kindly woman,
and his progeny, consisting of stout boys and blooming
girls, and there, though wonderfully cramped for want
of room, he feasted bards, who requited his hospitality
with alliterative odes very difficult to compose, and
which at the present day only a few bookworms understand. There he dwelt for many years, the virtual, if
not the nominal, king of North Wales; occasionally,
no doubt, looking down with self-complaisance from
the top of his fastness on the parks and fish-ponds, of
which he had several; his mill, his pigeon tower, his
ploughed lands, and the cottages of a thousand re-
tainers, huddled round the lower part of the hill, or
strewn about the valley; and there he might have lived
and died, had not events caused him to draw the sword
and engage in a war, at the termination of which
Sycharth was a fire-scathed ruin, and himself a broken-
hearted old man in anchorite's weeds, living in a cave
on the estate of Sir John Scudamore, the great Herefordshire proprietor, who married his daughter Elen,
his only surviving child.

After I had been a considerable time on the hill,
looking about me and asking questions of my guide,
I took out a piece of silver and offered it to him, thanking him at the same time for the trouble he had taken
in showing me the place. He refused it, saying that
I was quite welcome.

I tried to force it upon him.

"I will not take it," said he; "but if you come to my house and have a cup of coffee, you may give sixpence to my old woman."

"I will come," said I, "in a short time. In the meanwhile, do you go; I wish to be alone."

"What do you want to do?"

"To sit down and endeavour to recall Glendower, and the times that are past."

The fine fellow looked puzzled; at last he said, "Very well," shrugged his shoulders, and descended the hill.

When he was gone I sat down on the brow of the hill, and with my face turned to the east, began slowly to chant a translation made by myself in the days of my boyhood of an ode to Sycharth, composed by Iolo Goch when upwards of a hunderd years old, shortly after his arrival at that place, to which he had been invited by Owen Glendower :—

Twice have I pledg'd my word to thee
To come thy noble face to see;
His promises let every man
Perform as far as e'er he can!
Full easy is the thing that's sweet,
And sweet this journey is and meet;
I've vowed to Owain's court to go,
And I'm resolv'd to keep my vow;
So thither straight I'll take my way
With blithesome heart, and there I'll stay,
Respect and honour, whilst I breathe,
To find his honour'd roof beneath.
My chief of long lin'd ancestry
Can harbour sons of poesy;
I've heard, for so the muse has told,
He's kind and gentle to the old;
Yes, to his castle I will hie;
There's none to match it 'neath the sky :
It is a baron's stately court,
Where bards for sumptuous fare resort;
There dwells the lord of Powis land,
Who granteth every just demand.
Its likeness now I'll limn you out :
'Tis water girdled wide about;
It shows a wide and stately door
Reached by a bridge the water o'er;
'Tis form'd of buildings coupled fair,
Coupled is every couple there;

Within a quadrate structure tall
Muster the merry pleasures all.
Conjointly are the angles bound—
No flaw in all the place is found.
Structures in contact meet the eye
Upon the hillock's top on high;
Into each other fastened they
The form of a hard knot display.
There dwells the chief we all extol
In timber house on lightsome knoll;
Upon four wooden columns proud
Mounteth his mansion to the cloud;
Each column's thick and firmly bas'd,
And upon each a loft is plac'd;
In these four lofts, which coupled stand,
Repose at night the minstrel band;
Four lofts they were in pristine state,
But now partitioned form they eight.
Tiled is the roof, on each house-top
Rise smoke-ejecting chimneys up.
All of one form there are nine halls
Each with nine wardrobes in its walls
With linen white as well supplied
As fairest shops of fam'd Cheapside.
Behold that church with cross uprais'd
And with its windows neatly glaz'd;
All houses are in this comprest—
An orchard's near it of the best,
Also a park where void of fear
Feed antler'd herds of fallow deer.
A warren wide my chief can boast,
Of goodly steeds a countless host.
Meads where for hay the clover grows,
Corn-fields which hedges trim inclose,
A mill a rushing brook upon,
And pigeon tower fram'd of stone;
A fish-pond deep and dark to see
To cast nets in when need there be,
Which never yet was known to lack
A plenteous store of perch and jack.
Of various plumage birds abound;
Herons and peacocks haunt around.
What luxury doth his hall adorn,
Showing of cost a sovereign scorn;
His ale from Shrewsbury town he brings;
His usquebaugh is drink for kings;
Bragget he keeps, bread white of look,
And, bless the mark! a bustling cook.
His mansion is the minstrels' home,
You'll find them there whene'er you come
Of all her sex his wife's the best;
The household through her care is blest.
She's scion of a knightly tree,
She's dignified, she's kind and free.

His bairns approach me, pair by pair,
O what a nest of chieftains fair !
Here difficult it is to catch
A sight of either bolt or latch ;
The porter's place here none will fill ;
Here largess shall be lavish'd still,
And ne'er shall thirst or hunger rude
In Sycharth venture to intrude.
A noble leader, Cambria's knight,
The lake possesses, his by right,
And midst that azure water plac'd,
The castle, by each pleasure grac'd.

And when I had finished repeating these lines I said,
" How much more happy, innocent and holy I was in
the days of my boyhood, when I translated Iolo's ode,
than I am at the present time!" Then covering my
face with my hands, I wept like a child.

CHAPTER LXVII

Cup of Coffee—Gwen—Bluff old Fellow—A Rabble Rout—
All from Wrexham.

AFTER a while I arose from my seat, and descending
the hill, returned to the house of my honest friends,
whom I found sitting by their fire, as I had first seen
them.

" Well," said the man, " did you bring back Owen
Glendower?"

" Not only him," said I, " but his house, family,
and all relating to him."

" By what means?" said the man.

" By means of a song made a long time ago, which
describes Sycharth as it was in his time, and his
manner of living there."

Presently Gwen, who had been preparing coffee in
expectation of my return, poured out a cupful, which
she presented to me, at the same time handing me some
white sugar in a basin.

I took the coffee, helped myself to some sugar, and
returned her thanks in her own language.

" Ah," said the man, in Welsh, " I see you are a
Cumro. Gwen and I have been wondering whether

you were Welsh or English; but I see you are one of ourselves."

"No," said I in the same language, "I am an Englishman, born in a part of England the farthest of any from Wales. In fact, I am a Carn Sais."

"And how came you to speak Welsh?" said the man.

"I took it into my head to learn it when I was a boy," said I. "Englishmen sometimes do strange things."

"So I have heard," said the man, "but I never heard before of an Englishman learning Welsh."

I proceeded to drink my coffee, and having finished it, and had a little more discourse, I got up, and having given Gwen a piece of silver, which she received with a smile and a curtsey, I said I must now be going.

"Won't you take another cup?" said Gwen, "you are welcome."

"No, thank you," said I; "I have had enough."

"Where are you going?" said the man in English.

"To Llan Rhyadr," said I, "from which I came this morning."

"Which way did you come?" said the man.

"By Llan Gedwln," I replied, "and over the hill. Is there another way?"

"There is," said the man; "by Llan Silin."

"Llan Silin!" said I; "is not that the place where Huw Morris is buried?"

"It is," said the man.

"I will return by Llan Silin," said I, "and in passing through pay a visit to the tomb of the great poet. Is Llan Silin far off?"

"About half-a-mile," said the man. "Go over the bridge, turn to the right, and you will be there presently."

I shook the honest couple by the hand, and bade them farewell. The man put on his hat, and went with me a few yards from the door, and then proceeded towards the factory. I passed over the bridge, under which was a streamlet, which a little below the bridge received the brook which once turned Owen Glendower's corn-mill. I soon reached Llan Silin, a village or townlet, having some high hills at a short distance to the westward, which form part of the Berwyn.

I entered the kitchen of an old-fashioned public-house, and sitting down by a table, told the landlord, a red-nosed, elderly man, who came bowing up to me, to bring me a pint of ale. The landlord bowed and departed. A bluff-looking old fellow, somewhat under the middle size, sat just opposite to me at the table. He was dressed in a white frieze coat, and had a small hat on his head, set rather consequentially on one side. Before him on the table stood a jug of ale, between which and him lay a large crabstick. Three or four other people stood or sat in different parts of the room. Presently the landlord returned with the ale.

"I suppose you come on sessions business, sir?" said he, as he placed it down before me.

"Are the sessions being held here to-day?" said I.

"They are," said the landlord, "and there is plenty of business; two bad cases of poaching. Sir Watkin's keepers are up at court, and hope to convict."

"I am not come on sessions business," said I; "I am merely strolling a little about to see the country."

"He is come from South Wales," said the old fellow in the frieze coat to the landlord, "in order to see what kind of country the north is. Well, at any rate, he has seen a better country than his own."

"How do you know that I come from South Wales?" said I.

"By your English," said the old fellow; "anybody may know you are South Welsh by your English; it is so cursedly bad. But let's hear you speak a little Welsh; then I shall be certain as to who you are."

I did as he bade me, saying a few words in Welsh.

"There's Welsh," said the old fellow, "who but a South Welshman would talk Welsh in that manner? It's nearly as bad as your English."

I asked him if he had ever been in South Wales.

"Yes," said he; "and a bad country I found it; just like the people."

"If you take me for a South Welshman," said I, "you ought to speak civilly both of the South Welsh and their country."

"I am merely paying tit for tat," said the old fellow. "When I was in South Wales your people laughed at my folks and country, so when I meet one of them here I serve him out as I was served out there."

I made no reply to him, but addressing myself to the landlord, inquired whether Huw Morris was not buried in Llan Silin churchyard. He replied in the affirmative.

" I should like to see his tomb," said I.

" Well, sir," said the landlord, " I shall be happy to show it to you whenever you please."

Here again the old fellow put in his word.

" You never had a prydydd like Huw Morris in South Wales," said he; " nor Twm o'r Nant either."

" South Wales has produced good poets," said I.

" No, it hasn't," said the old fellow; " it never produced one. If it had you wouldn't have needed to come here to see the grave of a poet; you would have found one at home."

As he said these words he got up, took his stick, and seemed about to depart. Just then in burst a rabble rout of gamekeepers and river-watchers, who had come from the petty sessions, and were in high glee, the two poachers whom the landlord had mentioned having been convicted and heavily fined. Two or three of them were particularly boisterous, running against some of the guests who were sitting or standing in the kitchen, and pushing the landlord about, crying at the same time that they would stand by Sir Watkin to the last, and would never see him plundered. One of them, a fellow of about thirty, in a hairy cap, black coat, dirty yellow breeches, and dirty-white top-boots, who was the most obstreperous of them all, at last came up to the old chap who disliked South Welshmen and tried to knock off his hat, swearing that he would stand by Sir Watkin; he, however, met a Tartar. The enemy of the South Welsh, like all crusty people, had lots of mettle, and with the stick which he held in his hand forthwith aimed a blow at the fellow's poll, which, had he not jumped back, would probably have broken it.

" I will not be insulted by you, you vagabond," said the old chap, " nor by Sir Watkin either; go and tell him so."

The fellow looked sheepish, and turning away, proceeded to take liberties with other people less dangerous to meddle with than old crabstick. He, however, soon desisted, and sat down, evidently disconcerted.

"Were you ever worse treated in South Wales by the people there than you have been here by your own countrymen?" said I to the old fellow.

"My countrymen?" said he; "this scamp is no countryman of mine; nor is one of the whole kit. They are all from Wrexham, a mixture of broken house-keepers, and fellows too stupid to learn a trade; a set of scamps fit for nothing in the world but to swear bodily against honest men. They say they will stand up for Sir Watkin, and so they will, but only in a box in the Court to give false evidence. They won't fight for him on the banks of the river. Countrymen of mine, indeed! they are no countrymen of mine; they are from Wrexham, where the people speak neither English nor Welsh, not even South Welsh as you do."

Then giving a kind of flourish with his stick, he departed.

CHAPTER LXVIII

Llan Silin Church—Tomb of Huw Morris—Barbara and Richard —Welsh Country Clergyman—The Swearing Lad—Anglo-Saxon Devils.

HAVING discussed my ale, I asked the landlord if he would show me the grave of Huw Morris. "With pleasure, sir," said he; "pray follow me." He led me to the churchyard, in which several enormous yew trees were standing, probably of an antiquity which reached as far back as the days of Henry the Eighth, when the yew bow was still the favourite weapon of the men of Britain. The church fronts the south, the portico being in that direction. The body of the sacred edifice is ancient, but the steeple, which bears a gilded cock on its top, is modern. The innkeeper led me directly up to the southern wall, then pointing to a broad discoloured slab, which lay on the ground just outside the wall, about midway between the portico and the oriel end, he said:

"Underneath this stone lies Huw Morris, sir."

Forthwith taking off my hat, I went down on my knees

and kissed the cold slab covering the cold remains of
the mighty Huw, and then, still on my knees, proceeded to examine it attentively. It is covered over
with letters three parts defaced. All I could make out
of the inscription was the date of the poet's death,
1709. "A great genius, a very great genius, sir," said
the innkeeper, after I had got on my feet and put on
my hat.

"He was indeed," said I; "are you acquainted with
his poetry?"

"O yes," said the innkeeper, and then repeated the
four lines composed by the poet shortly before his
death, which I had heard the intoxicated stonemason
repeat in the public-house of the Pandy, the day I went
to visit the poet's residence with John Jones.

"Do you know any more of Huw's poetry?" said I.

"No," said the innkeeper. "Those lines, however,
I have known ever since I was a child, and repeated
them, more particularly of late, since age has come
upon me, and I have felt that I cannot last long."

It was very odd how few of the verses of great
poets are in people's mouths. Not more than a dozen
of Shakespear's lines are in people's mouths; of those
of Pope not more than half that number. Of Addison's
poetry, two or three lines may be in people's mouths,
though I have never heard one quoted, the only line
which I ever heard quoted as Addison's not being his,
but Garth's:

> "'Tis best repenting in a coach and six."

Whilst of the verses of Huw Morris I never knew any
one but myself, who am not a Welshman, who could
repeat a line beyond the four which I have twice had
occasion to mention, and which seem to be generally
known in North, if not in South Wales.

From the flagstone I proceeded to the portico, and
gazed upon it intensely. It presented nothing very remarkable, but it had the greatest interest for me, for
I remembered how many times Huw Morris had walked
out of that porch at the head of the congregation, the
clergyman yielding his own place to the inspired bard.
I would fain have entered the church, but the landlord
had not the key, and told me that he imagined there

would be some difficulty in procuring it. I was therefore obliged to content myself with peeping through a window into the interior, which had a solemn and venerable aspect.

"Within there," said I to myself, "Huw Morris, the greatest songster of the seventeenth century, knelt every Sunday during the latter thirty years of his life, after walking from Pont y Meibion across the bleak and savage Berwyn. Within there was married Barbara Wynn, the Rose of Maelai, to Richard Middleton, the handsome cavalier of Maelor, and within there she lies buried, even as the songster who lamented her untimely death in immortal verse lies buried out here in the graveyard. What interesting associations has this church for me, both outside and in; but all connected with Huw; for what should I have known of Barbara the Rose and gallant Richard but for the poem on their affectionate union and untimely separation, the dialogue between the living and the dead, composed by humble Huw, the farmer's son of Pont y Meibion?"

After gazing through the window till my eyes watered, I turned to the innkeeper, and inquired the way to Llan Rhyadr. Having received from him the desired information, I thanked him for his civility, and set out on my return.

Before I could get clear of the town, I suddenly encountered my friend R——, the clever lawyer and magistrate's clerk of Llangollen.

"I little expected to see you here," said he.

"Nor I you," I replied.

"I came in my official capacity," said he; "the petty sessions have been held here to-day."

"I know they have," I replied; "and that two poachers have been convicted. I came here in my way to South Wales to see the grave of Huw Morris, who, as you know, is buried in the churchyard."

"Have you seen the clergyman?" said R——.

"No," I replied.

"Then come with me," said he; "I am now going to call upon him. I know he will be rejoiced to make your acquaintance."

He led me to the clergyman's house, which stood at the south-west end of the village within a garden fenced with iron paling. We found the clergyman in a nice comfortable parlour, or study, the sides of which were decorated with books. He was a sharp, clever-looking man, of about the middle age. On my being introduced to him, he was very glad to see me, as my friend R—— told me he would be. He seemed to know all about me, even that I understood Welsh. We conversed on various subjects: on the power of the Welsh language; its mutable letters; on Huw Morris, and likewise on ale, with an excellent glass of which he regaled me. I was much pleased with him, and thought him a capital specimen of the Welsh country clergyman. His name was Walter Jones.

After staying about half-an-hour I took leave of the good kind man, who wished me all kind of happiness, spiritual and temporal, and said that he should always be happy to see me at Llan Silin. My friend R—— walked with me a little way and then bade me farewell. It was now late in the afternoon, the sky was grey and gloomy, and a kind of half wintry wind was blowing. In the forenoon I had travelled along the eastern side of the valley, which I will call that of Llan Rhyadr, directing my course to the north, but I was now on the western side of the valley journeying towards the south. In about half-an-hour I found myself nearly parallel with the high crag which I had seen from a distance in the morning. It was now to the east of me. Its western front was very precipitous, but on its northern side it was cultivated nearly to the summit. As I stood looking at it from near the top of a gentle acclivity a boy with a team, whom I had passed a little time before, came up. He was whipping his horses, who were straining up the ascent, and was swearing at them most frightfully in English. I addressed him in that language, inquiring the name of the crag, but he answered Dim Saesneg, and then again fell to cursing his horses in English. I allowed him and his team to get to the top of the ascent, and then overtaking him I said in Welsh: " What do you mean by saying you have no English? you were talking English just now to your horses."

" Yes," said the lad, " I have English enough for my horses, and that is all."

"You seem to have plenty of Welsh," said I; "why don't you speak Welsh to your horses?"

"It's of no use speaking Welsh to them," said the boy; "Welsh isn't strong enough."

"Isn't Myn Diawl tolerably strong?" said I.

"Not strong enough for horses," said the boy; "if I were to say Myn Diawl to my horses, or even Cas András they would laugh at me."

"Do the other carters," said I, "use the same English to their horses which you do to yours?"

"Yes," said the boy, "they all use the same English words; if they didn't the horses wouldn't mind them."

"What a triumph," thought I, "for the English language that the Welsh carters are obliged to have recourse to its oaths and execrations to make their horses get on!"

I said nothing more to the boy on the subject of language, but again asked him the name of the crag. "It is called Craig y Gorllewin," said he. I thanked him, and soon left him and his team far behind.

Notwithstanding what the boy said about the milk-and-water character of native Welsh oaths, the Welsh have some very pungent execrations, quite as efficacious, I should say, to make a horse get on as any in the English swearing vocabulary. Some of their oaths are curious, being connected with heathen times and Druidical mythology; for example that Cas András mentioned by the boy, which means hateful enemy or horrible András. András or Andraste was the fury or Demigorgon of the Ancient Cumry, to whom they built temples and offered sacrifices out of fear. Curious that the same oath should be used by the Christian Cumry of the present day, which was in vogue amongst their pagan ancestors some three thousand years ago. However, the same thing is observable amongst us Christian English: we say the Duse take you! even as our heathen Saxon forefathers did, who worshipped a kind of Devil so called and named a day of the week after him, which name we still retain in our hebdomadal calendar like those of several other Anglo-Saxon devils. We also say: Go to old Nick! and Nick or Nikkur was a surname of Woden, and also the name of a spirit which haunted fords and was in the habit of drowning passengers.

Night came quickly upon me after I had passed the swearing lad. However, I was fortunate enough to reach Llan Rhyadr, without having experienced any damage or impediment from Diawl, András, Duse or Nick.

CHAPTER LXIX

Church of Llan Rhyadr—The Clerk—The Tablet-Stone—First View of the Cataract.

THE night was both windy and rainy like the preceding one, but the morning which followed, unlike that of the day before, was dull and gloomy. After breakfast I walked out to take another view of the little town. As I stood looking at the church a middle-aged man of a remarkably intelligent countenance came up and asked me if I should like to see the inside. I told him I should, whereupon he said that he was the clerk and would admit me with pleasure. Taking a key out of his pocket he unlocked the door of the church and we went in. The inside was sombre, not so much owing to the gloominess of the day as the heaviness of the architecture. It presented something in the form of a cross. I soon found the clerk, what his countenance represented him to be, a highly intelligent person. His answers to my questions were in general ready and satisfactory.

" This seems rather an ancient edifice," said I; " when was it built?"

" In the sixteenth century," said the clerk; " in the days of Harry Tudor."

" Have any remarkable men been clergymen of this church?"

" Several, sir; amongst its vicars was Doctor William Morgan the great South Welshman, the author of the old Welsh version of the Bible, who flourished in the time of Queen Elizabeth. Then there was Doctor Robert South, an eminent divine, who though not a Welshman spoke and preached Welsh better than many of the native clergy. Then there was the last vicar, Walter D——, a great preacher and writer, who styled himself in print Gwalter Mechain."

" Are Morgan and South buried here?" said I.

" They are not, sir," said the clerk; " they had been transferred to other benefices before they died."

I did not inquire whether Walter D—— was buried there, for of him I had never heard before, but demanded whether the church possessed any ancient monuments.

" This is the oldest which remains, sir," said the clerk, and he pointed with his finger to a tablet-stone over a little dark pew on the right side of the oriel window. There was an inscription upon it, but owing to the darkness I could not make out a letter. The clerk however read as follows.

1694. 21 Octr.
Hic Sepultus Est.
Sidneus Bynner.

" Do you understand Latin?" said I to the clerk.

" I do not, sir; I believe, however, that the stone is to the memory of one Bynner."

" That is not a Welsh name," said I.

" It is not, sir," said the clerk.

" It seems to be radically the same as Bonner," said I, " the name of the horrible Popish Bishop of London in Mary's time. Do any people of the name of Bynner reside in the neighbourhood at present?"

" None, sir," said the clerk; " and if the Bynners are the descendants of Bonner, it is, perhaps, well that there are none."

I made the clerk, who appeared almost fit to be a clergyman, a small present, and returned to the inn. After paying my bill I flung my satchel over my shoulder, took my umbrella by the middle in my right hand, and set off for the Rhyadr.

I entered the narrow glen at the western extremity of the town and proceeded briskly along. The scenery was romantically beautiful: on my left was the little brook, the waters of which run through the town; beyond it a lofty hill; on my right was a hill covered with wood from the top to the bottom. I enjoyed the scene, and should have enjoyed it more had there been a little sunshine to gild it.

I passed through a small village, the name of which I think was Cynmen, and presently overtook a man and boy. The man saluted me in English and I entered into conversation with him in that language. He told me that he came from Llan Gedwin, and was going to a place called Gwern something in order to fetch home some sheep. After a time he asked me where I was going.

" I am going to see the Pistyll Rhyadr," said I.

We had then just come to the top of a rising ground.

" Yonder's the Pistyll!" said he, pointing to the west.

I looked in the direction of his finger, and saw something at a great distance, which looked like a strip of grey linen, hanging over a crag.

" That is the waterfall," he continued, " which so many of the Saxons come to see. And now I must bid you good-bye, master; for my way to the Gwern is on the right."

Then followed by the boy he turned aside into a wild road at the corner of a savage, precipitous rock.

CHAPTER LXX

Mountain Scenery—The Rhyadr—Wonderful Feat.

AFTER walking about a mile with the cataract always in sight, I emerged from the glen into an oblong valley extending from south to north, having lofty hills on all sides, especially on the west, from which direction the cataract comes. I advanced across the vale till within a furlong of this object, when I was stopped by a deep hollow or nether vale into which the waters of the cataract tumble. On the side of this hollow I sat down, and gazed before me and on either side. The water comes spouting over a crag of perhaps two hundred feet in altitude between two hills, one south-east and the other nearly north. The southern hill is wooded from the top, nearly down to where the cataract burst forth; and so, but not so thickly, is the northern hill, which bears a singular resemblance to a hog's back. Groves of pine are on the lower parts of both; in front of a grove low down on the northern hill is a small white house of a picturesque appearance. The water of the cataract, after reaching the bottom of the precipice, rushes in a narrow brook down the vale in the direction of Llan. Rhyadr. To the north-east, between the hog-backed hill and another strange-looking mountain, is a wild glen, from which comes a brook to swell the waters discharged by the Rhyadr. The south-west side of the vale is steep, and from a cleft of a hill in that quarter a slender stream rushing impetuously joins the brook of the Rhyadr, like the rill of the northern glen. The principal object of the whole is of course the Rhyadr. What shall I liken it to? I scarcely know, unless to an immense skein of silk agitated and disturbed by tempestuous blasts, or to the long tail of a grey courser at furious speed. Through the profusion of long silvery threads or hairs, or what looked such, I could here and there see the black sides of the crag down which the Rhyadr precipitated itself with something between a boom and a roar.

After sitting on the verge of the hollow for a considerable time I got up, and directed my course towards the house in front of the grove. I turned down the path which brought me to the brook which runs from the northern glen into the waters discharged by the Rhyadr, and crossing it by stepping-stones found myself on the lowest spur of the hog-backed hill. A steep path led towards the house. As I drew near, two handsome dogs came rushing to welcome the stranger. Coming to a door on the northern side of the house I tapped and a handsome girl of about thirteen making her appearance I enquired in English the nearest way to the waterfall; she smiled, and in her native language said that she had no Saxon. On my telling her in Welsh that I was come to see the Pistyll she smiled again, and said that I was welcome, then taking me round the house she pointed to a path and bade me follow it. I followed the path which led downwards to a tiny bridge of planks, a little way below the fall. I advanced to the middle of the bridge, then turning to the west looked at the wonderful object before me.

There are many remarkable cataracts in Britain and the neighbouring isles, even the little Celtic Isle of Man has its remarkable waterfall; but this Rhyadr, the grand cataract of North Wales, far exceeds them all in altitude and beauty, though it is inferior to several of them in the volume of its flood. I never saw water falling so gracefully, so much like thin beautiful threads as here. Yet even this cataract has its blemish. What beautiful object has not something which more or less mars its loveliness? There is an ugly black bridge or semicircle of rock, about two feet in diameter and about twenty feet high, which rises some little way below it, and under which the water, after reaching the bottom, passes, which intercepts the sight, and prevents it from taking in the whole fall at once. This unsightly object has stood where it now stands since the day of creation, and will probably remain there to the day of judgment. It would be a desecraton of nature to remove it by art, but no one could regret if nature in one of her floods were to sweep it away.

As I was standing on the planks a woman plainly but neatly dressed came from the house. She addressed me in very imperfect English, saying that she was the mistress of the house and should be happy to show me about. I thanked her for her offer and told her that she might speak Welsh, whereupon she looked glad and said in that tongue that she could speak Welsh much better than Saesneg. She took me by a winding path up a steep bank on the southern side of the fall to a small plateau, and told me that was the best place to see the Pistyll from. I did not think so, for we were now so near that we were almost blinded by the spray, though, it is true, the semicircle of rock no longer impeded the sight; this object we now saw nearly laterally rising up like a spectral arch, spray and foam above it, and water rushing below. " That is a bridge rather for ysprydoedd [1] to pass over than men," said I.

" It is," said the woman; " but I once saw a man pass over it."

" How did he get up?" said I. " The sides are quite steep and slippery."

[1] Spirits.

" He wriggled up the side like a llysowen,[1] till he got to the top, when he stood upright for a minute, and then slid down on the other side."

" Was he any one from these parts?" said I.

" He was not. He was a dyn dieithr, a Russian; one of those with whom we are now at war."

" Was there as much water tumbling then as now?"

" More, for there had fallen more rain."

" I suppose the torrent is sometimes very dreadful?" said I.

" It is indeed, especially in winter; for it is then like a sea, and roars like thunder or a mad bull."

After I had seen all I wished of the cataract, the woman asked me to come to the house and take some refreshment. I followed her to a neat little room where she made me sit down and handed me a bowl of buttermilk. On the table was a book in which she told me it was customary for individuals who visited the cataract to insert their names. I took up the book which contained a number of names mingled here and there with pieces of poetry. Amongst these compositions was a Welsh englyn on the Rhyadr, which though incorrect in its prosody I thought stirring and grand. I copied it, and subjoin it with a translation which I made on the spot.

" Crychiawg, ewynawg anian—yw y Rhyadr
Yn rhuo mal taran;
Colofn o dwr, gloyw-dwr glan,
Gorwyllt, un lliw ag arian."

" Foaming and frothing from mountainous height,
Roaring like thunder the Rhyadr falls;
Though its silvery splendour the eye may delight,
Its fury the heart of the bravest appals."

CHAPTER LXXI

Wild Moors—The Guide—Scientific Discourse—The Land of Arthur—The Umbrella—Arrival at Bala.

WHEN I had rested myself and finished the buttermilk I got up, and, making the good woman a small com-

[1] Eel.

pensation for her civility, inquired if I could get to Bala
without returning to Llan Rhyadr.

" O yes," said she, " if you cross the hills for about
five miles you will find yourself upon a road which will
take you straight to Bala."

" Is there any one here," said I, " who will guide me
over the hills provided I pay him for his trouble?"

" O yes," said she; " I know one who will be
happy to guide you whether you pay him or not."

She went out and presently returned with a man
about thirty-five, stout and well-looking, and dressed
in a waggoner's frock.

" There," said she, " this is the man to show you
over the hills; few know the paths better."

I thanked her, and telling the man I was ready, bade
him lead the way. We set out, the two dogs of which
I have spoken attending us and seemingly very glad to
go. We ascended the side of the hog-backed hill to the
north of the Rhyadr. We were about twenty minutes
in getting to the top, close to which stood a stone or
piece of rock, very much resembling a church altar, and
about the size of one. We were now on an extensive
moory elevation, having the brook which forms the
Rhyadr a little way on our left. We went nearly due
west, following no path, for path there was none, but
keeping near the brook. Sometimes we crossed water-
courses which emptied their tribute into the brook,
and every now and then ascended and descended
hillocks covered with gorse and whin. After a little
time I entered into conversation with my guide. He
had not a word of English. " Are you married?"
said I.

" In truth I am, sir."

" What family have you?"

" I have a daughter."

" Where do you live?"

" At the house of the Rhyadr."

" I suppose you live there as servant?"

" No, sir, I live there as master."

" Is the good woman I saw there your wife?"

" In truth, sir, she is."

" And the young girl I saw your daughter?"

" Yes, sir, she is my daughter."

"And how came the good woman not to tell me you were her husband?"

"I suppose, sir, you did not ask who I was, and she thought you did not care to know."

"But can you be spared from home?"

"O yes, sir, I was not wanted at home."

"What business are you?"

"I am a farmer, sir."

"A sheep farmer?"

"Yes, sir."

"Who is your landlord?"

"Sir Watkin."

"Well, it was very kind of you to come with me."

"Not at all, sir; I was glad to come with you, for we are very lonesome at Rhyadr, except during a few weeks in the summer, when the gentry come to see the Pistyll. Moreover, I have sheep lying about here which need to be looked at now and then, and by coming hither with you I shall have an opportunity of seeing them."

We frequently passed sheep feeding together in small numbers. In two or three instances my guide singled out individuals, caught them, and placing their heads between his knees examined the inside of their eyelids, in order to learn by their colour whether or not they were infected with the pwd or moor disorder. We had some discourse about that malady. At last he asked me if there was a remedy for it.

"O yes," said I; "a decoction of hoarhound."

"What is hoarhound?" said he.

"Llwyd y Cwn," said I. "Pour some of that down the sheep's throat twice a day, by means of a horn, and the sheep will recover, for the bitterness, do you see, will destroy the worm [1] in the liver, which learned men say is the cause of the disorder."

We left the brook on our left hand and passed by some ruined walls which my guide informed me had once belonged to houses but were now used as sheep-folds. After walking several miles, according to my computation, we began to ascend a considerable eleva-

---

[1] For an account of this worm, which has various denominations, see article Fasciola Hepatica in any encyclopædia.

tion covered with brown heath and ling. As we went on the dogs frequently put up a bird of a black colour, which flew away with a sharp whirr.

" What bird is that?" said I.

" Ceiliog y grug, the cock of the heath," replied my guide. " It is said to be very good eating, but I have never tasted it. The ceiliog y grug is not food for the like of me. It goes to feed the rich Saxons in Caer Ludd."

We reached the top of the elevation.

" Yonder," said my guide, pointing to a white bare place a great way off to the west, " is Bala road."

" Then I will not trouble you to go any further," said I; " I can find my way thither."

" No, you could not," said my guide; " if you were to make straight for that place you would perhaps fall down a steep, or sink into a peat hole up to your middle, or lose your way and never find the road, for you would soon lose sight of that place. Follow me, and I will lead you into a part of the road more to the left, and then you can find your way easily enough to that bare place, and from thence to Bala." Thereupon he moved in a southerly direction down the steep and I followed him. In about twenty minutes we came to the road.

" Now," said my guide, " you are on the road; bear to the right and you cannot miss the way to Bala."

" How far is it to Bala?" said I.

" About twelve miles," he replied.

I gave him a trifle, asking at the same time if it was sufficient. " Too much by one half," he replied; " many, many thanks." He then shook me by the hand, and accompanied by his dogs departed, not back over the moor, but in a southerly direction down the road.

Wending my course to the north, I came to the white bare spot which I had seen from the moor, and which was in fact the top of a considerable elevation over which the road passed. Here I turned and looked at the hills I had come across. There they stood, darkly blue, a rain cloud, like ink, hanging over their summits. O, the wild hills of Wales, the land of old renown and of wonder, the land of Arthur and Merlin.

The road now lay nearly due west. Rain came on, but it was at my back, so I expanded my umbrella, flung it over my shoulder and laughed. O, how a man laughs who has a good umbrella when he has the rain at his back, aye and over his head too, and at all times when it rains except when the rain is in his face, when the umbrella is not of much service. O, what a good friend to a man is an umbrella in rain time, and likewise at many other times. What need he fear if a wild bull or a ferocious dog attacks him, provided he has a good umbrella? he unfurls the umbrella in the face of the bull or dog, and the brute turns round quite scared, and runs away. Or if a footpad asks him for his money, what need he care provided he has an umbrella? he threatens to dodge the ferrule into the ruffian's eye, and the fellow starts back and says, " Lord, sir ! I meant no harm. I never saw you before in all my life. I merely meant a little fun." Moreover, who doubts that you are a respectable character provided you have an umbrella? you go into a public-house and call for a pot of beer, and the publican puts it down before you with one hand without holding out the other for the money, for he sees that you have an umbrella and consequently property. And what respectable man, when you overtake him on the way and speak to him, will refuse to hold conversation with you, provided you have an umbrella? No one. The respectable man sees you have an umbrella and concludes that you do not intend to rob him, and with justice, for robbers never carry umbrellas. O, a tent, a shield, a lance and a voucher for character is an umbrella. Amongst the very best friends of man must be reckoned an umbrella.[1]

The way lay over dreary, moory hills : at last it began to descend and I saw a valley below me with a narrow river running through it to which wooded hills sloped down ; far to the west were blue mountains. The scene was beautiful but melancholy ; the rain had passed

---

[1] As the umbrella is rather a hackneyed subject two or three things will of course be found in the above eulogium on an umbrella which have been said by other folks on that subject ; the writer, however, flatters himself that in his eulogium on an umbrella two or three things will also be found which have never been said by any one else about an umbrella.

away, but a gloomy almost November sky was above, and the mists of night were coming down apace.

I crossed a bridge at the bottom of the valley and presently saw a road branching to the right. I paused, but after a little time went straight forward. Gloomy woods were on each side of me and night had come down. Fear came upon me that I was not in the right road, but I saw no house at which I could inquire, nor did I see a single individual for miles of whom I could ask. At last I heard the sound of hatchets in a dingle on my right, and catching a glimpse of a gate at the head of a path, which led down into it, I got over it. After descending some time I hallooed. The noise of the hatchets ceased. I hallooed again, and a voice cried in Welsh, " What do you want?" " To know the way to Bala," I replied. There was no answer, but presently I heard steps, and the figure of a man drew nigh half undistinguishable in the darkness and saluted me. I returned his salutation, and told him I wanted to know the way to Bala. He told me, and I found I had been going right. I thanked him and regained the road. I sped onward and in about half an hour saw some houses, then a bridge, then a lake on my left, which I recognised as the lake of Bala. I skirted the end of it, and came to a street cheerfully lighted up, and in a minute more was in the White Lion Inn.

CHAPTER LXXII

Cheerful Fire—Immense Man—Doctor Jones—Recognition—A Fast Young Man—Excellent Remarks—Disappointment.

I was conducted into the coffee-room of the White Lion by a little freckled maid whom I saw at the bar, and whom I told that I was come to pass the night at the inn. The room presented an agreeable contrast to the gloomy, desolate places through which I had lately come. A good fire blazed in the grate, and there were four lights on the table. Lolling in a chair by one side of the fire was an individual at the sight of whom I almost started. He was an immense man, weighing I should say at least eighteen stone, with brown hair, thinnish whiskers, half-ruddy, half-tallowy complexion, and dressed in a brown sporting coat, drab breeches and yellow-topped boots—in every respect the exact image of the Wolverhampton gent or hog-merchant who had appeared to me in my dream at Llangollen, whilst asleep before the fire. Yes, the very counterpart of the same gent looked this enormous fellow, save and except that he did not appear to be more than seven or eight and twenty, whereas the hog-merchant looked at least fifty. Laying my satchel down I took a seat and ordered the maid to get some dinner for me, and then asked what had become of the waiter Tom Jenkins.

" He is not here at present, sir," said the freckled maid; " he is at his own house."

" And why is he not here?" said I.

" Because he is not wanted, sir; he only comes in summer when the house is full of people."

And having said this the little freckled damsel left the room.

" Reither a cool night, sir!" said the enormous man after we had been alone together a few minutes.

I again almost started, for he spoke with the same kind of half-piping, half-wheezing voice, with which methought the Wolverhampton gent had spoken to me in my dream.

" Yes," said I; " it is rather cold out abroad, but I don't care, as I am not going any farther to-night."

" That's not my case," said the stout man, " I have got to go ten miles, as far as Cerrig Drudion, from which place I came this afternoon in a wehicle."

" Do you reside at Cerrig Drudion?" said I.

" No," said the stout man, whose dialect I shall not attempt further to imitate, " but I have been staying there some time; for happening to go there a month or two ago I was tempted to take up my quarters at the inn. A very nice inn it is, and the landlady a very agreeable woman, and her daughters very agreeable young ladies."

" Is this the first time you have been at Bala?"

" Yes, the first time. I had heard a good deal about it, and wished to see it. So to-day, having the offer of a vehicle at a cheap rate I came over with two or three other gents, amongst whom is Doctor Jones."

" Dear me," said I ; " is Doctor Jones in Bala?"

" Yes," said the stout man; " do you know him?"

" Oh yes," said I, " and have a great respect for him; his like for politeness and general learning is scarcely to be found in Britain."

" Only think," said the stout man. " Well, I never heard that of him before."

Wishing to see my sleeping room before I got my dinner, I now rose and was making for the door, when it opened, and in came Doctor Jones. He had a muffler round his neck, and walked rather slowly and disconsolately, leaning upon a cane. He passed without appearing to recognise me, and I, thinking it would be as well to defer claiming acquaintance with him till I had put myself a little to rights, went out without saying anything to him. I was shown by the freckled maid to a nice sleeping apartment, where I stayed some time adjusting myself. On my return to the coffee-room I found the doctor sitting near the fire-place. The stout man had left the room. I had no doubt that he told Doctor Jones that I had claimed acquaintance with him, and that the doctor not having recollected me had denied that he knew anything of me, for I observed that he looked at me very suspiciously.

I took my former seat, and after a minute's silence said to Doctor Jones, " I think, sir, I had the pleasure of seeing you some time ago at Cerrig Drudion?"

" It's possible, sir," said Doctor Jones in a tone of considerable hauteur, and tossing his head so that the end of his chin was above his comforter, " but I have no recollection of it."

I held my head down for a little time, then raising it and likewise my forefinger I looked Doctor Jones full in the face and said, " Don't you remember talking to me about Owen Pugh and Coll Gwynfa?"

" Yes, I do," said Doctor Jones in a very low voice, like that of a person who deliberates; " yes, I do. I remember you perfectly, sir," he added almost immediately in a tone of some animation; " you are the gentleman with whom I had a very interesting conversation one evening last summer in the bar of the inn at Cerrig Drudion. I regretted very much that our con-

versation was rather brief, but I was called away to
attend to a case, a professional case, sir, of some deli-
cacy, and I have since particularly regretted that I was
unable to return that night, as it would have given
me much pleasure to have been present at a dialogue
which, I have been told by my friend the landlady, you
held with a certain Italian who was staying at the
house, which was highly agreeable and instructive to
herself and her daughter."

"Well," said I, "I am rejoiced that fate has brought
us together again. How have you been in health since
I had the pleasure of seeing you?"

"Rather indifferent, sir, rather indifferent. I have
of late been afflicted with several ailments the original
cause of which, I believe, was a residence of several
years in the Ynysoedd y Gorllewin—the West-India
Islands—where I had the honour of serving her present
gracious Majesty's gracious uncle, George the Fourth—
in a medical capacity, sir. I have likewise been afflicted
with lowness of spirits, sir. It was this same lowness
of spirits which induced me to accept an invitation made
by the individual lately in the room to accompany him
in a vehicle with some other people to Bala. I shall
always consider my coming as a fortunate circumstance
inasmuch as it has given me an opportunity of renewing
my acquaintance with you."

"Pray," said I, "may I take the liberty of asking
who that individual is?"

"Why," said Doctor Jones, "he is what they call a
Wolverhampton gent."

"A Wolverhampton gent," said I to myself; "only
think!"

"Were you pleased to make any observation, sir?"
said the doctor.

"I was merely saying something to myself," said I.
"And in what line of business may he be? I suppose
in the hog line."

"O no," said Doctor Jones. "His father it is true
is a hog-merchant, but as for himself he follows no
business; he is what is called a fast young man, and
goes about here and there on the spree, as I think they
term it, drawing, whenever he wants money, upon his
father, who is in affluent circumstances. Some time

ago he came to Cerrig Drudion, and was so much pleased with the place, the landlady and her daughters that he has made it his head-quarters ever since. Being frequently at the house I formed an acquaintance with him, and have occasionally made one in his parties and excursions, though I can't say I derive much pleasure from his conversation, for he is a person of little or no literature."

"The son of a hog-merchant," thought I to myself. "Depend upon it, that immense fellow whom I saw in my dream purchase the big hog at Llangollen fair, and who wanted me to give him a poond for his bargain, was this gent's father. O there is much more in dreams than is generally dreamt of by philosophy!"

Doctor Jones presently began to talk of Welsh literature, and we were busily engaged in discussing the subject when in walked the fast young man, causing the floor to quake beneath his ponderous tread. He looked rather surprised at seeing the doctor and me conversing, but Doctor Jones turning to him said, "O I remember this gentleman perfectly."

"Oh!" said the fast young man; "very good!" then flinging himself down in a chair with a force that nearly broke it and fixing his eyes upon me said, "I think I remember the gentleman too. If I am not much mistaken, sir, you are one of our principal engineers at Wolverhampton. O yes! I remember you now perfectly. The last time I saw you was at a public dinner given to you at Wolverhampton, and there you made a speech, and a capital speech it was."

Just as I was about to reply Doctor Jones commenced speaking Welsh, resuming the discourse on Welsh literature. Before, however, he had uttered a dozen words he was interrupted by the Wolverhampton gent, who exclaimed in a blubbering tone: "O Lord, you are surely not going to speak Welsh. If I had thought I was to be bothered with Welsh I wouldn't have asked you to come."

"If I spoke Welsh, sir," said the Doctor, "it was out of compliment to this gentleman, who is a proficient in the ancient language of my country. As, however, you dislike Welsh, I shall carry on the conversation with him in English, though peradventure you may not be more edified by it in that language than if it were held in Welsh.''

He then proceeded to make some very excellent remarks on the history of the Gwedir family, written by Sir John Wynn; to which the Wolverhampton gent listened with open mouth and staring eyes. My dinner now made its appearance, brought in by the little freckled maid—the cloth had been laid during my absence from the room. I had just begun to handle my knife and fork, Doctor Jones still continuing his observations on the history of the Gwedir family, when I heard a carriage drive up to the inn, and almost immediately after two or three young fellows rollicked into the room. '' Come, let's be off,'' said one of them to the Wolverhampton gent; '' the carriage is ready.'' '' I'm glad of it,'' said the fast young man, '' for it's rather slow work here. Come, doctor! are you going with us or do you intend to stay here all night?'' Thereupon the doctor got up, and coming towards me, leaning on his cane, said : '' Sir! it gives me infinite pleasure that I have met a second time a gentleman of so much literature. That we shall ever meet a third time I may wish but can scarcely hope, owing to certain ailments under which I suffer, brought on, sir, by a residence of many years in the Occidental Indies. However, at all events I wish you health and happiness.'' He then shook me gently by the hand and departed with the Wolverhampton gent and his companions; the gent as he stumped out of the room saying, '' Good night, sir; I hope it will not be long before I see you at another public dinner at Wolverhampton, and hear another speech from you as good as the last.'' In a minute or two I heard them drive off.

Left to myself 1 began to discuss my dinner. Of the dinner I had nothing to complain, but the ale which accompanied it was very bad. This was the more mortifying, for remembering the excellent ale I had drunk at Bala some months previously I had, as I came along the gloomy roads the present evening, been promising myself a delicious treat on my arrival.

'' This is very bad ale!'' said I to the freckled maid, '' very different from what I drank in the summer, when I was waited on by Tom Jenkins.''

" It is the same ale, sir," said the maid, " but the last in the cask; and we shan't have any more for six months, when he will come again to brew for the summer; but we have very good porter, sir, and first-rate Allsopp."

" Allsopp's ale," said I, " will do for July and August, but scarcely for the end of October. However, bring me a pint; I prefer it at all times to porter."

My dinner concluded, I trifled away the time till about ten o'clock, and then went to bed.

CHAPTER LXXIII

Breakfast—The Freckled Maid—Llan uwch Llyn—The Landlady —Llewarch Hen—Conversions to the Church.

AWAKING occasionally in the night I heard much storm and rain. The following morning it was gloomy and lowering. As it was Sunday I determined to pass the day at Bala, and accordingly took my prayer-book out of my satchel, and also my single white shirt, which I put on.

Having dressed myself I went to the coffee-room and sat down to breakfast. What a breakast! pot of hare; ditto of trout; pot of prepared shrimps; dish of plain shrimps; tin of sardines; beautiful beef-steak; eggs, muffin; large loaf, and butter, not forgetting capital tea. There's a breakfast for you!

As the little freckled maid was removing the break-fast things I asked her how old she was.

" Eighteen, sir, last Candlemas," said the freckled maid.

" Are your parents alive?"

" My mother is, sir, but my father is dead."

" What was your father?"

" He was an Irishman, sir! and boots to this inn."

" Is your mother Irish?"

" No, sir, she is of this place; my father married her shortly after he came here."

" Of what religion are you?"

" Church, sir, church."

" Was your father of the church?"

" Not always, sir; he was once what is called a Cartholic. He turned to the church after he came here."

" A'n't there a great many Methodists in Bala?"

" Plenty, sir, plenty."

" How came your father not to go over to the Methodists instead of the church?"

" 'Cause he didn't like them, sir; he used to say they were a trumpery, cheating set; that they wouldn't swear, but would lie through a three-inch board."

" I suppose your mother is a churchwoman?"

" She is now, sir; but before she knew my father she was a Methodist."

" Of what religion is the master of the house?"

" Church, sir, church; so is all the family."

" Who is the clergyman of the place?"

" Mr. Pugh, sir!"

" Is he a good preacher?"

" Capital, sir! and so is each of his curates; he and they are converting the Methodists left and right."

" I should like to hear him."

" Well, sir! that you can do. My master, who is going to church presently, will be happy to accommodate you in his pew."

I went to the church with the landlord, a tall gentlemanly man of the name of Jones—O that eternal name of Jones! Rain was falling fast, and we were glad to hold up our umbrellas. We did not go to the church at Bala, at which there was no service that morning, but to that of a little village close by, on the side of the lake, the living of which is incorporated with that of Bala. The church stands low down by the lake at the bottom of a little nook. Its name, which is Llan uwch Llyn, is descriptive of its position, signifying the Church above the Lake. It is a long, low, ancient edifice, standing north-east by south-west. The village is just above it on a rising ground, behind which are lofty hills pleasantly dotted with groves, trees and houses. The interior of the edifice has a somewhat dilapidated appearance. The service was in Welsh. The clergyman was about forty years of age, and had a highly-intelligent look. His voice was remarkably clear and distinct. He preached an excellent practical sermon, text 14th chapter 22nd verse of Luke, about sending out servants to invite people to the supper. After the sermon there was a gathering for the poor.

As I returned to the inn I had a good deal of conversation with the landlord on religious subjects. He told me that the Church of England, which for a long time had been a down-trodden Church in Wales, had of late begun to raise its head, and chiefly owing to the zeal and activity of its present ministers; that the former ministers of the Church were good men but had not energy enough to suit the times in which they lived; that the present ministers fought the Methodist preachers with their own weapon, namely extemporary preaching, and beat them, winning shoals from their congregations. He seemed to think that the time was not far distant when the Anglican Church would be the popular as well as the established church of Wales.

Finding myself rather dull in the inn I went out again notwithstanding that it rained. I ascended the toman or mound which I had visited on a former occasion. Nothing could be more desolate and dreary than the scene around. The woods were stript of their verdure and the hills were half shrouded in mist. How unlike was this scene to the smiling, glorious prospect which had greeted my eyes a few months before. The rain coming down with redoubled violence I was soon glad to descend and regain the inn.

Shortly before dinner I was visited by the landlady, a fine tall woman of about fifty with considerable remains of beauty in her countenance. She came to ask me if I was comfortable. I told her that it was my own fault if I was not. We were soon in very friendly discourse. I asked her her maiden name.

"Owen," said she laughing, "which after my present name of Jones is the most common name in Wales."

"They were both one and the same originally," said I, "Owen and Jones both mean John."

She too was a staunch member of the Church of England, which she said was the only true church. She spoke in terms of high respect and admiration of her minister, and said that a new church was being

built, the old one not being large enough to accommodate the numbers who thronged to hear him.

I had a noble goose for dinner to which I did ample
justice.   About four o'clock the weather having cleared
up I took a stroll.   It was a beautiful evening, though
rain clouds still hovered about.   I wandered to the
northern end of Llyn Tegid which I had passed in the
preceding evening.   The wind was blowing from the
south, and tiny waves were beating against the shore
which consisted of small brown pebbles.   The lake has
certainly not its name, which signifies Lake of Beauty,
for nothing.   It is a beautiful sheet of water, and
beautifully situated.   It is oblong and about six miles
in length.   On all sides, except to the north, it is
bounded by hills.   Those at the southern end are very
lofty; the tallest of which is Arran, which lifts its head
to the clouds like a huge loaf.   As I wandered on the
strand I thought of a certain British prince and poet,
who in the very old time sought a refuge in the vicinity
of the lake from the rage of the Saxons.   His name
was Llewarch Hen, of whom I will now say a few
words.

Llewarch Hen, or Llewarch the Aged, was born about
the commencement of the sixth and died about the
middle of the seventh century, having attained to the
prodigious age of one hundred and forty or fifty years,
which is perhaps the lot of about forty individuals in the
course of a millenium.   If he was remarkable for the
number of his years he was no less so for the number
of his misfortunes.   He was one of the princes of the
Cumbrian Britons; but Cumbria was invaded by the
Saxons, and a scene of horrid war ensued.   Llewarch
and his sons, of whom he had twenty-four, put themselves at the head of their forces, and in conjunction
with the other Cumbrian princes made a brave but fruit-
less opposition to the invaders.   Most of his sons were
slain, and he himself with the remainder sought shelter
in Powys in the hall of Cynddylan its prince.   But the
Saxon bills and bows found their way to Powys too.
Cynddylan was slain, and with him the last of the sons
of Llewarch, who, reft of his protector, retired to a hut
by the side of the lake of Bala, where he lived the life
of a recluse and composed elegies on his sons and

slaughtered friends, and on his old age, all of which abound with so much simplicity and pathos that the heart of him must be hard indeed who can read them unmoved. Whilst a prince he was revered for his wisdom and equity, and he is said in one of the historical triads to have been one of the three consulting warriors of Arthur.

In the evening I attended service in the old church at Bala. The interior of the edifice was remarkably plain; no ornament of any kind was distinguishable; the congregation was overflowing, amongst whom I observed the innkeeper and his wife, the little freckled maid and the boots. The entire service was in Welsh. Next to the pew in which I sat was one filled with young singing women, all of whom seemed to have voices of wonderful power. The prayers were read by a strapping young curate at least six feet high. The sermon was preached by the rector, and was a continuation of the one which I had heard him preach in the morning. It was a very comforting discourse, as the preacher clearly proved that every sinner will be pardoned who comes to Jesus. I was particularly struck with one part. The preacher said that Jesus' arms being stretched out upon the cross was emblematic of his surprising love and his willingness to receive anybody. The service concluded with the noble anthem Teyrnasa Jesu Mawr, " May Mighty Jesus reign !"

The service over I returned to the parlour of the inn. There I sat for a long time lone and solitary, staring at the fire in the grate. I was the only guest in the house; a great silence prevailed both within and without; sometimes five minutes elapsed without my hearing a sound, and then perhaps the silence would be broken by a footstep at a distance in the street—at length finding myself yawning I determined to go to bed. The freckled maid, as she lighted me to my room, inquired how I liked the sermon. "Very much," said I. "Ah," said she, "did I not tell you that Mr. Pugh was a capital preacher?" She then asked me how I liked the singing of the gals who sat in the next pew to mine. I told her that I liked it exceedingly. "Ah!" said she, "them gals have the best voices in Bala. They were once Methody gals, and sang in the chapels, but were converted, and are now as good Church as myself. Them gals have been the cause of a great many conversions, for all the young fellows of their acquaintance amongst the Methodists——"

"Follow them to church," said I, "and in time become converted. That's a thing of course. If the Church gets the girls she is quite sure of the fellows."

CHAPTER LXXIV

Proceed on Journey—The Lad and Dog—Old Bala—The Pass—Extensive View—The Two Men—The Tap Nyth—The Meeting of the Waters—The Wild Valley—Dinas Mawddwy.

THE Monday morning was gloomy and misty, but it did not rain, a circumstance which gave me no little pleasure, as I intended to continue my journey without delay. After breakfast I bade farewell to my kind hosts and also to the freckled maid, and departed, my sachel o'er my shoulder and my umbrella in my hand.

I had consulted the landlord on the previous day as to where I had best make my next halt, and had been advised by him to stop at Mallwyd. He said that if I felt tired I could put up at Dinas Mawddwy, about two miles on this side of Mallwyd, but that if I were not he would advise me to go on, as I should find very poor accommodation at Dinas. On my inquiring as to the nature of the road he told me that the first part of it was tolerably good, lying along the eastern side of the lake, but that the greater part of it was very rough, over hills and mountains belonging to the great chain of Arran, which constituted upon the whole the wildest part of all Wales.

Passing by the northern end of the lake I turned to the south and proceeded along a road a little way above the side of the lake. The day had now to a certain extent cleared up, and the lake was occasionally gilded by beams of bright sunshine. After walking a little way I overtook a lad dresser in a white great coat and attended by a tolerably large black dog. I addressed him in English, but finding that he did not understand me I began to talk to him in Welsh.

" That's a fine dog," said I.

Lad.—Very fine, sir, and a good dog; though young, he has been known to kill rats.

Myself.—What is his name?

Lad.—His name is Toby, sir.

Myself.—And what is your name?

Lad.—John Jones, sir.

Myself.—And what is your father's?

Lad.—Waladr Jones, sir.

Myself.—Is Waladr the same as Cadwaladr?

Lad.—In truth, sir, it is.

Myself.—That is a fine name.

Lad.—It is, sir; I have heard my father say that it was the name of a king.

Myself.—What is your father?

Lad.—A farmer, sir.

Myself.—Does he farm his own land?

Lad.—He does not, sir; he is tenant to Mr. Price of Hiwlas.

Myself.—Do you live far from Bala?

Lad.—Not very far, sir.

Myself.—Are you going home now?

Lad.—I am not, sir; our home is on the other side of Bala. I am going to see a relation up the road.

Myself.—Bala is a nice place.

Lad.—It is, sir; but not so fine as old Bala.

Myself.—I never heard of such a place. Where is it?

Lad.— Under the lake, sir.

Myself.—What do you mean?

Lad.—It stood in the old time where the lake now is, and a fine city it was, full of fine houses, towers and castles, but with neither church nor chapel, for the people neither knew God nor cared for Him, and thought of nothing but singing and dancing and other wicked things. So God was angry with them, and one night, when they were all busy at singing and dancing and the like, God gave the word and the city sank down into Unknown, and the lake boiled up where it once stood.

Myself.—That was a long time ago.

Lad.—In truth, sir, it was.

Myself.—Before the days of King Cadwaladr.

Lad.—I dare say it was, sir.

I walked fast, but the lad was a shrewd walker, and

though encumbered with his great coat contrived to keep tolerably up with me. The road went over hill and dale, but upon the whole more upward than downward. After proceeding about an hour and a half we left the lake, to the southern extremity of which we had nearly come, somewhat behind, and bore away to the south-east, gradually ascending. At length the lad pointing to a small farm-house on the side of a hill told me he was bound thither, and presently bidding me farewell turned aside up a footpath which led towards it.

About a minute afterwards a small delicate furred creature with a white mark round its neck and with a little tail trailing on the ground ran swiftly across the road. It was a weasel or something of that genus; on observing it I was glad that the lad and the dog were gone, as between them they would probably have killed it. I hate to see poor wild animals persecuted and murdered, lose my appetite for dinner at hearing the screams of a hare pursued by greyhounds, and am silly enough to feel disgust and horror at the squeals of a rat in the fangs of a terrier, which one of the sporting tribe once told me were the sweetest sounds in " natur."

I crossed a bridge over a deep gulley which discharged its waters into a river in a valley on the right. Arran rose in great majesty on the farther side of this vale, its head partly shrouded in mist. The day now became considerably overcast. I wandered on over much rough ground till I came to a collection of houses at the bottom of a pass leading up a steep mountain. Seeing the door of one of the houses open I peeped in, and a woman who was sitting knitting in the interior rose and came out to me. I asked the name of the place. The name which she told me sounded something like Tŷ Capel Saer—the House of the Chapel of the Carpenter. I inquired the name of the river in the valley. Cynllwyd, hoary-headed, she seemed to say; but here as well as with respect to her first answer I speak under correction, for her Welsh was what my old friends the Spaniards would call muy cerrado, that is close or indistinct. She asked me if I was going up the bwlch. I told her I was.

" Rather you than I," said she, looking up to the

heavens which had assumed a very dismal, not to say awful appearance.

Presently I began to ascend the pass or bwlch, a green hill on my right intercepting the view of Arran, another very lofty hill on my left with wood towards the summit. Coming to a little cottage which stood on the left I went to the door and knocked. A smiling young woman opened it, of whom I asked the name of the house.

" Tŷ Nant—the House of the Dingle," she replied.

" Do you live alone?" said I.

" No; mother lives here."

" Any Saesneg?"

" No," said she with a smile, " S'sneg of no use here."

Her face looked the picture of kindness, I was now indeed in Wales amongst the real Welsh. I went on some way. Suddenly there was a moaning sound, and rain came down in torrents. Seeing a deserted cottage on my left I went in. There was fodder in it, and it appeared to serve partly as a barn, partly as a cowhouse. The rain poured upon the roof and I was glad I had found shelter. Close behind this place a small brook precipitated itself down rocks in four successive falls.

The rain having ceased I proceeded and after a considerable time reached the top of the pass. From thence I had a view of the valley and lake of Bala, the lake looking like an immense sheet of steel. A round hill, however, somewhat intercepted the view of the latter. The scene in my immediate neighbourhood was very desolate; moory hillocks were all about me of a wretched russet colour; on my left, on the very crest of the hill up which I had so long been toiling, stood a black pyramid of turf, a pole on the top of it. The road now wore nearly due west down a steep descent. Arran was slightly to the north of me. I, however, soon lost sight of it, as I went down the farther side of the hill which lies over against it to the south-east. The sun, now descending, began to shine out. The pass down which I was now going was yet wilder than the one up which I had lately come. Close on my right was the steep hill's side out of which the road or path had been cut, which was here and there overhung by crags of wondrous forms; on my left was a very deep glen, beyond which was a black, precipitous, rocky wall, from a chasm near the top of which tumbled with a rushing sound a slender brook seemingly the commencement of a mountain stream which hurried into a valley far below towards the west. When nearly at the bottom of the descent I stood still to look around me. Grand and wild was the scenery. On my left were noble green hills, the tops of which were beautifully gilded by the rays of the setting sun. On my right a black, gloomy, narrow valley or glen showed itself; two enormous craggy hills of immense altitude, one to the west and the other to the east of the entrance; that to the east terminating in a peak. The background to the north was a wall of rocks forming a semicircle, something like a bent bow with the head downward; behind this bow, just in the middle, rose the black loaf of Arran. A torrent tumbled from the lower part of the semicircle, and after running for some distance to the south turned to the west, the way I was going.

Observing a house a little way within the gloomy vale I went towards it in the hope of finding somebody in it who could give me information respecting this wild locality. As I drew near the door two tall men came forth, one about sixty, and the other about half that age. The elder had a sharp, keen look; the younger a lumpy and a stupid one. They were dressed like farmers. On my saluting them in English the elder returned my salutation in that tongue, but in rather a gruff tone. The younger turned away his head and said nothing.

" What is the name of this house?" said I, pointing to the building.

" The name of it," said the old man, " is Tŷ Mawr."

" Do you live in it?" said I.

" Yes, I live in it."

" What waterfall is that?" said I, pointing to the torrent tumbling down the crag at the farther end of the gloomy vale.

" The fountain of the Royal Dyfi."

"Why do you call the Dyfy royal?" said I.

" Because it is the king of the rivers in these parts."

" Does the fountain come out of a rock?"

" It does not; it comes out of a lake, a llyn."

" Where is the llyn?"

" Over that crag at the foot of Aran Vawr."

" Is it a large lake?"

" It is not; it is small."

" Deep?"

" Very."

" Strange things in it?"

" I believe there are strange things in it." His English now became broken.

" Crocodiles?"

" I do not know what cracadailes be."

" Efync?"

" Ah! No I do not tink there be efync dere. Hu Gadarn in de old time kill de efync dere and in all de lakes in Wales. He draw them out of the water with his ychain banog his humpty oxen, and when he get dem out he burn deir bodies on de fire, he good man for dat."

" What do you call this allt?" said I, looking up to the high pinnacled hill on my right.

" I call that Tap Nyth yr Eryri."

" Is not that the top nest of the eagles?"

" I believe it is. Ha, I see you understand Welsh."

" A little," said I; " are there eagles there now?"

" No, no eagle now."

" Gone like avanc?"

" Yes, gone like avanc, but not so long. My father see eagle on Tap Nyth, but my father never see avanc in de llyn."

" How far to Dinas?"

" About three mile."

" Any thieves about?"

" No, no thieves here, but what come from England," and he looked at me with a strange, grim smile.

" What is become of the red-haired robbers of Mawddwy?"

" Ah," said the old man, staring at me, " I see you are a Cumro. The red-haired thieves of Mawddwy! I see you are from these parts."

" What's become of them?"

" Oh, dead, hung. Lived long time ago; long before eagle left Tap Nyth."

He spoke true. The red-haired banditti of Mawddwy were exterminated long before the conclusion of the sixteenth century, after having long been the terror not only of these wild regions but of the greater part of North Wales. They were called the red-haired banditti because certain leading individuals amongst them had red foxy hair.

" Is that young man your son?" said I, after a little pause.

" Yes, he my son."

" Has he any English?"

" No, he no English, but he plenty of Welsh—that is if he see reason."

I spoke to the young man in Welsh, asking him if he had ever been up to the Tap Nyth, but he made no answer.

" He no care for your question," said the old man; " ask him price of pig." I asked the young fellow the price of hogs, whereupon his face brightened up, and he not only answered my question, but told me that he had a fat hog to sell. " Ha, ha," said the old man; " he plenty of Welsh now, for he see reason. To other question he no Welsh at all, no more than English, for he see no reason. What business he on Tap Nyth with eagle? His business down below in sty with pig. Ah, he look lump, but he no fool; know more about pig than you or I, or any one 'twixt here and Mahuncleth."

He now asked me where I came from, and on my telling him from Bala, his heart appeared to warm towards me, and saying that I must be tired, he asked me to step in and drink buttermilk, but I declined his offer with thanks, and bidding the two adieu returned to the road.

I hurried along and soon reached a valley which abounded with trees and grass; I crossed a bridge over a brook, not what the old man had called the Dyfi, but the stream whose source I had seen high up the bwlch, and presently came to a place where the two waters joined. Just below the confluence on a fallen tree was seated a man decently dressed; his eyes were fixed on the rushing stream. I stopped and spoke to him.

He had no English, but I found him a very sensible man. I talked to him about the source of the Dyfi. He said it was a disputed point which was the source. He himself was inclined to believe that it was the Pistyll up the bwlch. I asked him of what religion he was. He said he was of the Church of England, which was the Church of his father and his grandfather, and which he believed to be the only true Church. I inquired if it flourished. He said it did, but that it was dreadfully persecuted by all classes of dissenters, who though they were continually quarrelling with one another agreed in one thing namely to persecute the Church. I asked him if he ever read. He said he read a great deal, especially the works of Huw Morris, and that reading them had given him a love for the sights of nature. He added that his greatest delight was to come to the place where he then was, of an evening, and look at the waters and hills. I asked him what trade he was. "The trade of Joseph," said he smiling. "Saer. Farewell, brother," said I; "I am not a carpenter, but like you I read the works of Huw Morris and am of the Church of England." I then shook him by the hand and departed.

I passed a village with a stupendous mountain just behind it to the north, which I was told was called Moel Vrith or the party-coloured moel. I was now drawing near to the western end of the valley. Scenery of the wildest and most picturesque description was rife and plentiful to a degree: hills were here, hills were there; some tall and sharp, others huge and humpy; hills were on every side; only a slight opening to the west seemed to present itself. "What a valley!" I exclaimed. But on passing through the opening I found myself in another, wilder and stranger, if possible. Full to the west was a long hill rising up like the roof of a barn, an enormous round hill on its north-east side, and on its south-east the tail of the range which I had long had on my left—there were trees and groves and running waters, but all in deep shadow, for night was now close at hand.

"What is the name of this place?" I shouted to a man on horseback, who came dashing through a brook with a woman in a Welsh dress behind him.

"Aber Cowarch, Saxon!" said the man in a deep guttural voice, and lashing his horse disappeared rapidly in the shades of night.

"Aber Cywarch!" I cried, springing half a yard into the air. "Why that's the place where Ellis Wynn composed his immortal *Sleeping Bard*, the book which I translated in the blessed days of my youth. O no wonder that the *Sleeping Bard* is a wild and wondrous work, seeing that it was composed amidst the wild and wonderful scenes which I here behold."

I proceeded onwards up an ascent; after some time I came to a bridge across a stream which a man told me was called Avon Gerres. It runs into the Dyfi, coming down with a rushing sound from a wild vale to the north-east between the huge barn-like hill and Moel Vrith. The barn-like hill I was informed was called Pen Dyn. I soon reached Dinas Mawddwy which stands on the lower part of a high hill connected with the Pen Dyn. Dinas, though at one time a place of considerable importance, if we may judge from its name which signifies a fortified city, is at present little more than a collection of filthy huts. But though a dirty squalid place, I found it anything but silent and deserted. Fierce-looking red-haired men, who seemed as if they might be descendants of the red-haired banditti of old, were staggering about, and sounds of drunken revelry echoed from the huts. I subsequently learned that Dinas was the head-quarters of miners, the neighbourhood abounding with mines both of lead and stone. I was glad to leave it behind me. Mallwyd is to the south of Dinas—the way to it is by a romantic gorge down which flows the Royal Dyfi. As I proceeded along this gorge the moon rising above Moel Vrith illumined my path. In about half-an-hour I found myself before the inn at Mallwyd.

CHAPTER LXXV

Inn at Mallwyd—A Dialogue—The *Cumro*.

I ENTERED the inn and seeing a comely-looking damsel at the bar I told her that I was in need of supper and a bed. She conducted me into a neat sanded parlour where a good fire was blazing and asked me what I would have for supper. " Whatever you can most readily provide," said I; " I am not particular." The maid retired, and taking off my hat, and disencumbering myself of my satchel I sat down before the fire and fell into a doze, in which I dreamed of some of the wild scenes through which I had lately passed.

I dozed and dozed till I was roused by the maid touching me on the shoulder and telling me that supper was ready. I got up and perceived that during my doze she had laid the cloth and put supper upon the table. It consisted of bacon and eggs. During supper I had some conversation with the maid.

Myself.—Are you a native of this place?

Maid.—I am not, sir; I come from Dinas.

Myself.—Are your parents alive?

Maid.—My mother is alive, sir, but my father is dead.

Myself.—Where does your mother. live?

Maid.—At Dinas, sir.

Myself.—How does she support herself?

Maid.—By letting lodgings to miners, sir.

Myself.—Are the miners quiet lodgers?

Maid.—Not always, sir; sometimes they get up at night and fight with each other.

Myself.—What does your mother do on those occasions?

Maid.—She draws the quilt over her head, and says her prayers, sir.

Myself.—Why doesn't she get up and part them?

Maid.—Lest she should get a punch or a thwack for her trouble, sir.

Myself.—Of what religion are the miners?

Maid.—They are Methodists, if they are anything; but they don't trouble their heads much about religion.

Myself.—Of what religion are you?

Maid.—I am of the Church, sir.

Myself.—Did you always belong to the Church?

Maid.—Not always. When I was at Dinas I used to hear the preacher, but since I have been here I have listened to the clergyman.

Myself.—Is the clergyman here a good man?

Maid.—A very good man indeed, sir. He lives close by. Shall I go and tell him you want to speak to him?

Myself.—O dear me, no! He can employ his time much more usefully than in waiting upon me.

After supper I sat quiet for about an hour. Then ringing the bell I inquired of the maid whether there was a newspaper in the house. She told me there was not, but that she thought she could procure me one. In a little time she brought me a newspaper, which she said she had borrowed at the parsonage. It was the *Cumro,* an excellent Welsh journal written in the interest of the Church. In perusing its columns I passed a couple of hours very agreeably, and then went to bed.

CHAPTER LXXVI

Mallwydd and its Church—Sons of Shoemakers—Village Inn—Dottings.

THE next day was the thirty-first of October, and was rather fine for the season. As I did not intend to journey farther this day than Machynlleth, a principal town in Montgomeryshire, distant only twelve miles, I did not start from Mallwyd till just before noon.

Mallwyd is a small but pretty village. The church is a long edifice standing on a slight elevation on the left of the road. Its pulpit is illustrious from having for many years been occupied by one of the very celebrated men of Wales, namely Doctor John Davies, author of the great Welsh and Latin dictionary, an imperishable work. An immense yew tree grows in the churchyard, and partly overshadows the road with its branches. The parsonage stands about a hundred yards to the south near a grove of firs. The village is overhung on the north by the mountains of the Arran range, from which it is separated by the murmuring Dyfi. To

the south for many miles the country is not mountainous, but presents a pleasant variety of hill and dale.

After leaving the village a little way behind me I
turned round to take a last view of the wonderful
region from which I had emerged on the previous
evening. Forming the two sides of the pass down which
comes "the royal river" stood the Dinas mountain
and Cefn Coch, the first on the left, and the other on the
right. Behind, forming the background of the pass,
appearing, though now some miles distant, almost in
my close proximity, stood Pen Dyn. This hill has
various names, but the one which I have noted here,
and which signifies the head of a man, perhaps
describes it best. From where I looked at it on that
last day of October it was certainly like an enormous
head, and put me in mind of the head of Mambrino
mentioned in the master work which commemorates the
achievements of the Manchegan knight. This mighty
mountain is the birth-place of more than one river.
If the Gerres issues from its eastern side, from its
western springs the Maw that singularly picturesque
stream, which enters the ocean at the place which the
Saxons corruptly call Barmouth and the Cumry with
great propriety Aber Maw or the disemboguement of
the Maw.

Just as I was about to pursue my journey, two boys
came up, bound in the same direction as myself. One
was a large boy, dressed in a waggoner's frock, the
other was a little fellow, in a brown coat and yellowish
trowsers. As we walked along together, I entered into
conversation with them. They came from Dinas
Mawddwy. The large boy told me that he was the son
of a man who carted mwyn, or lead ore, and the little
fellow that he was the son of a shoemaker. The latter
was by far the cleverest, and no wonder, for the sons
of shoemakers are always clever, which assertion,
should anybody doubt, I beg him to attend the examina-
tions at Cambridge, at which he will find that in three
cases out of four the senior wranglers are the sons of
shoemakers. From this little chap I got a great deal of
information about Pen Dyn, every part of which he
appeared to have traversed. He told me, amongst other
things, that there was a castle upon it. Like a true son

of a shoemaker, however, he was an arch rogue. Coming to a small house, with a garden attached to it, in which there were apple-trees, he stopped, whilst I went on with the other boy, and after a minute or two came running up with a couple of apples in his hand.

" Where did you get those apples?" said I ; " I hope you did not steal them."

He made no reply, but bit one, then making a wry face, he flung it away, and so he served the other. Presently afterwards, coming to a side lane, the future senior wrangler—for a senior wrangler he is destined to be, always provided he finds his way to Cambridge—darted down it like an arrow, and disappeared.

I continued my way with the other lad, occasionally asking him questions about the mines of Mawddwy. The information, however, which I obtained from him was next to nothing, for he appeared to be as heavy as the stuff which his father carted. At length we reached a village, forming a kind of semicircle on a green, which looked something like a small English common. To the east were beautiful green hills ; to the west the valley, with the river running through it, beyond which rose other green hills, yet more beautiful than the eastern ones. I asked the lad the name of the place, but I could not catch what he said, for his answer was merely an indistinct mumble, and before I could question him again he left me, without a word of salutation, and trudged away across the green.

Descending a hill, I came to a bridge, under which ran a beautiful river, which came foaming down from a gulley between two of the eastern hills. From a man whom I met I learned that the bridge was called Pont Coomb Linau, and that the name of the village I had passed was Linau. The river carries an important tribute to the Dyfi—at least it did when I saw it, though perhaps in summer it is little more than a dry water-course.

Half-an-hour's walking brought me from this place to a small town, or large village, with a church at the entrance, and the usual yew-tree in the churchyard. Seeing a kind of inn, I entered it, and was shown by a lad-waiter into a large kitchen, in which were several people. I had told him in Welsh that I wanted

some ale, and as he opened the door he cried with a
loud voice, "Cumro!" as much as to say, Mind what
you say before this chap, for he understands Cumraeg—
that word was enough. The people, who were talking
fast and eagerly as I made my appearance, instantly
became silent, and stared at me with most suspicious
looks. I sat down, and when my ale was brought I took
a hearty draught, and observing that the company were
still watching me suspiciously, and maintaining the
same suspicious silence, I determined to comport myself
in a manner which should, to a certain extent, afford
them ground for suspicion. I therefore slowly and deliberately drew my note-book out of my waistcoat
pocket, unclasped it, took my pencil from the loops at
the side of the book, and forthwith began to dot down
observations upon the room and company, now looking
to the left, now to the right, now aloft, now alow,
now skewing at an object, now leering at an individual,
my eyes half closed, and my mouth drawn considerably
aside. Here follow some of my dottings :—

"A very comfortable kitchen with a chimney-corner
on the south side—immense grate and brilliant fire—
large kettle hanging over it by a chain attached to a
transverse iron bar—a settle on the left-hand side of the
fire—seven fine large men near the fire—two upon the
settle, two upon chairs, one in the chimney-corner
smoking a pipe, and two standing up—table near the
settle with glasses, amongst which is that of myself,
who sit nearly in the middle of the room a little way on
the right-hand side of the fire.

"The floor is of slate; a fine brindled greyhound
lies before it on the hearth, and a shepherd's dog wan-
ders about, occasionally going to the door and scratching as if anxious to get out. The company are dressed
mostly in the same fashion—brown coats, broad-
brimmed hats, and yellowish corduroy breeches with
gaiters. One who looks like a labouring man has
a white smock and a white hat, patched trowsers,
and highlows covered with gravel—one has a blue
coat.

"There is a clock on the right-hand side of the
kitchen; a warming-pan hangs close by it on the projecting side of the chimney-corner. On the same side

is a large rack containing many plates and dishes of Staffordshire ware. Let me not forget a pair of fire-irons which hang on the right-hand side of the chimney-corner!''

I made a great many more dottings, which I shall not insert here. During the whole time I was dotting the most marvellous silence prevailed in the room, broken only by the occasional scratching of the dog against the inside of the door, the ticking of the clock, and the ruttling of the smoker's pipe in the chimney-corner. After I had dotted to my heart's content I closed my book, put the pencil into the loops, then the book into my pocket, drank what remained of my ale, got up, and, after another look at the apartment and its furniture and a leer at the company, departed from the house without ceremony, having paid for the ale when I received it. After walking some fifty yards down the street I turned half round and beheld, as I knew I should, the whole company at the door staring after me. I leered sideways at them for about half a minute, but they stood my leer stoutly. Suddenly I was inspired by a thought. Turning round I confronted them, and pulling my note-book out of my pocket, and seizing my pencil, I fell to dotting vigorously. That was too much for them. As if struck by a panic, my quondam friends turned round and bolted into the house; the rustic-looking man with the smock-frock and gravelled highlows nearly falling down in his eagerness to get in.

The name of the place where this adventure occurred was Cemmaes.

CHAPTER LXXVII

The Deaf Man—Funeral Procession—The Lone Family—The Welsh and their Secrets—The Vale of the Dyfi—The Bright Moon.

A LITTLE way from Cemmaes I saw a respectable-looking old man, like a little farmer, to whom I said:

" How far to Machynlleth?''

Looking at me in a piteous manner in the face, he pointed to the side of his head and said:

" Dim clywed."

It was no longer no English, but no hearing.

Presently I met one yet more deaf. A large procession of men came along the road. Some distance behind them was a band of women, and between the two bands was a kind of bier, drawn by a horse, with plumes at each of the four corners. I took off my hat, and stood close against the hedge on the right-hand side till the dead had passed me some way to its final home.

Crossed a river, which, like that on the other side of Cemmaes, streamed down from a gully between two hills into the valley of the Dyfi. Beyond the bridge on the right-hand side of the road was a pretty cottage, just as there was in the other locality. A fine, tall woman stood at the door, with a little child beside her. I stopped and inquired in English whose body it was that had just been borne by.

" That of a young man, sir, the son of a farmer, who lives a mile or so up the road."

Myself.—He seems to have plenty of friends.

Woman.—O yes, sir, the Welsh have plenty of friends both in life and death.

Myself.—An't you Welsh, then?

Woman.—O no, sir, I am English, like yourself, as I suppose.

Myself.—Yes, I am English. What part of England do you come from?

Woman.—Shropshire, sir.

Myself.—Is that little child yours?

Woman.—Yes, sir, it is my husband's child and mine.

Myself.—I suppose your husband is Welsh?

Woman.—O no, sir, we are all English.

Myself.—And what is your husband?

Woman.—A little farmer, sir; he farms about forty acres under Mrs. ——.

Myself.—Well, are you comfortable here?

Woman.—O dear me, no, sir! we are anything but comfortable. Here we are three poor lone creatures in a strange land, without a soul to speak to but one another. Every day of our lives we wish we had never left Shropshire.

Myself.—Why don't you make friends amongst your neighbours?

Woman.—O, sir, the English cannot make friends amongst the Welsh. The Welsh won't neighbour with them, or have anything to do with them, except now and then in the way of business.

Myself.—I have occasionally found the Welsh very civil.

Woman.—O yes, sir, they can be civil enough to passers-by, especially those who they think want nothing from them—but if you came and settled amongst them you would find them, I'm afraid, quite the contrary.

Myself.—Would they be uncivil to me if I could speak Welsh?

Woman.—Most particularly, sir; the Welsh don't like any strangers, but least of all those who speak their language.

Myself.—Have you picked up anything of their language?

Woman.—Not a word, sir, nor my husband neither. They take good care that we shouldn't pick up a word of their language. I stood the other day and listened whilst two women were talking just where you stand now, in the hope of catching a word, and as soon as they saw me they passed to the other side of the bridge, and began buzzing there. My poor husband took it into his head that he might possibly learn a word or two at the public-house, so he went there, called for a jug of ale and a pipe, and tried to make himself at home just as he might in England, but it wouldn't do. The company instantly left off talking to one another, and stared at him, and before he could finish his pot and pipe took themselves off to a man, and then came the landlord, and asked him what he meant by frightening away his customers. So my poor husband came home as pale as a sheet, and sitting down in a chair said, " Lord, have mercy upon me !"

Myself.—Why are the Welsh afraid that strangers should pick up their language?

Woman.—Lest, perhaps, they should learn their secrets, sir !

Myself.—What secrets have they?

Woman.—The Lord above only knows, sir !

Myself.—Do you think they are hatching treason against Queen Victoria?

Woman.—O dear no, sir.

Myself.—Is there much murder going on amongst them?

Woman.—Nothing of the kind, sir.

Myself.—Cattle-stealing?

Woman.—O no, sir !

Myself.—Pig-stealing?

Woman.—No, sir !

Myself.—Duck or hen stealing?

Woman.—Haven't lost a duck or hen since I have been here, sir.

Myself.—Then what secrets can they possibly have?

Woman.—I don't know, sir ! perhaps none at all, or at most only a pack of small nonsense, that nobody would give three farthings to know. However, it is quite certain they are as jealous of strangers hearing their discourse as if they were plotting gunpowder treason, or something worse.

Myself.—Have you been long here?

Woman.—Only since last May, sir ! and we hope to get away by next, and return to our own country, where we shall have some one to speak to.

Myself.—Good bye !

Woman.—Good bye, sir, and thank you for your conversation; I haven't had such a treat of talk for many a weary day.

The Vale of the Dyfi became wider and more beautiful as I advanced. The river ran at the bottom amidst green and seemingly rich meadows. The hills on the farther side were cultivated a great way up, and various neat farm-houses were scattered here and there on their sides. At the foot of one of the most picturesque of these hills stood a large white village. I wished very much to know its name, but saw no one of whom I could inquire. I proceeded for about a mile, and then perceiving a man wheeling stones in a barrow for the repairing of the road, I thought I would inquire of him. I did so, but the village was then out of sight, and though I pointed in its direction, and described its situation, I could not get its name out of him. At length I said hastily, "Can you tell me your own name?"

"Dafydd Tibbot, sir," said he.

"Tibbot, Tibbot," said I; "why, you are a Frenchman."

"Dearie me, sir," said the man, looking very pleased, "am I indeed?"

"Yes, you are," said I, rather repenting of my haste, and giving him sixpence, I left him.

"I'd bet a trifle," said I to myself, as I walked away, "that this poor creature is the descendant of some desperate Norman Tibault who helped to conquer Powisland under Roger de Montgomery, or Earl Baldwin. How striking that the proud old Norman names are at present only borne by people in the lowest station. Here's a Tibbot, or Tibault, barrowing stones on a Welsh road, and I have known a Mortimer munching poor cheese and bread under a hedge on an English one. How can we account for this save by the supposition that the descendants of proud, cruel and violent men—and who so proud, cruel and violent as the old Normans—are doomed by God to come to the dogs?"

Came to Pont Velin Cerrig, the bridge of the mill of the Cerrig, a river which comes foaming down from between two rocky hills. This bridge is about a mile from Machynlleth, at which place I arrived at about five o'clock in the evening—a cool, bright moon shining upon me. I put up at the principal inn, which was of course called the Wynstay Arms.

CHAPTER LXXVIII

Welsh Poems—Sessions Business—The Lawyer and his Client—
The Court—The Two Keepers—The Defence.

During supper I was waited upon by a brisk, buxom maid, who told me that her name was Mary Evans. The repast over, I ordered a glass of whiskey-and-water, and when it was brought I asked the maid if she could procure me some book to read. She said she was not aware of any book in the house which she could lay her hand on except one of her own, which if I pleased she would lend me. I begged her to do so. Whereupon she went out, and presently returned with a very small volume, which she laid on the table and then retired. After taking a sip of my whiskey-and-water, I proceeded to examine it. It turned out to be a volume of Welsh poems entitled *Blodau Glyn Dyfi*, or, Flowers of Glyn Dyfi, by one Lewis Meredith, whose poetical name is Lewis Clyn Dyfi. The author indites his preface from Cemmaes, June, 1852. The best piece is called " Dyffryn Dyfi "; and is descriptive of the scenery of the vale through which the Dyfi runs. It commences thus :

> " Heddychol ddyffryn tlws,"
> Peaceful, pretty vale,

and contains many lines breathing a spirit of genuine poetry.

The next day I did not get up till nine, having no journey before me, as I intended to pass that day at Machynlleth. When I went down to the parlour I found another guest there, breakfasting. He was a tall, burly, and clever looking man of about thirty-five. As we breakfasted together at the same table, we entered into conversation. I learned from him that he was an attorney from a town at some distance, and was come over to Machynlleth to the petty sessions, to be held that day, in order to defend a person accused of spearing a salmon in the river. I asked him who his client was.

" A farmer," said he, " a tenant of Lord V——, who will probably preside over the bench which will try the affair."

" O," said I, " a tenant spearing his landlord's fish —that's bad."

" No," said he, " the fish which he speared—that is, which he is accused of spearing—did not belong to his landlord, but to another person; he hires land of Lord V——, but the fishing of the river which runs through that land belongs to Sir Watkin."

" O, then," said I, " supposing he did spear the salmon, I shan't break my heart if you get him off; do you think you shall?"

" I don't know," said he. " There's the evidence of

two keepers against him; one of whom I hope, however, to make appear a scoundrel, in whose oath the slightest confidence is not to be placed. I shouldn't wonder if I make my client appear a persecuted lamb. The worst is, that he has the character of being rather fond of fish—indeed, of having speared more salmon than any other six individuals in the neighbourhood."

"I really should like to see him," said I; "what kind of person is he? some fine, desperate-looking fellow, I suppose?"

"You will see him presently," said the lawyer; "he is in the passage, waiting till I call him in to take some instructions from him; and I think I had better do so now, for I have breakfasted, and time is wearing away."

He then got up, took some papers out of a carpet bag, sat down, and after glancing at them for a minute or two, went to the door and called to somebody in Welsh to come in. Forthwith in came a small, mean, wizened-faced man of about sixty, dressed in a black coat and hat, drab breeches and gaiters, and looking more like a decayed Methodist preacher than a spearer of imperial salmon.

"Well," said the attorney, "this is my client; what do you think of him?"

"He is rather a different person from what I had expected to see," said I; "but let us mind what we say, or we shall offend him."

"Not we," said the attorney; "that is, unless we speak Welsh, for he understands not a word of any other language."

Then sitting down at the farther table, he said to his client in Welsh: "Now, Mr. So-and-so, have you learnt anything more about that first keeper?"

The client bent down, and placing both his hands upon the table, began to whisper in Welsh to his professional adviser. Not wishing to hear any of their conversation, I finished my breakfast as soon as possible, and left the room. Going into the inn-yard, I had a great deal of learned discourse with an old ostler about the glanders in horses. From the inn-yard I went to my own private room, and made some dottings in my note-book, and then went down again to the parlour, which I found unoccupied. After sitting some time before the fire, I got up, and strolling out, presently came to a kind of market-place, in the middle of which stood an old-fashioned-looking edifice supported on pillars. Seeing a crowd standing round it, I asked what was the matter, and was told that the magistrates were sitting in the town-hall above, and that a grand poaching-case was about to be tried. "I may as well go and hear it," said I.

Ascending a flight of steps, I found myself in the hall of justice, in the presence of the magistrates, and amidst a great many people, amongst whom I observed my friend the attorney and his client. The magistrates upon the whole were rather a fine body of men. Lord V—— was in the chair, a highly-intelligent-looking person, with fresh complexion, hooked nose, and dark hair. A policeman very civilly procured me a commodious seat. I had scarcely taken possession of it when the poaching case was brought forward. The first witness against the accused was a fellow dressed in a dirty snuff-coloured suit, with a debauched look, and having much the appearance of a town shack. He deposed that he was a hired keeper, and went with another to watch the river at about four o'clock in the morning; that they placed themselves behind a bush, and that a little before daylight they saw the farmer drive some cattle across the river. He was attended by a dog. Suddenly they saw him put a spear upon a stick which he had in his hand, run back to the river, and plunging the spear in, after a struggle pull out a salmon; that they then ran forward, and he himself asked the farmer what he was doing, whereupon the farmer flung the salmon and spear into the river, and said that if he did not take himself off he would fling him in too. The attorney then got up, and began to cross-question him. "How long have you been a keeper?"

"About a fortnight."

"What do you get a week?"

"Ten shillings."

"Have you not lately been in London?"

"I have."

"What induced you to go to London?"

"The hope of bettering my condition."

" Were you not driven out of Machynlleth?"

" I was not."

" Why did you leave London?"

" Because I could get no work, and my wife did not like the place."

" Did you obtain possession of the salmon and the spear?"

" I did not."

" Why didn't you?"

" The pool was deep where the salmon was struck, and I was not going to lose my life by going into it."

" How deep was it?"

" Over the tops of the houses," said the fellow, lifting up his hands.

The other keeper then came forward; he was brother to the former, but had much more the appearance of a keeper, being rather a fine fellow and dressed in a wholesome, well-worn suit of velveteen. He had no English, and what he said was translated by a sworn interpreter. He gave the same evidence as his brother about watching behind the bush, and seeing the farmer strike a salmon. When cross-questioned, however, he said that no words passed between the farmer and his brother, at least, that he heard. The evidence for the prosecution being given, my friend the attorney entered upon the defence. He said that he hoped the court were not going to convict his client, one of the most respect-able farmers in the county, on the evidence of two such fellows as the keepers, one of whom was a well-known bad one, who for his evil deeds had been driven from Machynlleth to London, and from London back again to Machynlleth, and the other, who was his brother, a fellow not much better, and who, moreover, could not speak a word of English—the honest lawyer forgetting, no doubt, that his own client had just as little English as the keeper. He repeated that he hoped the court would not convict his respectable client on the evidence of these fellows, more especially as they flatly contra-dicted each other in one material point, one saying that words had passed between the farmer and himself, and the other that no words at all had passed, and were unable to corroborate their testimony by anything visible or tangible. If his client speared the salmon, and then flung the salmon with the spear sticking in its body into the pool, why didn't they go into the pool and recover the spear and salmon? They might have done so with perfect safety, there being an old proverb —he need not repeat it—which would have secured them from drowning had the pool been not merely over the tops of the houses, but over the tops of the steeples. But he would waive all the advantage which his client derived from the evil character of the witnesses, the discrepancy of their evidence, and their not producing the spear and salmon in court. He would rest the issue of the affair with confidence, on one argument, on one question; it was this. Would any man in his senses— and it was well known that his client was a very sensible man—spear a salmon not his own, when he saw two keepers close at hand watching him—staring at him? Here the chairman observed that there was no proof that he saw them—that they were behind a bush. But my friend the attorney very properly, having the interest of his client and his own character for consistency in view, stuck to what he had said, and insisted that the farmer must have seen them, and he went on reiterating that he must have seen them, notwithstanding that several magistrates shook their heads.

Just as he was about to sit down, I moved up behind him and whispered, " Why don't you mention the dog? Wouldn't the dog have been likely to have scented the fellows out, even if they had been behind the bush."

He looked at me for a moment, and then said with a kind of sigh, " No, no! twenty dogs would be of no use here. It's no go—I shall leave the case as it is."

The court was cleared for a time, and when the audience were again admitted, Lord V—— said that the Bench found the prisoner guilty; that they had taken into consideration what his counsel had said in his defence, but that they could come to no other conclusion, more especially as the accused was known to have been frequently guilty of similar offences. They fined him four pounds, including costs.

As the people were going out I said to the farmer in Welsh, " A bad affair this."

" Drwg iawn—very bad indeed," he replied.

" Did those fellows speak truth?" said I.

"Nage—Dim ond celwydd—not they! nothing but lies."

"Dear me!" said I to myself, "what an ill-treated individual!"

CHAPTER LXXIX

Machynlleth—Remarkable Events—Ode to Glendower—Dafydd Gam—Lawdden's Hatchet.

MACHYNLLETH, pronounced Machuncleth, is one of the principal towns of the district which the English call Montgomeryshire, and the Welsh Shire Trefaldwyn, or the Shire of Baldwin's town; Trefaldwyn, or the town of Baldwin, being the Welsh name for the town which is generally termed Montgomery. It is situated in nearly the centre of the valley of the Dyfi, amidst pleasant green meadows, having to the north the river, from which, however, it is separated by a gentle hill. It possesses a stately church, parts of which are of considerable antiquity, and one or two good streets. It is a thoroughly Welsh town, and the inhabitants, who amount in number to about four thousand, speak the ancient British language with considerable purity.

Machynlleth has been the scene of remarkable events, and is connected with remarkable names, some of which have rung through the world. At Machynlleth in 1402 Owen Glendower, after several brilliant victories over the English, held a parliament in a house which is yet to be seen in the Eastern Street, and was formally crowned King of Wales; in his retinue was the venerable bard Iolo Goch, who, imagining that he now saw the old prophecy fulfilled, namely that a prince of the race of Cadwaladr should rule the Britons, after emancipating them from the Saxon yoke, greeted the chieftain with an ode to the following effect:—

> Here's the life I've sigh'd for long :
> Abash'd is now the Saxon throng,
> And Britons have a British lord
> Whose emblem is the conquering sword ;
> There's none I trow but knows him well
> The hero of the watery dell,

Owain of bloody spear in field,
Owain his country's strongest shield;
A sovereign bright in grandeur drest,
Whose frown affrights the bravest breast.
Let from the world upsoar on high
A voice of splendid prophecy !
All praise to him who forth doth stand
To 'venge his injured native land !
Of him, of him a lay I'll frame
Shall bear through countless years his name :
In him are blended portents three,
Their glories blended sung shall be :
There's Owain meteor of the glen,
The head of princely generous men ;
Owain the lord of trenchant steel,
Who makes the hostile squadrons reel ;
Owain besides of warlike look,
A conqueror who no stay will brook ;
Hail to the lion leader gay,
Marshaller of Griffith's war array ;
The scourger of the flattering race,
For them a dagger has his face ;
Each traitor false he loves to smite,
A lion is he for deeds of might ;
Soon may he tear, like lion grim,
All the Lloegrians limb from limb !
May God and Rome's blest father high
Deck him in surest panoply !
Hail to the valiant carnager,
Worthy three diadems to bear !
Hail to the valley's belted king !
Hail to the widely conquering,
The liberal, hospitable, kind,
Trusty and keen as steel refined !
Vigorous of form he nations bows,
Whilst from his breast-plate bounty flows.
Of Horsa's seed on hill and plain
Four hundred thousand he has slain.
The cope-stone of our nation's he,
In him our weal, our all we see ;
Though calm he looks his plans when breeding,
Yet oaks he'd break his clans when leading.
Hail to this partisan of war,
This bursting meteor flaming far !
Where'er he wends Saint Peter guard him,
And may the Lord five lives award him !

To Machynlleth on the occasion of the parliament
came Dafydd Gam, so celebrated in after time; not,
however, with the view of entering into the counsels
of Glendower, or of doing him homage, but of assassin-
ating him. This man, whose surname Gam signifies

crooked, was a petty chieftain of Breconshire. He was small of stature, and deformed in person, though possessed of great strength. He was very sensitive of injury, though quite as alive to kindness; a thorough-going enemy and a thorough-going friend. In the earlier part of his life he had been driven from his own country for killing a man, called Big Richard of Slwch, in the High Street of Aber Honddu, or Brecon, and had found refuge in England, and kind treatment in the house of John of Gaunt, for whose son Henry, generally called Bolingbroke, he formed one of his violent friendships. Bolingbroke, on becoming King Henry the Fourth, not only restored the crooked little Welshman to his possessions, but gave him employments of great trust and profit in Herefordshire. The insurrection of Glendower against Henry was quite sufficient to kindle against him the deadly hatred of Dafydd, who swore " by the nails of God " that he would stab his countryman for daring to rebel against his friend King Henry, the son of the man who had received him in his house and comforted him, when his own countrymen were threatening his destruction. He therefore went to Machynlleth with the full intention of stabbing Glendower, perfectly indifferent as to what might subsequently be his own fate. Glendower, however, who had heard of his threat, caused him to be seized and conducted in chains to a prison which he had in the mountains of Sycharth. Shortly afterwards, passing through Breconshire with his host, he burnt Dafydd's house, a fair edifice called the Cyrnigwen, situated on a hillock, near the river Honddu, to the ground, and seeing one of Gam's dependents gazing mournfully on the smouldering ruins, he uttered the following taunting englyn :—

> " Shouldst thou a little red man descry
> Asking about his dwelling fair,
> Tell him it under the bank doth lie,
> And its brow the mark of the coal doth bear."

Dafydd remained confined till the fall of Glendower, shortly after which event he followed Henry the Fifth to France, where he achieved that glory which will for ever bloom, dying covered with wounds in the field of

Agincourt after saving the life of the king, to whom
in the dreadest and most critical moment of the fight
he stuck closer than a brother, not from any abstract
feeling of loyalty, but from the consideration that King
Henry the Fifth was the son of King Henry the Fourth,
who was the son of the man who received and comforted him in his house, after his own countrymen had
hunted him from house and land.

Connected with Machynlleth is a name not so widely
celebrated as those of Glendower and Dafydd Gam,
but well known to and cherished by the lovers of Welsh
song. It is that of Lawdden, a Welsh bard in holy
orders, who officiated as priest at Machynlleth from
1440 to 1460. But though Machynlleth was his place of
residence for many years, it was not the place of his
birth, Llychwr in Carmarthenshire being the spot where
he first saw the light. He was an excellent poet, and
displayed in his compositions such elegance of language, and such a knowledge of prosody, that it was
customary long after his death, when any master-piece
of vocal song or eloquence was produced, to say that
it bore the traces of Lawdden's hatchet. At the request
of Griffith ap Nicholas, a powerful chieftain of South
Wales, and a great patron of the muse, he drew up a
statute relating to poets and poetry, and at the great
Eisteddfod, or poetical congress, held at Carmarthen,
in the year 1450, under the auspices of Griffith, which
was attended by the most celebrated bards of the north
and south, he officiated as judge in conjunction with
the chieftain upon the compositions of the bards who
competed for the prize, a little silver chair. Not without
reason, therefore, do the inhabitants of Machynlleth
consider the residence of such a man within their walls,
though at a far, bygone period, as conferring a lustre
on their town, and Lewis Meredith has probability on
his side when, in his pretty poem on Glen Dyfi, he
says :—

> " Whilst fair Machynlleth decks thy quiet plain
> Conjoined with it shall Lawdden's name remain."

CHAPTER LXXX

The Old Ostler—Directions—Church of England Man—The Deep
Dingle—The Two Women—The Cutty Pipe—Waen y Bwlch
—The Deaf and Dumb—The Glazed Hat.

I ROSE on the morning of the 2nd of November intending to proceed to the Devil's Bridge, where I proposed
halting a day or two in order that I might have an
opportunity of surveying the far-famed scenery of that
locality.   After paying my bill, I went into the yard
to my friend the old ostler, to make inquiries with
respect to the road.

"What kind of road," said I, "is it to the Devil's
Bridge?"

"There are two roads, sir, to the Pont y Gwr Drwg;
which do you mean to take?"

"Why do you call the Devil's Bridge the Pont y
Gwr Drwg, or the bridge of the evil man?"

"That we may not bring a certain gentleman upon
us, sir, who doesn't like to have his name taken in
vain."

"Is there much difference between the roads?"

"A great deal, sir; one is over the hills, and the
other round by the valleys."

"Which is the shortest?"

"O, that over the hills, sir; it is about twenty miles
from here to the Pont y Gwr Drwg over the hills, but
more than twice that by the valleys."

"Well, I suppose you would advise me to go by the
hills."

"Certainly, sir.   That is, if you wish to break your
neck, or to sink in a bog, or to lose your way, or perhaps, if night comes on, to meet the Gwr Drwg himself
taking a stroll.   But to talk soberly.   The way over the
hills is an awful road, and indeed for the greater part
is no road at all."

"Well, I shall go by it.   Can't you give me some
directions?"

"I'll do my best, sir; but I tell you again that the
road is a horrible one, and very hard to find."

He then went with me to the gate of the inn, where

he began to give me directions, pointing to the south,
and mentioning some names of places through which I
must pass, amongst which were Waen y Bwlch and
Long Bones; at length he mentioned Pont Erwyd, and
said, "If you can but get there you are all right, for
from thence there is a very fair road to the bridge of
the evil man. Though I dare say if you get to Pont
Erwyd—and I wish you may get there—you will have
had enough of it, and will stay there for the night,
more especially as there is a good inn."

Leaving Machynlleth, I ascended a steep hill which
rises to the south of it. From the top of this hill there
is a fine view of the town, the river and the whole
valley of Dyfi. After stopping for a few minutes to
enjoy the prospect I went on. The road at first was
exceedingly good, though up and down, and making
frequent turnings. The scenery was beautiful to a
degree, lofty hills were on either side clothed most
luxuriantly with trees of various kinds, but principally
oaks. "This is really very pleasant," said I, "but I
suppose it is too good to last long." However, I went
on for a considerable way, the road neither deteriorating
nor the scenery decreasing in beauty; "surely I can't
be in the right road," said I; "I wish I had an opportunity of asking." Presently seeing an old man working with a spade in a field near a gate, I stopped and
said in Welsh, "Am I in the road to the Pont y Gwr
Drwg?" The old man looked at me for a moment,
then shouldering his spade he came up to the gate,
and said in English, "In truth, sir, you are."

"I was told that the road thither was a very bad
one," said I, "but this is quite the contrary."

"This road does not go much farther, sir," said he;
"it was made to accommodate grand folks who live
about here."

"You speak very good English," said I; "where
did you get it?"

He looked pleased, and said that in his youth he
had lived some years in England.

"Can you read?" said I.

"O yes," said he, "both Welsh and English."

"What have you read in Welsh?" said I.

"The Bible and Twm O'r Nant."

" What pieces of Twm O'r Nant have you read?"

" I have read two of his interludes and his life."

" And which do you like best—his life or his interludes."

" O, I like his life best."

" And what part of his life do you like best?"

" O, I like that part best where he gets the ship into the water at Abermarlais."

" You have a good judgment," said I; " his life is better than his interludes, and the best part of his life is where he describes his getting the ship into the water. But do the Methodists about here in general read Twm O'r Nant?"

" I don't know," said he; " I am no Methodist."

" Do you belong to the Church?"

" I do."

" And why do you belong to the Church?"

" Because I believe it is the best religion to get to heaven by."

" I am much of your opinion," said I. " Are there many Church-people about here?"

" Not many," said he, " but more than when I was young."

" How old are you?"

" Sixty-nine."

" You are not very old," said I.

" Ain't I? I only want one year of fulfilling my proper time on earth."

" You take things very easily," said I.

" Not so very easily, sir; I have often my quakings and fears, but then I read my Bible, say my prayers, and find hope and comfort."

" I really am very glad to have seen you," said I; " and now can you tell me the way to the bridge?"

" Not exactly, sir, for I have never been there, but you must follow this road some way farther, and then bear away to the right along yon hill "—and he pointed to a distant mountain.

I thanked him, and proceeded on my way. I passed through a deep dingle, and shortly afterwards came to the termination of the road; remembering, however, the directions of the old man, I bore away to the right, making for the distant mountain. My course lay now over very broken ground, where there was no path—at least that I could perceive. I wandered on for some time; at length, on turning round a bluff, I saw a lad tending a small herd of bullocks. " Am I in the road," said I, " to the Pont y Gwr Drwg?"

" Nis gwn ! I don't know," said he sullenly. " I am a hired servant, and have only been here a little time."

" Where's the house," said I, " where you serve?" But as he made no answer I left him. Some way further on I saw a house on my left, a little way down the side of a deep dingle, which was partly overhung with trees, and at the bottom of which a brook murmured. Descending a steep path, I knocked at the door. After a little time it was opened, and two women appeared, one behind the other. The first was about sixty; she was very powerfully made, had stern grey eyes and harsh features, and was dressed in the ancient Welsh female fashion, having a kind of riding-habit of blue, and a high conical hat like that of the Tyrol. The other seemed about twenty years younger; she had dark features, was dressed like the other, but had no hat. I saluted the first in English, and asked her the way to the Bridge. Whereupon she uttered a deep guttural " augh " and turned away her head, seemingly in abhorrence. I then spoke to her in Welsh, saying I was a foreign man I did not say a Saxon—was bound to the Devil's Bridge, and wanted to know the way. The old woman surveyed me sternly for some time, then turned to the other and said something, and the two began to talk to each other, but in a low, buzzing tone, so that I could not distinguish a word. In about half-a-minute the eldest turned to me, and extending her arm, and spreading out her five fingers wide, motioned to the side of the hill in the direction which I had been following.

" If I go that way shall I get to the bridge of the evil man?" said I; but got no other answer than a furious grimace and violent agitations of the arm and fingers in the same direction. I turned away, and scarcely had I done so when the door was slammed to behind me with great force, and I heard two " aughs," one not quite so deep and abhorrent as the other, probably proceeding from the throat of the younger female.

" Two regular Saxon-hating Welsh women," said I, philosophically; " just the same sort, no doubt, as those who played such pranks on the slain bodies of the English soldiers, after the victory achieved by Glendower over Mortimer on the Severn's side."

I proceeded in the direction indicated, winding round the side of the hill, the same mountain which the old man had pointed out to me some time before. At length, on making a turn, I saw a very lofty mountain in the far distance to the south-west, a hill right before me to the south, and on my left a meadow overhung by the southern hill, in the middle of which stood a house, from which proceeded a violent barking of dogs. I would fain have made immediately up to it for the purpose of inquiring my way, but saw no means of doing so, a high precipitous bank lying between it and me. I went forward and ascended the side of the hill before me, and presently came to a path running east and west. I followed it a little way towards the east. I was now just above the house, and saw some children and some dogs standing beside it. Suddenly I found myself close to a man who stood in a hollow part of the road from which a narrow path led down to the house; a donkey with panniers stood beside him. He was about fifty years of age, with a carbuncled countenance, high but narrow forehead, grey eyebrows, and small, malignant grey eyes. He had a white hat with narrow eaves, and the crown partly knocked out, a torn blue coat, corduroy breeches, long stockings and highlows. He was sucking a cutty pipe, but seemed unable to extract any smoke from it. He had all the appearance of a vagabond, and of a rather dangerous vagabond. I nodded to him, and asked him in Welsh the name of the place. He glared at me malignantly, then taking the pipe out of his mouth, said that he did not know, that he had been down below to inquire and light his pipe, but could get neither light nor answer from the children. I asked him where he came from, but he evaded the question by asking where I was going to.

" To the Pont y Gwr Drwg," said I.

He then asked me if I was an Englishman.

" O yes !" said I, " I am Carn Sais ;" whereupon
with a strange mixture in his face of malignity and
contempt, he answered in English that he didn't understand me.

" You understood me very well," said I, without
changing my language, " till I told you I was an
Englishman. Harkee, man with the broken hat, you
are one of the bad Welsh, who don't like the English
to know the language, lest they should discover your
lies and rogueries." He evidently understood what I
said, for he gnashed his teeth though he said nothing.
" Well," said I, " I shall go down to those children
and inquire the name of the house," and I forthwith
began to descend the path, the fellow uttering a con-
temptuous " humph " behind me, as much as to say,
much you'll make out down there. I soon reached the
bottom, and advanced towards the house. The dogs
had all along been barking violently; as I drew near
to them, however, they ceased, and two of the largest
came forward wagging their tails. " The dogs were
not barking at me," said I, " but at that vagabond
above." I went up to the children ; they were four in
number, two boys and two girls, all red-haired, but
tolerably good-looking. They had neither shoes nor
stockings. " What is the name of this house?" said
I to the eldest, a boy about seven years old. He looked
at me, but made no answer. I repeated my question ;
still there was no answer, but methought I heard a
humph of triumph from the hill. " Don't crow quite
yet, old chap," thought I to myself, and putting my
hand into my pocket, I took out a penny ; and offering
it to the child, said, " Now, small man, Peth wy y enw
y lle hwn?" Instantly the boy's face became intelligent,
and putting out the fat little hand, he took the ceiniog,
and said in an audible whisper, " Waen y Bwlch." " I
am all right," said I to myself, " that is one of the
names of the places which the old ostler said I must
go through." Then addressing myself to the child, I
said, " Where's your father and mother?"

" Out on the hill," whispered the child.

" What's your father?"

" A shepherd."

" Good," said I. " Now can you tell me the way to the bridge of the evil man?" But the features became blank, the finger was put to the mouth, and the head was hung down. That question was evidently beyond the child's capacity. " Thank you!" said I, and turning round, I regained the path on the top of the bank. The fellow and his donkey were still there. " I had no difficulty," said I, " in obtaining information; the place's name is Waen y Bwlch. But oes genoch dim Cumraeg—you have no Welsh." Thereupon I proceeded along the path in the direction of the east. Forthwith the fellow said something to his animal, and both came following fast behind. I quickened my pace, but the fellow and his beast were close in my rear. Presently I came to a place where another path branched off to the south. I stopped, looked at it, and then went on, but scarcely had done so when I heard another exulting " humph " behind. " I am going wrong," said I to myself; " that other path is the way to the Devil's Bridge, and the scamp knows it, or he would not have grunted." Forthwith I faced round, and brushing past the fellow without a word turned into the other path and hurried along it. By a side glance which I cast I could see him staring after me; presently, however, he uttered a sound very much like a Welsh curse, and kicking his beast proceeded on his way, and I saw no more of him. In a little time I came to a slough which crossed the path. I did not like the look of it at all; and to avoid it ventured upon some green mossy-looking ground to the left, and had scarcely done so when I found myself immersed to the knees in a bog. I, however, pushed forward, and with some difficulty got to the path on the other side of the slough. I followed the path, and in about half-an-hour saw what appeared to be houses at a distance. " God grant that I may be drawing near some inhabited place," said I. The path now grew very miry, and there were pools of water on either side. I moved along slowly. At length I came to a place where some men were busy in erecting a kind of building. I went up to the nearest and asked him the name of the place. He had a crow-bar in his hand, was half-naked, had a

wry mouth and only one eye. He made me no answer,
but moved and gibbered at me.

"For God's sake," said I, "don't do so, but tell me
where I am!" He still uttered no word, but mowed
and gibbered yet more frightfully than before. As I
stood staring at him another man came to me and said
in broken English, "It is of no use speaking to him,
sir, he is deaf and dumb."

"I am glad he is no worse," said I, "for I really
thought he was possessed with the evil one. My good
person, can you tell me the name of this place?"

"Esgyrn Hirion, sir," said he.

"Esgyrn Hirion," said I to myself; "Esgyrn means
bones, and Hirion means long. I am doubtless at the
place which the old ostler called Long Bones. I
shouldn't wonder if I get to the Devil's Bridge to-night
after all." I then asked the man if he could tell me the
way to the bridge of the evil man, but he shook his
head and said that he had never heard of such a place,
adding, however, that he would go with me to one of
the overseers, who could perhaps direct me. He then
proceeded towards a row of buildings, which were in
fact those objects which I had guessed to be houses in
the distance. He led me to a corner house, at the door
of which stood a middle-aged man, dressed in a grey
coat, and saying to me, "This person is an overseer,"
returned to his labour. I went up to the man, and
saluting him in English, asked whether he could direct
me to the devil's bridge, or rather to Pont Erwyd.

"It would be of no use directing you, sir," said he,
"for with all the directions in the world it would be
impossible for you to find the way. You would not
have left these premises five minutes before you would
be in a maze, without knowing which way to turn.
Where do you come from?"

"From Machynlleth," I replied.

"From Machynlleth!" said he. "Well, I only wonder you ever got here, but it would be madness to go
farther alone."

"Well," said I, "can I obtain a guide?"

"I really don't know," said he; "I am afraid all the
men are engaged."

As we were speaking a young man made his appearance at the door from the interior of the house. He was dressed in a brown short coat, had a glazed hat on his head, and had a pale but very intelligent countenance.

" What is the matter?" said he to the other man.

" This gentleman," replied the latter, " is going to Pont Erwyd, and wants a guide."

" Well," said the young man, " we must find him one. It will never do to let him go by himself."

" If you can find me a guide," said I, " I shall be happy to pay him for his trouble."

" O, you can do as you please about that," said the young man; " but, pay or not, we would never suffer you to leave this place without a guide, and as much for our own sake as yours, for the directors of the company would never forgive us if they heard we had suffered a gentleman to leave these premises without a guide, more especially if he were lost, as it is a hundred to one you would be if you went by yourself."

" Pray," said I, " what company is this, the directors of which are so solicitous about the safety of strangers?"

" The Potosi Mining Company," said he, " the richest in all Wales. But pray walk in and sit down, for you must be tired."

CHAPTER LXXXI

The Mining Compting Room—Native of Aberystwyth—Story of a Bloodhound—The Young Girls—The Miner's Tale—Gwen Frwd—The Terfyn.

I FOLLOWED the young man with the glazed hat into a room, the other man following behind me. He of the glazed hat made me sit down before a turf fire, apologising for its smoking very much. The room seemed half compting room, half apartment. There was a wooden desk with a ledger upon it by the window which looked to the west, and a camp bedstead extended from the southern wall nearly up to the desk. After I had sat for about a minute the young man asked

me if I would take any refreshment. I thanked him for
his kind offer, which I declined, saying, however, that
if he would obtain me a guide I should feel much
obliged. He turned to the other man and told him to
go and inquire whether there was any one who would
be willing to go. The other nodded, and forthwith went
out.

" You think, then," said I, " that I could not find the
way by myself?"

" I am sure of it," said he, " for even the people best
acquainted with the country frequently lose their way.
But I must tell you that if we do find you a guide it
will probably be one who has no English."

" Never mind," said I, " I have enough Welsh to
hold a common discourse."

A fine girl about fourteen now came in, and began
bustling about.

" Who is this young lady?" said I.

" The daughter of a captain of a neighbouring mine,"
said he; " she frequently comes here with messages,
and is always ready to do a turn about the house, for
she is very handy."

" Has she any English?" said I.

" Not a word," he replied. " The young people of
these hills have no English, except they go abroad to
learn it."

" What hills are these?" said I.

" Part of the Plynlimmon range," said he.

" Dear me," said I, " am I near Plynlimmon?"

" Not very far from it," said the young man, " and
you will be nearer when you reach Pont Erwyd."

" Are you a native of these parts?" said I.

" I am not," he replied. " I am a native of Aberystwyth, a place on the sea-coast about a dozen miles
from here."

" This seems to be a cold, bleak spot," said I; " is
it healthy?"

" I have reason to say so," said he; " for I came
here from Aberystwyth about four months ago very
unwell, and am now perfectly recovered. I do not
believe there is a healthier spot in all Wales."

We had some further discourse. I mentioned to him
the adventure which I had on the hill with the fellow

with the donkey. The young man said that he had no doubt that he was some prowling thief.

"The dogs of the shepherd's house," said I, "didn't seem to like him, and dogs generally know an evil customer. A long time ago I chanced to be in a posada, or inn, at Valladolid in Spain. One hot summer's afternoon I was seated in a corridor which ran round a large open court in the middle of the inn; a fine yellow, three-parts-grown bloodhound was lying on the ground beside me, with whom I had been playing a little time before. I was just about to fall asleep, when I heard a 'hem' at the outward door of the posada, which was a long way below at the end of a passage which communicated with the court. Instantly the hound started upon his legs, and with a loud yell, and with eyes flashing fire, ran nearly round the corridor down a flight of steps and through the passage to the gate. There was then a dreadful noise, in which the cries of a human being and the yells of the hound were blended. I forthwith started up and ran down, followed by several other guests who came rushing out of their chambers round the corridor. At the gate we saw a man on the ground, and the hound trying to strangle him. It was with the greatest difficulty, and chiefly through the intervention of the master of the dog, who happened to be present, that the animal could be made to quit his hold. The assailed person was a very powerful man, but had an evil countenance, was badly dressed, and had neither hat, shoes nor stockings. We raised him up and gave him wine, which he drank greedily, and presently without saying a word disappeared. The guests said they had no doubt that he was a murderer flying from justice, and that the dog by his instinct, even at a distance, knew him to be such. The master said that it was the first time the dog had ever attacked any one or shown the slightest symptom of ferocity. Not the least singular part of the matter was, that the dog did not belong to the house, but to one of the guests from a distant village; the creature therefore could not consider itself the house's guardian."

I had scarcely finished my tale when the other man came in and said that he had found a guide, a young man from Pont Erwyd, who would be glad of such an opportunity to go and see his parents; that he was then dressing himself and would shortly make his appearance. In about twenty minutes he did so. He was a stout young fellow with a coarse blue coat, and coarse white felt hat; he held a stick in his hand. The kind young book-keeper now advised us to set out without delay as the day was drawing to a close, and the way was long. I shook him by the hand, told him that I should never forget his civility, and departed with the guide.

The fine young girl, whom I have already mentioned, and another about two years younger, departed with us. They were dressed in the graceful female attire of old Wales.

We bore to the south down a descent, and came to some moory quaggy ground intersected with water-courses. The agility of the young girls surprised me; they sprang over the water-courses, some of which were at least four feet wide, with the ease and alacrity of fawns. After a short time we came to a road, which, however, we did not long reap the benefit of as it only led to a mine. Seeing a house on the top of a hill, I asked my guide whose it was.

"Ty powdr," said he, "a powder house," by which I supposed he meant a magazine of powder used for blasting in the mines. He had not a word of English.

If the young girls were nimble with their feet, they were not less so with their tongues, as they kept up an incessant gabble with each other and with the guide. I understood little of what they said, their volubility preventing me from catching more than a few words. After we had gone about two miles and a half they darted away with surprising swiftness down a hill towards a distant house, where as I learned from my guide the father of the eldest lived. We ascended a hill, passed between two craggy elevations, and then wended to the south-east over a strange miry place, in which I thought any one at night not acquainted with every inch of the way would run imminent risk of perishing. I entered into conversation with my guide. After a little time he asked me if I was a Welshman. I told him no.

" You could teach many a Welshman," said he.

" Why do you think so?" said I.

" Because many of your words are quite above my comprehension," said he.

" No great compliment," thought I to myself, but putting a good face upon the matter, I told him that I knew a great many old Welsh words.

" Is Potosi an old Welsh word?" said he.

" No," said I; " it is the name of a mine in the Deheubarth of America."

" Is it a lead mine?"

" No!" said I; " it is a silver mine."

" Then why do they call our mine, which is a lead mine, by the name of a silver mine?"

" Because they wish to give people to understand," said I, " that it is very rich, as rich in lead as Potosi in silver. Potosi is, or was, the richest silver mine in the world, and from it has come at least one-half of the silver which we use in the shape of money and other things."

" Well," said he, " I have frequently asked, but could never learn before, why our mine was called Potosi."

" You did not ask at the right quarter," said I; " the young man with the glazed hat could have told you as well as I." I inquired why the place where the mine was bore the name of Esgyrn Hirion, or Long Bones. He told me that he did not know, but believed that the bones of a cawr, or giant, had been found there in ancient times. I asked him if the mine was deep.

" Very deep," he replied.

" Do you like the life of a miner?" said I.

" Very much," said he, " and should like it more, but for the noises of the hill."

" Do you mean the powder blasts?" said I.

" O no!" said he; " I care nothing for them, I mean the noises made by the spirits of the hill in the mine. Sometimes they make such noises as frighten the poor fellow who works underground out of his senses. Once on a time I was working by myself very deep underground, in a little chamber to which a very deep shaft led. I had just taken up my light to survey my work, when all of a sudden I heard a dreadful rushing noise,

as if an immense quantity of earth had come tumbling
down. ' O God !' said I, and fell backwards, letting the
light fall, which instantly went out. I thought the
whole shaft had given way, and that I was buried alive.
I lay for several hours half stupefied, thinking now and
then what a dreadful thing it was to be buried alive.
At length I thought I would get up, go to the mouth of
the shaft, feel the mould with which it was choked up,
and then come back, lie down and die. So I got up and
tottered to the mouth of the shaft, put out my hand and
felt—nothing. All was clear. I went forward and presently felt the ladder. Nothing had fallen; all was just
the same as when I came down. I was dreadfully afraid
that I should never be able to get up in the dark without
breaking my neck; however, I tried, and at last, with
a great deal of toil and danger, got to a place where
other men were working. The noise was caused by the
spirits of the hill in the hope of driving the miner out
of his senses. They very nearly succeeded. I shall
never forget how I felt when I thought I was buried
alive. If it were not for those noises in the hill the
life of a miner would be quite heaven below."

We came to a cottage standing under a hillock,
down the side of which tumbled a streamlet close by
the northern side of the building. The door was open,
and inside were two or three females and some children.
" Have you any enwyn?" said the lad, peeping in.

" O yes !" said a voice—" digon ! digon !" Presently
a buxom laughing girl brought out two dishes of buttermilk, one of which she handed to me and the other to
the guide. I asked her the name of the place.

"Gwen Frwd : the Fair Rivulet," said she.

" Who lives here?"

" A shepherd."

" Have you any English?"

" Nagos !" said she, bursting into a loud laugh.
" What should we do with English here?" After we
had drunk the buttermilk I offered the girl some money,
but she drew back her hand angrily, and said, " We
don't take money from tired strangers for two drops of
buttermilk ; there's plenty within, and there are a thousand ewes on the hill. Farvel !"

" Dear me !" thought I to myself as I walked away,

"that I should once in my days have found shepherd life something as poets have represented it!"

I saw a mighty mountain at a considerable distance on the right, the same I believe which I had noted some hours before. I inquired of my guide whether it was Plynlimmon.

"O no!" said he, "that is Gaverse; Pumlimmon is to the left."

"Plynlimmon is a famed hill," said I; "I suppose it is very high."

"Yes!" said he, "it is high, but it is not famed because it is high, but because the three grand rivers of the world issue from its breast; the Hafren, the Rheidol, and the Gwy."

Night was now coming rapidly on, attended with a drizzling rain. I inquired if we were far from Pont Erwyd. "About a mile," said my guide; "we shall soon be there." We quickened our pace. After a little time he asked me if I was going farther than Pont Erwyd.

"I am bound for the bridge of the evil man," said I; "but I dare say I shall stop at Pont Erwyd to-night."

"You will do right," said he; "it is only three miles from Pont Erwydd to the bridge of the evil man, but I think we shall have a stormy night."

"When I get to Pont Erwyd," said I, "how far shall I be from South Wales?"

"From South Wales!" said he; "you are in South Wales now; you passed the Terfyn of North Wales a quarter of an hour ago."

The rain now fell fast, and there was so thick a mist that I could only see a few yards before me. We descended into a valley, at the bottom of which I heard a river roaring.

"That's the Rheidol," said my guide, "coming from Pumlimmon, swollen with rain."

Without descending to the river we turned aside up a hill, and after passing by a few huts came to a large house, which my guide told me was the inn of Pont Erwyd.

CHAPTER LXXXII

Consequential Landlord—Cheek—Darfel Gatherel—Dafydd Nanmor—Sheep Farms—Wholesome Advice—The Old Postman—
The Plant de Bat—The Robber's Cavern.

My guide went to a side door, and opening it without
ceremony, went in. I followed, and found myself in a
spacious and comfortable-looking kitchen; a large fire
blazed in a huge grate, on one side of which was a
settle; plenty of culinary utensils, both pewter and
copper, hung around on the walls, and several goodly
rows of hams and sides of bacon were suspended from
the roof. There were several people present, some on
the settle, and others on chairs in the vicinity of the
fire. As I advanced a man arose from a chair and came
towards me. He was about thirty-five years of age,
well and strongly made, with a fresh complexion, a
hawk nose and a keen grey eye. He wore top boots
and breeches, a half-jockey coat, and had a round cap
made of the skin of some animal on his head.

"Servant, sir!" said he in rather a sharp tone, and
surveying me with something of a supercilious air.

"Your most obedient humble servant!" said I; "I
presume you are the landlord of this house."

"Landlord!" said he, "landlord! It is true I receive guests sometimes into my house, but I do so
solely with the view of accommodating them; I do not
depend upon innkeeping for a livelihood. I hire the
principal part of the land in this neighbourhood."

"If that be the case," said I, "I had better continue
my way to the Devil's Bridge; I am not at all tired,
and I believe it is not very far distant."

"O, as you are here," said the farmer-landlord, "I
hope you will stay. I should be very sorry if any
gentleman should leave my house at night after coming
with an intention of staying, more especially in a night
like this. Martha!" said he, turning to a female between thirty and forty, who I subsequently learned was
the mistress—"prepare the parlour instantly for this
gentleman, and don't fail to make up a good fire."

Martha forthwith hurried away, attended by a much younger female.

" Till your room is prepared, sir," said he, " perhaps you will have no objection to sit down before our fire?"

" Not in the least," said I; "nothing gives me greater pleasure than to sit before a kitchen fire. First of all, however, I must settle with my guide, and likewise see that he has something to eat and drink."

" Shall I interpret for you?" said the landlord; " the lad has not a word of English; I know him well."

" I have not been under his guidance for the last three hours," said I, " without knowing that he cannot speak English; but I want no interpreter."

" You do not mean to say, sir," said the landlord, with a surprised and dissatisfied air, " that you understand Welsh?"

I made no answer, but turning to the guide, thanked him for his kindness, and giving him some money, asked him if that was enough.

" More than enough, sir," said the lad; " I did not expect half as much. Farewell!"

He was then about to depart, but I prevented him, saying:

" You must not go till you have eaten and drunk. What will you have?"

" Merely a cup of ale, sir," said the lad.

" That won't do," said I; " you shall have bread and cheese and as much ale as you can drink. Pray," said I to the landlord, " let this young man have some bread and cheese and a large quart of ale."

The landlord looked at me for a moment, then turning to the lad he said:

" What do you think of that, Shon? It is some time since you had a quart of ale to your own cheek."

" Cheek," said I, " cheek! Is that a Welsh word? Surely it is an importation from the English, and not a very genteel one."

" O come, sir!" said the landlord, " we can dispense with your criticisms. A pretty thing indeed for you, on the strength of knowing half-a-dozen words of Welsh, to set up for a Welsh critic in the house of a person who knows the ancient British language perfectly."

" Dear me !" said I, " how fortunate I am ! a person
thoroughly versed in the ancient British language is
what I have long wished to see. Pray what is the
meaning of Darfel Gatherel?"

" O sir," said the landlord, " you must answer that
question yourself; I don't pretend to understand
gibberish !"

" Darfel Gatherel," said I, " is not gibberish; it was
the name of the great wooden image at Ty Dewi, or
Saint David's, in Pembrokeshire, to which thousands
of pilgrims in the days of popery used to repair for the
purpose of adoring it, and which at the time of the
Reformation was sent up to London as a curiosity,
where it eventually served as firewood to burn the monk
Forrest upon, who was sentenced to the stake by Henry
the Eighth for denying his supremacy. What I want
to know is, the meaning of the name, which I could
never get explained, but which you who know the
ancient British language perfectly can doubtless
interpret."

" O sir," said the landlord, " when I said I knew
the British language perfectly, I perhaps went too far;
there are of course some obsolete terms in the British
tongue, which I don't understand. Dar, Dar—what is
it? Darmod Cotterel amongst the rest, but to a general
knowledge of the Welsh language I think I may lay
some pretensions; were I not well acquainted with it
I should not have carried off the prize at various
eisteddfodau, as I have done. I am a poet, sir, a
prydydd."

" It is singular enough," said I, " that the only two
Welsh poets I have seen have been innkeepers—one is
yourself, the other a person I met in Anglesey. I suppose the Muse is fond of cwrw da."

" You would fain be pleasant, sir," said the landlord;
" but I beg leave to inform you that I am not fond of
pleasantries; and now as my wife and the servant are
returned, I will have the pleasure of conducting you to
the parlour."

" Before I go," said I, " I should like to see my
guide provided with what I ordered." I stayed till the
lad was accommodated with bread and cheese and a
foaming tankard of ale, and then bidding him farewell,

I followed the landlord into the parlour, where I found a fire kindled, which, however, smoked exceedingly. I asked my host what I could have for supper, and was told that he did not know, but that if I would leave the matter to him he would send the best he could. As he was going away, I said, " So you are a poet. Well, I am very glad to hear it, for I have been fond of Welsh poetry from my boyhood. What kind of verse do you employ in general? Did you ever write an awdl in the four-and-twenty measures? What are the themes of your songs? The deeds of the ancient heroes of South Wales, I suppose, and the hospitality of the great men of the neighbourhood who receive you as an honoured guest at their tables. I'll bet a guinea that however clever a fellow you may be you never sang anything in praise of your landlord's housekeeping equal to what Dafydd Nanmor sang in praise of that of Ryce of Twyn four hundred years ago :

'For Ryce if hundred thousands plough'd,
The lands around his fair abode;
Did vines of thousand vineyards bleed,
Still corn and wine great Ryce would need;
If all the earth had bread's sweet savour,
And water all had cyder's flavour,
Three roaring feasts in Ryce's hall
Would swallow earth and ocean all.'

Hey?"
" Really, sir," said the landlord, " I don't know how to reply to you, for the greater part of your discourse is utterly unintelligible to me. Perhaps you are a better Welshman than myself; but however that may be, I shall take the liberty of retiring in order to give orders about your supper."
In about half-an-hour the supper made its appearance in the shape of some bacon and eggs; on tasting them I found them very good, and calling for some ale I made a very tolerable supper. After the things had been removed I drew near to the fire, but, as it still smoked, I soon betook myself to the kitchen. My guide had taken his departure, but the others whom I had left were still there. The landlord was talking in Welsh to a man in a rough great-coat about sheep. Setting myself down near the fire I called for a glass of whiskey-

and-water, and then observing that the landlord and
his friend had suddenly become silent, I said, " Pray go
on with your discourse ! Don't let me be any hindrance
to you."

" Yes, sir," said the landlord snappishly, "go on
with our discourse; for your edification, I suppose?"

" Well," said I, " suppose it is for my edification,
surely you don't grudge a stranger a little edification
which will cost you nothing?"

" I don't know that, sir," said the landlord; " I don't
know that. Really, sir, the kitchen is not the place for
a gentleman."

" Yes, it is," said I, " provided the parlour smokes.
Come, come, I am going to have a glass of whiskey-
and-water; perhaps you will take one with me."

" Well, sir !" said the landlord in rather a softened
tone, " I have no objection to take a glass with you."

Two glasses of whiskey-and-water were presently
brought, and the landlord and I drank to each other's
health.

" Is this a sheep district?" said I, after a pause of
a minute or two.

" Yes, sir !" said the landlord ; " it may to a certain
extent be called a sheep district."

" I suppose the Southdown and Norfolk breeds
would not do for these here parts," said I with a
regular Norfolk whine.

" No, sir ! I don't think they would exactly," said
the landlord, staring at me. " Do you know anything
about sheep?"

" Plenty, plenty," said I ; " quite as much indeed as
about Welsh words and poetry." Then in a yet more
whining tone than before, I said, " Do you think that
a body with money in his pocket could hire a comfortable sheep farm hereabouts?"

" O sir !" said the landlord in a furious tone, " you
have come to look out for a farm, I see, and to outbid
us poor Welshmen; it is on that account you have
studied Welsh; but, sir, I would have you know——"

" Come," said I, " don't be afraid; I wouldn't have
all the farms in your country, provided you would tie
them in a string and offer them to me. If I talked about
a farm it was because I am in the habit of talking about

everything, being versed in all matters, do you see, or affecting to be so, which comes much to the same thing. My real business in this neighbourhood is to see the Devil's Bridge and the scenery about it."

"Very good, sir!" said the landlord; "I thought so at first. A great many English go to see the Devil's Bridge and the scenery near it, though I really don't know why, for there is nothing so very particular in either. We have a bridge here too quite as good as the Devil's Bridge; and as for scenery, I'll back the scenery about this house against anything of the kind in the neighbourhood of the Devil's Bridge. Yet everybody goes to the Devil's Bridge and nobody comes here."

"You might easily bring everybody here," said I, "if you would but employ your talent. You should celebrate the wonders of your neighbourhood in cowydds, and you would soon have plenty of visitors; but you don't want them, you know, and prefer to be without them."

The landlord looked at me for a moment, then taking a sip of his whiskey-and-water, he turned to the man with whom he had previously been talking, and recommenced the discourse about sheep. I made no doubt, however, that I was a restraint upon them; they frequently glanced at me, and soon fell to whispering. At last both got up and left the room; the landlord finishing his glass of whiskey-and-water before he went away.

"So you are going to the Devil's Bridge, sir!" said an elderly man, dressed in a grey coat with a broad-brimmed hat, who sat on the settle smoking a pipe in company with another elderly man with a leather hat, with whom I had heard him discourse, sometimes in Welsh, sometimes in English, the Welsh which he spoke being rather broken.

"Yes!" said I, "I am going to have a sight of the bridge and the neighbouring scenery."

"Well, sir, I don't think you will be disappointed, for both are wonderful."

"Are you a Welshman?" said I.

"No, sir! I am not; I am an Englishman from Durham, which is the best county in England."

" So it is," said I,; " for some things, at any rate.
For example, where do you find such beef as in
Durham?"

" Ah, where indeed, sir? I have always said that
neither the Devonshire nor the Lincolnshire beef is to
be named in the same day with that of Durham."

" Well," said I, " what business do you follow in
these parts? I suppose you farm?"

" No, sir! I do not; I am what they call a mining
captain."

" I suppose that gentleman," said I, motioning to
the man in the leather hat, " is not from Durham?"

" No, sir, he is not; he is from the neighbourhood."

" And does he follow mining?"

" No, sir, he does not; he carries about the letters."

" Is your mine near this place?" said I.

" Not very, sir; it is nearer the Devil's Bridge."

" Why is the bridge called the Devil's Bridge?"
said I.

" Because, sir, 'tis said that the Devil built it in the
old time, though that I can hardly believe, for the
Devil, do ye see, delights in nothing but mischief, and
it is not likely that such being the case he would have
built a thing which must have been of wonderful service
to people by enabling them to pass in safety over a
dreadful gulf."

" I have heard," said the old postman with the
leather hat, " that the Devil had no hand in de work
at all, but that it was built by a Mynach, or monk, on
which account de river over which de bridge is built is
called Afon y Mynach—dat is de Monk's River."

" Did you ever hear," said I, " of three creatures
who lived a long time ago near the Devil's Bridge
called the Plant de Bat?"

" Ah, master!" said the old postman, " I do see
that you have been in these parts before; had you not
you would not know of the Plant de Bat."

" No," said I, " I have never been here before; but
I heard of them when I was a boy from a Cumro who
taught me Welsh, and had lived for some time in these
parts. Well, what do they say here about the Plant de
Bat? for he who mentioned them to me could give me
no further information about them than that they were

horrid creatures who lived in a cave near the Devil's Bridge several hundred years ago."

"Well, master," said the old postman, thrusting his forefinger twice or thrice into the bowl of his pipe, "I will tell you what they says here about the Plant de Bat. In de old time two, three hundred year ago, a man lived somewhere about here called Bat, or Bartholomew; this man had three children, two boys and one girl, who, because their father's name was Bat, were generally called Plant de Bat, or Bat's children. Very wicked children they were from their cradle, giving their father and mother much trouble and uneasiness; no good in any one of them, neither in the boys nor the girl. Now the boys, once when they were rambling idly about, lighted by chance upon a cave near the Devil's Bridge. Very strange cave it was, with just one little hole at top to go in by. So the boys said to one another, ' Nice cave this for thief to live in. Suppose we come here when we are a little more big and turn thief ourselves.' Well, they waited till they were a little more big, and then leaving their father's house they came to de cave and turned thief, lying snug there all day, and going out at night to rob upon the roads. Well, there was soon much talk in the country about the robberies which were being committed, and people often went out in search of de thieves, but all in vain; and no wonder, for they were in a cave very hard to light upon, having as I said before merely one little hole at top to go in by. So Bat's boys went on swimmingly for a long time, lying snug in cave by day and going out at night to rob, letting no one know where they were but their sister, who was as bad as themselves, and used to come to them and bring them food, and stay with them for weeks, and sometimes go out and rob with them. But as de pitcher which goes often to de well comes home broke at last, so it happened with Bat's children. After robbing people upon the roads by night many a long year and never being found out, they at last met one great gentleman upon the roads by night, and not only robbed but killed him, leaving his body all cut and gashed near to Devil's Bridge. That job was the ruin of Plant de Bat, for the great gentleman's friends gathered together and hunted after his murderers with dogs, and at length came to the cave, and going in found it stocked with riches, and the Plant de Bat sitting upon the riches, not only the boys but the girl also. So they took out the riches and the Plant de Bat, and the riches they did give to churches and spyttys, and the Plant de Bat they did execute, hanging the boys and burning the girl. That, master, is what they says in dese parts about the Plant de Bat."

"Thank you!" said I. "Is the cave yet to be seen?"

"O yes! it is yet to be seen, or part of it, for it is not now what it was, having been partly flung open to hinder other thieves from nestling in it. It is on the bank of the river Mynach, just before it joins the Rheidol. Many gentlefolk in de summer go to see the Plant de Bat's cave."

"Are you sure?" said I, "that Plant de Bat means Bat's children?"

"I am not sure, master; I merely says what I have heard other people say. I believe some says that it means the wicked children, or the Devil's children. And now, master, we may as well have done with them, for should you question me through the whole night I could tell you nothing more about the Plant de Bat."

After a little farther discourse, chiefly about sheep and the weather, I retired to the parlour, where the fire was now burning brightly; seating myself before it, I remained for a considerable time staring at the embers and thinking over the events of the day. At length I rang the bell and begged to be shown to my chamber, where I soon sank to sleep, lulled by the pattering of rain against the window and the sound of a neighbouring cascade.

CHAPTER LXXXIII

Wild Scenery—Awful Chasm—John Greaves—Durham County—Queen Philippa—The Two Aldens—Welsh Wife—The Noblest Business—The Welsh and the Salve—The Lad John.

A RAINY and boisterous night was succeeded by a bright and beautiful morning. I arose, and having ordered breakfast, went forth to see what kind of country I had

got into. I found myself amongst wild, strange-looking hills, not, however, of any particular height. The
house, which seemed to front the east, stood on the
side of a hill on a wide platform abutting on a deep
and awful chasm, at the bottom of which chafed and
foamed the Rheidol. This river enters the valley of
Pont Erwyd from the north-west, then makes a variety
of snake-like turns, and at last bears away to the
south-east just below the inn. The banks are sheer
walls from sixty to a hundred feet high, and the bed of
the river has all the appearance of a volcanic rent. A
brook running from the south past the inn, tumbles
into the chasm at an angle, and forms the cascade
whose sound had lulled me to sleep the preceding
night.

After breakfasting, I paid my bill, and set out for
the Devil's Bridge without seeing anything more of
that remarkable personage in whom were united landlord, farmer, poet, and mighty fine gentleman—the
master of the house. I soon reached the bottom of the
valley, where are a few houses, and the bridge from
which the place takes its name, Pont Erwyd signifying
the Bridge of Erwyd. As I was looking over the bridge
near which are two or three small waterfalls, an elderly
man in a grey coat, followed by a young lad and dog,
came down the road which I had myself just descended.

" Good day, sir," said he, stopping, when he came
upon the bridge. " I suppose you are bound my
road?"

" Ah," said I, recognising the old mining captain
with whom I had talked in the kitchen the night before,
" is it you? I am glad to see you. Yes! I am bound
your way, provided you are going to the Devil's
Bridge."

" Then, sir, we can go together, for I am bound to
my mine, which lies only a little way t'other side of
the Devil's Bridge."

Crossing the bridge of Erwyd, we directed our course
to the south-east.

" What young man is that?" said I, " who is following behind us?"

" The young man, sir, is my son John, and the dog
with him is his dog Joe."

"And what may your name be, if I may take the liberty of asking?"

"Greaves, sir; John Greaves from the county of Durham."

"Ah! a capital county that," said I.

"You like the county, sir! God bless you! John!" said he in a loud voice, turning to the lad, "why don't you offer to carry the gentleman's knapsack?"

"Don't let him trouble himself," said I. "As I was just now saying, a capital county is Durham county."

"You really had better let the boy carry your bag, sir."

"No!" said I; "I would rather carry it myself. I question upon the whole whether there is a better county in England."

"Is it long since your honour was in Durham county?"

"A good long time. A matter of forty years."

"Forty years! why that's the life of a man. That's longer than I have been out of the county myself. I suppose your honour can't remember much about the county."

"O yes I can, I remember a good deal."

"Please your honour tell me what you remember about the county. It would do me good to hear it."

"Well, I remember it was a very fine county in more respects than one. One part of it was full of big hills and mountains, where there were mines of coal and lead with mighty works with tall chimneys spouting out black smoke, and engines roaring and big wheels going round, some turned by steam, and others by what they called forces, that is brooks of water dashing down steep channels. Another part was a more level country with beautiful woods, happy-looking farmhouses, well-filled fields and rich glorious meadows, in which stood stately with brown sides and short horns the Durham ox."

"O dear, O dear!" said my companion. "Ah, I see your honour knows everything about Durham county. Forces! none but one who had been in Durham county would have used that word. I haven't heard it for five-and-thirty years. Forces! there was a force

close to my village. I wonder if your honour has ever
been in Durham city."

"O yes! I have been there."

"Does your honour remember anything about
Durham city?"

"O yes! I remember a good deal about it."

"Then, your honour, pray tell us what you remember about it—pray do! perhaps it will do me good."

"Well, then, I remember that it was a fine old city
standing on a hill with a river running under it, and
that it had a fine old church, one of the finest in the
whole of Britain; likewise a fine old castle; and last,
not least, a capital old inn, where I got a capital
dinner off roast Durham beef, and a capital glass of ale,
which I believe was the cause of my being ever after
fond of ale."

"Dear me! Ah, I see your honour knows all about
Durham city. And now let me ask one question. How
came your honour to Durham city and county? I don't
think your honour is a Durham man, either of town or
field."

"I am not; but when I was a little boy I passed
through Durham county with my mother and brother
to a place called Scotland."

"Scotland! a queer country that, your honour!"

"So it is," said I; "a queerer country I never saw
in all my life."

"And a queer set of people, your honour."

"So they are," said I; "a queerer set of people than
the Scotch you would scarcely see in a summer's day."

"The Durham folks, neither of town or field, have
much reason to speak well of the Scotch, your honour."

"I dare say not," said I; "very few people have."

"And yet the Durham folks, your honour, generally
contrived to give them as good as they brought."

"That they did," said I; "a pretty licking the
Durham folks once gave the Scots under the walls
of Durham city, after the scamps had been plundering
the country for three weeks—a precious licking they
gave them, slaying I don't know how many thousands,
and taking their king prisoner."

"So they did, your honour, and under the command
of a woman too."

" Very true," said I ; " Queen Philippa. "

" Just so, your honour ! the idea that your honour should know so much about Durham, both field and town ! "

" Well," said I, " since I have told you so much about Durham, perhaps you will now tell me something about yourself. How did you come here ? "

" I had better begin from the beginning, your honour. I was born in Durham county close beside the Great Force, which no doubt your honour has seen. My father was a farmer and had a bit of a share in a mining concern. I was brought up from my childhood both to farming and mining work, but most to mining, because, do you see, I took most pleasure in it, being the more noble business of the two. Shortly after I had come to man's estate my father died leaving me a decent little property, whereupon I forsook farming altogether and gave myself up, body, soul and capital, to mining, which at last I thoroughly understood in all its branches. Well, your honour, about five-and-thirty years ago, that was when I was about twenty-eight, a cry went through the north country that a great deal of money might be made by opening Wales, that is, by mining in Wales in the proper fashion, which means the north-country fashion, for there is no other fashion of mining good for much—there had long been mines in Wales, but they had always been worked in a poor, weak, languid manner, very different from that of the north country. So a company was formed, at the head of which were the Aldens, George and Thomas, for opening Wales, and they purchased certain mines in these districts, which they knew to be productive, and which might be made yet more so, and settling down here called themselves the Rheidol United. Well, after they had been here a little time they found themselves in want of a man to superintend their concerns, above all in the smelting department. So they thought of me, who was known to most of the mining gentry in the north country, and they made a proposal to me through George Alden, afterwards Sir George, to come here and superintend. I said no, at first, for I didn't like the idea of leaving Durham county to come to such an outlandish place as Wales ; howsomever, I at last allowed myself to be overpersuaded by George Alden, afterwards Sir George, and here I came with my wife and family, for I must tell your honour I had married a respectable young woman of Durham county, by whom I had two little ones—here I came and did my best for the service of the Rheidol United. The company was terribly set to it for a long time, spending a mint of money and getting very poor returns. To my certain knowledge the two Aldens, George and Tom, spent between them thirty thousand pounds—the company, however, persevered, chiefly at the instigation of the Aldens, who were in the habit of saying ' Never say die !' and at last got the better of all their difficulties and rolled in riches, and had the credit of being the first company that ever opened Wales, which they richly deserved, for I will uphold it that the Rheidol United, particularly the Aldens, George and Thomas, were the first people who really opened Wales. In their service I have been for five-and-thirty years, and dare say shall continue so till I die. I have been tolerably comfortable, your honour, though I have had my griefs, the bitterest of which was the death of my wife, which happened about eight years after I came to this country. I thought I should have gone wild at first, your honour ! Having, however, always plenty to do, I at last got the better of my affliction. I continued single till my English family grew up and left me, when feeling myself rather lonely I married a decent young Welshwoman, by whom I had one son, the lad John, who is following behind with his dog Joe. And now your honour knows the whole story of John Greaves, miner from the county of Durham.''

" And a most entertaining and instructive history it is," said I. " You have not told me, however, how you contrived to pick up Welsh : I heard you speaking it last night with the postman."

" Why, through my Welsh wife, your honour ! Without her I don't think I should ever have picked up the Welsh manner of discoursing—she is a good kind of woman, my Welsh wife, though——''

" The loss of your Durham wife must have been a great grief to you," said I.

" It was the bitterest grief, your honour, as I said

before, that I ever had—my next worst I think was the death of a dear friend."

" Who was that?" said I.

" Who was it, your honour? why, the Duke of New-castle."

" Dear me!" said I; " how came you to know him?"

" Why, your honour, he lived at a place not far from here, called Hafod, and so——"

" Hafod!" said I; " I have often heard of Hafod and its library; but I thought it belonged to an old Welsh family called Johnes."

" Well, so it did, your honour! but the family died away, and the estate was put up for sale, and purchased by the Duke, who built a fine house upon it, which he made his chief place of residence—the old family house, I must tell your honour, in which the library was had been destroyed by fire: well, he hadn't been long settled there before he found me out and took wonderfully to me, discoursing with me and consulting me about his farming and improvements. Many is the pleasant chat and discourse I have had with his Grace for hours and hours together, for his Grace had not a bit of pride, at least he never showed any to me, though, perhaps, the reason of that was that we were both north-country people. Lord! 1 would have laid down my life for his Grace and have done anything but one which he once asked me to do: ' Greaves,' said the Duke to me one day, ' I wish you would give up mining and become my steward.' ' Sorry I can't oblige your Grace,' said I; ' but give up mining I cannot. I will at any time give your Grace all the advice I can about farming and such like, but give up mining I cannot: because why? I conceive mining to be the noblest business in the 'versal world.' Whereupon his Grace laughed, and said he dare say I was right, and never mentioned the subject again."

" Was his Grace very fond of farming and improving?"

" O yes, your honour! like all the great gentry, especially the north-country gentry, his Grace was wonderfully fond of farming and improving—and a wonderful deal of good he did, reclaiming thousands of acres of land which was before good for nothing, and building capital farm-houses and offices for his tenants. His grand feat, however, was bringing the Durham bull into this country, which formed a capital cross with the Welsh cows. Pity that he wasn't equally fortunate with the north-country sheep."

" Did he try to introduce them into Wales?"

" Yes; but they didn't answer, as I knew they wouldn't. Says I to the Duke, ' It won't do, your Grace, to bring the north-country sheep here : because why? the hills are too wet and cold for their constitutions;' but his Grace, who had sometimes a will of his own, persisted and brought the north-country sheep to these parts, and it turned out as I said : the sheep caught the disease and the wool parted and——"

" But," said I, " you should have told him about the salve made of bran, butter and oil; you should have done that."

" Well, so I did, your honour; I told him about the salve, and the Duke listened to me, and the salve was made by these very hands; but when it was made, what do you think? the foolish Welsh wouldn't put it on, saying that it was against their laws and statties and religion to use it, and talked about Devil's salves and the Witch of Endor, and the sin against the Holy Ghost, and such-like nonsense. So to prevent a regular rebellion, the Duke gave up the salve and the poor sheep pined away and died, till at last there was not one left."

" Who holds the estate at present?" said I.

" Why, a great gentleman from Lancashire, your honour, who bought it when the Duke died; but he doesn't take the same pleasure in it which the Duke did, nor spend so much money about it, the consequence being that everything looks very different from what it looked in the Duke's time. The inn at the Devil's Bridge and the grounds look very different from what they looked in the Duke's time, for you must know that the inn and the grounds form part of the Hafod estate, and are hired from the proprietor."

By this time we had arrived at a small village, with a toll-bar and a small church or chapel at some little distance from the road, which here made a turn nearly full south. The road was very good, but the country was wild and rugged; there was a deep vale on the

right, at the bottom of which rolled the Rheidol in its
cleft, rising beyond which were steep, naked hills.

"This village," said my companion, "is called
Ysbytty Cynfyn. Down on the right, past the church,
is a strange bridge across the Rheidol, which runs
there through a horrid kind of a place. The bridge is
called Pont yr Offeiriad, or the Parson's Bridge, because in the old time the clergyman passed over it every
Sunday to do duty in the church here."

"Why is this place called Ysbytty Cynfyn?" said I,
"which means the hospital of the first boundary; is
there a hospital of the second boundary near here?"

"I can't say anything about boundaries, your
honour; all I know is, that there is another Spytty
farther on beyond Hafod called Ysbytty Ystwyth, or
the 'Spytty upon the Ystwyth. But to return to the
matter of the Minister's Bridge: I would counsel your
honour to go and see that bridge before you leave
these parts. A vast number of gentry go to see it in
the summer time. It was the bridge which the landlord
was mentioning last night, though it scarcely belongs
to his district, being quite as near the Devil's Bridge
inn, as it is to his own, your honour."

We went on discoursing for about half-a-mile farther,
when, stopping by a road which branched off to the
hills on the left, my companion said, "I must now
wish your honour good day, being obliged to go a little
way up here to a mining work on a small bit of business; my son, however, and his dog Joe will show your
honour the way to the Devil's Bridge, as they are
bound to a place a little way past it. I have now
but one word to say, which is, that should ever
your honour please to visit me at my mine, your
honour shall receive every facility for inspecting the
works, and moreover have a bellyfull of drink and
victuals from Jock Greaves, miner from the county of
Durham."

I shook the honest fellow by the hand and went on
in company with the lad John and his dog as far as the
Devil's Bridge. John was a highly intelligent lad, spoke
Welsh and English fluently, could read, as he told me,
both languages, and had some acquaintance with the
writings of Twm o'r Nant, as he showed by repeating

the following lines of the carter poet, certainly not the
worst which he ever wrote :—

> " Twm o'r Nant mae cant a'm galw
> Tomas Edwards yw fy enw.
>
> Tom O Nant is a nickname I've got,
> My name's Thomas Edwards, I wot."

CHAPTER LXXXIV

The Hospice—The Two Rivers—The Devil's Bridge—
Pleasant Recollections.

I ARRIVED at the Devil's Bridge at about eleven o'clock
of a fine but cold day, and took up my quarters at the
inn, of which I was the sole guest during the whole time
that I continued there, for the inn, standing in a lone,
wild district, has very few guests except in summer,
when it is thronged with tourists, who avail themselves
of that genial season to view the wonders of Wales, of
which the region close by is considered amongst the
principal.

The inn, or rather hospice, for the sounding name of
hospice is more applicable to it than the common one
of inn, was built at a great expense by the late Duke
of Newcastle. It is an immense lofty cottage with projecting eaves, and has a fine window to the east which
enlightens a stately staircase and a noble gallery. It
fronts the north and stands in the midst of one of the
most remarkable localities in the world, of which it
would require a far more vigorous pen than mine to
convey an adequate idea.

Far to the west is a tall, strange-looking hill, the top
of which bears no slight resemblance to that of a battle-
mented castle. This hill, which is believed to have been
in ancient times a stronghold of the Britons, bears the
name of Bryn y Castell or the hill of the castle. To the
north-west are russet hills, to the east two brown paps,
whilst to the south is a high, swelling mountain. To
the north and just below the hospice is a profound
hollow with all the appearance of the crater of an
extinct volcano; at the bottom of this hollow the waters
of two rivers unite; those of the Rheidol from the north,

and those of the Afon y Mynach, or the Monks' River,
from the south-east. The Rheidol falling over a rocky
precipice at the northern side of the hollow forms a
cataract very pleasant to look upon from the middle
upper window of the inn. Those of the Mynach which
pass under the celebrated Devil's Bridge are not visible,
though they generally make themselves heard. The
waters of both, after uniting, flow away through a
romantic glen towards the west. The sides of the
hollow, and indeed of most of the ravines in the neighbourhood, which are numerous, are beautifully clad
with wood.

Penetrate now into the hollow above which the hospice stands. You descend by successive flights of
steps, some of which are very slippery and insecure.
On your right is the Monks' River, roaring down its
dingle in five successive falls, to join its brother the
Rheidol. Each of the falls has its own peculiar basin,
one or two of which are said to be of awful depth.
The length which these falls with their basins occupy is
about five hundred feet. On the side of the basin of
the last but one is the cave, or the site of the cave, said
to have been occupied in old times by the Wicked
Children, the mysterious Plant de Bat, two brothers
and a sister, robbers and murderers. At present it is
nearly open on every side, having, it is said, been destroyed to prevent its being the haunt of other evil
people : there is a tradition in the country that the fall
at one time tumbled over its mouth. This tradition,
however, is evidently without foundation, as from the
nature of the ground the river could never have run
but in its present channel. Of all the falls the fifth or
last is the most considerable : you view it trom a kind
of den, to which the last flight of steps, the ruggedest
and most dangerous of all, has brought you; your
position here is a wild one. The fall, which is split
into two, is thundering beside you; foam, foam, foam
is flying all about you; the basin or cauldron is boiling
frightfully below you; hirsute rocks are frowning
terribly above you, and above them forest trees, dank
and wet with spray and mist, are distilling drops in
showers from their boughs.

But where is the bridge, the celebrated bridge of the

Evil Man? From the bottom of the first flight of steps
leading down into the hollow you see a modern-looking
bridge bestriding a deep chasm or cleft to the south-
east, near the top of the dingle of the Monks' River;
over it lies the road to Pont Erwyd. That, however, is
not the Devil's Bridge—but about twenty feet below
that bridge and completely overhung by it, don't you
see a shadowy, spectral object, something like a bow,
which likewise bestrides the chasm? You do! Well!
that shadowy, spectral object is the celebrated Devil's
Bridge, or, as the timorous peasants of the locality call
it, the Pont y Gwr Drwg. It is now merely preserved
as an object of curiosity, the bridge above being alone
used for transit, and is quite inaccessible except to
birds, and the climbing wicked boys of the neighbourhood, who sometimes at the risk of their lives contrive
to get upon it from the frightfully steep northern bank,
and snatch a fearful joy, as, whilst lying on their
bellies, they poke their heads over its sides worn by
age, without parapet to prevent them from falling into
the horrid gulf below. But from the steps in the hollow the view of the Devil's Bridge, and likewise of the
cleft, is very slight and unsatisfactory. To view it
properly, and the wonders connected with it, you must
pass over the bridge above it, and descend a precipitous
dingle on the eastern side till you come to a small platform in a crag. Below you now is a frightful cavity,
at the bottom of which the waters of the Monks' River,
which comes tumbling from a glen to the east, whirl,
boil and hiss in a horrid pot or cauldron, called in the
language of the country Twll yn y graig, or the hole in
the rock, in a manner truly tremendous. On your
right is a slit, probably caused by volcanic force,
through which the waters after whirling in the cauldron
eventually escape. The slit is wonderfully narrow considering its altitude, which is very great, considerably
upwards of a hundred feet—nearly above you, crossing
the slit, which is partially wrapped in darkness, is the
far-famed bridge, the Bridge of the Evil Man, a work
which though crumbling and darkly grey does much
honour to the hand which built it, whether it was the
hand of Satan or of a monkish architect, for the arch
is chaste and beautiful, far superior in every respect,

except in safety and utility, to the one above it, which from this place you have not the mortification of seeing. Gaze on these objects, namely, the horrid seething pot or cauldron, the gloomy volcanic slit, and the spectral, shadowy Devil's Bridge for about three minutes, allowing a minute to each, then scramble up the bank and repair to your inn, and have no more sight-seeing that day, for you have seen enough.   And if pleasant recollections do not haunt you through life of the noble falls and the beautiful wooded dingles to the west of the Bridge of the Evil One, and awful and mysterious ones of the monks' boiling cauldron, the long, savage, shadowy cleft, and the grey, crumbling spectral bridge, I say boldly that you must be a very unpoetical person indeed.

CHAPTER LXXXV

Dinner at the Hospice—Evening Gossip—A Day of Rain—A
Scanty Flock—The Bridge of the Minister—Legs in Danger.

I DINED in a parlour of the inn commanding an excel-lent view of the hollow and the Rheidol fall.   Shortly after I had dined a fierce storm of rain and wind came on.   It lasted for an hour, and then everything again became calm.   Just before evening was closing in I took a stroll to a village which stands a little way to the west of the inn.   It consists only of a few ruinous edifices, and is chiefly inhabited by miners and their families. I saw no men, but plenty of women and children. Seeing a knot of women and girls chatting I went up and addressed them—some of the girls were very good-looking—none of the party had any English; all of them were very civil.   I first talked to them about religion, and found that without a single exception they were Calvinistic Methodists.   I next talked to them about the Plant de Bat.   They laughed heartily at the first mention of their name, but seemed to know very little about their history.   After some twenty minutes' discourse I bade them good-night and returned to my inn.

The night was very cold; the people of the house,

however, made up for me a roaring fire of turf, and I felt very comfortable. About ten o'clock I went to bed, intending next morning to go and see Plynlimmon, which I had left behind me on entering Cardiganshire. When the morning came, however, I saw at once that I had entered upon a day by no means adapted for excursions of any considerable length, for it rained terribly; but this gave me very little concern; my time was my own, and I said to myself, " If I can't go to-day I can perhaps go to-morrow." After breakfast I passed some hours in a manner by no means disagreeable, sometimes meditating before my turf fire with my eyes fixed upon it, and sometimes sitting by the window with my eyes fixed upon the cascade of the Rheidol, which was every moment becoming more magnificent. At length, about twelve o'clock, fearing that if I stayed within I should lose my appetite for dinner, which has always been one of the greatest of my enjoyments, I determined to go and see the Minister's Bridge which my friend the old mining captain had spoken to me about. I knew that I should get a wetting by doing so, for the weather still continued very bad, but I don't care much for a wetting provided I have a good roof, a good fire and good fare to betake myself to afterwards.

So I set out. As I passed over the bridge of the Mynach River I looked down over the eastern balustrade. The Bridge of the Evil One, which is just below it, was quite invisible. I could see, however, the pot or crochan distinctly enough, and a horrible sight it presented. The waters were whirling round in a manner to describe which any word but frenzied would be utterly powerless. Half-an-hour's walking brought me to the little village through which I had passed the day before. Going up to a house I knocked at the door, and a middle-aged man opening it, I asked him the way to the Bridge of the Minister. He pointed to the little chapel to the west and said that the way lay past it, adding that he would go with me himself, as he wanted to go to the hills on the other side to see his sheep.

We got presently into discourse. He at first talked broken English, but soon began to speak his native language. I asked him if the chapel belonged to the Methodists.

"It is not a chapel," said he, "it is a church."

"Do many come to it?" said I.

"Not many, sir, for the Methodists are very powerful here. Not more than forty or fifty come."

"Do you belong to the Church?" said I.

"I do, sir, thank God!"

"You may well be thankful," said I, "for it is a great privilege to belong to the Church of England."

"It is so, sir!" said the man, "though few, alas! think so."

I found him a highly intelligent person : on my talking to him about the name of the place, he said that some called it Spytty Cynfyn, and others Spytty Cynwyl, and that both Cynwyl and Cynfyn were the names of people, to one or other of which the place was dedicated, and that like the place farther on called Spytty Ystwyth, it was in the old time a hospital or inn for the convenience of the pilgrims going to the great monastery of Ystrad Flur or Strata Florida.

Passing through a field or two we came to the side of a very deep ravine, down which there was a zigzag path leading to the bridge. The path was very steep, and, owing to the rain, exceedingly slippery. For some way it led through a grove of dwarf oaks, by grasping the branches of which I was enabled to support myself tolerably well; nearly at the bottom, however, where the path was most precipitous, the trees ceased altogether. Fearing to trust my legs I determined to slide down, and put my resolution in practice, arriving at a little shelf close by the bridge without any accident. The man, accustomed to the path, went down in the usual manner. The bridge consisted of a couple of planks and a pole flung over a chasm about ten feet wide, on the farther side of which was a precipice with a path at least quite as steep as the one down which I had come, and without any trees or shrubs, by which those who used it might support themselves. The torrent rolled about nine feet below the bridge; its channel was tortuous; on the south-east side of the bridge was a cauldron, like that on which I had looked down from the bridge over the river of the monks.

The man passed over the bridge and I followed him;
on the other side we stopped and turned round. The
river was rushing and surging, the pot was boiling
and roaring, and everything looked wild and savage;
but the locality for awfulness and mysterious gloom
could not compare with that on the east side of the
Devil's Bridge, nor for sublimity and grandeur with
that on the west.

"Here you see, sir," said the man, "the Bridge of
the Offeiriad, called so, it is said, because the popes
used to pass over it in the old time; and here you
have the Rheidol, which, though not so smooth nor so
well off for banks as the Hafren and the Gwy, gets to
the sea before either of them, and as the pennill says
is quite as much entitled to honour :—

> "'Hafren a Wy yn hyfryd eu wêdd
> A Rheidol vawr ei anrhydedd.'

Good rhyme, sir, that. I wish you would put it into
Saesneg."

"I am afraid I shall make a poor hand of it," said
I; "however, I will do my best.

> "'O pleasantly do glide along the Severn and the Wye;
> But Rheidol's rough, and yet he's held by all in honour
> high.'"

"Very good rhyme that, sir! though not so good as
the pennill Cymraeg. Ha, I do see that you know the
two languages and are one poet. And now, sir, I must
leave you, and go to the hills to my sheep, who I am
afraid will be suffering in this dreadful weather. However, before I go, I should wish to see you safe over
the bridge."

I shook him by the hand, and retracing my steps
over the bridge began clambering up the bank on my
knees.

"You will spoil your trowsers, sir!" cried the man
from the other side.

"I don't care if I do," said I, "provided I save my
legs, which are in some danger of this place, as well
as my neck, which is of less consequence."

I hurried back amidst rain and wind to my friendly
hospice, where, after drying my wet clothes as well as

I could, I made an excellent dinner on fowl and bacon. Dinner over I took up a newspaper which was brought me, and read an article about the Russian war, which did not seem to be going on much to the advantage of the allies. Soon flinging the paper aside I stuck my feet on the stove, one on each side of the turf fire, and listened to the noises without. The bellowing of the wind down the mountain passes and the roaring of the Rheidol fall at the north side of the valley, and the rushing of the five cascades of the river Mynach, were truly awful. Perhaps I ought not to have said the five cascades of the Mynach, but the Mynach cascade, for now its five cascades had become one, extending from the chasm over which hung the bridge of Satan to the bottom of the valley.

After a time I fell into a fit of musing. I thought of the Plant de Bat : I thought of the spitties or hospitals connected with the great monastery of Ystrad Flur or Strata Florida : I thought of the remarkable bridge close by, built by a clever monk of that place to facilitate the coming of pilgrims with their votive offerings from the north to his convent : I thought of the convent built in the time of our Henry the Second by Ryce ab Gruffyd, prince of South Wales; and lastly I thought of a wonderful man who was buried in its precincts, the greatest genius which Wales, and perhaps Britain, ever produced, on whose account, and not because of old it had been a magnificent building, and the most celebrated place of popish pilgrimage in Wales, I had long ago determined to visit it on my journey, a man of whose life and works the following is a brief accoun

CHAPTER LXXXVI

Birth and Early Years of Ab Gwilym—Morfudd—Relic of Druidism—The Men of Glamorgan—Legend of Ab Gwilym—Ab Gwilym as a Writer—Wonderful Variety—Objects of Nature —Gruffydd Gryg.

DAFYDD AB GWILYM was born about the year 1320 at a place called Bro Gynnin in the county of Cardigan. Though born in wedlock he was not conceived legitimately. His mother being discovered by her parents to be pregnant was turned out of doors by them, whereupon she went to her lover, who married her, though in so doing he acted contrary to the advice of his relations. After a little time, however, a general reconciliation took place. The parents of Ab Gwilym, though highly connected, do not appear to have possessed much property. The boy was educated by his mother's brother, Llewelyn ab Gwilym Fychan, a chief of Cardiganshire; but his principal patron in after life was Ifor, a cousin of his father, surnamed Hael or the bountiful, a chieftain of Glamorganshire. This person received him within his house, made him his steward and tutor to his daughter. With this young lady Ab Gwilym speedily fell in love, and the damsel returned his passion. Ifor, however, not approving of the connection, sent his daughter to Anglesey and eventually caused her to take the veil in a nunnery of that island. Dafydd pursued her, but not being able to obtain an interview he returned to his patron, who gave him a kind reception. Under Ifor's roof he cultivated poetry with great assiduity and wonderful success. Whilst very young, being taunted with the circumstances of his birth by a brother bard called Rhys Meigan, he retorted in an ode so venomously bitter that his adversary, after hearing it, fell down and expired. Shortly after this event he was made head bard of Glamorgan by universal acclamation.

After a stay of some time with Ifor he returned to his native county and lived at Bro Gynnin. Here he fell in love with a young lady of birth called Dyddgu, who did not favour his addresses. He did not break his heart, however, on her account, but speedily bestowed it on the fair Morfudd, whom he first saw at Rhosyr in Anglesey, to which place both had gone on a religious account. The lady after some demur consented to become his wife. Her parents refusing to sanction the union their hands were joined beneath the greenwood tree by one Madawg Benfras, a bard and a great friend of Ab Gwilym. The joining of people's hands by bards, which was probably a relic of Druidism, had long been practised in Wales, and marriages of this kind were generally considered valid, and seldom set aside. The ecclesiastical law, however, did not recognise these poetical marriages, and the parents of Morfudd by appealing to the law soon severed the union. After confining the lady for a short time they bestowed her hand in legal fashion upon a chieftain of the neighbourhood, very rich but rather old, and with a hump on his back, on which account he was nick-named bow-back or little hump-back. Morfudd, however, who passed her time in rather a dull manner with this person, which would not have been the case had she done her duty by endeavouring to make the poor man comfortable, and by visiting the sick and needy around her, was soon induced by the bard to elope with him. The lovers fled to Glamorgan, where Ifor Hael, not much to his own credit, received them with open arms, probably forgetting how he had immured his *own* daughter in a convent rather than bestow her on Ab Gwilym. Having a hunting-lodge in a forest on the banks of the lovely Taf, he allotted it to the fugitives as a residence. Ecclesiastical law, however, as strong in Wild Wales as in other parts of Europe, soon followed them into Glamorgan, and, very properly, separated them. The lady was restored to her husband, and Ab Gwilym fined to a very high amount. Not being able to pay the fine he was cast into prison; but then the men of Glamorgan arose to a man, swearing that their head bard should not remain in prison. "Then pay his fine!" said the ecclesiastical law, or rather the ecclesiastical lawyer. "So we will!" said the men of Glamorgan; and so they did. Every man put his hand into his pocket; the amount was soon raised, the fine paid, and the bard set free.

Ab Gwilym did not forget this kindness of the men of Glamorgan, and to requite it wrote an address to the sun, in which he requests that luminary to visit Glamorgan, to bless it and to keep it from harm. The piece concludes with some noble lines somewhat to this effect :—

> " If every strand oppression strong
> Should arm against the son of song,
> The weary wight would find, I ween,
> A welcome in Glamorgan green."

Some time after his release he meditated a second

elopement with Morfudd, and even induced her to consent to go off with him. A friend to whom he disclosed what he was thinking of doing, asking him whether he would venture a second time to take such a step, " I will," said the bard, " in the name of God and the men of Glamorgan." No second elopement, however, took place, the bard probably thinking, as has been well observed, that neither God nor the men of Glamorgan would help him a second time out of such an affair. He did not attain to any advanced age, but died when about sixty, some twenty years before the rising of Glendower. Some time before his death his mind fortunately took a decidedly religious turn.

He is said to have been eminently handsome in his youth, tall, slender, with yellow hair falling in ringlets down his shoulders. He is likewise said to have been a great libertine. The following story is told of him :—

" In a certain neighbourhood he had a great many mistresses, some married and others not. Once upon a time in the month of June he made a secret appointment with each of his lady-loves, the place and hour of meeting being the same for all; each was to meet him at the same hour beneath a mighty oak which stood in the midst of a forest glade. Some time before the appointed hour he went, and climbing up the oak, hid himself amidst the dense foliage of its boughs. When the hour arrived he observed all the nymphs tripping to the place of appointment; all came, to the number of twenty-four, not one stayed away. For some time they remained beneath the oak staring at each other. At length an explanation ensued, and it appeared that they had all come to meet Ab Gwilym.

" ' Oh, the treacherous monster !' cried they with one accord; ' only let him show himself and we will tear him to pieces.'

" ' Will you?' said Ab Gwilym from the oak; ' here I am ! let her who has been most wanton with me make the first attack upon me !'

" The females remained for some time speechless; all of a sudden, however, their anger kindled, not against the bard, but against each other. From harsh and taunting words they soon came to actions: hair

was torn off; faces were scratched; blood flowed from
cheek and nose. Whilst the tumult was at its fiercest
Ab Gwilym slipped away."

The writer merely repeats this story, and he repeats
it as concisely as possible, in order to have an opportunity of saying that he does not believe one particle
of it. If he believed it he would forthwith burn the
most cherished volume of the small collection of books
from which he derives delight and recreation, namely,
that which contains the songs of Ab Gwilym, for he
would have nothing in his possession belonging to such
a heartless scoundrel as Ab Gwilym must have been
had he got up the scene above described. Any common
man who would expose to each other and the world
a number of hapless, trusting females who had favoured
him with their affections, and from the top of a tree
would feast his eyes upon their agonies of shame and
rage would deserve to be . . . emasculated. Had Ab
Gwilym been so dead to every feeling of gratitude and
honour as to play the part which the story makes him
play, he would have deserved not only to be emasculated, but to be scourged with harp-strings in every
market-town in Wales, and to be dismissed from the
service of the Muse. But the writer repeats that he
does not believe one tittle of the story, though Ab
Gwilym's biographer, the learned and celebrated
William Owen, not only seems to believe it, but rather
chuckles over it. It is the opinion of the writer that the
story is of Italian origin, and that it formed part of
one of the many rascally novels brought over to England after the marriage of Lionel Duke of Clarence,
the third son of Edward the Third, with Violante,
daughter of Galeazzo, Duke of Milan.

Dafydd Ab Gwilym has been in general considered
as a songster who never employed his muse on any subject save that of love, and there can be no doubt that
by far the greater number of his pieces are devoted
more or less to the subject of love. But to consider
him merely in the light of an amatory poet would be
wrong. He has written poems of wonderful power on
almost every conceivable subject. Ab Gwilym has been
styled the Welsh Ovid, and with great justice, but not
merely because like the Roman he wrote admirably on

love. The Roman was not merely an amatory poet : let the shade of Pythagoras say whether the poet who embodied in immortal verse the oldest, the most wonderful and at the same time the most humane of all philosophy was a mere amatory poet. Let the shade of blind Homer be called up to say whether the bard who composed the tremendous line—

" Surgit ad hos clypei dominus septemplicis Ajax "—

equal to any save *one* of his own, was a mere amatory songster. Yet, diversified as the genius of the Roman was, there was no species of poetry in which he shone in which the Welshman may not be said to display equal merit. Ab Gwilym then has been fairly styled the Welsh Ovid. But he was something more—and here let there be no sneers about Welsh ; the Welsh are equal in genius, intellect and learning to any people under the sun, and speak a language older than Greek, and which is one of the immediate parents of the Greek. He was something more than the Welsh Ovid ; he was the Welsh Horace, and wrote light, agreeable, sportive pieces, equal to any things of the kind composed by Horace in his best moods. But he was something more ; he was the Welsh Martial, and wrote pieces equal in pungency to those of the great Roman epigrammatist, perhaps more than equal, for we never heard that any of Martial's epigrams killed anybody, whereas Ab Gwilym's piece of vituperation on Rhys Meigan—pity that poets should be so virulent—caused the Welshman to fall down dead. But he was yet something more ; he could, if he pleased, be a Tyrtæus ; he was no fighter —where was there ever a poet that was ?—but he wrote an ode on a sword, the only warlike piece that he ever wrote, the best poem on the subject ever written in any language. Finally, he was something more ; he was what not one of the great Latin poets was, a Christian ; that is, in his latter days, when he began to feel the vanity of all human pursuits, when his nerves began to be unstrung, his hair to fall off, and his teeth to drop out, and he then composed sacred pieces entitling him to rank with—we were going to say Cædmon—had we done so we should have done wrong ; no uninspired poet ever handled sacred subjects like the grand Saxon

Skald—but which entitle him to be called a great
religious poet, inferior to none but the *protégé* of
Hilda.

Before ceasing to speak of Ab Gwilym, it will be
necessary to state that his amatory pieces, which con-
stitute more than one-half of his productions, must be
divided into two classes, the purely amatory, and those
only partly devoted to love. His poems to Dyddgu,
and the daughter of Ifor Hael, are productions very
different from those addressed to Morfudd. There can
be no doubt that he had a sincere affection for the two
first; there is no levity in the cowydds which he addressed to them, and he seldom introduces any other
objects than those of his love. But in his cowydds
addressed to Morfudd is there no levity? Is Morfudd
ever prominent? His cowydds to that woman abound
with humorous levity, and for the most part have far
less to do with her than with natural objects—the
snow, the mist, the trees of the forest, the birds of the
air, and the fishes of the stream. His first piece to
Morfudd is full of levity quite inconsistent with true
love. It states how, after seeing her for the first time
at Rhosyr in Anglesey, and falling in love with her, he
sends her a present of wine by the hands of a servant,
which present she refuses, casting the wine contemptuously over the head of the valet. This commencement
promises little in the way of true passion, so that we
are not disappointed when we read a little farther on
that the bard is dead and buried, all on account of love,
and that Morfudd makes a pilgrimage to Mynyw to
seek for pardon for killing him, nor when we find him
begging the popish image to convey a message to her.
Then presently we almost lose sight of Morfudd amidst
birds, animals and trees, and we are not sorry that we
do; for though Ab Gwilym is mighty in humour, great
in describing the emotions of love and the beauties of
the lovely, he is greatest of all in describing objects of
nature; indeed in describing them he has no equal, and
the writer has no hesitation in saying that in many of
his cowydds in which he describes various objects of
nature, by which he sends messages to Morfudd, he
shows himself a far greater poet than Ovid appears in
any one of his Metamorphoses. There are many poets

who attempt to describe natural objects without being intimately acquainted with them, but Ab Gwilym was not one of these. No one was better acquainted with nature; he was a stroller, and there is every probability that during the greater part of the summer he had no other roof than the foliage, and that the voices of birds and animals were more familiar to his ears than was the voice of man. During the summer months, indeed, in the early part of his life, he was, if we may credit him, generally lying perdue in the woodland or mountain recesses near the habitation of his mistress, before or after her marriage, awaiting her secret visits made, whenever she could escape the vigilance of her parents, or the watchful jealousy of her husband, and during her absence he had nothing better to do than to observe objects of nature and describe them. His ode to the Fox, one of the most admirable of his pieces, was composed on one of these occasions.

Want of space prevents the writer from saying as much as he could wish about the genius of this wonderful man, the greatest of his country's songsters, well calculated by nature to do honour to the most polished age and the most widely-spoken language. The bards his contemporaries, and those who succeeded him for several hundred years, were perfectly convinced of his superiority not only over themselves but over all the poets of the past, and one, and a mighty one, old Iolo the bard of Glendower, went so far as to insinuate that after Ab Gwilym it would be of little avail for any one to make verses :—

> " Aed lle mae'r eang dangneff,
> Ac aed y gerdd gydag ef."

> To Heaven's high peace let him depart,
> And with him go the minstrel art.

He was buried at Ystrad Flur, and a yew tree was planted over his grave, to which Gruffydd Gryg, a brother bard, who was at one time his enemy, but eventually became one of the most ardent of his admirers, addressed an ode, of part of which the following is a paraphrase :—

> Thou noble tree ; who shelt'rest kind
> The dead man's house from winter's wind ;

May lightnings never lay thee low,
Nor archer cut from thee his bow;
Nor Crispin peel thee pegs to frame,
But may thou ever bloom the same,
A noble tree the grave to guard
Of Cambria's most illustrious bard !

CHAPTER LXXXVII

Start for Plynlimmon—Plynlimmon's Celebrity—Troed
Rhiw Goch.

THE morning of the fifth of November looked rather
threatening. As, however, it did not rain, I determined
to set off for Plynlimmon, and returning at night to the
inn, resume my journey to the south on the following
day. On looking into a pocket almanac I found it was
Sunday. This very much disconcerted me, and I
thought at first of giving up my expedition. Eventually, however, I determined to go, for I reflected that
I should be doing no harm, and that I might acknowledge the sacredness of the day by attending morning
service at the little Church of England chapel which lay
in my way.

The mountain of Plynlimmon to which I was bound
is the third in Wales for altitude, being only inferior to
Snowdon and Cadair Idris. Its proper name is Pum
or Pump Lumon, signifying the five points, because
towards the upper part it is divided into five hills or
points. Plynlimmon is a celebrated hill on many accounts. It has been the scene of many remarkable
events : in the tenth century a dreadful battle was
fought on one of its spurs between the Danes and the
Welsh, in which the former sustained a bloody overthrow, and in 1401 a conflict took place in one of its
valleys between the Welsh under Glendower and the
Flemings of Pembrokeshire, who, exasperated at having
their homesteads plundered and burned by the chieftain,
who was the mortal enemy of their race, assembled in
considerable numbers and drove Glendower and his
forces before them to Plynlimmon, where the Welshmen standing at bay a contest ensued, in which, though
eventually worsted, the Flemings were at one time all

but victorious. What, however, has more than anything else contributed to the celebrity of the hill is the
circumstance of its giving birth to three rivers. The
first of which, the Severn, is the principal stream in
Britain; the second, the Wye, the most lovely river,
probably, which the world can boast of; and the third,
the Rheidol, entitled to high honour from its bold-
ness and impetuosity, and the remarkable banks between which it flows in its very short course, for there
are scarcely twenty miles between the ffynnon or source
of the Rheidol and the aber or place where it disembogues itself into the sea.

I started about ten o'clock on my expedition, after
making, of course, a very hearty breakfast. Scarcely
had I crossed the Devil's Bridge when a shower of hail
and rain came on. As, however, it came down nearly
perpendicularly, I put up my umbrella and laughed.
The shower pelted away till I had nearly reached Spytty
Cynwyl, when it suddenly left off, and the day became
tolerably fine. On arriving at the Spytty I was sorry
to find that there would be no service till three in the
afternoon. As waiting till that time was out of the
question, I pushed forward on my expedition. Leaving
Pont Erwyd at some distance on my left, I went duly
north till I came to a place amongst hills where the
road was crossed by an angry-looking rivulet, the
same I believe which enters the Rheidol near Pont
Erwyd, and which is called the Castle River. I was
just going to pull off my boots and stockings in order
to wade through, when I perceived a pole and a rail
laid over the stream at a little distance above where I
was. This rustic bridge enabled me to cross without
running the danger of getting a regular sousing, for
these mountain streams, even when not reaching so
high as the knee, occasionally sweep the wader off his
legs, as I know by my own experience. From a lad
whom I presently met I learned that the place where I
crossed the water was called Troed rhiw goch, or the
Foot of the Red Slope.

About twenty minutes' walk from hence brought me
to Castell Dyffryn, an inn about six miles distant from
the Devil's Bridge, and situated near a spur of the
Plynlimmon range. Here I engaged a man to show me

the sources of the rivers and the other wonders of the mountain. He was a tall, athletic fellow, dressed in brown coat, round buff hat, corduroy trowsers, linen leggings and highlows, and though a Cumro had much more the appearance of a native of Tipperary than a Welshman. He was a kind of shepherd to the people of the house, who like many others in South Wales followed farming and inn-keeping at the same time.

CHAPTER LXXXVIII

The Guide—The Great Plynlimmon—A Dangerous Path—Source of the Rheidol—Source of the Severn—Pennillion—Old Times and New—The Corpse-Candle—Supper.

LEAVING the inn my guide and myself began to ascend a steep hill just behind it. When we were about half way up I asked my companion, who spoke very fair English, why the place was called the Castle.

" Because, sir," said he, " there was a castle here in the old time."

" Whereabouts was it?" said I.

" Yonder," said the man, standing still and pointing to the right. " Don't you see yonder brown spot in the valley? There the castle stood."

" But are there no remains of it?" said I. " I can see nothing but a brown spot."

" There are none, sir! but there a castle once stood, and from it the place we came from had its name, and likewise the river that runs down to Pont Erwyd."

" And who lived there?" said I.

" I don't know, sir," said the man. " But I suppose they were grand people or they would not have lived in a castle."

After ascending the hill and passing over its top we went down its western side and soon came to a black frightful bog between two hills. Beyond the bog and at some distance to the west of the two hills rose a brown mountain, not abruptly but gradually, and looking more like what the Welsh call a rhiw or slope than a mynydd or mountain.

R

" That, sir," said my guide, " is the great Plyn-limmon."

" It does not look much of a hill," said I.

" We are on very high ground, sir, or it would look much higher. I question, upon the whole, whether there is a higher hill in the world. God bless Pumlummon Mawr!" said he, looking with reverence towards the hill. " I am sure I have a right to say so, for many is the good crown I have got by showing gentle-folks, like yourself, to the top of him."

" You talk of Plynlimmon Mawr, or the great Plyn-limmon," said I; " where are the small ones?"

" Yonder they are," said the guide, pointing to two hills towards the north—" one is Plynlimmon Canol, and the other Plynlimmon Bach. The middle and the small Plynlimmon."

" Pumlummon," said I, " means five summits. You have pointed out only three—now, where are the other two?"

" Those two hills which we have just passed make up the five. However, I will tell your worship that there is a sixth summit. Don't you see that small hill con-nected with the big Pumlummon, on the right?"

" I see it very clearly," said I.

" Well, your worship, that's called Bryn y Llo—the Hill of the Calf, or the Calf Plynlimmon, which makes the sixth summit."

" Very good," said I, " and perfectly satisfactory. Now let us ascend the Big Pumlummon."

In about a quarter of an hour we reached the sum-mit of the hill, where stood a large carn or heap of stones. I got up on the top and looked around me.

A mountainous wilderness extended on every side, a waste of russet-coloured hills, with here and there a black, craggy summit. No signs of life or cultivation were to be discovered, and the eye might search in vain for a grove or even a single tree. The scene would have been cheerless in the extreme had not a bright sun lighted up the landscape.

" This does not seem to be a country of much society," said I to my guide.

" It is not, sir. The nearest house is the inn we came from, which is now three miles behind us. Straight

before you there is not one for at least ten, and on
either side it is an anialwch to a vast distance. Plun-
lummon is not a sociable country, sir; nothing to be
found in it, but here and there a few sheep or a
shepherd.''

"Now," said I, descending from the carn, "we will
proceed to the sources of the rivers."

" The ffynnon of the Rheidol is not far off," said the
guide; "it is just below the hill."

We descended the western side of the hill for some
way; at length, coming to a very craggy and precipitous place my guide stopped, and pointing with his
finger into the valley below, said:

" There, sir, if you look down you can see the source
of the Rheidol.''

I looked down, and saw far below what appeared
to be part of a small sheet of water.

" And that is the source of the Rheidol?" said I.

" Yes, sir," said my guide; " that is the ffynnon of
the Rheidol."

" Well," said I, " is there no getting to it?"

" O yes ! but the path, sir, as you see, is rather steep
and dangerous. ''

" Never mind," said I. " Let us try it."

" Isn't seeing the fountain sufficient for you, sir?"

" By no means," said I. " It is not only necessary
for me to see the sources of the rivers, but to drink of
them, in order that in after times I may be able to
harangue about them with a tone of confidence and
authority."

" Then follow me, sir; but please to take care, for
this path is more fit for sheep or shepherds than
gentlefolk.''

And a truly bad path I found it; so bad indeed that
before I had descended twenty yards I almost repented
having ventured. I had a capital guide, however, who
went before and told me where to plant my steps.
There was one particularly bad part, being little better
than a sheer precipice; but even here I got down in
safety with the assistance of my guide, and a minute
afterwards found myself at the source of the Rheidol.

The source of the Rheidol is a small, beautiful lake,
about a quarter of a mile in length. It is overhung on

the east and north by frightful crags, from which it is fed by a number of small rills. The water is of the deepest blue and of very considerable depth. The banks, except to the north and east, slope gently down, and are clad with soft and beautiful moss. The river, of which it is the head, emerges at the south-western side, and brawls away in the shape of a considerable brook, amidst moss and rushes down a wild glen tending to the south. To the west the prospect is bounded, at a slight distance, by high, swelling ground. If few rivers have a more wild and wondrous channel than the Rheidol, fewer still have a more beautiful and romantic source.

After kneeling down and drinking freely of the lake I said :

" Now, where are we to go to next?"

" The nearest ffynnon to that of the Rheidol, sir, is the ffynnon of the Severn."

" Very well," said I; " let us now go and see the ffynnon of the Severn !"

I followed my guide over a hill to the north-west into a valley, at the farther end of which I saw a brook streaming apparently to the south, where was an outlet.

" That brook," said the guide, " is the young Severn." The brook came from round the side of a very lofty rock, singularly variegated, black and white, the northern summit presenting something of the appearance of the head of a horse. Passing round this crag we came to a fountain surrounded with rushes, out of which the brook, now exceedingly small, came murmuring.

" The crag above," said my guide, " is called Crag y Cefyl, or the Rock of the Horse, and this spring at its foot is generally called the ffynnon of the Hafren. However, drink not of it, master; for the ffynnon of the Hafren is higher up the nant. Follow me, and I will presently show you the real ffynnon of the Hafren."

I followed him up a narrow and very steep dingle. Presently we came to some beautiful little pools of water in the turf, which was here remarkably green.

" These are very pretty pools, an't they, master?"

said my companion. " Now, if I was a false guide I might bid you stoop and drink, saying that these were the sources of the Severn; but I am a true cyfarwydd and therefore tell you not to drink, for these pools are not the sources of the Hafren, no more than the spring below. The ffynnon of the Severn is higher up the nant. Don't fret, however, but follow me, and we shall be there in a minute."

So I did as he bade me, following him without fretting higher up the nant. Just at the top he halted and said, " Now, master, I have conducted you to the source of the Severn. I have considered the matter deeply, and have come to the conclusion that here, and here only, is the true source. Therefore stoop down and drink, in full confidence that you are taking possession of the Holy Severn."

The source of the Severn is a little pool of water some twenty inches long, six wide, and about three deep. It is covered at the bottom with small stones, from between which the water gushes up. It is on the left-hand side of the nant, as you ascend, close by the very top. An unsightly heap of black turf-earth stands just above it to the north. Turf-heaps, both large and small, are in abundance in the vicinity.

After taking possession of the Severn by drinking at its source, rather a shabby source for so noble a stream, I said, " Now let us go to the fountain of the Wye."

" A quarter of an hour will take us to it, your honour," said the guide, leading the way.

The source of the Wye, which is a little pool, not much larger than that which constitutes the fountain of the Severn, stands near the top of a grassy hill which forms part of the Great Plynlimmon. The stream after leaving its source runs down the hill towards the east, and then takes a turn to the south. The fountains of the Severn and the Wye are in close proximity to each other. That of the Rheidol stands somewhat apart from both, as if, proud of its own beauty, it disdained the other two for their homeliness. All three are contained within the compass of a mile.

" And now, I suppose, sir, that our work is done, and we may go back to where we came from," said my guide, as I stood on the grassy hill after drinking copiously of the fountain of the Wye.

"We may," said I; "but before we do I must repeat some lines made by a man who visited these sources, and experienced the hospitality of a chieftain in this neighbourhood four hundred years ago." Then taking off my hat I lifted up my voice and sang :—

> "From high Plynlimmon's shaggy side
> Three streams in three directions glide,
> To thousands at their mouth who tarry
> Honey, gold and mead they carry.
> Flow also from Plynlimmon high
> Three streams of generosity ;
> The first, a noble stream indeed,
> Like rills of Mona runs with mead ;
> The second bears from vineyards thick
> Wine to the feeble and the sick ;
> The third, till time shall be no more,
> Mingled with gold shall silver pour."

"Nice pennillion, sir, I dare say," said my guide, "provided a person could understand them. What's meant by all this mead, wine, gold and silver?"

"Why," said I, "the bard meant to say that Plynlimmon, by means of its three channels, sends blessings and wealth in three different directions to distant places, and that the person whom he came to visit, and who lived on Plynlimmon, distributed his bounty in three different ways, giving mead to thousands at his banquets, wine from the vineyards of Gascony to the sick and feeble of the neighbourhood, and gold and silver to those who were willing to be tipped, amongst whom no doubt was himself, as poets have never been above receiving a present."

"Nor above asking for one, your honour; there's a prydydd in this neighbourhood, who will never lose a shilling for want of asking for it. Now, sir, have the kindness to tell me the name of the man who made those pennillion."

"Lewis Glyn Cothi," said I; "at least, it was he who made the pennillion from which those verses are translated."

"And what was the name of the gentleman whom he came to visit?"

" His name," said I, " was Dafydd ab Thomas
Vychan."

" And where did he live?"

" Why, I believe, he lived at the castle, which you
told me once stood on the spot which you pointed out
as we came up. At any rate, he lived somewhere upon
Plynlimmon."

" I wish there was some such rich gentleman at
present living on Plynlimmon," said my guide; " one
of that sort is much wanted."

" You can't have everything at the same time," said
I : " formerly you had a chieftain who gave away wine
and mead, and occasionally a bit of gold or silver, but
then no travellers and tourists came to see the wonders
of the hills, for at that time nobody cared anything
about hills; at present you have no chieftain, but
plenty of visitors who come to see the hills and the
sources and scatter plenty of gold about the neighbourhood."

We now bent our steps homeward, bearing slightly
to the north, going over hills and dales covered with
gorse and ling. My guide walked with a calm and
deliberate gait, yet I had considerable difficulty in keeping up with him. There was, however, nothing surprising in this; he was a shepherd walking on his own
hill, and having first-rate wind, and knowing every inch
of the ground, made great way without seeming to be
in the slightest hurry : I would not advise a road-
walker, even if he be a first-rate one, to attempt to
compete with a shepherd on his own, or indeed any
hill; should he do so, the conceit would soon be taken
out of him.

After a little time we saw a rivulet running from the
west.

" This ffrwd," said my guide, " is called Frennig.
It here divides shire Trefaldwyn from Cardiganshire,
one in North and the other in South Wales."

Shortly afterwards we came to a hillock of rather a
singular shape.

" This place, sir," said he, " is called Eisteddfa."

" Why is it called so?" said I.   " Eisteddfa means
the place where people sit down."

" It does so," said the guide, " and it is called the

place of sitting because three men from different quarters of the world once met here, and one proposed that they should sit down.''

"And did they?" said I.

"They did, sir; and when they had sat down they told each other their histories.''

"I should be glad to know what their histories were," said I.

"I can't exactly tell you what they were, but I have heard say that there was a great deal in them about the Tylwith Teg or fairies.''

"Do you believe in fairies?" said I.

"I do, sir; but they are very seldom seen, and when they are they do no harm to anybody. I only wish there were as few corpse-candles as there are Tylwith Teg, and that they did as little harm.''

"They foreshow people's deaths, don't they?" said I.

"They do, sir? but that's not all the harm they do. They are very dangerous for anybody to meet with. If they come bump up against you when you are walking carelessly it's generally all over with you in this world. I'll give you an example: A man returning from market from Llan Eglos to Llan Curig, not far from Plynlimmon, was struck down dead as a horse not long ago by a corpse-candle. It was a rainy, windy night, and the wind and rain were blowing in his face, so that he could not see it, or get out of its way. And yet the candle was not abroad on purpose to kill the man. The business that it was about was to prognosticate the death of a woman who lived near the spot and whose husband dealt in wool—poor thing! she was dead and buried in less than a fortnight. Ah, master, I wish that corpse-candles were as few and as little dangerous as the Tylwith Teg or fairies.''

We returned to the inn where I settled with the honest fellow, adding a trifle to what I had agreed to give him. Then sitting down I called for a large measure of ale and invited him to partake of it. He accepted my offer with many thanks and bows, and as we sat and drank our ale we had a great deal of discourse about the places we had visited. The ale being finished I got up and said:

" I must now be off for the Devil's Bridge!"

Whereupon he also arose, and offering me his hand,
said :

" Farewell, master; I shall never forget you: were
all the gentlefolks who come here to see the sources
like you, we should indeed feel no want in these hills
of such a gentleman as is spoken of in the pennillion."

The sun was going down as I left the inn. I re-
crossed the streamlet by means of the pole and rail.
The water was running with much less violence than in
the morning, and was considerably lower. The evening
was calm and beautifully cool, with a slight tendency
to frost. I walked along with a bounding and elastic
step, and never remember to have felt more happy and
cheerful.

I reached the hospice at about six o'clock, a bright
moon shining upon me, and found a capital supper
awaiting me, which I enjoyed exceedingly.

How one enjoys one's supper at one's inn, after a
good day's walk, provided one has the proud and
glorious consciousness of being able to pay one's
reckoning on the morrow !

CHAPTER LXXXIX

A Morning View — Hafod Ychdryd — The Monument — Fairy-
looking Place—Edward Lhuyd.

THE morning of the sixth was bright and glorious. As
I looked from the window of the upper sitting-room of
the hospice the scene which presented itself was wild
and beautiful to a degree. The oak-covered tops of the
volcanic crater were gilded with the brightest sunshine,
whilst the eastern sides remained in dark shade and
the gap or narrow entrance to the north in shadow yet
darker, in the midst of which shone the silver of the
Rheidol cataract. Should I live a hundred years I shall
never forget the wild fantastic beauty of that morning
scene.

I left the friendly hospice at about nine o'clock to
pursue my southern journey. By this time the morning
had lost much of its beauty, and the dull grey sky

characteristic of November began to prevail. The way lay up a hill to the south-east; on my left was a glen down which the river of the Monk rolled with noise and foam. The country soon became naked and dreary and continued so for some miles. At length coming to the top of a hill I saw a park before me, through which the road led after passing under a stately gateway. I had reached the confines of the domain of Hafod.

Hafod Ychdryd, or the summer mansion of Uchtryd, has from time immemorial been the name of a dwelling on the side of the hill above the Ystwyth, looking to the east. At first it was a summer boothie or hunting lodge to Welsh chieftains, but subsequently expanded into the roomy, comfortable dwelling of Welsh squires, where hospitality was much practised and bards and harpers liberally encouraged. Whilst belonging to an ancient family of the name of Johnes, several members of which made no inconsiderable figure in literature, it was celebrated, far and wide, for its library, in which was to be found, amongst other treasures, a large collection of Welsh manuscripts on various subjects—history, medicine, poetry and romance. The house, however, and the library were both destroyed in a dreadful fire which broke out. This fire is generally called the great fire of Hafod, and some of those who witnessed it have been heard to say that its violence was so great that burning rafters mixed with flaming books were hurled high above the summits of the hills. The loss of the house was a matter of triviality compared with that of the library. The house was soon rebuilt, and probably, phœnix-like, looked all the better for having been burnt, but the library could never be restored. On the extinction of the family, the last hope of which, an angelic girl, faded away in the year 1811, the domain became the property of the late Duke of Newcastle, a kind and philanthropic nobleman and a great friend of agriculture, who held it for many years and considerably improved it. After his decease it was purchased by the head of an ancient Lancashire family, who used the modern house as a summer residence, as the Welsh chieftains had used the wooden boothie of old.

I went to a kind of lodge, where I had been told that I should find somebody who would admit me to the church, which stood within the grounds and contained a monument which I was very desirous of seeing, partly from its being considered one of the masterpieces of the great Chantrey, and partly because it was a memorial to the lovely child, the last scion of the old family who had possessed the domain. A good-looking young woman, the only person whom I saw, on my telling my errand forthwith took a key and conducted me to the church. The church was a neat edifice with rather a modern look. It exhibited nothing remarkable without, and only one thing remarkable within, namely the monument, which was indeed worthy of notice, and which, had Chantrey executed nothing else, might well have entitled him to be considered, what the world has long pronounced him, the prince of British sculptors.

This monument, which is of the purest marble, is placed on the eastern side of the church, below a window of stained glass, and represents a truly affecting scene : a lady and gentleman are standing over a dying girl of angelic beauty who is extended on a couch, and from whose hand a volume, the Book of Life, is falling. The lady is weeping.

Beneath is the following inscription :——

> To the Memory of
> Mary
> The only child of Thomas and Jane Johnes
> Who died in 1811
> After a few days' sickness
> This monument is dedicated
> By her parents.

An inscription worthy, by its simplicity and pathos, to stand below such a monument.

After presenting a trifle to the woman, who to my great surprise could not speak a word of English, I left the church, and descended the side of the hill, near the top of which it stands. The scenery was exceedingly beautiful. Below me was a bright green valley, at the bottom of which the Ystwyth ran brawling, now hid amongst groves, now showing a long stretch of water. Beyond the river to the east was a noble mountain, richly wooded. The Ystwyth, after a circuitous course, joins the Rheidol near the strand of the Irish Channel, which the united rivers enter at a place called Aber

Ystwyth, where stands a lovely town of the same name, which sprang up under the protection of a baronial castle, still proud and commanding even in its ruins, built by Strongbow the conqueror of the great western isle. Near the lower part of the valley the road tended to the south, up and down through woods and bowers, the scenery still ever increasing in beauty. At length, after passing through a gate and turning round a sharp corner, I suddenly beheld Hafod on my right hand, to the west at a little distance above me, on a rising ground, with a noble range of mountains behind it.

A truly fairy place it looked, beautiful but fantastic, in the building of which three styles of architecture seemed to have been employed. At the southern end was a Gothic tower; at the northern an Indian pagoda; the middle part had much the appearance of a Grecian villa. The walls were of resplendent whiteness, and the windows which were numerous shone with beautiful gilding. Such was modern Hafod, a strange contrast, no doubt, to the hunting lodge of old.

After gazing at this house of eccentric taste for about a quarter of an hour, sometimes with admiration, sometimes with a strong disposition to laugh, I followed the road, which led past the house in nearly a southerly direction. Presently the valley became more narrow, and continued narrowing till there was little more room than was required for the road and the river, which ran deep below it on the left-hand side. Presently I came to a gate, the boundary in the direction in which I was going of the Hafod domain.

Here, when about to leave Hafod, I shall devote a few lines to a remarkable man whose name should be ever associated with the place. Edward Lhuyd was born in the vicinity of Hafod about the period of the Restoration. His father was a clergyman, who after giving him an excellent education at home sent him to Oxford, at which seat of learning he obtained an honourable degree, officiated for several years as tutor, and was eventually made custodiary of the Ashmolean Museum. From his early youth he devoted himself with indefatigable zeal to the acquisition of learning. He was fond of natural history and British antiquities, but his favourite pursuit and that in which he principally distinguished himself was the study of the Celtic dialects; and it is but doing justice to his memory to say, that he was not only the best Celtic scholar of his time, but that no one has arisen since worthy to be considered his equal in Celtic erudition. Partly at the expense of the university, partly at that of various powerful individuals who patronised him, he travelled through Ireland, the Western Highlands, Wales, Cornwall and Armorica, for the purpose of collecting Celtic manuscripts. He was partially successful in Ireland and Wales. Several of the most precious Irish manuscripts in Oxford and also in the Chandos Library were of Lhuyd's collection, and to him the old hall at Hafod was chiefly indebted for its treasures of ancient British literature. Shortly after returning to Oxford from his Celtic wanderings he sat down to the composition of a grand work in three parts, under the title of Archæologia Britannica, which he had long projected. The first was to be devoted to the Celtic dialects; the second to British Antiquities, and the third to the natural history of the British Isles. He only lived to complete the first part. It contains various Celtic grammars and vocabularies, to each of which there is a preface written by Lhuyd in the particular dialect to which the vocabulary or grammar is devoted. Of all these prefaces the one to the Irish is the most curious and remarkable. The first part of the Archæologia was published at Oxford in 1707, two years before the death of the author. Of his correspondence, which was very extensive, several letters have been published, all of them relating to philology, antiquities, and natural history.

CHAPTER XC

An Adventure—Spytty Ystwyth—Wormwood.

SHORTLY after leaving the grounds of Hafod I came to a bridge over the Ystwyth. I crossed it, and was advancing along the road which led apparently to the south-east, when I came to a company of people who seemed to be loitering about. It consisted entirely of young men and women, the former with crimson favours, the latter in the garb of old Wales, blue tunics and sharp crowned hats. Going up to one of the young women I said, " Peth yw? what's the matter?"

" Priodas (a marriage)," she replied, after looking at me attentively. I then asked her the name of the bridge, whereupon she gave a broad grin, and after some little time replied : " Pont y Groes ; (the bridge of the cross)." I was about to ask her some other question when she turned away with a loud chuckle, and said something to another wench near her, who grinning yet more uncouthly, said something to a third, who grinned too, and lifting up her hands and spreading her fingers wide said : " Dyn oddi dir y Gogledd—a man from the north country, hee, hee!" Forthwith there was a general shout—the wenches crying : " A man from the north country, hee, hee!" and the fellows crying : " A man from the north country, hoo, hoo!"

" Is this the way you treat strangers in the south?" said I. But I had scarcely uttered the words when with redoubled shouts the company exclaimed : " There's Cumraeg ! there's pretty Cumraeg. Go back, David, to shire Fon ! That Cumraeg won't pass here."

Finding they disliked my Welsh I had recourse to my own language. " Really," said I in English, " such conduct is unaccountable. What do you mean?" But this only made matters worse, for the shouts grew louder still, and every one cried : " There's pretty English ! Well, if I couldn't speak English better than that I'd never speak English at all. No, David; if you must speak at all, stick to Cumraeg." Then forthwith all the company set themselves in violent motion : the women rushing up to me with their palms and fingers spread out in my face, without touching me, however, as they wheeled round me at about a yard's distance, crying : " A man from the north country, hee, hee!" and the fellows acting just in the same way, rushing up with their hands spread out, and then wheeling round me with cries of " A man from the north country, hoo, hoo!" I was so enraged that I made for a heap of stones by the road-side, intending to take some up and fling them at the company. Reflecting, however, that I had but one pair of hands and the company at least forty, and that by such an attempt at revenge I should only make myself ridiculous, I gave up my intention, and continued my journey at a rapid pace, pursued for a long way by " hee, hee," and " hoo, hoo," and, " Go back, David, to your goats in Anglesey, you are not wanted here."

I began to ascend a hill forming the eastern side of an immense valley, at the bottom of which rolled the river. Beyond the valley to the west was an enormous hill, on the top of which was a most singular-looking crag, seemingly leaning in the direction of the south. On the right-hand side of the road were immense works of some kind in full play and activity, for engines were clanging and puffs of smoke were ascending from tall chimneys. On inquiring of a boy the name of the works I was told that they were called the works of Level Vawr, or the Great Level, a mining establishment; but when I asked him the name of the hill with the singular peak, on the other side of the valley, he shook his head and said he did not know. Near the top of the hill I came to a village consisting of a few cottages and a shabby-looking church. A rivulet descending from some crags to the east crosses the road, which leads through the place, and tumbling down the valley, joins the Ystwyth at the bottom. Seeing a woman standing at the door I enquired the name of the village.

" Spytty Ystwyth," she replied, but she, no more than the boy down below, could tell me the name of the strange-looking hill across the valley. This second Spytty or monastic hospital, which I had come to, looked in every respect an inferior place to the first. Whatever its former state might have been, nothing but dirt and wretchedness were now visible. Having reached the top of the hill I entered upon a wild moory region. Presently I crossed a little bridge over a rivulet, and seeing a small house on the shutter of which was painted ' cwrw,' I went in, sat down on an old chair which I found vacant, and said in English to an old woman who sat knitting by the window : " Bring me a pint of ale !"

" Dim Saesneg !" said the old woman.

" I told you to bring me a pint of ale," said I to her in her own language.

" You shall have it immediately, sir," said she; and going to a cask, she filled a jug with ale, and after handing it to me resumed her seat and knitting.

" It is not very bad ale," said I, after I had tasted it.

" It ought to be very good," said the old woman, " for I brewed it myself."

" The goodness of ale," said I, " does not so much depend on who brews it as on what it is brewed of. Now there is something in this ale which ought not to be. What is it made of?"

" Malt and hop."

" It tastes very bitter," said I. " Is there no chwerwlys[1] in it?"

" I do not know what chwerwlys is," said the old woman.

" It is what the Saxons call wormwood," said I.

" O, wermod. No, there is no wermod in my beer, at least not much."

" O, then there is some; I thought there was. Why do you put such stuff into your ale?"

" We are glad to put it in sometimes when hops are dear, as they are this year. Moreover, wermod is not bad stuff, and some folks like the taste better than that of hops."

" Well, I don't. However, the ale is drinkable. What am I to give you for the pint?"

" You are to give me a groat."

" That is a great deal," said I, " for a groat I ought to have a pint of ale made of the best malt and hops."

" I give you the best I can afford. One must live by what one sells. I do not find that easy work."

" Is this house your own?"

" O no! I pay rent for it, and not a cheap one."

" Have you a husband?"

" I had, but he is dead."

" Have you any children?"

" I had three, but they are dead too, and buried with my husband at the Monastery."

" Where is the Monastery?"

---

[1] Bitter root.

" A good way farther on, at the strath beyond Rhyd Fendigaid."

" What is the name of the little river by the house?"

" Avon Marchnad (Market River)."

" Why is it called Avon Marchnad?"

" Truly, gentleman, I cannot tell you."

I went on sipping my ale and finding fault with its bitterness till I had finished it, when getting up I gave the old lady her groat, bade her farewell and departed.

CHAPTER XCI

Pont y Rhyd Fendigaid—Strata Florida—The Yew-Tree—
Idolatry—The Teivi—The Llostlydan.

AND now for the resting-place of Dafydd Ab Gwilym ! After wandering for some miles towards the south over a bleak moory country I came to a place called Fair Rhos, a miserable village, consisting of a few half-ruined cottages, situated on the top of a hill. From the hill I looked down on a wide valley of a russet colour, along which a river ran towards the south. The whole scene was cheerless. Sullen hills were all around. Descending the hill I entered a large village divided into two by the river, which here runs from east to west, but presently makes a turn. There was much mire in the street; immense swine lay in the mire, who turned up their snouts at me as I passed. Women in Welsh hats stood in the mire, along with men without any hats at all, but with short pipes in their mouths; they were talking together; as I passed, however, they held their tongues, the women leering contemptuously at me, the men glaring sullenly at me, and causing tobacco smoke to curl in my face; on my taking off my hat, however, and enquiring the way to the Monachlog, everybody was civil enough, and twenty voices told me the way to the Monastery. I asked the name of the river.

" The Teivi, sir : the Teivi."

" The name of the bridge?"

" Pont y Rhyd Fendigaid—the Bridge of the Blessed Ford, sir."

I crossed the Bridge of the Blessed Ford, and presently leaving the main road I turned to the east by a dung-hill, up a narrow lane parallel with the river. After proceeding a mile up the lane, amidst trees and copses, and crossing a little brook, which runs into the Teivi, out of which I drank, I saw before me in the midst of a field, in which were tombstones and broken ruins, a rustic-looking church; a farm-house stood near it, in the garden of which stood the framework of a large gateway. I crossed over into the churchyard, ascended a green mound, and looked about me. I was now in the very midst of the Monachlog Ystrad Flur, the celebrated monastery of Strata Florida, to which in old times Popish pilgrims from all parts of the world repaired. The scene was solemn and impressive : on the north side of the river a large bulky hill looked down upon the ruins and the church, and on the south side, some way behind the farm-house, was another which did the same. Rugged mountains formed the background of the valley to the east, down from which came murmuring the fleet but shallow Teivi. Such is the scenery which surrounds what remains of Strata Florida : those scanty broken ruins compose all which remains of that celebrated monastery, in which kings, saints and mitred abbots were buried, and in which, or in whose precincts, was buried Dafydd Ab Gwilym, the greatest genius of the Cimbric race and one of the first poets of the world.

After standing for some time on the mound I descended, and went up to the church. I found the door fastened, but obtained through the window a tolerable view of the interior, which presented an appearance of the greatest simplicity. I then strolled about the churchyard looking at the tomb-stones, which were humble enough and for the most part modern. I would give something, said I, to know whereabouts in this neighbourhood Ab Gwilym lies. That, however, is a secret that no one can reveal to me. At length I came to a yew-tree which stood just by the northern wall which is at a slight distance from the Teivi. It was one of two trees, both of the same species, which stood in the churchyard, and appeared to be the oldest of the two Who knows, said I, but this is the tree that was planted over Ab Gwilym's grave, and to which Gruffyd Gryg wrote an ode? I looked at it attentively, and thought that there was just a possibility of its being the identical tree. If it was, however, the benison of Gruffyd Gryg had not had exactly the effect which he intended, for either lightning or the force of wind had splitten off a considerable part of the head and trunk, so that though one part of it looked strong and blooming, the other was white and spectral. Nevertheless, relying on the possibility of its being the sacred tree, I behaved just as I should have done had I been quite certain of the fact: Taking off my hat I knelt down and kissed its root, repeating lines from Gruffydd Gryg, with which I blended some of my own in order to accommodate what I said to circumstances:

> " O tree of yew, which here I spy,
> By Ystrad Flur's blest monast'ry,
> Beneath thee lies, by cold Death bound,
> The tongue for sweetness once renown'd.
>
> Better for thee thy boughs to wave,
> Though scath'd, above Ab Gwilym's grave,
> Than stand in pristine glory drest
> Where some ignobler bard doth rest;
> I'd rather hear a taunting rhyme
> From one who'll live through endless time,
> Than hear my praises chanted loud
> By poets of the vulgar crowd."

I had left the churchyard, and was standing near a kind of garden, at some little distance from the farmhouse, gazing about me and meditating, when a man came up attended by a large dog. He had rather a youthful look, was of the middle size and dark complexioned. He was respectably drest, except that upon his head he wore a common hairy cap.

" Good evening," said I to him in Welsh.

" Good evening, gentleman," said he in the same language.

" Have you much English?" said I.

" Very little; I can only speak a few words."

" Are you the farmer?"

" Yes! I farm the greater part of the Strath."

" I suppose the land is very good here?"

" Why do you suppose so?"

" Because the monks built their house here in the old time, and the monks never built their houses except on good land."

" Well, I must say the land is good; indeed I do not think there is any so good in Shire Aberteifi."

" I suppose you are surprised to see me here; I came to see the old Monachlog."

" Yes, gentleman! I saw you looking about it."

" Am I welcome to see it?"

" Croesaw! gwr boneddig, croesaw! many, many welcomes to you, gentleman!"

" Do many people come to see the monastery?"

Farmer.—Yes! many gentlefolk come to see it in the summer time.

Myself.—It is a poor place now.

Farmer.—Very poor, I wonder any gentlefolks come to look at it.

Myself.—It was a wonderful place once; you merely see the ruins of it now. It was pulled down at the Reformation.

Farmer.—Why was it pulled down then?

Myself.—Because it was a house of idolatry to which people used to resort by hundreds to worship images. Had you lived at that time you would have seen people down on their knees before stocks and stones, worshipping them, kissing them and repeating pennillion to them.

Farmer.—What fools! How thankful I am that I live in wiser days. If such things were going on in the old Monachlog it was high time to pull it down.

Myself.—What kind of a rent do you pay for your land?

Farmer.—O, rather a stiffish one.

Myself.—Two pound an acre?

Farmer.—Two pound an acre! I wish I paid no more.

Myself.—Well! I think that would be quite enough. In the time of the old monastery you might have had the land at two shillings an acre.

Farmer.—Might I? Then those couldn't have been such bad times, after all.

Myself.—I beg your pardon! They were horrible times—times in which there were monks and friars and graven images, which people kissed and worshipped and sang pennillion to. Better pay three pounds an acre and live on crusts and water in the present enlightened days than pay two shillings an acre and sit down to beef and ale three times a day in the old superstitious times.

Farmer.—Well, I scarcely know what to say to that.

Myself.—What do you call that high hill on the other side of the river?

Farmer.—I call that hill Bunk Pen Bannedd.

Myself.—Is the source of the Teivi far from here?

Farmer.—The head of the Teivi is about two miles from here high up in the hills.

Myself.—What kind of place is the head of the Teivi?

Farmer.—The head of the Teivi is a small lake about fifty yards long and twenty across.

Myself.—Where does the Teivi run to?

Farmer.—The Teivi runs to the sea, which it enters at a place which the Cumry call Aber Teivi and the Saxons Cardigan.

Myself.—Don't you call Cardiganshire Shire Aber Teivi?

Farmer.—We do.

Myself.—Are there many gleisiaid in the Teivi?

Farmer.—Plenty, and salmons too—that is, farther down. The best place for salmon and gleisiaid is a place, a great way down the stream, called Dinas Emlyn.

Myself.—Do you know an animal called Llostlydan?

Farmer.—No, I do not know that beast.

Myself.—There used to be many in the Teivi.

Farmer.—What kind of beast is the Llostlydan?

Myself.—A beast with a broad tail, on which account the old Cumry did call him Llostlydan. Clever beast he was; made himself house of wood in middle of the river, with two doors, so that when hunter came upon him he might have good chance of escape. Hunter often after him, because he had skin good to make hat.

Farmer.—Ha, I wish I could catch that beast now in Teivi.

Myself.—Why so?

Farmer.—Because I want hat. Would make myself hat of his skin.

Myself.—O, you could not make yourself a hat even if you had the skin.

Farmer.—Why not? Shot coney in Bunk Pen Blanedd; made myself cap of his skin. So, why not make hat of skin of broadtail, should I catch him in Teivi?

Myself.—How far is it to Tregaron?

Farmer.—'Tis ten miles from here, and eight from the Rhyd Fendigaid.

Myself.—Must I go back to Rhyd Fendigaid to get to Tregaron?

Farmer.—You must.

Myself.—Then I must be going, for the night is coming down. Farewell!

Farmer.—Farvel, Saxon gentleman!

CHAPTER XCII

Nocturnal Journey—Maes y Llyn—The Figure—Earl of Leicester—Twm Shone Catti—The Farmer and Bull—Tom and the Farmer—The Cave—The Threat—Tom a Justice—The Big Wigs—Tregaron.

It was dusk by the time I had regained the highroad by the village of the Rhyd Fendigaid.

As I was yet eight miles from Tregaron, the place where I intended to pass the night, I put on my best pace. In a little time I reached a bridge over a stream which seemed to carry a considerable tribute to the Teivi.

" What is the name of this bridge?" said I to a man riding in a cart whom I met almost immediately after I had crossed the bridge.

" Pont Vleer," methought he said, but as his voice was husky and indistinct, very much like that of a person somewhat the worse for liquor, I am by no means positive.

It was now very dusk, and by the time I had advanced about a mile farther dark night settled down, which compelled me to abate my pace a little, more especially as the road was by no means first-rate. I had come, to the best of my computation, about four miles from the Rhyd Fendigaid when the moon began partly to show itself, and presently by its glimmer I saw some little way off on my right hand what appeared to be a large sheet of water. I went on, and in about a minute saw two or three houses on the left, which stood nearly opposite to the object which I had deemed to be water, and which now appeared to be about fifty yards distant in a field which was separated from the road by a slight hedge. Going up to the principal house I knocked, and a woman making her appearance at the door, I said—

" I beg pardon for troubling you, but I wish to know the name of this place."

" Maes y Llyn—The Field of the Lake," said the woman.

" And what is the name of the lake?" said I.

" I do not know," said she; " but the place where it stands is called Maes Llyn, as I said before."

" Is the lake deep?" said I.

" Very deep," said she.

" How deep?" said I.

" Over the tops of the houses," she replied.

" Any fish in the lake?"

" O yes! plenty."

" What fish?"

" O there are llysowen, and the fish we call ysgetten."

" Eels and tench," said I; " anything else?"

" I do not know," said the woman; " folks say that there used to be queer beast in the lake, water-cow used to come out at night and eat people's clover in the fields."

" Pooh," said I, " that was merely some person's cow or horse, turned out at night to fill its belly at other folks' expense."

" Perhaps so," said the woman; " have you any more questions to ask?"

" Only one," said I; " how far is it to Tregaron?"

" About three mile: are you going there?"

" Yes, I am going to Tregaron."

" Pity that you did not come a little time ago," said the woman; " you might then have had pleasant company on your way; pleasant man stopped here to light his pipe; he too going to Tregaron."

"It doesn't matter," said I; "I am never happier than when keeping my own company." Bidding the woman good night, I went on. The moon now shone tolerably bright, so that I could see my way, and I sped on at a great rate. I had proceeded nearly half-a-mile, when I thought I heard steps in advance, and presently saw a figure at some little distance before me. The individual, probably hearing the noise of my approach, soon turned round and stood still. As I drew near I distinguished a stout burly figure of a man, seemingly about sixty, with a short pipe in his mouth.

"Ah, is it you?" said the figure, in English, taking the pipe out of his mouth; "good evening, I am glad to see you." Then shaking some burning embers out of his pipe, he put it into his pocket, and trudged on beside me.

"Why are you glad to see me?" said I, slackening my pace; "I am a stranger to you; at any rate, you are to me."

"Always glad to see English gentleman," said the figure; "always glad to see him."

"How do you know that I am an English gentleman?" said I.

"O, I know Englishman at first sight; no one like him in the whole world."

"Have you seen many English gentlemen?" said I.

"O yes, have seen plenty when I have been up in London."

"Have you been much in London?"

"O yes; when I was a drover was up in London every month."

"And were you much in the society of English gentlemen when you were there?"

"O yes; a great deal."

"Whereabouts in London did you chiefly meet them?"

"Whereabouts? Oh, in Smithfield."

"Dear me!" said I; "I thought that was rather a place for butchers than gentlemen."

"Great place for gentlemen, I assure you," said the figure; "met there the finest gentlemen I ever saw in

my life; very grand, but kind and affable, like every
true gentleman. Talked to me a great deal about
Anglesey runts, and Welsh legs of mutton, and at
parting shook me by the hand, and asked me to look
in upon him, if I was ever down in his parts, and see
his sheep and taste his ale."

" Do you know who he was?" said I.

" O yes; know all about him; Earl of Leicester,
from county of Norfolk; fine old man indeed—you
very much like him—speak just in same way."

" Have you given up the business of drover long?"
said I.

" O yes; given him up a long time ever since
domm'd railroad came into fashion."

" And what do you do now?" said I.

" O, not much; live upon my means; picked up a
little property, a few sticks, just enough for old crow to
build him nest with—somctimes, however, undertake a
little job for neighbouring people and get a little money.
Can do everything in small way, if necessary; build
little bridge, if asked;—Jack of all Trades—live very
comfortably."

" And where do you live?"

" O, not very far from Tregaron."

" And what kind of place is Tregaron?"

" O, very good place; not quite so big as London,
but very good place."

" What is it famed for?" said I.

" O, famed for very good ham; best ham at
Tregaron in all Shire Cardigan."

" Famed for anything else?"

" O yes! famed for great man, clever thief, Twm
Shone Catti, who was born there."

" Dear me!" said I; " when did he live?"

" O, long time ago, more than two hundred year."

" And what became of him?" said I; " was he
hung?"

" Hung, no! only stupid thief hung. Twm Shone
clever thief; died rich man, justice of the peace and
mayor of Brecon."

" Very singular," said I, " that they should make
a thief mayor of Brecon."

" O, Twm Shone Catti very different from other

thieves; funny fellow, and so good-natured that everybody loved him—so they made him magistrate, not, however, before he had become very rich man by marrying great lady who fell in love with him."

"Ah, ah," said I; "that's the way of the world. He became rich, so they made him a magistrate; had he remained poor they would have hung him in spite of all his fun and good-nature. Well, can't you tell me some of the things he did?"

"O yes, can tell you plenty. One day in time of fair Tom Shone Catti goes into ironmonger's shop in Llandovery. 'Master,' says he, 'I want to buy a good large iron porridge pot; please to show me some.' So the man brings out three or four big iron porridge pots, the very best he has. Tom takes up one and turns it round. 'This looks very good porridge pot,' said he; 'I think it will suit me.' Then he turns it round and round again, and at last lifts it above his head and peaks into it. 'Ha, ha,' says he; 'this won't do; I see one hole here. What mean you by wanting to sell article like this to stranger?' Says the man, 'there be no hole in it.' 'But there is,' says Tom, holding it up and peaking into it again; 'I see the hole quite plain. Take it and look into it yourself.' So the man takes the pot, and having held it up and peaked in, 'as I hope to be saved,' says he, 'I can see no hole.' Says Tom, 'good man, if you put your head in, you will find that there is a hole.' So the man tries to put in his head, but having some difficulty Tom lends him a helping hand by jamming the pot quite down over the man's face, then whisking up the other pots Tom leaves the shop, saying as he goes, 'Friend, I suppose you now see that there is a hole in the pot, otherwise how could you have got your head inside?'"

"Very good," said I; "can you tell us something more about Twm Shone Catti?"

"O yes; can tell you plenty about him. The farmer at Newton, just one mile beyond the bridge at Brecon, had one very fine bull, but with a very short tail. Says Tom to himself: 'By God's nails and blood I will steal the farmer's bull, and then sell it to him for other bull in open market place.' Then Tom makes one fine tail, just for all the world such a tail as the bull ought to

have had, then goes by night to the farmer's stall at
Newton, steals away the bull, and then sticks to the
bull's short stump the fine bull's tail which he himself
had made. The next market day he takes the bull to
the market-place at Brecon and calls out : ' Very fine
bull this, who will buy my fine bull?' Quoth the farmer
who stood nigh at hand, ' That very much like my bull,
which thief stole t'other night; I think I can swear to
him.' Says Tom, ' What do you mean? This bull is
not your bull, but mine.' Says the farmer, ' I could
swear that this is my bull but for the tail. The tail of my
bull was short, but the tail of this is long. I would fain
know whether the tail of this be real tail or not.' ' You
would?' says Tom; ' well, so you shall.' Thereupon
he whips out big knife and cuts off the bull's tail, some
little way above where the false tail was joined on.
' Ha, ha,' said Tom, as the bull's stump of tail bled,
and the bit of tail bled, too, to which the false tail was
stuck, and the bull kicked and bellowed. ' What say
you now? Is it a true tail or no?' ' By my faith !'
says the farmer, ' I see that the tail is a true tail, and
that the bull is not mine. I beg pardon for thinking
that he was.' ' Begging pardon,' says Tom, ' is all
very well; but will you buy the bull?' ' No,' said the
farmer, ' I should be loth to buy a bull with tail cut off
close to the rump.' ' Ha,' says Tom, ' who made me
cut off the tail but yourself? Did you not force me to
do so in order to clear my character? Now as you
made me cut off my bull's tail, I will make you buy my
bull without his tail.' 'Yes, yes,' cried the mob; ' as
he forced you to cut off the tail, do you now force
him to buy the bull without the tail.' Says the farmer,
' What do you ask for the bull?' Says Tom, ' I ask
for him ten pound.' Says the farmer, ' I will give you
eight.' ' No,' says Tom; ' you shall give me ten, or
I will have you up before the justice.' ' That is right,'
cried the mob. ' If he won't pay you ten pound, have
him up before the justice.' Thereupon the farmer,
becoming frightened, pulled out the ten pounds and
gave it for his own bull to Tom Shone Catti, who
wished him joy of his bargain. As the farmer was
driving the bull away he said to Tom : ' Won't you
give me the tail?' ' No,' said Tom; ' I shall keep it

against the time I steal another bull with a short tail; ' and thereupon he runs off."

"A clever fellow," said I; "though it was rather cruel in him to cut off the poor bull's tail. Now, perhaps, you will tell me how he came to marry the rich lady?"

"O yes; I will tell you. One day as he was wandering about, dressed quite like a gentleman, he heard a cry, and found one very fine lady in the hands of one highwayman, who would have robbed and murdered her. Tom kills the highwayman and conducts the lady home to her house and her husband, for she was a married lady. Out of gratitude to Tom for the service he has done, the gentleman and lady invite him to stay with them. The gentleman, who is a great gentleman, fond of his bottle and hunting, takes mightily to Tom for his funny sayings, and because Tom's a good hand at a glass when at table, and a good hand at a leap when in field; the lady also takes very much to Tom, because he one domm'd handsome fellow, with plenty of wit and what they call boetry,— for Tom amongst other things was no bad boet, and could treat a lady to pennillion about her face and her ancle, and the tip of her ear. At last Tom goes away upon his wanderings, not, however, before he has got one promise from the lady, that if ever she becomes disengaged she will become his wife. Well, after some time the lady's husband dies and leaves her all his property, so that all of a sudden she finds herself one great independent lady, mistress of the whole of Strath Feen, one fair and pleasant valley far away there over the Eastern hills; by the Towey; on the borders of Shire Car. Tom, as soon as he hears the news of all this, sets off for Strath Feen and asks the lady to perform her word; but the lady, who finds herself one great and independent lady, and moreover does not quite like the idea of marrying one thief, for she had learnt who Tom was, does hum and hah, and at length begs to be excused, because she has changed her mind. Tom begs and entreats, but quite in vain, till at last she tells him to go away and not trouble her any more. Tom goes away, but does not yet lose hope. He takes up his quarters in one strange little cave, nearly at the

top of one wild hill, very much like sugar loaf, which
does rise above the Towey, just within Shire Car. I
have seen the cave myself, which is still called Ystafell
Twm Shone Catty. Very queer cave it is, in strange
situation : steep rock just above it, Towey river roaring
below. There Tom takes up his quarters, and from
there he often sallies forth, in hope of having interview
with fair lady and making her alter her mind, but she
will have nothing to do with him, and at last shuts
herself up in her house and will not go out. Well,
Tom nearly loses all hope; he, however, determines to
make one last effort; so one morning he goes to the
house and stands before the door, entreating with one
loud and lamentable voice that the lady will see him
once more, because he is come to bid her one eternal
farewell, being about to set off for the wars in the
kingdom of France. Well, the lady who hears all he
says relents one little, and showing herself at the
window before which are very strong iron bars she
says : ' Here I am ! whatever you have to say, say it
quickly, and go your way.' Says Tom : ' I am come
to bid you one eternal farewell, and have but one last
slight request to make, which is that you vouchsafe to
stretch out of the window your lily-white hand, that I
may impress one last burning kiss of love on the same.'
Well, the lady hesitates one little time; at last, having
one woman's heart, she thinks she may grant him this
last little request, and stretching her hand through the
bars she says : ' Well, there's my hand, kiss it once
and begone.' Forthwith Tom seizing her wrist with
his left hand says : ' I have got you now, and will never
let you go till you swear to become my wife.' ' Never,'
said the lady, ' will I become the wife of one thief,' and
strives with all her might to pull her hand free, but
cannot, for the left hand of Tom is more strong than
the right of other man. Thereupon Tom with his right
hand draws forth his sword, and with one dreadful
shout does exclaim : ' Now will you swear to become
my wife, for if you don't, by God's blood and nails, I
will this moment smite off your hand with this sword.'
Then the lady being very much frightened, and having
one sneaking kindness for Tom, who though he looked
very fierce looked also very handsome, said : ' Well,

well! a promise is a promise; I promised to become your wife, and so I will; I swear I will; by all I hold holy I swear; so let go my hand, which you have almost pulled off, and come in and welcome!' So Tom lets go her hand, and the lady opens her door, and before night they were married, and in less than one month Tom, being now very rich and lord of Ystrad Feen, was made justice of the peace and chairman at quarter session."

"And what kind of justice of the peace did Tom make?"

"Ow, the very best justice of the peace that there ever was. He made the old saying good: you must set one thief to catch one thief. He had not been a justice three year before there was not a thief in Shire Brecon nor in Shire Car, for they also made him justice of Carmarthenshire, and a child might walk through the country quite safe with a purse of gold in its hand. He said that as he himself could not have a finger in the pie, he would take care nobody else should. And yet he was not one bloody justice either; never hanged thief without giving him a chance to reform; but when he found him quite hardened he would say: 'Hang up de rogue!' O Tom was not a very hard man, and had one grateful heart for any old kindness which had been shown him. One day as Tom sat on de bench with other big wigs, Tom the biggest wig of the lot, a man was brought up charged with stealing one bullock. Tom no sooner cast eye on the man than he remembered him quite well. Many years before Tom had stole a pair of oxen, which he wished to get through the town of Brecon, but did not dare to drive them through, for at that very time there was one warrant out against Tom at Brecon for something he had done. So Tom stands with his oxen on the road, scratching his head and not knowing what to do. At length there comes a man along the road, making towards Brecon, to whom Tom says: 'Honest man, I want these two oxen to be driven to such and such a public-house two miles beyond Brecon; I would drive them myself only I have business to do elsewhere of more importance. Now if you will drive them for me there and wait till I come, which will not be long, I will give you a groat.'

Says the man : ' I will drive them for nothing, for as my way lies past that same public-house I can easily afford to do so.' So Tom leaves the oxen with the man, and by rough and roundabout road makes for the public-house beyond Brecon, where he finds the man waiting with the oxen, who hands them over to him and goes on his way. Now, in the man brought up before him and the other big wigs on the bench for stealing the bullock, Tom does recognise the man who had done him that same good turn. Well! the evidence was heard against the man, and it soon appeared quite clear that the man did really steal the bullock. Says the other big wigs to Tom : ' The fact has been proved quite clear. What have we now to do but to adshudge at once that the domm'd thief be hung?' But Tom, who remembered that the man had once done him one good turn, had made up his mind to save the man. So says he to the other big wigs : ' My very worthy esteemed friends and coadshutors, I do perfectly agree with you that the fact has been proved clear enough, but with respect to de man, I should be very much grieved should he be hung for this one fact, for I did know him long time ago, and did find him to be one domm'd honest man in one transaction which I had with him. So my wordy and esteemed friends and coadshutors I should esteem it one great favour if you would adshudge that the man should be let off this one time. If, however, you deem it inexpedient to let the man off, then of course the man must be hung, for I shall not presume to set my opinions and judgments against your opinions and judgments, which are far better than my own.' Then the other big wigs did look very big and solemn, and did shake their heads and did whisper to one another that they were afraid the matter could not be done. At last, however, they did come to the conclusion that as Tom had said that he had known the fellow once to be one domm'd honest man, and as they had a great regard for Tom, who was one domm'd good magistrate and highly respectable gentleman with whom they were going to dine the next day—for Tom I must tell you was in the habit of giving the very best dinners in all Shire Brecon—it might not be incompatible with the performance of their duty to let

the man off this one time, seeing as how the poor
fellow had probably merely made one slight little mistake.
Well: to make the matter short, the man was let off
with only a slight reprimand, and left the court.
Scarcely, however, had he gone twenty yards, when
Tom was after him, and tapping him on the shoulder
said: 'Honest friend, a word with you!' Then the
man turning round, Tom said: 'Do you know me,
pray?' 'I think I do, your honour,' said the man. 'I
think your honour was one of the big wigs, who were
just now so kind as to let me off.' 'I was so,' said
Tom; 'and it is well for you that I was the biggest of
those big wigs before whom you stood placed, otherwise
to a certainty you would have been hung up on high;
but did you ever see me before this affair?' 'No, your
honour,' said the man, 'I don't remember ever to have
seen your honour before.' Says Tom, 'Don't you
remember one long time ago driving a pair of oxen
through Brecon for a man who stood scratching his
head on the road?' 'O yes,' says the man; 'I do
remember that well enough.' 'Well,' said Tom, 'I
was that man. I had stolen that pair of oxen, and I
dared not drive them through Brecon. You drove them
for me; and for doing me that good turn I have this
day saved your life. I was thief then, but am now big
wig. I am Twm Shone Catti. Now lookee! I have
saved your life this one time, but I can never save it
again. Should you ever be brought up before me
again, though but for stealing one kid, I will hang you
as high as ever Haman was hung. One word more:
here are five pieces of gold. Take them: employ them
well, and reform as I have done, and perhaps in time
you may become one big wig, like myself.' Well: the
man took the money, and laid it out to the best advantage, and became at last so highly respectable a
character that they made him constable. And now, my
gentleman, we are close upon Tregaron."

After descending a hill we came to what looked a
small suburb, and presently crossed a bridge over the
stream, the waters of which sparkled merrily in the
beams of the moon which was now shining bright over
some lofty hills to the south-east. Beyond the bridge
was a small market-place, on the right-hand side of

which stood an ancient-looking church. The place upon the whole put me very much in mind of an Andalusian village overhung by its sierra. "Where is the inn?" said I to my companion.

"Yonder it be," said he, pointing to a large house at the farther end of the market-place. "Very good inn that—Talbot Arms—where they are always glad to see English gentlemans." Then touching his hat, and politely waving his hand, he turned on one side, and I saw him no more.

CHAPTER XCIII

Tregaron Church—The Minister—Good Morning—Tom Shone's Disguises—Tom and the Lady—Klim and Catti.

I EXPERIENCED very good entertainment at the Tregaron Inn, had an excellent supper and a very comfortable bed. I arose at about eight in the morning. The day was dull and misty. After breakfast, according to my usual fashion, I took a stroll to see about. The town, which is very small, stands in a valley, near some wild hills called the Berwyn, like the range to the south of Llangollen. The stream, which runs through it and which falls into the Teivi at a little distance from the town, is called the Brennig, probably because it descends from the Berwyn hills. These southern Berwyns form a very extensive mountain region, extending into Brecon and Carmarthenshire, and contain within them, as I long subsequently found, some of the wildest solitudes and most romantic scenery in Wales. High up amidst them, at about five miles from Tregaron, is a deep broad lake which constitutes the source of the Towy, a very beautiful stream, which, after many turnings and receiving the waters of numerous small streams, discharges itself into Carmarthen Bay.

I did not fail to pay a visit to Tregaron church. It is an antique building with a stone tower. The door being open, as the door of a church always should be, I entered, and was kindly shown by the clerk, whom I met in the aisle, all about the sacred edifice. There

S

was not much to be seen. Amongst the monuments was a stone tablet to John Herbert, who died 1690. The clerk told me that the name of the clergyman of Tregaron was Hughes; he said that he was an excellent charitable man, who preached the Gospel, and gave himself great trouble in educating the children of the poor. He certainly seemed to have succeeded in teaching them good manners : as I was leaving the church, I met a number of little boys belonging to the church school : no sooner did they see me than they drew themselves up in a rank on one side, and as I passed took off their caps and simultaneously shouted " Good morning !"

And now something with respect to the celebrated hero of Tregaron, Tom Shone Catti, concerning whom I picked up a good deal during my short stay there, and of whom I subsequently read something in printed books.[1]

According to the tradition of the country, he was the illegitimate son of Sir John Wynn of Gwedir, by one Catharine Jones of Tregaron, and was born at a place called Fynnon Lidiart, close by Tregaron, towards the conclusion of the sixteenth century. He was baptised by the name of Thomas Jones, but was generally called Tom Shone Catti, that is Tom Jones, son of Catti, or Catharine. His mother, who was a person of some little education, brought him up, and taught him to read and write. His life, till his eighteenth year, was

---

[1] Amongst others a kind of novel called *The Adventures of Twm Shon Catty, a Wild Wag of Wales*. It possesses considerable literary merit, the language being pure, and many of the descriptions graphic. By far the greater part of it, however, would serve for the life of any young Welsh peasant, quite as well as for that of Twm Shone Catti. Its grand fault is endeavouring to invest Twm Shone with a character of honesty, and to make his exploits appear rather those of a wild young waggish fellow than of a robber. This was committing a great mistake. When people take up the lives of bad characters the more rogueries and villanies they find, the better are they pleased, and they are very much disappointed and consider themselves defrauded by any attempt to apologise for the actions of the heroes. If the thieves should chance to have reformed, the respectable readers wish to hear nothing of their reformation till just at the close of the book, when they are very happy to have done with them for ever.

much like that of other peasant boys; he kept crows, drove bullocks, and learned to plough and harrow, but always showed a disposition to roguery and mischief. Between eighteen and nineteen, in order to free himself and his mother from the poverty which they had long endured, he adopted the profession of a thief, and soon became celebrated through the whole of Wales for the cleverness and adroitness which he exercised in his calling; qualities in which he appears to have trusted much more than in strength and daring, though well endowed with both. His disguises were innumerable, and all impenetrable; sometimes he would appear as an ancient crone : sometimes as a begging cripple; sometimes as a broken soldier. Though by no means scrupulous as to what he stole, he was particularly addicted to horse and cattle stealing, and was no less successful in altering the appearance of animals than his own, as he would frequently sell cattle to the very persons from whom he had stolen them, after they had been subject to such a metamorphosis, by means of dyes and the scissors, that recognition was quite impossible. Various attempts were made to apprehend him, but all without success; he was never at home to people who particularly wanted him, or if at home he looked anything but the person they came in quest of. Once a strong and resolute man, a farmer, who conceived, and very justly, that Tom had abstracted a bullock from his stall, came to Tregaron well armed in order to seize him. Riding up to the door of Tom's mother, he saw an aged and miserable-looking object, with a beggar's staff and wallet, sitting on a stone bench beside the door. "Does Tom Shone Catti live here?" said the farmer. "O yes: he lives here," replied the beggar. "Is he at home?" "O yes, he is at home." "Will you hold my horse whilst I go in and speak to him?" "O yes, I will hold your horse." Thereupon the man dismounted, took a brace of pistols out of his holsters, gave the cripple his horse's bridle and likewise his whip, and entered the house boldly. No sooner was he inside than the beggar, or rather Tom Shone Catti, for it was he, jumped on the horse's back, and rode away to the farmer's house, which was some ten miles distant, altering his dress and appearance as he rode along, having various articles of disguise in his wallet. Arriving at the house he told the farmer's wife that her husband was in the greatest trouble, and wanted fifty pounds, which she was to send by him, and that he came mounted on her husband's horse, and brought his whip, that she might know he was authorised to receive the money. The wife seeing the horse and the whip delivered the money to Tom without hesitation, who forthwith made the best of his way to London, where he sold the horse, and made himself merry with the price, and with what he got from the farmer's wife, not returning to Wales for several months. Though Tom was known by everybody to be a thief, he appears to have lived on very good terms with the generality of his neighbours, both rich and poor. The poor he conciliated by being very free of the money which he acquired by theft and robbery, and with the rich he ingratiated himself by humorous jesting, at which he was a proficient, and by being able to sing a good song. At length, being an extremely good-looking young fellow, he induced a wealthy lady to promise to marry him. This lady is represented by some as a widow, and by others as a virgin heiress. After some time, however, she refused to perform her promise, and barred her doors against him. Tom retired to a cave on the side of a steep wild hill near the lady's house, to which he frequently repaired, and at last, having induced her to stretch her hand to him through the window bars, under the pretence that he wished to imprint a parting kiss upon it, he won her by seizing her hand and threatening to cut it off unless she performed her promise. Then, as everything at the time at which he lived could be done by means of money, he soon obtained for himself a general pardon, and likewise a commission as justice of the peace, which he held to the time of his death, to the satisfaction of everybody except thieves and ill-doers, against whom he waged incessant war, and with whom he was admirably qualified to cope, from the knowledge he possessed of their ways and habits, from having passed so many years of his life in the exercise of the thieving trade. In his youth he was much addicted to poetry, and a great many pennillion of his composition, chiefly on his own thievish exploits, are yet recited by the inhabitants of certain districts of the Shires of Brecon, Carmarthen, and Cardigan.

Such is the history, or rather the outline of the history of Twm Shone Catti. Concerning the actions attributed to him it is necessary to say that the greater part consist of myths which are told of particular individuals of every country, from the Indian Ocean to the Atlantic: for example, the story of cutting off the bull's tail is not only told of him but of the Irish thief Delany, and is to be found in the " Lives of Irish Rogues and Rapparees; " certain tricks related of him in the printed tale bearing his name are almost identical with various rogueries related in the story-book of Klim the Russian robber,[1] and the most poetical part of Tom Shone's history, namely, that in which he threatens to cut off the hand of the reluctant bride unless she performs her promise, is, in all probability, an offshoot of the grand myth of " the severed hand," which in various ways figures in the stories of most nations, and which is turned to considerable account in the tale of the above-mentioned Russian worthy Klim.

CHAPTER XCIV

Llan Ddewi Brefi— Pelagian Heresy—Hu Gadarn—God of Agriculture—The Silver Cup—Rude Tablet.

IT was about eleven o'clock in the morning when I started from Tregaron; the sky was still cloudy and heavy. I took the road to Lampeter, distant about eight miles, intending, however, to go much farther ere I stopped for the night. The road lay nearly south-west. I passed by Aber Coed, a homestead near the bottom of a dingle down which runs a brook into the Teivi, which flows here close by the road; then by Aber Carvan, where another brook disembogues. Aber, as perhaps the reader already knows, is a disembogue-ment, and wherever a place commences with Aber there to a certainty does a river flow into the sea or a brook or rivulet into a river. I next passed through

[1] Skazka O Klimkie. Moscow, 1829.

Nant Derven, and in about three quarters of an hour after leaving Tregaron reached a place of old renown called Llan Ddewi Brefi.

Llan Ddewi Brefi is a small village situated at the entrance of a gorge leading up to some lofty hills which rise to the east and belong to the same mountain range as those near Tregaron. A brook flowing from the hills murmurs through it and at length finds its way into the Teivi—an ancient church stands on a little rising ground just below the hills, multitudes of rooks inhabit its steeple and fill throughout the day the air with their cawing. The place wears a remarkable air of solitude, but presents nothing of gloom and horror, and seems just the kind of spot in which some quiet pensive man, fatigued but not soured by the turmoil of the world, might settle down, enjoy a few innocent pleasures, make his peace with God and then compose himself to his long sleep.

It is not without reason that Llan Ddewi Brefi has been called a place of old renown. In the fifth century, one of the most remarkable ecclesiastical convocations which the world has ever seen was held in this secluded spot. It was for the purpose of refuting certain doctrines which had for some time past caused much agitation in the Church, and which originated with one Morgan, a native of North Wales, who left his country at an early age and repaired to Italy, where having adopted the appellation of Pelagius, which is a Latin translation of his own name Morgan, which signifies " by the seashore," he soon became noted as a theological writer. It is not necessary to enter into any detailed exposition of his opinions; it will, however, be as well to state that one of the points which he was chiefly anxious to inculcate was that it is possible for a man to lead a life entirely free from sin by obeying the dictates of his own reason without any assistance from the grace of God—a dogma certainly to the last degree delusive and dangerous. When the convocation met there were a great many sermons preached by various learned and eloquent divines, but nothing was produced which was pronounced by the general voice a satisfactory answer to the doctrines of the heresiarch. At length it was resolved to send for Dewi,

a celebrated teacher of theology at Mynyw in Pembrokeshire, who from motives of humility had not appeared
in the assembly. Messengers therefore were despatched
to Dewi, who after repeated entreaties was induced
to repair to the place of meeting, where after three
days' labour in a cell he produced a treatise in writing
in which the tenets of Morgan were so triumphantly
overthrown that the convocation unanimously adopted
it and sent it into the world with a testimony of
approbation as an antidote to the heresy, and so great
was its efficacy that from that moment the doctrines
of Morgan fell gradually into disrepute.[1]

Dewi shortly afterwards became primate of Wales,
being appointed to the see of Minevai or Mynyw,
which from that time was called Ty Ddewi or David's
House, a name which it still retains amongst the
Cumry, though at present called by the Saxons Saint
David's. About five centuries after his death, the
crown of canonisation having been awarded to Dewi,
various churches were dedicated to him, amongst which
was that now called Llan Ddewi Brefi, which was built
above the cell in which the good man composed his
celebrated treatise.

If this secluded gorge or valley is connected with a
remarkable historical event it is also associated with
one of the wildest tales of mythology. Here according
to old tradition died one of the humped oxen of the
team of Hu Gadarn. Distracted at having lost its
comrade, which perished from the dreadful efforts
which it made along with the others in drawing the
avanc hen or old crocodile from the lake of lakes, it
fled away from its master, and wandered about till
coming to the glen now called that of Llan Ddewi Brefi
it fell down and perished after excessive bellowing,
from which noise the place probably derived its name
of Brefi, for Bref in Cumric signifies a mighty bellowing or lowing. Horns of enormous size, said to have
belonged to this humped ox or bison, were for many
ages preserved in the church.

Many will exclaim who was Hu Gadarn? Hu
Gadarn in the Gwlad yr Haf or summer country, a
certain region of the East, perhaps the Crimea, which

[1] Hanes Crefydd Yn Nghymru.

seems to be a modification of Cumria, taught the Cumry the arts of cvilised life, to build comfortable houses, to sow grain and reap, to tame the buffalo and the bison, and turn their mighty strength to profitable account, to construct boats with wicker and the skins of animals, to drain pools and morasses, to cut down forests, cultivate the vine and encourage bees, make wine and mead, frame lutes and fifes and play upon them, compose rhymes and verses, fuse minerals and form them into various instruments and weapons, and to move in masses against their enemies, and finally when the summer country became over-populated led an immense multitude of his countrymen across many lands to Britain, a country of forests in which bears, wolves and bisons wandered, and of morasses and pools full of dreadful efync or crocodiles, a country inhabited only by a few savage Gauls, but which shortly after the arrival of Hu and his people became a smiling region, forests being thinned, bears and wolves hunted down, efync annihilated, bulls and bisons tamed, corn planted and pleasant cottages erected. After his death he was worshipped as the God of agriculture and war by the Cumry and the Gauls. The Germans paid him divine honours under the name of Heus, from which name the province of Hesse in which there was a mighty temple devoted to him derived its appellation. The Scandinavians worshipped him under the name of Odin and Gautr, the latter word a modification of Cadarn or mighty. The wild Finns feared him as a wizard and honoured him as a musician under the name of Wainoemoinen, and it is very probable that he was the wondrous being whom the Greeks termed Odysses. Till a late period the word Hu amongst the Cumry was frequently used to express God—Gwir Hu, God knows, being a common saying. Many Welsh poets have called the Creator by the name of the creature, amongst others Iolo Goch in his ode to the ploughman :—

> The Mighty Hu who lives for ever,
> Of mead and wine to men the giver,
> The emperor of land and sea,
> And of all things that living be,
> Did hold a plough with his good hand,
> Soon as the Deluge left the land,

To show to men both strong and weak,
The haughty-hearted and the meek,
Of all the arts the heaven below
The noblest is to guide the plough.

So much for Hu Gadarn or Hu the Mighty, whose name puts one strangely in mind of the Al Kader Hu or the Almighty He of the Arabians.

I went to see the church. The inside was very rude and plain—a rough table covered with a faded cloth served for an altar—on the right-hand side was a venerable-looking chest.

" What is there in that box?" said I to the old sexton who attended me.

" The treasure of the church, sir," he replied in a feeble quaking voice.

" Dear me!" said I, " what does the treasure consist of?"

" You shall see, sir," said he, and drawing a large key out of his pocket he unlocked the chest and taking out a cup of silver he put it into my hand saying:—" This is the treasure of the church, sir!"

I looked at the cup. It was tolerably large and of very chaste workmanship. Graven upon it were the following words:—

" Poculum Eclesie De LXXN Dewy Brefy 1574."

" Do you always keep this cup in that chest?" said I.

" Yes, sir! we have kept it there since the cup was given to us by de godly Queen Elizabeth."

I said nothing, but I thought to myself:—" I wonder how long a cup like this would have been safe in a crazy chest in a country church in England."

I kissed the sacred relic of old times with reverence and returned it to the old sexton.

" What became of the horns of Hu Gadarn's bull?" said I after he had locked the cup again in its delapidated coffer.

" They did dwindle away, sir, till they came to nothing."

" Did you ever see any part of them?" said I.

" O no, sir; I did never see any part of them, but one very old man who is buried here did tell me shortly

before he died that he had seen one very old man who
had seen of dem one little tip.''

'' Who was the old man who said that to you?''
said I.

'' I will show you his monument, sir,'' then taking
me into a dusky pew he pointed to a small rude tablet
against the church wall and said:—'' That is his
monument, sir.''

The tablet bore the following inscription, and below
it a rude englyn on death not worth transcribing :—

Coffadwriaeth am
Thomas Jones
Diweddar o'r Draws Llwyn yn y Plwyf hwn :
Bu farw Chwefror 6 fed 1830
Yn 92 oed.

To the Memory of
Thomas Jones
Of Traws Llwyn (across the Grove) in this
parish who died February the sixth, 1830.
Aged 92.

After copying the inscription I presented the old man
with a trifle and went my way.

CHAPTER XCV

Lampeter—The Monk Austin—The Three Publicans—The Tombstone—Sudden Change—Trampers—A Catholic—The Bridge
of Twrch.

THE country between Llan Ddewi and Lampeter
presented nothing remarkable, and I met on the road
nothing worthy of being recorded. On arriving at
Lampeter I took a slight refreshment at the inn, and
then went to see the college which stands a little to the
north of the town. It was founded by Bishop Burgess
in the year 1820, for the education of youths intended
for the ministry of the Church of England. It is a
neat quadrate edifice with a courtyard in which stands
a large stone basin. From the courtyard you enter a
spacious dining-hall, over the door of which hangs a
well-executed portrait of the good bishop. From the
hall you ascend by a handsome staircase to the library,

a large and lightsome room, well stored with books in various languages. The grand curiosity is a manuscript Codex containing a Latin synopsis of Scripture which once belonged to the monks of Bangor Is Coed. It bears marks of blood with which it was sprinkled when the monks were massacred by the heathen Saxons, at the instigation of Austin the Pope's missionary in Britain. The number of students seldom exceeds forty.

It might be about half-past two in the afternoon when I left Lampeter. I passed over a bridge, taking the road to Llandovery which, however, I had no intention of attempting to reach that night, as it was considerably upwards of twenty miles distant. The road lay, seemingly, due east. After walking very briskly for about an hour I came to a very small hamlet consisting of not more than six or seven houses; of these three seemed to be public-houses, as they bore large flaming signs. Seeing three rather shabby-looking fellows standing chatting with their hands in their pockets, I stopped and inquired in English the name of the place.

" Pen- something," said one of them, who had a red face and a large carbuncle on his nose, which served to distinguish him from his companions, who though they had both very rubicund faces had no carbuncles.

" It seems rather a small place to maintain three public-houses," said I; " how do the publicans manage to live?"

" O, tolerably well, sir; we get bread and cheese and have a groat in our pockets. No great reason to complain; have we, neighbours?"

" No! no great reason to complain," said the other two.

" Dear me!" said I; " are you the publicans?"

" We are, sir," said the man with the carbuncle on his nose, " and shall be each of us glad to treat you to a pint in his own house in order to welcome you to Shire Car—shan't we, neighbours?"

" Yes, in truth we shall," said the other two.

" By Shire Car," said I, " I suppose you mean Shire Cardigan?"

" Shire Cardigan!" said the man; " no indeed; by

Shire Car is meant Carmarthenshire. Your honour
has left beggarly Cardigan some way behind you.
Come, your honour, come and have a pint; this is my
house," said he, pointing to one of the buildings.

"But," said I, "I suppose if I drink at your expense
you will expect to drink at mine?"

"Why, we can't say that we shall have any objection, your honour; I think we will arrange the matter
in this way : we will go into my house, where we will
each of us treat your honour with a pint, and for each
pint we treat your honour with your honour shall treat
us with one."

"Do you mean each?" said I.

"Why, yes! your honour, for a pint amongst three
would be rather a short allowance."

"Then it would come to this," said I, "I should
receive three pints from you three, and you three would
receive nine from me."

"Just so, your honour; I see your honour is a
ready reckoner."

"I know how much three times three make," said
I. "Well, thank you, kindly, but I must decline your
offer; I am bound on a journey."

"Where are you bound to, master?"

"To Llandovery, but if I can find an inn a few
miles farther on I shall stop there for the night."

"Then you will put up at the ' Pump Saint,' master;
well, you can have your three pints here and your three
pipes too, and yet get there easily by seven. Come in,
master, come in! If you take my advice you will think
of your pint and your pipe and let all the rest go to the
devil."

"Thank you," said I, "but I can't accept your
invitation, I must be off;" and in spite of yet more
pressing solicitations I went on.

I had not gone far when I came to a point where the
road parted in two; just at the point where a house and
premises belonging apparently to a stone-mason, as a
great many pieces of half-cut granite were standing
about, and not a few tombstones. I stopped, and
looked at one of the latter. It was to the memory of
somebody who died at the age of sixty-six, and at the
bottom bore the following bit of poetry :—

" Ti ddaear o ddaear ystyria mewn braw,
Mai daear i ddaear yn fuan a ddaw ;
A ddaear mewn ddaear raid aros bob darn
Nes daear o ddaear gyfrodir i farn."

" Thou earth from earth reflect with anxious mind
That earth to earth must quickly be consigned,
And earth in earth must lie entranced enthralled
Till earth from earth to judgment shall be called."

" What conflicting opinions there are in this world,"
said I, after I had copied the quatrain and translated
it. " The publican yonder tells me to think of my pint
and pipe and let everything else go to the devil, and the
tombstone here tells me to reflect with dread—a much
finer expression by the bye than reflect with anxious
mind, as I have got it—that in a very little time I must
die, and lie in the ground till I am called to judgment.
Now, which is most right, the tombstone or the
publican? Why, I should say the tombstone decidedly.
The publican is too sweeping when he tells you to think
of your pint and pipe and nothing else. A pint and pipe
are good things. I don't smoke myself, but I dare
say a pipe is a good thing for them who like it, but
there are certainly things worth being thought of in this
world besides a pint and pipe—hills and dales, woods
and rivers, for example—death and judgment too are
worthy now and then of very serious thought. So it
won't do to go with the publican the whole hog. But
with respect to the tombstone, it is quite safe and right
to go with it its whole length. It tells you to think of
death and judgment—and assuredly we ought to think
of them. It does not, however, tell you to think of
nothing but death and judgment and to eschew every
innocent pleasure within your reach. If it did it would
be a tombstone quite as sweeping in what it says as
the publican, who tells you to think of your pint and pipe
and let everything else go to the devil. The wisest
course evidently is to blend the whole of the philosophy
of the tombstone with a portion of the philosophy of the
publican and something more, to enjoy one's pint and
pipe and other innocent pleasures, and to think every
now and then of death and judgment—that is what
I intend to do, and indeed is what I have done for the
last thirty years."

I went on—desolate hills rose in the east, the way I was going, but on the south were beautiful hillocks adorned with trees and hedge-rows. I was soon amongst the desolate hills, which then looked more desolate than they did at a distance. They were of a wretched russet colour, and exhibited no other signs of life and cultivation than here and there a miserable field and vile-looking hovel; and if there was here nothing to cheer the eye, there was also nothing to cheer the ear. There were no songs of birds, no voices of rills; the only sound I heard was the lowing of a wretched bullock from a far-off slope.

I went on slowly and heavily; at length I got to the top of this wretched range—then what a sudden change! Beautiful hills in the far east, a fair valley below me, and groves and woods on each side of the road which led down to it. The sight filled my veins with fresh life, and I descended this side of the hill as merrily as I had come up the other side despondingly. About half-way down the hill I came to a small village. Seeing a public-house I went up to it, and inquired in English of some people within the name of the village.

"Dolwen," said a dark-faced young fellow of about four-and-twenty.

"And what is the name of the valley?" said I.

"Dolwen," was the answer, "the valley is named after the village."

"You mean that the village is named after the valley," said I, "for Dolwen means fair valley."

"It may be," said the young fellow, "we don't know much here."

Then after a moment's pause he said:

"Are you going much farther?"

"Only as far as the 'Pump Saint.'"

"Have you any business there?" said he.

"No," I replied, "I am travelling the country, and shall only put up there for the night."

"You had better stay here," said the young fellow. "You will be better accommodated here than at the 'Pump Saint.'"

"Very likely," said I; "but I have resolved to go there, and when I once make a resolution I never alter it."

Then bidding him good evening I departed. Had I
formed no resolution at all about stopping at the
" Pump Saint " I certainly should not have stayed in
this house, which had all the appearance of a tramper's
hostelry, and though I am very fond of the conversation
of trampers, who are the only people from whom you
can learn anything, I would much rather have the
benefit of it abroad than in their own lairs. A little
farther down I met a woman coming up the ascent.
She was tolerably respectably dressed, seemed about
five-and-thirty, and was rather good-looking. She
walked somewhat slowly, which was probably more
owing to a large bundle which she bore in her hand than
to her path being up-hill.

" Good evening," said I, stopping.

" Good evening, your honour," said she, stopping
and slightly panting.

" Do you come from far?" said I.

" Not very far, your honour, but quite far enough for
a poor feeble woman."

" Are you Welsh?" said I.

" Och no ! your honour ; I am Mary Bane from
Dunmanway in the kingdom of Ireland."

" And what are you doing here?" said I.

" Och sure ! I am travelling the country with soft
goods."

" Are you going far?" said I.

" Merely to the village a little farther up, your
honour."

" I am going farther," said I ; " I am thinking of
passing the night at the ' Pump Saint.' "

" Well, then, I would just advise your honour to do
no such thing, but to turn back with me to the village
above, where there is an illigant inn where your honour
will be well accommodated."

" O, I saw that as I came past," said I ; " I don't
think there is much accommodation there."

" O, your honour is clane mistaken ; there is always
an illigant fire and an illigant bed too."

" Is there only one bed?" said I.

" O yes, there are two beds, one for the accommodation of the people of the house and the other for that
of the visitors."

" And do the visitors sleep together then?" said I.

" O yes! unless they wish to be unsociable. Those who are not disposed to be sociable sleeps in the chimney-corners."

" Ah," said I, " I see it is a very agreeable inn; however, I shall go on to the ' Pump Saint.' "

" I am sorry for it, your honour, for your honour's sake; your honour won't be half so illigantly served at the ' Pump Saint ' as there above."

" Of what religion are you?" said I.

" O, I'm a Catholic, just like your honour, for if I am not clane mistaken your honour is an Irishman."

" Who is your spiritual director?" said I.

" Why then, it is jist Father Toban, your honour, whom of course your honour knows."

" O yes!" said I; " when you next see him present my respects to him."

" What name shall I mention, your honour?"

" Shorsha Borroo," said I.

" Oh, then I was right in taking your honour for an Irishman. None but a raal Paddy bears that name. A credit to your honour is your name, for it is a famous name,[1] and a credit to your name is your honour, for it is a neat man without a bend you are. God bless your honour and good night! and may you find dacent quarters in the ' Pump Saint.' "

Leaving Mary Bane I proceeded on my way. The evening was rather fine but twilight was coming rapidly on. I reached the bottom of the valley and soon overtook a young man dressed something like a groom. We entered into conversation. He spoke Welsh and a little English. His Welsh I had great difficulty in understanding, as it was widely different from that which I had been accustomed to. He asked me where I was going to; I replied to the " Pump Saint," and then inquired if he was in service.

" I am," said he.

" With whom do you live?" said I.

" With Mr. Johnes of Dol Cothi," he answered.

Struck by the word Cothi, I asked if Dol Cothi was ever called Glyn Cothi.

[1] The good gentlewoman was probably thinking of the celebrated king Brian Boromhe slain at the battle of Clontarf.

" O yes," said he, " frequently."

" How odd," thought I to myself, " that I should have stumbled all of a sudden upon the country of my old friend Lewis Glyn Cothi, the greatest poet after Ab Gwilym of all Wales !"

" Is Cothi a river?" said I to my companion.

" It is," said he.

Presently we came to a bridge over a small river.

" Is this river the Cothi?" said I.

" No," said he, " this is the Twrch; the bridge is called Pont y Twrch."

" The bridge of Twrch or the hog," said I to myself; " there is a bridge of the same name in the Scottish Highlands, not far from the pass of the Trossachs. I wonder whether it has its name from the same cause as this, namely, from passing over a river called the Twrch or Torck, which word in Gaelic signifies boar or hog even as it does in Welsh." It had now become nearly dark. After proceeding some way farther I asked the groom if we were far from the inn of the " Pump Saint."

" Close by," said he, and presently pointing to a large building on the right-hand side he said : " This is the inn of the ' Pump Saint,' sir. Nos Da'chi !"

CHAPTER XCVI

Pump Saint—Pleasant Residence—The Watery Coom—
Philological Fact—Evening Service—Meditation.

I ENTERED the inn of the " Pump Saint." It was a comfortable old-fashioned place, with a very large kitchen and a rather small parlour. The people were kind and attentive, and soon set before me in the parlour a homely but savoury supper, and a foaming tankard of ale. After supper I went into the kitchen, and sitting down with the good folks in an immense chimney-corner, listened to them talking in their Carmarthenshire dialect till it was time to go to rest, when I was conducted to a large chamber where I found an excellent and clean bed awaiting me, in which I enjoyed a refreshing sleep occasionally visited by dreams in which some of the scenes of the preceding day again appeared before me, but in an indistinct and misty manner.

Awaking in the very depth of the night I thought I heard the murmuring of a river; I listened and soon found that I had not been deceived. " I wonder whether that river is the Cothi," said I, " the stream of the immortal Lewis. I will suppose that it is "—and rendered quite happy by the idea, I soon fell asleep again.

I arose about eight and went out to look about me. The village consists of little more than half-a-dozen houses. The name " Pump Saint " signifies " Five Saints." Why the place is called so I know not. Perhaps the name originally belonged to some chapel which stood either where the village now stands or in the neighbourhood. The inn is a good specimen of an ancient Welsh hostelry. Its gable is to the road and its front to a little space on one side of the way. At a little distance up the road is a blacksmith's shop. The country around is interesting : on the north-west is a fine wooded hill—to the south a valley through which flows the Cothi, a fair river, the one whose murmur had come so pleasingly upon my ear in the depth of night.

After breakfast I departed for Llandovery. Presently I came to a lodge on the left-hand beside an ornamental gate at the bottom of an avenue leading seemingly to a gentleman's seat. On inquiring of a woman who sat at the door of the lodge to whom the grounds belonged, she said to Mr. Johnes, and that if I pleased I was welcome to see them. I went in and advanced along the avenue, which consisted of very noble oaks; on the right was a vale in which a beautiful brook was running north and south. Beyond the vale to the east were fine wooded hills. I thought I had never seen a more pleasing locality, though I saw it to great disadvantage, the day being dull, and the season the latter fall. Presently, on the avenue making a slight turn, I saw the house, a plain but comfortable gentleman's seat with wings. It looked to the south down the dale. " With what satisfaction I could live in that house," said I to myself, " if backed by a couple of thousands a-year.

With what gravity could I sign a warrant in its library,
and with what dreamy comfort translate an ode of
Lewis Glyn Cothi, my tankard of rich ale beside me.
I wonder whether the proprietor is fond of the old
bard and keeps good ale. Were I an Irishman instead
of a Norfolk man I would go in and ask him.''

Returning to the road I proceeded on my journey.
I passed over Pont y Rhanedd or the bridge of the
Rhanedd, a small river flowing through a dale, then by
Clas Hywel, a lofty mountain which appeared to have
three heads. After walking for some miles I came to
where the road divided into two. By a sign-post I saw
that both led to Llandovery, one by Porth y Rhyd and
the other by Llanwrda. The distance by the first was
six miles and a half, by the latter eight and a half.
Feeling quite the reverse of tired I chose the longest
road, namely the one by Llanwrda, along which I sped
at a great rate.

In a little time I found myself in the heart of a
romantic winding dell overhung with trees of various
kinds, which a tall man whom I met told me was called
Cwm Dwr Llanwrda, or the Watery Coom of Llanwrda;
and well might it be called the Watery Coom, for there
were several bridges in it, two within a few hundred
yards of each other. The same man told me that the
war was going on very badly, that our soldiers were
suffering much, and that the snow was two feet deep
at Sebastopol.

Passing through Llanwrda, a pretty village with a
singular-looking church, close to which stood an enormous yew, I entered a valley which I learned was the
valley of the Towey. I directed my course to the north,
having the river on my right, which runs towards the
south in a spacious bed which, however, except in times
of flood, it scarcely half fills. Beautiful hills were on
either side, partly cultivated, partly covered with wood,
and here and there dotted with farm-houses and gentlemen's seats; green pastures which descended nearly
to the river occupying in general the lower parts.
After journeying about four miles amid this kind of
scenery I came to a noble suspension bridge, and
crossing it found myself in about a quarter of an hour
at Llandovery.

It was about half-past two when I arrived. I put up at the Castle Inn and forthwith ordered dinner, which was served up between four and five. During dinner I was waited upon by a strange old fellow who spoke Welsh and English with equal fluency.

"What countryman are you?" said I.

"An Englishman," he replied.

"From what part of England?"

"From Herefordshire."

"Have you been long here?"

"O yes! upwards of twenty years."

"How came you to learn Welsh?"

"O, I took to it and soon picked it up."

"Can you read it?" said I.

"No, I can't."

"Can you read English?"

"Yes, I can; that is, a little."

"Why didn't you try to learn to read Welsh?"

"Well, I did; but I could make no hand of it. It's one thing to speak Welsh and another to read it."

"I can read Welsh much better than I can speak it," said I.

"Ah, you are a gentleman—gentlefolks always find it easier to learn to read a foreign lingo than to speak it, but it's quite the contrary with we poor folks."

"One of the most profound truths ever uttered connected with language," said I to myself. I asked him if there were many Church of England people in Llandovery.

"A good many," he replied.

"Do you belong to the Church?" said I.

"Yes, I do."

"If this were Sunday I would go to church," said I.

"O, if you wish to go to church you can go to-night. This is Wednesday, and there will be service at half-past six. If you like I will come for you."

"Pray do," said I; "I should like above all things to go."

Dinner over I sat before the fire occasionally dozing, occasionally sipping a glass of whiskey-and-water. A little after six the old fellow made his appearance with a kind of Spanish hat on his head. We set out, the night was very dark; we went down a long street seemingly in the direction of the west. "How many churches are there in Llandovery?" said I to my companion.

"Only one, but you are not going to Llandovery Church, but to that of Llanfair, in which our clergyman does duty once or twice a week."

"Is it far?" said I.

"O no; just out of the town, only a few steps farther."

We seemed to pass over a bridge and began to ascend a rising ground. Several people were going in the same direction.

"There," said the old man, "follow with these, and a little farther up you will come to the church, which stands on the right hand."

He then left me. I went with the rest and soon came to the church. I went in and was at once conducted by an old man who I believe was the sexton to a large pew close against the southern wall. The inside of the church was dimly lighted; it was long and narrow, and the walls were painted with a yellow colour. The pulpit stood against the northern wall near the altar, and almost opposite to the pew in which I sat. After a little time the service commenced; it was in Welsh. When the litanies were concluded the clergyman, who appeared to be a middle-aged man, and who had rather a fine voice, began to preach. His sermon was from the 119th Psalm: "Am hynny hoffais dy gorchymynion yn mwy nag aur;" "Therefore have I loved thy commandments more than gold." The sermon, which was extempore, was delivered with great earnestness, and I make no doubt was a very excellent one, but owing to its being in South Welsh I did not derive so much benefit from it as I otherwise might have done. When it was over a great many got up and went away. Observing, however, that not a few remained, I determined upon remaining too. When everything was quiet the clergyman descending from the pulpit repaired to the vestry, and having taken off his gown went into a pew, and standing up began a discourse, from which I learned that there was to be a sacrament on the ensuing Sabbath. He spoke with much fervency, enlarging upon the high importance of the holy communion and exhorting people to come to it in a fit state of mind. When he had finished a man in a neighbouring pew got up and spoke about his own unworthiness, saying this and that about himself, his sins of commission and omission, and dwelling particularly on his uncharitableness and the malicious pleasure which he took in the misfortunes of his neighbours. The clergyman listened attentively, sometimes saying " Ah !" and the congregation also listened attentively, a voice here and there frequently saying " Ah." When the man had concluded the clergyman again spoke, making observations on what he had heard and hoping that the rest would be visited with the same contrite spirit as their friend. Then there was a hymn and we went away.

The moon was shining on high and cast its silvery light on the tower, the church, some fine trees which surrounded it, and the congregation going home ; a few of the better dressed were talking to each other in English, but with an accent and pronunciation which rendered the discourse almost unintelligible to my ears.

I found my way back to my inn and went to bed after musing awhile on the concluding scene of which I had been witness in the church.

CHAPTER XCVII

Llandovery—Griffith ap Nicholas—Powerful Enemies—Last Words
—Llandovery Church—Rees Pritchard—The Wiser Creature
—" God's Better than All "—The Old Vicarage.

THE morning of the ninth was very beautiful, with a slight tendency to frost. I breakfasted, and having no intention of proceeding on my journey that day, I went to take a leisurely view of Llandovery and the neighbourhood.

Llandovery is a small but beautiful town, situated amidst fertile meadows. It is a water-girdled spot, whence its name Llandovery or Llanymdyfri, which signifies the church surrounded by water. On its west is the Towey, and on its east the river Bran or Brein, which descending from certain lofty mountains to the north-east runs into the Towey a little way below the

town. The most striking object which Llandovery can
show is its castle, from which the inn, which stands
near to it, has its name. This castle, majestic though
in ruins, stands on a green mound, the eastern side of
which is washed by the Bran. Little with respect to
its history is known. One thing, however, is certain,
namely that it was one of the many strongholds, which
at one time belonged to Griffith ap Nicholas, Lord of
Dinevor, one of the most remarkable men which South
Wales has ever produced, of whom a brief account here
will not be out of place.

Griffith ap Nicholas flourished towards the concluding
part of the reign of Henry the Sixth. He was a powerful chieftain of South Wales and possessed immense
estates in the counties of Carmarthen and Cardigan.
King Henry the Sixth, fully aware of his importance
in his own country, bestowed upon him the commission
of the peace, an honour at that time seldom vouchsafed
to a Welshman, and the captaincy of Kilgarran, a
strong royal castle situated on the southern bank of the
Teivi a few miles above Cardigan. He had many
castles of his own, in which he occasionally resided,
but his chief residence was Dinevor, half way between
Llandovery and Carmarthen, once a palace of the
kings of South Wales, from whom Griffith traced
lineal descent. He was a man very proud at heart,
but with too much wisdom to exhibit many marks of
pride, speaking generally with the utmost gentleness
and suavity, and though very brave never addicted to
dashing into danger for the mere sake of displaying his
valour. He was a great master of the English tongue,
and well acquainted with what learning it contained,
but nevertheless was passionately attached to the language and literature of Wales, a proof of which he
gave by holding a congress of bards and literati at
Carmarthen, at which various pieces of eloquence and
poetry were recited, and certain alterations introduced
into the canons of Welsh versification. Though holding
offices of trust and emolument under the Saxon, he in
the depths of his soul detested the race and would have
rejoiced to see it utterly extirpated from Britain. This
hatred of his against the English was the cause of his
doing that which cannot be justified on any principle of

honour, giving shelter and encouragement to Welsh thieves who were in the habit of plundering and ravaging the English borders. Though at the head of a numerous and warlike clan which was strongly attached to him on various accounts, Griffith did not exactly occupy a bed of roses. He had amongst his neighbours four powerful enemies who envied him his large possessions, with whom he had continual disputes about property and privilege. Powerful enemies they may well be called, as they were no less personages than Humphrey Duke of Buckingham, Richard Duke of York, who began the contest for the crown with King Henry the Sixth, Jasper Earl of Pembroke, son of Owen Tudor, and half-brother of the king, and the Earl of Warwick. These accused him at court of being a comforter and harbourer of thieves, the result being that he was deprived not only of the commission of the peace but of the captaincy of Kilgarran which the Earl of Pembroke, through his influence with his half-brother, procured for himself. They moreover induced William Borley and Thomas Corbet, two justices of the peace for the county of Hereford, to grant a warrant for his apprehension on the ground of his being in league with the thieves of the Marches. Griffith in the bosom of his mighty clan bade defiance to Saxon warrants, though once having ventured to Hereford he nearly fell into the power of the ministers of justice, only escaping by the intervention of Sir John Scudamore, with whom he was connected by marriage. Shortly afterwards the civil war breaking out the Duke of York apologised to Griffith and besought his assistance against the king, which the chieftain readily enough promised, not out of affection for York but from the hatred which he felt, on account of the Kilgarran affair, for the Earl of Pembroke, who had sided, very naturally, with his half-brother the king and commanded his forces in the west. Griffith fell at the great battle of Mortimer's Cross, which was won for York by a desperate charge made right at Pembroke's banner by Griffith and his Welshmen when the rest of the Yorkists were wavering. His last words were, " Welcome, Death ! since honour and victory make for us."

The power and wealth of Griffith ap Nicholas and

also parts of his character have been well described
by one of his bards, Gwilym ab Ieuan Hen, in an ode
to the following effect :—

" Griffith ap Nicholas, who like thee
For wealth and power and majesty !
Which most abound, I cannot say,
On either side of Towey gay,
From hence to where it meets the brine,
Trees or stately towers of thine?
The chair of judgment thou didst gain,
But not to deal in judgments vain—
To thee upon thy judgment chair
From near and far do crowds repair ;
But though betwixt the weak and strong
No questions rose of right and wrong,
The strong and weak to thee would hie ;
The strong to do thee injury,
And to the weak thou wine wouldst deal
And wouldst trip up the mighty heel.
A lion unto the lofty thou,
A lamb unto the weak and low.
Much thou resemblest Nudd of yore,
Surpassing all who went before ;
Like him thou'rt fam'd for bravery,
For noble birth and high degree.
Hail, captain of Kilgarran's hold !
Lieutenant of Carmarthen old !
Hail chieftain, Cambria's choicest boast !
Hail Justice at the Saxon's cost !
Seven castles high confess thy sway,
Seven palaces thy hands obey.
Against my chief, with envy fired,
Three dukes and judges two conspired,
But thou a dauntless front didst show,
And to retreat they were not slow.
O, with what gratitude is heard
From mouth of thine the whispered word ;
The deepest pools in rivers found
In summer are of softest sound ;
The sage concealeth what he knows,
A deal of talk no wisdom shows ;
The sage is silent as the grave,
Whilst of his lips the fool is slave ;
Thy smile doth every joy impart,
Of faith a fountain is thy heart ;
Thy hand is strong, thine eye is keen,
Thy head o'er every head is seen."

The church of Llandovery is a large edifice standing
at the southern extremity of the town in the vicinity of
the Towey.   The outside exhibits many appearances of

antiquity, but the interior has been sadly modernised.
It contains no remarkable tombs; I was pleased, however, to observe upon one or two of the monuments
the name of Ryce, the appellation of the great clan to
which Griffith ap Nicholas belonged; of old the regal
race of South Wales. On inquiring of the clerk, an
intelligent young man who showed me over the sacred
edifice, as to the state of the Church of England at
Llandovery, he gave me a very cheering account,
adding, however, that before the arrival of the present
incumbent it was very low indeed. "What is the
clergyman's name?" said I; "I heard him preach last
night."

"I know you did, sir," said the clerk bowing, "for
I saw you at the service at Llanfair—his name is
Hughes."

"Any relation of the clergyman at Tregaron?"
said I.

"Own brother, sir."

"He at Tregaron bears a very high character,"
said I.

"And very deservedly, sir," said the clerk, "for he
is an excellent man; he is, however, not more worthy
of his high character than his brother here is of the
one which he bears, which is equally high, and which
the very dissenters have nothing to say against."

"Have you ever heard," said I, "of a man of the
name of Rees Pritchard, who preached within these
walls some two hundred years ago?"

"Rees Pritchard, sir! Of course I have—who hasn't
heard of the old vicar—the Welshman's candle? Ah,
he was a man indeed! We have some good men in the
Church, very good; but the old vicar—where shall we
find his equal?"

"Is he buried in this church?" said I. "No, sir,
he was buried out abroad in the churchyard, near the
wall by the Towey."

"Can you show me his tomb?" said I. "No, sir,
nor can any one; his tomb was swept away more than
a hundred years ago by a dreadful inundation of the
river, which swept away not only tombs but dead bodies
out of graves. But there's his house in the market-place,
the old vicarage, which you should go and see. I would

go and show it you myself, but I have church matters
just now to attend to—the place of church clerk at
Llandovery, long a sinecure, is anything but that under
the present clergyman, who though not a Rees Pritchard is a very zealous Christian, and not unworthy to
preach in the pulpit of the old vicar.''

Leaving the church I went to see the old vicarage,
but, before saying anything respecting it, a few words
about the old vicar.

Rees Pritchard was born at Llandovery, about the
year 1575, of respectable parents. He received the rudi-
ments of a classical education at the school of the place,
and at the age of eighteen was sent to Oxford, being
intended for the clerical profession. At Oxford he did
not distinguish himself in an advantageous manner,
being more remarkable for dissipation and riot than
application in the pursuit of learning. Returning to
Wales he was admitted into the ministry, and after the
lapse of a few years was appointed vicar of Llandovery.
His conduct for a considerable time was not only un-
becoming a clergyman but a human being in any
sphere. Drunkenness was very prevalent in the age in
which he lived, but Rees Pritchard was so inordinately
addicted to that vice that the very worst of his parish-
ioners were scandalised and said : '' Bad as we may be
we are not half so bad as the parson.''

He was in the habit of spending the greater part of
his time in the public-house, from which he was generally trundled home in a wheelbarrow in a state of utter
insensibility. God, however, who is aware of what
every man is capable of, had reserved Rees Pritchard
for great and noble things, and brought about his
conversion in a very remarkable manner.

The people of the tavern which Rees Pritchard frequented had a large he-goat, which went in and out
and mingled with the guests. One day Rees in the
midst of his orgies called the goat to him and offered
it some ale; the creature, far from refusing it, drank
greedily, and soon becoming intoxicated fell down upon
the floor, where it lay quivering, to the great delight
of Rees Pritchard, who made its drunkenness a subject
of jest to his boon companions, who, however, said
nothing, being struck with horror at such conduct in a

person who was placed among them to be a pattern and example. Before night, however, Pritchard became himself intoxicated, and was trundled to the vicarage in the usual manner. During the whole of the next day he was ill and kept at home, but on the following one he again repaired to the public-house, sat down and called for his pipe and tankard. The goat was now perfectly recovered and was standing nigh. No sooner was the tankard brought than Rees, taking hold of it, held it to the goat's mouth. The creature, however, turned away its head in disgust and hurried out of the room. This circumstance produced an instantaneous effect upon Rees Pritchard. "My God!" said he to himself, "is this poor dumb creature wiser than I? Yes, surely; it has been drunk, but having once experienced the wretched consequences of drunkenness, it refuses to be drunk again. How different is its conduct to mine! I, after having experienced a hundred times the filthiness and misery of drunkenness, have still persisted in debasing myself below the condition of a beast. O, if I persist in this conduct what have I to expect but wretchedness and contempt in this world and eternal perdition in the next? But, thank God, it is not yet too late to amend; I am still alive—I will become a new man—the goat has taught me a lesson." Smashing his pipe, he left his tankard untasted on the table, went home, and became an altered man.

Different as an angel of light is from the fiend of the pit was Rees Pritchard from that moment from what he had been in former days. For upwards of thirty years he preached the Gospel as it had never been preached before in the Welsh tongue since the time of Saint Paul, supposing the beautiful legend to be true which tells us that Saint Paul in his wanderings found his way to Britain and preached to the inhabitants the inestimable efficacy of Christ's blood-shedding in the fairest Welsh, having like all the other apostles the miraculous gift of tongues. The good vicar did more. In the short intervals of relaxation which he allowed himself from the labour of the ministry during those years he composed a number of poetical pieces, which after his death were gathered together into a volume and published, under the title of "Canwyll y Cymry; or, the Candle of the Welshman." This work, which has gone through almost countless editions, is written in two common easy measures, and the language is so plain and simple that it is intelligible to the homeliest hind who speaks the Welsh language. All of the pieces are of a strictly devotional character, with the exception of one, namely a welcome to Charles, Prince of Wales, on his return from Spain, to which country he had gone to see the Spanish ladye whom at one time he sought as bride. Some of the pieces are highly curious, as they bear upon events at present forgotten; for example, the song upon the year 1629, when the corn was blighted throughout the land, and " A Warning to the Cumry to repent when the Plague of Blotches and Boils was prevalent in London." Some of the pieces are written with astonishing vigour, for example, " The Song of the Husbandman," and " God's Better than All," of which last piece the following is a literal translation.

GOD'S BETTER THAN ALL.

God's better than heaven or aught therein,
Than the earth or aught we there can win,
Better than the world or its wealth to me—
God's better than all that is or can be.

Better than father, than mother, than nurse,
Better than riches, oft proving a curse,
Better than Martha or Mary even—
Better by far is the God of heaven.

If God for thy portion thou hast ta'en
There's Christ to support thee in every pain,
The world to respect thee thou wilt gain,
To fear the fiend and all his train.

Of the best of portions thou choice didst make
When thou the high God to thyself didst take,
A portion which none from thy grasp can rend
Whilst the sun and the moon on their course shall wend.

When the sun grows dark and the moon turns red,
When the stars shall drop and millions dread,
When the earth shall vanish with its pomps in fire,
Thy portion still shall remain entire.

Then let not thy heart though distressed, complain !
A hold on thy portion firm maintain.
Thou didst choose the best portion, again I say—
Resign it not till thy dying day.

The old vicarage of Llandovery is a very large mansion of dark red brick, fronting the principal street or market-place, and with its back to a green meadow bounded by the river Bran. It is in a very dilapidated condition, and is inhabited at present by various poor families. The principal room, which is said to have been the old vicar's library, and the place where he composed his undying Candle, is in many respects a remarkable apartment. It is of large dimensions. The roof is curiously inlaid with stucco or mortar, and is traversed from east to west by an immense black beam. The fire-place, which is at the south, is very large and seemingly of high antiquity. The windows, which are two in number and look westward into the street, have a quaint and singular appearance. Of all the houses in Llandovery the old vicarage is by far the most worthy of attention, irrespective of the wonderful monument of God's providence and grace who once inhabited it.

The reverence in which the memory of Rees Pritchard is still held in Llandovery the following anecdote will show. As I was standing in the principal street staring intently at the antique vicarage, a respectable-looking farmer came up and was about to pass, but observing how I was employed he stopped, and looked now at me and now at the antique house. Presently he said :

" A fine old place, is it not, sir? but do you know who lived there?"

Wishing to know what the man would say provided he thought I was ignorant as to the ancient inmate, I turned a face of inquiry upon him; whereupon he advanced towards me two or three steps, and placing his face so close to mine that his nose nearly touched my cheek, he said in a kind of piercing whisper :

" The Vicar."

Then drawing his face back he looked me full in the eyes as if to observe the effect of his intelligence, gave me two nods as if to say, " He did, indeed," and departed.

The Vicar of Llandovery had then been dead nearly two hundred years. Truly the man in whom piety and genius are blended is immortal upon earth.

CHAPTER XCVIII

Departure from Llandovery—A Bitter Methodist—North and South
—The Caravan—Captain Bosvile—Deputy Ranger—A Scrimmage—The Heavenly Gwynfa—Dangerous Position.

ON the tenth I departed from Llandovery, which I
have no hesitation in saying is about the pleasantest
little town in which I have halted in the course of my
wanderings.   I intended to sleep at Gutter Vawr, a
place some twenty miles distant, just within Glamorganshire, to reach which it would be necessary to pass over
part of a range of wild hills, generally called the Black
Mountains.   I started at about ten o'clock; the morning
was lowering, and there were occasional showers of
rain and hail.   I passed by Rees Pritchard's church,
holding my hat in my hand as I did so, not out of
respect for the building, but from reverence for the
memory of the sainted man who of old from its pulpit
called sinners to repentance, and whose remains slum-
ber in the churchyard unless washed away by some
frantic burst of the neighbouring Towey.   Crossing a
bridge over the Bran just before it enters the greater
stream, I proceeded along a road running nearly south
and having a range of fine hills on the east.   Presently
violent gusts of wind came on, which tore the sear
leaves by thousands from the trees of which there were
plenty by the roadsides.   After a little time, however,
this elemental hurly-burly passed away, a rainbow
made its appearance and the day became comparatively
fine.   Turning to the south-east under a hill covered
with oaks, I left the vale of the Towey behind me, and
soon caught a glimpse of some very lofty hills which I
supposed to be the Black Mountains.   It was a mere
glimpse, for scarcely had I descried them when mist
settled down and totally obscured them from my
view.

In about an hour I reached Llangadog, a large
village.   The name signifies the Church of Gadog.
Gadog was a British saint of the fifth century, who
after labouring amongst his own countrymen for their
spiritual good for many years, crossed the sea to

Brittany, where he died. Scarcely had I entered Llan-gadog when a great shower of rain came down. Seeing an ancient-looking hostelry I at once made for it. In a large and comfortable kitchen I found a middle-aged woman seated by a huge deal table near a blazing fire, with a couple of large books open before her. Sitting down on a chair I told her in English to bring me a pint of ale. She did so and again sat down to her books, which on inquiry I found to be a Welsh Bible and Concordance. We soon got into discourse about religion, but did not exactly agree, for she was a bitter Methodist, as bitter as her beer, only half of which I could get down.

Leaving Llangadog I pushed forward. The day was now tolerably fine. In two or three hours I came to a glen, the sides of which were beautifully wooded. On my left was a river, which came roaring down from a range of lofty mountains right before me to the south-east. The river, as I was told by a lad, was the Sawdde or Southey, the lofty range the Black Mountains. Passed a pretty village on my right standing something in the shape of a semi-circle, and in about half-an-hour came to a bridge over a river which I supposed to be the Sawdde which I had already seen, but which I subsequently learned was an altogether different stream. It was running from the south, a wild fierce flood amidst rocks and stones, the waves all roaring and foaming.

After some time I reached another bridge near the foot of a very lofty ascent. On my left to the east upon a bank was a small house, on one side of which was a wheel turned round by a flush of water running in a little artificial canal; close by it were two small cas-cades, the waters of which and also those of the canal passed under the bridge in the direction of the west. Seeing a decent-looking man engaged in sawing a piece of wood by the roadside, I asked him in Welsh whether the house with the wheel was a flour-mill.

"Nage," said he, "it is a pandy, fulling mill."

"Can you tell me the name of a river," said I, "which I have left about a mile behind me? Is it the Sawdde?"

"Nage," said he. "It is the Lleidach."

Then looking at me with great curiosity he asked me if I came from the north country.

" Yes," said I, " I certainly come from there."

" I am glad to hear it," said he, " for I have long wished to see a man from the north country."

" Did you never see one before?" said I.

" Never in my life," he replied: " men from the north country seldom show themselves in these parts."

" Well," said I; " I am not ashamed to say that I come from the north."

" Ain't you? Well, I don't know that you have any particular reason to be ashamed, for it is rather your misfortune than your fault; but the idea of any one coming from the north—ho, ho!"

" Perhaps in the north," said I, " they laugh at a man from the south."

" Laugh at a man from the south! No, no; they can't do that."

" Why not?" said I; " why shouldn't the north laugh at the south as well as the south at the north?"

" Why shouldn't it? why, you talk like a fool. How could the north laugh at the south as long as the south remains the south and the north the north? Laugh at the south! you talk like a fool, David, and if you go on in that way I shall be angry with you. However, I'll excuse you; you are from the north, and what can one expect from the north but nonsense? Now tell me, do you of the north eat and drink like other people? What do you live upon?"

" Why, as for myself," said I, " I generally live on the best I can get."

" Let's hear what you eat; bacon and eggs?"

" O yes! I eat bacon and eggs when I can get nothing better."

" And what do you drink? Can you drink ale?"

" O yes," said I; " I am very fond of ale when it's good. Perhaps you will stand a pint?"

" H'm," said the man looking somewhat blank; " there is no ale in the Pandy and there is no public-house near at hand, otherwise——. Where are you going to-night?"

" To Gutter Vawr."

" Well, then, you had better not loiter. Gutter Vawr

T

is a long way off over the mountain. It will be dark, I am afraid, long before you get to Gutter Vawr. Good evening, David! I am glad to have seen you, for I have long wished to see a man from the north country. Good evening! you will find plenty of good ale at Gutter Vawr!"

I went on my way. The road led in a south-eastern direction gradually upward to very lofty regions. After walking about half-an-hour I saw a kind of wooden house on wheels drawn by two horses coming down the hill towards me. A short black-looking fellow in brown top boots, corduroy breeches, jockey coat and jockey cap sat on the box, holding the reins in one hand and a long whip in the other. Beside him was a swarthy woman in a wild flaunting dress. Behind the box out of the fore part of the caravan peered two or three children's black heads. A pretty little foal about four months old came frisking and gambolling now before now beside the horses, whilst a colt of some sixteen months followed more leisurely behind. When the caravan was about ten yards distant I stopped, and, raising my left hand with the little finger pointed aloft, I exclaimed:

"Shoon, Kaulomengro, shoon! In Dibbel's nav, where may tu be jawing to?"

Stopping his caravan with considerable difficulty the small black man glared at me for a moment like a wild cat, and then said in a voice partly snappish, partly kind:

"Savo shan tu? Are you one of the Ingrines?"

"I am the chap what certain folks calls the Romany Rye."

"Well, I'll be jiggered if I wasn't thinking so and if I wasn't penning so to my juwa as we were welling down the chong."

"It is a long time since we last met, Captain Bosvile, for I suppose I may call you Captain now?"

"Yes! the old man has been dead and buried this many a year, and his sticks and titles are now mine. Poor soul, I hope he is happy; indeed I know he is, for he lies in Cockleshell churchyard, the place he was always so fond of, and has his Sunday waistcoat on him with the fine gold buttons, which he was always so proud of. Ah, you may well call it a long time since we met—why, it can't be less than thirty year.''

" Something about that—you were a boy then of about fifteen.''

" So I was, and you a tall young slip of about twenty ; well, how did you come to jin mande ?''

" Why, I knew you by your fighting mug—there an't such another mug in England.''

" No more there an't—my old father always used to say it was of no use hitting it for it always broke his knuckles. Well, it was kind of you to jin mande after so many years. The last time I think I saw you was near Brummagem, when you were travelling about with Jasper Petulengro and—I say, what's become of the young woman you used to keep company with ?''

" I don't know.''

" You don't ? Well, she was a fine young woman and a vartuous. I remember her knocking down and giving a black eye to my old mother, who was wonderfully deep in Romany, for making a bit of a gillie about you and she. What was the song ? Lord, how my memory fails me. O, here it is :—

" Ando berkho Rye canó
Oteh pivò teh khavó.—
Tu lerasque ando berkho piranee
Teh corbatcha por pico.''

" Have you seen Jasper Petulengro lately ?'' said I.

" Yes, I have seen him, but it was at a very considerable distance. Jasper Petulengro doesn't come near the likes of we now. Lord ! you can't think what grand folks he and his wife have become of late years, and all along of a trumpery lil which some body has written about them. Why, they are hand and glove with the Queen and Prince, and folks say that his wife is going to be made dame of honour, and Jasper Justice of the Peace and Deputy Ranger of Windsor Park.''

" Only think,'' said I. " And now tell me, what brought you into Wales ?''

" What brought me into Wales ? I'll tell you ; my own fool's head. I was doing nicely in the Kaulo Gav and the neighbourhood, when I must needs pack up and come into these parts with bag and baggage, wife and childer. I thought that Wales was what it was some thirty years agone when our foky used to say—for I was never here before—that there was something to be done in it; but I was never more mistaken in my life. The country is overrun with Hindity mescrey, woild Irish, with whom the Romany foky stand no chance. The fellows underwork me at tinkering, and the women outscream my wife at telling fortunes—moreover, they say the country is theirs and not intended for niggers like we, and as they are generally in vast numbers what can a poor little Roman family do but flee away before them? a pretty journey I have made into Wales. Had I not contrived to pass off a poggado bav engro—a broken-winded horse—at a fair, I at this moment should be without a tringoruschee piece in my pocket. I am now making the best of my way back to Brummagem, and if ever I come again to this Hindity country may Calcraft nash me."

"I wonder you didn't try to serve some of the Irish out," said I.

"I served one out, brother; and my wife and childer helped to wipe off a little of the score. We had stopped on a nice green, near a village over the hills in Glamorganshire, when up comes a Hindity family, and bids us take ourselves off. Now it so happened that there was but one man and a woman and some childer, so I laughed, and told them to drive us off. Well, brother, without many words, there was a regular scrimmage. The Hindity mush came at me, the Hindity mushi at my juwa, and the Hindity chaves at my chai. It didn't last long, brother. In less than three minutes I had hit the Hindity mush, who was a plaguey big fellow, but couldn't fight, just under the point of the chin, and sent him to the ground with all his senses gone. My juwa had almost scratched an eye out of the Hindity mushi, and my chai had sent the Hindity childer scampering over the green. 'Who has got to quit now?' said I to the Hindity mush after he had got on his legs, looking like a man who has been cut down after hanging just a minute and a half. 'Who has got notice to quit now, I wonder?' Well, brother, he didn't say anything, nor did any of them, but after a little time they all took themselves off, with a cart they had, to the south. Just as they got to the edge of the green, however, they turned round and gave a yell which made all our blood cold. I knew what it meant, and said, ' This is no place for us.' So we got everything together and came away, and, though the horses were tired, never stopped till we had got ten miles from the place; and well it was we acted as we did, for, had we stayed, I have no doubt that a whole Hindity clan would have been down upon us before morning and cut our throats.''

" Well,'' said I, " farewell. I can't stay any longer. As it is, I shall be late at Gutter Vawr.''

" Farewell, brother!'' said Captain Bosvile; and, giving a cry, he cracked his whip and set his horses in motion.

" Won't you give us sixpence to drink?'' cried Mrs. Bosvile, with a rather shrill voice.

" Hold your tongue, you she-dog,'' said Captain Bosvile. " Is that the way in which you take leave of an old friend? Hold your tongue, and let the Ingrine gentleman jaw on his way.''

I proceeded on my way as fast as I could, for the day was now closing in. My progress, however, was not very great; for the road was steep, and was continually becoming more so. In about half-an-hour I came to a little village, consisting of three or four houses; one of them, at the door of which several carts were standing, bore the sign of a tavern.

" What is the name of this place?'' said I to a man who was breaking stones on the road.

" Capel Gwynfa,'' said he.

Rather surprised at the name, which signifies in English the Chapel of the place of bliss, I asked the man why it was called so.

" I don't know,'' said the man.

" Was there ever a chapel here?'' said I.

" I don't know, sir; there is none now.''

" I dare say there was in the old time,'' said I to myself, as I went on, " in which some holy hermit prayed and told his beads, and occasionally received benighted strangers. What a poetical word that Gwynfa, place of bliss, is. Owen Pugh uses it in his translation of *Paradise Lost* to express Paradise, for he

has rendered the words Paradise Lost by Coll Gwynfa
—the loss of the place of bliss. I wonder whether the
old scholar picked up the word here. Not unlikely.
Strange fellow that Owen Pugh. Wish I had seen him.
No hope of seeing him now, except in the heavenly
Gwynfa. Wonder whether there is such a place. Tom
Payne thinks there's not. Strange fellow that Tom
Payne. Norfolk man. Wish I had never read him."

Presently I came to a little cottage with a toll-bar.
Seeing a woman standing at the door, I inquired of her
the name of the gate.

"Cowslip Gate, sir."

"Has it any Welsh name?"

"None that I know of, sir."

This place was at a considerable altitude, and commanded an extensive view to the south, west, and
north. Heights upon heights rose behind it to the
east. From here the road ran to the south for a little
way nearly level, then turned abruptly to the east, and
was more steep than ever. After the turn, I had a huge
chalk cliff towering over me on the right, and a chalk
precipice on my left. Night was now coming on fast,
and, rather to my uneasiness, masses of mist began to
pour down the sides of the mountain. I hurried on, the
road making frequent turnings. Presently the mist
swept down upon me, and was so thick that I could
only see a few yards before me. I was now obliged
to slacken my pace, and to advance with some degree of
caution. I moved on in this way for some time, when
suddenly I heard a noise, as if a number of carts were
coming rapidly down the hill. I stopped, and stood
with my back close against the high bank. The noise
drew nearer, and in a minute I saw indistinctly through
the mist, horses, carts, and forms of men passing.
In one or two cases the wheels appeared to be within
a few inches of my feet. I let the train go by, and then
cried out in English, "Am I right for Gutter Vawr?"

"Hey?" said a voice, after a momentary interval.

"Am I right for Gutter Vawr?" I shouted yet louder.

"Yes, sure!" said a voice, probably the same.

Then instantly a much rougher voice cried, "Who
the Devil are you?"

I made no answer, but went on, whilst the train con-

tinued its way rumbling down the mountain. At length
I gained the top, where the road turned and led down
a steep descent towards the south-west. It was now
quite night, and the mist was of the thickest kind. I
could just see that there was a frightful precipice on my
left, so I kept to the right, hugging the side of the hill.
As I descended I heard every now and then loud noises
in the vale probably proceeding from stone quarries. I
was drenched to the skin, nay, through the skin, by
the mist, which I verily believe was more penetrating
than that described by Ab Gwilym. When I had proceeded about a mile I saw blazes down below, resembling those of furnaces, and soon after came to the foot
of the hill. It was here pouring with rain, but I did not
put up my umbrella as it was impossible for me to
be more drenched than I was. Crossing a bridge over
a kind of torrent, I found myself amongst some houses.
I entered one of them from which a blaze of light and
a roar of voices proceeded, and, on inquiring of an old
woman who confronted me in the passage, I found
that I had reached my much needed haven of rest, the
tavern of Gutter Vawr in the county of Glamorgan.

CHAPTER XCIX

Inn at Gutter Vawr—The Hurly-burly—Bara y Caws—Change of
Manner—Welsh Mistrust—Wonders of Russia—The Emperor
—The grand Ghost Story.

THE old woman who confronted me in the passage of
the inn turned out to be the landlady. On learning
that I intended to pass the night at her house, she conducted me into a small room on the right-hand side of
the passage, which proved to be the parlour. It was
cold and comfortless, for there was no fire in the grate.
She told me, however, that one should be lighted, and
going out presently returned with a couple of buxom
wenches, who I soon found were her daughters. The
good lady had little or no English; the girls, however,
had plenty, and of a good kind too. They soon lighted
a fire and then the mother inquired if I wished for any
supper.

"Certainly," said I, "for I have not eaten any-thing since I left Llandovery. What can I have?"

"We have veal and bacon," said she.

"That will do," said I; "fry me some veal and bacon, and I shan't complain. But pray tell me what prodigious noise is that which I hear on the other side of the passage?"

"It is only the miners and the carters in the kitchen making merry," said one of the girls.

"Is there a good fire there?" said I.

"O yes," said the girl, "we have always a good fire in the kitchen."

"Well then," said I, "I shall go there till supper is ready, for I am wet to the skin, and this fire casts very little heat."

"You will find them a rough set in the kitchen," said the girl.

"I don't care if I do," said I; "when people are rough I am civil, and I have always found that civility beats roughness in the long run." Then going out I crossed the passage and entered the kitchen.

It was nearly filled with rough unkempt fellows smoking, drinking, whistling, singing, shouting or jabbering, some in a standing, some in a sitting posture. My entrance seemed at once to bring everything to a dead stop; the smokers ceased to smoke, the hand that was conveying the glass or the mug to the mouth was arrested in air, the hurly-burly ceased and every eye was turned upon me with a strange inquiring stare. Without allowing myself to be disconcerted I advanced to the fire, spread out my hands before it for a minute, gave two or three deep ahs of comfort, and then turning round said: "Rather a damp night, gentlemen—fire cheering to one who has come the whole way from Llandovery—Taking a bit of a walk in Wales, to see the scenery and to observe the manners and customs of the inhabitants—Fine country, gentlemen, noble prospects, hill and dale—Fine people too—open-hearted and generous; no wonder! descendants of the Ancient Britons—Hope I don't intrude—other room rather cold and smoking—If I do will retire at once—don't wish to interrupt any gentlemen in their avocations or de-liberations—scorn to do anything ungenteel or calcu-

lated to give offence—hope I know how to behave
myself—ought to do so—learnt grammar at the High
School at Edinburgh."

" Offence, intrusion!" cried twenty voices. "God
bless your honour! no intrusion and no offence at all
—sit down—sit here—won't you drink?"

" Please to sit here, sir," said an old grimy-looking
man, getting up from a seat in the chimney-corner—
" this is no seat for me whilst you are here, it belongs
to you—sit down in it," and laying hold of me he
compelled me to sit down in the chair of dignity,
whilst half-a-dozen hands pushed mugs of beer towards
my face; these, however, I declined to partake of on
the very satisfactory ground that I had not taken
supper, and that it was a bad thing to drink before
eating, more especially after coming out of a mist.

" Have you any news to tell of the war, sir?" said
a large rough fellow, who was smoking a pipe.

" The last news that I heard of the war," said I,
" was that the snow was two feet deep at Sebastopol."

" I heard three," said the man; " however, if there
be but two it must be bad work for the poor soldiers.
I suppose you think that we shall beat the Russians in
the end."

" No, I don't," said I; " the Russians are a young
nation and we are an old; they are coming on and we
are going off; every dog has its day."

" That's true," said the man, " but I am sorry that
you think we shall not beat the Russians, for the
Russians are a bad set."

" Can you speak Welsh?" said a darkish man with
black bristly hair and a small inquisitive eye.

" O, I know two words in Welsh," said I, "bara
y caws."

" That's bread and cheese," said the man, then turning to a neighbour of his he said in Welsh: " He
knows nothing of Cumraeg, only two words; we may
say anything we please; he can't understand us. What
a long nose he has!"

" Mind that he an't nosing us," said his neighbour.
" I should be loth to wager that he doesn't understand
Welsh; and after all he didn't say that he did not, but
got off by saying he understood those two words."

" No, he doesn't understand Welsh," said the other;
" no Sais understands Welsh, and this is a Sais. Now
with regard to that piece of job-work which you and
I undertook." And forthwith he and the other entered
into a disquisition about the job-work.

The company soon got into its old train, drinking
and smoking and making a most terrific hullabaloo.
Nobody took any farther notice of me. I sat snug in
the chimney-corner, trying to dry my wet things, and
as the heat was very great partially succeeded. In
about half-an-hour one of the girls came to tell me
that my supper was ready, whereupon I got up and said :
" Gentlemen, I thank you for your civility; I am now
going to supper; perhaps before I turn in for the night
I may look in upon you again." Then without waiting
for an answer I left the kitchen and went into the other
room, where I found a large dish of veal cutlets and
fried bacon awaiting me, and also a smoking bowl of
potatoes. Ordering a jug of ale I sat down, and what
with hunger and the goodness of the fare, for everything was first-rate, made one of the best suppers I ever
made in my life.

Supper over, I called for a glass of whiskey-and-
water, over which I trifled for about half-an-hour and
then betook myself again to the kitchen. Almost as
soon as I entered, the company, who seemed to be discussing some point, and were not making much hurly-
burly, became silent and looked at me in a suspicious
and uneasy manner. I advanced towards the fire. The
old man who had occupied the seat in the chimney-
corner and had resigned it to me, had again taken
possession of it. As I drew near to the fire he looked
upon the ground, and seemed by no means disposed to
vacate the place of honour; after a few moments, however, he got up and offered me the seat with a slight
motion of his hand and without saying a word. I did
not decline it, but sat down, and the old gentleman
took a chair near. Universal silence now prevailed;
sullen looks were cast at me; and I saw clearly enough
that I was not welcome. Frankness was now my only
resource. " What's the matter, gentlemen?" said I;
" you are silent and don't greet me kindly; have I
given you any cause of offence?" No one uttered a

word in reply for nearly a minute, when the old man
said slowly and deliberately : " Why, sir, the long and
short of it is this : we have got it into our heads that
you understand every word of our discourse; now, do
you or do you not?"

" Understand every word of your discourse," said I;
" I wish I did; I would give five pounds to understand
every word of your discourse."

" That's a clever attempt to get off, sir," said the
old man, " but it won't exactly do. Tell us whether
you know more Welsh than bara y caws; or to speak
more plainly, whether you understand a good deal of
what we say."

" Well," said I, " I do understand more Welsh than
bara y caws—I do understand a considerable part of a
Welsh conversation—moreover, I can read Welsh, and
have the life of Tom O'r Nant at my fingers' ends."

" Well, sir, that is speaking plain, and I will tell you
plainly that we don't like to have strangers among us
who understand our discourse, more especially if they
be gentlefolks."

" That's strange," said I; " a Welshman or foreigner,
gentle or simple, may go into a public-house in Eng
land, and nobody cares a straw whether he understands
the discourse of the company or not."

" That may be the custom in England," said the old
man; " but it is not so in Wales."

" What have you got to conceal?" said I. " I suppose you are honest men."

" I hope we are, sir," said the old man; " but I
must tell you, once for all, that we don't like strangers
to listen to our discourse."

" Come," said I, " I will not listen to your discourse,
but you shall listen to mine. I have a wonderful deal
to say if I once begin; I have been everywhere."

" Well, sir," said the old man, " if you have anything to tell us about where you have been and what
you have seen we shall be glad to hear you."

" Have you ever been in Russia?" shouted a voice,
that of the large rough fellow who asked me the question about the Russian war.

" O yes, I have been in Russia," said I.

" Well, what kind of a country is it?"

" Very different from this," said I, " which is a little country up in a corner, full of hills and mountains; that is an immense country, extending from the Baltic Sea to the confines of China, almost as flat as a pancake, there not being a hill to be seen for nearly two thousand miles."

" A very poor country, isn't it, always covered with ice and snow?"

" O no; it is one of the richest countries in the world, producing all kinds of grain, with noble rivers intersecting it, and in some parts covered with stately forests.   In the winter, which is rather long, there is a good deal of ice and snow, it is true, but in the summer the weather is warmer than here."

" And are there any towns and cities in Russia, sir, as there are in Britain?" said the old man, who had resigned his seat in the chimney-corner to me; " I suppose not, or, if there be, nothing equal to Hereford or Bristol, in both of which I have been."

" O yes," said I, " there are plenty of towns and cities.   The two principal ones are Moscow and Saint Petersburg, both of which are capitals.   Moscow is a fine old city, far up the country, and was the original seat of empire.   In it there is a wonderful building called the Kremlin, situated on a hill.   It is partly palace, partly temple, and partly fortress.   In one of its halls are I don't know how many crowns, taken from various kings, whom the Russians have conquered. But the most remarkable thing in the Kremlin is a huge bell in a cellar or cave, close by one of the churches; it is twelve feet high, and the sound it gives when struck with an iron bar, for there are no clappers to Russian bells, is so loud that the common Russians say it can be heard over the empire.   The other city, Saint Petersburg, where the court generally reside, is a modern and very fine city; so fine indeed, that I have no hesitation in saying that neither Bristol nor Hereford is worthy to be named in the same day with it.   Many of the streets are miles in length and straight as an arrow.   The Nefsky Prospect, as it is called, a street which runs from the grand square, where stands the Emperor's palace, to the monastery of Saint Alexander Nefsky, is nearly three miles in length and is full of noble shops and houses. The Neva, a river twice as broad and twice as deep as the Thames, and whose waters are clear as crystal, runs through the town, having on each side of it a superb quay, fenced with granite, which affords one of the most delightful walks imaginable. If I had my choice of all the cities of the world to live in, I would chose Saint Petersburg."

"And did you ever see the Emperor?" said the rough fellow, whom I have more than once mentioned, "did you ever see the Emperor Nicholas?"

"O yes; I have seen him frequently."

"Well, what kind of a man is he? we should like to know."

"A man of colossal stature, with a fine, noble, but rather stern and severe aspect. I think I now see him, with his grey cloak, cocked hat, and white waving plumes, striding down the Nefsky Prospect, and towering by a whole head over other people."

"Bravo! Did you ever see him at the head of his soldiers?"

"O yes! I have seen the Emperor review forty thousand of his chosen troops in the Champs de Mars, and a famous sight it was. There stood the great, proud man looking at his warriors as they manœuvred before him. Two-thirds of them were cavalry, and each horseman was mounted on a beautiful blood charger of Cossack or English breed, and arrayed in a superb uniform. The blaze, glitter and glory were too much for my eyes, and I was frequently obliged to turn them away. The scene upon the whole put me in mind of an immense field of tulips of various dyes, for the colours of the dresses, of the banners and the plumes, were as gorgeous and manifold as the hues of those queenly flowers."

"Bravo!" said twenty voices; "the gentleman speaks like an areithiwr. Have you been in other countries besides Russia?"

"O yes! I have been in Turkey, the people of which are not Christians, but frequently put Christians to shame by their good faith and honesty. I have been in the land of the Maugrabins, or Moors—a people who live on a savoury dish, called couscousoo, and have the gloomiest faces and the most ferocious hearts under

heaven. I have been in Italy, whose people, though
the most clever in the world, are the most unhappy,
owing to the tyranny of a being called the Pope, who,
when I saw him, appeared to be under the influence of
strong drink. I have been in Portugal, the people of
which supply the whole world with wine, and drink only
water themselves. I have been in Spain, a very fine
country, the people of which are never so happy as
when paying other folks' reckonings. I have been——
but the wind is blowing wildly without, and the rain
pelting against the windows;—this is a capital night
for a ghost story : shall I tell you a ghost story which
I learnt in Spain?''

'' Yes, sir, pray do; we all love ghost stories. Do
tell us the ghost story of Spain.''

Thereupon I told the company Lope de Vega's ghost
story, which is decidedly the best ghost story in the
world.

Long and loud was the applause which followed the
conclusion of the grand ghost story of the world, in
the midst of which I got up, bade the company good
night, and made my exit. Shortly afterwards I desired
to be shown to my sleeping apartment. It was a very
small room upstairs, in the back part of the house;
and I make no doubt was the chamber of the two poor
girls, the landlady's daughters, as I saw various articles
of female attire lying about. The spirit of knight-
errantry within me was not, however, sufficiently
strong to prevent me from taking possession of the
female dormitory; so, forthwith divesting myself of
every portion of my habiliments, which were steaming
like a boiling tea-kettle, I got into bed between the
blankets, and in a minute was fast in the arms of
Morpheus.

CHAPTER C

Morning—A Cheerless Scene—The Carter—Ode to Glamorgan—
Startling Halloo—One-sided Liberty—Clerical Profession—De
Courcy—Love of the Drop—Independent Spirit—Another
People.

I SLEPT soundly through the night. At about eight
o'clock on the following morning I got up and looked

out of the window of my room, which fronted the
north. A strange scene presented itself: a roaring
brook was foaming along towards the west, just under
the window. Immediately beyond it was a bank, not of
green turf, grey rock, or brown mould, but of coal
rubbish, coke and cinders; on the top of this bank was
a fellow performing some dirty office or other, with a
spade and barrow; beyond him, on the side of a hill,
was a tramway, up which a horse was straining, drawing a load of something towards the north-west.
Beyond the tramway was a grove of yellow-looking
firs; beyond the grove a range of white houses with
blue roofs, occupied, I supposed, by miners and their
families; and beyond these I caught a sight of the
mountain on the top of which I had been the night
before, only a partial one, however, as large masses of
mist were still hanging about it. The morning was
moist and dripping, and nothing could look more cheerless and uncomfortable than the entire scene.

I put on my things, which were still not half dry,
and went down into the little parlour, where I found an
excellent fire awaiting me, and a table spread for breakfast. The breakfast was delicious, consisting of excellent tea, buttered toast and Glamorgan sausages, which
I really think are not a whit inferior to those of Epping.
After breakfast I went into the kitchen, which was now
only occupied by two or three people. Seeing a large
brush on a dresser, I took it up, and was about to
brush my nether habiliments, which were terribly be-
spattered with half-dried mire. Before, however, I
could begin, up started one of the men, a wild shock-
headed fellow dressed like a carter, in rough blue frieze
coat, yellow broad corduroy trowsers, grey woollen
stockings and highlows, and snatching the brush out of
my hand, fell to brushing me most vigorously, purring
and blowing all the time in a most tremendous manner.
I did not refuse his services, but let him go on, and
to reward him, as I thought, spoke kindly to him,
asking him various questions. "Are you a carter?"
said I. No answer. "One of Twm O'r Nant's
people?" No answer. "Famous fellow that Twm
O'r Nant, wasn't he? Did you ever hear how he got
the great tree in at Carmarthen Gate? What is wood

per foot at present? Whom do you cart for? Or are you your own master? If so, how many horses do you keep?"

To not one of these questions, nor to a dozen others which I put, both in English and Welsh, did my friend with the brush return any verbal answer, though I could occasionally hear a kind of stifled giggle proceeding from him. Having at length thoroughly brushed not only my clothes, but my boots and my hat, which last article he took from my head, and placed on again very dexterously, after brushing it, he put the brush down on the dresser, and then advancing to me made me a bow, and waving his forefinger backwards and forwards before my face, he said, with a broad grin: "Nice gentleman—will do anything for him but answer questions, and let him hear my discourse. Love to listen to his pleasant stories of foreign lands, ghosts and tylwith teg; but before him deem it wise to be mum, quite mum. Know what he comes about. Wants to hear discourse of poor man, that he may learn from it poor man's little ways and invirmities, and mark them down in one small, little book to serve for fun to Lord Palmerston and the other great gentlefolks in London. Nice man, civil man, I don't deny; and clebber man too, for he knows Welsh, and has been everywhere—but fox—old fox—lives at Plas y Cadno."[1]

Having been informed that there was a considerable iron foundry close by, I thought it would be worth my while to go and see it. I entered the premises, and was standing and looking round, when a man with the appearance of a respectable mechanic came up and offered to show me over the place. I gladly accepted his offer, and he showed me all about the iron-foundry. I saw a large steam-engine at full play, terrible furnaces, and immense heaps of burning, crackling cinders, and a fiery stream of molten metal rolling along. After seeing what there was to be seen, I offered a piece of silver to my kind conductor, which he at once refused. On my asking him, however, to go to the inn and have a friendly glass, he smiled, and said he had no objection. So we went to the inn, and had two friendly glasses of whiskey-and-water together, and also some

[1] Fox's Court—perhaps London.

discourse. I asked him if there were any English employed on the premises. " None," said he, " nor Irish either; we are all Welsh." Though he was a Welshman, his name was a very common English one.

After paying the reckoning, which only amounted to three and sixpence, I departed for Swansea, distant about thirteen miles. Gutter Vawr consists of one street, extending for some little way along the Swansea road, the foundry, and a number of huts and houses scattered here and there. The population is composed almost entirely of miners, the workers at the foundry, and their families. For the first two or three miles the country through which I passed did not at all pre-possess me in favour of Glamorganshire : it consisted of low, sullen, peaty hills. Subsequently, however, it improved rapidly, becoming bold, wild, and pleasantly wooded. The aspect of the day improved, also, with the appearance of the country. When I first started the morning was wretched and drizzly, but in less than an hour it cleared up wonderfully, and the sun began to flash out. As I looked on the bright luminary I thought of Ab Gwilym's ode to the sun and Glamorgan, and with breast heaving and with eyes full of tears, I began to repeat parts of it, or rather of a translation made in my happy boyish years :

> " Each morn, benign of countenance,
> Upon Glamorgan's pennon glance!
> Each afternoon in beauty clear
> Above my own dear bounds appear !
> Bright outline of a blessèd clime,
> Again, though sunk, arise sublime—
> Upon my errand, swift repair,
> And unto green Glamorgan bear
> Good days and terms of courtesy
> From my dear country and from me !
> Move round—but need I thee command?—
> Its chalk-white halls, which cheerful stand—
> Pleasant thy own pavilions too—
> Its fields and orchards fair to view.

> " O, pleasant is thy task and high
> In radiant warmth to roam the sky,
> To keep from ill that kindly ground,
> Its meads and farms, where mead is found,
> A land whose commons live content,
> Where each man's lot is excellent.

Where hosts to hail thee shall upstand,
Where lads are bold and lasses bland,
A land I oft from hill that's high
Have gazed upon with raptur'd eye;
Where maids are trained in virtue's school,
Where duteous wives spin dainty wool;
A country with each gift supplied,
Confronting Cornwall's cliffs of pride."

Came to Llanguick, a hamlet situated near a tremendous gorge, the sides of which were covered with wood. Thence to the village of Tawy Bridge, at the bottom of a beautiful valley, through which runs the Tawy, which, after the Taf, is the most considerable river in Glamorganshire. Continuing my course, I passed by an enormous edifice which stood on my right hand. It had huge chimneys, which were casting forth smoke, and from within I heard the noise of a steam-engine and the roar of furnaces.

"What place is this?" said I to a boy.

"Gwaith haiarn, sir; ym perthyn i Mr. Pearson. Mr. Pearson's iron works, sir."

I proceeded, and in about half-an-hour saw a man walking before me in the same direction in which I was. He was going very briskly, but I soon came up to him. He was a small, well-made fellow, with reddish hair and ruddy, determined countenance, somewhat tanned. He wore a straw hat, checkered shirt, open at the neck, canvas trowsers, and blue jacket. On his feet were shoes remarkably thin, but no stockings, and in his hand he held a stout stick, with which, just before I overtook him, he struck a round stone which lay on the ground, sending it flying at least fifty yards before him on the road, and following it in its flight with a wild and somewhat startling halloo.

"Good day, my friend," said I; "you seem to be able to use a stick."

"And sure I ought to be, your honour, seeing as how my father taught me, who was the best fighting man with a stick that the Shanavests ever had. Many is the head of a Caravaut that he has broken with some such an Alpeen wattle as the one I am carrying with me here."

"A good thing," said I, "that there are no Old

Waistcoats and Cravats at present, at least bloody
factions bearing those names."

"Your honour thinks so! Faith! I am clane of a
contrary opinion. I wish the ould Shanavests and
Caravauts were fighting still; and I among them.
Faith! there was some life in Ireland in their days."

"And plenty of death too," said I. "How fortunate
it is that the Irish have the English among them, to
prevent their cutting each other's throats."

"The English prevent the Irish from cutting each
other's throats! Well! if they do, it is only that they
may have the pleasure of cutting them themselves. The
bloody tyrants! too long has their foot been upon the
neck of poor old Ireland."

"How do the English tyrannise over Ireland?"

"How do they tyrannise over her? Don't they prevent her from having the free exercise of her Catholic
religion, and make her help to support their own
Protestant one?"

"Well, and don't the Roman Catholics prevent the
Protestants from having the free exercise of their
religion, whenever they happen to be the most numerous, and don't they make them help to support the
Roman Catholic religion?"

"Of course they do, and quite right. Had I my will
there shouldn't be a place of Protestant worship left
standing, or a Protestant churl allowed to go about
with a head unbroken."

"Then why do you blame the Protestants for keeping the Romans a little under?"

"Why do I blame them? A purty question! Why,
an't they wrong, and an't we right?"

"But they say that they are right and you wrong."

"They say! who minds what they say? Havn't we
the word of the blessed Pope that we are right?"

"And they say that they have the word of the
blessed Gospel that you are wrong."

"The Gospel! who cares for the Gospel? Surely you
are not going to compare the Gospel with the Pope?"

"Well, they certainly are not to be named in the
same day."

"They are not? Then good luck to you! We are
both of the same opinion. Ah, I thought your honour

was a rale Catholic. Now, tell me from what kingdom
of Ireland does your honour hail?"

" Why, I was partly educated in Munster."

" In Munster ! Hoorah ! Here's the hand of a
countryman to your honour. Ah, it was asy to be
seen from the learning which your honour shows, that
your honour is from Munster. There's no spot in
Ireland like Munster for learning. What says the old
song ?

> " ' Ulster for a soldier
> Connaught for a thief,
> Munster for learning,
> And Leinster for beef.' "

" Hoorah for learned Munster ! and down with beggarly, thievish Connaught ! I would that a Connaught
man would come athwart me now, that I might break
his thief's head with my Alpeen."

" You don't seem to like the Connaught men,"
said I.

" Like them ! who can like them? a parcel of beggarly thievish blackguards. So your honour was edicated in Munster, I mane partly edicated. I suppose
by your saying that you were partly edicated, that your
honour was intended for the clerical profession, but
being over fond of the drop was forced to lave college
before your edication was quite completed, and so for
want of a better profession took up with that of mer-
chandise. Ah, the love of the drop at college has prevented many a clever young fellow from taking holy
orders. Well, it's a pity, but it can't be helped. I am
fond of a drop myself, and when we get to —— shall
be happy to offer your honour a glass of whiskey. I
hope your honour and I shall splice the mainbrace
together before we part."

" I suppose," said I, " by your talking of splicing
the mainbrace that you are a sailor."

" I am, your honour, and hail from the Cove of Cork
in the kingdom of Munster."

" I know it well," said I. " It is the best sea-basin
in the world. Well, how came you into these parts?"

" I'll tell your honour; my ship is at Swansea, and
having a relation working at the foundry behind us,
I came to see him."

"Are you in the royal service?"

"I am not, your honour; I was once in the royal service, but having a dispute with the boatswain at Spithead, I gave him a wipe, jumped overboard and swam ashore. After that I sailed for Cuba, got into the merchants' service there and made several voyages to the Black Coast. At present I am in the service of the merchants of Cork."

"I wonder that you are not now in the royal service," said I, "since you are so fond of fighting. There is hot work going on at present up the Black Sea, and brave men, especially Irishmen, are in great request."

"Yes, brave Irishmen are always in great request with England when she has a battle to fight. At other times they are left to lie in the mud with the chain round their necks. It has been so ever since the time of De Courcy, and I suppose always will be so, unless Irishmen all become of my mind, which is not likely. Were the Irish all of my mind, the English would find no Irish champion to fight their battles when the French or the Russians come to beard them."

"By De Courcy," said I, "you mean the man whom the King of England confined in the Tower of London after taking him from his barony in the county of Cork."

"Of course, your honour, and whom he kept in the Tower till the King of France sent over a champion to insult and beard him, when the king was glad to take De Courcy out of the dungeon to fight the French champion, for divil a one of his own English fighting men dared take the Frenchman in hand."

"A fine fellow that De Courcy," said I.

"Rather too fond of the drop though, like your honour and myself, for after he had caused the French champion to flee back into France he lost the greater part of the reward which the King of England promised him solely by making too free with the strong drink. Does your honour remember that part of the story?"

"I think I do," said I, "but I should be very glad to hear you relate it."

"Then your honour shall. Right glad was the King

of England when the French champion fled back to
France, for no sooner did the dirty spalpeen hear that
they were going to bring De Courcy against him, the
fame of whose strength and courage filled the whole
world, than he betook himself back to his own country
and was never heard of more. Right glad, I say, was
the King of England, and gave leave to De Courcy
to return to Ireland, 'And you shall have,' said he, ' of
the barony which I took from you all that you can ride
round on the first day of your return.' So De Courcy
betook himself to Ireland and to his barony, but he
was anything but a lucky man, this De Courcy, for
his friends and relations and tenantry, hearing of his
coming, prepared a grand festival for him with all
kinds of illigant viands and powerful liquors, and when
he arrived there it was waiting for him, and down to it
he sat, and ate and drank, and for joy of seeing himself
once more amongst his friends and tenantry in the hall
of his forefathers and for love of the drop, which he
always had, he drank of the powerful liquors more than
he ought, and the upshot was that he became drunk,
agus do bhi an duine maith sin misgeadh do ceathar o
glog; the good gentleman was drunk till four o'clock,
and when he awoke he found that he had but two hours
of day remaining to win back his brave barony. However, he did not lose heart, but mounted his horse and
set off riding as fast as a man just partly recovered
from intoxication could be expected to do, and he contrived to ride round four parishes, and only four, and
these four parishes were all that he recovered of his
brave barony, and all that he had to live upon till his
dying day, and all that he had to leave to his descendants, so that De Courcy could scarcely be called a very
lucky man, after all.''

Shortly after my friend the sailor had concluded his
account of De Courcy we arrived in the vicinity of a
small town or rather considerable village. It stood on
the right-hand side of the road, fronting the east,
having a high romantic hill behind it on the sides of
which were woods, groves, and pleasant-looking white
houses.

"What place is this?" said I to my companion.

"This is ——, your honour; and here, if your honour

will accept a glass of whiskey we will splice the main-brace together.''

'' Thank you,'' said I; '' but I am in haste to get to Swansea. Moreover, if I am over fond of the drop, as you say I am, the sooner I begin to practise abstinence the better.''

'' Very true, your honour! Well, at any rate, when your honour gets to Swansea you will not be able to say that Pat Flannagan walked for miles with your honour along the road without offering your honour a glass of whiskey.''

'' Nor shall Pat Flannagan be able to say the same thing of my honour. I have a shilling in my pocket at Pat Flannagan's service, if he chooses to splice with it the mainbrace for himself and for me.''

'' Thank your honour; but I have a shilling in my own pocket, and a dollar too, and a five-pound note besides; so I needn't be beholden for drink money to anybody under the sun.''

'' Well then, farewell! Here's my hand!—Slan leat a Phatraic ui Flannagan!''

'' Slan leat a dhuine-uasail!'' said Patrick, giving me his hand; '' and health, hope and happiness to ye.''

Thereupon he turned aside to ——, and I continued my way to Swansea. Arrived at a place called Glandwr, about two miles from Swansea, I found that I was splashed from top to toe, for the roads were frightfully miry, and was sorry to perceive that my boots had given way at the soles, large pieces of which were sticking out. I must, however, do the poor things the justice to say that it was no wonder that they were in this dilapidated condition, for in those boots I had walked at least two hundred miles, over all kinds of paths, since I had got them soled at Llangollen. '' Well,'' said I to myself, '' it won't do to show myself at Swansea in this condition, more especially as I shall go to the best hotel; I must try and get myself made a little decent here.'' Seeing a little inn on my right I entered it, and addressing myself to a neat, comfortable landlady, who was standing within the bar, I said—

'' Please to let me have a glass of ale!—and hearkee; as I have been walking along the road, I should be glad of the services of the ' boots.' ''

"Very good, sir," said the landlady with a curtsey.
Then showing me into a nice little sanded parlour,
she brought me the glass of ale, and presently sent in
a lad with a boot-jack to minister to me. O, what
can't a little money effect? For sixpence in that small
nice inn I had a glass of ale, my boots cleaned and the
excrescences cut off, my clothes wiped with a dwile,
and then passed over with a brush, and was myself
thanked over and over again. Starting again with all
the spirited confidence of one who has just cast off his
slough, I soon found myself in the suburbs of Swansea.
As I passed under what appeared to be a railroad
bridge I inquired in Welsh of an ancient-looking man,
in coaly habiliments, if it was one. He answered in the
same language that it was, then instantly added in
English—

"You have taken your last farewell of Wales, sir;
it's no use speaking Welsh farther on."

I passed some immense edifices, probably manufac-
tories, and was soon convinced that, whether I was in
Wales or not, I was no longer amongst Welsh. The
people whom I met did not look like Welsh. They were
taller and bulkier than the Cambrians, and were speaking a dissonant English jargon. The women had much
the appearance of Dutch fisherwomen; some of them
were carrying huge loads on their heads. I spoke in
Welsh to two or three whom I overtook.

"No Welsh, sir!"

"Why don't you speak Welsh?" said I.

"Because we never learnt it. We are not Welsh."

"Who are you then?"

"English; some call us Flamings."

"Ah, ah!" said I to myself, "I had forgot."

Presently I entered the town, a large, bustling,
dirty, gloomy place, and inquiring for the first hotel
was directed to the "Mackworth Arms," in Wine
Street.

As soon as I was shown into the parlour I summoned
the "boots," and on his making his appearance I said
in a stern voice: "My boots want soling; let them
be done by to-morrow morning."

"Can't be, sir; it's now Saturday afternoon, and
the shoemaker couldn't begin them to-night!"

" But you must make him !" said I; " and look here,
I shall give him a shilling extra, and you an extra
shilling for seeing after him."

" Yes, sir; I'll see after him—they shall be done, sir.
Bring you your slippers instantly. Glad to see you
again in Swansea, sir, looking so well."

CHAPTER CI

Swansea—The Flemings—Towards England.

SWANSEA is called by the Welsh Abertawé, which signifies the mouth of the Tawy. Aber, as I have more
than once had occasion to observe, signifies the place
where a river enters into the sea or joins another. It
is a Gaelic as well as a Cumric word, being found in
the Gaelic names Aberdeen and Lochaber, and there
is good reason for supposing that the word harbour
is derived from it. Swansea or Swansey is a compound word of Scandinavian origin, which may mean
either a river abounding with swans, or the river of
Swanr, the name of some northern adventurer who
settled down at its mouth. The final ea or ey is the
Norwegian aa, which signifies a running water; it is
of frequent occurrence in the names of rivers in
Norway, and is often found, similarly modified, in
those of other countries where the adventurous Nor-
wegians formed settlements.

Swansea first became a place of some importance
shortly after the beginning of the twelfth century. In
the year 1108 the greater part of Flanders having been
submerged by the sea [1] an immense number of Flemings
came over to England, and entreated of Henry the First,
the king then occupying the throne, that he would allot
to them lands in which they might settle. The king
sent them to various parts of Wales which had been
conquered by his barons or those of his predecessors :
a considerable number occupied Swansea and the neighbourhood; but far the greater part went to Dyfed,
generally but improperly called Pembroke, the south-
eastern part of which, by far the most fertile, they

[1] Drych y Prif Oesoedd, p. 100.

entirely took possession of, leaving to the Welsh the rest, which is very mountainous and barren.

I have already said that the people of Swansea stand out in broad distinctness from the Cumry, differing from them in stature, language, dress, and manners, and wish to observe that the same thing may be said of the inhabitants of every part of Wales which the Flemings colonised in any considerable numbers.

I found the accommodation very good at the "Mackworth Arms;" I passed the Saturday evening very agreeably, and slept well throughout the night. The next morning to my great joy I found my boots, capitally repaired, awaiting me before my chamber door. O the mighty effect of a little money! After breakfast I put them on, and as it was Sunday went out in order to go to church. The streets were thronged with people; a new mayor had just been elected, and his worship, attended by a number of halbert and javelin men, was going to church too. I followed the procession, which moved with great dignity and of course very slowly. The church had a high square tower and looked a very fine edifice on the outside and no less so within, for the nave was lofty with noble pillars on each side. I stood during the whole of the service as did many others, for the congregation was so great that it was impossible to accommodate all with seats. The ritual was performed in a very satisfactory manner and was followed by an excellent sermon. I am ashamed to say that I have forgot the text, but I remember a good deal of the discourse. The preacher said amongst other things that the Gospel was not preached in vain, and that he very much doubted whether a sermon was ever delivered which did not do some good. On the conclusion of the services I strolled about in order to see the town and what pertained to it. The town is of considerable size with some remarkable edifices, spacious and convenient quays, and a commodious harbour into which the river Tawy flowing from the north empties itself. The town and harbour are overhung on the side of the east by a lofty green mountain with a Welsh name, no doubt exceedingly appropriate, but which I regret to say has escaped my memory.

After having seen all that I wished I returned to my inn and discharged all my obligations. I then departed, framing my course eastward towards England, having traversed Wales nearly from north to south.

CHAPTER CII

Leave Swansea—The Pandemonium—Neath Abbey—
Varied Scenery.

IT was about two o'clock of a dull and gloomy afternoon when I started from Abertawy or Swansea, intending to stop at Neath, some eight miles distant. As I passed again through the suburbs I was struck with their length and the evidences of enterprise which they exhibited—enterprise, however, evidently chiefly connected with iron and coal, for almost every object looked awfully grimy. Crossing a bridge I proceeded to the east up a broad and spacious valley, the eastern side of which was formed by russet-coloured hills, through a vista of which I could descry a range of tall blue mountains. As I proceeded I sometimes passed pleasant groves and hedgerows, sometimes huge works; in this valley there was a singular mixture of nature and art, of the voices of birds and the clanking of chains, of the mists of heaven and the smoke of furnaces.

I reached Llan——, a small village half-way between Swansea and Neath, and without stopping continued my course, walking very fast. I had surmounted a hill and had nearly descended that side of it which looked towards the east, having on my left, that is to the north, a wooded height, when an extraordinary scene presented itself to my eyes. Somewhat to the south rose immense stacks of chimneys surrounded by grimy diabolical-looking buildings, in the neighbourhood of which were huge heaps of cinders and black rubbish. From the chimneys, notwithstanding it was Sunday, smoke was proceeding in volumes, choking the atmosphere all around. From this pandemonium, at the distance of about a quarter of a mile to the southwest, upon a green meadow, stood, looking darkly grey, a ruin of vast size with window holes, towers, spires, and arches. Between it and the accursed pandemonium, lay a horrid filthy place, part of which was swamp and part pool : the pool black as soot, and the swamp of a disgusting leaden colour. Across this place of filth stretched a tramway leading seemingly from the abominable mansions to the ruin. So strange a scene I had never beheld in nature. Had it been on canvas, with the addition of a number of diabolical figures, proceeding along the tramway, it might have stood for Sabbath in Hell—devils proceeding to afternoon worship, and would have formed a picture worthy of the powerful but insane painter Jerome Bos.

After standing for a considerable time staring at the strange spectacle I proceeded. Presently meeting a lad, I asked him what was the name of the ruin.

" The Abbey," he replied.

" Neath Abbey?" said I.

" Yes !"

Having often heard of this abbey, which in its day was one of the most famous in Wales, I determined to go and inspect it. It was with some difficulty that I found my way to it. It stood, as I have already observed, in a meadow, and was on almost every side surrounded by majestic hills. To give any clear description of this ruined pile would be impossible, the dilapidation is so great, dilapidation evidently less the effect of time than of awful violence, perhaps that of gunpowder. The southern is by far the most perfect portion of the building ; there you see not only walls but roofs. Fronting you full south, is a mass of masonry with two immense arches, other arches behind them : entering, you find yourself beneath a vaulted roof, and passing on you come to an oblong square which may have been a church ; an iron-barred window on your right enables you to look into a mighty vault, the roof of which is supported by beautiful pillars. Then——but I forbear to say more respecting these remains for fear of stating what is incorrect, my stay amongst them having been exceedingly short.

The Abbey of Glen Neath was founded in the twelfth century by Richard Grenfield, one of the followers of Robert Fitzhamon, who subjugated Glamorgan. Neath

Abbey was a very wealthy one, the founder having endowed it with extensive tracts of fertile land along the banks of the rivers Neath and Tawy. In it the unfortunate Edward of Carnarvon sought a refuge for a few days from the rage of his revolted barons, whilst his favourite the equally unfortunate Spencer endeavoured to find a covert amidst the thickets of the wood-covered hill to the north. When Richmond landed at Milford Haven to dispute the crown with Richard the Second, the then Abbot of Neath repaired to him and gave him his benediction, in requital for which the adventurer gave him his promise that in the event of his obtaining the crown he would found a college in Glen Neath, which promise, however, after he had won the crown, he forgot to perform.[1] The wily abbot, when he hastened to pay worship to what he justly conceived to be the rising sun, little dreamt that he was about to bless the future father of the terrible man doomed by Providence to plant the abomination of desolation in Neath Abbey and in all the other nests of monkery throughout the land.

Leaving the ruins I proceeded towards Neath. The scenery soon became very beautiful; not that I had left machinery altogether behind, for I presently came to a place where huge wheels were turning and there was smoke and blast, but there was much that was rural and beautiful to be seen, something like park scenery, and then there were the mountains near and in the distance. I reached Neath at about half-past four, and took up my quarters at an inn which had been recommended to me by my friend the boots at Swansea.

CHAPTER CIII

Town of Neath—Hounds and Huntsman—Spectral Chapel—The Glowing Mountain.

NEATH is a place of some antiquity, for it can boast of the remains of a castle and is a corporate town. There is but little Welsh spoken in it. It is situated on the Neath, and exports vast quantities of coal and iron, of

[1] Y Greal, p. 279.

both of which there are rich mines in the neighbourhood. It derives its name from the river Nedd or Neth on which it stands. Nedd or Neth is the same word as Nith the name of a river in Scotland, and is in some degree connected with Nidda the name of one in Germany. Nedd in Welsh signifies a dingle, and the word in its various forms has always something to do with lowness or inferiority of position. Amongst its forms are Nether and Nieder. The term is well applied to the Glamorganshire river, which runs through dingles and under mountains.

The Neath has its source in the mountains of Brecon, and enters the sea some little way below the town of Neath.

On the Monday morning I resumed my journey, directing my course up the vale of Neath towards Merthyr Tydvil, distant about four-and-twenty miles. The weather was at first rainy, misty, and miserable, but improved by degrees. I passed through a village which I was told was called Llanagos; close to it were immense establishments of some kind. The scenery soon became exceedingly beautiful; hills covered with wood to the tops were on either side of the dale. I passed an avenue leading somewhere through groves, and was presently overtaken and passed by hounds and a respectable-looking old huntsman on a black horse; a minute afterwards I caught a glimpse of an old redbrick mansion nearly embosomed in groves, from which proceeded a mighty cawing. Probably it belonged to the proprietor of the dogs, and certainly looked a very fit mansion for a Glamorganshire squire, justice of the peace, and keeper of a pack of hounds.

I went on, the vale increasing in beauty; there was a considerable drawback, however: one of those detestable contrivances a railroad was on the farther side— along which trains were passing, rumbling and screaming.

I saw a bridge on my right hand with five or six low arches over the river, which was here full of shoals. Asked a woman the name of the bridge.

"*Pont Fawr* ei galw, sir."

I was again amongst the real Welsh—this woman had no English.

I passed by several remarkable mountains, both on the south and northern side of the vale. Late in the afternoon I came to the eastern extremity of the vale and ascended a height. Shortly afterwards I reached Rhigos, a small village.

Entering a public-house I called for ale and sat down amidst some grimy fellows, who said nothing to me and to whom I said nothing—their discourse was in Welsh and English. Of their Welsh I understood but little, for it was a strange corrupt jargon. In about half-an-hour after leaving this place I came to the beginning of a vast moor. It was now growing rather dusk and I could see blazes here and there; occasionally I heard horrid sounds. Came to Irvan, an enormous mining-place with a spectral-looking chapel, doubtless a Methodist one. The street was crowded with rough savage-looking men. " Is this the way to Merthyr Tydvil?" said I to one.

" Yes!" bawled the fellow at the utmost stretch of his voice.

" Thank you!" said I, taking off my hat and passing on.

Forward I went, up hill and down dale. Night now set in. I passed a grove of trees and presently came to a collection of small houses at the bottom of a little hollow. Hearing a step near me I stopped and said in Welsh: " How far to Merthyr Tydvil?"

" Dim Cumrag, sir!" said a voice, seemingly that of a man.

" Good-night!" said I, and without staying to put the question in English, I pushed on up an ascent and was presently amongst trees. Heard for a long time the hooting of an owl or rather the frantic hollo. Appeared to pass by where the bird had its station. Toiled up an acclivity and when on the top stood still and looked around me. There was a glow on all sides in the heaven except in the north-east quarter. Striding on I saw a cottage on my left-hand, and standing at the door the figure of a woman. " How far to Merthyr?" said I in Welsh.

" Tair milltir—three miles, sir."

Turning round a corner at the top of a hill I saw blazes here and there and what appeared to be a glowing mountain in the south-east. I went towards it down a descent which continued for a long, long way; so great was the light cast by the blazes and that wonderful glowing object that I could distinctly see the little stones upon the road. After walking about half-an-hour, always going downwards, I saw a house on my left hand and heard a noise of water opposite to it. It was a pistyll. I went to it, drank greedily, and then hurried on, more and more blazes and the glowing object looking more terrible than ever. It was now above me at some distance to the left, and I could see that it was an immense quantity of heated matter like lava, occupying the upper and middle parts of a hill and descending here and there almost to the bottom in a zigzag and tortuous manner. Between me and the hill of the burning object lay a deep ravine. After a time I came to a house, against the door of which a man was leaning.

"What is all that burning stuff above, my friend?"

"Dross from the iron forges, sir!"

I now perceived a valley below me full of lights, and descending reached houses and a tramway. I had blazes now all around me. I went through a filthy slough, over a bridge, and up a street, from which dirty lanes branched off on either side, passed throngs of savage-looking people talking clamorously, shrank from addressing any of them, and finally undirected found myself before the Castle Inn at Merthyr Tydvil.

CHAPTER CIV

Iron and Coal—The Martyred Princess—Cyfartha Fawr— Diabolical Structure.

MERTHYR TYDVIL is situated in a broad valley through which roll the waters of the Taf. It was till late an inconsiderable village, but is at present the greatest mining place in Britain, and may be called with much propriety the capital of the iron and coal.

It bears the name of Merthyr Tydvil, which signifies the Martyr Tydvil, because in the old time a Christian British princess was slain in the locality which it occupies. Tydvil was the daughter of Brychan Prince of Brecon, surnamed Brycheiniawg, or the Breconian, who flourished in the fifth century and was a contemporary of Hengist. He was a man full of Christian zeal and a great preacher of the Gospel, and gave his children, of which he had many both male and female by various wives, an education which he hoped would not only make them Christians, but enable them to preach the Gospel to their countrymen. They proved themselves worthy of his care, all of them without one exception becoming exemplary Christians, and useful preachers. In his latter days he retired to a hermitage in Glamorganshire near the Taf and passed his time in devotion, receiving occasionally visits from his children. Once, when he and several of them, amongst whom was Tydvil, were engaged in prayer a band of heathen Saxons rushed in upon them and slew Tydvil with three of her brothers. Ever since that time the place has borne the name of Martyr Tydvil.[1]

The Taf, which runs to the south of Merthyr, comes down from Breconshire, and enters the Bristol Channel at Cardiff, a place the name of which in English is the city on the Taf. It is one of the most beautiful of rivers, but is not navigable on account of its numerous shallows. The only service which it renders to commerce is feeding a canal which extends from Merthyr to Cardiff. It is surprising how similar many of the Welsh rivers are in name : Taf, Tawey, Towey, Teivi, and Duffy differ but very little in sound. Taf and Teivi have both the same meaning, namely a tendency to spread out. The other names, though probably expressive of the properties or peculiarities of the streams to which they respectively belong, I know not how to translate.

The morning of the fourteenth was very fine. After breakfast I went to see the Cyfartha Fawr iron works, generally considered to be the great wonder of the place. After some slight demur I obtained permission from the superintendent to inspect them. I was attended by an intelligent mechanic. What shall I say about the Cyfartha Fawr? I had best say but very little. I saw enormous furnaces. I saw streams of

[1] Hanes Crefydd Yn NGhymru.

U

molten metal. I saw a long ductile piece of red-hot iron being operated upon. I saw millions of sparks flying about. I saw an immense wheel impelled round with frightful velocity by a steam engine of two hundred and forty horse power. I heard all kinds of dreadful sounds. The general effect was stunning. These works belong to the Crawshays, a family distinguished by a strange kind of eccentricity, but also by genius and enterprising spirit, and by such a strict feeling of honour that it is a common saying that the word of any one of them is as good as the bond of other people.

After seeing the Cyfartha I roamed about making general observations. The mountain of dross which had startled me on the preceding night with its terrific glare, and which stands to the north-west of the town, looked now nothing more than an immense dark heap of cinders. It is only when the shades of night have settled down that the fire within manifests itself, making the hill appear an immense glowing mass. All the hills around the town, some of which are very high, have a scorched and blackened look. An old Anglesea bard, rather given to bombast, wishing to extol the abundant cheer of his native isle, said : " The hills of Ireland are blackened by the smoke from the kitchens of Mona." With much more propriety might a bard of the banks of the Taf who should wish to apologise for the rather smutty appearance of his native vale exclaim : " The hills around the Taf once so green are blackened by the smoke from the chimneys of Merthyr." The town is large and populous. The inhabitants for the most part are Welsh, and Welsh is the language generally spoken, though all have some knowledge of English. The houses are in general low and mean, and built of rough grey stone. Merthyr, however, can show several remarkable edifices, though of a gloomy, horrid Satanic character. There is the hall of the Iron, with its arches, from whence proceeds incessantly a thundering noise of hammers. Then there is an edifice at the foot of a mountain, half way up the side of which is a blasted forest, and on the top an enormous crag. A truly wonderful edifice it is, such as Bos would have imagined had he wanted to paint the palace of Satan. There it stands; a house of reddish brick with a slate roof—four horrid black towers behind, two of them belching forth smoke and flame from their tops—holes like pigeon holes here and there —two immense white chimneys standing by themselves. What edifice can that be of such strange mad details? I ought to have put that question to some one in Tydvil, but did not, though I stood staring at the diabolical structure with my mouth open. It is of no use putting the question to myself here.

After strolling about for some two hours with my hands in my pockets, I returned to my inn, called for a glass of ale, paid my reckoning, flung my satchel over my shoulder, and departed.

CHAPTER CV

Start for Caerfili—Johanna Colgan—Alms-Giving—The Monstrous Female—The Evil Prayer—The Next Day—The Aifrionn—Unclean Spirits — Expectation — Wreaking Vengeance — A Decent Alms.

I LEFT Merthyr about twelve o'clock for Caerfili. My course lay along the valley to the south-east. I passed a large village called Troed y Rhiw, or the foot of the slope, from its being at the foot of a lofty elevation, which stands on the left-hand side of the road, and was speeding onwards fast, with the Taf at some distance on my right, when I saw a strange-looking woman advancing towards me. She seemed between forty and fifty, was bare-footed and bare-headed, with grizzled hair hanging in elf locks, and was dressed in rags and tatters. When about ten yards from me, she pitched forward, gave three or four grotesque tumbles, heels over head, then standing bolt upright, about a yard before me, she raised her right arm, and shouted in a most discordant voice—" Give me an alms, for the glory of God."

I stood still, quite confounded. Presently, however, recovering myself, I said :—" Really, I don't think it would be for the glory of God to give you alms."

" Ye don't ! Then, Biadh an taifronn——however, I'll give ye a chance yet. Am I to get my alms or not?"

" Before I give you alms I must know something about you. Who are you?"

" Who am I? Who should I be but Johanna Colgan, a bedivilled woman from the county of Limerick?"

" And how did you become bedevilled?"

" Because a woman something like myself said an evil prayer over me for not giving her an alms, which prayer I have at my tongue's end, and unless I get my alms will say over you. So for your own sake, honey, give me my alms, and let me go on my way."

" O, I am not to be frightened by evil prayers! I shall give you nothing till I hear all about you."

" If I tell ye all about me will ye give me an alms?"

" Well, I have no objection to give you something if you tell me your story."

" Will ye give me a dacent alms?"

" O, you must leave the amount to my free will and pleasure. I shall give you what I think fit."

" Well, so ye shall, honey; and I make no doubt ye will give me a dacent alms, for I like the look of ye, and knew ye to be an Irishman half-a-mile off. Only four years ago, instead of being a bedivilled woman, tumbling about the world, I was as quiet and respectable a widow as could be found in the county of Limerick. I had a nice little farm at an aisy rint, horses, cows, pigs, and servants, and, what was better than all, a couple of fine sons, who were a help and comfort to me. But my black day was not far off. I was a mighty charitable woman, and always willing to give to the bacahs and other beggars that came about. Every morning, before I opened my door, I got ready the alms which I intended to give away in the course of the day to those that should ask for them, and I made so good a preparation that, though plenty of cripples and other unfortunates wandering through the world came to me every day, part of the alms was sure to remain upon my hands every night when I closed my door. The alms which I gave away consisted of meal; and I had always a number of small measures of male standing ready on a board, one of which I used to empty into the poke of every bacah or other unfortunate who used to place himself at the side of my door and cry out ' Ave Maria!' or ' In the name of God!' Well, one morning I sat within my door spinning, with a little bit of a colleen beside me who waited upon me as servant. My measures of meal were all ready for the unfortunates who should come, filled with all the meal in the house; for there was no meal in the house save what was in those measures—divil a particle, the whole stock being exhausted; though by evening I expected plenty more, my two sons being gone to the ballybetagh, which was seven miles distant, for a fresh supply, and for other things. Well, I sat within my door, spinning, with my servant by my side to wait upon me, and my measures of male ready for the unfortunates who might come to ask for alms. There I sat, quite proud, and more happy than I had ever felt in my life before; and the unfortunates began to make their appearance. First came a bacah on crutches; then came a woman with a white swelling; then came an individual who had nothing at all the matter with him, and was only a poor unfortunate, wandering about the world; then came a far cake,[1] a dark man, who was led about by a gossoon; after him a simpley, and after the simpleton somebody else as much or more unfortunate. And as the afflicted people arrived and placed themselves by the side of the door and said 'Ave Mary,' or 'In the name of God,' or crossed their arms, or looked down upon the ground, each according to his practice, I got up and emptied my measure of male into his poke, or whatever he carried about with him for receiving the alms which might be given to him; and my measures of male began to be emptied fast, for it seemed that upon that day, when I happened to be particularly short of meal, all the unfortunates in the county of Limerick had conspired together to come to ask me for alms. At last every measure of meal was emptied, and there I sat in my house with nothing to give away provided an unfortunate should come. Says I to the colleen: 'What shall I do provided any more come, for all the meal is gone and there will be no more before the boys come home at night from the ballybetagh.' Says the colleen: 'If any more come, can't ye give them something else?' Says I: 'It has always been my practice to give in meal, and loth should I be to alter

[1] Fear caoch : vir cæcus.

it; for if once I begin to give away other things, I may
give away all I have.' Says the colleen: 'Let's hope
no one else will come: there have been thirteen of them
already.' Scarcely had she said these words, when a
monstrous woman, half-naked, and with a long staff
in her hand, on the top of which was a cross, made her
appearance; and placing herself right before the door,
cried out so that you might have heard her for a mile,
'Give me an alms for the glory of God.'

"'Good woman,' says I to her, 'you will be kind
enough to excuse me: all the preparation I had made
for alms has been given away, for I have relieved
thirteen unfortunates this blessed morning—so may the
Virgin help ye, good woman!' 'Give me an alms,'
said the Beanvore, with a louder voice than before, 'or
it will be worse for you.' 'You must excuse me, dear
mistress,' says I, 'but I have no more meal in the
house. Those thirteen measures which you see there
empty were full this morning, for what was in them I
have given away to unfortunates. So the Virgin and
Child help you.' 'Do you choose to give me an alms?'
she shrieked, so that you might have heard her to
Londonderry. 'If ye have no male give me something
else.' 'You must excuse me, good lady,' said I: 'it
is my custom to give alms in meal, and in nothing else.
I have none in the house now; but if ye come on the
morrow ye shall have a triple measure. In the meanwhile may the Virgin, Child, and the Holy Trinity
assist ye!' Thereupon she looked at me fixedly for a
moment, and then said, not in a loud voice, but in a
low, half-whispered way, which was ten times more
deadly—

"'Biaidh an taifrionn gan sholas duit a bhean shalach!'

Then turning from the door she went away with long
strides. Now, honey, can ye tell me the meaning of
those words?"

"They mean," said I, "unless I am much mistaken:
'May the Mass never comfort ye, you dirty quean!'"

"Ochone! that's the maning of them, sure enough.
They are cramped words, but I guessed that was the
meaning, or something of the kind. Well, after hearing
the evil prayer, I sat for a minute or two quite stunned;

at length recovering myself a bit I said to the colleen :
' Get up, and run after the woman and tell her to
come back and cross the prayer.' I meant by crossing
that she should call it back or do something that would
take the venom out of it. Well, the colleen was rather
loth to go, for she was a bit scared herself, but on
my beseeching her, she got up and ran after the woman,
and being rather swift of foot, at last, though with
much difficulty, overtook her, and begged her to come
back and cross the prayer, but the divil of a woman
would do no such thing, and when the colleen persisted
she told her that if she didn't go back, she would say
an evil prayer over her too. So the colleen left her,
and came back crying and frightened. All the rest of
the day I remained sitting on the stool speechless,
thinking of the prayer which the woman had said, and
wishing I had given her everything I had in the world,
rather than she should have said it. At night came
home the boys, and found their mother sitting on the
stool, like one stupefied. ' What's the matter with you,
mother?' they said. ' Get up and help us to unpack.
We have brought home plenty of things on the car, and
amongst others a whole boll of meal.' ' You might as
well have left it behind you,' said I ; ' this morning a
single measure of male would have been to me of all
the assistance in the world, but I quistion now if I shall
ever want meal again.' They asked me what had happened to me, and after some time I told them how a
monstrous woman had been to me, and had said an evil
prayer over me, because having no meal in the house
I had not given her an alms. ' Come, mother,' said
they, ' get up and help us to unload ! never mind the
prayer of the monstrous woman—it is all nonsense.'
Well, I got up and helped them to unload, and cooked
them a bit and sat down with them, and tried to be
merry, but felt that I was no longer the woman that I
was. The next day I didn't seem to care what became
of me, or how matters went on, and though there was
now plenty of meal in the house, not a measure did I
fill with it to give away in the shape of alms ; and
when the bacahs, and the liprous women, and the dark
men, and the other unfortunates placed themselves at
the side of the door, and gave me to understand that

they wanted alms, each in his or her particular manner, divil an alms did I give them, but let them stand and took no heed of them, so that at last they took themselves off grumbling and cursing. And little did I care for their grumblings and cursings. Two days before I wouldn't have had an unfortunate grumble at me, or curse me, for all the riches below the sun; but now their grumblings and curses didn't give me the slightest uneasiness, for I had an evil prayer spoken against me in the Shanna Gailey by the monstrous woman, and I knew that I was blighted in this world and the next. In a little time I ceased to pay any heed to the farming business, or to the affairs of the house, so that my sons had no comfort in their home. And I took to drink and induced my eldest son to take to drink too—my youngest son, however, did not take to drink, but conducted himself well, and toiled and laboured like a horse, and often begged me and his brother to consider what we were about, and not to go on in a way which would bring us all to ruin, but I paid no regard to what he said, and his brother followed my example, so that at last seeing things were getting worse every day, and that we should soon be turned out of house and home, for no rint was paid, every penny that could be got being consumed in waste, he bade us farewell and went and listed for a sodger. But if matters were bad enough before he went away, they became much worse after; for now when the unfortunates came to the door for alms, instead of letting them stand in pace till they were tired, and took themselves off, I would mock them and point at them, and twit them with their sores and other misfortunes, and not unfrequently I would fling scalding water over them, which would send them howling and honing away, till at last there was not an unfortunate but feared to come within a mile of my door. Moreover, I began to misconduct myself at chapel, more especially at the Aifrionn or Mass, for no sooner was the bell rung, and the holy corpus raised, than I would shout and hoorah, and go tumbling and toppling along the floor before the holy body, as I just now tumbled along the road before you, so that the people were scandalised, and would take me by the shoulders and turn me out of doors, and

began to talk of ducking me in the bog. The priest
of the parish, however, took my part, saying that I
ought not to be persecuted, for that I was not account-
able for what I did, being a possessed person, and
under the influence of divils. 'These, however,' said
he, 'I'll soon cast out from her, and then the woman
will be a holy cratur, much better than she ever was
before.' A very learned man was Father Hogan, especially in casting out divils, and a portly good-looking
man too, only he had a large rubicon nose, which people
said he got by making over free with the cratur in
sacret. I had often looked at the nose, when the divil
was upon me, and felt an inclination to seize hold of
it, jist to see how it felt. Well, he had me to his house
several times, and there he put holy cloths upon me,
and tied holy images to me, and read to me out of holy
books, and sprinkled holy water over me, and put questions to me, and at last was so plased with the answers
I gave him, that he prached a sermon about me in the
chapel, in which he said that he had cast six of my
divils out of me, and should cast out the seventh, which
was the last, by the next Sabbath, and then should
present me to the folks in the chapel as pure a vessel
as the blessed Mary herself—and that I was destined to
accomplish great things, and to be a mighty instrument
in the hands of the Holy Church, for that he intended
to write a book about me describing the miracle he had
performed in casting the seven divils out of me, which
he should get printed at the printing-press of the blessed
Columba, and should send me through all Ireland to sell
the copies, the profits of which would go towards the
support of the holy society for casting out unclane
spirits, to which he himself belonged. Well, the people
showed that they were plased by a loud shout, and
went away longing for the next Sunday when I was to
be presented to them without a divil in me. Five times
the next week did I go to the priest's house, to be read
to, and be sprinkled, and have cloths put upon me, in
order that the work of casting out the last divil, which
it seems was stronger than all the rest, might be made
smooth and aisy, and on the Saturday I came to have
the last divil cast out, and found his riverince in full
canonicals, seated in his aisy chair. 'Daughter,' said

he when he saw me, ' the work is nearly over. Now
kneel down before me, and I will make the sign of the
cross over your forehead, and then you will feel the
last and strongest of the divils, which have so long
possessed ye, go out of ye through your eyes, as I
expect you will say to the people assembled in the
chapel to-morrow.' So I put myself on my knees before
his reverence, who after muttering something to himself, either in Latin or Shanna Gailey—I believe it was
Latin, said, ' Look me in the face, daughter !' Well,
I looked his reverence in the face, and there I saw his
nose looking so large, red, and inviting that I could
not resist the temptation, and before his reverence could
make the sign of the cross, which doubtless would have
driven the divil out of me, I made a spring at it, and
seizing hold of it with fore-finger and thumb, pulled
hard at it. Hot and inctious did it feel. O, the yell
that his reverence gave ! However, I did not let go my
hold, but kept pulling at the nose, till at last to avoid
the torment his reverence came tumbling down upon
me, causing me by his weight to fall back upon the
floor. At the yell which he gave, and at the noise of
the fall, in came rushing his reverence's housekeeper
and stable-boy, who seeing us down on the floor, his
reverence upon me and my hand holding his reverence's
nose, for I felt loth to let it go, they remained in
astonishment and suspense. When his reverence, however, begged them, for the Virgin's sake, to separate
him from the divil of a woman, they ran forward, and
having with some difficulty freed his reverence's nose
from my hand, they helped him up. The first thing
that his reverence did, on being placed on his legs, was
to make for a horsewhip, which stood in one corner of
the room, but I guessing how he meant to use it,
sprang up from the floor, and before he could make a
cut at me, ran out of the room, and hasted home. The
next day, when all the people for twenty miles round
met in the chapel, in the expectation of seeing me presented to them a purified and holy female, and hearing
from my mouth the account of the miracle which his
reverence had performed, his reverence made his appearance in the pulpit with a dale of gould-bater's leaf
on his nose, and from the pulpit he told the people how

I had used him, showing them the gould-bater's leaf on
his feature as testimony of the truth of his words,
finishing by saying that if at first there were seven
devils there were now seven times seven within me.
Well, when the people heard the story, and saw his nose
with the bater's leaf upon it, they at first began to
laugh, but when he appealed to their consciences, and
asked them if such was fitting tratement for a praist,
they said it was not, and that if he would only but
curse me, they would soon do him justice upon me.
His reverence then cursed by book, bell, and candle,
and the people, setting off from the chapel, came in a
crowd to the house where I lived, to wrake vengeance
upon me.   Overtaking my son by the way, who was
coming home in a state of intoxication, they bate him
within an inch of his life, and left him senseless on the
ground, and no doubt would have served me much
worse, only seeing them coming, and guessing what
they came about, though I was a bit intoxicated myself,
I escaped by the back of the house out into the bog,
where I hid myself amidst a copse of hazels.   The
people coming to the house, and not finding me there,
broke and destroyed every bit of furniture, and would
have pulled the house down, or set fire to it, had not
an individual among them cried out that doing so would
be of no use, for that the house did not belong to me,
and that destroying it would merely be an injury to
the next tenant.   So the people, after breaking my furniture and ill-trating two or three dumb beasts, which
happened not to have been made away with, went away,
and in the dead of night I returned to the house, where
I found my son, who had just crawled home covered
with blood and bruises.   We hadn't, however, a home
long, for the agents of the landlord came to seize for
rent, took all they could find, and turned us out upon
the wide world.   Myself and son wandered together for
an hour or two, then, having a quarrel with each
other, we parted, he going one way and I another.
Some little time after I heard that he was transported.
As for myself, I thought I might as well take a leaf
out of the woman's book, who had been the ruin of me.
So I went about bidding people give me alms for the
glory of God, and threatening those who gave me

nothing that the mass should never comfort them. It's a dreadful curse that, honey; and I would advise people to avoid it even though they give away all they have. If you have no comfort in the mass, you will have comfort in nothing else. Look at me: I have no comfort in the mass, for as soon as the priest's bell rings I shouts and hoorahs, and performs tumblings before the blessed corpus, getting myself kicked out of chapel, and as little comfort as I have in the mass have I in other things, which should be a comfort to me. I have two sons who ought to be the greatest comfort to me, but are they so? We'll see—one is transported, and of course is no comfort to me at all. The other is a sodger. Is he a comfort to me? not a bit. A month ago when I was travelling through the black north, tumbling and toppling about, and threatening people with my prayer, unless they gave me alms, a woman, who knew me, told me that he was with his regiment at Cardiff, here in Wales, whereupon I determined to go and see him, and crossing the water got into England, from whence I walked to Cardiff asking alms of the English in the common English way, and of the Irish, and ye are the first Irish I have met, in the way in which I asked them of you. But when I got to Cardiff did I see my son? I did not, for the day before he had sailed with his regiment to a place ten thousand miles away, so I shall never see his face again nor derive comfort from him. Oh, if there's no comfort from the mass there's no comfort from anything else, and he who has the evil prayer in the Shanna Gailey breathed upon him, will have no comfort from the mass. Now, honey, ye have heard the story of Johanna Colgan, the bedivilled woman. Give her now a dacent alms and let her go!"

"Would you consider sixpence a decent alms?"

"I would. If you give me sixpence, I will not say my prayer over ye."

"Would you give me a blessing?"

"I would not. A bedivilled woman has no blessing to give."

"Surely if you are able to ask people to give you alms for the glory of God, you are able to give a blessing."

"Bodderation! are ye going to give me six-pence?"

"No! here's a shilling for you! Take it and go in peace."

"There's no pace for me," said Johanna Colgan, taking the money. "What did the monstrous female say to me? Biadh an taifrionn gan sholas duit a bhean shalach.[1] This is my pace—hoorah! hoorah!" then giving two or three grotesque topples she hurried away in the direction of Merthyr Tydvil.

CHAPTER CVI

Pen y Glas—Salt of the Earth—The Quakers' Yard—The Rhugylgroen.

As I proceeded on my way the scenery to the south on the farther side of the river became surprisingly beautiful. On that side noble mountains met the view, green fields and majestic woods, the latter brown it is true, for their leaves were gone, but not the less majestic for being brown. Here and there were white farm-houses : one of them, which I was told was called Pen y Glas, was a truly lovely little place. It stood on the side of a green hill with a noble forest above it, and put me wonderfully in mind of the hunting lodge, which Ifor Hael allotted as a retreat to Ab Gwilym and Mor-fydd, when they fled to him from Cardigan to avoid the rage of the Bow Bach, and whose charming ap-pearance made him say to his love :

"More bliss for us our fate propounds
On Tat's green banks than Telvy's bounds."

On I wandered. After some time the valley assumed the form of an immense basin, enormous mountains composed its sides. In the middle rose hills of some altitude, but completely overcrowned by the mountains

---

[1] Curses of this description, or evil prayers as they are called, are very common in the Irish language, and are frequently turned to terrible account by that most singular class or sect the Irish mendicants. Several cases have occurred corresponding in many respects with the one detailed above.

around. These hills exhibited pleasant inclosures, and were beautifully dotted with white farm-houses. Down below meandered the Taf, its reaches shining with a silver-like splendour. The whole together formed an exquisite picture, in which there was much sublimity, much still, quiet life, and not a little of fantastic fairy loveliness.

The sun was hastening towards the west as I passed a little cascade on the left, the waters of which, after running under the road, tumbled down a gulley into the river. Shortly afterwards meeting a man I asked him how far it was to Caerfili.

" When you come to the Quakers' Yard, which is a little way further on, you will be seven miles from Caerfili. ''

" What is the Quakers' Yard?''

" A place where the people called Quakers bury their dead. ''

" Is there a village near it ?''

" There is, and the village is called by the same name. ''

" Are there any Quakers in it?''

" Not one, nor in the neighbourhood, but there are some, I believe, in Cardiff. ''

" Why do they bury their dead there?''

" You should ask them, not me. I know nothing about them, and don't want; they are a bad set of people. ''

" Did they ever do you any harm?''

" Can't say they did. Indeed I never saw one in the whole of my life. ''

" Then why do you call them bad?''

" Because everybody says they are. ''

" Not everybody. I don't; I have always found them the salt of the earth. ''

" Then it is salt that has lost its savour. But perhaps you are one of them?''

" No, I belong to the Church of England. ''

" O you do. Then good night to you. I am a Methodist. I thought at first that you were one of our ministers, and had hoped to hear from you something profitable and conducive to salvation, but——''

" Well, so you shall. Never speak ill of people of

whom you know nothing. If that isn't a saying conducive to salvation I know not what is. Good evening to you."

I soon reached the village. Singularly enough, the people of the very first house, at which I inquired about the Quakers' Yard, were entrusted with the care of it. On my expressing a wish to see it a young woman took down a key, and said that if I would follow her she would show it me. The Quakers' burying-place is situated on a little peninsula or tongue of land, having a brook on its eastern and northern sides, and on its western the Taf. It is a little oblong yard, with low walls, partly overhung with ivy. The entrance is a porch to the south. The Quakers are no friends to tombstones, and the only visible evidence that this was a place of burial was a single flagstone, with a half-obliterated inscription, which with some difficulty I deciphered, and was as follows :—

> To the Memory of Thomas Edmunds
> Who died April the ninth 1802 aged 60
> years
> And of Mary Edmunds
> Who died January the fourth 1810 aged 70.

The beams of the descending sun gilded the Quakers' burial-ground as I trod its precincts. A lovely resting-place looked that little oblong yard on the peninsula, by the confluence of the waters, and quite in keeping with the character of the quiet Christian people who sleep within it. The Quakers have for some time past been a decaying sect, but they have done good work in their day, and when they are extinct they are not destined to be soon forgotten. Soon forgotten! How should a sect ever be forgotten, to which have belonged three such men as George Fox, William Penn and Joseph Gurney?

Shortly after I left the Quakers' Yard the sun went down and twilight settled upon the earth. Pursuing my course I reached some woodlands, and on inquiring of a man, whom I saw standing at the door of a cottage, the name of the district, was told that it was called Ystrad Manach—the Monks' Strath or valley. This name it probably acquired from having belonged in times of old to some monkish establishment. The moon now arose, and the night was delightful. As I was wandering along I heard again the same wild noise which I had heard the night before, on the other side of Merthyr Tydvil. The cry of the owl afar off in the woodlands. O that strange bird! O that strange cry! The Welsh as I have said on a former occasion call the owl Dylluan. Amongst the cowydds of Ab Gwilym there is one to the dylluan. It is full of abuse against the bird, with whom the poet is very angry for having with its cry frightened Morfydd back, who was coming to the wood to keep an assignation with him, but not a little of this abuse is wonderfully expressive and truthful. He calls the owl a grey thief—the haunter of the ivy bush—the chick of the oak, a blinking-eyed witch, greedy of mice, with a visage like the bald forehead of a big ram, or the dirty face of an old abbess, which bears no little resemblance to the chine of an ape. Of its cry he says that it is as great a torment as an agonising recollection, a cold shrill laugh from the midst of a kettle of ice; the rattling of sea-pebbles in an old sheep-skin, on which account many call the owl the hag of the Rhugylgroen. The Rhugylgroen, it will be as well to observe, is a dry sheep-skin containing a number of pebbles, and is used as a rattle for frightening crows. The likening the visage of the owl to the dirty face of an old abbess is capital, and the likening the cry to the noise of the Rhugylgroen is anything but unfortunate. For, after all, what does the voice of the owl so much resemble as a diabolical rattle! I'm sure I don't know. Reader, do you?

I reached Caerfili at about seven o'clock, and went to the " Boar's Head," near the ruins of a stupendous castle, on which the beams of the moon were falling.

CHAPTER CVII

Caerfili Castle—Sir Charles—The Waiter—Inkerman.

I SLEPT well during the night. In the morning after breakfast I went to see the castle, over which I was conducted by a woman who was intrusted with its care.

It stands on the eastern side of the little town, and is a truly enormous structure, which brought to my recollection a saying of our great Johnson, to be found in the account of his journey to the Western Islands, namely " that for all the castles which he had seen beyond the Tweed the ruins yet remaining of some one of those which the English built in Wales would find materials." The original founder was one John De Bryse, a powerful Norman, who married the daughter of Llewellyn Ap Jorwerth, the son-in-law of King John, and the most warlike of all the Welsh princes, whose exploits, and particularly a victory which he obtained over his father-in-law, with whom he was always at war, have been immortalised by the great war-bard, Dafydd Benfras. It was one of the strongholds which belonged to the Spencers, and served for a short time as a retreat to the unfortunate Edward the Second. It was ruined by Cromwell, the grand foe of the baronial castles of Britain, but not in so thorough and sweeping a manner as to leave it a mere heap of stones. There is a noble entrance porch fronting the west—a spacious courtyard, a grand banqueting-room, a corridor of vast length, several lofty towers, a chapel, a sally-port, a guard-room, and a strange underground vaulted place called the mint, in which Caerfili's barons once coined money, and in which the furnaces still exist which were used for melting metal. The name Caerfili is said to signify the Castle of Haste, and to have been bestowed on the pile because it was built in a hurry. Caerfili, however, was never built in a hurry, as the remains show. Moreover the Welsh word for haste is not fil but ffrwst. Fil means a scudding or darting through the air, which can have nothing to do with the building of a castle. Caerfili signifies Philip's City, and was called so after one Philip, a saint. It no more means the castle of haste than Tintagel in Cornwall signifies the castle of guile, as the learned have said it does, for Tintagel simply means the house in the gill of the hill, a term admirably descriptive of the situation of the building.

I started from Caerfili at eleven for Newport, distant about seventeen miles. Passing through a toll-gate I ascended an acclivity, from the top of which I obtained a full view of the castle, looking stern, dark, and majestic. Descending the hill I came to a bridge over a river called the Rhymni or Rumney, much celebrated in Welsh and English song—thence to Pentref Bettws, or the village of the bead-house, doubtless so called from its having contained in old times a house in which pilgrims might tell their beads.

The scenery soon became very beautiful—its beauty, however, was to a certain extent marred by a horrid black object, a huge coal work, the chimneys of which were belching forth smoke of the densest description. "Whom does that work belong to?" said I to a man nearly as black as a chimney sweep.

"Who does it belong to? Why, to Sir Charles."

"Do you mean Sir Charles Morgan?"

"I don't know. I only know that it belongs to Sir Charles, the kindest heart and richest man in Wales and in England too."

Passing some cottages I heard a group of children speaking English. Asked an intelligent-looking girl if she could speak Welsh.

"Yes," said she, "I can speak it, but not very well. There is not much Welsh spoken by the children hereabout. The old folks hold more to it."

I saw again the Rhymni river, and crossed it by a bridge; the river here was filthy and turbid owing of course to its having received the foul drainings of the neighbouring coal works—shortly afterwards I emerged from the coom or valley of the Rhymni and entered upon a fertile and tolerably level district. Passed by Llanawst and Machen. The day which had been very fine now became dark and gloomy. Suddenly, as I was descending a slope, a brilliant party consisting of four young ladies in riding habits, a youthful cavalier, and a servant in splendid livery—all on noble horses, swept past me at full gallop down the hill. Almost immediately afterwards seeing a road-mender who was standing holding his cap in his hand—which he had no doubt just reverentially doffed—I said in Welsh: "Who are those ladies?"

"Merched Sir Charles—the daughters of Sir Charles," he replied.

"And is the gentleman their brother?"

" No ! The brother is in the Crim—fighting with the Roosiaid. I don't know who yon gentleman be."

" Where does Sir Charles live?"

" Down in the Dyfryn, not far from Basallaig."

" If I were to go and see him," I said, " do you think he would give me a cup of ale?"

" I dare say he would; he has given me one many a time."

I soon reached Basallaig, a pleasant village standing in a valley and nearly surrounded by the groves of Sir Charles Morgan. Seeing a decent public-house I said to myself, " I think I shall step in and have my ale here, and not go running after Sir Charles, whom perhaps after all I shouldn't find at home." So I went in and called for a pint of ale. Over my ale I trifled for about half-an-hour, then paying my groat I got up and set off for Newport in the midst of a thick mist which had suddenly come on and which speedily wetted me nearly to the skin.

I reached Newport at about half-past four and put up at a large and handsome inn called the King's Head. During dinner the waiter unasked related to me his history. He was a short thick fellow of about forty, with a very disturbed and frightened expression of countenance. He said that he was a native of Brummagem, and had lived very happily at an inn there as waiter, but at length had allowed himself to be spirited away to an establishment high up in Wales amidst the scenery. That very few visitors came to the establishment, which was in a place so awfully lonesome that he soon became hipped and was more than once half in a mind to fling himself into a river which ran before the door and moaned dismally. That at last he thought his best plan would be to decamp, and accordingly took French leave early one morning. That after many frights and much fatigue he had found himself at Newport and taken service at the King's Head, but did not feel comfortable and was frequently visited at night by dreadful dreams. That he should take the first opportunity of getting to Brummagem, though he was afraid that he should not be able to get into his former place owing to his ungrateful behaviour. He then uttered a rather eloquent eulogium on the beauties of the black capital, and wound up all by saying that he would rather be a brazier's dog at Brummagem than head waiter at the best establishment in Wales.

After dinner I took up a newspaper and found in it an account of the battle of Inkerman, which appeared to have been fought on the fifth of November, the very day on which I had ascended Plinlymmon. I was sorry to find that my countrymen had suffered dreadfully, and would have been utterly destroyed but for the opportune arrival of the French. " In my childhood," said I, " the Russians used to help us against the French; now the French help us against the Russians. Who knows but before I die I may see the Russians helping the French against us?"

CHAPTER CVIII

Town of Newport—The Usk—Note of Recognition—An Old Acquaintance—Connamara Quean—The Wake—The Wild Irish—The Tramping Life—Business and Prayer—Methodists —Good Counsel.

NEWPORT is a large town in Monmouthshire, and had once walls and a castle. It is called in Welsh Cas Newydd ar Wysg, or the New Castle upon the Usk. It stands some miles below Caerlleon ar Wysg, and was probably built when that place, at one time one of the most considerable towns in Britain, began to fall into decay. The Wysg or Usk has its source among some wild hills in the south-west of Breconshire, and, after absorbing several smaller streams, amongst which is the Hondu, at the mouth of which Brecon stands, which on that account is called in Welsh Aber Hondu, and traversing the whole of Monmouthshire, enters the Bristol Channel near Newport, to which place vessels of considerable burden can ascend. Wysg or Usk is an ancient British word, signifying water, and is the same as the Irish word uisge or whiskey, for whiskey, though generally serving to denote a spirituous liquor, in great vogue amongst the Irish, means simply water. The proper term for the spirit is uisquebaugh, literally acqua vitæ, but the compound being abbreviated by the English, who have always been notorious for their habit of clipping words, one of the strongest of spirits is now generally denominated by a word which is properly expressive of the simple element water.

Monmouthshire is at present considered an English county, though certainly with little reason, for it not only stands on the western side of the Wye, but the names of almost all its parishes are Welsh, and many thousands of its population still speak the Welsh language. It is called in Welsh Sir, or Shire, Fynwy, and takes its name from the town Mynwy or Monmouth, which receives its own appellation from the river Mynwy or Minno on which it stands. There is a river of much the same name, not in Macedon, but in the Peninsula, namely the Minho, which probably got its denomination from that race cognate to the Cumry, the Gael, who were the first colonisers of the Peninsula, and whose generic name yet stares us in the face and salutes our ears in the words Galicia and Portugal.

I left Newport at about ten o'clock on the 16th, the roads were very wet, there having been a deluge of rain during the night. The morning was a regular November one, dull and gloomy. Desirous of knowing whereabouts in those parts the Welsh language ceased I interrogated several people whom I met. First spoke to Esther Williams. She told me she came from Pennow some miles farther on, that she could speak Welsh, and that indeed all the people could for at least eight miles to the east of Newport. This latter assertion of hers was, however, anything but corroborated by a young woman, with a pitcher on her head, whom I shortly afterwards met, for she informed me that she could speak no Welsh, and that for one who could speak it, from where I was to the place where it ceased altogether, there were ten who could not. I believe the real fact is that about half the people for seven or eight miles to the east of Newport speak Welsh, more or less, as about half those whom I met and addressed in Welsh answered me in that tongue.

Passed through Penow or Penhow, a small village. The scenery in the neighbourhood of this place is highly interesting. To the north-west at some distance is Mynydd Turvey, a sharp-pointed blue mountain. To the south-east, on the right, much nearer, are two beautiful green hills, the lowest prettily wooded, and having on its top a fair white mansion called Penhow Castle, which belongs to a family of the name of Cave. Thence to Llanvaches, a pretty little village. When I was about the middle of this place I heard an odd sound something like a note of recognition, which attracted my attention to an object very near to me, from which it seemed to proceed, and which was coming from the direction in which I was going. It was the figure seemingly of a female, wrapped in a coarse blue cloak, the feet bare and the legs bare also nearly up to the knee, both terribly splashed with the slush of the road. The head was surmounted by a kind of hood which just permitted me to see coarse red hair, a broad face, grey eyes, a snubbed nose, blubber lips and great white teeth—the eyes were staring intently at me. I stopped and stared too, and at last thought I recognised the features of the uncouth girl I had seen on the green near Chester with the Irish tinker Tourlough and his wife.

"Dear me!" said I, "did I not see you near Chester last summer?"

"To be sure ye did; and ye were going to pass me without a word of notice or kindness had I not given ye a bit of a hail."

"Well," said I, "I beg your pardon. How is it all wid ye?"

"Quite well. How is it wid yere hanner?"

"Tolerably. Where do you come from?"

"From Chepstow, yere hanner."

"And where are you going to?"

"To Newport, yere hanner."

"And I come from Newport, and am going to Chepstow. Where's Tourlough and his wife?"

"At Cardiff, yere hanner; I shall join them again to-morrow."

"Have you been long away from them?"

"About a week, yere hanner."

"And what have you been doing?"

"Selling my needles, yere hanner."

"Oh! you sell needles. Well, I am glad to have met you. Let me see. There's a nice little inn on the right : won't you come in and have some refreshment?"

" Thank yere hanner; I have no objection to take a glass wid an old friend."

" Well, then, come in; you must be tired, and I shall be glad to have some conversation with you."

We went into the inn—a little tidy place. On my calling a respectable-looking old man made his appearance behind a bar. After serving my companion with a glass of peppermint, which she said she preferred to anything else, and me with a glass of ale, both of which I paid for, he retired, and we sat down on two old chairs beneath a window in front of the bar.

" Well," said I, " I suppose you have Irish: here's slainte——"

" Slainte yuit a shaoi," said the girl, tasting her peppermint.

" Well, how do you like it?"

" It's very nice indeed."

" That's more than I can say of the ale, which, like all the ale in these parts, is bitter. Well, what part of Ireland do you come from?"

" From no part at all. I never was in Ireland in my life. I am from Scotland Road, Manchester."

" Why, I thought you were Irish!"

" And so I am; and all the more from being born where I was. There's not such a place for Irish in all the world as Scotland Road."

" Were your father and mother from Ireland?"

" My mother was from Ireland; my father was Irish of Scotland Road, where they met and married."

" And what did they do after they married?"

" Why, they worked hard, and did their best to get a livelihood for themselves and children, of which they had several besides myself, who was the eldest. My father was a bricklayer, and my mother sold apples and oranges and other fruits, according to the season, and also whiskey, which she made herself, as she well knew how; for my mother was not only a Connacht woman, but an out-and-out Connamara quean, and when only thirteen had wrought with the lads who used to make the raal cratur on the islands between Ochterard and Bally na hinch. As soon as I was able, I helped my mother in making and disposing of the whiskey and in selling the fruit. As for the other children, they all died when young, of favers, of which there is always plenty in Scotland Road. About four years ago—that is, when I was just fifteen—there was a great quarrel among the workmen about wages. Some wanted more than their masters were willing to give; others were willing to take what was offered them. Those who were dissatisfied were called bricks; those who were not were called dungs. My father was a brick; and, being a good man with his fists, was looked upon as a very proper person to fight a principal man amongst the dungs. They fought in the fields near Salford for a pound a side. My father had it all his own way for the first three rounds, but in the fourth, receiving a blow under the ear from the dung, he dropped, and never got up again, dying suddenly. A grand wake my father had, for which my mother furnished usquebaugh galore; and comfortably and decently it passed over till about three o'clock in the morning, when, a dispute happening to arise—not on the matter of wages, for there was not a dung amongst the Irish of Scotland Road—but as to whether the O'Keefs or O'Kellys were kings of Ireland a thousand years ago, a general fight took place, which brought in the police, who, being soon dreadfully baten, as we all turned upon them, went and fetched the military, with whose help they took and locked up several of the party, amongst whom were my mother and myself, till the next morning, when we were taken before the magistrates, who, after a slight scolding, set us at liberty, one of them saying that such disturbances formed part of the Irish funeral service; whereupon we returned to the house, and the rest of the party joining us, we carried my father's body to the church-yard, where we buried it very dacently, with many tears and groanings."

"And how did your mother and you get on after your father was buried?"

"As well as we could, yere hanner; we sold fruit and now and then a drop of whiskey which we made; but this state of things did not last long, for one day mother seeing the dung who had killed my father she flung a large flint stone and knocked out his right eye, for doing which she was taken up and tried and

sentenced to a year's imprisonment, chiefly it was
thought because she had been heard to say that she
would do the dung a mischief the first time she met him.
She, however, did not suffer all her sentence, for before
she had been in prison three months she caught a
disorder which carried her off. I went on selling
fruit by myself whilst she was in trouble, and for some
time after her death, but very lonely and melancholy.
At last my uncle Tourlough, or as the English would
call him, Charles, chancing to come to Scotland Road
along with his family, I was glad to accept an invitation to join them which he gave me, and with them I
have been ever since, travelling about England and
Wales and Scotland, helping my aunt with the children
and driving much the same trade which she has driven
for twenty years past, which is not an unprofitable
one."

"Would you have any objection to tell me all you
do?"

"Why I sells needles, as I said before, and sometimes I buys things of servants, and sometimes I tells
fortunes."

"Do you ever do anything in the way of striopachas?"

"O, no! I never do anything in that line; I would
be burnt first. I wonder you should dream of such a
thing."

"Why surely it is not worse than buying things of
servants, who no doubt steal them from their employers,
or telling fortunes, which is dealing with the devil."

"Not worse? Yes a thousand times worse; there
is nothing so very particular in doing them things,
but striopachas—O dear!"

"It's a dreadful thing I admit, but the other things
are quite as bad; you should do none of them."

"I'll take good care that I never do one, and that
is striopachas; them other things I know are not quite
right, and I hope soon to have done wid them; any day
I can shake them off and look people in the face, but
were I once to do striopachas I could never hold up my
head."

"How comes it that you have such a horror of
striopachas?"

" I got it from my mother and she got it from hers. All Irish women have a dread of striopachas. It's the only thing that frights them; I manes the wild Irish, for as for the quality women I have heard they are no bit better than the English. Come, yere hanner, let's talk of something else."

" You were saying now that you were thinking of leaving off fortune-telling and buying things of servants. Do you mean to depend upon your needles alone?"

" No; I am thinking of leaving off tramping altogether and going to the Tir na Siar."

" Isn't that America?"

" It is, yere hanner; the land of the west is America."

" A long way for a lone girl."

" I should not be alone, yere hanner; I should be wid my uncle Tourlough and his wife."

" Are they going to America?"

" They are, yere hanner; they intends leaving off business and going to America next spring."

" It will cost money."

" It will, yere hanner; but they have got money, and so have I."

" Is it because business is slack that you are thinking of going to America?"

" O no, yere hanner; we wish to go there in order to get rid of old ways and habits, amongst which are fortune-telling and buying things of sarvants, which yere hanner was jist now checking me wid."

" And can't you get rid of them here?"

" We cannot, yere hanner. If we stay here we must go on tramping, and it is well known that doing them things is part of tramping."

" And what would you do in America?"

" O we could do plenty of things in America—most likely we should buy a piece of land and settle down."

" How came you to see the wickedness of the tramping life?"

" By hearing a great many sermons and preachings, and having often had the Bible read to us by holy women who came to our tent."

" Of what religion do you call yourselves now?"

" I don't know, yere hanner; we are clane unsettled

about religion. We were once Catholics and carried
Saint Colman of Cloyne about wid us in a box; but
after hearing a sermon at a church about images, we
went home, took the saint out of his box and cast him
into a river."

" O it will never do to belong to the Popish religion,
a religion which upholds idol-worship and persecutes
the Bible—you should belong to the Church of
England."

" Well, perhaps we should, yere hanner, if its
ministers were not such proud violent men. O, you
little know how they look down upon all poor people,
especially on us tramps. Once my poor aunt, Tourlough's wife, who has always had stronger convictions
than any of us, followed one of them home after he had
been preaching, and begged him to give her God, and
was told by him that she was a thief, and if she didn't
take herself out of the house he would kick her
out."

" Perhaps, after all," said I, " you had better join
the Methodists—I should say that their ways would
suit you better than those of any other denomination of
Christians."

" Yere hanner knows nothing about them, otherwise
ye wouldn't talk in that manner. Their ways would
never do for people who want to have done wth lying
and staling, and have always kept themselves clane
from striopachas. Their word is not worth a rotten
straw, yere hanner, and in every transaction which they
have with people they try to cheat and overreach—ask
my uncle Tourlough, who has had many dealings with
them. But what is far worse, they do that which the
wildest calleen t'other side of Ougteraarde would be
burnt rather than do. Who can tell ye more on that
point than I, yere hanner? I have been at their chapels
at nights and have listened to their screaming prayers,
and have seen what's been going on outside the chapels
after their services, as they call them, were over—I
never saw the like going on outside Father Toban's
chapel, yere hanner! Yere hanner's hanner asked me
if I ever did anything in the way of striopachas—now
I tell ye that I was never asked to do anything in that
line but by one of them folks—a great man amongst

them he was, both in the way of business and prayer, for he was a commercial traveller during six days of the week and a preacher on the seventh—and such a preacher. Well, one Sunday night after he had preached a sermon an hour and a half long, which had put half-a-dozen women into what they call static fits, he overtook me in a dark street and wanted me to do striopachas with him—he didn't say striopachas, yer hanner, for he had no Irish—but he said something in English which was the same thing."

" And what did you do?"

" Why I asked him what he meant by making fun of a poor ugly girl—for no one knows better than myself, yere hanner, that I am very ugly—whereupon he told me that he was not making fun of me, for it had long been the chief wish of his heart to commit strio-pachas with a wild Irish Papist, and that he beieved if he searched the world he should find none wilder than myself."

" And what did you reply?"

" Why I said to him, yere hanner, that I would tell the congregation, at which he laughed and said that he wished I would, for that the congregation would say they didn't believe me, though at heart they would, and would like him all the better for it."

" Well, and what did you say then?"

" Nothing at all, yere hanner; but I spat in his face and went home and told my uncle Tourlough, who forthwith took out a knife and began to sharp it on a whetstone, and I make no doubt would have gone and stuck the fellow like a pig, had not my poor aunt begged him not on her knees. After that we had nothing more to do with the Methodists as far as religion went."

" Did this affair occur in England or Wales?"

" In the heart of England, yere hanner; we have never been to the Welsh chapels, for we know little of the language."

" Well, I am glad it didn't happen in Wales; I have rather a high opinion of the Welsh Methodists. The worthiest creature I ever knew was a Welsh Methodist. And now I must leave you and make the best of my way to Chepstow."

" Can't yere hanner give me God before ye go?"

" I can give you half-a-crown to help you on your way to America."

" I want no half-crowns, yere hanner; but if ye would give me God I'd bless ye."

" What do you mean by giving you God?"

" Putting Him in my heart by some good counsel which will guide me through life."

" The only good counsel I can give you is to keep the commandments; one of them it seems you have always kept. Follow the rest and you can't go very wrong."

" I wish I knew them better than I do, yere hanner."

" Can't you read?"

" O no, yere hanner, I can't read, neither can Tourlough nor his wife."

" Well, learn to read as soon as possible. When you have got to America and settled down you will have time enough to learn to read."

" Shall we be better, yere hanner, after we have learnt to read?"

" Let's hope you will."

" One of the things, yere hanner, that have made us stumble is that some of the holy women, who have come to our tent and read the Bible to us, have afterwards asked my aunt and me to tell them their fortunes."

" If they have the more shame for them, for they can have no excuse. Well, whether you learn to read or not still eschew striopachas, don't steal, don't deceive, and worship God in spirit, not in image. That's the best counsel I can give you."

" And very good counsel it is, yere hanner, and I will try to follow it, and now, yere hanner, let us go our two ways."

We placed our glasses upon the bar and went out. In the middle of the road we shook hands and parted, she going towards Newport and I towards Chepstow. After walking a few yards I turned round and looked after her. There she was in the damp lowering afternoon wending her way slowly through mud and puddle, her upper form huddled in the rough frieze mantle, and her coarse legs bare to the top of the calves. " Surely," said I to myself, " there never was an object less promising in appearance. Who would think that there could be all the good sense and proper feeling in that uncouth girl which there really is?"

CHAPTER CIX

Arrival at Chepstow—Stirring Lyric—Conclusion.

I PASSED through Caer Went, once an important Roman station, and for a long time after the departure of the Romans a celebrated·British city, now a poor desolate place consisting of a few old-fashioned houses and a strange-looking dilapidated church. No Welsh is spoken at Caer Went, nor to the east of it, nor indeed for two or three miles before you reach it from the west.

The country between it and Chepstow, from which it is distant about four miles, is delightfully green, but somewhat tame.

Chepstow stands on the lower part of a hill, near to where the beautiful Wye joins the noble Severn. The British name of the place is Aber Wye or the disemboguement of the Wye. The Saxons gave it the name of Chepstow, which in their language signifies a place where a market is held, because even in the time of the Britons it was the site of a great cheap or market. After the Norman Conquest it became the property of De Clare, one of William's followers, who built near it an enormous castle, which enjoyed considerable celebrity during several centuries from having been the birthplace of Strongbow, the conqueror of Ireland, but which is at present chiefly illustrious from the mention which is made of it in one of the most stirring lyrics of modern times, a piece by Walter Scott, called the "Norman Horseshoe," commemorative of an expedition made by a De Clare of Chepstow with the view of insulting with the print of his courser's shoe the green meads of Glamorgan, and which commences thus :—

" Red glows the forge "—

I went to the principal inn, where I engaged a

private room and ordered the best dinner which the people could provide. Then leaving my satchel behind me I went to the castle, amongst the ruins of which I groped and wandered for nearly an hour, occasionally repeating verses of the " Norman Horseshoe." I then went to the Wye and drank of the waters at its mouth, even as sometime before I had drunk of the waters at its source. Then returning to my inn I got my dinner, after which I called for a bottle of port, and placing my feet against the sides of the grate I passed my time drinking wine and singing Welsh songs till ten o'clock at night, when I paid my reckoning, amounting to something considerable. Then shouldering my satchel I proceeded to the railroad station, where I purchased a first-class ticket, and ensconcing myself in a comfortable carriage was soon on the way to London, where I arrived at about four o'clock in the morning, having had during the whole of my journey a most uproarious set of neighbours a few carriages behind me, namely some hundred and fifty of Napier's tars returning from their expedition to the Baltic.

THE END